A textbook for

Medical assistants

A textbook for

Medical assistants

M. Murray Lawton, M.D.

Administrator of the Berkley School; Director,
In-Service Training, Berkley East Hospital,
Santa Monica, California

Donald F. Foy, B.S., M.S., M.P.H.

Director, Management Services Division,
American Medical Association,
Chicago, Illinois

THIRD EDITION

with 243 illustrations

The C. V. Mosby Company

Saint Louis 1975

THIRD EDITION

Printed in the United States of America

Library of Congress Cataloging in Publication Data

Lawton, M Murray, 1899-
A textbook for medical assistants.

Bibliography: p.
Includes index.
1. Medical assistants. I. Foy, Donald F., joint author. II. Title. [DNLM: 1. Medical secretaries. 2. Office Management. W80 L425t]
R728.8.L3 1975 610.69'53 75-15577
ISBN 0-8016-2892-X

CB/CB/B 9 8 7 6 5 4 3 2

dedicated to

Dorothy Tietz Lawton

A pioneer in the field
of medical assistant training
whose vision and devotion to the
principles of medical education
have made this book possible.

Preface

The basic philosophy underlying the first two editions of this book is continued in this edition. Its object is to impart the habits of thinking that enable medical assistants to obtain the fullest information from all sources of medical literature. We shall indeed feel happy if, in addition, we succeed in making this book attractive for use as a reference source. We hope that the suggestions offered here will provide the enthusiasm to motivate students to pursue this type of training throughout their lives.

The job of vocational education is to enable people to understand the basis of order and security in a world of rapid change and to build their goals realistically in fitting terms. Almost all adults require some help at particular times. It is an obligation of education to introduce people to careers, to help people understand their problems, discover the resources available to them, and find ways to resolve their problems and reach their goals under current circumstances. A formal education and preparation during youth, though beyond reproach, may be inadequate as one reaches adulthood and has to function in a changing world. Adults change, too, because they live in the midst of responsibility and are under pressure to make decisions and take action. In short, adults need contemporary education.

Current job requirements continue to uncover weaknesses in the knowledge and skills of many people. The opportunities to fill the gaps in order to keep people adequately equipped to meet contemporary standards must always be available. The changing world also arouses new interests and stimulates new aspirations that will be followed if opportunity exists. However, the one inescapable trend affecting all areas of human life and activity is to become more technical. Technology dominates our present civilization.

It is our intent to provide the most comprehensive and up-to-date work on the training of medical assistants, while not sacrificing clarity and practical application. We desire to provide a basic reference text for all those actively engaged in the career of medical assisting as well as those aspiring to enter the field.

In preparing this edition, we have made use of an eclectic approach—being guided by our own experiences as well as by all those with whom we have communicated. Care has been taken to make the text useful to students who are taking their initial training in medical assisting. We realize that students may not necessarily be required to master all of the material in this book, but we hope that as graduates they will find the book valuable as they continue to study and mature in their chosen field.

This revision updates the information contained in the second edition. In all areas, especially health insurance, new material has been added where indicated and old material has been deleted. New terms have been substituted for those that have fallen into disuse.

Keeping in mind the diverse backgrounds and preparation levels of our readers, we have attempted to accomplish the following: (1) to write a readable text that is within the reach of all; (2) to lay a broad basis of fact and principle in this field; (3) to provide orientation for the student by presenting a coherent, consistent, meaningful analysis of the major issues encountered; (4) to present the best thought on the subject in such a way as to form a sound basis for teaching procedures; and (5) to challenge the student so as to arouse a permanent interest in the medical field.

The curriculum of the medical assistant is quite diversified, but so are the methods of instruction. The well-constructed curriculum should be student-centered and should use all types of teaching methods, including formal lectures, group discussions, individual tutoring, laboratory practice, clinical demonstration, personal conferences, and both individual and group projects. Such methods of instruction must be varied but should be supplemented with the numerous audiovisual aids designed to help reinforce a learning situation.

We believe that the training of the medical assistant demands a maximum of individual instruction and attention. This situation can be achieved only by limiting the size of all classes, thus giving the instructor the opportunity to study the characteristics and personality of each student and to aid the student's development along lines best suited to individual needs. The maximum of individual attention is thus possible when student-teacher relationships are on a personal basis. Whether in the classroom or in the laboratory, the instructional staff should develop within the student an intellectual curiosity and foster a better understanding and appreciation of the world in general.

Stress must be placed on proper grooming, dignified bearing, and the meticulous personal appearance of trainees, because it is absolutely essential that the medical assistant project a professional image. It is good practice to insist that students begin to groom professionally, behave professionally, and think professionally from the time they first enter training.

In the process of evaluation, major emphasis should be placed on the daily progress of the student rather than on the results of specific tests or examinations. This does not mean, however, that final or comprehensive examinations should not be given. Rather, it is meant that the final measure of a student is based on the sum total of demonstrated achievement.

Automation has made tremendous inroads into our economy, greatly reducing the number of unskilled jobs. Provided this present trend continues, succeeding decades will present a real challenge for vocational institutions. Those engaged in the various allied health professions can derive a certain sense of security in knowing that they should remain relatively immune from the replacement effects of automation. It is doubtful whether automation will exercise much influence in an occupation where the element of personal contact is so important.

A note of gratitude is due to all those who cooperated in permitting use of their forms, illustrations, and photographs, which contribute significantly to enrichment of the text.

M. Murray Lawton
Donald F. Foy

Contents

part one

Business practices

chapter 1

The medical assistant–role and function

HISTORICAL BACKGROUND

At one time the physician led a relatively simple professional existence, practicing with makeshift arrangements, with unskilled assistants, and with limited professional equipment and medications. This was the era of "kitchen-table surgery," the horse-and-buggy doctor with the battered black medical bag.

As more knowledge was gained over a period of years, improved equipment, better-trained assistants, and services of many types were made available. The instruments of medicine became innumerable. To use these instruments and to make available the accumulated knowledge from closely related and specialized sciences, other members were added to the health care team, such as nurses, dietitians, x-ray technicians, physical therapists, occupational therapists, medical record librarians, medical secretaries, laboratory technologists, and, of course, medical assistants.

As the private practice of medicine became more complex, the physician came to rely upon the help of allied medical personnel to assist in providing scientific medical services to an increasing volume of patients. These workers also made it possible for the physician to make more efficient use of professional time and skills.

Nevertheless, there still remained a need for someone trained to assist the physician —someone who could be trained in a relatively short period of time to relieve many of the routine responsibilities of running an office.

The answer to this manpower need is today's medical assistant, whose main function is to care for the many needs of a physician's office. The medical assistant is often referred to as the "right hand of the medical profession," standing as the first point of contact with the medical care system, and as such can make or break a physician's practice. The medical assistant is a combination of secretary, nurse, x-ray assistant, and laboratory assistant and ideally is trained to perform a number of routine

---

Glossary

accreditation U. S. recognition of an academic institution as coming up to an official standard with regard to course credits and degrees
allied medical fields closely related to medicine
basal metabolism measurement of the rate at which the body burns foods for fuel (BMR)
blood count determination of the relative number of red and white blood cells present in the blood—RBC: red blood count; WBC: white blood count (The presence of an excessive amount of white blood cells is often indicative of bodily infection.)
catharsis an emotional purification or relief
diagnosis determination of a disease or ailment
electrocardiogram (EKG or ECG) measuring and recording heart action
empathetic entering by imagination into another's feelings or motives
flaunt to wave, display, parade in front of, or exhibit
lackadaisical listless, languid, dreamy
mundane earthly, of this world
rapport close harmony or accord among people
urinalysis (UA) test of urine content

functions in each of these areas. The medical assistant is not a qualified nurse, x-ray technician, or laboratory technologist, but generally does have enough basic knowledge in all these fields to serve the common office needs of most practitioners.

Although a physician may start out practice with only one part-time or full-time medical office assistant, as the practice grows the office staff may be augmented to include others—perhaps a registered nurse, a laboratory or x-ray technician, depending upon the nature of the practice and the needs of the office.

The role of the medical assistant differs from that of the registered nurse in that the medical assistant is trained especially for the physician's office, whereas the nurse is trained primarily for hospital work. Despite the depth of the nurse's training, there are some functions associated with the physician's office that the medical assistant is trained to perform but for which the nurse receives little or no training. For instance, most medical assistants are instructed in the techniques of routine laboratory work, taking electrocardiograms, and in medical office management.

The great majority of physicians are usually reluctant to spend much time and energy on the nonmedical, more mundane aspects of running their offices. The handling of fees, the collection of delinquent accounts, the mechanics of a smoothly functioning appointment schedule, and the efficient utilization of office space and personnel are all tasks that most physicians prefer to leave to someone else to handle. This leaves a great deal of responsibility to the medical assistant.

Thus medical assistants should not underestimate the importance of their jobs. Unless it is a large office where the responsibility for assisting the physician is divided among several people, their duties are numerous. The medical assistant is not only the nurse in the examining room and the secretary in the reception room, but, and just as important, the morale officer for both the physician and the patients. The assistant also serves as a public relations officer, an accountant and bookkeeper, and a friend in need to take a patient's mind off his worries. If ever a job called for one to be both an assistant and alter ego, this is it.

Maintaining the necessary office supplies and keeping prescription pads at hand are no less important than keeping the physician's instruments and medications ready for use. In the midst of all of this the assistant must see that appointments are made and kept and that patients move smoothly from reception room to examining rooms.

In no place must the art of human relations be practiced with more grace and skill than in the physician's office. People who are sick, afraid, or worried need a ready smile and show of confidence to give them hope and assurance. In many cases, this can be of almost as much value to the sick person as the physician's knowledge and skill.

The medical assistant career field has become a distinct health care occupation, despite some evidence that the career field is not clearly understood throughout the health care delivery system. Confusion regarding the role of the medical assistant has been, in part, the result of three factors: (1) recent rapid growth in formal medical assistant training programs, (2) wide use of the medical assistant in many functional areas, and (3) generalized training given to the medical assistant in an industry characterized by growing specialization.

Although medical assistants are being utilized in a wide variety of employment settings, including physicians' offices, hospitals (in various departments), and large medical clinics, it is clear that the medical assistant is best utilized in a private physician's office where the capabilities of such a generalist can be best applied.

SPECIFIC DUTIES OF THE MEDICAL ASSISTANT

The tempo of activities in a busy office creates a great amount of tension and exposes the medical assistant to constant stress. It is necessary for the medical assistant to possess a high stress tolerance. Above all, however, there must be organization. In order to survive the day, conserve time, and perform efficiently, it is imperative that some sort of work schedule be maintained.

For example, the medical assistant arrives at the office in the morning prior to the arrival of the physician. The office is aired, anything out of order, such as magazines, furniture, books on the physician's professional bookshelf, and medications, are arranged, and the equipment and instruments in the examination rooms are secured.

Several of the immediate duties the organized medical assistant performs in the morning are to review the appointments and messages for the day and to read any written instructions left by the physician. The physician's answering service must be checked and calls returned when necessary.

Before the physician begins office hours, the medical assistant answers the phone and keeps an account of where he can be located in an emergency. As home and hospital calls are made, the doctor can usually be expected to keep the assistant informed of his whereabouts.

Typing reports and letters, completing patients' records, and ordering supplies can also be done before office hours. The assistant could also utilize this time to perform routine laboratory tests of specimens left by patients.

During office hours the assistant is very busy. In some offices the physician's entire time in the office is scheduled with appointments made well in advance. In other offices where patients are served in the order of their arrival at the office, it is up to the assistant to keep an account of these arrivals so that patients will be served in the proper order, although this procedure would seldom function well in a large and busy office.

Before a patient enters the examination room or the physician's private office, the assistant secures the medical record maintained by the doctor for each patient. As each patient is ushered into the inner office, this record is placed on the physician's desk. If a new patient arrives, the assistant makes out a new file containing the personal data considered necessary by the doctor. The assistant may choose to file patients' charts after they leave the office or at the end of the day. However, this procedure will vary from office to office.

As the patient leaves, the assistant records the charges incurred on the patient's ledger and may even collect the fee at this time. In any event, the process of recording charges at this time ensures proper billing at the end of the month.

Physicians may have one examination room or several separate ones. It is usually the job of the assistant to prepare the patient for an examination. The physician indicates the type of examination to be performed, and the assistant may aid or direct the patient in preparing for the examination.

The assistant also sets out the necessary instruments, using accepted sterile methods for handling them if not all are disposables. The office sterilizer is prepared in advance with the instruments most commonly used by the physician so that they are available for immediate use. If rubber gloves are used by the physician, they should be properly prepared and sterilized.

A female assistant should be present during the examination of female patients unless otherwise directed. She may assist by handling instruments, making notes, positioning patients, and performing other simple duties and tests. When the examination is over, she may assist the patient in dressing and may repeat directions and comments made by the physician. The assistant then gets the room ready for the next patient by straightening or replacing the sheet on the examination table, cleaning the instruments and placing them in a cabinet or in a sterilizer. Specimens from patients for laboratory examinations may have been obtained and should be processed quickly.

After office hours, it may be necessary

for the assistant to sterilize all instruments used, file patients' folders, receive orders from the physician, and rearrange all the rooms used. Normally, this is a good time to make hospital arrangements for patients, return telephone calls, perform clerical and bookkeeping duties, and complete laboratory tests.

The laboratory tests performed by the assistant usually consist of relative routine screening examinations such as urinalyses, glucose tolerance tests, electrocardiograms, and blood counts.

A routine urine test can be accomplished with a test tube, a chemical tablet, and heat from a Bunsen burner or an alcohol lamp when more modern devices are not available. The blood count takes considerable skill and experience to secure quick and accurate results. The assistant may take this blood sample from the patient under the physician's supervision, or the physician may do it during the examination. The required blood sample may be secured through a vein-puncture procedure, as is the case with most adults, or through the finger-puncture technique, which is more commonly used with children.

The glucose tolerance test and electrocardiogram are relatively simple procedures to administer, but the interpretation of findings must be done by a physician. These simple but important tests are done in the physician's office so that more immediate information will be available to make a quick diagnosis. If the nature of the required test calls for more complex equipment than the office has on hand or greater knowledge than that possessed by the medical assistant, the material to be tested is sent to a larger, more specialized laboratory.

The assistant should be endowed with special personality qualities since most patients are not truly themselves when they come to the doctor's office. They are ill and therefore sensitive, anxious, and more irritable than usual. The assistant with the right attitude can do much to relieve the anxieties of patients.

Occasionally it will be necessary for the assistant to employ special talents in dealing with moaning, groaning, crying, depressed, and ill-tempered patients. The assistant will also occasionally need to clean up after patients who have vomited or soiled.

Duties vary, depending upon the type of the physician's practice and whether or not the assistant is the only employee. It is quite common for physicians engaged in group practice to have a suite of offices and employ a number of different types of allied medical personnel. In such cases the assistant might specialize in any one or more areas, such as front office duty, examination room duty, or laboratory and x-ray duty.

WORKING CONDITIONS

The physical surroundings of the medical office are normally quite pleasant and conducive to comfort and good health. The working hours of the medical assistants are usually established by the employer. The eight-hour day five days a week is common, but it often difficult for the conscientious assistant to adhere to a strictly hourly schedule. Although hours are often irregular and long, the work is interesting and varied. Since few days are ever the same, the office should never become a source of boredom.

There is no room for "clock-watchers" in the medical profession. There will be times when the assistant will be expected to stay late in case of an emergency or possibly work overtime just to catch up. Working on Saturday may also be required. Nevertheless, most understanding physicians make arrangements for their personnel to take corresponding time off at less hectic times.

PERSONAL ADJUSTMENT

According to a recent study that served as the subject for an unpublished master's thesis entitled *A Job Analysis of Medical Secretaries in California,* a genuine affection for people and a sincere desire to help them appear to be the principal reasons why individuals choose careers in medical offices. Besides having a keen interest in medicine generally, other reasons include an admiration for physicians and a desire for the high prestige enjoyed by those connected with the medical profession. From a more practical standpoint, respondents in the survey further cited the advantage of the shorter training programs for medical assistants and medical secretaries as opposed to nursing programs and the period required to obtain a college degree.

Many medical assistants who were interviewed indicated that they had originally been interested in nursing and laboratory work but for various reasons decided to train as medical assistants, primarily because the shorter course better fitted their personal needs. The fact that work in a physician's office is rewarding and challenging were additional reasons given, as was the opportunity to utilize varied skills.

The length of training of the medical assistant certainly is not an excuse for lack of those attributes of personality that make for success in the medical profession. Such values are not taught per se but are nurtured and developed over a long period of time. Perhaps one of the more important of these is self-discipline which must originate from within. It must arise from one's own desire for self-control and not simply because its development is suggested. A medical office affords an excellent opportunity to practice self-discipline. There are countless activities, responsibilities, relationships, and irritants that will test the medical assistant's ability to exercise this quality.

The assistant must learn to perform duties that may be personally distasteful. Some necessary duties may be considered less than stimulating but must nevertheless be performed. It may sometimes help to analyze why some people react so strongly to certain tasks to discover why they make countless excuses to avoid them. It may be simply the sheer monotony of the work involved, but more than likely such individuals probably have never taken the time to really determine an efficient and rapid method for accomplishment of an undesirable task.

Whatever the reason for procrastination, one should take the time to analyze the job, determine a way to solve it, and discipline oneself to tackle it regularly at the most opportune time. The sense of satisfaction and achievement resulting from the accomplishment of difficult tasks tends to minimize their future repugnance and is more than repayment for the expended effort.

The medical profession is in great need of trained workers who are able to take orders or develop the ability to do so. Such a cooperative attitude demonstrates a sense of dedication and purpose that is characteristic of the mature, well-adjusted individual. Every efficient organization and institution must maintain a code of rules or regulations in order to preclude confusion and ensure the realization of its aims and purposes. The observance of established standards of professional conduct and behavior is absolutely essential in the medical field, which is, by its very nature, highly structured.

The ability to get along with people is one of those intangible assets that not everyone possesses. And getting along well is not something that just happens. It is the result of conscious effort and practice. It can spell the difference between a mediocre medical assistant and a better-than-average one. The person with a well-adjusted personality is able to get along with people both in intimate, personal relationships and in larger, more formal relationships. Success in this area requires the ability to see the other person's side and to understand his problems. It implies the ability to consider the other person's happiness and needs —in other words, the ability to reflect an empathetic attitude.

Well-adjusted individuals understand their own limitations and capacities and do not take themselves too seriously. They should possess a lively sense of humor and be ready to display it whenever the occasion warrants.

Such a person is able to evaluate a given situation as a whole without jumping to hasty conclusions and attaching too much significance to any one factor.

It bears mentioning here that no individual can be expected to get along with everyone or necessarily work well in every group. A well-integrated personality does not unduly worry about being liked by everyone. The old axiom, "You can please some of the people some of the time, but you can't please all of the people all of the time," is well substantiated in everyday life.

Making an effort to get along with an individual one dislikes may be a difficult task, but with self-discipline one can find the courage to make the effort. As Aldous Huxley once stated, "There is only one corner of the universe one is certain of improving and that's his own."

Self-discipline enables one to control criticism of others. One should never criticize except when there is no other alternative. At this juncture silence is golden.

On the other hand, the assistant should not be so smug as to feel an expert in all matters affecting the office. It may very well be that a great deal could be learned from someone with a fresh new approach. Longevity on the job is no excuse for becoming rigid and inflexible. Serious problems can arise from the attitude of a medical assistant who happens to possess superior education and academic degrees and does not hesitate to flaunt them before co-workers.

Each of us must be amenable to personal preferences as well as suggested changes for the improvement in methods of operation. When a new physician joins the practice it is always a good idea for the medical assistant to ask for suggestions and recommendations concerning the handling of the office routine. Misunderstandings are frequently the result of a lack of communication between individuals.

While it is sometimes admittedly difficult to remain tolerant of the irritating habits of associates and co-workers, it requires an even greater amount of restraint to overcome one's own shortcomings once they are recognized. The removal of an individual's most objectionable traits calls for a large dose of self-discipline.

Criticism is part of our lives since few of us can claim perfection. We must therefore learn to accept constructive criticism without becoming overly sensitive. In the interests of office harmony, the medical assistant must develop a "thick skin."

Few physicians will deny the fact that the value and worth of a medical assistant are largely dependent upon an ability to deal with people and an enjoyment of the challenge of dealing with a great variety of individuals. Some basic principles pertaining to getting along with people bear mentioning at this point.

1. Keep restraint on your voice and try to say less than you are thinking. The cultivation of a low, persuasive voice can be helpful, for how you say something is often more important than what you say.
2. Make few promises but keep those you do make.
3. Take advantage of each opportunity to say kind and encouraging things to and about those with whom you are dealing. Praise work well done; criticize constructively when necessary.
4. Be genuinely interested in others regardless of their position, but don't become involved personally with patients. It is too easy to become upset and depressed over favorite patients who are seriously ill.
5. Always try to be cheerful and smile.
6. Keep an open mind on all debatable questions. When necessary, discuss, but don't argue.
7. Discourage gossip. Make it a habit to not talk of another's faults and to say nothing about someone else unless it is something positive.
8. Don't expect immediate and constant praise and recognition for doing your job well. Be patient and your efforts will be rewarded eventually.

THE PHYSICIAN AND THE ASSISTANT

A close working relationship between the physician and assistant must be maintained at all times. It should be quite obvious that assistants must possess the utmost confidence in their employers and in themselves before they can impart confidence to patients. They must be able to follow directions carefully and even anticipate them. They should be so accustomed to the physician's method of response that a single word will immediately make them aware of what is needed. There is no room in medicine for guessing; therefore the assistant must not be afraid to ask questions about carrying out directions. When possible, directions should be followed quickly and to the letter.

The language of medical ethics is expressly clear and concise. A physician is obliged not to reveal the secrets of the examining room and is ethically bound not to discuss one patient's case with another. The code is exactly the same for the medical assistant who is duty-bound to keep all office business as well as patient revelations confidential. Special diligence must be used in handling the telephone so as never to cause embarrassment to the physician, a patient on the telephone, or another patient in the office who might overhear the conversation. It must be emphasized that medical information should never be revealed to anyone except the patient involved, and then only by the physician. Medical ethics is discussed in greater detail in Chapter 6.

The medical assistant should never hesitate to speak to the doctor about the condition of the instruments and office equipment, since one of the principal duties is the preparation of the office for the examination and treatment of patients. It is quite obvious that a harmonious relationship between the doctor and the assistant is necessary for efficient and professional performance of duties. A satisfactory rapport is not possible when the physician feels the assistant is not putting in an honest day's work. The physician also will have reason to be annoyed with an assistant who is habitually late in arriving in the morning, overstaying the lunch hour, or closing the office early when the physician is not present. The assistant should be ready to correct any mistakes whenever they have been pointed out.

The medical assistant must always exercise discretion in office behavior. Nothing is more irritating to a physician, or to any employer, than to find someone has been hired who utilizes office facilities and time to conduct personal business. The medical assistant should be discouraged from either making or receiving personal telephone calls in the office. The typing of personal letters is also taboo. A resourceful assistant can always find something to do in the office during any slack periods that occur.

On the other side of the coin, if the assistant suspects the physician is taking unfair advantage of dedication and goodwill, this also tends to create an atmosphere of resentment and tension that affects office harmony. Should the assistant be conscientious and dependable in the conduct of duties and obligations to the physician and yet feel that too much is expected, what should be done about it? Rather than harbor a smoldering grudge, which invariably will exercise an unfavorable influence upon the attitude toward patients and overall job performance, the assistant should discuss grievances with the physician. In most cases the physician is probably unaware of being guilty of expecting or demanding too much. Moreover, a good catharsis now and then promotes healthy adjustment and is good medicine for everyone. The great majority of misunderstandings arise because of a lack of communication between people. A clarification of such matters as duties and hours can often preclude a great deal of misunderstanding between the physician and the assistant.

An employee may have all the essential qualities for the job yet lack the necessary drive. Though a doctor may not fire a lackadaisical assistant who puts off small chores, she is not likely to reach a high salary level or be entrusted with a position of greater responsibility. Thus the selection of an intelligent and poised medical assistant may represent to the physician the difference between peace of mind and continual worry and concern over the conduct of office affairs. Since much of the physican's time is spent outside the office, he must feel assured that matters that come up in his absence will be handled with tact, intelligence, and dispatch.

Intelligence is probably the first characteristic the physician seeks in a medical assistant. Educational background, tact, and a charming and pleasant manner will all prove of importance in welcoming patients, in gaining confidence, in making bearable any waiting that would ordinarily prove irksome, and in effecting satisfactory financial arrangements. Through experience the assistant gradually develops intuitive ways with patients, making them feel comfortable and aiding them to adjust to the treatment they are undergoing. In short, a basic understanding of psychology will prove invaluable to the medical assistant. Other desirable or required skills are neatness and orderliness in keeping records, familiarity with the routine of keeping records accurate and up-to-date, and a thorough knowledge of medical office procedures and terminology. These should be supplemented by an acquaintance with the resources of the medical dictionary.

INTEROFFICE RELATIONS

As we mentioned previously, the smooth functioning of the physician's office relieves a great burden from his shoulders and contributes significantly to his peace of mind. Whenever there are several people working together in an office, minor irritations are bound to arise. In a busy office the work load may be distributed among a number of persons. One person might only do laboratory or x-ray work, another might handle the front office, and another might deal with insurance and bookkeeping; all must work together to present the professional atmosphere that patients take for granted when they visit the doctor. Petty arguments and personality clashes can never be allowed to disrupt the cordial relationship and spirit of cooperation that must exist among all the office personnel. Potentially disruptive situations should be straightened out immediately. Sometimes discord can be held to a minimum by well-established personnel policies.

Too many clashes between office personnel are the result of jealousy. It is surprising how many people feel that their jobs are being threatened when someone intrudes into what they consider to be their private bailiwick. There is no room for a rigid caste system in the physician's office. Everyone must work together as a team in order to accomplish the professional objectives of the physician. If the secretary is busy or out to lunch, the bookkeeper may be expected to assist. Likewise, the secretary may be expected to come to the aid of the bookkeeper if necessary. Each individual should be capable and willing to function in a limited way in other capacities for there will always be instances when each must help out the other. Cooperation is the key.

EDUCATION—A CONTINUING PROCESS

In the past, adult education placed most of its emphasis upon remedial education. Today, however, the emphasis has shifted to the broad idea of "continuing education." In other words, adult education is no longer almost exclusively devoted to the process of making up but is now stressing the necessity of keeping up and going ahead. Throughout the country there appear signs of an awakening to the importance and the possibilities of education at the adult level. This awakening has engendered the rebirth of the forgotten proverb, "It's never too late to learn."

Everyone naturally learns from experience to a certain degree, for on-the-job learning is a must. Nevertheless, nondirective or chance learning is certainly not the optimum method of acquiring knowledge. In fact, all of us experience occasions when we become frustrated or discouraged as a result of discovering something new and not having the time to investigate it.

The diligent medical assistant is constantly seeking to increase overall knowledge through daily intellectual curiosity and investigation. It is just such an attitude that will promote a professional value and ultimately increase financial remuneration. There is no shortcut to proper learning. True learning results from conscious and deliberate concentration, and a surplus of time is required to facilitate this situation. The secret, of course, is planning one's time adequately.

Assuming that one desires to improve upon his education, the first step to take in planning is to decide what one wishes to study. The second step to consider in planning is to decide just how one wants to go about studying.

In the event that circumstances make it impossible for the assistant to attend classes regularly, the possibility of taking correspondence courses might be considered. The advantage of correspondence courses is that one can work and study at home and at a convenient pace. Of course, one misses the interchange of ideas that results from classroom discussions.

There are many private, independent, correspondence schools as well as colleges and universities that offer correspondence instruction. The great majority of such institutions specialize in business and vocational subjects. Universities and colleges have added study programs in the liberal arts and technical fields to their list of offerings. Further information about the accredited correspondence schools in existence and the courses they offer may be obtained by writing to any one of the following associations:

National Home Study Council
1601 18th Street, N.W.
Washington, D. C. 20009

National University Extension Association
One Dupont Circle, Suite 360
Washington, D. C. 20036

Adult Education Association
810 18th Street, N.W.
Washington, D. C. 20006

National Education Association
Division of Adult Education
1201 16th Street, N.W.
Washington, D. C. 20036

National Vocational Guidance Association
1607 New Hampshire Avenue, N.W.
Washington, D. C. 20009

American Association of Medical Assistants
One East Wacker Drive
Chicago, Ill. 60601

National Health Council
1740 Broadway
New York, N. Y. 10019

No self-study program would be complete without the inclusion of periodical literature, particularly professional publications and journals. Periodicals provide contemporary information, enabling the reader to keep up with the latest developments in his field of interest. These may be subscribed to and mailed to one's home. However, if cost is an obstacle, one could stop by the library from time to time and read them there. Many libraries allow readers to check out periodicals for use at home for short periods of time. The official journal of the American Association of Medical Assistants, the *Professional Medical Assistant,* also stresses education. In addition to the current news and views of the profession each issue offers clinical refreshers, medical terminology quizzes, and office management tips.

A self-study program requires a great deal of determination but can prove to be very fruitful. Regardless of the form of study, the increased learning will supply the physician's assistant with a great deal of self-satisfaction and at the same time increase the value as a medical assistant.

Review questions

1. List at least five functions of the medical assistant.
2. How does the training of the medical assistant differ from that of the registered nurse?
3. Name several reasons why individuals choose careers as medical assistants.
4. Explain why self-discipline is such an important quality for the medical assistant to possess.
5. Why is a close working relationship between physician and medical assistant so necessary?
6. What is meant by "continuing education"? Why is it important?

Suggested readings

Alsop, G. F., and McBride, M. F.: She's off to work: a guide to successful earnings and living, New York, 1971, Vanguard Press, Inc.

Whitcomb, H., and Lang, R.: Charm: the career girl's guide to personal and business success, New York, 1968, McGraw-Hill Book Co.

Winter, E. L.: Women at work: every woman's guide to successful employment, New York, 1967, Simon & Schuster, Inc.

chapter 2
Obtaining the job

SELF-ANALYSIS

Before the medical assistant has the opportunity to display knowledge and training in a practical situation, a job must first be obtained; little else matters at this point. Securing the right position, particularly the first one, is an important consideration for any prospective employee; a person's initial experience in a chosen field often permanently shapes attitudes toward all aspects of that field.

Those considering careers as medical assistants should first engage in a certain amount of introspection. According to the consensus of opinion, the following general attributes are most often associated with successful achievement in a physician's office.

1. A natural interest in the sciences
2. Accuracy
3. Reliability
4. Enthusiasm
5. A capacity for patience through effort
6. A certain amount of manual dexterity
7. Steady nerves
8. Loyalty
9. Intelligence

Although everyone may not be suited for a career as a medical assistant, there is little need for a psychologic test to confirm or deny one's suitability. Fitness for the field can invariably be determined through personal interviews with a candidate and an objective evaluation of high school records. Perhaps the most important attributes are the so-called intangible ones, which do not lend themselves to measurement. Personality, appearance, and the ability to get along with people are personal assets that largely determine the extent of an individual's success in the physician's office. Moreover, tests should be administered only by those with the proper educational background. Test results by themselves are meaningless unless properly interpreted in the light of other related information. Motivation and potential for success in the medical field are difficult to measure quantitatively.

What a job has to offer in the way of incentives and rewards is always an important consideration in seeking employment. For the individual contemplating whether or not to change positions, the challenge offered by a job is also an im-

---

Glossary

attributes those things that belong especially to someone; his own peculiar possessions

axiom a self-evident or necessary truth; any proposition or principle that is universally accepted

extraneous something that is not intrinsic or essential; foreign

fringe benefits additional rewards given to an employee over and above a regular salary

idiosyncrasy a fundamental peculiarity; a distinctive mental quality or characteristic

introspection the act of looking within, self-examination

plaudit an expression of praise or applause

résumé a recapitulation or summary of one's training, employment experiences, etc.

portant determinant. Realistic job applicants should recognize their aptitudes, their personal characteristics, and the interests and talents they can develop that may be useful to an employer. They owe it to themselves to be aware of failings and handicaps, making every attempt to overcome them, or at the very least to face them squarely. Most introspective questions actually can be reduced to one: Would I hire myself?

Experience indicates that the majority of employers seem to place a premium on an assistant's insight, initiative, tact, and understanding—qualifications that have little to do with basic skills, which apparently most employers take for granted. These intangible qualities, which extend beyond mere competence on the job, can be summarized in three general attributes: courage, decisiveness, and energy.

Courage is a quality employers are always seeking but rarely find in any appreciable degree. It has been truthfully said that fear defeats more people than any other one thing in the world. Worry is so closely akin to fear that only a hairline divides them. The individual whose mind is beset by worries, large or small, cannot do a good job. The only way to stop worrying is to recognize fear and the fact that fear can and must be overcome.

There are on-the-job situations that call for courage, too. We are all familiar with the yes-man and his philosophy. Actually, there are very few employers who really respect a yes-man. The meek soul dreads new responsibility and consequently keeps any ability he might possess a secret.

Along with courage comes the second attribute: decisiveness. The ability to make a decision and stick by it is a rare and highly regarded quality. Nobody admires a person who is unable to make up his mind or who is swayed by every wind of chance and every stray opinion. Firm decisions, based on careful reasoning and a well-calculated risk, are the sign of a person who knows what the job is about and who has the courage to act on that knowledge.

Energy is the third attribute. Mental or physical laziness is inherent in the human makeup, and it is as detrimental to success as a lack of courage or decisiveness. Yet it, too, can be overcome. The way to do this is to assign definite tasks for specific times, if one needs this strict routine in the beginning. The heartening thing about forcing oneself to perform a specific task is that once it is begun it does not seem difficult at all.

One of the surest cures for mental laziness is to have a sense of direction and a goal toward which one is eagerly working. The assistant will find that everything comes more easily when having a definite, clear-cut purpose in life and then working steadily toward that purpose with determination and faith.

Every person has something of his own to give to his job. The "average man" that we so glibly speak about exists only on paper in the form of statistics. Nobody is average; everyone is in some special way himself, possessing qualities and abilities peculiar only to himself.

MAKING THE PROPER APPEARANCE

Naturally, the medical assistant will want to impress a potential employer with qualifications. First, however, he must be impressed, and favorably so, by the assistant's appearance. The fact that first impressions are so lasting makes proper appearance an absolute necessity. The applicant most likely to succeed in obtaining the job is the one who is properly groomed.

Although styles change frequently, good grooming never does; it is always in fashion. Grooming is more a matter of discretion and common sense than a matter of money. Good grooming involves daily upkeep—the day-by-day practice of looking one's best.

Whether we like it or not, first impressions are often lasting ones. This happens to be one of the facts of life we cannot seem to avoid or change. Most of us are well aware of the presence of this phenomenon in our own positive and negative reactions to people. However, these implications take on ever greater proportions for the individual who is job-hunting.

Most firms do not want to spend the time and money to test a potential employee who does not appear to be someone they would want to hire. Moreover, since there are generally more than enough applicants for every available job, employers can afford to be somewhat selective.

Appearance, then, can be and often is the deciding factor in a job interview, for one who does not look the part of an employee, may not become one. Of course, the medical assistant needs more than a well-groomed exterior to land a job. A neat appearance helps get a foot in the door, so to speak, but by itself it is no guarantee of a job.

The impression one makes in an interview depends upon many things: grooming, appearance, personal mannerisms, alertness, interest, and preparation. In order to convey a good impression the applicant should have a carefully groomed look. A woman's hair should be attractively arranged but simply styled and her makeup should be subdued. Dress should be simple and conservative but in good taste. If one doesn't have a comfortable, appropriate business suit or dress, it sometimes pays to invest in one. Some observers even suggest that, whenever practical, a female medical assistant report for an interview in a white uniform. This gives the doctor an opportunity to see how she would look on the job and also serves as an indication of her readiness to go to work.

The applicant's good manners, or the lack thereof, can also exercise a profound effect upon both social contacts and potential employers.

LETTERS OF APPLICATION

The logical way to answer an advertisement for an interesting job or to follow up any other lead that comes one's way is to write a letter of application. There are other ways, of course: telephoning, sending a telegram, and making a personal call. But by far the best way is to write a letter. The cost of a letter is small, and, if directed toward sources that will do the most good, a letter provides an individual with a wider scope for self-description and the selling of services to a prospective employer.

Writing letters of application is therefore a highly important part of an applicant's job-hunting campaign. Setting out with a definite letter-writing strategy in mind, the applicant should attempt to write the perfect letter of application. This perfect letter of application can be sent to every likely employer in the locality as well as to everyone who advertises the kind of job desired.

The primary purpose of a letter of application is not so much to secure a job but to secure an interview. One cannot hope to include a life history in a single letter. Hopefully, enough ground may be covered in the letter of application to intrigue the prospective employer and make him want to see and speak to the applicant, and find out more about personal background. It takes more than a good letter to land a good job; it takes ability, specific experience, and good character. But the letter opens the door and gives one the chance to sell oneself. Letters of application should be kept simple, human, personal, and brief; the briefer they are the better. An effective technique is to say something interesting in the first sentence or two.

Every year millions of letters are sent out by people looking for jobs. An appalling percentage of these letters are a complete waste, for they receive little or no attention. Why? Because they look alike, read alike, and are alike; they show no evidence of creative ability nor any understanding of the qualities required for the job involved. This is precisely the reason a good letter stands apart from the competition.

The prudent medical assistant responding to an advertisement or seeking to initiate a contact will accompany the letter of application with a more detailed account of experience and background in the form of a résumé. A résumé is nothing more than a brief inventory, in outline form, of one's complete background slanted to the job being sought and written as concisely and interesting as possible.

Many employers prefer to study an applicant's résumé before making an appointment for an interview. The résumé saves time by supplying, in advance, answers to pertinent facts such as an applicant's age, social and educational background, health, marital status, employment experience, and any particularly outstanding accomplishments. A résumé should be kept almost as direct and simple as a calling card; its neat and attractive appearance is of the utmost importance.

A campaign of solid, well-written letters of application, each accompanied by a factual one-page résumé, should be enough to secure the assistant more than an adequate number of interviews.

When structuring letters of application and original inquiry, applicants should take note of the following specific points.

1. Letters should be neat, concise, and courteous and should possess good form and content.
2. They should be typewritten whenever possible. If handwritten, the applicant must be careful about penmanship. How one writes is just as important as what one writes.
3. Normally, letters should be no longer than one page (two if absolutely necessary).
4. The applicant should be careful to state the position being sought.
5. The applicant should state the source of information regarding the position.
6. The applicant should very briefly indicate the extent of education, practical training, and experience. The résumé is there for more detailed information.
7. The applicant might include the names and addresses of several references that may be contacted. About three names are sufficient; more than five should not be given. Friends and relatives are not considered objective references.
8. The applicant should include a complete address and telephone number. Health and availability of transportation may also be given.
9. The applicant should request a personal interview to be arranged at the convenience of the employer.

PREPARING FOR THE INTERVIEW

Before going on an interview, the assistant should take the time to find out as much as possible about the physician who plans to interview her and the nature of the practice. This gives her a distinct advantage, for she can then discuss herself in terms of the needs and requirements of the doctor's practice.

Here are a few reminders gathered from employers that could help an applicant in getting ready for an interview.

1. Have all the important facts such as address, telephone number, and Social Security number readily available.
2. Have the necessary papers ready; Social Security card for verification, military discharge papers (if applicable), and diplomas, certificates, and licenses.
3. Be thoroughly familiar with previous work record and educational background. If you did not include a résumé with your original letter of aplication, it is sometimes a good idea to take a résumé along on an interview to help fill in any memory gaps.
4. Know the type of practice the physician engages in and why you want to work for him.
5. Be ready to talk about kinds of work previously performed, training and experience in relation to the job you are seeking, and school record (subjects taken, grades, activities, accomplishments, and so on).
6. Allow plenty of time for missing trains and buses or being delayed in traffic.

Excuses are of little value when you are late for an interview.

7. Personal appearance is all-important. Be extremely careful about grooming and looking professional.

THE INTERVIEW

One of the most important things for the applicant to remember during an interview is to exhibit self-confidence, confidence in one's knowledge and training, and the ability to apply them. During an interview you become your own public relations representative. You are your own best salesman, especially when you are selling yourself. No one else can perform this task quite as effectively.

Personnel studies reveal that a lack of confidence is the most common cause of applicants failing to obtain jobs. Other significant causes include: applying for jobs without having the necessary qualifications, poor appearance and conduct during the personal interview, and overselling one's abilities.

Most management consultants advise physicians to use an imaginative approach to employment interviews. Although the majority of physicians probably have not done enough interviewing to have developed a skilled technique, the applicant should be prepared to deal with leading questions.

The majority of judgmental mistakes in the selection of personnel have been traced to faulty interviewing techniques. A surprising number of experienced interviewers merely rehash data already recorded on the application form, instead of trying to dig behind the facts as presented and study the applicant's attitudes and personality traits. The interviewer's objectives should include weighing the accuracy and truthfulness of an applicant's statements and questioning any gaps or apparent contradictions in the history.

It is equally important to look for self-assurance, personal motivation, realistic thinking, mature self-evaluation, and the candidate's ability for self-expression. The attitudes reflected in the responses may be far more revealing than the actual responses themselves. One of the most valuable tools in the hiring process is a good employment application form.

In order to expose true attitudes, it is often necessary for the physician to ask more penetrating questions than the usual ones concerning previous work experience, education, family and financial responsibilities, and so on. Such questions might include any of the following.

1. Describe a typical day on your present or previous job.
2. Which of your previous bosses did you like best and why?
3. Why do you think you would be successful in this job?
4. What might cause you to fail on the job being discussed?
5. If you get this job, how will you want me to assist you in your work?

Since most physicians know the requirements of the position to be filled, they will usually assume the initiative and ask the questions. Thus it is quite proper to allow the interviewer to conduct the interview. The applicant should display interest in the physician's practice but should avoid an aggressive approach or asking a barrage of questions about such things as fringe benefits, coffee breaks, and vacations. The interviewer will usually cover these items.

The applicant should wait for the interviewer to introduce the subject of salary, for this is sometimes a ticklish problem. When faced with the question of salary, one should try to be realistic and reasonably flexible. The best advice on the matter is to get the physician to make an offer by asking, "How much does your budget afford?" or "How much do you feel I can be worth to you in the position where you can use me?" If the physician presses the issue and desires the applicant to counter with a flat statement, the reply may be, "If you want to know what value others have placed on my services, I earned ________ on that job, and I am presently earning ________ on my current job." The medical assistant who is applying for a first position might refer to the average beginning salaries in the area of those comparably trained.

From there, the discussion can move in either of two directions. The applicant can say, "I would not like to start for less than ________, but I will if necessary." Or "I wouldn't care to make a change for less than ________, or this is less than I really feel I can be worth to you." Such a response leaves the subject open and up to the physician. An applicant should always keep in mind that some jobs may offer less money to start but often prove to be better in the long run because they provide a greater opportunity for advancement.

Employment agencies are continually amazed by the large number of applicants who fail to show up or arrive late for interviews. When an applicant cannot keep an appointment, the interviewer should always be called and so informed.

The medical assistant should take note of the following suggested rules of behavior when reporting for an employment interview.

1. Act self-confident but not overly so. Try not to act too nervous; however, most interviewers expect an applicant to be a bit nervous at first.
2. Be on time. Never be late, but do not be too early, either. Arrive approximately 10 to 15 minutes before the appointed time. Have a pen or pencil handy.
3. Let the physician take the lead in the interview and adjust to his conversation.
4. Be businesslike and brief.
5. Ask for a specific job or type of work Don't say, "I'll take anything." Be flexible and willing, but indicate preferences. Never beg for a job.
6. Stress your qualifications for the job and your interest in it.
7. Give only the information asked for.
8. Pick up clues given you by the physician's questions or statements and use them as evidence that you fit the requirements.
9. Have your papers arranged for easy reference.
10. Avoid mention of your personal, domestic, or financial problems. Discuss only matters related to the job.
11. Watch personal mannerisms such as gum chewing, smoking, fiddling with your purse, or jingling coins.
12. Have a definite understanding as to what is to be required of you before you are hired. This will avoid disappointment for you and the employer.
13. Be sure you pronounce the physician's name correctly.
14. Smile occasionally, but try not to laugh nervously. Speak softly and pleasantly.
15. Use good English and avoid slang.
16. Be as natural as you can. Be yourself.
17. Make no rash promises.
18. Make no complaint about a former employer.
19. Be sure you understand hours, salary, vacations clearly.
20. When the doctor wants to end the interview, take the hint.
21. If possible, be ready to go to work immediately if you are asked.
22. Keep up your courage if the employer doesn't take you. You may not get the first job you seek.
23. As you leave, thank the physician for the courtesy of seeing you.
24. No matter what the outcome, do not show too much enthusiasm or disappointment.
25. If you are not interested in the position, say so in a courteous manner and leave.

If nothing is settled during the interview, it is a good practice for the applicant to follow up the interview with a letter of appreciation, thanking the prospective employer for the courtesy shown and suggesting the availability for further questioning. Such a letter arriving when the employer is considering four or five applicants may influence the final decision.

PRACTICING EFFECTIVE HUMAN RELATIONS

Obtaining the job is one thing; retaining it is quite another matter. The successful medical assistant is one who, recognizing any flaws and weaknesses, constantly strives to improve upon them. This kind of perseverance can only bring plaudits from an employer.

An association of long standing is to be encouraged, for it provides the physician with a feeling of security; he realizes that his assistant not only understands his methods but also his personal idiosyncrasies. With time, the medical assistant should become more and more of an asset to the physician who employs her.

It is to the physician's advantage to select someone who not only has the attributes previously mentioned but also possesses particular qualities that complement his own. For instance, if he forgets appointments and dislikes writing letters, his assistant should have a good memory, be faithful with reminders, and be able to express herself both in writing and verbally. Furthermore, if he is poor with figures and considers himself awkward at collecting fees and securing payments, his assistant should be able to keep an adequate set of books and handle financial arrangements with patients.

Though it would be extremely difficult to obtain the services of such a paragon, it is sometimes possible to find a person in whom will be united a sufficient number of desirable qualities. Once chosen, however, to do an effective job, the assistant must be imbued with a sense of responsibility, a feeling of freedom and independence, and the certainty that the service being performed is eminently worth doing.

It is of the utmost importance that all medical office personnel, especially medical assistants, know what is expected of them. Too many physicians hire an office assistant, then heave a great sigh of relief and say, "Now go to work." To do the job well an assistant must be thoroughly trained in the specific office routine and the duties clearly outlined. This is particularly important in an office with more than one employee. In order to avoid misunderstanding, each office should have posted a written personnel policy covering sick leave, vacations, raises, holidays, and so on. If there are more than one or two employees, there should be posted a written statement documenting the primary responsibilities of each of the employees.

Once a specific task has been assigned to an employee, overzealous supervision on the part of the employer frequently acts as a hindrance to performance. The employee who is aware that every move is being watched is placed under a nervous strain that often interferes with intelligent effort. Office work proceeds better without thoughtless interference.

Harsh discipline, demands for stringent observance of rules, frequent loss of temper, overwork, and underpay eventually react to the disadvantage of the physician-employer. The average physician's office employs a very small staff, and, provided they were selected carefully and diligently, the sincere cooperation of all should be channeled toward effective achievement. The physician cannot afford to allow a personality clash in the office to disrupt its smooth operation. This is one of the most frequent causes for dismissal of office personnel.

The physician should not expect the same acumen in an employee that he himself might exhibit under similar circumstances. Breakage, mistakes, and misunderstandings should be tolerated within certain bounds as being human and to some extent inevitable. An employer who is easily aroused and impulsive must learn to control his emotions and temper his judgment before acting.

"Praise in public, but always criticize in private," is a worthwhile axiom for any employer to keep in mind. If an employee has been scolded unjustly, it is only fair for the doctor to apologize and attempt to make amends. The doctor should always be careful not to show favoritism, for it can become a constant source of jealousy and friction in his office. The physician who shows consideration and sympathy in dealing with the staff may reasonably expect to receive their full cooperation in return, and as a consequence will find many of the burdens of professional life lessened.

Human relations is by no means a "one-way street." Every employee is ethically bound to display a certain sense of loyalty and responsibility to the employer and the job, even after the position has become unsatisfactory. There is more to quitting a job than mere laying down one's pencil, telling off the boss, and walking out. Incidentally, whether an assistant holds a job while looking for another or has plans to quit first, there is an obligation to the job, the employer, and any co-workers. There is a moral duty to continue doing the work just as efficiently and cheerfully as if the present job were going to be permanent.

OPPORTUNITIES AVAILABLE

Regardless of one's ambitions, preparing for a career is like an insurance policy. Should a woman, for example, desire to work later on, or should she want to go back to work after her children are grown, adequate preparation will increase her chances for obtaining interesting and well-paying jobs.

The curricula of those institutions engaged in training medical assistants are primarily designed to prepare young people to deal with the daily occurrences in the physician's office. Although the majority of opportunities are in the physician's office, the medical assistant or medical secretary is not necessarily limited to the doctor's office. For those who possess a working knowledge of medical terminology, anatomy and physiology, medical office procedures, and have good secretarial skills, the opportunities are unlimited. Furthermore, physicians are always on the lookout for competent medical secretaries capable of assuming front office responsibilities only.

The following is a list of potential employment settings for well-qualified medical assistants and secretaries.

1. The physician's office
2. Hospitals
3. Clinics
4. Insurance companies
5. Dentists' offices
6. Public health agencies
7. Public school districts
8. Social Security Administration
9. Research foundations
10. Medical supply houses, drug firms, and so on
11. Convalescent homes
12. County welfare agencies
13. University medical schools
14. Medical research and assisting writers in the preparation of manuscripts
15. Medical publishing houses

It is readily apparent from the foregoing list that a career in this field is hardly devoid of variety. However, this list is by no means an exhaustive one. The opportunities for trained allied medical personnel are continually growing. The increased demand for medical services resulting from the numerous innovations in medicine is no doubt partly responsible for the existing state of affairs. The advent of Medicare and Medicaid has further increased the demand for medical services and consequently expanded the opportunities for well-trained medical assistants. A national health insurance system will add to this demand.

The graduate medical assistant in search of a job should register with the school's placement department. Almost all of the reputable private schools as well as the public institutions maintain free placement services for their graduates. This then becomes the applicant's source of primary contact. Other channels for making job contacts include the following.

1. The business offices of local medical societies.
2. Medical supply houses
3. State department of employment
4. Detail men and medical supply salesmen
5. Newspaper advertisements

6. Family physicians
7. Medical journals
8. Commercial employment agencies
9. Local medical assistants organizations

Review questions

1. List several attributes possessed by the majority of successful medical assistants.
2. What intangible qualities do employers look for in a prospective employee?
3. Why is proper grooming so essential to a successful interview?
4. What is the purpose of the letter of application? Why do so many go unanswered?
5. Compare a letter of application with a résumé as to function and content.
6. What advantage does an applicant gain by preparing for an interview?
7. When an employer raises the question of salary during the interview, what should be the reaction of the applicant?
8. Describe the employment outlook for those entering a career in any of the allied medical fields.

Suggested readings

Winter, E. L.: Women at work: every woman's guide to successful employment, New York, 1967, Simon & Schuster, Inc.

Vogel, E.: How to write your job-getting résumé and covering letter, Brooklyn, N. Y., 1971, Copy-Write Artograph Co.

chapter 3

Development of medical science

PRIMITIVE MEDICINE

Primitive medicine resulted from man's superstitious interpretation of the facts of nature. Over the years, his thinking in medical matters has been greatly influenced by religious, moral, economic, and philosophic considerations. In many instances these influences have produced favorable scientific results, such as when the church pressed for the construction of hospitals for the sick, as well as results detrimental to science, such as when it was considered immoral to violate a corpse for purposes of dissection. It is interesting to take note that each step in the progress of medicine was the product of the culture of the times.

In the earliest days of civilization, mystery, magic, and medicine were synonymous. Primitive man was curiously imaginative, and he believed that evil spirits and angry gods were responsible for diseases. Without having sufficient facts to explain cause-and-effects relationships, primitive man assumed many things. He therefore attributed many of the unexplained phenomena in his environment to supernatural powers or those beyond his control. We find that very little of his thinking could be classified as rational and scientific even in the broad sense.

Witch doctors were thought to have special powers to drive away evil spirits. Throughout the ages gullible people have fallen victim to the unorthodox healer. In many instances the patent medicine man of today is as guilty of taking advantage of the credulity of his customers as was the witch doctor.

Coincidentally, primitive physicians discovered and used many drugs that form the basis for many of our modern medicines. Their motivation, however, in treating the afflicted was to rid the patient of evil spirits that were thought to be responsible for his symptoms. Today's physicians treat the sick in order to destroy bacteria and other natural causes of disease. Thus it was accidentally discovered that chewing leaves of the foxglove plant, which was eventually discovered to contain digitalis, could slow a rapidly beating heart. The bark of certain

---

Glossary

archeologist one who studies history from relics and remains of antiquities

caduceus symbol of the medical profession

detriment something that impairs or injures or causes damage or loss

gullible capable of being persuaded to believe anything

Hellenistic resembling Greek thought or style; Greek with a mixture of foreign elements

hieroglyphics a form of picture-writing, especially of the ancient Egyptians

noxious causing or tending to cause injury, as to health or morals

precursor one who or that which precedes and gives intimation of a coming event

primitive pertaining to the beginning or origin; earliest; simplest form

supernatural existing or occurring through some agency above the forces of nature; caused miraculously or by the immediate exercise of divine power

unorthodox not in agreement with accepted standards

trees (quinine) was found to help control fever. Juice was squeezed from the belladonna plant (atropine) and used in the relief of pain caused by abdominal cramps.

Superstition played a dominant role in the healing arts from early antiquity. This type of practice was characteristic of the civilizations that thrived in the so-called fertile crescent area of the Middle East—the Mesopotamians, the Babylonians, the Assyrians, and, of course, the Egyptians. Interestingly enough, the healing methods that were developed and used by a group of primitive savages in one part of the world were very similar to those of another group of primitives residing in a distant land. In fact, to go a step further, the practices of the primitive healers of thousands of years ago are still in existence and are used today by primitive peoples in backward parts of Africa, New Guinea, and Yucatan.

From the earliest times for which we possess historical documents, in primitive drawings, in popular songs, and in epic legends the serpents has occupied a most important place among supernatural beings. Traces of serpent worship (ophiolatry) have been found in every country of the world and survive even today in India, Egypt, and many other countries. In America the worship of the serpent has been preserved among some Indian groups, thus sustaining faith in the miraculous power of the serpent.

The reason for this worship is easily explained. The serpent alone, of all animals without limbs, moves with singular speed. Its motion is a continued progression in the most graceful curves; its form is full of elegance; the eyes are bright and piercing and seem to possess a fascinating power. The serpent seems to appear and disappear in an inexplicable way and to prefer the deep regions of the earth; one of its most remarkable qualities is that it periodically casts its skin, and the ancients obviously concluded that it renewed its youth.

The deadly action of the poisonous fang of the snake was well known among primitive peoples. The first conception of the serpent and its supernatural power was probably connected with this fact.

In Greek legend, Asclepius (the Romans called him Aesculapius) was the god of healing and was always represented with the serpent coiled around his staff, the symbol of power. Hence the serpent became permanently connected with Aesculapius, and serpents were protected and fed in many of the ancient sanctuaries.

It is quite apparent that the serpent was considered a living deity, capable of interfering in the affairs of man. Since the first attribute believers demand instinctively of any divinity is the power to cure disease and to prolong human life, the serpent was the first of all healing gods and perhaps the one whose reign has been most lasting. The symbol of the serpent as a healer has been universally accepted.

In modern times the serpent has found its official recognition and place as the symbol of the medical profession itself and on the emblem of the medical corps in the various armies of the world. The caduceus, as it is called, consists of a staff with two snakes twined around it and a pair of wings on top.

Primitive medicine represents the expression of a philosophy that arises from the natural reactions of all ignorant men who find themselves in strange and hazardous surroundings. Long before any form of civilization appeared, savage man was not, as some people believe, a carefree creature living a free and idealistic life in the midst of abundance. Instead, however, this precursor of modern man was a terror-driven, ignorant savage facing a hostile environment. By day he was forced to slink through the rough terrain in search of food in constant fear of death by stronger men and wild animals. When darkness fell, he hid from unseen terrors. He trembled before the lightning and fell prostrate before the thunder. When convulsed in the agony of disease he reacted like a dumb beast; when injured he would retreat to his lair to either die of hunger or be murdered by his stronger adversaries.

Obviously, the lot of early man was not a bright one. Those experiences he was unable to understand he attributed to ghosts and spirits. The savage of yesterday believed that supernatural forces brought disease. Thus it was only natural that in order to prevent or cure disease the evil spirits would have to be controlled or driven away.

The medicine man of ancient times is known to have treated some patients who suffered from severe headaches by performing an operation known as trephining. This operation involved opening an area of the patient's skull, which was accomplished with crude stone instruments. The opening in the skull known as the trephine was supposed to allow the evil spirit responsible for all the trouble to escape. Strangely enough this operation had the desirable effect of relieving a certain amount of pressure on the brain. Archeologists examining the skulls of primitive men have discovered that in some cases there was evidence of healing around the opening in the skull, indicating that not only did some individuals survive the operation, but that they also probably lived for some time afterwards.

As the centuries passed and tribal organization grew, the medicine man grew in stature both as priest and doctor. Few people dared to doubt the wisdom of his teachings, which only more firmly entrenched his position.

Even before man discovered how to make and use fire, he had unearthed certain roots. These, he realized, served not only as nourishment but also as relaxers and stimulants. Gradually it was found that combining many of these herbs and substances produced more spectacular results. Thus the herbalist, the soothsayer, the conjurer, and the wizard came into existence to assume positions of tribal leadership and power.

Although most of the earliest remedies were not grounded, to say the least, in scientific fact, they offered the patient hope. Those who were strong believers sometimes were cured. These early traces of psychosomatic medicine help to substantiate the fact that it is not a totally new phenomenon; yet it still remains one of the greatest of medical mysteries.

An old Greek idea still popular in certain rural areas in this country is that of rubbing a toad on a wart in order to make it fall off. The Romans would hang red coral about their necks to ward off the evil eye. The contemporary practice of wrapping a sore throat with red flannel material had its origin in England during the reign of Edward II. Apparently his son was afflicted with smallpox and was placed in a room where a red cloth was hung from the ceiling. His subsequent recovery and cure were therefore attributed to the flannel, and the color red was thought to be effective in driving away evil spirits.

Few, if any, of these practices have any basis in scientific fact, and yet many of them are still in widespread use. The world of today is far from being free of superstitions and magic. There is much wisdom in the observation of William James that, "As long as people believe in ghosts there are ghosts." Although the witchcraft trials of the seventeenth century were replete with false accusations and utter nonsense, the fact remains that many of the accused witches were able, through the power of suggestion, to render their victims helpless and, in certain instances, cause death with their curses.

CONCEPTS AMONG THE ANCIENTS

The first civilization of which we have any extensive knowledge is that of the Egyptians. Most history texts begin their treatises of modern man with the development of hieroglyphics (a crude form of picture writing). Very little was actually known about the Egyptians until the early part of the nineteenth century. Some troops of Napoleon accidentally discovered the Rosetta stone, which was captured by the British in 1801 and which later unlocked the key to the mystery of translating hieroglyphics.

The medicine of the Egyptians constituted

a combination of superstition, religion, and some practical considerations. The gods were invoked to heal, but they also administered medicines to the sick and used splints for fractures. Burnt sponge was used to treat conditions similar to goiter. Today doctors use iodine, a medication similar in many aspects. The Egyptian physicians were quite adept in the diagnosis and treatment of numerous diseases. They also performed many different kinds of operations, including surgery to relieve cranial pressure (trephining).

The first step toward scientific inquiry and break with the pure superstition and mysticism of the primitives was made by the Greeks. They attempted to study nature objectively by considering the human body and its diseases as a definite part of nature. Thus they were the first people to formulate lucid descriptions of the body and its ailments without resorting to the supernatural. The Greeks became the first civilization to enunciate principles of scientific medicine and effect a separation of religion and medicine. It was they who first removed mystery from medicine, helping to make it not a practice of magic or religion but one of common sense, observation, and logical reasoning. They also were first to realize the importance of research in medical practice.

Hippocrates, who is often referred to as the father of medicine and who lived during the golden age of Greek culture (circa 400 B.C.), developed great skill in diagnosis. Hippocrates was careful to record case histories noting the symptoms of the various diseases. Although crude, Hippocrates' concepts of treatment were far superior to the prevalent exorcistic practices of the times. In fact, many doctors today still refer to his descriptions of certain diseases, such as pneumonia and pleurisy.

Hippocrates was chiefly responsible for establishing a high standard of ethics for the physician. There is much in the spirit of the ethical code introduced by Hippocrates, known as the Oath of Hippocrates, that is applicable to the present day practice of medicine.

According to Hippocrates, the world consisted of four essential elements: fire, air, earth, and water. He reasoned that the human body consisted of four similar elements, which could be demonstrated by observation of the blood. Disease, he thought, created an imbalance in these four elements of the blood and therefore disease was caused by a faulty mixture of body fluids. As a result, blood-letting was used as a therapeutic device to remove the noxious materials from the body and restore normalcy. Patients were encouraged to drink a great amount of water with the idea that the toxic body fluids could be diluted and neutralized.

Greek philosophers Plato and Aristotle wrote extensively concerning the individual's responsibility in criminal actions. Plato clearly felt that the mentally disturbed person was not responsible for his acts and should not receive punishment in the same manner as normal persons. Through his writings Plato contributed a better understanding of human behavior by pointing out that man, as well as other forms of life, was motivated by physiologic needs or natural appetites.

Unfortunately, the Greeks did not engage in dissection of the human body, and the little knowledge they did possess regarding anatomy and physiology was derived primarily from bedside observation of patients. Greek physicians would note certain symptoms and the eventual disposition of the patient, endeavoring to correlate other experiences wherever they applied.

The Romans became the cultural descendants of the Greeks. The Romans inherited their knowledge of medicine from the Greeks and developed it further. Greek physicians were practicing in Rome around 300 B.C. In 46 B.C., recognizing the potential contribution of the Greek methods, Julius Caesar granted Roman citizenship to all freeborn Greek physicians in Rome.

The Greeks must be given credit for establishing the importance of personal hygiene, but it remained for the Romans to develop public health. From a medical standpoint the greatest contribution of the Roman period was sanitation. Recognizing the urgent need for a system of sanitary engineering, they set about draining swamps, building aqueducts to carry fresh water to their cities, and constructing a system of sewers to carry off wastes.

Surgery was a highly developed art in Rome, as was substantiated by the unearthing of some 200 or more surgical instruments near Pompeii. Unfortunately, the dissection of the human body was considered to be a sacrilegious act by the Romans, just as it was by the Greeks.

Most medical historians rank Galen as the most famous of Roman physicians. He performed many experiments that served to demonstrate the facts of physiology. In A.D. 162 Galen brilliantly described both the involuntary and autonomic central nervous systems. Galen studied anatomy extensively at the medical school in Alexandria and was the physician of the Roman gladiators. Despite his great contributions, Galen misconstrued the actual function of the heart and blood vessels and thus retarded knowledge concerning the circulatory system.

EFFECTS OF THE RENAISSANCE (1350-1650)

For all practical purposes the fall of Rome occurred around A.D. 475. Immediately following the collapse of the Roman Empire, there ensued a period during which very little progress of any kind was made. During this period, known as the Dark Ages (A.D. 400 to A.D. 800), life was extremely difficult for civilized man. Great hordes of barbarians roamed the Western world plundering, murdering, and destroying. People lived in continual fear for their lives. Small wonder that under such circumstances the lamp of learning was practically extinguished except for that carried on by the monks. Incidentally, it was the conditions of the Dark Ages that precipitated the development of the feudal system of the medieval period.

Historians disagree as to the exact dates of the Middle Ages, also known as the medieval period. However, for purposes of this discussion, we will accept A.D. 800 to A.D. 1400 as constituting medieval times, the dividing line between ancient and modern history. During this period medicine continued to be practiced largely in the great monasteries. The monks grew herbs which they used for treatment. We owe them a debt of gratitude for collecting and translating the work of Greek and Roman physicians. The medieval period witnessed a tremendous destruction of human life caused by the relentless spread of the bubonic plague, better known as the black death. It is estimated that the plague killed some 20,000,000 people in Europe. Other diseases, such as syphilis and smallpox, took their silent toll of life. Doctors had little defense against these diseases.

As the Renaissance, the period of great cultural and scientific activity, began to make itself felt throughout Europe, there were several developments that profoundly influenced the course of medicine. The university was established during this period, and along with it the medical school. At long last an environment was provided where research and instruction in the medical arts could thrive in a more systematic manner. Several well-known medical schools were founded, all of which served as disseminators of past medical knowledge. The great discoveries of the Hellenistic culture and Roman, Hebrew, and Arabian medicine were taught there.

Another important development that also strongly modified the evolution of medicine was the change in man's pattern of thought. He began to develop more confidence in his own ability to cope with mundane problems. Many truths that had been handed down from century to century were questioned and challenged by the Renaissance man. This constituted a revolt against tradition and the authority of the church. Man was no longer merely satisfied with reading about the works of the ancients; he wanted to explore things for himself.

The third major development of this period was the invention of printing. Until the fifteenth century the only sources of books were the monasteries, where often a single monk would devote his entire life to the copying of an original ancient manuscript or book. This was the only way books could be multiplied and knowledge transmitted. With the invention of the printing press, the written word became available to a multitude of readers.

Galileo is credited with establishing the method of scientific inquiry that produced principles fundamental to the workings of other branches of science. Francis Bacon also typified the prevailing thirst for additional knowledge. He was probably the first scientist to fully utilize the so-called inductive method of analyzing scientific problems. This method involves the collecting and tabulating of all recorded and observable facts in an experiment, paving the way for general conclusions concerning related phenomena. No aspect of knowledge or the arts escaped the spirit of the Renaissance.

Philippus Paracelsus, a Swiss physician, contributed much understanding to the treatment of diseases with drugs. Often referred to as the Martin Luther of medicine, he helped to overthrow the dominance of ancient medical authority. Most doctors of his time used drugs in the treatment of all diseases. Usually these medicines consisted of numerous different ingredients. Paracelsus pointed out that when one ingredient was combined with another one they would cancel out each other's effectiveness. He persuaded his colleagues to find the drug that was most effective against a particular disease.

Through his travels, Paracelsus learned a great deal about medical practice from barbers, executioners, bath keepers, gypsies, midwives, and fortune-tellers. Paracelsus discarded the herb medicines of Galen and substituted strong mineral medicines such as mercury, lead, sulphur, iron, and arsenic. While preaching for revolt against dogmatic authority, he advocated man's right to individual judgment.

Andreas Vesalius was the first true anatomist. During the 1500s he served as a professor of anatomy and physiology at the University of Padua. His research findings were published in a book that furnished the first complete descriptions of the human body. Although many of his ideas were eventually proved wrong, his work helped to destroy many of the false beliefs about the structure of the body.

Vesalius was not the first to dissect the human body. His predecessor was the great artist and scientist Leonardo da Vinci. Da Vinci pioneered in dissection and studied the human body in detail in order to enhance the accuracy of his drawings. His pictures of the various parts of the human anatomy were truly magnificent.

The fact that relatively few physicians had intelligently examined the internal organs of the body was perhaps the most serious handicap to the advancement of medical science down through the ages and into the medieval period. The social stigma attached to the dissection of the dead lingered despite the needless waste of human life and general cruelty that characterized the times. The spirit of scientific inquiry engendered by the Renaissance was chiefly responsible for overcoming this prejudice. The Renaissance man finally came to realize that only through scientific examination of the dead could knowledge of anatomy and physiology be advanced.

POST-RENAISSANCE CONTRIBUTIONS

It was not enough to know the structure of the human body. The scientific physician also needed to understand the internal functioning of bodily organs. Man's knowledge of physiology remained in the embryonic stages until the 1600s when William Harvey, an English physician, accurately described the manner in which the blood circulates through the body. For centuries men believed that the blood flowed back and forth in the body, much like the ebb and flow of ocean tides. Harvey demonstrated that the heart pumps blood into the arteries and that the veins return the blood back to the heart. Experimenting with animals, he actually viewed and felt the heart beating. He was the first to apply mathematical measurements in his medical research. Harvey's great contribution to medical knowledge helped to substantiate the close interdependence between the structure of the body and its internal workings.

In spite of the detail of Harvey's animal experiments and use of mathematics, he failed to describe the linkage between the arteries and veins that permitted blood to flow from one to the other. In 1661, four years after Harvey's death, an Italian anatomist, Marcello Malpighi, showed that capillaries connect the arteries to the veins.

Although the Renaissance had generated a great deal of scientific inquiry and logical thinking, the majority of physicians merely paid lip service to this spirit, never allowing it to transcend the philosophical level. Their speculations remained vague, and their medications were administered more because of their presumed qualities than their actual medical effects.

A British physician named Thomas Sydenham appeared on the scene and called for a return to the principles of Hippocrates. Because of his outspoken manner, he was not held in high esteem by his contemporaries. Much of his work was left to posterity, not to be appreciated until the eighteenth century. Sydenham sought to restore clinical medicine back to the simple scientific principles of observation and logical reasoning. Many of his clinical descriptions remain fundamental, such as his clear-cut distinction between measles and scarlet fever and his distinction between chorea and gout.

The discovery of the microscope provided doctors with a method of studying bacteria. Anton van Leeuwenhoek, a Dutch lens maker and amateur scientist, produced the early forerunner of the microscope. He saw many kinds of bacteria through his crude microscope, such as the *Streptococcus spirillum* and others, but was not able to associate them with any particular disease. However, the role of bacteria in the cause of disease was not to be recognized until about 150 years later.

The seventeenth and eighteenth centuries were characterized by a tremendous increase in the accumulation of factual knowledge. Edward Jenner, an English physician, was the man responsible for relieving humanity of one of its greatest scourges. In the latter part of the 1700s Jenner made one of the greatest contributions toward the prevention of disease when he discovered a method of vaccination against smallpox. He was never quite sure why this prophylactic technique worked, but he did prove that people could be saved from smallpox even after they had been exposed to the disease.

The importance of Jenner's work became more apparent as time went on. In 1779, some 15,000 persons died from smallpox. In 1823, only 37 people were victims of the dread disease. Jenner's discovery led to the science of immunology, the prevention of disease by building up a bodily resistance to it, which started people to think more seriously about public health and preventive medicine.

Medicine progressed quite rapidly during the nineteenth century. In fact, preventive medicine was actually launched during the nineteenth century. Great discoveries in chemistry and physics were applied to research in physiologic problems. The medical advances of the nineteenth century, particularly those arising from the demonstration of the bacterial cause of infection, made medicine a social necessity and a guiding force in modern civilization.

Although Leeuwenhoek and several other seventeenth century pioneers in the use of the microscope described some very small forms of life that they were able to see through their lenses, the real significance and origin of these bodies was not actually understood until they were investigated by Louis Pasteur. Pasteur was a French bacteriologist and chemist whose work closely paralleled that of a German physician named Koch. Koch is generally credited with discovering the tubercle bacillus. The research of both men showed that bacteria exist everywhere simultaneous and do not necessarily come into being in the patient's body as a result of his illness. Both men proved that sterilization kills bacteria.

Pasteur studied the process of fermentation, demonstrating that yeast cells were partly responsible for this phenomenon. Of course, his name is most commonly associated with pasteurization, the process that bears his name, whereby food is heated to prevent the growth of bacteria.

The identification and classification of the various organisms were greatly facilitated by the work of Paul Ehrlich. Ehrlich is credited with developing the technique of differential staining of bacteria and the various types of cells.

The conquering of diphtheria and of typhoid fever stand out as shining examples of man's determination in the fight against disease. It is common knowledge that during the Spanish-American War many more soldiers died of typhoid fever than were actually killed in battle. The same situation existed during the Crimean War, where more soldiers were casualties of disease than of actual combat. Typhoid fever has now been brought under complete control.

DEVELOPMENT OF SURGERY

Because surgery is primarily dependent upon a knowledge of anatomy, it remained relatively primitive until the Renaissance. Later, Joseph Lister, born in 1827, made use of the new knowledge of bacteria to make surgery safe. He understood the relationship of bacteria to operative wounds and thus introduced the idea of antisepsis. Lister searched for a substance that, if applied to wounds, would kill the bacteria present without inflicting serious injury to the tissue and that at the same time would prevent the entrance of other bacteria from the outside. He thought he found this in carbolic acid, which he used for cleaning out wounds and dressing them. This form of dressing wounds proved unsatisfactory since carbolic acid also did damage to surrounding tissue. Since it was generally thought that bacteria also came from the air in the operating room, Lister ordered the operating room to be sprayed with carbolic acid. This was not without its adverse effects, for the air frequently became saturated with the substance, which rendered surgeons ill and hampered their performance. Later he discovered that contamination by instruments and transmission of bacteria from one person to another were much more important causes of infection.

For centuries surgery remained in the hands of barber-surgeons, who were certainly not at the top of the social scale. It is interesting to note that the stripes on the poles outside barber shops represent strips of bandages as they were worn by patients. The surgeon did not attain any degree of respectability until the eighteenth century.

Besides Joseph Lister no other single individual made more of a contribution to the advancement of surgery than John Hunter. Often referred to as the father of modern surgery, Dr. Hunter, a British practitioner, helped to elevate the status of surgery to the level of medicine. He performed a great number of experimental operations on the grounds of his estate, where he housed a great many different kinds of animals. Hunter also founded the English School of Surgery, which remains in existence to this day.

Until the early 1840s the necessity for speed to reduce the pain and shock of operations precluded the development of the accuracy and precision that are characteristic of modern surgery. In the United States, Dr. Crawford Long, a physician, and Dr. William Morton, a dentist, helped to make anesthesia safe for surgery. Apparently, both men began to use ether as an anesthetic at about the same time. The use of anesthetics has made possible the performance of many operations that otherwise could not have been previously undertaken. Moreover, surgery became a practical way of conquering many diseases.

The twofold advancement of alleviation

of pain and freedom from infection enabled surgery to progress rapidly. Speed was no longer a primary concern, and surgical operations could be allowed to last longer, thus increasing precision and care. The penetration by surgeons of parts of the body that were previously considered inaccessible was also made possible.

The extent to which surgery had progressed was best illustrated by the achievements of World War II, especially in surgery of the heart. Furthermore, very few of the wounded died if they survived long enough to reach an aid station. The great strides made in surgical techniques are due in large part to the many improvements made in postoperative care.

PROGRESS IN NURSING

The professional career of nursing is a comparatively recent development. However, nursing has been practiced by women outside of their own homes since the early days of Christianity. Noblewomen, including the wives of the emperors, helped care for the ill in ancient Rome. During the crusades, militant groups of monks and knights tended the sick and wounded.

St. Vincent de Paul was the first to encourage the formal training of nurses. The initial hospital training school for nurses was established in 1836 at Kaiserswerth, Germany. It was here that Florence Nightingale received her training. The efforts of Florence Nightingale and her gallant troop of dedicated women did a great deal to alleviate the suffering of the ill and wounded during the Crimean War (1853-1856).

Doctors looked upon her work with disdain and thought her to be little more than a busybody and a meddler. After many disappointments and a long struggle, Florence Nightingale succeeded in mobilizing public opinion behind her efforts to improve the care of the sick. The principles she established have served as a fundamental guide for nursing progress, and the school she established at St. Thomas's Hospital, London, has served as a pattern for subsequent nursing schools. The first nursing schools in the United States were established in 1873 at Massachusetts General Hospital in Boston, New Haven Hospital in Connecticut, and Bellevue Hospital in New York City.

Prior to the middle half of the nineteenth century hospitals were not exactly the place to go if one was seriously ill. Most hospitals were constructed for charity patients and staffed by untrained and often disreputable women. Needless to say, wealthy people did not go to hospitals to seek treatment. Preventive medicine was in its infant stages, and the necessity for sanitation and cleanliness was unknown. Hospital personnel were not aware that they were contributing to the spread of disease, and many contracted contagious diseases from their patients.

There were others besides Florence Nightingale who made outstanding contributions to the advancement of nursing. Rating high among these is Lillian Wald, who is credited with placing public health nursing on a firm and practical foundation. She championed the idea that the health needs of patients were closely related to their social needs. She was instrumental in founding the Henry Street Settlement House in New York City, which served as an example of all communities to observe and emulate.

The passage of the Bolton Act in 1941 illustrated the government's concern for a corps of trained nurses and is considered a tribute to the importance of their work. According to this act, Congress appropriated $1,250,000 to finance a training program for nurses in the interests of national defense.

The contribution of the professional registered nurse to the progress of medicine has been basically dependent upon the raising of standards in nursing education. Legislation regulating the practice of nursing was initiated in the twentieth century. The registered nurse was gradually accorded true professional status not only because of an ability to perform in an excellent manner but because it was proved to the physician that an educated nurse is far superior to an uneducated one. Nursing education has continually improved and expanded in scope to meet modern needs. The federal government, realizing the critical shortage of trained nurses, has provided funds to stimulate the construction of training schools and has made loans available to qualified candidates.

For centuries nursing was regarded by most people as consisting almost entirely of bedside care, baths, and bedpans. However, with the ability of the nurse to demonstrate a skill and comprehension of medical matters, came an increasing measure of responsibility.

Today's registered nurse is prepared to relieve the physician of scores of duties and functions that were formerly his sole responsibility. A visit to a modern hospital reflects significant changes in nursing personnel and functions. Much of the actual bedside care has been taken over by nurses' aides or practical nurses.

Public health nurses have made significant contributions in caring for the sick and in the prevention of disease. They work in a variety of places: homes, clinics, schools, and industrial plants. Public health nurses may be employed by city, county, or state health departments. They are often involved in teaching patients with chronic illnesses how to care for themselves. They also instruct patients and their families about proper diet, personal cleanliness, and other methods of preventing disease. They often take part in community health projects such as polio vaccination and chest x-ray campaigns. The public health nurse has been a strong educational force.

The fields of industrial medicine and industrial hygiene have provided new vistas for the registered nurse, and the demand for nurses in industry is a continuing one. Company-wide programs stressing the importance and desirability of safety practices by employees have given indirect impetus to this need. Industrial firms over the years have assumed a greater share of responsibility in providing medical treatment and first aid for their employees.

All states have registration laws requiring the registered nurse to pass a written examination and obtain a license before being allowed to practice. These laws are for the protection of both the nurse and the patient. The registered nurse therefore becomes legally responsible for the consequences of any professional act.

The American Nurses' Association, an organization for professional registered nurses, was first organized in 1896. The *American Journal of Nursing* is the official publication for nurses in the United States.

The majority of practicing registered nurses in the United States and Canada have received their professional training in hospital-based schools of nursing. More commonly referred to as "diploma schools," they offer a three-year program of study. In recent years, however, there has been a marked shift in emphasis from programs that are hospital-based to those based in colleges and universities having clinical affiliations with hospitals. This trend has resulted in the phasing out of many diploma schools and the rapid growth of collegiate programs, both the two-year technical and the four-year baccalaureate nursing curricula. Perhaps the main reason for this development is economic. Hospital costs are now subject to much closer scrutiny, making it more difficult for the hospital to pass along the costs of education to its patients.

Nursing is currently in a state of evolution. The pressure of striving for recognition as a profession, combined with the changes in duties, in responsibilities, and in the attitudes of nurses themselves, have caused conflicts with physicians and auxiliary workers.

The nurse is often responsible for coordinating the services of a variety of auxiliary workers into the patient's regimen of care. Because of this change in role there is frequently not enough time to give direct nursing care.

As a direct result of the overburdening of the professional registered nurse—brought about by the increase of administrative duties, paper work, and patient care—most states today have adopted licensing programs to regulate practical or vocational nurses. Many public and private vocational nursing schools have developed a one-year curricula that qualify graduates to take the licensing examination of their respective states. Upon successful completion of the examination, they are designated as licensed practical nurses (LPN) or licensed vocational nurses (LVN) (some states use the LPN designation, others use the LVN designation).

The practical nurse assumes many of the duties of the professional registered nurse, such as the administration of medications and oxygen, supervision of nurse aides, recording of patients' charts, and general bedside care of the patient. Thus these licensed personnel relieve the professional registered nurse of these duties, which permits the registered nurse to devote more time to administration, supervision, and specialized nursing care.

In addition to the various state licensing programs there are several national organizations that accredit qualified schools for the training of licensed vocational/practical nurses. The National Association for Practical Nurse Education and Service, 122 East 42nd St., New York, New York 10017, is one of the major associations accrediting LVN/LPN personnel and training institutions.

Tradition has defined nursing as the direct personal care of the sick. In present-day practice, the nurse is concerned more and more with technical, supervisory, and administrative duties, and is less and less able to be at the bedside of patients. This conflict between what professional nurses have been taught and what they now find themselves doing is a major problem confronting nursing today.

One of the more recent innovative developments in nursing is the concept of progressive patient care. In order to make more efficient use of personnel and equipment, most hospitals are grouping patients according to the care that they need. This system of progressive patient care includes an intensive care unit for the critically ill, a recovery room for patients immediately following surgery, regular care for the average patient, and minimal care or self-care units for convalescent patients and others who are ambulatory.

The development of medical assisting as a separate and distinct career field is a relatively recent phenomenon. For many years physicians hired only nurses and secretaries to assist them in their offices. However, because the training of the nurse was a preparation primarily for work in the hospital, a period of transition and adjustment was required for the nurse who wished to take up duties in a physician's office. Most nursing curricula still omit such items of instruction as office management, laboratory technique, x-ray technique, and electrocardiography.

The idea to train personnel specifically for work in the physician's office was germinated by Dr. M. M. Mandl, a biologist and former teacher in the New York City Public Schools. Dr. Mandl established the first such school of its kind in 1934. Several other good schools pioneered this type of training shortly thereafter. Today there are many such private and public junior colleges throughout the country engaged in the training of medical assistants.

As the shortage of registered nurses grew in recent years, physicians came to rely more and more upon the services of trained medical assistants. There are still some doctors, usually located in rural communities, who prefer to train their own assistants. Such doctors generally do not have the busy practices of their urban counterparts and may be less involved in specialization.

According to a continuing survey conducted by *Medical Economics,* solo practitioners without a medical assistant typically average about 71 patient visits per week, but could raise the number to 113 visits by merely hiring one assistant. Practitioners with two assistants can count on about 43%

more patient visits generally, depending on other factors such as field of practice.

Medical assisting has moved from the position of being just a job to that of a full-fledged career. Efforts are being made to more clearly define qualifications and establish minimum standards of education and training. Foremost in this movement has been the 15,000 member American Association of Medical Assistants. Now over sixteen years old, this organization operates on the premise that—as the right hand of the physician—each medical assistant must share the physician's obligation to update and improve patient care. Despite its relatively small membership, the AAMA has made substantial progress in fostering a professional image for medical assisting. The organization publishes a professional journal, holds an annual convention, conducts educational workshops and study groups, and disseminates information through its state and local chapters scattered throughout the country.

Not surprisingly, this emphasis has fostered a close working relationship between the AAMA and the American Medical Association. The two organizations collaborate in a number of activities, among them the accreditations of post secondary programs for medical assistants. Many of these programs have been accredited since the AMA House of Delegates adopted the first set of program essentials in 1969.

In an effort to upgrade clinical as well as clerical skills among employed medical assistants, the AAMA administers a certification program. While membership in the AAMA is not a requirement for eligibility to take an examination, annual examinations are administered by the Certifying Board of the AAMA. Successful candidates are granted certification and the old program has seen a good number of medical assistants achieve certified medical assistant (CMA) status. Certification is given in several areas including Administrative (CMA-A), Clinical (CMA-C) and Administrative/Clinical (CMA-A/C) as well as in some of the medical specialties. For information on certification examinations, short-term educational loans, and scholarships (the AAMA administers the Maxine Williams Scholarship Fund for medical-assisting students in need of financial aid), one may contact the American Association of Medical Assistants, One East Wacker Drive, Chicago, Illinois 60601.

TWENTIETH CENTURY ACHIEVEMENTS

In this chapter we have mentioned the two basic philosophies underlying the practice of medicine—the primitive or superstitious and the modern or rational. They are diametrically opposed to one another. The former involves the belief that disease is caused by supernatural forces, associates disease with sin, and is an aspect of religion. On the other hand, rational medicine is based on the concept that disease arises from natural causes that are within the power of man to control. The civilized or rational man endeavors to exercise control over the forces causing disease through material means. He recognizes that increased knowledge is man's best weapon in combating and preventing the spread of disease.

It is small wonder that so much time and money are now expended on scientific experimentation and investigation. During the eighteenth and nineteenth centuries most of the scientists and inventors were independently wealthy. They worked in their own private laboratories, which were usually located on the grounds of estates. These individuals possessed the time to tinker and experiment because they did not have to be concerned with earning a living. Consequently, a great many of their discoveries were more the result of accident than of conscious, deliberate purpose. Furthermore, organized experimentation did not have public support. In fact, for centuries scientific investigation was frowned upon by society. Society's attitude toward human dissection, for instance, forced medical students to steal bodies from graves in order to study anatomy.

Today we acknowledge the important contribution of experimentation to our everyday lives as well as our increased life expectancy. It is no longer necessary for scientifically oriented individuals to conduct their investigations as a hobby in private. There are special agencies and organizations whose sole function is that of research and experimentation.

In spite of the fantastic scientific accomplishments of the twentieth century, we can still find primitive people in certain parts of the world practicing primitive medicine in much the same superstitious manner as their primitive ancestors of centuries ago. Also, unfortunately, quackery is still practiced widely all over the world, and we can find traces of its acceptance in many levels of society.

Research in physics, chemistry, bacteriology, and biochemistry has enabled medicine to advance to its present state. But perhaps the most outstanding feature of twentieth century medicine has been the cooperative efforts of civilized people all over the world in working to prevent disease. The present World Health Organization (WHO), an important agency of the United Nations, has performed a great service to humanity since its inception. Practically all civilized nations recognize the necessity of abiding by the basic laws of preventive medicine. In so doing they protect themselves from the importation of infectious diseases by utilizing quarantine methods.

Improved methods of sanitation have wrought striking results. Our experience in Cuba following the end of the Spanish-American War in 1898 offers an excellent example of what improved sanitation methods can accomplish. At that time Havana possessed the reputation of being a very unhealthy city. Typhoid fever was widespread, taking its daily toll in life. There was also a high incidence of yellow fever. The United States felt a responsibility to take steps to correct the situation. The government selected Army Major William Gorgas to work with General Leonard Wood in cleaning up Havana's sanitation. Although their efforts to improve sanitation were successful in cleaning up the city, yellow fever did not disappear. Later, a commission headed by Dr. Walter Reed was appointed to investigate the yellow fever problem.

American history books present an interesting account of this investigation. It makes for fascinating reading, for it is a story of heroism, dedication, and persistence in tracing the disease to its actual source. Investigation showed that yellow fever was carried from person to person by the *Aedes* mosquito. Further study revealed that the natural habitat of this mosquito was human dwelling places and that it laid its eggs in water. By 1901 the disease had been brought under control and the incidence of yellow fever greatly reduced.

In 1904 Major Gorgas was requested by the United States government to exercise his talents in ridding the Panama Canal Zone of the dread disease. Conditions were so bad in Panama that it was often referred to as the "white man's grave." Ten years after Major Gorgas began his program to clean up the Canal Zone, the death rate of its inhabitants was greatly reduced and yellow fever was all but eliminated.

The most outstanding contribution to the treatment of infections has been the discovery of penicillin. The discovery was made in 1929 by an English bacteriologist, Dr. Alexander Fleming, who noted that the growth of bacteria was inhibited by a contaminating mold, later identified as *Penicillium notatum.* In the first clinical trials on severely ill patients, penicillin was found to be many times more effective than the sulfonamide drugs. For many years afterward penicillin remained in short supply because it was difficult to produce in large quantities. British scientists received help from the United States in producing penicillin in large quantities as the need increased during World War II.

Subsequent clinical studies conducted with penicillin have revealed that it is not equally effective against all bacteria. However, the effectiveness of his antibiotic in the therapy of *Staphylococcus* infection, subacute bacterial endocarditis, gonorrhea, and syphilis has revolutionized the treatment of these diseases. In the case of venereal disease, penicillin has provided a cure where previously no actual cure existed.

Another antibiotic, streptomycin, was discovered by the American biochemist, Selman Waksman. Streptomycin has proved to be very useful in the fight against tuberculosis. Numerous other antibiotics of an improved nature have since been developed.

Similarly, in the treatment and suppression of malaria, quinacrine or Atabrine was found to be superior to quinine. Much experience was gained with the use of these drugs during World War II and after.

Influenza has always been an endemic disease with frequent epidemics throughout the United States, and of course, all over the world. In the fall of 1943, researchers discovered that a single dose of influenza vaccine (gamma globulin), contained certain antibodies. The administration of gamma globulin proved to be useful in preventing or at least reducing the effect of measles. This vaccine has also been shown to be effective against hepatitis. The administration of gamma globulin to an expectant mother who has been exposed to measles is almost a must in precluding congenital deformities in the offspring.

Other extraordinary achievements have been developed more recently. Medical researchers have produced machines that are able to perform the work of a defective or missing body organ. The iron lung, for example, can keep a polio victim alive for years. It takes over the work of the paralyzed muscles of the patient's diaphragm. Other devices such as the artificial kidney and mechanical heart are utilized by surgeons to pump body fluids during operations involving these vital organs. The successful transplantation of organs such as kidneys, lungs, livers, spleens, and hearts is being conducted with increasing frequency. In many instances severed limbs have been reattached successfully.

The development of strong, lightweight materials has provided doctors with a method of replacing damaged body parts. It is now possible for orthopedic surgeons to insert a plastic plate to replace a shattered portion of one's skull. New substitute plastic and metal materials developed after World War II have made possible the use of artificial limbs for amputees. These artificial limbs have been perfected to such an extent that they can function almost as well as the real thing. Mechanical hands made of metal can take the place of amputated hands. The mechanical parts are covered with a plastic material so lifelike that it even has fingerprints and hairs.

Another important discovery resulting from experimentation pertains to the reduction of shock through freezing. Surgeons have found it possible to perform many operations without administering any anesthetic by merely anesthetizing the surrounding tissue through a process of freezing.

The strides of medicine since 1900 have been truly magnificent. The French physicists Marie and Pierre Curie discovered radium, a weapon used against cancer. X-rays, discovered by the German physicist Wilhelm Röntgen, provided a way to diagnose many different maladies and provided a method for treatment of cancer.

Briefly, here are a few less spectacular but nonetheless significant medical accomplishments of the century.

1. The discovery of new methods for detecting cancer and other diseases by the use of radioactive isotopes and tracers
2. Development of techniques for the storage of blood and blood plasma used in transfusions
3. Introduction of insulin shock, electrical shock, and tranquilizing drugs for the treatment of mental patients
4. The discovery of large numbers of new vitamins and the synthesization of cortisone for use in rheumatoid arthritis
5. Development of psychosomatic medicine

based upon recognition of the importance of anxiety, fear, and other psychologic factors in causing ulcers, asthma, high blood pressure, and diseases of the heart

Medical experts generally agree that the four major challenges to present medical research are cancer, hypertension, arteriosclerosis (hardening of the arteries), and geriatrics (old age).

Despite all of the marvelous achievements, doctors are not yet able to control many of man's most common ailments. Researchers are constantly seeking better methods of destroying viruses without destroying body cells. If they succeed, doctors may be able to conquer such diseases as the common cold and influenza. Physicians also need to learn a great deal more about the causes of mental illness and heart disease. Additional knowledge in these areas would provide ways of minimizing the incidence of these ailments.

Review questions

1. What was the most important single factor inhibiting the scientific advancement of anatomy and physiology?
2. Describe a caduceus. Explain the significance of the snake in the symbol.
3. What Greek physician developed descriptive methods of diagnosis that are still referred to by physicians?
4. Discuss two developments occurring during the Renaissance that exercised a strong influence on medicine.
5. Compare primitive medicine with modern medicine as to philosophy and motivation.
6. Describe briefly the contribution of each of the following to medical science: William Harvey, Thomas Sydenham, Anton van Leeuwenhoek, Edward Jenner, Louis Pasteur, Paul Ehrlich, Joseph Lister, John Hunter, William C. Gorgas, and Florence Nightingale.
7. Name several ways in which the nurse has aided the physician in the development of medical science.
8. What was the significance of the Bolton Act of 1941?
9. Discuss the duties of a licensed practical nurse; differentiate between those duties and those of the professional registered nurse.
10. Contrast the scientific experimentation of the eighteenth and nineteenth centuries with that of today.
11. What are the four future challenges to medical research?

Suggested readings

Boyd, W.: An introduction to the study of disease, ed. 5, Philadelphia, 1962, Lea & Febiger.

Hanlon, J. J.: Public health: administration and practice, ed. 6, St. Louis, 1974, The C. V. Mosby Co.

Mathison, R. R.: The eternal search, New York, 1958, G. P. Putnam's Sons.

Young, C. A., and Barger, J.: Introduction to medical science, ed. 2, St. Louis, 1973, The C. V. Mosby Co.

chapter 4
Medical specialization

GROWTH OF SPECIALIZATION

Specialization is a relatively recent phenomenon in the history of medicine, although a few instances of it were recorded back as far as the time of Galen. Today only the very sparsely settled or remote areas of the world have managed to remain immune from the effects of specialization.

The initial impetus to this division of function occurred during the past one hundred years. The industrial and technologic revolution of the nineteenth century accelerated the advancement of the so-called natural sciences, notably biology, physics, and chemistry. This development resulted in the establishment of numerous hospitals for the treatment of specific diseases. For example, the Royal Ophthalmic Hospital was established in London in 1804, and the Royal Hospital for Diseases of the Chest was founded in 1814. A Fever Hospital was founded in New York in 1825, and the Boston Lying-In Hospital was founded in 1832. It then followed that the doctors who practiced in these hospitals became specialists in these respective fields. Since these physicians were exposed daily to particular types of cases, it also followed that they became consultants to those with more limited experience.

Another important factor in hastening specialization was the development of various instruments of precision, which required more than average skill to operate. Experts in the handling of precision apparatus found that they had little time for other aspects of medicine. Such instruments as the ophthalmoscope, the laryngoscope, the sphygmograph, the cystoscope, the bronchoscope, and other diagnostic devices, because of their complexity, required the full attention of experts. Thus those individuals who worked with these instruments quite naturally became specialists.

Perhaps the greatest impetus to the age of specialization was World War II. The number of specialists prior to the war was rather small and usually a matter of accident. The war created a tremendous upheaval in the lives of those it touched as well as in the methods of doing things. The military, in critical need of well-trained personnel, soon discovered that the average practitioner seldom pursued postgraduate

---

Glossary

allay to put at rest; to quiet or relieve

certification the process of providing oneself with a certificate of training, qualifications, etc.; authorization

holistic pertaining to a theory or an approach which holds that the whole organism is a more fruitful field of study than its individual parts

impetus a driving force; incentive

meticulous extremely or excessively careful about minute details

therapeutic having to do with the treatment or curing of disease; curative

upheaval a sudden or violent agitation in a society; social turmoil

urbanization the process of taking on the characteristics of a city or town study. The concept of "continuing education" was unknown at this time, and many were so far removed from their original training that they were unfamiliar with even the most common diagnostic techniques and procedures. Medical educators were partly to blame for this state of affairs, for they were too involved with the advancing knowledge of the times and the education of their medical undergraduates to pay much heed to needs of the many physicians already in practice. The war, in calling attention to this lack of foresight, also provided direction in remedying the situation. The Army Medical Corps, for instance, organized and administered brief but intensive refresher courses for its personnel.

With the advent of postgraduate study, specialization was an inevitable outcome. Those physicians who had been conscientious enough to seek out advanced study in one of the specialties tended to restrict their practices to the treatment of ailments falling into that class. This trend was further stimulated by the construction and staffing of large hospitals. The magnitude and patient load of these institutions pointed their staffs into even greater degrees of differentiation of functions.

The great majority of today's medical students are directed and strongly influenced by their professors into selecting a specialty. Although the number of those choosing family practice residencies is increasing, the majority of young physicians still gravitate into the more glamorous specialties. As a result, the role of family physician has frequently been assumed principally by internists and pediatricians.

More science and more knowledge mean increased specialization, which in turn brings subdivision of labor and interdependence of personnel. No one man can possess the skills needed to remove a brain tumor, treat diabetic coma, and care for a psychotic patient. No one man can even keep up with the avalanche of current medical literature. In other words, technologic developments, more than patient demand, have provided the major impetus toward both specialism and combined practice.

The importance of technology in determining the nature and limits of our lives is so obvious that it is sometimes overlooked. Fast-moving science and technology are at the root of the current revolution in medical care. The autoanalyzer, the artificial kidney, the cardiac pacemaker, the atomic absorption spectrophotometer, and the equipment for echoencephalography, for angiocardiography, for cardiac resuscitation and monitoring—these and dozens of other highly sophisticated, expensive, life-saving and life-supporting instruments are rapidly becoming indispensable to comprehensive medical care.

It is almost impossible for the individual physician to practice good medicine alone. Inescapably medicine has become a team or group enterprise. In place of a one-to-one relationship between doctor and patient, optimum medical care has become a complicated, and necessarily expensive, undertaking involving many different disciplines and institutions. As a matter of fact, the present ratio of physicians to other health personnel is about 1 to 13.

It is interesting to note that the trend toward specialization is not without its socioeconomic overtones since it is closely associated with the urbanization of our society. The need for the general practioner would appear to be greater in smaller communities and in rural areas with less dense populations. The specialist, on the other hand, is generally attracted to the larger cities over 100,000 in population and in particular to cities over 1,000,000 in population, where he finds affluence and the facilities for practicing scientific medicine.

With the elevation of family practice to the level of a board specialty and sustained funding of family practice residencies by the federal government, the number of family practitioners is gradually increasing. Unfortunately this may not represent the total answer to the problem since large numbers of doctors are still lured into other specialties because of more regularized hours as well as the promise of greater financial reward.

The most vocal champion of a better trained general practitioner is the American Academy of Family Practice. Its chief objective is the upgrading of its members through specialized graduate training and better hospital affiliations. It demands two years of family practice following internship as a prerequisite for membership, and members are required to complete 150 hours of accredited postgraduate study every three years to maintain their accreditation. Some of its members are difficult to distinguish from specialists in internal medicine except that they usually do a considerable amount of pediatrics and obstetrics. The gap between their earnings and those of specialists is gradually being reduced.

SPECIALIZATION AND THE MEDICAL ASSISTANT

The selection of a specialty by a physician is a highly personal matter; the choice is dictated by personal preference, interest, and special abilities. In selecting a specialty the physician must be completely honest, remaining ever mindful of the fact that excellent training and a thorough knowledge of the subject field do not of themselves guarantee success. The physician's personality is an important ingredient for achieving a successful practice and must be given due consideration.

The physician who decides to pursue a specialty must plan on spending an additional three to six years of study following internship. In order to legally practice in a specialty, the physician must be registered with the national board that has been established to set up standards and certify the competency of its members. The physician applying for certification in a specialty must fulfill certain requirements in regard to education, training, and practical experience and is also expected to pass an examination. Upon successful passage of the examination the physician is granted a certificate or diploma attesting to competency in the specialty and becomes known as a diplomate or one who has been certifed in a field of specialization by any of the various medical boards.

The most recently published directory of diplomates lists the following 22 recognized medical specialty boards:

- Allergy and immunology
- Anesthesiology
- Colon and rectal surgery
- Dermatology
- Family practice
- Internal medicine
- Neurologic surgery
- Nuclear medicine
- Obstetrics and gynecology
- Ophthalmology
- Orthopedic surgery
- Otolaryngology
- Pathology
- Pediatrics
- Physical medicine and rehabilitation
- Plastic surgery
- Preventive medicine
- Psychiatry and neurology
- Radiology
- Surgery
- Thoracic surgery
- Urology

The introduction of new diagnostic procedures and equipment created the need for the expert in diagnosing all kinds of disorders. This relatively new specialty is called *internal medicine* and confines itself primarily to consultation and the diagnosis of complex diseases. In addition to consultation services, however, many internists also maintain a general practice and the line of distinction is very narrow. Branches of internal medicine include pediatrics, cardiology, and gastroenterology. Even these fields are practiced as separate specialties since each field is quite extensive in itself. In the remaining pages of this chapter we will attempt to briefly discuss some of the recognized board specialties and some of their subspecialties that commonly employ medical assistants.

Working for a general practitioner or an internist affords an assistant the opportunity to make use of almost every facet of training and preparation. Variety in duties and responsibilities is the rule and certainly not the exception.

Cardiology is subspecialty of internal medicine dealing with the functions and disorders of the human heart. The patient suffering from heart disease is usually quite tense and apprehensive; consequently he must be put at ease and given reassurance. Patients who visit a cardiologist's office are usually referred by their family physicians. It is only natural in such cases for the cardiologist and the referring physician to work in close harmony; the referring physician should be supplied with regular reports concerning the patient's treatment and progress.

The most important functions of the medical assistant in the cardiologist's office are the administration of electrocardiograms (ECG) and the taking of blood pressures. The results of these examinations enable the specialist to determine the condition of the patient's heart and hence the prognosis and treatment. In addition to being able to take accurate electrocardiograms and blood pressures, the assistant must also be prepared to perform certain routine laboratory work (CBC, urinalysis, prothrombin time), take case histories and prepare them for the doctor, and type letters to referring physicians along with complete reports of findings.

In the strict sense, *surgery* is not a separate branch of medicine but a function of medical practice. Almost all physicians are capable of performing some kind of surgery. Surgery involves the treatment of pathologic conditions or disease by operative means.

Within the field of surgery there are different areas of specialization or subdivisions because of the requirement of special skills and techniques. A surgeon may specialize in one branch or may be classified as a general surgeon and operate for various ailments. Some of the most important of these divisions are: general surgery, neurosurgery (brain and nerves), thoracic surgery (chest), plastic (repair and/or restoration of tissues), abdominal surgery (stomach and intestines), pelvic surgery (reproductive organs), urinary surgery (kidneys, ureters, and bladder), and orthopedic surgery (skeleton and muscles).

Since many surgeons are equipped to perform minor surgical operations in their offices, the medical assistant must be prepared to assist in such cases. The assistant must be thoroughly familiar with sterile technique, sterilization, and operative procedures as well as adept at changing dressings and at bandaging. Since most operations are performed in a hospital, the surgeon spends relatively little time in the office. This means the medical assistant who is alone in the office for long periods of time must therefore also be skilled in telephone technique, in the processing of insurance forms, and in the general techniques of medical office management.

Endocrinology is a medical subspecialty (not a board-certified specialty) that deals with the ductless glands and their disorders. It was formerly included as a part of internal medicine, but because of the expanding complexity in the diagnosis of glandular disorders, it has become necessary to establish it as a separate and distinct discipline.

The endocrinologist is frequently involved in the treatment of obesity but also often deals with special conditions of sterility, menopause, diabetes, and diseases of the adrenal and thyroid glands. The endocrinologist must possess a great deal of knowledge about a patient's condition before making a diagnosis and rendering treatment. Hence a large number of laboratory tests must be carried out to provide this information. The appointment schedule should be arranged by the medical assistant to allow for the time involved in these tests.

The medical assistant who hopes to work for an endocrinologist must be prepared to administer a great number of injections. The medication used in the treatment of affected patients usually requires the use of many types of injections, and therefore it is necessary that the assistant keep an adequate supply of needles and syringes on hand.

Many of the patients visiting the endocrinologist may be physically atypical and hence quite sensitive about their appearance. The medical assistant must be aware of this situation and strive to avoid creating any embarrassing situations. Those patients who are extremely repugnant in appearance should be scheduled for appointments at different times from other patients, preferably at the end of the day.

Dermatology is concerned with the proper care of the skin as well as the treatment of diseases affecting the skin. Treatments are frequently extended over long periods of time, and is not always necessary for the doctor to see the patient on each visit. Many of the routine treatments can be performed by the experienced medical assistant, including use of the x-ray machine for x-ray therapy, the electrolysis machine, and the ultraviolet lamp.

Just as the assistant who works for the endocrinologist must be conscious of patients' vanity and sensitivity, so also must the assistant who works in the dermatologist's office. Even well-adjusted people possessing skin diseases tend to become embarrassed about their afflictions if placed in an uncompromising situation. The assistant must be careful not to display obvious revulsion in dealing with skin diseases. Such patients are easily upset if attention is directed to their misfortunes.

The medical assistant is charged with the responsibility of obtaining accurate and detailed case histories from patients. The responses given to a predetermined pattern of questions constitutes an extremely important part of the dermatologist's diagnosis. The early symptoms of the various skin diseases possess very similar physical characteristics. The danger of infection from skin patients is minimal since even contagious skin diseases, contrary to popular belief, are not easily communicated through casual contact.

Patients suffering from allergic reactions are frequent visitors to the dermatologist, especially as these reactions affect the skin. Allergic patients are often subjected to the so-called patch test or scratch test in order to test susceptibility and reaction to a group of substances. Sometimes it is necessary to test numerous substances to find the one or ones responsible for the allergic reaction.

The nature of the practice makes the dermatologist particularly prone to malpractice suits. Therefore malpractice insurance coverage with high limits of indemnity is usually sought. Everyone working in a dermatologist's office must be meticulous and diligent in following the proper safety procedures in order to avoid possible injury to patients.

Gastroenterology is a subspecialty of internal medicine dealing with disorders of the digestive system. In arriving at a diagnosis the gastroenterologist makes great use of x-ray examinations and fluoroscopy. The person whose duties are primarily in the front office (medical secretary) as well as the medical assistant in the back office should be trained to work with the physician in carrying out diagnostic procedures and administering medications. It will often be necessary for the medical secretary to temporarily replace the medical assistant in the event of vacation or illness.

The medical assistant working for the gastroenterologist should be prepared to do a considerable amount of light laboratory work. Such laboratory technique might include the examination of stool specimens for blood and the detection of intestinal parasites. Complicated tests requiring more extensive knowledge and equipment are usually performed by the larger commercial laboratories. The only problem here is that the doctor and the patient must wait for the report of the results before a diagnosis can be achieved.

In order to facilitate x-ray and fluoroscopic examinations of the stomach and intestines, various substances that serve to illuminate these organs are administered to the patient. Barium sulfate is the substance most often used for the upper and lower G.I. series. In certain cases requiring a series of x-ray pictures at specified intervals, the patient may have to return to the office on the same day. The appointment schedule should be arranged accordingly.

The word *neurology* comes from the Greek *neuron,* meaning a nerve, and *logos,* meaning a treatise or the total knowledge in the field. It is interesting to note that Aristotle was the first to limit the word to the nerves; prior to his limiting influences it had been widely used to describe any cordlike tissue and even ureters. The terminology involved in neurology is the most troublesome of all for the student. The birth of modern clinical neurology occurred in the middle of the nineteenth century and was soon followed by wide advances in neuropathology and neurophysiology. Many new words can be expected to be added as more and more is learned of the chemistry and pharmacology of the nervous system.

The neurologist deals with disorders of the nervous system that may be caused by organic injury, disease, or infection and is primarily concerned with the diagnosis and treatment of conditions by other than operative procedures. In examining a patient the neurologist tests the reactions of the sensory system and the motor system as well as the various reflexes. The medical assistant should allow about an hour in the appointment schedule for diagnostic examinations and must be prepared to record the physician's findings during the course of the examination if it is desired.

The medical assistant is expected to give patients every help since the great majority of those visiting the neurologist are physically handicapped and are usually suffering from impaired motor functions. The epileptic patient may be a frequent visitor to the neurologist's office; therefore, the assistant must be familiar with epilepsy and the procedures to follow in cases of seizure.

Many of the neurotic or nervous symptoms exhibited by patients may have either an organic or a functional cause. The distinction is difficult and sometimes even impossible to make. It is necessary, then, that there be an exchange of knowledge between the neurologist and the psychiatrist; the neurologist should also be familiar with psychologic influencing factors and the psychiatrist must be able to recognize the symptoms connected with organically caused factors. The specialties of neurology and psychiatry are closely related and in fact are quite often combined; many neurologists also practice psychiatry.

The field of neurologic surgery, a board specialty, is a rapidly expanding one and is very closely related to both neurology and psychiatry. Neurologic surgery (neurosurgery) concerns the surgical treatment of diseases and disorders of the nervous system. Doctors who specialize in this field are known as neurosurgeons. Many physicians are either neurologists and psychiatrists or neurologists and neurologic surgeons. Some practice only one of the three specialties.

The electroencephalogram (EEG) is commonly used in the diagnosing of neurologic conditions. The electroencephalograph is a machine designed to record brain waves. By comparing the tracings of the patient's brain waves with those of a normal model, the various pathologic conditions can be discovered. Conditions of epilepsy and brain tumors are frequently detected in this manner, making early treatment possible.

Psychiatry is a branch of medicine dealing with the understanding, diagnosis, treatment, and prevention of mental disorders. Whereas the neurologist is chiefly concerned with diseases of the nervous system that are of an organic origin, the psychiatrist deals with mental disorders of a functional nature. By functional we mean those symptoms that originate from the various psychologic stresses associated with the patient's total environment. Organic symptoms are those resulting from some type of brain pathology.

Generally speaking, the prognosis for organically caused disorders is less favorable than that for functional disorders. Treatment consists of any one or combination of drugs, electroshock therapy, and psychotherapy. Although electroshock therapy appears to be the chief method for obtaining a rapid alleviation of symptoms, if used it is usually combined now with antidepressant and various other drugs. The best results have been obtained using a combination of the physical or medical methods of treatment followed by psychotherapy. Mental disorders create a certain amount of damage to the personality, creating marked personality decompensation. Psychotherapy seeks to repair this damage and to enable the patient to make a more satisfactory adjustment to his environment. Psychotherapy is discussed in more detail in Chapter 5.

The assistant or secretary to the psychiatrist has a minimum of contact with patients. The confidential nature of their problems often precludes the presence of anyone except the physician. Psychiatric patients are anxious enough and should not be kept waiting for long periods of time. The appointment schedule should reflect an awareness of this fact and allow sufficient intervals between appointments in case of overlapping.

Although mental disease has recently achieved a more general public acceptance and understanding there still remains a certain social stigma connected with being under the care of a psychiatrist. Consequently, most patients are sensitive about their problems and wish to keep others from discovering them. The office assistant must respect their wishes, which can be facilitated by arranging for patients to enter and leave by different exits.

The secretary or the assistant who seeks employment from a psychiatrist should be a well-adjusted person and should be broad-minded and a realist. The assistant will become well acquainted (through typing) with many of the aspects of patients' problems brought out in interviews with the doctor. Many of these details are likely to be sordid and bizarre. The individual who is employed in the office of a psychiatrist cannot be overly sensitive, dogmatic in beliefs, or prone to render value judgments. The psychiatrist looks for an aide who is flexible, and, perhaps most important of all, does not become emotionally involved with the problems of patients.

The word *gynecology* is derived from the Greek *gyne,* meaning woman, and *logos,* meaning discourse or treatise. The origin of obstetrics is somewhat more surprising in that it comes from the Latin *obstare,* meaning to stand before, as the obstetrician does. In Rome *obstetricia* meant the management of childbirth, and an *obstetrix* was a midwife.

Obstetrics and gynecology are specialties dealing with the study and treatment of the female reproductive system. Obstetricians are primarily concerned with treating women during pregnancy and labor. The gynecologist is more concerned with female disorders. However, the two specialties are almost always combined and one seldom finds them practiced separately. It is probably safe to say that all gynecologists are obstetricians, but the reverse is not always true. Most general practitioners practice obstetrics and refer to an obstetrician only those cases in which complications are anticipated. The specialist's fee is considerably larger, and very few are found in rural communities.

Obviously, the medical assistant who works in a gynecologist's office must possess a good working knowledge of the processes of pregnancy and childbirth and should be familiar with the anatomy and physiology of the female reproductive system, in order to render explanations and give reassurance to patients without bothering the physician in every case.

The assistant will be expected to be familiar with the technique of draping patients, since pelvic examinations are quite routine. The majority of young women who come into the office for their first pelvic examination are usually self-conscious and easily embarrassed, especially if the doctor is young. The situation must be handled with care, and every precaution should be taken to respect the patient's modesty. Nevertheless, the impression should be conveyed that such an examination is relatively routine. The attitude and office manner of the assistant are very important in giving the patient confidence and allaying her fears.

Good medical ethics dictates that a female assistant be present during such examinations. This serves to protect both the doctor and the patient, especially when the patient happens to be a complete stranger. Prior to the pelvic examination, the assistant should instruct the patient to empty her bladder and rectum. During the examination the assistant should remain quiet and never converse unnecessarily with the patient. She should be there primarily to help alleviate fear by an assuring look or a pat of the hand, but she should not talk and should remain relatively quiet and in the background. Let the doctor converse with the patient.

The conscientious obstetrician's assistant takes it upon herself to become thoroughly acquainted with the routine instructions given to women during pregnancy. In most cases, patients feel freer to discuss female problems with another female.

The assistant should be prepared to do a certain amount of laboratory work. For instance, she should be able to perform a simple test for detecting the presence of albumin in urine. The physician will usually want this information before consulting with the patient. The physician may also wish the assistant to be familiar with the techniques for cervical and vaginal smears.

When the pregnant patient visits the doctor for the first time, she should be informed of the fee schedule. Most obstetricians have an overall fee that includes care during pregnancy, normal delivery, and one or more postnatal visits. It is often the assistant's responsibility to explain to the patient the nature of each visit, how often she is to visit, and exactly what the physician's fee includes and excludes. The doctor may wish to quote a special fee for other than normal deliveries.

Since most maternity patients in this country are admitted to hospitals, the doctor's assistant possesses the important function of making reservations and attending to the details involved. This procedure is discussed in more detail in Chapter 12.

Orthopedics is a field of specialization chiefly concerned with the various parts of the skeletal system, including bones, joints, and ligaments. Persons suffering from various muscular and skeletal diseases such as poliomyelitis, displaced disks, muscular dystrophy, fractures, and deformities are likely to visit the orthopedist's office.

Physical therapy is a very important aspect of the treatment rendered by the orthopedist. The medical assistant should understand the value of physical therapy in the treatment of orthopedic problems. Many orthopedic specialists refer their patients to qualified physical therapists for supplementary treatment. It is the medical assistant's responsibility to make arrangements for these treatments. The assistant may also help the physician in placing casts on patients as well as removing them.

In routine examinations the patient should be given a gown that opens down the back. The doctor often uses a special percussion instrument and a needle to test the patient's reflexes and reactions to sensation. The assistant's duties might also include the shaving and preparing of the patient's skin prior to application of a brace or other supportive device. From time to time patients with orthopedic braces must visit the office to have the physician check and adjust them. The appointment schedule must be flexible enough to allow for this.

The specially trained or interested medical assistant can be a valuable asset to the orthopedist. Patients must be given instructions in the proper use of crutches. It may also be necessary to demonstrate corrective exercises. If the assistant is at least knowledgeable in these areas, with a minimum of training the physician can delegate these tasks to be free to attend to other professional activities.

Orthopedic surgery is a board specialty that seeks to treat pathologic conditions of the skeletal system (bones, joints, and ligaments) by operative means. An orthopedist may or may not be an orthopedic surgeon, for this requires board certification. The position of the medical assistant working for an orthopedic surgeon would vary little from that of an assistant employed in an orthopedist's office.

The common acronym for *otolaryngology* (E.N.T.) is somewhat smaller than one might anticipate in view of the fact that otology, rhinology, and laryngology are included under this heading. These specialties, involving disorders of the ear, nose, and throat, are usually combined and practiced together.

The medical assistant who is involved in the practice of either one or all of these specialties should be ready to assist with all examinations and treatments and usually bears the responsibility for sterilizing and laying out the necessary instruments for the doctor.

A good deal of minor surgery is performed in the office, particularly in connection with the nose and throat. The assistant must be thoroughly familiar with the techniques of sterilization and of assisting the physician.

The assistant often has the responsibility of conducting hearing tests with an audiometer. The audiometer produces a graphic record of a patient's hearing capacity, which is then placed in the patient's folder for future reference. Patients with hearing difficulties can create special problems in the office. The assistant should be resourceful enough to discover the most effective methods of communicating with such patients.

One of the great steps in the advance of medicine and science in general was achieved in 1895, when Röntgen, a German physicist, first observed the phenomenon of the so-called X rays. In 1925 the term roentgen was established as the name of the international unit of radiation intensity.

The radiologist is a specialist who uses roentgenograms and radium to diagnose and treat disease. The physician who elects to specialize and take a residency in *radiology* should possess a high language facility. The radiologist not only has to learn the specialized terms having to do with the intricacies of the apparatus being used, but must also be familiar with the terminology of many other fields of medicine including anatomy, pathology, physiology, medicine, and surgery, to name only a few.

The assistant who works for a radiologist must be an excellent stenographer and typist and also will have to have a sound grounding in the terminology of many fields of medicine, especially those pertaining to anatomy and the skeletal structure.

The practice of radiology is now divided into two areas, diagnostic and therapeutic. The diagnostic practice of radiology is primarily limited to the taking of x-ray pictures, interpreting their results, and submitting reports of findings to the referring physician. It is not necessary for the physician to take x-ray pictures and develop them provided a qualified technologist is employed or the medical assistant is capable enough. However, only a physician is permitted to interpret results and make a diagnosis.

The therapeutic branch of radiology is a rapidly expanding one. As more knowledge is accumulated and new techniques are developed, the use of x-ray therapy and radium in the treatment of disease is achieving a new prominence. The administration of radium therapy in the early stages of cancer has produced significant results. Some success has also been achieved with the use of cobalt and radioisotopes in arresting certain well-established types of cancer. However, because of the danger of radioactivity from these substances great care must be taken to ensure the safety of both the patient and the technician. Usually only large hospitals and medical centers presently possess the equipment and trained personnel to administer such therapy.

The specialty of *pediatrics* is concerned with the treatment of children and diseases more commonly associated with children. It is interesting to note that pediatrics has very little terminology of its own, for it employs the terminology of all the basic sciences and also that of medicine.

In seeking an office assistant, the pediatrician looks for someone who is fond of children and enjoys the challenge of working with them. An understanding of child psychology is a great help to an assistant who may strive to control the behavior of children in the office.

The pediatrician receives many emergency calls and probably makes more house calls than other specialists. Before seeking employment in a pediatrician's office, the medical assistant will want to become totally familiar with the serious and the not-too-serious symptoms of childhood disorders.

The newly employed assistant should always check with the physician first to find out how telephone calls should be handled and must know the exact limits of the position and just how much advice she is authorized to dispense to mothers over the telephone. Children often develop nosebleeds, vomiting, high temperatures, and convulsions in the absence of serious causes. A simple suggestion to the parents is often sufficient to allay their fears until the doctor arrives, the child is brought to the office, or it is determined that the child is not seriously ill. It is always a good practice to invite the parent to call back and report on the child's progress.

The medical assistant should arrange the appointment schedule so that a minimum of time is spent in the waiting room. The fewer the number of children in the waiting room, the better for all concerned. Children are hyperactive, and it is difficult to keep them quiet and occupied for long periods of time. Furthermore, mothers are apprehensive and fearful that their child will contract some contagious disease from other children.

Urology is principally concerned with disorders of the genitourinary tract. In the course of practice the urologist treats many cases of venereal disease, particularly gonorrhea, since it invades the genitourinary tract. Surgery of the kidney, bladder, and prostate is performed by the urologist.

Since the great preponderance of patients who visit a urologist are males, it is questionable whether of not the female medical assistant is required to assist the doctor during examinations. The feelings of the patient often govern the physician's decision.

The two major types of diagnostic procedures carried out in the urologist's office are catheterization and cystoscopy. Catheterization is a process whereby the bladder is emptied of its contents by means of a rubber tube known as a catheter. A cystoscopy is an examination of the inner surface of the bladder and ureter by means of an instrument called a cystoscope. Patients suspected of having kidney diseases are frequently examined by means of cystoscopy.

Proctology is concerned with diseases of the colon, the rectum, and the anus. The American Medical Association no longer refers to this specialty as proctology; it is now referred to in the list of board specialties as colon and rectal surgery. The practice of the proctologist is chiefly involved with the treatment of such ailments as hemorrhoids, ulcers of the sigmoid, and fissures of the anus. The diagnostic instruments most commonly used by the proctologist are the sigmoidoscope and the proctoscope, which make close inspection of the colon and rectum possible.

In the case of male patients the female assistant usually is not required to assist the doctor in these examinations. However, she is generally expected to prepare the room and the instruments for conducting examinations.

Ophthalmology is a medical specialty in every sense of the word; it deals with the study of the eye and its diseases. Ophthalmology has a considerable amount of terminology of its own, with most of it being derived from the Greek rather than Latin. In the days of Celsus, an eye specialist was termed an *ocularius medicus,* and only a generation ago a specialist in this field was called an oculist. Today he goes under the more impressive name of ophthalmologist, while one who makes optical instruments or glasses is termed an optician. An optometrist is an expert in optometry, which is the measurement of the powers of vision and the adaptation of lenses or prisms for the eye.

The assistant who aspires to work for an ophthalmologist should be familiar with sterilization and surgical techniques since a considerable amount of eye surgery is performed in the office. The ophthalmologist makes use of a great deal of highly complex diagnostic equipment. The assistant, in order to perform efficiently, should be acquainted with the mechanics of this equipment.

In the broad sense, the physician who engages in full-time *medical research* may also be considered a specialist. However, research may be carried on in a host of theoretical branches of medicine. The true researcher sees few, if any, patients, but devotes most of his time to working in a hospital or institution investigating various problems and seeking their solutions. These findings are usually recorded and later published in books and journals. The duties of the individual who assists a physician in this type of work consist of handling correspondence and aiding in the preparation of manuscripts. The job requires an assistant who not only can take care of routine office work but who also is interested in research and writing. She should enjoy the search for information and the satisfaction of finding the desired material.

The major portion of medical research is carried on in what is known as preclinical subjects. Preclinical applies to those subjects that are taught as basic sciences, supposedly before the medical student reaches the clinical stage of his training. This distinction, however, is rapidly disappearing as the problem of the patient is being introduced earlier into the curriculum. The following subjects are classified as preclinical and are the object of most research: anatomy, physiology, biology, physiologic chemistry, pharmacology and therapeutics, pathology, bacteriology, and parasitology.

At this point it is probably apparent to the reader that a number of the board specialties listed in the beginning of this chapter have thus far been omitted from discussion. Instead we have included those subspecialties and areas of specialization that more frequently employ the services of medical assistants. There are a number of board specialties that do not normally employ medical assistants; among them are the fields of anesthesiology, pathology, physical medicine and rehabilitation, plastic surgery, preventive medicine, and thoracic surgery.

Anesthesiology is the study of anesthesia and anesthetics. Physicians who elect to take advanced training in this field are known as anesthesiologists. During minor operations they usually direct the administration of anesthetics by anesthetists; the more serious operations require their direct participation. Few, if any, anesthesiologists maintain an office, for the great majority are full-time hospital staff physicians.

Pathology deals with the nature of disease. Pathologists study changes in the body that cause disease or are caused by disease. Clinical pathologists make use of laboratory tests to diagnose diseases and generally employ medical technologists and technicians.

Physical medicine and rehabilitation or physiatrics treats diseases by such physical means as exercises or light, heat, or water therapy. Doctors who limit their practice to this field are known as physiatrists. Like orthopedists they normally employ and direct the work of physical therapists and occupational therapists.

Plastic surgery is concerned with the rebuilding of certain parts of the body that are imperfect or have been damaged. The duties of a medical assistant employed by a plastic surgeon would be much the same as those of a medical assistant working in a dermatologist's office.

Preventive medicine deals with the prevention of disease. Physicians and surgeons in this field may limit their practice to such fields as public health, aviation medicine, or industrial medicine. Specialists in this field are generally employed by various health departments and agencies, which require the bachelor's degree as a minimum for those who work under the direction of a health officer or physician.

Thoracic surgery deals with the surgical treatment of diseases of the thorax (chest). Thoracic surgeons normally perform their surgical operations in well-equipped hospitals. The role of the medical assistant working for a thoracic surgeon would be little different from that of the assistant who is employed by a general surgeon with the exception that few, if any, operations would be conducted in the office of a thoracic surgeon.

PROFESSIONAL SYMBOLS AND ABBREVIATIONS

In the course of performing professional duties the medical assistant encounters many abbreviations and titles. The conscientious assistant will want to understand the meaning and full import of each, for it will be a valuable aid in rendering the proper social and professional courtesies. A brief list of some of the more commonly used professional symbols and abbreviations is given on p. 49.

RELICENSURE AND RECERTIFICATION

Should a physician, whose license to practice usually lasts for life, face relicensing? And should medical specialists periodically prove they know the latest about brain surgery, broken bone repair or cancer cures? An increasing number of consumerists and other critics of medicine say they certainly should. Many physicians are beginning to agree there is a need for more public accountability by the profession.

At present, a student becomes a licensed physician by finishing medical school and passing a test administered by a state medical examining board. After advanced training and more examinations by one of twenty-two medical specialty boards, a physician gains recognition as a "board certified" specialist. Although not legally required to practice a specialty, board certification is frequently necessary before a hospital will grant a doctor staff privileges. About half of the 238,000 specialists in the United States are board certified.

Many proponents of relicensing and recertification argue that such requirements will promote higher quality medical care by forcing all physicians to maintain their skills and keep up with rapidly changing medical knowledge. The 1970 Carnegie Commission on Higher Education report pointed out that physicians who do not remain lifelong students "face partial obsolescence in five to ten years."

In 1971, New Mexico became the first state to pass a relicensing law. Now its physicians will lose their right to practice unless they take 120 hours of continuing medical education every three years.

Three other states (Maryland, Kentucky, and Kansas) have passed relicensing laws, although Maryland has been the only other one to implement it so far, beginning in September, 1974. Several other states, including California, Colorado, Michigan and Virginia, are considering adopting relicensing statutes.

Nineteen of the twenty-two medical specialty boards have endorsed recertification. This endorsement is seen as giving the greatest impetus to the relicensing trend, since so many physicians are board certified. Four specialty boards (family practice, internal medicine, plastic surgery, and ophthalmology) already have announced dates for their initial recertification procedures.

While all but one of these reexamining steps are presently voluntary in nature some experts believe recertification eventually will come to have the same importance as certification had originally. Seven state medical associations and two medical specialty societies now require members to take continuing education courses or forfeit their membership. As more specialty societies institute this requirement, this will affect many medical specialists who are not board certified but do belong to the societies, medical observers say.

A.A.	Associate of Arts	**Ob.**	obstetrics
A.S.	Associate of Science	**Gyn.**	gynecology or gynecologist
A.B. or B.A.	Bachelor of Arts	**G.U.**	genitourinary
B.S.	Bachelor of Science	**G.I.**	gastrointestinal
M.A.	Master of Arts	**D & C**	dilation and curettage
M.S.	Master of Science	**B.M.R.**	basal metabolic rate
Ph.D.	Doctor of Philosophy	**E.C.G.**	electrocardiogram
M.D.	Doctor of Medicine	**E.E.G.**	electroencephalogram
D.D.S.	Doctor of Dental Surgery	**Ca.**	carcinoma or malignant growth
D.D.	Doctor of Divinity	**L.P.T.**	Licensed Physical Therapist
D.S.C.	Doctor of Surgical Chiropody	**R.P.T.**	Registered Physical Therapist
LL.D.	Doctor of Laws or honorary Doctor of Letters	**M.T.(A.S.C.P.)**	Medical Technologist; certified by registry of the American Society of Clinical Pathologist
D.O.	Doctor of Osteopathy		
D.C.	Doctor of Chiropractic	**O.T.**	Occupational Therapist
V.D. or D.V.M.	Doctor of Veterinary Medicine	**C.O.T.A.**	Certified Occupational Therapy Assistant
M.P.H.	Master of Public Health	**R.T.**	Radiologic Technologist
Dr.P.H.	Doctor of Public Health	**R.R.L.**	Registered Record Librarian
A.M.A.	American Medical Association	**A.R.T.**	Accredited Record Technician
D.D.Sc.	Doctor of Dental Science	**M.S.W.**	Master of Social Work
D.E.	Doctor of Entomology	**I.T. or R.T.**	Inhalation Therapist or Respiration Therapist
D.Hy.	Doctor of Hygiene		
D.T.M.	Doctor of Tropical Medicine	**L.P.N.**	Licensed Practical Nurse
D.Z.	Doctor of Zoology	**L.V.N.**	Licensed Vocational Nurse
Ed.D	Doctor of Education	**C.L.A.**	Certified Laboratory Assistant
Opt.D.	Doctor of Optometry	**C.M.A.**	Certified Medical Assistant
R.N.	Registered Nurse	**C.M.A.—A.**	Certified Medical Assistant—Administrative
Pharm.D.	Doctor of Pharmacy		
Pod.D.	Doctor of Podiatry	**C.M.A.—C.**	Certified Medical Assistant—Clinical
S.F.	Senior Fellow		
F.A.C.S.	Fellow of the American College of Surgeons; highest honor that can be conferred on a surgeon	**C.M.A.—A/C.**	Certified Medical Assistant—Administrative/Clinical
		P.A.	Physician's Assistant
		Medex	Designation of former military corpsmen provided specialized preceptorship type training enabling them to assist physicians in rural practice
F.A.C.P.	Fellow of the American College of Physicians; highest honor that can be conferred upon a physician		
O.P.D.	Outpatient Department		
E.E.N.T.	eye, ear, nose, and throat		

The Oregon Medical Association, the first state society to begin such a program in 1970, has already expelled eleven doctors who did not keep up. Another fifteen resigned from the society rather than comply with the requirement.

The trend toward making physicians' continued proficiency more accountable is expected to spread. Recertification and relicensing will probably be a fact of life within the next decade. The American College of Surgeons is among those specialty societies now considering requiring continuing education for membership.

Since 1967, one Presidential commission and two top-level U. S. Health, Education, and Welfare reports have strongly urged relicensing of all health professionals. A number of states responded to this pressure, and now require it for dentists, nurses, pharmacists, and podiatrists, among others. Moreover, the advent of Medicare, Medicaid, and the strong likelihood of national health insurance has convinced many that a physician's eligibility for remuneration by the federal government may soon be related to demonstration of continued competence.

Review questions

1. Name and discuss at least two developments that have contributed to the growth of specialization in medicine.
2. What recent development is helping increase the number of physicians who become family practitioners?
3. Describe the specialties of cardiology and endocrinology and list three functions of a medical assistant working under each specialty.
4. Why are neurology and psychiatry closely related specialties?
5. What should be the personal qualifications of the medical assistant who desires to work for a psychiatrist?
6. Medical research is carried on in the so-called preclinical subjects. List them.
7. Explain the difference (if any) between orthopedics and orthopedic surgery. How do they relate to physiatry?

Suggested readings

Corey, L., Saltman, S., and Epstein, M.: Medicine in a changing society, St. Louis, 1972, The C. V. Mosby Co.

Stevens, R.: American medicine and the public interest, New Haven, Conn., 1971, Yale University Press.

Vahovich, S. G.: Reference data on the profile of medical practice, Chicago, 1973, AMA Center for Health Services Research and Development.

chapter 5
Mental health

THE MENTAL HYGIENE MOVEMENT

The mental hygiene movement was launched in 1908 with the publication of a book by Clifford Beers entitled *A Mind That Found Itself*. A former mental patient himself, Beers sought to focus public attention on the deplorable conditions that then existed in mental institutions and the horrible treatment accorded to patients. The book contains accounts of his own mental collapse, the bad treatment he received in the three mental hospitals where he was a patient, and his subsequent recovery in the home of a sympathetic attendant.

According to Beers, the plight of the mental patient at the turn of the century was no better than it had been a hundred years earlier. The asylums of his day were little different from penal institutions, for the inmates were treated more like wild animals than sick human beings. Patients were flogged regularly, placed in filthy cells with primitive sanitary conditions, starved, and indiscriminately placed in straitjackets. The straitjacket was a widely used device for restraining violent patients. Beers presents a vivid description of his own reaction to being placed in a straitjacket which, instead of quieting the patient, tends to further intensify his internal excitement.

Following his own recovery, Beers resolved that he would devote the rest of his life to directing attention to the necessity of improving existing conditions in mental institutions and promoting measures for the understanding and prevention of mental disorders. His efforts aroused the interest of many scientists and public-spirited citizens, among them William James, the great psychologist, and Adolph Meyer, the eminent psychiatrist. At Meyer's suggestion, Beers applied the term *mental hygiene* to the movement. In 1909 the National Committee for Mental Hygiene was organized and

Glossary

aberration a wandering from the right path or usual course of action
anxiety a state of fear and mental tension commonly occurring in mental disorders
coherent logically connected; consistent in thought
congenial agreeable; suitable; getting along well with others
eminent distinguished, prominent
emotion a strong feeling such as fear, anger, joy, love, and grief; disturbance
involutional having to do with a decline in bodily activity, especially sexual activity, in old age
maladjusted not in a healthy or harmonious relationship with one's environment
manifestation showing plainly; revealing
neurosis a mild nervous disorder; emotional disturbance with no apparent organic change
psychosis any severe form of mental disturbance or disease with deep and far-reaching disorders of behavior
psychosomatic having to do with both mind and body
regression the act of going back; a way of trying to escape difficult problems by casting off responsibility and assuming characteristics of an earlier period of development
succumb to give way; to yield; to die

under his able leadership the movement became worldwide in 1919 with the formation of the International Committee for Mental Hygiene.

Beginning primarily as a reform movement designed to improve the lot of the mentally ill, it sought to ensure humane treatment, better living conditions, more intelligent commitment laws, and a tolerant attitude on the part of the general public toward mental illness. The movement then changed its direction and became quite successful in projecting the importance of using medical skills in the treatment of disturbed individuals. The efforts expended by the mental hygiene movement have played an instrumental role in the development of modern psychiatry and psychology.

The National Committee for Mental Hygiene, through its quarterly periodical *Mental Hygiene,* has disseminated a great deal of valuable information dealing with behavior problems, the recognition of individual needs, the effects of environmental factors upon personality development, and the preservation of mental health. The work of the Committee has been both influential and broad in scope. From its earlier concern with humanitarian activities, it shifted its attention to medical techniques for the treatment of the mentally ill. The major area of interest today is what may be termed "social reconstruction," which enlists the cooperation of psychiatry, psychology, medicine, social work, education, business, and industry in maintaining and improving the mental health of society in general.

PRINCIPLES OF MENTAL HEALTH

The fact that so many people in our society today are what might be termed maladjusted is indeed unfortunate. There is, however, no easy explanation. While it is true that there is an awareness that the rapid development of science and technology has increased life's pressures, both challenging and threatening the individual's stress tolerance, this is not the entire answer. Equally as important have been the number of psychologic studies and investigations that have produced more effective means for recognizing maladaptive behavior. Improved methods for gathering, quantifying, and classifying data have provided psychologists with new insights into the many categories and causes of deviant behavior.

Since the term *abnormal* refers to something that is other than normal, it implies a deviation from some clearly apparent norm. Perhaps such a model exists at the physical level, but there is certainly no agreement as to a norm at the psychologic level. No one as yet has been successful in determining exactly what constitutes normal behavior. If the term *abnormal* were considered in the strict sense, statistical evidence would suffice. In this case any deviation from the numeric norm would be abnormal. A genius would have to be considered just as abnormal as one who is mentally retarded. Clearly, then, a satisfactory definition of abnormality must be along behavioral lines, taking into consideration the variations in cultures and environments.

Life is a continuous process of adjustment in which the individual strives to satisfy his needs and maintain a harmonious relationship with his environment. Individuals who deal effectively with their problems are generally thought to be well adjusted. On the other hand, there are those individuals who are overwhelmed by their problems and unable to cope with them. This inability to manage one's problems usually manifests itself in such neurotic symptoms as anxiety, unhappiness, inefficiency, or even more serious symptoms. Persons exhibiting such behavior are said to be maladjusted.

The incidence of mental ill health is rather startling. At least one in every ten Americans manifests some form of mental illness. World War II provided an excellent training laboratory for the study of mental health problems resulting from abnormal behavior. Approximately 18% of those rejected for military service during the war period were turned down because of mental illness or personality disturbances. Moreover, World War II furnished clinical evidence that even well-adjusted and emotionally stable individuals who had made adequate adjustments in civilian life might manifest psychologic symptoms when exposed to severe and prolonged combat experience. There were numerous battles during the war that taxed the individual soldier's stress tolerance to the breaking point, causing many to succumb. Thus there can be little doubt that even those persons who possess high thresholds of frustration and tolerance and who have generally well-integrated personalties will manifest symptoms of neurotic behavior when exposed to extreme situations.*

It must be pointed out that statistics relating to the number of patients in mental hospitals provide an incomplete picture of the actual incidence of serious personality disorders. First of all, many patients are never institutionalized, receiving all of their treatment from private clinicians. Only those who are deemed to be severely disturbed are hospitalized. Secondly, those individuals with milder degrees of disturbances are often cared for by relatives and consequently are not included in statistical data.*

More and more informed general practitioners and internists are becoming aware that there are psychologic factors present in many aspects of illness—whether they emerge as clear-cut physical or psychiatric difficulties or as a subtle blending of both. Progressive general practitioners and internists are acknowledging the psychosocial determinants of illness, particularly the impact of life—change—the incredible expansion of the extent, quality, and pace of change and the incredible pressures to adapt to change at accelerated rates not experienced in the slowly evolving societies of the past. In the face of this burgeoning awareness, it is vital that the primary physician understand and extend the efforts of science and academic medicine to find ways of strengthening man's capacity to adapt to stress.

Most people are familiar with physical hygiene; we are continually being reminded of the need for proper food, sleep, rest, exercise, and so on. Mental hygiene is similar in many respects, but it is more concerned with the mental or psychologic aspects such as mental ability, emotional reactions, personality traits, character and moral development, and attitudes. The individual's conduct is related to a large extent to his mental attitude, which is often referred to as his pattern of thinking. Whether or not he possesses such desirable traits as honesty and trustworthiness or has a respect for the property rights of others will depend upon his frame of reference. Since actions are merely the outward expressions of thoughts and emotions, the only way one can detect mental activity is by observing physical responses or behavior patterns. Therefore we may say that one responds to a given situation or stimulus because of his attitudes. If an individual is to be taught to guide and direct his own conduct in a wholesome and normal manner and if he is to become well adjusted, it is imperative that his attitudes be studied as the controlling factor. Helping individuals to better adjust to their respective environments and enabling them to be better able to control their own conduct is the main task and purpose of mental hygiene.

Adults are constantly being confronted with problems and situations that require them to choose a definite course of action. Inability to make a decision or the mere avoidance of making decisions is a frequent sign of maladjustment. It is possible that an individual may be better adjusted in some respects than in others. For instance, an individual may be well adjusted to his employment situation but not well adjusted socially. Mental soundness is best described as the individual's ability to react to his environment in a coherent, consistent, and efficient manner.

*From Thorpe, L. P.: The psychology of mental health, New York, 1960, The Ronald Press Co., pp. 12-15.

A large number of psychologists feel that man is strictly a product of his environment. These environmentalists hold that an individual's environment may possess a variety of inherent factors responsible for internal conflicts, emotional disturbances, retreats from reality, excessive daydreaming, immoral or dishonest activities, avoidance of solving difficult problems, and the substitution of lesser goals for those which are impossible to attain. Problem situations themselves are not always the cause of abnormal behavior. The individual's total environment has to be considered, including the friends he makes, the way he spends his leisure time, his hobbies, and various other factors. The more frequent causes of abnormal behavior patterns stem from family influences such as troubles in the home or a lack of self-confidence fostered by an overly protective mother.

Individuals have both tissue needs and social needs. Tissue needs include hunger, thirst, self-protection or the urge to defend oneself, and sex or the urge to preserve the human species. While social needs may not be considered as high in priority as tissue needs, their importance to the individual's total well-being must not be overlooked.

Each person feels a need to achieve something or attain mastery over something. Normal people derive a deep sense of satisfaction in being able to do something well; they want to be master of a situation or to be able to perform some skill well. Occasional mastery would seem to be a necessity. The occasional mastery of what appear to be trivial experiences provides definite assistance in the maintenance of mental health, while continual frustrations can often result in maladjustment.

People are continually seeking to gain position. Normal individuals, whether they admit it or not, desire status or standing among their peers. It is one thing to be master of a situation; it is quite another thing to be recognized as such by others. A great many of our actions are governed by what others may think of us. Consequently, mental health is significantly affected by what we think others think of us. This is an extremely important principle for the understanding of mental hygiene.

Every individual requires a certain degree of sympathetic understanding and affection. Almost everyone is able to look back to some event in his lifetime that precipitated the need for sympathy and affection. Oftentimes a kind word or a gesture of friendship to a troubled individual provides reassurance and even hope that enables him to overcome his difficulties. There is much clinical evidence to suggest that love possesses a good deal of therapeutic value. We are not referring here to merely conjugal love as between husband and wife but to a genuine concern for another person's welfare. The highest manifestation of love implies the element of self-sacrifice. One individual derives a great sense of pleasure in striving to please another and ensure his happiness. A more impersonal conception of love consists of treating an individual as a person and recognizing his right to realize all his capacities.

Witherington suggests a number of symptoms indicative of mental health in adults. These descriptive items are by no means exhaustive but merely serve to aid in the recognition of what might generally be considered normal behavior. The mentally well person:

1. Feels that others like to be with him
2. Feels secure in the presence of strangers
3. Has a wholesome sense of humor
4. Sleeps well
5. Feels that he has reasonable freedom and liberty
6. Expresses himself freely and appropriately
7. Has some wholesome hobby or recreation that will probably continue after retirement
8. Has a sense of belonging in the community
9. Feels at ease in groups
10. Feels that he received fair treatment at home and among other people
11. Enjoys living; has a good philosophy of life

12. Is emotionally well balanced
13. Is congenial with those of his own age
14. Accepts his own age gracefully
15. Feels that his services are worthwhile
16. Has a wholesome attitude toward the opposite sex
17. Appears relaxed, calm, serene; is not often tired
18. Is contented (not satisfied) with his economic status; is a good sport
19. Is self-dependent and is not always asking favors
20. Likes people; takes interest in them*

There is no clear line of demarcation between normal and abnormal behavior; the distinction is one of degree rather than kind. As was pointed out earlier, most normal (mentally healthy) persons, if subjected to severely disturbing pressures over a period of time, will display symptoms of deviant behavior. Therefore mental health denotes the achievement of a satisfactory adjustment to the requirements of reality. In other words, the mentally healthy or well-adjusted individual has satisfied his primary needs in harmony with the requirements of social living, thus developing and increasing his tolerance for stress.

CLASSIFICATION OF MENTAL DISORDERS

Everyone experiences frustrations from time to time, for frustrating situations cannot be wholly avoided. While consistent frustrations often result in maladjusted behavior patterns, occasional frustration may prove both healthy and stimulating. Generally speaking, however, all behavior that does not follow the principles of motivation with the realization and satisfaction of perceived or institutionally established goals, can result in some form of undesirable reaction. One or more of the following situations are often found to be causative factors in a large number of maladjustment cases:

1. Frustrated desires
2. Overprotection
3. Conflict of norms
4. Rejection
5. Physical handicaps
6. School or work environment
7. Sense of failure
8. Indecision
9. Social prohibitions

Abnormal behavior patterns manifest themselves in symptoms of psychoses or psychoneuroses. It is interesting to note that the term *insanity,* as used in reference to psychotic patients, is not a medical one. Actually, insanity is a legal and social term denoting mental disorders so severe that they render an individual incapable of managing his affairs, performing social duties, or being held responsible for his actions.

Mental disorders of the psychotic variety are classified according to their origin under two broad headings: organic and functional. Organic disorders evolve from structural or physiologic conditions. Closely associated with organic pathology are the symptoms of brain damage, neurologic disorders (diseases of the nervous system), mental retardation, and metabolic and nutritional disorders. By definition, an organic psychosis is a serious personality disturbance related to some physical aberration or structural defect of the body that can be treated as such.

Some 80% of all patients who are first admissions to mental hospitals, whether suffering from organic or functional psychoses, are subsequently discharged as recovered or improved. In fact, more than half of this number returned home after one or two months of hospital treatment, and the rest of them return home within one year.

Generally speaking, the prognosis for functional psychosis is more favorable than that for the organic type. However, of greatest importance to the long-range prognosis is the environment to which the patient returns. There is no substitute for early diagnosis and treatment of mental disorders, and, therefore, the longer the patient prolongs treatment the less favorable will be his prognosis for recovery.

The functional psychoses are those that

*From Witherington, H. C.: Educational psychology, Boston, 1952, Ginn and Company, pp. 350-351.

have their origin in the patient's environment, resulting from complete failure to cope with psychologic stresses and the nature of reality. They are divided into four main groups or types: schizophrenic reactions, paranoid reactions, affective reactions, and involutional psychotic reactions.

Hypochondria is a psychosomatic condition in which the individual exhibits excessive preoccupation with bodily functions with a tendency to exaggerate complaints about physical ailments. Through his concern with physical symptoms the individual solicits sympathy and attention from others, which provides him with a certain degree of security. Hypochondriacs are prone to do a great deal of reading of health literature and may be extremely careful about the foods they eat.

COPING

Those who are afflicted with mental disorders consciously or unconsciously strive to attain an avenue of escape from the feeling of frustration. The frustration, of course, results from their inability to effectively deal with problems and satisfy basic needs. Everyone at some time in his life employs psychologic mechanisms in defense of real or imagined threats to himself. However, it should be emphasized that the psychologic method of relieving tension and emotional stress is not necessarily the best way. In fact, many modes of adjustment are not really solutions at all but rather only ways of escape from frustrating or annoying situations. Some of these reactions are more desirable than others, and practically all of them are employed in normal behavior. The danger arises when some of the less desirable defense mechanisms are used to a great extent. If at all possible, when an individual encounters a frustrating situation, he should face the issue and attempt to establish a healthy defense.

One of the best means of adjustment is through compensation. The individual who fails in one pursuit may make up for it by excelling in another. The chief concern of the individual must not be the nature of the achievement but rather his success and accompanying social approval. The individual who is prevented from pursuing a chosen activity because of a mental or physical weakness may seek to alleviate his frustration by developing some skill or trait to offset feelings of inadequacy.

Compensatory adjustments are a necessary part of the overall behavior of society. Everyone is probably capable of achieving some kind of distinction or personal satisfaction. Most people have one field in which they do very well. The problem, of course, is to discover this capacity and not persist in the pursuit of one activity while success lies in another field. Both the mental health worker and vocational guidance counselor are vitally concerned with aiding young people in identifying their aptitudes and directing them into areas where they may be best utilized.

Just as there are desirable methods of dealing with emotional conflicts and frustrations, there are those less desirable responses, which are sometimes referred to as escape mechanisms. These defense mechanisms represent defenses against anxiety that result from a failure on the part of the individual to satisfy perceived or established goals. They represent unhealthy reactions to frustrations and if resorted to frequently can result in maladjustment on the part of an individual. Examples of such undesirable defense mechanisms include aggression, withdrawal, denial, repression, rationalization, projection, intellectualization, regression, and displacement.

Alcoholism and drug abuse are popular forms of escape. DeVito defines alcoholism as "an illness highlighted by impairments to physical health, socio-occupational functioning and interpersonal adaptation owing to excessive alcoholic intake, when such intake has become a prerequisite to normal functioning."*

*From DeVito, R. A.: Alcoholism, current therapy, Philadelphia, 1973, W. B. Saunders Company, p. 826.

Scientists are now hopeful that they are on the track of developing drugs that can control alcoholism—a disease that affects more than nine million Americans. The two drugs that have produced promising results are lithium, a compound that is highly effective in treating manic-depressive mental disorders, and propranolol, a drug used to prevent irregular heart beats. Both drugs appear to have the effect of relieving the drinker's depression that often begets further drinking.

Thorpe presents a lucid definition of an adequate coping mechanism. According to this definition, the healthy defense mechanism is one that "enables the individual to achieve a goal which is related in an integrated fashion to the satisfaction of a need, with a minimum expenditure of vital energy and without self—or other—destructiveness."* Many maladjusted individuals approach practically every situation with anxiety and fear. In an effort to overcome these threats to their adequacy they tend to adopt defensive measures that aid in coping with such unpleasant circumstances.

People must prepare themselves to meet the major catastrophes that are bound to occur in everyone's life. Examples include death of a loved one or the loss of home and possessions. Many people break up emotionally under the blows of adversity and never fully recover their stability.

PERSONAL ADJUSTMENT

The doctor's office is a prime location to spot potential suicide victims. According to suicide prevention experts more than 60% of all persons who commit suicide have visited a physician's office within 90 days of their time of death. Consequently, medical assistants are in a key position to detect the situational clues of potential suicide victims and bring them to the attention of the physician.

Suicide is a major public health problem —but one that is both treatable and preventable. Despite popular misconception, many persons who are thwarted in their attempt and receive treatment go on to live full lives. Suicide prevention centers are widespread throughout the country. A complete list of such community resources should be available in every medical office.

All of us, regardless of our degree of adjustment, experience emotions. Some people tend to regard them as shameful or a sign of weakness. There are several facts about emotions that warrant clarification.

First of all, emotions are physical phenomena; emotions will occur and we must expect them. It is possible to talk oneself out of a notion when a crisis arrives, but it is not likely that one can preclude an immediate emotion. Once an emotion seizes a person, regardless of whether it is pleasant or unpleasant, the only further emotional control a person has is by means of the attitude he adopts and the thinking he does at that time, which determine to a great extent his next emotion. It is well to know that the physical reaction (which is the emotion) will come. But we can be prepared for it so that it will not unnerve us.

At the moment of such a crisis the event pulls the trigger that brings on the emotion. Unless one understands just what is going on inside oneself, that is, the emotion one is feeling, apprehension and alarm may, and often do, increase.

Even though one cannot avoid these feelings, he should not be alarmed by them. These feelings are the emotion unavoidably triggered by the event. Starting at this point an individual should work out his own strategy and mature attitude for meeting the stressful situation.

An anxiety state may be conditioned and brought on by a certain room, a certain place, a certain object, a certain circumstance, or a certain train of thinking. In other words, the fear or anxiety, once established as a conditioned physical event, is no longer a notion; it is an emotion. An emo-

---

*From Thorpe, L. P.: The psychology of mental health, ed. 2, New York, 1960, The Ronald Press Co., p. 98.

tion cannot be dispelled by analyzing the fear and reasoning that the substance of the fear does not justify the reaction. However, it can be deconditioned by following these steps.

1. Realize that the physical symptoms (which are the emotion of fear or anxiety) switch on automatically whenever the switch is tripped by any one of many conditioning factors.
2. Tell oneself constantly not to be afraid of the symptoms of the emotion—the pounding heart, the trembling limbs, the difficult breathing. All these things are nothing bad, serious, or harmful but are merely the manifestations of a conditioned emotion.
3. If possible, one should deliberately expose himself to the conditioning factor, whatever it is, to bring on the fear. Tell yourself in a triumphant, determined way, "I'm going to lick this thing." Then deliberately repeat and repeat the exposure, maintaining the same triumphant and determined attitude. A feeling of confidence grows each time the fear is successfully handled. Each time the fear is managed it grows weaker, and the courage grows stronger. In this way fear or anxiety can be deconditioned.

Review questions

1. Define abnormal behavior.
2. Why are statistics pertaining to the mentally ill derived from hospital admissions generally incomplete?
3. Cite at least ten symptoms of mental well-being.
4. Name and describe the two major categories of psychosis.
5. What are the four main types of functional psychosis.
6. What are the healthy mechanisms of adjustment open to the individual?
7. Name at least four defense mechanisms of the less desirable variety.
8. What is the best method for dealing with emotions?
9. What role can the medical assistant play in suicide prevention?

Suggested readings

Coelho, G. V., Hamburg, D. A., Moos, R., and Randolph R., editors: Coping and adaptation, a behavioral sciences bibliography, U. S. Department of Health Education and Welfare, Public Health Service, Washington, D. C., 1970, Government Printing Office.

Committee on Medicolegal Problems: Alcohol and the impaired driver, ed. 2, Chicago, 1973, American Medical Association.

Current therapy 1973, Philadelphia, 1973, W. B. Saunders Co.

Fann, W. E., and Goshen, C. E.: The language of mental health, St. Louis, 1973, The C. V. Mosby Co.

Heck, E. T. et al.: A guide to mental health services, Pittsburgh, 1973, University of Pittsburgh Press.

Lindgren, H.: Psychology of personal development, ed. 2, New York, 1969, Van Nostrand Reinhold Co.

chapter 6

Medical ethics

ETHICS DEFINED

Ethics, a form of moral philosophy, is the study of human actions with regard to their being right or wrong. In other words, ethics may be considered the basic principles of correct conduct. The conduct of individuals as well as groups constitutes the subject matter of ethics.

In any discussion of ethics we must distinguish between voluntary actions or those we do intentionally and those actions that are considered involuntary. Ethical systems are primarily concerned with voluntary acts that presuppose sufficient knowledge and freedom of choice. The term *ethics* has its origin in the Greek word *ethos,* meaning custom or habitual mode of conduct, and the Latin word *ethicus,* meaning related to moral character.

It bears mentioning that true ethical reflection has rarely been carried on outside the context of religious conviction. Religions have always played a dominant role in coloring the moral judgments of both individuals and communities. In fact, the religions of ancient Assyria and Egypt embodied definite moral codes that were designed to regulate the conduct and decisions of their leaders, especially when moral matters were involved.

Even the earliest of man's tribal organizations attempted to establish rules of conduct for the guidance of its members. It is not surprising, then, that the various occupations have devised principles to regulate the behavior of those who join their ranks.

Over the years it has been necessary from time to time to modify the more specific rules of professional practice in order to make them conform to changing conditions. For example, the technology of practice set forth by the earlier physicians has long since fallen into disuse because it no longer courts the approval of modern medicine. The advancement of medical knowledge has rendered these earlier medical practices obsolete, and in some cases they would actually be harmful if applied. This does not apply to medical ethics, which has remained essentially standardized and relatively unchanged over a prolonged period of time.

There is, however, one rule of conduct

Glossary

adage a saying that has been much used; a well-known proverb

admonition advice concerning the faults a person has shown or may show; warning; counsel

indulgence to yield, usually unduly or unwisely, to wishes or inclinations

pilfering to take by petty theft; practice of petty stealing

zealousness filled with or incited by enthusiasm

that has remained unaltered throughout the ages. It has survived the test of time and usage. It is probably the most widely used rule, finding expression in many different forms from various sources. Often referred to as the Golden Rule, its origin has been credited to the ancient Chinese teacher-politician Confucius. "Do not do to others what you would not have them do to you." The spirit that permeates the teachings of Jesus Christ is an expression of this rule in another form.

The Golden Rule is the very embodiment of conduct that should serve as the cornerstone for the actions of all men regardless of their station in life. It not only serves as the basis for most of the rules of medical ethics but for most other codes of conduct as well. It is rather unfortunate that everyone does not abide by the wisdom contained in this basic rule of conduct, for certainly the world would be a much better place in which to live.

The ethics of a particular profession is the code by which it attempts to regulate the actions of its members and establish general standards. There are always a few persons in every line of endeavor, including the medical profession, who fail to uphold the tenets of their calling. This does not in any way excuse them from the responsibility of their wanderings. One of the chief purposes of formulating a professional code is to elevate the standard of competence in a given field by strengthening the relationships among its members, thereby benefiting the entire community.

Obviously, the mere formulation of a professional code of conduct does not automatically achieve these ends, but it does serve as a constant reminder and a guide. Most professional codes contain provisions authorizing the governing body to take disciplinary action against those members who violate the professional ethics of the group. In cases where the public interest is involved there are certain public laws in effect that serve to regulate professional practice. There are some professional codes that can boast of a long history requiring performance in accordance with high ethical standards.

The obligations of the physician were specified in a rigid code of behavior quite early in the history of medicine. This popular code, known as the Hippocratic Oath, is supposed to have been propounded by the Greek physician Hippocrates. The oath sought to pledge members of the medical profession to the preservation of life and the service of mankind. It has remained for centuries as an ethical ideal. It has also functioned as a basic frame of reference for much of the jurisprudence connected with the practice of medicine.

MEDICAL ETHICS

After the Oath of Hippocrates the most outstanding contribution to the development of medical ethics was made by Thomas Percival, a British physician, philosopher, and author. In 1803 he published his *Code of Ethics.* His interest in sociologic progress and his close association with the Manchester Infirmary led to the preparation of a code of conduct relative to hospitals. The code of ethics first adopted by the A.M.A. in 1847 was clearly based on Percival's Code.

Using the Hippocratic Oath and Percival's Code as frames of reference, the American Medical Association was able to adopt its own Principles of Medical Ethics. Although certain revisions have been necessary in order to reflect the temper of contemporary thought, the concepts originally adopted by the Association have remained unchanged.

Every medical assistant should be familiar with the Principles of Medical Ethics adopted by the American Medical Association. With the permission of the American Medical Association, a brief summary of these basic Principles is reprinted for the reader's consideration.

Principles of medical ethics

Preamble. These principles are intended to aid physicians individually and collectively in maintaining a high level of ethical conduct. They are not laws but standards by which a physician may determine the propriety of his conduct in his relationship with patients, with colleagues, with members of allied professions, and with the public.

Section 1. The principal objective of the medical profession is to render service to humanity with full respect for the dignity of man. Physicians should merit the confidence of patients entrusted to their care, rendering to each a full measure of service and devotion.

Section 2. Physicians should strive continually to improve medical knowledge and skill, and should make available to their patients and colleagues the benefits of their professional attainments.

Section 3. A physician should practice a method of healing founded on a scientific basis; and he should not voluntarily associate professionally with anyone who violates this principle.

Section 4. The medical profession should safeguard the public and itself against physicians deficient in moral character or professional competence. Physicians should observe all laws, uphold the dignity and honor of the profession and accept its self-imposed disciplines. They should expose, without hesitation, illegal or unethical conduct of fellow members of the profession.

Section 5. A physician may choose whom he will serve. In an emergency, however, he should render service to the best of his ability. Having undertaken the care of a patient, he may not neglect him; and unless he has been discharged he may discontinue his services only after giving adequate notice. He should not solicit patients.

Section 6. A physician should not dispose of his services under terms or conditions which tend to interfere with or impair the free and complete exercise of his medical judgment and skill or tend to cause a deterioration of the quality of medical care.

Section 7. In the practice of medicine a physician should limit the source of his professional income to medical services actually rendered by him or under his supervision, to his patients. His fee should be commensurate with the services rendered and the patient's ability to pay. He should neither pay nor receive a commission for referral of patients. Drugs, remedies or appliances may be dispensed or supplied by the physician provided it is in the best interests of the patient.

Section 8. A physician should seek consultation upon request; in doubtful or difficult cases; or whenever it appears that the quality of medical service may be enhanced thereby.

Section 9. A physician may not reveal the confidences entrusted to him in the course of medical attendance, or the deficiencies he may observe in the character of patients, unless he is required to do so by law or unless it becomes necessary in order to protect the welfare of the individual or of the community.

Section 10. The honored ideals of the medical profession imply that the responsibilities of the physician extend not only to the individual, but also to society where these responsibilities deserve his interest and participation in activities which have the purpose of improving both the health and the well-being of the individual and the community.*

The functions of the medical assistant are largely dependent upon the nature of the physician's practice, the amount of authority the physician wishes to delegate, and a willingness to demonstrate initiative and assume responsibility. Once these essentials have been determined, it is most important that both the physician and the assistant clearly agree on the extent of duties.

With increased efficiency the assistant will be in a position to take on additional tasks and further reduce the physician's burden. The assistant must be certain that these added tasks have been specifically outlined by the employer and are not merely taken for granted.

OFFICE ETHICS

The medical assistant is an extremely important factor in the success of a physician's practice. The physician bears responsibility for the consequences of any action of an assistant acting within the scope of set duties. The legal significance of the assistant's position is obvious. If the medical assistant behaves in any way that is acting in violation of the principles of medical ethics, the physician-employer may be subjected not only to an embarrassing situation but to an eventual lawsuit as well.

The assistant must be very careful not to jeopardize the trust of the physician. It is absolutely essential that the assistant also be cognizant of those aspects of the job that pertain to the application of good medical ethics and the legal limits of responsibility.

---

*From American Medical Association: Principles of medical ethics, Opinions and Reports, Chicago, 1973, American Medical Association, pp. VI-VII.

Most admonitions mentioned in the following pages are an outgrowth of the experience obtained from the study of numerous claims and legal actions filed against physicians involving the conduct of their office personnel. Each one will be treated briefly but separately.

The medical assistant must never forget that the work is strictly confidential. Since there is easy access to a great deal of confidential information, there must be no disclosure, either directly or indirectly, of a patient's confidential revelations. The law amply safeguards the rights of the patient in his relationship with the physician and likewise the rights of the physician in relationships with patients. The consequences of revealing patient confidences should be quite apparent.

As the involvement of government and other third party payers in the delivery of medical care grows, so also does the demand for accountability. An amendment to the Social Security Act now requires the establishment of Professional Standard Review Organizations (PSROs) to evaluate the medical care provided under federally financed programs such as Medicare and Medicaid. Patient's records provide the basis for evaluating quality of care. The PSRO law provides the government with access to physicians' offices to examine patients' records. The national network of PSROs currently being implemented by the Department of Health, Education, and Welfare will undoubtedly liberalize the laws with respect to confidentiality of patient records and therefore exercise a profound influence on medical ethics.

The assistant should always be polite and courteous to patients regardless of the circumstances involved. Any knowledge of the patient's financial condition must in no way reflect in the assistant's attitude toward the patient. Discussing the delinquent account of a patient within earshot of other patients is strictly taboo.

A great deal of aggravation can be prevented if the assistant, in handling a large fee to be charged to a patient, will make sure that the patient understands exactly what services he is to receive and any extra charges that may be anticipated. The physician is not obligated to send out an itemized bill, but it is a good idea to do so in order to reduce the number of telephone inquiries.

The ailments of patients should never be the subject of an office discussion. The patient comes to the office to discuss his medical problems with the doctor. One patient's condition should never be discussed with another patient. In talking about a patient's problems with him, the assistant may happen to say the wrong thing. Anxious patients have been known to misconstrue harmless comments. The medical assistant must always bear in mind that the physician is the only one permitted to make a diagnosis.

The relative merits of various forms of therapy or treatment should never be discussed with patients. Again, such comments are often misinterpreted and could lead to embarrassment for the physician, the assistant, and possibily other office personnel.

There is an old saying that a little knowledge can be a dangerous thing. The medical assistant's training provides a minimal amount of practical medical knowledge and sometimes there is an eagerness to dispense it. The temptation must be resisted. The assistant must never offer patients suggestions of possible medication or treatment without consulting the physician first. The individual who attempts to prescribe is guilty of practicing medicine, and it is unlawful for anyone to practice medicine without a license.

It is equally unethical, if not more so, for a medical assistant to discuss other physicians with patients. Patients frequently solicit criticism of former physicians in seeking to substantiate their own hostile feelings. No matter how angry a patient may be at another physician, the assistant will not furnish the irate patient with the fuel to kindle his flame.

Should a doctor tell the assistant in confidence that he thinks a patient was treated incorrectly, such information must not be revealed to anyone since it would be considered privileged communication. Practically all information regarding patients learned in the office must be treated as being confidential. Information should rarely, if ever, be given over the telephone in the absence of specific instructions from the doctor.

In cases requiring consultation with specialists, if one physician seeks the advice of another it is considered unethical for the second physician (consultant) to return part of the fee to the doctor in charge of the case. This is known as fee-splitting. The Judicial Council of the American Medical Association has held that the division of a fee constitutes the giving and receiving of a commission, which is completely contrary to the principles of good medical ethics. Fee-splitting, whenever done, is usually secretive, for it is generally done without the patient's knowledge. Perhaps the most objectionable aspect of fee-splitting is the fact that the patient assumes that the fee charged is reimbursement for the services of only one person.

Physicians are prohibited from advertising or soliciting patients in any form, even indirectly. This is a very delicate problem among members of the medical profession. The American Medical Association feels quite strongly about this matter. In fact, in 1936, its House of Delegates expressed the opinion that member physicians should be discouraged from permitting their names to be listed in a commercial advertising directory because it could be interpreted to constitute the indirect solicitation of patients. As for the medical assistant's role, care must be exercised not to publicly boast or advertise the accomplishments of the physician-employer.

Efficient medical assistants always think ahead and try to anticipate things before they occur. They try to keep track of the many details that must be attended to in a smoothly functioning office. They must not forget to remind their employer that the written consent of the parents or legal guardian is required before any surgery can be performed on a minor. Actually, for the physician's own protection, it is imperative that the consent of any patient, minor or otherwise, be obtained prior to an operation. In the case of a major surgical operation, a written consent should be signed by the patient. It is the duty of the medical assistant to protect the physician by having these consent forms available and bringing them to his attention.

The medical profession, among others, should assume a leadership role in determining the criteria of death and exactly what constitutes death with dignity. Enactment of legislation without appropriate medical input could lead to much more of medical practice being mandated in the form of statutes or regulations. Laws and courts alone cannot determine satisfactorily such matters as the criteria of death, the determination of the time of death, or what is death with dignity.

Good medical ethics dictates that a referred patient be treated only for the condition for which he was originally referred. If the physician in charge of the case is unable to accompany the patient in person, the consultant should be provided with a history of the case, together with the original physician's opinion and outline of the treatment given thus far. The medical assistant is usually charged with the responsibility of ensuring that such reports are forwarded to the consulting physician. Moreover, immediately following discussion with the patient, the consultant should communicate with the referring physician and advise him of the results of his findings.

Should a patient not wish to return to the referring physician, the medical assistant should pass this information on to the consulting physician-employer so that the matter can be discussed with the patient and the ethics involved explained. It is unethical for a doctor to treat a patient for any condition while he is being treated by another physician. If a patient happens to confide to the assistant that he has been under the care of another physician, it is the assistant's duty to report this information to the employer at once.

The assistant is cautioned to gain the goodwill of the patient and make his contact with the office as pleasant and beneficial as possible. Misunderstandings often result in ill feeling and undesirable consequences. When hospitalization is required for a patient, it is advisable to explain the physician's fee well in advance of admission. The patient should be informed about additional charges that may be made by the hospital such as charges for operating room, laboratory, anesthesia, pharmacy, and hospital room. Being furnished with this information enables the patient to make the necessary financial arrangements ahead of time. Nothing should be taken for granted.

All office personnel should be safety-conscious and on the lookout for any hazards that could cause injury to patients, the physician, or themselves. An alert assistant is watchful for loose wires, rugs or carpets that may curl up at the edges, rickety chairs, slippery floors, and protruding objects.

PERSONAL ETHICS

Accuracy in a medical office is absolutely essential and can never be taken for granted. Although the patient load in most offices demands speed, accuracy must receive overriding consideration. The consequences of not placing the proper emphasis on accuracy could be considerable.

Accuracy implies precision, exactness, and the absence of mistakes or errors. Accuracy presupposes two important elements: (1) a willingness to examine details along with the ability to think ahead and (2) a continual awareness of the necessity of such caution. Neatness is a very important aspect of accuracy along with intelligent thought. One should never be reluctant to ask questions or to double-check detailed work. The assistant should get into the habit of proofreading all written work before it leaves the office. Accurate reports and correspondence that is free from spelling and grammatical errors are a reflection of the physician's integrity and must be the norm rather than the exception in any office.

The cooperation of everyone connected with the medical team is most essential to the practice of good medicine. Cooperation implies getting along well with others. Cooperation among co-workers is particularly necessary in promoting office harmony and for the successful completion of those tasks which require the skills of more than one person. Even though office personnel may not like each other, they still must overcome their personal feelings and be cordial and pleasant to one another for the sake of providing a friendly atmosphere for patients.

The acid test of a good employee is a willingness to perform unliked or seemingly unimportant jobs. It must be borne in mind that the physician's chief concern is that of providing the best possible care and treatment for patients. In light of this fact it is his prerogative to ask his office aides to carry out any task or adhere to any schedule, within reason, that will enable him to satisfy his ends. The physician is the boss and it is he who makes the decisions and pays the office salaries. Whether or not one agrees with the reasoning behind them, all tasks should be performed with a spirit of cooperation and some semblance of enthusiasm. If the assistant feels so strongly about some of the duties, the matter can always be discussed with the physician or resignation could be offered. Every job has its disagreeable aspects, but if pursued with the idea that certain tasks are necessary and essential, the job becomes much easier to perform.

Dependability is expected of all employees. The dependable person is one who completes all assignments promptly, pays attention to orders and instructions, and reports to work on time. Routine assignments are performed by the dependable employee faithfully and with a minimum of supervision.

The physician should never have reason

to worry about whether the assistant called the hospital to make the necessary arrangements for surgery or made travel reservations to attend a meeting. On the other hand, he should also feel confident that while he is away from the office the more routine chores of posting and filing, ordering supplies, scheduling appointments, and completing insurance forms will be carried on. To finish some of these tasks, it may sometimes be necessary for the assistant to stay a few minutes overtime. However, a good assistant budgets time to be able to leave at the proper hour.

A most important aspect of dependability, especially in the case of the physician's office, is regular attendance. The physician must be able to count on the assistant to be on the job every day. Since the assistant plays such an integral part in the functioning of the office, irregular attendance cannot be tolerated for long.

The person who wishes to get ahead in a career, whatever it may be, must display initiative. Initiative is often described as consisting of original thinking and independent action. The assistant who shows initiative constantly seeks better ways of doing things in order that the physician-employer may be served more effectively. The physician's needs should be anticipated and the next major assignment prepared for.

Every employer considers himself fortunate to have a conscientious and energetic assistant who is capable of thinking ahead and relieving him from the burden of routine tasks. This type of efficiency does not go unrewarded. The more responsibility the medical assistant is able to assume, the more value the physician places upon the assistant and consequently there is likely to be greater financial remuneration.

If the assistant knows that the physician is scheduled to present a talk, pertinent material for him to examine can be gathered. If the physician plans to attend an out-of-town meeting the assistant should go ahead and make all the necessary reservations and travel arrangements before being reminded to do so. The office aide who takes this kind of action is obviously the aide who doesn't wait to be instructed what to do next.

One of the most necessary and desirable of all personality attributes is loyalty. Loyalty implies many things, but most important of all it presupposes that the assistant will speak well of the physician-employer at all times, that his interest is placed above any personal ones, and that office confidences are never betrayed.

All of the aforementioned qualities form a part of loyalty. As long as the physician pays the salary he is entitled to complete support from all of his employees, which includes both their unspoken as well as their spoken attitudes. Facial expressions often reveal more than the spoken word. Failure to respond to a question or not making a comment when one is called for also can result in creating a false or unfavorable impression.

Loyalty demands that one abstain from joining in the spread of office rumors via the grapevine. Passing on rumors is destructive to the morale of the entire office. All personnel should make it a practice to refute any rumor they know to be unfounded. Rumors can be destroyed at the outset by obtaining an immediate clarification of the facts.

The assistant usually has a hand on the pulsebeat of the physician's practice. The assistant occupies a position of trust and confidence, and is sometimes in a better position than the physician to make an objective assessment of his practice. Contacts with patients are generally longer and on a more informal basis than those of the doctor.

Usefulness as a public relations representative would be seriously weakened if it were not possible to communicate important information to the physician. If physician and assistant are able to communicate with one another freely, any information obtained by the assistant in the pursuit of the job should be passed on. The responsibility for evaluating the information and making decisions is then put squarely in the physician's lap where it belongs.

There still exists the popular misconception that people are generally born honest. No one is actually born honest; it is a character trait that can only be acquired through conditioning or education. Unfortunately, petty thievery accounts for a great amount of dollars lost each year to industry. As a matter of fact, many businesses count upon a certain percentage to occur each year and even go so far as to budget for it. It has become a far more serious problem for hospitals, which are constantly striving to operate in the the black.

The problem of petty theft arises in part from the fact that many individuals possess a double standard of honesty. There are some people who would never think of stealing money or possessions from anyone except their employer. In the case of those employed in the medical field, some think nothing of pilfering supplies from doctors' offices and hospitals. Petty thievery greatly increases the expenses of maintaining a private practice or running a hospital. Those who engage in this practice probably reason that supplies are not the property of any one person and thus belong to no one in particular. Nevertheless, pilfering is the same as stealing and represents dishonesty. Worst of all, it signifies disloyalty to one's employer.

It is certainly not as easy as it would first appear to be honest in our dealings with others. Many people choose the path of least resistance and select the easy way out, which is evasiveness. When the medical assistant leaves her position, does she just leave and not show up after payday or does she give her doctor-employer adequate notice (at least two weeks)? When confronted with the embarrassing question as to why she is leaving her job, does she fabricate an answer that she is sure will be readily acceptable for fear that the true reason would hurt the doctor's feelings? Once having left her position, does her bitterness and resentment permit her to openly criticize her former doctor-employer in the presence of others? All of the foregoing are important elements of honesty and personal integrity.

Those individuals who fail to see the reasoning behind the high standards of conduct and performance expected of medical personnel should voluntarily exempt themselves from a career in this field. In short, physicians want an assistant who:

- Likes the job.
- Knows the job.
- Wants to get ahead.
- Wants to do a day's work for a day's pay.
- Is cheerful, not sullen.
- Is always on the job, unless excused.
- Gets along with fellow workers.
- Enjoys doing a job well.
- Tries to avoid waste and cut expenses.
- Is always neat.
- Tells the truth and is sincere.
- Is willing to face any personal problems.
- Has a spirit of teamwork.
- Tries to put herself into the employer's place now and then.
- Feels that the job is a privilege, not a right.

In connection with the type of behavior expected of the medical assistant, reference is made to the so-called "Ten Demandments" of an employer. The majority of these are applicable to the medical assistant.

1. Don't lie; it wastes my time and yours. I'm sure to catch you in the end.
2. Watch your work, not the clock. A long day's work makes a long day short, and a day's short work makes my face long.
3. Give me more than I expect and I will pay you more than you expect. I can afford to increase your pay if you increase my profits.
4. You owe so much to yourself, you can't afford to owe anybody else.
5. Mind your own business, and in time you will have a business of your own to mind.
6. Dishonesty is never an accident. A

good person recognizes temptation.

7. Don't do anything here that hurts your self-respect. The employee who is willing to steal for me is capable of stealing from me.
8. It is none of my business what you do at night, but if dissipation affects what you do the next day and you do half as much as I demand, you'll last half as long as you hope.
9. Don't tell me what I like to hear but what I ought to hear. I don't want a valet to my vanity, but I need one for my dollars.
10. Don't worry if I kick; if you're worth correcting, you're worth keeping. I don't waste time cutting.

Just as the physician graduating from medical school subscribes to the principles of the Hippocratic Oath, so also should the medical assistant be dedicated to the ideals pertinent to the position. If it were possible to standardize an oath for the medical assistant it should include, at least, the following essentials:

Medical assistant's oath

To exalt my work and consider it an opportunity to serve the profession of medicine and people in need of medical care.

To increase my knowledge of medicine as it relates to health and medical service.

To remember that my success is the success of the office in which I work; therefore I shall be loyal to my employer and concerned for the welfare of this office and these patients.

To develop a sense of protection for the health and well-being of patients by complete and careful sterilization and sanitary precautions.

To comply with prevailing medical laws.

To increase my effectiveness by constant self-improvement.

To add to my effectiveness by following the important rules of personal hygiene and developing a sympathetic and pleasing personality.

To deport myself with a dignity in keeping with professional standards.

To refrain from critical discussion of other assistants, of physicians and their practices, of the patients, or of the business or professional affairs of my own or any other physician's office.

To speak with pride of my employer when out with my friends.

Review questions

1. What is the Golden Rule and how is it applicable to the medical profession?
2. What is the purpose in formulating a professional code?
3. What serves as the foundation for the Principles of Medical Ethics?
4. In your own words, briefly summarize the ten Principles of Medical Ethics.
5. What is the potential impact of PSRO on the confidentiality of medical records?
6. Why is it wrong for the medical assistant to discuss patients' ailments with them?
7. What is the physician's chief concern and how can the assistant help in this regard?
8. Describe dependability and tell why it is such an important quality for the medical assistant to possess.
9. What do we mean by a double standard of honesty?

Suggested readings

American Medical Association: Principles of medical ethics, Opinions and Reports, Chicago, 1971, The Association.

Roth, R. B.: Medicine's ethical responsibilities, J.A.M.A. **215:** 1956-1958, 1971.

Torrey, E. F.: Ethical issues in medicine: the role of the physician in today's society, Boston, 1968, Little, Brown and Co.

chapter 7
Medical jurisprudence

RELATIONSHIP BETWEEN PHYSICIAN AND PATIENT

A contract is a mutual agreement, upon sufficient consideration, to do or not to do certain things. Contracts may be of two types: expressed or implied. An expressed contract is formulated in distinct oral or written language. An implied contract is one not necessarily created or evidenced by the explicit agreement of the parties but one which can be inferred by law, as a matter of reason and justice, from the conduct and actions of the parties involved. The relationship between physician and patient falls into the latter category.

To be enforceable in law a contract must meet the following criteria.

1. The parties must be capable of contracting.
2. There must be agreement (a meeting of the minds).
3. There must be mutual consent.
4. There must be no mistake or fraud.
5. There must be valid consideration.

Infants, of course, cannot legally contract. A minor's contract remains voidable until he becomes of age, at which time he can, within a reasonable time, render the same contract cancelled or not cancelled.

An individual who claims to be physician is legally charged with the responsibility of possessing the required knowledge. The patient has a right to assume this to be a fact. The physician contracts, by implication, that he possesses the ordinary degree of skill and learning commonly held by reputable physicians in the same general line of practice in the the same locality or in similar localities. He is further obligated to use his degree of learning, skill, and best judgment for the benefit of the patient. In keeping with his position of trust and confidence with regard to the patient, the physician is obligated to act in good faith. If he

---

Glossary

accessory a person who, even if not present, is concerned, either before or after, in the perpetration of a felonious act

consideration a legal term referring to the thing given or done, or to be given, done, or abstained from, by one party to a contract, in exchange for the act or promise of another

disparagement the act of speaking of someone slightingly and undervaluing his worth

libel slanderous statements that are printed

malpractice the treatment by a surgeon or physician in a manner contrary to accepted rules and with injurious results to the patient

morbidity the relative incidence of disease

reciprocity granting equal status to physicians of two different states with respect to the privilege of practicing medicine

res ipsa loquitur "The thing speaks for itself." The general law of negligence; applies whenever a patient is injuried by an instrumentality entirely under the control of the physician.

respondeat superior "Let the master answer." This means that an employer is liable in certain cases for wrongful acts of his employees.

revocation the cancellation of an instrument or an act; also the summoning back of a license

slander spoken statements that tend to damage a person's reputation

statutory pertains to a statute or law; a law created by or dependent upon legislative enactment knows a case to be beyond the scope of his competency, it is his duty to so inform the patient and advise him accordingly.

Because the physician-patient relationship is predicated on the assumption that a contract, either expressed or implied, has been voluntarily entered into by both parties, a physician is never obligated to accept a patient. This is true even where there is clear evidence that an obvious emergency exists.

Most decisions involving questions of the creation of the physician-patient relationship are logically those involving emergencies. The question rarely arises otherwise. When a patient presents himself to a physician in a nonemergency situation and asks that physician to treat him, whether the physician accepts the patient or refuses to do so, both parties generally understand clearly whether or not the relationship was established. On the other hand, in an emergency the fact may be so confused that, in good faith, there may be a complete absence of understanding between them.*

The physician is legally obligated to complete his responsibilities to patients even in situations where financial remuneration is delinquent or not anticipated. Should the physician abandon a case, he leaves himself open to suit.

Under ordinary circumstances the physician practices within the bounds of an implied contract with his patient. While practicing within the sphere of his implied contract with the patient the physician *is not* bound contractually:

1. To accept employment from anyone who solicits his services (He is free to use his own discretion.)
2. To restore the patient to the same condition as he was before treatment.
3. To possess the highest skill or the maximum education
4. To effect a recovery with every patient (The physician who fails to effect a recovery cannot be condemned for lack of skill.)
5. To be familiar with the various reactions of patients to anesthetics or drugs of any kind
6. To be as skilled as the specialist if he is a general practitioner
7. To make a correct diagnosis
8. To be free from mistakes of judgment in difficult cases
9. To display infallibility of judgment
10. To continue his services after he has been discharged by the patient or by some responsible person, even if harm should come to his patient
11. To guarantee the successful result of any treatment or operation

A physician has the right, after agreeing to accept an individual as his patient, to make reasonable limitations on the relationship. He is under no legal obligation whatever to treat patients who may wish him to exceed those limitations. A specialist, for instance, most certainly does not have to practice outside his specialty and, in fact, would doubtless be severely criticized for doing so except in an emergency where no other physician was available. The mere fact that a patient grows progressively worse while under the physician's care and shows improvement when he withdraws from a case does not necessarily constitute liability.

In consulting a physician a patient has a right to expect that the treatment rendered will be in accordance with the principles of the system or school of medicine to which the physician belongs. Legally it is the duty of the physician "to exercise that degree of care, judgment, and skill, which other physicians of good standing of the same school or system of practice usually exercise in the same or similar localities under like or similar circumstances."* More specifically, this

*From American Medical Association: Law and medicine—creation of the physical-patient relationship, J.A.M.A. **226**:1391-1392, 1973.

*From Morris, R. C. and Moritz, A. R.: Doctor and patient and the law, ed. 5, St. Louis, 1971, The C. V. Mosby Co., p. 327.

contract between patient and physician obligates the physician to:

1. Use due care, skill, and diligence in treating patients and to keep informed as to the best modern methods of diagnosis and treatment
2. Perform to the best of his ability whether he is to receive a fee or not
3. Exercise his best professional judgment in all cases, particularly in those where there is considerable doubt involved
4. Consider the established customary treatment of the profession in similar cases
5. Abstain from performing experiments on a patient without securing the patient's complete understanding and approval
6. Provide proper instructions for a patient's care to the person responsible in order that proper treatment can be given the patient in the doctor's absence
7. Furnish proper and complete instructions to each patient
8. Take every precaution to prevent the spread of contagious diseases
9. Advise patients against the performance of needless or unwise operations

As we can see, the legal relationship between physician and patient is governed by an implied contract requiring certain obligations on the part of both contracting parties. At first glance it would seem that most of the responsibilities in this contractual agreement become the burden of the physician, but actually the patient also has certain implied duties.

The patient is obliged to cooperate with the physician and to follow any instructions given. Should an incorrect diagnosis be made because the patient fails to give the proper information, the physician is not liable. The patient is obligated to follow the physician's treatment and orders, provided the treatment is similar to the system or school of medicine to which such physician belongs.

The physician is not responsible for the negligence of hospital or other attendants over whom he exercises little or no control. Moreover, if a patient either willfully or negligently fails to follow the physician's instructions, the patient has little legal recourse. It is interesting to note that the failure or inability of the patient to follow the physician's instructions does not alter the fact that the instructions were correct in the first place. A patient, who when requested by the physician to return for further treatment fails to do so, has no legal recourse against his physician.

The physician-patient relationship could be construed to end with a missed appointment. For example in a recent ruling the Ohio Supreme Court held that when a patient failed to keep an appointment with a surgeon for postoperative care and declined to see the surgeon again, the physician-patient relationship was terminated no later than the date of the missed appointment.*

THE LAW OF MEDICAL PRACTICE

All states including the District of Columbia license doctors of medicine (M.D.) and most also license doctors of osteopathy (D.O.). The license itself is issued in each state by a licensing board either after a candidate has passed his initial examination or by an agreement of reciprocity with another state. Depending upon the state, the license must be renewed every year or every two years. The Medical Practice Act of each state defines the limitations of medical practice and prescribes the penalties for practicing without a valid license.

Physicians serving on active duty with the Armed Forces and with the United States Public Health Service are not required to possess a license while providing health services to federal beneficiaries within federal facilities. Nevertheless, the law of medical malpractice applies with equal force to all professional medical employees, whether in private practice or employed by federal, state, county, or city authorities. However, the federal government is obliged to provide for the federal physician's defense.

*From The Citation **26**:9, October 15, 1972, The American Medical Association.

Thus a medical error that would give rise to a suit against a private physician could likewise result in a suit against a federal physician. Whether in private practice or governmental practice, all professional medical personnel should be familiar with the legal principles applicable to malpractice claims.

A physician's license may be revoked under certain conditions. The Medical Practice Act of each state specifies the conditions that would warrant the revocation of a physician's license. The following are some of the more common reasons for revocation.

1. Drug addiction
2. Unprofessional conduct
3. Fraud in application
4. Alcoholism
5. Unethical advertising
6. Producing or aiding in an illegal abortion*
7. Conviction of a felony
8. Crime involving moral turpitude
9. Mental illness
10. Betrayal of professional secrets
11. Loss of a malpractice suit*
12. Promiscuous prescribing of drugs for known addicts and police characters

The physician should, whenever possible, try to avoid a court appearance, either as a plaintiff or a defendant. The publicity connected with testimony in court is seldom advantageous and usually results in damage to his reputation. Court proceedings are always annoying and tedious, and unless there is a great issue at stake, it is hardly worthwhile for the physician to initiate a suit.

*The Judicial Council of the American Medical Association has offered the following commentary on the Association's policy on abortion as reaffirmed by the House of Delegates in June, 1973: "The Judicial Council is charged with interpreting the Principles of Medical Ethics as adopted by the House of Delegates of the AMA.

The Principles of Medical Ethics of the AMA do not prohibit a physician from performing an abortion that is performed in accordance with good medical practice and under circumstances that do not violate the laws of the community in which he practices.

In the matter of abortions, as of any other medical procedure, the Judicial Council becomes involved whenever there is alleged violation of the Principles of Medical Ethics as established by the House of Delegates."

Malpractice

Black's Law Dictionary defines malpractice as "the failure upon the part of the physician to properly perform the duty which devolves upon him in his professional relation to his patient, a failure which results in some injury to the patient. Thus, malpractice has two essential parts to it: first, that the physician fails to do his duty; and second, that definite injury to the patient is the result of his failure."*

Although it would be difficult to pinpoint a definition of malpractice to cover all phases of conduct, the law is quite explicit with regard to malpractice. The physician who does not adhere to the standards of medical practice expected of him and as a result inflicts injury upon the patient becomes legally liable for money damages.

Malpractice suits arise both from the quality of medical care given and from indirect influences of a sociologic nature. The family doctor has given way to the busy specialist, who generally sees the patient after referral by another physician. The specialist seldom gets to know the patient intimately.

The less personal the patient-physician relationship, the more likely the patient will think of suing for damages when he is dissatisfied with the results of treatment. Most patients want to be treated as individuals, and react best to treatment when they know their physician has a genuine interest and concern for their welfare.

Medical assistants can help physicians make up for any shortcomings in communication. Again the role of the medical assistant as a bridge between physician and patient is most important. If the assistant is able to soothe a patient's feelings when

*From Shindell, S.: Highlights of the law of medical practice, AAMA Bulletin **9**:46, 1965.

minor mistakes have been made and convince him that the physician is his friend, the patient will be less tempted to sue.

Unfortunately for the physician, a patient may institute a malpractice suit against any physician who formerly attended him in a professional capacity. Obviously, the mere filing of an action does not imply that the claim has any merit. In fact, the majority of all the malpractice claims brought against physicians are often without merit. However, in any malpractice suit the physician is the loser in the end, both financially when the decision is unfavorable and in terms of damage to his reputation unless he has taken steps to protect himself. The vulnerable position of the physician exposes him to the constant peril of malpractice litigation.

Practically every physician carries malpractice insurance, since a patient can sue a physician if the patient is injured as a result of negligence or an accident caused by the physician or his employees. Of course, the patient must prove negligence, which in most cases is not an easy matter.

Should a patient win a damage suit, the physician's insurance would be liable up to the amount of indemnity or the limits of coverage. It is incumbent upon certain high-risk specialists to carry greater amounts of coverage. Malpractice insurance premiums are excessively high where available and are usually paid annually or semiannually.

Physicians are finding it increasingly more difficult to obtain malpractice insurance, especially those practicing in "high-risk" specialties. The growing volume of malpractice claims has gradually forced many insurance underwriters out of the business. Thus the number of companies currently writing such insurance has been reduced to only a handful who, out of necessity, charge exorbitant premiums. This is one of the factors contributing to the high cost of medical care.

Malpractice insurance policies should never be allowed to lapse as long as the doctor is practicing, nor should policies be thrown away. The physician's assistant should assume the responsibility of reminding the physician about renewal dates. Malpractice actions may be initiated many years after an injury is supposed to have occurred, and therefore the physician's liability as well as that of the insurance carrier is retroactive.

The physician who is involved in a lawsuit has two immediate sources of assistance available—the medical society of which he is a member and his insurance carrier. While the medical society chiefly furnishes advice, there are a number of state societies that sponsor their own professional liability programs. Not only is the trend in this direction, but several carriers who write individual policies have announced recently that they will not write a physican's professional liability insurance unless he is a member of some level of organized medicine.

Maryland has a unique new law that now requires professional liability insurance carriers to report details of all medical malpractice claims or actions to a central agency. Under this new procedure trends can be observed and providers of care alerted to be extra careful.

A malpractice alert system such as that established in Maryland is of obvious value to both physicians and hospitals. If a physician knows that a particular type of malpractice claim is on the rise, he will make a special effort to avoid it.

The law creating the system was promoted by the Maryland State Medical Society. Under it, carriers report malpractice claims and actions to the Maryland Commission on Medical Discipline, a state agency composed of physicians. This committee then conveys the data to the state medical society for evaluation and analysis.*

Obtaining the patient's written or oral consent prior to an operation is an absolute must. A physician who administers treat-

*From Carlova, J.: A new way to stay on top of malpractice mistakes, Medical Economics, January 7, 1974, p. 80.

ment or performs surgery on a patient without having the necessary authority is guilty of committing assault and battery for which he may be held criminally or civilly liable. In most instances the authority to treat or perform an operation results from the consent of the patient or someone eligible to act in his behalf. For consent to be legally valid it must be intelligent and informed. In other words, the patient or person responsible must fully understand what is to be accomplished and the nature of the risk involved. If the patient is a minor or is incompetent, the consent of his parent or legal guardian will suffice. The only exception to this practice pertains to emergency cases, where time is of the essence.

The most common grounds for suits against physicians are: nonfulfillment of contract, negligence, incompetence, lack of informed consent, abandonment, and invasion of privacy. By far the great majority of suits result from surgical procedures, x-ray therapy, and the repair of fractures.

In order to preclude suits for infringement or nonfulfillment of contract, a physician should always avoid making any positive promise as to certainty of cure or as to the outcome of treatment. Such caution is especially necessary in plastic surgery, for instance, where cosmetic results can never be guaranteed.

Defenses against malpractice

The patient's records may be the most important evidence in any medical professional liability suit, regardless of the factual issues involved. Either hospital or physician's office records may demonstrate the presence or absence or professional conduct that corroborates the patient's claim. Maintaining complete and up-to-date records is, of course, time-consuming and difficult. However, a physician confronted by a negligence suit who can demonstrate that what was done in treating the patient was proper, will consider the efforts of record keeping worthwhile.

During the course of an operation, should the physician find some other condition he considers immediately remediable by operative means and attempt to correct it, the patient, as has been determined in the courts, can sue the doctor for having performed some portion of the operation in a manner not in accordance with that previously agreed upon. This issue can be prevented by requesting the patient to sign a written agreement giving consent to everything that, in the doctor's professional judgment, is necessary.

The essential requirements of a written consent form are that it state clearly the nature and extent of the operative procedure authorized and that it be signed by a person legally qualified to give such consent. The sample consent form seen in Fig. 7-1 may be used for any type of surgery and can easily be modified to suit an individual case by adding or deleting appropriate sections.

If the form is to cover voluntary sterilization or skin grafting, all parties involved should be requested to sign the consent form. The important thing is that the patient acknowledge his understanding of the nature and scope of a surgical procedure in writing and that it become part of his medical record. For the consent to be considered informed, the physician must supplement the form by explaining in simple language the procedure, the risks, and the possible complications of the proposed treatment.

In some jurisdictions voluntary sterilization may be illegal without adequate medical justification. Unfortunately, many states have produced no clear-cut authority on this issue, leaving it to the educated guesses of attorneys. The preponderance of advice has been of a conservative nature, and many hospitals today will not permit sterilizations for nonmedical reasons to be performed within their operating rooms. Such operations are therefore left to be carried out in physicians' offices, where the best possible conditions do not always exist.

The doctor's assistant should be familiar with the various consent forms and ensure that a ready supply of all types is available

A.M.
Date __________________________ Time ____________P.M.

1. I authorize the performance upon ____
(myself or name of patient)

of the following operation ____,
(state nature and extent of operation)

to be performed under the direction of Dr. ____.

2. I consent to the performance of operations and procedures in addition to or different from those now contemplated, whether or not arising from presently unforeseen conditions, which the above-named doctor or his associates or assistants may consider necessary or advisable in the course of the operation.

3. I consent to the administration of such anesthetics as may be considered necessary or advisable by the physician responsible for this service, with the exception of

_______________________________________.
(state "none," "spinal anesthesia," etc.)

4. I consent to the photographing or televising of the operations or procedures to be performed, including appropriate portions of my body, for medical, scientific or educational purposes, provided my identity is not revealed by the pictures or by descriptive texts accompanying them.

5. For the purpose of advancing medical education, I consent to the admittance of observers to the operating room.

6. I consent to the disposal by hospital authorities of any tissues or parts that may be removed.

7. I am aware that sterility may result from this operation. I know that a sterile person is incapable of becoming a parent.

8. The nature and purpose of the operation, possible alternative methods of treatment, the risks involved, and the possibility of complications have been fully explained to me. No guarantee or assurance has been given by anyone as to the results that may be obtained.

(cross out any paragraphs above that do not apply)

Signed __________________________________
(patient or person authorized to consent for patient)

Witness __________________________________

Fig. 7-1. Consent to operation, anesthetics, and other medical services. This is a general form of consent, used with various procedures; the portions that are inapplicable may be deleted. (From Morris, R. C., and Moritz, A. R.: Doctor and patient and the law, ed. 5, St. Louis, 1971, The C. V. Mosby Co.)

To whatever medical authority it may concern:

In the event that you are unable, after diligent effort, to obtain parental consent, then please perform any and all medical treatment requested or needed by my minor child, ------------------------------------, that you, in the exercise of your best professional judgment, deem necessary under the circumstances.

We hereby consent in advance to such treatment and agree to hold you harmless from any action or claim based on lack of parental consent that may arise in connection with such treatment.

Precautions: --

(list known problems, such as diabetes, asthma, heart condition, aller-

----

gies, blood type, special medications or diets, all tetanus shots and dates of each, etc.)

Signed --

(mother)

Signed --

(father)

Fig. 7-2. Parental consent to medical treatment of a minor. (From Morris, R. C., and Moritz, A. R.: Doctor and patient and the law, ed. 5, St. Louis, 1971, The C. V. Mosby Co.)

in the office. Pertinent paragraphs may be added or deleted where applicable.

In the case of autopsies, prior to performance the consent of the person who possesses legal rights to the dead body must be obtained. The only exception applies to cases involving crime, sudden death, suspicious circumstances, and reasons of public policy. Permission to perform an autopsy should be secured from the relatives of the deceased in order of the nearness of the relation: surviving husband or wife, children, parents of the deceased, and so on to the next of kin. The nearer the relationship, obviously the stronger the right of consent.

The general law of negligence is commonly referred to as res ipsa loquitur, "The thing speaks for itself." The doctrine of res ipsa loquitur has been held applicable in the malpractice field chiefly in the following kind of cases: (1) infections resulting from broken glassware, needles, or unsterilized instruments; (2) burns from electrical machines, hot-water bottles, hot compresses, and so on; (3) slipping of surgical instruments causing injury; (4) leaving foreign bodies in tissues; (5) burns and injurious effects from diathermy or ultraviolet lamps; and (6) injury to a portion of anesthetized patient's body outside the field of treatment of operation.

Ordinarily the complaining party in a medical malpractice case has the responsibility to prove that the physician or other medical employee was negligent. However, when an injury occurs that ordinarily does not occur except for someone's negligence, the legal doctrine of res ipsa loquitur comes into play. Under the circumstances, the law permits an inference of negligence on the part of the medical worker involved, who then must prove that he was not negligent.

Res ipsa loquitur would apply in the case of burns or other injuries suffered while a patient was under anesthesia. Usually in malpractice suits, expert medical testimony is necessary to prove medical negligence, but where the doctrine of res ipsa loquitur is applicable, expert testimony is not necessary.

A.M.
Date ____________________________ Time ____________P.M.

I (We) request and authorize the physicians and surgeons in attendance at the ______________________________ Hospital to perform a complete autopsy on the remains of ________________________________ and I (we) authorize the removal and retention or use for diagnostic, scientific, or therapeutic purposes of such organs, tissues, and parts as such physicians and surgeons deem proper.

This authority is granted subject to the following restrictions:

____

____

(if no restrictions, write "none")

The following special examinations shall be made:

____

____

I (We) wish the remains to be released to:

_____________________________________ __________________________ _____________

(name of undertaking establishment) (city) (state)

I (We) represent that I am (we are) the ________________________ of the deceased
(relationship)
and entitled by law to control the disposition of the remains.

Signed _________________________________

Signed _________________________________

Witnesses:

____

____

(name of person obtaining authorization)

____

Witness

Fig. 7-3. Authorization for autopsy. This form should be signed by the surviving spouse or if there is no surviving spouse, by the next of kin in accordance with the applicable state law. If the deceased was a minor who lived with both parents, it is desirable that the authorization of both be obtained. (From Morris, R. C., and Moritz, A. R.: Doctor and patient and the law, ed. 5, St. Louis, 1971, The C. V. Mosby Co.)

A physician is usually not liable for the negligence of a substitute physician whom he has referred to take his place. He is merely expected to have exercised reasonable care in his choice and to have secured the consent of the patient to the substitution. His responsibility ceases once the substitute has been accepted by the patient.

The law is quite lenient in dealing with incompetency. The physician is expected to possess only the average amount of learning and skill comparable to that evidenced by physicians and surgeons in the locality where he practices.

There is no fixed method by which to determine the duty of a physician. The physician is obligated only to use his best judgment and to apply the most approved modern methods, but he is neither required nor expected to perform the miraculous. Should he employ the ordinary diagnostic methods and aids at his disposal and at the same time make an incorrect diagnosis, neither is he to be held accountable nor has he violated any standard of practice. Nevertheless, the allegation by a patient that in arriving at his diagnosis the physician did not use all the necessary and obtainable diagnostic aids is a firm basis for malpractice action.

The prudent practitioner or specialist avoids any case he considers to be beyond the scope of his competency. In cases where there is some doubt as to the actual procedure involved, consultation with another physician should always be sought and x-ray photographs taken as a precautionary measure whenever they can be used to aid in the certitude of a diagnosis. It is a good practice to take x-ray photographs again after treatment in order to determine the degree of success.

The fact that a patient died is not a suffi-

A.M.
Date ____________________________ Time __________P.M.

I have been fully informed by Dr. __________________________ of the risks, possible alternative methods of treatment, and possible consequences involved in treatment by

means of ____

____

____

for the relief of ____________________. Nevertheless, I authorize Dr. __________________ to administer such treatment to me.

Signed ________________________________
(patient or person authorized to consent for patient)

Witness ________________________________

Fig. 7-4. Consent to treatment. This is a general form of consent that is primarily used with the administration of hazardous drugs and treatment normally provided in the physician's office. (From Morris, R. C., and Moritz, A. R.: Doctor and patient and the law, ed. 5, St. Louis, 1971, The C. V. Mosby Co.)

cient basis for a charge of homicide. However, if it can be shown that the gross ignorance or negligent care administered by the doctor resulted in the patient's death, the doctor can be held criminally responsible.

Physicians could avoid most damage cases if they would take the time to warn patients of unfavorable possibilities, expressly stipulating that in the event of an unfavorable reaction they would not be responsible. This procedure could be further secured by a written notice such as that seen in Fig. 7-4, a copy of which should be given to the patient and the original placed in the patient's file.

The laws of most states are designed to protect the confidential nature of the physician-patient relationship. In the course of his contact with a physician the patient reveals many facts about his innermost feelings and physical condition that he assumes will not be divulged to anyone. To reveal these confidential communications without the express consent of the patient constitutes a violation of medical ethics. In order to protect himself the physician should always take the precaution of securing the patient's written authorization before disclosing confidential information (Fig. 7-5).

Normally a physician's records are not subject to subpoena, and all information obtained from patients is regarded as strictly confidential and secret. This right to privacy may usually only be waived by the patient concerned, a chief exception to this rule being when a malpractice suit is brought against a physician. The initiation of the suit is held to constitute a waiver of privilege on the part of the patient, thus enabling the physician to produce his evidence.

In actual practice, however, the obligation to keep secret any information relating to a patient's illness is based first on ethics and only secondarily on law. According to the principles of medical ethics of the American Medical Association, a physician may not reveal the confidences entrusted to

1. I authorize Dr. ____________________ to disclose complete information to ______ ________________ concerning his medical findings and treatment of the undersigned from on or about ____________________, 19____, until date of the conclusion of such treatment.

2. Further, I authorize him to testify, without limitation, as to all of his medical findings and the treatment administered to the undersigned, in any legal action, suit, or proceedings to which I am or may become a party; and I waive, on behalf of myself and any persons who may have an interest in the matter, all provisions of law relating to the disclosure of confidential medical information.

Signed ____

Place ____

Date ____

Witness ____

Fig. 7-5. Authorization for disclosure of information by patient's physician. (From Morris, R. C., and Moritz, A. R.: Doctor and patient and the law, ed. 5, St. Louis, 1971, The C. V. Mosby Co.)

him in the course of medical attention, nor may he release the deficiencies he may observe in the character of his patients unless he is required to do so by law (PSRO) or unless it becomes necessary in order to protect the welfare of the individual or of the community.

The greatest number of requests for releasing information do not come from legal sources but from the patient himself, his family or relatives, neighbors, other physicians, employers, governmental agencies, insurance companies, and attorneys. The release of any information concerning patients' conditions should come directly from the physician with the written consent of the patients involved. A prudent medical assistant will insulate herself against the pressure of these requests. It is important to bear in mind that, simply because an employer arranges for the medical care of employees and even has agreed to pay for it, this agreement does not act as a waiver of the confidential relationship between the patient and physician.

There are a number of conditions that must be reported to the local public health department by private practicing physicians. Public health departments are primarily engaged in preventive medicine and in protecting the health of the community. The health officer as an administrative agent is required to enforce the law, and the private practitioner is expected to fulfill his legal responsibility in the proper and adequate reporting of certain conditions. As a matter of fact, there are some twenty communicable diseases that should be reported by telephone and confirmed in writing. The local health authority generally prints and has available a supply of confidential morbidity forms. These forms often list all of the communicable diseases that are required by law to be reported.

X-ray films can serve as valuable items of evidence. Films, like all medical records, become the permanent property of the physician who orders them. It is important that they be retained by the doctor so that in the event of a lawsuit they may be produced as demonstrable evidence.

In a malpractice action there must exist a causal relationship between the alleged negligence and the injury suffered. A patient is obliged to exercise the care of a reasonably prudent man and cannot recover damages from a physician if injury resulted from his own negligence.

The patient who willfully or negligently fails to follow a physician's instructions is barred from recovering damages in court. This is known as contributory negligence.

Dear Mr. ____:

At the time that you brought your son, William, to me for examination this afternoon, I informed you that I was unable to determine without x-ray study whether a fracture exists in his injured right arm. I strongly urge you to permit me or some other physician of your choice to make this x-ray examination without further delay.

Your neglect in not permitting a proper x-ray examination to be made of William's arm may result in serious consequences if in fact a fracture does exist.

Very truly yours,

____, M.D.

Fig. 7-6. Letter to patient who fails to follow advice. (From Morris, R. C., and Moritz, A. R.: Doctor and patient and the law, ed. 5, St. Louis, 1971, The C. V. Mosby Co.)

If a patient fails to cooperate with a physician and refuses to heed sound medical advice or discharges a physician, the physician should be able to prove that he did not abandon the patient. In order to protect himself, the physician should send a letter to the patient relating the pertinent facts involved confirming the discharge or failure to follow medical instructions. It is always a good idea to send such letters by registered mail and retain copies for the office files. An example of a letter to a patient who fails to follow advice is shown in Fig. 7-6.

A letter confirming discharge of a physician by the patient could read as shown in Fig. 7-7.

Once the physician-patient relationship has been established, the physician cannot arbitrarily abandon his patient and still remain immune from legal action. Even in cases where his chances of financial remuneration are doubtful, he may not withhold his professional services. The doctor has little choice in such instances but to continue to attend his patient.

"The relationship between physician and patient continues until ended by mutual consent of the parties, revoked by dismissal of the physician by the patient, or until the physician determines that his services are no longer needed and then only upon reasonable notice."*

For purposes of legal protection, before withdrawing from a case the physician is required to notify the patient of his intention and allow the patient a reasonable length of time to obtain another physician. This notification of intention to withdraw from a case should take the form of a letter sent to the patient by registered mail with one copy being retained for the files. A letter of withdrawal may be drafted by the doctor or his secretary to fit the individual case. In any event, in addition to giving the reason for withdrawal, the letter should also contain the following essentials: reasonable notice, the date of severance, the willingness to treat, and the need for further medical care. A sample letter is shown in Fig. 7-8.

The statute of limitations may sometimes, under certain conditions, be considered to constitute a defense against a malpractice action. The statute of limitations fixes a period of time or a deadline for instituting legal action to prosecute claims or enforce judgments. After the lapse of the prescribed period of time, which varies from state to

*Quoted in Holder, A. R.: Law and medicine, abandonment, J.A.M.A. **225**:1572, 1973.

Dear Mr. ____:

This will confirm our telephone conversation of today in which you discharged me from attending you as your physician in your present illness. In my opinion your condition requires continued medical treatment by a physician. If you have not already done so, I suggest that you employ another physician without delay. You may be assured that, at your request, I will furnish him with information regarding the diagnosis and treatment that you have received from me.

Very truly yours,

____, M.D.

Fig. 7-7. Letter to confirm discharge by patient. (From Morris, R. C., and Moritz, A. R.: Doctor and patient and the law, ed. 5, St. Louis, 1971, The C. V. Mosby Co.)

state, this law serves as a barrier to legal action.

Frequently, a disgruntled patient hires an unscrupulous attorney to file a malpractice suit as a counteraction to a physician's suit for his fee. Since most states possess statutes that specify the interval during which malpractice suits may be filed, the physician is sometimes wise not to press his suit for the recovery of his fee until the malpractice issue is no longer available to the patient as a defense. In most cases it is difficult for a claimant to sustain a malpractice suit against a physician after one year.

The statute of limitations does not offer protection to the physician who fraudulently conceals his malpractice guilt from an injured patient. The weight of authority has been that the statute begins to run against an action of this kind from the date of the discovery of the injury rather than from the date the injury was caused. The mere fact that the patient was not aware of his injuries or of his right to a cause of action for malpractice, at least in the absence of fraudulent concealment, has been held to be immaterial. The statute does not apply in a case where there is said to be continuing negligence, as, for example, when a foreign body has been left in the patient's tissues.*

Continued vigilance on the part of both physician and assistant is the best defense against the accusation of negligence. From a legal standpoint, actions are evaluated by the courts in light of what an average, ordinary, and reasonably prudent physician would do in similar circumstances.

The prudent physician will not undertake any major operations at the office as long as there exists any possibility of danger. The physician and the assistant should always be on the alert in order to avert accidents. Instruments and office equipment should be maintained in safe and proper working order. Patients have been known to bring suit because of alleged injuries sustained in falls from operating tables and beds.

In a well-managed office all types of equipment, especially those of an electrical and mechanical nature, should be checked

*From Regan, L. J.: Doctor and patient and the law, ed. 2, St. Louis, 1949, The C. V. Mosby Co., pp. 185-186.

Dear Mr. ____:

I find it necessary to inform you that I am withdrawing from further professional attendance upon you for the reason that you have persisted in refusing to follow my medical advice and treatment. Since your condition requires medical attention, I suggest that you place yourself under the care of another physician without delay. If you so desire, I shall be available to attend you for a reasonable time after you have received this letter, but in no event for more than five days. This should give you ample time to select a physician of your choice from the many competent practitioners in this city. With your approval, I will make available to this physician your case history and information regarding the diagnosis and treatment which you have received from me.

Very truly yours,

____, M.D.

Fig. 7-8. Letter of withdrawal from case. (From Morris, R. C., and Moritz, A. R.: Doctor and patient and the law, ed. 5, St. Louis, 1971, The C. V. Mosby Co.)

and tested regularly. The medical assistant will want to keep a record of all service calls and note any defects discovered.

THE MEDICAL ASSISTANT AND THE LAW

A basic understanding of the essential legal principles governing the performance of the medical assistant's professional duties will be of great assistance in avoiding legal action, both against herself and against her employer. She must be knowledgeable of just how far her professional duties will carry her within the protection of common and statute laws. Consideration will be given here to the employer-employee relationship, which is the only legal principle applicable to the medical assistant since she is not a licensed worker.

Liability for negligence has been recognized to imply the physician's responsibility not only for his own acts but also for those employed by him. The doctrine of *respondeat superior,* more commonly known as the Law of Agency, is the legal statute that holds the physician liable for the actions of his assistants. While acting within her capacity the medical assistant becomes the agent of the physician-employer.

In summary, then, the physician is liable for the negligent acts or omissions of employees providing such acts occur during the course and within the scope of the employment agreement. On the other hand, the physician may not be held responsible for the wrongful acts of his licensed employees even though they may be working under his direction if it is within their competence to know the true nature and outcome of the acts. For example, the physician is not held responsible for the negligent acts of interns, nurses, and other hospitals employees, especially when he is not an owner of said hospital, except when these acts are committed under his immediate direction and control. Moreover, since the landmark decision in the case of Darling vs. Charleston Memorial Hospital, hospitals are now being held responsible for the negligent acts or omissions of those within their employ. The effect of this decision was to make the hospital along with the physician liable for damages and responsible for the quality of medical care rendered.

The physician exerts direct control and supervision over the assistant's activities, and therefore a certain degree of responsibility is assumed for some but not necessarily all of the assistant's actions. The medical practice acts of most states require that only a licensed individual be allowed to administer an injection or withdraw blood from a patient's vein. The assistant, therefore, should be familiar, for self protection as well as for the physician-employer's protection, with the Medical Practice Act of the state. Broadly speaking, the legal obligations of the medical assistant in performing those functions that fall within the scope of the job include:

1. Carrying out all the reasonable and legal orders of her employing physician
2. Avoiding all acts which in her judgment pose a danger to the patient
3. In an emergency situation when a physician is not at hand, doing everything within her capacity to sustain and prolong life.*

It is imperative for each physician to assure himself that his assistants are adequately trained to perform the tasks delegated to them. The medicolegal risk to the physician can be minimized when assistants have some guidelines as to what is expected of them and how they are to go about it. Such duties should be defined in writing by the physician-employer, as well as what duties assistants are not permitted to perform.

It is interesting to note that a recently concluded study in Minnesota of office-based physicians shows how heavily they rely on their medical assistants. For instance the study revealed that one patient in five is seen only by medical assistants, and more

*From Wolf, G. D.: The physician's business, Philadelphia, 1938, J. B. Lippincott Co., p. 342.

than half of the physicians polled, delegate such tasks as injections, routine history taking, applying dressings, and removing casts. Nearly half permit their assistants to give telephone advice, and one physician in twenty-five even permits medical assistants to make hospital visits for him.*

As a rule, a physician should not delegate those functions that require professional judgment leading to diagnosis or treatment. Scope of practice is clearly spelled out in the licensing statutes for those medical disciplines to whom they apply. However, the medical assistant is placed in a difficult situation in the absence of licensure because what can and cannot be done is not clearly established.

In most instances, the physician's malpractice insurance policy can also cover the medical assistant; this should always be checked, and a rider can be added if necessary. The physician may not know the extent of coverage and therefore the assistant should always verify this fact with the employer or the insurance agent.

Another way of looking at the problem is that if a physician can remove some burdens by delegating many tedious, time-consuming tasks to assistants, the chances of malpractice may actually be lessened. An important factor in malpractice suits is not so much what the physician did wrong, but rather what he failed to do, often because he was overburdened with the routine aspects of medical care not requiring his expertise. An assistant, by assuming some of these tasks, can help the physician upgrade the quality of his practice, which in turn helps prevent malpractice claims from arising.

There is a significant legal difference between performing acts on the doctor's orders and performing them under his supervision. The medical assistant must not carry out the doctor's orders if, in her judgment: (1) she is instructed to perform what she believes or knows to be an illegal act and (2) she is aware of a gross error in the doctor's orders that could result in harm to the patient.

Emergencies are considered somewhat differently. Accidents usually create the need for swift action in the form of first aid. First aid is best defined as the emergency treatment given to the victim of an accident before regular medical care can be administered or the services of a physician can be obtained. In serious emergency cases, time is often of the essence, and first aid procedures are those that are needed to preserve and prolong life. The good first-aider deals with the whole situation, the person, and the injury. He knows what to do as well as what not to do. Thus he avoids the errors so commonly made through well-meaning but misguided efforts. He confines his procedures to what is necessary, recalling that the handling of injured parts should be kept to a minimum.

Since many physicians are reluctant to give voluntary emergency care to injured persons at the scene of a highway accident because of their fear of malpractice suits, many states have enacted so-called Good Samaritan statutes to encourage such voluntary help by protecting physicians from legal liability for any negligence which may occur under such circumstances. These statutes generally make the physician immune from any suit arising out of emergency care, provided such care is given in good faith and with due care under the circumstances. A few states extend this protection to registered nurses. The statutes are not uniform in scope or coverage, but generally apply only to roadside or highway accidents.

Unfortunately, the genuine good Samaritan who undertakes first aid procedures beyond his competence, which result in further injury to the victim, is liable to suit. Many individuals have been known to shy away from rendering aid at the scene of an accident for fear of legal implications. However, the medical assistant sometimes has a

*From Professional Briefs: Medical Economics, November 12, 1973, p. 47.

moral obligation to take some legal risks.

The medical assistant is often called upon to make a medical judgment in the absence of the physician, but medical treatment should be rendered only when it is reasonably certain that a delay would not be acceptable. In an actual emergency, the law permits anyone to do whatever is reasonably necessary, provided that the action taken is within his skill and competence. This would certainly apply to the medical assistant in an office emergency, but suits against medical assistants for this reason are virtually nonexistent.*

In handling office emergencies the medical assistant must exercise great discretion. It is a good idea, however, to have a general plan of action worked out in advance that can be applied to all emergency situations. It is the responsibility of the physician to determine the competence of a medical assistant. Titles and certificates are not necessarily an adequate indication of preparation.

Such acts as introducing sutures and trimming wounds are not considered proper first aid procedures necessary for the preservation of life. If the medical assistant, in the course of administering emergency treatment, makes an honest and reasonable error in judgment, it is usually not considered a cause for liability.

The medical assistant who supports the physician-employer in performing a felonious act is considered, in the eyes of the law, to be an accessory before the fact. Even if the assistant had nothing to do with the commission of the crime but possesses knowledge to the effect that the crime has been committed and attempts to shield the physician by concealing the facts, the assistant is none the less considered guilty and liable to prosecution as an accessory after the fact.

The charge of conspiracy is very closely related to that of being an accessory before the fact, the difference being one of degree rather than kind. An individual may be charged as an accessory before the fact if he merely aids, supports, or encourages another in the commission of a crime. To be guilty of conspiracy, an individual must actually assist another in the commission of a crime. The medical assistant who knowingly assists the physician in performing an illegal act may be liable to prosecution for conspiracy.

The position of the medical assistant makes her especially vulnerable to charges of slander and libel. Not only must she be careful not to reveal confidential information, but she must make a special effort not to make thoughtless remarks. Slander and libel both carry the liability of punitive damages. Slander refers only to spoken statements which tend to damage an individual's reputation. Libel, often referred to as written slander, applies only to those statements that are written or printed. In order to qualify as being slanderous or libelous, belittling statements must be untrue and made to a third party. Any false statement made in disparagement of the professional ability of a physician by a disgruntled employee is a sufficient basis for a charge of slander.

Likewise, it is very easy for suit to be brought against a physician or medical assistant because of loose talk. Statements to patients by medical assistants such as, "I can't understand why the doctor didn't put you in the hospital for that ailment," or "It's too bad you didn't come to see Dr. X first," may sound rather harmless but are actually potentially dangerous. Even though criticism of the patient's former physician may not be intended, a disgruntled patient is apt to interpret such remarks as inferring that malpractice was committed.

The volume and size of malpractice suits are steadily increasing and becoming a constant source of irritation. The best safeguard against a malpractice suit is an efficiently run office where scrupulous attention is paid to details. In this connection, here are a few axioms every office should observe.

---

*From Bergen, R.: Is some legal risk inevitable? AAMA Bulletin **9**(2):36-40, 1965.

1. Claims can sometimes be prevented by the establishment and continuation of a good patient-physician relationship. Be particularly aware of the need for that relationship if a poor medical result has occurred. A suit-prone patient is usually an emotionally immature person who mistrusts doctors, does not state his complaint honestly, and is generally uncooperative in the treatment process.
2. The physician should be familiar with the nature and amount of insurance coverage.
3. Insurance policies should be filed in a safe place but be available for easy reference.
4. The physician should see to it that exceptionally detailed records are maintained.
5. Always be available to assist a patient in getting on and off the examining table.
6. Check all equipment frequently to make certain that everything is in perfect working order.
7. Always double-check before administering medication to patients.
8. Adhere to proper sterilization techniques.
9. When examining a female patient, the presence of a female medical assistant should be required.
10. Keep a sufficient inventory of supplies.
11. Do not leave prescription pads lying about.
12. Make no critical statements or remarks about the treatment administered by another physician.

REPORTS REQUIRED BY LAW

The medical assistant must be aware that from time to time the physician is required to submit reports to the various governmental agencies and should take the initiative to learn when and where to submit these reports and keep an adequate supply of the necessary forms in the office. Then if an up-to-date calendar is kept, it will be possible to remind the physician when a particular report is due. Since the laws vary so much from state to state and even from county to county, the assistant should find out exactly what statutory reports are required in the area by contacting the local department of public health.

Practically every state requires reports of births and deaths as well as reports of certain types of communicable diseases. Report forms and deadlines for filing may vary from state to state. Generally speaking, the physician is required to report all injuries and deaths resulting from violence to the local police department. "In the following instances, deaths must be reported to a coroner or medical examiner:

1. Sudden and unexpected natural deaths
2. Deaths occurring without medical attendance
3. Deaths due to violence
4. Deaths occurring under suspicious or unusual circumstances
5. Deaths occurring while in custody of the law
6. Deaths due to industrial diseases or injuries
7. Deaths associated with diagnostic, therapeutic and anesthetic procedures
8. Deaths from diseases thought to be of a contagious nature."*

As mentioned earlier in this chapter, most states require that certain diseases be reported to the appropriate government agency, usually the health department. Reports of this type are used in formulating quarantine laws and instituting appropriate preventive measures. The purpose of filing these reports is quite obvious: to protect the health of the community. Physicians dealing with these diseases must complete and submit reports as soon as possible after making a positive diagnosis. Failure to comply warrants severe penalties.†

---

*From Shindell, S.: Highlights of the law of medical practice, AAMA Bulletin **9**(2):48, 1965.

†From Statutory reports, M.S. for Medical Secretaries, Vol. IV, No. 21, Waterford, Conn., 1965, Bureau of Business Practice, Division of Prentice-Hall, Inc.

A report must contain, in addition to the attending physician's signature, the name and address of the patient, the nature of his disease, and the approximate time of onset. Reports of venereal disease should include the following personal information: the patient's sex, marital status and whether a pregnancy exists, the diagnostic laboratory tests performed and their results, whether or not the patient is under treatment, the identity of the patient's possible contacts, and whether or not these contacts have been examined. The appropriate forms are obtainable from state and local health departments.*

A physician who administers, prescribes, or dispenses any drugs listed under the Controlled Substances Act of 1970 must register annually with the Bureau of Narcotics and Dangerous Drugs, Registration Branch, P. O. Box 28083, Central Station, Washington, D. C. 20005. In a few states physicians must also register with the appropriate state agency. Both the registration and issuance of triplicate order forms are the responsibility of BNDD, a branch of the Department of Justice. For a complete listing of all controlled drugs, contact the nearest regional office of BNDD.

It is most important for the medical assistant to be aware that only a physician may prescribe drugs and only a physician or a licensed pharmacist may dispense drugs. In many cases it is necessary to distinguish between prescribing, dispensing, and administering. Prescribing is often defined as the selection of a particular remedy to alleviate a particular symptom or group of symptoms. Prescribing is held to be the prerogative of physicians and dentists in most states. Such acts as labeling, mixing, compounding, and transferring from bulk storage are considered dispensing; prescription drugs may not be dispensed by a nurse or attendant.

*From Statutory reports, M.S. for Medical Secretaries, Vol. IV, No. 21, Waterford, Conn., 1965. Bureau of Business Practice, Division of Prentice-Hall, Inc.

In most states only a licensed nurse may administer medication to a patient. When a nonlicensed worker such as a medical assistant administers medication, it is assumed that it is done under the direct supervision of the physician-employer.

Druggists are compelled by law to keep a record of each prescription sale, and such records must be maintained for two years subject to inspection at any time.

A prescription for the specific drugs named in the Harrison Narcotic Law must be originated in triplicate form and bear the following information:

1. The physician's name, address, and registry number
2. The name, address, and age of the patient involved
3. The date the prescription was written

Two copies of the prescription are given to the patient, which he in turn gives to his pharmacist. The pharmacist forwards a copy to the Federal Narcotics Bureau and retains one for his records. The physician keeps the third copy for his files.

It is unlawful for a pharmacist to refill a prescription for narcotic drugs regulated by this law. A new prescription must be originated in each case following the same procedure. The penalty for violation of the Harrison Law is a fine of not more than $2,000 or imprisonment for not more than five years or both.

The law does not permit the gradual withdrawal of ambulatory narcotic addicts, and the sympathetic physician who administers small doses of narcotics to a patient to ease the effects of withdrawal is open to prosecution. There are, however, experiments currently under way with a synthetic drug known as methadone. Methadone, although addictive, is supposedly cheaper and less harmful than heroin. The drug is being used to facilitate the withdrawal of addicts from the more dangerous drugs, but federal guidelines require that methadone be dispensed only under the direction of a physician.

The Drug Abuse Control Amendments of

1965 added a new classification of prescription-legend drugs which includes those which have a potential for abuse because of their depressant or stimulant effect on the central nervous system or because of their hallucinogenic effect. The law specifically mentions amphetamines and barbiturates and gives the Food and Drug Administration authority to add additional drugs by regulation.

Practically all states require the physician to report to the proper authorities suspected cases of parental neglect and injuries sustained from parental beatings. Animal bites should also be reported in order to determine the presence of rabies in the guilty animal.

The medical assistant should be alert to helping detect and diagnose instances of the so-called parent–infant trauma syndrome. Although the Federal Department of Health, Education, and Welfare has developed a model act to be adopted by the states, few states have uniform reporting laws. The medical assistant should not only be acquainted with the laws of the state but also inform the physician-employer regarding such laws.

Review questions

1. Define a contract and list the essential elements that should be included to make it enforceable.
2. If a physician knows he is not going to be paid for his services, what should he do?
3. Describe the Medical Practice Act and name ten reasons for revoking a physician's license.
4. Explain why it is necessary for every physician to carry malpractice insurance. Why do some physicians carry more insurance than others?
5. What are the common causes for malpractice suits? Why is the doctor always the loser in a malpractice suit?
6. Name some of the ways by which the doctor can protect himself against malpractice suits.
7. What is contributory negligence? If a patient refuses to follow medical advice, should the physician withdraw from the case? Explain your answer.
8. What is the statute of limitations? How does it affect the doctor's practice?
9. State the legal obligations of the medical assistant in performing her job.
10. List and describe at least three different types of statutory reports that originate in the physician's office.

Suggested readings

American Medical Association: Consent forms with legal analyses, Chicago, 1962, The Association.

Black's law dictionary, ed. 4, St. Paul, 1968, West Publishing Co.

Hanlon, J. J.: Public health: administration and practice, ed. 6, St. Louis, 1974, The C. V. Mosby Co.

Morris, R. C. and Moritz, A. R.: Doctor and patient and the law, ed. 5, St. Louis, 1971, The C. V. Mosby Co.

Moritz, A. R., and Morris, R. C.: Handbook of legal medicine, ed. 4, St. Louis, 1975, The C. V. Mosby Co.

chapter 8
Public relations

PUBLIC RELATIONS AND THE MEDICAL ASSISTANT

Public relations is still a growing field. In fact, it is so encompassing that practically every segment of our economy uses it to foster the goodwill of clients.

If we were given the difficult task of isolating one of the many functions of the medical assistant as being the single most important aspect of the job, we would have to say it is public relations or perhaps patient relations.

The physician depends upon the assistant in many ways, but most of all he depends upon an ability to practice the kind of public relations in the office that will generate more and happier patients. The assistant's responsibility in this area is an essential one, whether the official title or duties in the office are those of medical secretary, receptionist, assistant, or just plain office worker.

The medical assistant serves as the doctor's public relations representative. The assistant frequently spends time with the patient prior to his consultation with the physician and is often the first person the patient encounters when entering an office and sometimes the last one he sees. The initial impression conveyed to a patient at this time will, more often than not, have a great deal to do with whether or not that patient ever returns to the doctor. Many patients frequently become annoyed and leave the care of a physician simply because of the attitude of the assistant or because of the reception accorded them over the telephone.

"First impressions are sometimes lasting impressions," is certainly applicable to this particular situation. The medical assistant must be somewhat aggressive in the office and yet not overly so; must be able to take charge of things and be tactful and diplomatic; and at the same time, must always be cognizant of the necessity of promoting goodwill for the doctor.

For lack of a better analogy, we might compare the airline hostess and the medical assistant, for both have a great deal in common. The airline hostess greets passengers; the medical assistant greets patients in a friendly and courteous manner. Both the airline hostess and the medical assistant must meet any emergency with level-headed composure. Like the airline hostess, the medical assistant remains responsible for the

Glossary

brusque abrupt in manner or speech; blunt
ingenuity skill in planning, inventing; cleverness
kaleidoscope a constantly changing pattern, such as a pattern of bright colors or colored objects
pertinent related to the matter at hand or what is being considered
reticent disposed to keep silent or say little; reserved in speech

comfort and well-being of the doctor's patients until the end of their office visit.

The knowledgeable medical assistant reacts promptly and handles patients with confidence and firmness. For example, it may suddenly be discovered that during an extremely busy period a patient was somehow ushered into the wrong treatment room. Seeing another patient in the waiting room whose condition requires specialized treatment in the treatment room, the mistake is realized. The experienced assistant normally would indicate to the patient in a courteous but firm manner that a mistake has been made. It should be suggested that there is another more appropriate treatment room down the hall equally as comfortable. The assistant should then help the patient gather up his belongings, pick up his charge slip, and escort him out of the room. The incident is handled politely but firmly without any question as to who is in command of the situation.

One form of communication we often tend to forget about is the transmission of our attitudes. We tend to forget that some very important psychological exchanges take place between people without a written or spoken work. People communicate through facial expressions, hand gestures, and other more subtle forms of body language. In the larger sense, attitude is the manner in which one looks at his environment.

Physical appearance plays an equally important part in the formulation of first impressions. A neat, attractive assistant is certainly a good tonic for any patient. Presenting a good appearance is as much an ethical duty as is the use of tact and diplomacy.

Do you look like a professional person? The following are a few basic principles that a well-groomed medical assistant should consider important:

1. Abide by the standard health rules of getting plenty of sleep and exercise and eating balanced meals
2. Follow the rules of personal cleanliness
3. Wear comfortable shoes while working
4. A woman should wear a minimum amount of makeup in good taste
5. Shampoo hair regularly and arrange it neatly and attractively
6. Keep nails spotlessly clean
7. Avoid smoking while on duty

APPLYING THE TECHNIQUES OF PUBLIC RELATIONS

Helping patients pass waiting time pleasantly will be a great test for the medical assistant's ingenuity. Being responsible for patients' comfort from the time they enter the office until they see the doctor, the medical assistant's first thought should be to put them at ease. Whatever happens to a patient during this time might well make the difference between a successful or an unsuccessful session with the physician.

These first few minutes are most important because they should put the patient in the right frame of mind for his visit with the physician. The doctor's office is like a second home to those who work there, but it is easy to forget that it may be a strange and even frightening place to a patient, especially if he has never seen a doctor before. First of all, the patient might be worried about his complaint or condition. Second, he might be apprehensive about the consultation or examination and what the doctor may say to him. Finally, and just as important, he might be fearful of certain medical procedures, such as having an injection or having his skin punctured to obtain a blood sample.

Many patients will not show their fear in obvious ways. It is the medical assistant's job to recognize the less obvious indications—a nervous laugh, a restless or depressed attitude, and so on. Such patients require extra reassurance to be put at ease. Of course, giving special attention to anxious patients does not mean neglecting the patients who seem perfectly relaxed and familiar with the office environment. Regular patients are sometimes apt to resent being taken for granted or slighted in any way simply because of their long association with the doctor.

The management of patients before and during an examination is certainly an exacting and delicate responsibility. Here are some reminders and tips to help the medical assistant become more adept at patient management:

1. Try not to be brusquely efficient—efficient, yes; brusque, no. A detached, cold, or impersonal attitude will only intimidate or irritate patients.
2. Do not take anyone for granted. Patients should not be treated as objects on an assembly line to be manipulated by command; no complaint or ailment is routine to them. The medical assistant may see scores of patients during the week, but each one should be treated as an individual.
3. Keep examining rooms spotlessly clean at all times. Traces of a previous patient's visit should not be visible. It is also important to make sure the room temperature is adequate for patients who must disrobe for examinations.
4. The assistant should never show a patient to the examining room, tell him to disrobe, and then forget about him. Try to be helpful and attentive by showing him where to hang his clothes, how to put on the dressing gown, and where to sit while waiting to see the doctor. Be alert to the patient's needs; offer help with clothes removal if indicated. Never take it for granted that the patient knows the procedure.
5. Be sure to keep the door to the examining room closed while the patient is disrobing and waiting to see the doctor. Some patients may be too shy to close it themselves, yet they are embarrassed by the lack of privacy.
6. It is most important not to leave a patient in the examining room alone for long periods of time. He will only wonder if he has been forgotten, and become unnecessarily anxious. If the physician is unduly delayed with another patient or busy on the telephone, look in on the waiting patient from time to time and keep him informed. Try to let him know how long he may have to wait and offer him some reading material.
7. Give a nervous patient a few words of encouragement. Avoid making any reference to his complaint or reason for seeing the doctor. A friendly chat about some general topic will often relax a patient and make him feel more at ease.

Nothing is more distressing to patients than to be kept waiting for long periods of time. When a patient becomes visibly irritated at waiting, try to show him some personal attention. There are a variety of different techniques—his reading light can be adjusted, his ashtray emptied, or he may be offered another magazine. Perhaps the assistant could even chat with him for a few moments. In any event, a special effort should be made to work him into an inner office or treatment room. At least he will feel that he is making progress.

The following suggestions should serve as the foundation for a public relations program in any physician's office:

1. A medical assistant should always exhibit a pleasant, sympathetic, and friendly attitude.
2. A medical assistant should try to memorize names of patients. There is no more important person than the patient himself. Keeping a supply of memo pads is of invaluable service in helping to track down many of the office details. No one should trust too much to memory.
3. Confidences about patients, their illnesses, or their personal lives should never be repeated.
4. The assistant should always avoid mentioning the names of patients too loudly, for sometimes the physician's specialty reveals the patient's reason for consulting him.
5. The efficient and intelligent scheduling of the physician's appointments helps

avoid long waits by patients and is one of the medical assistant's chief duties.

6. Patients usually appreciate concern beyond the office visit. Show interest in the patient and his problems. As one learns some pertinent facts about a patient's personal life, it is a good idea to jot them down somewhere in the patient's folder. They can often serve as stimulants for making small conversation.
7. Many physicians, especially pediatricians, make a regular practice of sending birthday cards to their patients.
8. Many patients use up precious office time asking the same routine questions although there are things they want and need to know as well as office procedures that should be explained to them. Some physicians are dealing with this problem by writing an annual letter to every patient seen during the previous twelve months. Such a letter has proved to be an efficient way to anticipate and respond to common questions, thereby leaving the medical assistant as well as the doctor more time to devote to patient care.

COPING WITH CHILDREN

How does the assistant handle a waiting room filled with children and mothers with appointments? It certainly sounds challenging, and it is. Children are often noisy and restless. They may climb over the furniture and try to run through the corridors. This makes entirely too much noise and naturally disturbs some of the older patients.

Experience has demonstrated that there are several methods the assistant may employ to maintain a calm and orderly waiting room. Some offices suggest to mothers that they make an appointment at a better time, preferably when children are in school. Often the mother is merely reticent to suggest a different time herself, and this alternative is just what she is waiting for.

Some offices have a special room set aside for children. If the regular waiting room becomes too noisy or congested, the mother and her children can be moved into this room with the explanation that the children can play there while waiting to see the physician.

The more the assistant understands the needs and desires of children, the easier it is to cope with them. A knowledge of child psychology can be an invaluable asset. The assistant must realize that most children are active and full of energy. In fact, just watching them for a short length of time is enough to make any adult weary. Obviously, then, children cannot be expected to wait and sit quietly with nothing to do.

It is always a good practice to have a few toys in the office that can be passed out to the children to keep them busy. Such toys should be of the variety that can be easily cleaned, collected, and maintained in some sort of container that keeps them from becoming a problem. Most children enjoy scribbling and writing, and therefore a supply of scratch pads and pencils will prove very useful. Some children's books might prove invaluable as a time-filler for children. Try to purchase only those books that have cardboard pages; they cannot be torn out as easily. Sometimes it may be necessary to offer children drinks of water, lollipops, and balloons in order to persuade them to sit still and read or look at books.

Another technique that has proved successful in many offices is to furnish a corner of the room especially for children. This will naturally divert their attention to one particular area. Some possible amusements might include miniature cars, building blocks, coloring books, paper, and crayons. If the budget is limited, the accent can be put on a few time-consuming toys, such as wooden jigsaw puzzles, plastic maze games, and kaleidoscopes. The supply of books and toys may only have to be replaced several times a year, and most of these articles are relatively inexpensive.

Music is an inexpensive technique. The cost of an FM radio is the only item necessary except that consideration should be given to its location. It should be placed where young patients cannot tune in other stations or turn up the volume.

There are always a few children who frequently annoy the other patients. There is really no excuse for such a problem to exist. A normal child will generally respond immediately when corrected by an adult. Moreover it is usually possible to reason with children if one has a few moments to spare and uses the right approach.

SPECIAL PROBLEMS

Each patient presents a new challenge with a different need for care and the employment of a special technique. The deaf, the blind, the handicapped, the mute, emergency care situations, the geriatric, and the foreign born all offer a unique opportunity to be of assistance.

From time to time every medical assistant will have occasion to receive patients who speak in foreign tongues. In dealing with the patient who does not speak English, the main thing to remember is to smile and be cheerful. Dismay or a hint of frustration only increases the patient's tension. The assistant should avoid shouting, although it is almost instinctive to raise one's voice when one is not being understood. Shouting is hard on everyone's nerves and does not improve communication. Sign language, on the other hand, can and often will help both the assistant and the patient.

It is also helpful if the medical assistant will compile a list of clergymen, relatives, and friends who can be called upon to act as interpreters when a patient who does not speak English makes an appointment. Since interpreters are not always available, it might be a good idea to purchase dictionaries for some of the more common languages one encounters. Gathering together a file of pictures, drawings, and models that help to illustrate directions for the patient is quite useful. Incidentally, some surgical supply houses and x-ray companies sometimes supply such materials free of charge.

Those patients who understand and speak some English have to be handled with special care as well. Although the assistant will not need as many illustrations or as much sign language, she must speak slowly and distinctly. Only the simplest words should be chosen for this restricted vocabulary. Avoid using technical terms, and be brief and to the point.

It would be well worth a little time and effort for the assistant to learn a few key words in the patient's language; even if they are only "hello" and "goodbye." Patients will feel a little more secure if they hear a few familiar words. Tearing down this barrier to effective communication can be a real challenge. It can be accomplished, however, with just a little extra effort, common sense, and goodwill.

The deaf are truly a silent minority. It is often difficult to evaluate a deaf patient's problem. Each physician's office should be aware of the local registry for interpreters with the deaf in the area. Medical assistants may write to the Registry Interpreters for the Deaf (RID), 814 Thayer Avenue, Silver Spring, Maryland 20910 for information regarding communicating with the deaf.

The blind have a completely different set of problems as they cope in a world devoid of color and form. They often have sharpened other senses in compensating for their handicap. It is well to remember that caring can be translated in the tone of one's voice. The medical assistant should consider taking a moment to explain the physical location of furniture in the office and this will generally make the blind patient feel more comfortable. It might also be wise to keep one or two magazines in braille available in the reception room.

DEALING WITH THE PHYSICIAN'S FAMILY

Since the majority of physicians have families, the chances are quite good that the medical assistant will have some dealings with various family members. In order to diplomatically handle any situation, the assistant must be absolutely certain of the extent of the position and responsibilities to both the physician and the relatives.

Actually, both the assistant and the physician's spouse have a common interest—concern for the physician. This should be sufficient reason to motivate them to cooperate. This also applies to the doctor's parents who may from time to time enter the picture.

If a family member is used to dropping by the office frequently, the assistant should not object as long as the office routine is not disrupted. The physician should establish exactly how the assistant is expected to deal with these situations. The assistant should handle any telephone or office situations with the doctor's family with one objective in mind—to make things easy for the physician. Above all, in carrying out the physician's instructions, conveying either a disinterested view toward the family or an overprotective attitude toward the physician must be avoided.

Review questions

1. Why are first impressions so important in the physician's office?
2. Name at least five principles of good public relations.
3. What can the physician's assistant do to keep waiting children occupied and quiet?
4. Should the medical assistant resent frequent office visits by the physician's family? How should the assistant handle the situation?

Suggested readings

Chinoy, E.: Sociological perspective—basic concepts and their application, New York, 1964, Random House, Inc.

Committee on Trauma, American College of Surgeons, Chicago, Ill.

Fant, L. J., Jr.: Say it with hands, Department of Education, Gallaudet College, Washington, D. C.

Hall, E. T.: The silent language, Greenwich, Conn., 1963, Fawcett Publications, Inc.

Purtilo, R.: The allied health professional and the patient: technique of effective interaction, Philadelphia, 1973, W. B. Saunders Co.

Schmidt, F., and Weiner, H. M., editors: Public relations in health and welfare, New York, 1966, Columbia University Press.

Wolfe, E. W.: Basic guide interview, Strong Memorial Hospital, Rochester, N. Y.

chapter 9

Social and professional amenities

EFFICIENCY

Executive secretaries and their counterparts, medical assistants, are valued for their relative efficiency. Efficiency implies two necessary ingredients: organization, or a plan to accomplish required tasks, and an awareness that certain details must be attended to in the absence of specific instructions.

In Chapter 1 we emphasized the desirability of the physician choosing an assistant who possesses certain qualities that complement those of his own. If such a person can be found, an excellent medical team is thus formed.

Despite the fact that the physician is chiefly concerned with the care and treatment of patients, there are many other details that must be attended to in order to maintain a successful practice. Some of these require the personal attention of the physician, but others can be handled just as effectively by the office assistant whose main administrative function is to relieve the doctor of the burden of dealing with routine duties in order to free him to devote the full measure of his time to patient care. It should be left to the office assistant to remember things that the doctor is apt to forget, such as important engagements and special dates. An efficient assistant is a reservoir of information about many different things. Much of this handy knowledge is committed to memory or readily available. Although the possession of a good memory is an invaluable asset to the efficient individual, knowing where to seek and find certain information can be an equally useful tool.

If a person reaches his majority and lives to the ripe old age of 70, he will have invested 613,200 hours in the progress of life. Since the earning of one's living consumes a large portion of this time, the development of efficient and self-disciplined habits on the job can make this portion of life more satisfying.

The following check list of suggestions reflects an efficient and disciplined approach to office management.

1. Maintain an orderly desk and keep it neat. Putting things in their right places saves time when they are needed in a hurry.
2. Know exactly what to do before starting to work. Secure explicit instructions.
3. Simplify work by organizing it first. Always be alert to new and better methods for accomplishing tasks.
4. Take full advantage of periods when one feels like working.

Glossary

conscientious careful to do what one knows is right; done with care

itinerary a route of travel; a record or journal of travel

5. Take occasional breaks to avoid becoming groggy. It is always a good idea to stand up and walk around to help the circulation, especially when one is involved with monotonous work such as volume typing.
6. Concentrate on the work at hand, taking an interest in and recognizing the significance of the work.
7. Note things that the doctor is apt to forget, such as birthdays, expiration dates of insurance policies, and important renewal dates.
8. Maintain a list of reasonable hotels, motels, and rooming houses in the city for out-of-town patients and their families. Keep a card list of inexpensive restaurants, plane schedules, and bus and train schedules. Keep street guides and maps on hand in case the physician has to make a house call in an unfamiliar neighborhood.
9. Avoid getting involved in lengthy or personal conversations with patients; this wastes time and it may be regretted later. Explain all procedures to patients clearly.
10. Avoid speaking with patients and their relatives, either in person or on the telephone, where the conversation, even in part, may be overheard. This is often the way confidential information is passed out of the office.
11. Deal tactfully and in a businesslike manner with salesmen, insurance men, and other people who come to see the physician on business. Do not allow the physician's time to be wasted, but do not miss an opportunity to obtain valuable supplies, equipment, and information. Remember that courteous treatment of these people is also part of the physician's public relations program and that they may be valuable friends and potential patients.
12. In relationships with the physician, be efficient, professional, and eventempered. Carry out orders promptly. Learn to judge when the doctor wants an assistant in attendance or would welcome an interruption.
13. Keep cool in emergencies; work rapidly but not frantically. Learn steps to take in emergencies. Know where to contact your physician and whom to call when he is not available. Have emergency telephone numbers readily available. Avoid transmitting a feeling of panic to patients who may be in the office. If ambulance, undertaker or other emergency personnel come to the office, try to avoid making their identity known to patients.
14. Organize the work to save time and steps by getting everything in one trip and putting each item in the most convenient spot. Handle office supplies economically. Organize a schedule of activities (other than those concerned with patients) around the regular office hours. Remember, however, that your schedule must be flexible to allow for emergencies and the special needs of the physician. Do not make personal phone calls.
15. Make a tentative activities schedule for the office. Revise it from time to time as you become more familiar with the routine.
16. Take periodic inventory of laboratory and office supplies, drugs, instruments, and so on.
17. Stock your desk with necessary supplies in order to work efficiently and to conserve time.
18. Designate one drawer as your personal drawer and keep there any personal belongings.
19. Remember that the speed with which something is done, particularly typing a letter, is as important as the quality of the work.
20. Keep in mind that punctuality is most important in a doctor's office.

REMINDERS

In addition to being organized and knowing where to find certain information, the efficient medical assistant also possesses a good memory. A good memory is not necessarily an inherent trait but comes from following three simple rules: (1) Write it down. (2) Write it down where it can be found. (3) Remember to find it again. Since every assistant bears the responsibility of ensuring that certain things are attended to at specific times, it is obvious that some kind of orderly system of reminders is needed. There are various devices that can serve as reminders, such as calendars, tickler systems, come-up files, future files, and follow-up files. It is not a question of which system is the best but the preference of the person using the system.

The conscientious assistant will also want to maintain an up-to-date desk calendar for the physician that indicates all appointments other than those with patients, special dates, and important engagements. Although it is a good practice to enter reminders well before the actual date on her own calendar, it is usually not necessary for the assistant to enter the same information on the doctor's calendar. However, the assistant should be cautioned to inspect the physician's calendar daily for appointments that may have been made without her knowledge.

Good organization dictates that a list of those items that recur year after year be entered on a master calendar. The autumn of each year is an excellent time to enter all of the recurring items, events, and engagements for the forthcoming year on the new year's calendar. In preparing future calendars, one should avoid using the current calendar because the dates of the events change from year to year. One should, therefore, remember to work from the check list of recurring items. The following check list is intended to serve only as a guide since each office possesses its own requirements.

- Payment dates
  - Contributions, pledged or otherwise, to religious and charitable institutions
  - Insurance premium due dates, especially malpractice insurance
  - Interest due on notes payable and maturity dates of said notes
  - Interest due on notes receivable and their maturity dates
  - Periodic payments such as salaries, tuition, etc.
- Renewal dates
  - Automobile license
  - Narcotics license
  - Subscriptions to journals and periodicals
- Tax dates
  - Federal taxes
  - State and local taxes
  - Property taxes
- Important meetings
  - Board meetings
  - Medical society meetings
  - Club meetings
  - Committee meetings
  - Stockholder meetings
- Holidays
  - Legal holidays such as Christmas and Thanksgiving
  - Easter
  - Election Day
  - Religious days
- Family dates

The medical assistant must be very careful to keep an accurate record of the due dates for the doctor's insurance premiums. Most policies provide a 28- to 31-day period of grace after the due date during which payment may be made without lapse of the policy. However, the assistant should observe the due date on the policy as a guide for payment. Checks should be drawn and readied for the physician's signature and mailed prior to the due date.

TRAVEL ARRANGEMENTS

The average physician will certainly not travel as much as a business executive. Perhaps the easiest course to follow in handling the physician's travel is to enlist the services of a reputable travel agent. A travel agent is an expert in providing advice and offering suggestions in addition to scheduling and making all the necessary reservations. The travel agent can also provide the traveler with folders and booklets describing the locations to be visited. It is important to note that the traveler normally does not pay for the services of the travel agent since the agent receives a commission on all air and surface transportation from the various carriers as well as from the hotels used.

A travel service is able to assist the international traveler in particular in the following ways:

1. Prepare and submit a tentative intenerary that can be changed or modified at the discretion of the traveler.
2. Make all travel and hotel reservations and sight-seeing arrangements.
3. Inform the traveler as to the necessary documents needed such as passports, health certificates, and so on. The assistant could assume the responsibility of seeing that the physician has all the necessary papers.
4. Provide the client with a small amount of currency of the country to be visited in order to take care of the initial incidental expenses.
5. Provide information concerning current regulations and restrictions on currency and customs.

The medical assistant should be prepared to aid the physician in making arrangements should the need arise. A physician's trips may be quite varied in nature; they may be trips for business, pleasure, or a combination of both; they may be extensive or brief; they may be within the United States or extend into foreign countries.

The following is an outline of procedures to follow when arranging the physician's trip.

1. Obtain information about the kinds of transportation available and their time schedules.
2. After the physician decides on the method of travel, make the necessary transportation and hotel reservations.
3. Arrange for the tickets to be sent to the office or picked up.
4. Prepare a travel itinerary and appointment schedule for the physician's use and make a copy for the office.
5. Assemble any business data or materials that are to be taken.
6. Arrange for baggage identification labels if necessary.
7. If the physician so prefers, make financial arrangements for the trip.

In the event the physician does any amount of traveling, the following are good sources of information and schedules:

1. The *Official Airline Guide,* North American Edition, is published twice a month by the Reuben H. Donnelley Corporation, 2000 Clearwater Drive, Oak Brook, Illinois 60521. They also publish an International Edition monthly but the North American Edition is generally sufficient for determining rates and schedules between most domestic cities.
2. Individual airlines publish and distribute timetables of their own flights. Flight information can also be obtained directly by telephoning the local number of a specific airline. Airline passenger representatives will work out itineraries of connecting flights for their customers. It is often advantageous to become acquainted with one or more passenger resentatives since they are usually cooperative and can be very helpful in securing a last-minute reservation should an emergency arise.
3. The *Official Guide of the Railways* is published by the National Railway Publications Company. This publication is currently undergoing change and when available will be similar in format to the *Official Airline Guide.*

When making travel reservations, one should always inquire about the cost, how long the reservation will be held, and when the tickets should be picked up. If, for some reason, the physician cannot make the scheduled trip, it is common courtesy to cancel all reservations. Concerning baggage, the assistant should be informed about current regulations for airline travel within the United States as well as to foreign countries.

When making hotel reservations, it is necessary to give the name of the person for whom the reservation is being made, the estimated time of arrival and departure, and the type of accommodation desired. Information regarding check-in and check-out times should also be obtained and given to the physician. Reservations may be made by telephone or letter and, whenever possible, confirmations should be requested in writing to avert possible embarrassment and disappointment later on.

Application forms for traveler's checks and letters of credit may be obtained from the bank and completed by the assistant but it is necessary that they be signed by the applicant in the presence of a bank employee.

INVITATIONS

If the assistant is expected to handle the physician's social engagements as well as professional ones, this should be explained and agreed upon at the initial interview. When the assistant does act for the physician-employer in social matters, the established rules of etiquette should be followed. Although many of these rules have been relaxed somewhat in recent years, it is still essential to know many of them. Keeping good records makes the job of managing the social aspects of the physician's practice much easier. If the assistant is required to handle invitations for a social event, the latest edition of a standard etiquette handbook such as *Emily Post's Etiquette* or *Amy Vanderbilt's Etiquette* should be consulted.

When the physician receives an invitation, it is proper to answer it promptly and in the same format as it is received. Formal replies are usually written by hand on personal stationery while replies to invitations to business or professional functions may be made on office stationery. When time permits, it is a good practice to make an office copy of all incoming invitations especially those for nonprofessional functions. Should the invitation become lost or misplaced, all of the information pertaining to the occasion would be on file in the office.

If the physician requests the office assistant to handle the arrangements for a social function, the first step might be the making of a guest list. The names of the various invited guests are typed on the left hand side of the page and on the right are two columns headed "Accepts" and "Regrets." As the replies are received, the appropriate column opposite the respective names is checked. For further information regarding etiquette for social functions, again, a good etiquette handbook should be consulted.

PROFESSIONAL INFORMATION

In most medical offices it is the responsibility of the secretary or the assistant to prevent memberships and subscriptions from expiring. The same applies to insurance policies, particularly malpractice policies.

Further, it is the responsibility of the person handling the front desk to maintain a list of telephone numbers that are called frequently. The list should be kept close to the telephone for handy reference. For example, the name and number of each hospital where the physician enjoys staff privileges, together with any extensions where he may be located, are essential pieces of information and should be included on such a list. The assistant will want to be familiar with other hospital and clinic facilities in the area, their charges, check-in times, visiting hours, and so on, and have available any other pertinent information that may be helpful to patients.

Physicians invariably find it necessary to refer patients to outside agencies for special services or the purchase of medical supplies. Accordingly, in order to properly reply to patient inquiries, the medical assistant should maintain, for quick referral, a directory containing the names, addresses, and telephone numbers of those to whom the doctor might refer patients. If such a file does not exist, one should be compiled. An alphabetical card file is probably the most practical method, for it can be easily expanded and kept up to date without a great deal of effort.

Finding qualified persons to provide home health care services to patients, for instance, can be a time-consuming task. Suppose a patient needs a licensed nurse, a nurse's aide, an orderly, or a housekeeper. Where would you find such reliable personnel on short notice? Generally temporary health care personnel with the requisite skills are available through various metropolitan agencies such as the visiting nurses association or a home health agency. There are organizations that maintain extensive rosters of carefully selected and screened employees, each of whom are bonded and insured in the performance of their assignments. Because their employees include licensed nurses, orderlies, nurse aides, live-in companions, visiting home managers, and housekeepers, they are prepared to provide, on short notice, an almost unlimited variety of home health care services.

These services may also prove useful when the need for temporary additional office help is involved. The need could be precipitated by a seasonal flu epidemic resulting in a sudden increase in patient load. On the other hand, having temporary help for a day or two to maintain clerical functions in the office while you handle the monthly billings may result in greater office efficiency.

Since the recommendation of a physician is an important consideration to a patient in deciding whom to consult, cooperating specialists and agencies can easily be made a part of the list. The following list represents some of the services and goods that patients frequently inquire about:

- Ankle supports
- Arch supports
- Anesthesiologist
- Chiropodist
- Dentist
- Dermatologist
- Employment agencies
- Homes—convalescent, nursing, and homes for the aged
- Hospitals
- Internist
- Laboratories
- Masseur or masseuse
- Neurologist
- Nurses—registered and practical/vocational
- Obstetrician
- Ophthalmologist
- Orthopedic surgeon
- Pay clinics
- Pharmacies
- Pathologist
- Pediatrician
- Plastic surgeon
- Proctologist
- Psychiatrist
- Radiologist
- Social workers
- Surgeon
- Surgical appliances
- Urologist
- Welfare agencies

As an added service to patients who plan to make a trip to a foreign country the assistant might inform them about the work of the International Association for Medical Assistance to Travelers (IAMAT). This is a nonprofit organization made up of approximately 3,000 physicians located in some fifty countries of Europe, Asia, Africa, and South America. The majority of its member doctors have received their professional training in the United States, Canada, or Great Britain.

Many tourists become ill while traveling abroad, and it is always a great source of relief to be assured of receiving competent medical attention. The IAMAT publishes a regular list of its member physicians, a copy of which may be obtained by writing to IAMAT, 19 West 44th Street, New York, N. Y. 10036.

The World Medical Association, 10 Columbus Circle, New York, New York 10019, also distributes a pocket-size guide to English-speaking doctors in more than seventy countries around the world.

There is an added risk of modern travel that is a subtle hazard and produces some medical disasters to vulnerable individuals. Most modern travel schedules are planned for the able-bodied, and provide scant flexibility for adaptation to the temporary or partially disabled, who may therefore become casualties of the system. On the other hand, fear of travel, which is common, may be allayed by adequate preparation and protection of the traveler's health before departure. In this connection, a new pamphlet publication, *Physician's Guide to Medical Advice for Overseas Travelers,* is available for purchase from the American Medical Association, Order Department, 535 North Dearborn Street, Chicago, Illinois 60610. This guide attempts to furnish physicians with some suggestions for preventing casualties among their traveling patients.

The publications of the respective professional societies (membership lists and reports) provide an excellent source for locating names, addresses, and other personal data about professional people. One of the best known sources of biographical information is *Who's Who,* which is somewhat limited since it includes only those individuals who have made outstanding contributions in their respective fields. There are, however, several other more specialized publications or directories that list only the names of physicians and scientists. *Who's Who Among Physicians and Surgeons* and *American Men of Science* are two such publications.

The physician who feels very strongly about some aspect of his work or makes an important discovery may wish to share his ideas with his medical colleagues. Probably the most effective method for reaching the vast majority of them is by writing. In the course of his research the doctor may request his assistant to gather the facts for him on a particular subject. Most libraries of any size usually list references by subjects, titles of articles and publications, and authors. Specialized indexes to periodical literature may be found for a variety of fields. The most popular general reference source is *The Reader's Guide to Periodical Literature,* which is found in almost every library, and specifically for medical research, the *Index Medicus.*

Review questions

1. In a general sense, what is the main administrative function of the medical assistant?
2. Define *efficiency* and give at least five good examples of efficient office behavior.
3. If the physician informs the assistant of plans to spend a vacation touring the United States and requests an itinerary, what is the best course for the assistant to follow?
4. Why is it more efficient for the medical assistant to rely on a travel agent to handle all the physician's travel? What about the cost of using such an agent?

Suggested readings

Doris, L., and Miller, B. M.: Complete secretary's handbook, ed. 3, Englewood Cliffs, N. J., 1970, Prentice-Hall, Inc.

Medical criteria for passenger flying, Arch. Environ. Health **2**:124-138, 1961.

Physician's guide to medical advice for overseas travelers, Chicago, Ill., 1973, American Medical Association.

Post, E. L., editor: Emily Post's etiquette, ed. 12, New York, 1969, Funk & Wagnalls, Inc.

chapter 10
Effective written communications

WRITING CORRECTLY

The letters that emanate from the physician's office are a prime source of public relations. A neat and accurate letter is an absolute necessity for any office, especially a medical office. Well-written letters not only instill confidence, but they offer evidence of precision in thinking and performance. Each letter that leaves a medical office reveals subtle information about the intelligence, ability, and efficiency of the physician and the staff. The physician should settle for nothing less than perfection in professional correspondence in order to convey this image.

Since the assistant will frequently be expected to actually structure some of the more routine correspondence such as reports, simple letters, insurance forms, and supply orders, great care should be exercised in the choice of words. And, just because it is merely routine does not necessarily mean it is unimportant. Even a one-paragraph letter is reflective of the physician's office.

Everyone should be cognizant of the mechanics of grammar and spelling. The so-called gobbledygook and stilted phrases found in many contemporary publications have no place in a business letter. The knowledgeable medical assistant avoids, whenever possible, using medical terminology beyond the comprehension of the average person. Thus, medical terms should be explained in ordinary language. A writer must always be conscious of readers, and readers usually appreciate being able to comprehend the meaning of written material on the first reading.

It is important to always be courteous with the written word regardless of the circumstances involved. Caution should be exercised in using technical language. When it is necessary to use medical terms one should be absolutely certain of the choice of words and, even more important, be sure they are spelled correctly.

Style and effectiveness in writing can be improved by careful planning. The main purpose of any writer is to make contact with his reader and communicate his message in easily understood language. The following check list is designed to serve as a guide for assistants who wish to improve the quality of their letters:

Organization
1. Does the organization of the entire paper help carry out my original intent or purpose?
2. Do my beginning sentences present my topic clearly and interest my reader?
3. Are my sentences arranged in such a way as to show relationships?

Glossary

bibliography a list of the works of an author or the literature pertaining to a particular subject
eclectic selecting from different sources
emanate to flow forth or proceed from a source

4. Does each paragraph have a topic sentence and treat completely one phase of the subject?
5. Are my paragraphs properly linked, so that one follows logically after the other?
6. Does my conclusion adequately sum up the content of my paper?

Content

1. Have I covered every major phase of the subject related to my topic?
2. Have I chosen details to explain main ideas and given examples where they would help?

Style

1. Have I used exact words to convey meanings?
2. Have I checked in the dictionary for suitable synonyms I can use to avoid repetition of certain words?
3. Have I avoided trite or hackneyed expressions?
4. Have I used many words to say something when a few would do the job better?
5. Have I used concrete instead of abstract words?
6. Have I avoided stereotypes?
7. Are any of the sentences run-on sentences?
8. Do any of my sentences contain shifted constructions or misplaced modifiers?
9. Can I combine any of my sentences to make them more effective?

Mechanics

1. Have I written any incomplete sentences?
2. Is my punctuation correct throughout?
3. Have I capitalized the words that should be capitalized?
4. Is every word spelled correctly?

SOME FACTS ABOUT SPELLING

Accurate and correct spelling is necessary for intelligent communication. In fact, it is very much taken for granted. Many individuals, aware that their writing sometimes contains spelling errors, are embarrassed by doubts and apprehensions that their mistakes will create an unfavorable impression. Spelling mistakes do create confusion and misunderstanding; therefore everyone should strive for perfection in spelling.

Society expects those who have been exposed to educational opportunities to be able to spell correctly. The importance of accurate spelling by the medical assistant cannot be overemphasized. The physician should not have to proofread all outgoing correspondence. This is an individual responsibility and should remain so. It should be borne in mind that repeated spelling errors and typographic mistakes in the physician's correspondence reflect unfavorably upon his professional integrity. The security and maintenance of one's job could very well be jeopardized by continued lack of concern for accuracy.

It is an accepted fact of life that misspelling is the most frequently accepted sign of illiteracy. In our society we penalize the poor speller. He is sometimes prevented from obtaining good jobs and from moving up or advancing in most positions. The inability to spell is a real problem for some people—one that is often accompanied by emotional overtones. Anxiety resulting from distress over spelling inadequacies is as real as that which stems from concern over proper methods of dress or social behavior.

The uniformity required in spelling is unique and applies to no other aspect of the English language. A person is free to vary his choice of words or to combine them into complex and compound sentences using different punctuation. However, there generally is only one correct way to spell a particular word. Despite the fact that alternative spellings do exist, only one is usually judged correct for a given situation.

Why is it that so many people find spelling so difficult? Perhaps one reason is that English spelling and pronunciation are often very different. Actually, the spelling of a great number of words does not even approximate the sounds being represented. The truth of the matter is that our spoken word has gradually strayed from traditional writing, and this process is continuing. Since the English language is undergoing continual change, it is more than plausible that spelling will continue to differ more and more from pronunciation. Should this trend continue without reform or abatement, English spelling could very well progress to the point where some words become completely idiographic. In other words, a written symbol or the spelled word would represent a direct thought or idea rather than signify the actual sound of the word itself.

The fact that numerous words are not spelled as they sound is probably at the very root of the spelling problem. Also, to add to the confusion, there are many words that sound alike but are spelled differently. These are known as homonyms and create a great deal of difficulty for foreigners trying to master English. Typical homonyms include: principle, principal; accept, except; capitol, capital; break, brake; peace, piece.

The English language is largely an eclectic one; it possesses tremendous range and flexibility. During the past one thousand years of its development it has more than doubled its size. It has borrowed from French, Latin, Greek, Hebrew, Arabic, and many other tongues. Unfortunately, this borrowing compounds spelling problems.

No doubt most of us at one time or another have experienced a situation where a word we have been spelling correctly or using as part of our regular vocabulary suddenly looked totally unfamiliar. When one encounters the slightest suspicion concerning the spelling or meaning of a word, one should immediately look it up in the dictionary. It would be well for the medical assistant to become dictionary-conscious and get into the habit of consulting it whenever in doubt about a word.

Good spellers have a systematic method of approaching new words, while poor spellers commonly work at the task in a hit-or-miss manner. E. W. Dolch, commenting on the characteristics of a good speller, states, "A good speller (1) checks his guesses; (2) proofreads for spelling; (3) studies the spelling of new words, which means (a) he gets the exact pronunciation of each new word, (b) he asks if this sounding tells the letters, and (c) where it does not, he finds a means of remembering the exact letters at a difficult spot. He makes this rapid check in all subjects as a matter of habit and does it in a few seconds."*

*From Dolch, E. W.: Better spelling, Champaign, Ill., 1946, Garrard Publishing Co.

Any program for spelling improvement should include the following factors.

1. Mastery of most commonly used words
2. Consciousness of how words are built
3. Adequate methods of attacking the learning of new words
4. Independence in use of dictionary (where and how to check words that are doubtful)
5. Individual assumption of responsibility for spelling correctly all words used in writing

Evaluations of spelling performance on writing samples have caused both educators and laymen to express concern and dissatisfaction with the general spelling proficiency of a large segment of the student population. One of the greatest needs facing today's curriculum planners is to formulate a curriculum that develops a spelling conscience in students: the realization that spelling is important at all times and that it **does** count. Motivation far outranks method in significance when attempting to improve spelling.

One authoritative source on spelling has demonstrated that approximately 95% of all spelling errors occur in only 1,000 words. They further point out that about 90% of the average person's writing vocabulary consists of only 1,000 words. These figures are supposedly based on carefully controlled studies, but it must be remembered that each individual possesses his own unique writing vocabulary. One's writing vocabulary is comprised of simple, everyday words, the spelling of which can be easily mastered with a little effort.*

The medical assistant develops a distinct vocabulary of medical terms in addition to regular everyday writing vocabulary. The fact that daily use is made of medical terminology in no way minimizes use of everyday writing vocabulary. When using medical terms the assistant must be very careful to choose the correct term and spell it correctly.

*From Shaw, H.: Spell it right, New York, 1964, Barnes & Noble, Inc., p. 8.

There are several helpful aids available to the medical assistant who has difficulty with spelling. Such books include: *Better Spelling, Spell It Right, Word Finder,* and *20,000 Words.* Being small books and relatively inexpensive, they can be kept on the assistant's desk for ready reference. Each book seeks to identify and discuss the most common problems encountered by poor spellers. Spelling word lists, which illustrate the sources of spelling problems, are provided, the theory being that recognizing and understanding the problem involved in one word can help to correct the spelling of many other related words.

VOCABULARY

Laboratory studies have revealed that vocabulary and success are very much related. The possession of an extensive knowledge of the meaning and application of English words has been found to accompany outstanding success more often than any other single factor. The word vocabulary generally signifies a knowledge of the dictionary meaning of various words. According to laboratory experiments recently conducted, top-level executives scored considerably higher in the English vocabulary test than any other selected group.

Although success is a rather difficult term to define in a narrow sense, it seems apparent from these studies that a large vocabulary is typical not only of executives but of successful people in general. "The measured English vocabularies of executives correlate with their salaries. This does not mean that every high vocabulary person receives a large salary, but the relation is sufficiently close to show that a large vocabulary is one element of success, and seemingly an important one."*

Why is there such a positive correlation between socio-economic status and an outstanding vocabulary? A partial explanation may be that "Words are the instruments by means of which men and women grasp the thoughts of others and with which they do much of their own thinking. They are the tools of thought."*

*From O'Connor, J.: Vocabulary and success. In Modern English readings, New York, 1946, Holt, Rinehart & Winston, Inc., pp. 244-245.

*From O'Connor, J.: Vocabulary and success. In Modern English readings, New York, 1946, Holt, Rinehart & Winston, Inc., pp. 244-245.

Vocabulary building proceeds along the same lines as spelling improvement. It is rather difficult to learn how to correctly spell a word without also discovering its meaning. Getting into the habit of consulting a dictionary whenever one encounters a baffling word is the most effective method of building a better vocabulary.

MECHANICS OF WRITING

Time does not permit a thorough review of grammatical fundamentals. Besides, it is not the intention of this book to provide a review of the structural essentials of the language. Rather it is assumed that those individuals entering the field of medical assisting possess an adequate background in English, having already been exposed to some twelve years of formal education. We are interested in furnishing the reader with a very brief review of those elements that relate directly to the mechanics involved in the writing of letters, case histories, and reports. We are referring, of course, to the mechanics of grammar, namely, capitalization and punctuation.

It is difficult to dogmatically state the rules of capitalization because of the great number of deviations. Capitalization has always been based upon custom and many customs are not particularly logical. Moreover, there is much disagreement among authors and textbooks. How is it possible, in light of this lack of uniformity, to determine when to capitalize and when not to capitalize? The best advice is to follow the format established for each particular office or profession. Since firm rules cannot apply to every possible situation it may prove helpful for the assistant to refer to the following general principles as a guide. Of course, the dictionary is always available as a further reference source.

Rules of capitalization

1. Capitalize names of particular persons, places, and things; special titles and their abbreviations; and nicknames or other identifying names. Capitalize the names of relatives when used instead of a name or as part of a name and without a preceding possessive pronoun. *Example:* I asked Father for a dime. I asked my father for a dime.
2. Capitalize the names of the days of the week, months, and holidays but not seasons of year.
3. Capitalize the names of all political and geographic subdivisions and all nations, nationalities, tribes, and adjectives derived from such (proper adjectives).
4. Capitalize the names of streets, highways, squares, buildings, and other specific locations.
5. Capitalize names of rivers, oceans, islands, mountains, and other geographic features.
6. Capitalize words of direction *only* when they designate a specific area or location. *Example:* He lives in the South. (Place.) He went toward the south. (Direction.)
7. Capitalize the name of political parties, religious denominations, and their members.
8. Capitalize the names of business firms, organizations, and institutions.
9. Capitalize the word Bible and the names and designations of all sacred writings; also capitalize all nouns and pronouns that refer to the Supreme Being.
10. Capitalize the names of historical events, wars, treaties, laws, and documents.
11. Capitalize the names of divisions, departments, and instrumentalities of government.
12. Capitalize the names of classes and divisions in school or college and names of *specific* subjects. *Example:* Algebra 1.
13. Capitalize names of ships, trains, planes, submarines, and satellites.
14. Capitalize names of stars, planets, constellations, and so on.
15. Capitalize the first word in each line of poetry.
16. Capitalize the first word of a complete statement following a colon.
17. Capitalize the interjection "O."
18. Capitalize the first word of a direct quotation.
19. Capitalize the first word and all other *important* words in a title.
20. Capitalize the first word of a sentence, salutation, and complimentary close of a letter.

Most people today tend to overcapitalize in their writing. However, there is a trend to play down the use of capitals and to encourage less capitalization. One possible explanation for the present practice of overcapitalization is that many people carelessly make their small letters large enough to be interpreted as capitals. Also, people feel safe in adhering to the cliché, "When in doubt, capitalize."

Punctuation consists of the use of various marks in writing to convey the author's meaning more clearly. The advent of printing created the need for punctuation in order to make the structure and meaning of the written word clear to the reader. Aldus Manutius, an Italian maker of books, is generally considered to be the father of modern punctuation. Manutius is credited with systematizing the use of punctuation marks, which were formerly used by authors and printers without any conformity to standards or rules.

Just as there is a trend in capitalization today away from the use of capital letters, there is also a trend in punctuation to use fewer marks. Many of our modern writers have rebelled against the old steadfast rules of punctuation and adopted what is known as open punctuation (few marks). Perhaps they feel less bound and hence better able to express their thoughts and be more creative.

Everyone responsible for handling correspondence and reports should be familiar with the rules of punctuation and know how to use them intelligently. Business letters and reports demand a more formal use of grammar and adherence to the mechanics of language usage. The main purpose of punctuation is to substitute in writing for the pauses, the inflections, and the intonations of the spoken word. The rules of punctuation are simple to learn and use correctly; their principal object is clarity. A brief summary of the important marks of punctuation follows.

Rules of punctuation

The apostrophe

Use the apostrophe:
1. To show possession—John's book
2. To show omissions—Class of '64
3. To show contractions—o'clock, can't
4. To form plurals of letters that would be confusing if *s* alone were added—x's and y's

The colon

The colon suggests that something is to follow. Use the colon:
1. After an expression that anticipates enumeration of items—I want the following:
2. In a salutation—Dear Sir:

The comma

The comma is the most commonly used mark. Use the comma:
1. To separate words in a series—I like apples, peaches, and ice cream.
2. To separate quotations from the rest of the sentence—"I like you," Mr. Jones said.
3. With words in apposition—John Smith, our camp counselor, is a fine person.
4. To set off certain abbreviations—Joseph Martin, Jr.
5. Between parallel adjectives—pleasant, optimistic sales approach.
6. To set off year from month—July 1, 1974.
7. Before a conjunction that connects parts of a compound sentence unless parts are very short.
8. To set off a participial phrase that comes at beginning of a sentence—Feeling very foolish, he started all over again.
9. To set off an adverbial clause that comes first in a sentence—when it began to rain, we decided not to go.

The dash

The dash is used in writing to mark a sudden break in thought. The dash should not be used carelessly in place of commas, semicolons, and periods. Use the dash:
1. To indicate sharper separation than comma or semicolon.

The exclamation point

The exclamation point is an expression of strong feeling. Use the exclamation point:
1. After an emotional statement or word—Wow! Ouch! Hurrah!
2. Following single words, phases, or clauses of the same variety—Listen! You, over there! Trying to hide!

The hyphen

Use the hyphen:
1. To indicate division into syllables.
2. To join words into single expressions—well-developed; co-worker; thirty-six.
3. At the end of a line when a word is broken and part is carried over to the next line.

The parentheses

Parentheses are used to enclose parts of a sentence that might easily be omitted. Use parentheses:
1. To set off clarifying words explaining material—five dollars ($5.00).
2. To identify a source of information—the total number of Salt Lake City firms using our type of product is 442 (Chamber of Commerce Handbook).

The period

Use the period:
1. After a statement.
2. After an imperative request—"Come here."
3. After an abbreviation—Mr.; Mrs.; Ph.D.
4. As a decimal—$10.00.
5. Periods are placed inside quotation marks at the end of a sentence.

The question mark

The question mark is also called the interrogation mark or point. Use the question mark:
1. After a question—What have been the customer reactions to the new models?
2. After each of a series of questions—Will you be able to make more sales with Model 84? Model 86? Model 90?

The quotation mark

Use the quotation mark:

1. To identify the precise words of a speaker or writer—"The office machine," he says, "is here to stay."

2. To identify certain literary titles—Excerpts of his talk were taken from "The doctor in modern society" in *U. S. News & World Report.*

3. Quotation marks within quotation marks are enclosed in single quotation marks—"He answered, 'I will not,' when I asked him," she reported.

The semicolon

Use the semicolon:

1. To show omission of conjunction between complete thoughts of compound sentences—You may be satisfied with your record; the boss is not.

2. Between complete thoughts that contain commas—your sales, as we indicated last month, are far behind your quota; yet you are not making many calls.

3. The semicolon is used instead of a comma after items in a series when these items are long or complicated.

4. The semicolon is placed outside quotation marks.

The interrobang

The interrobang (interro for interrogation and bang, which is slang for an exclamation point) may someday be a part of our regular form of punctuation. It is an exclamation point accompanied by a query. It could be used after most rhetorical questions such as: "How about that?", "So what?", "Well, what do you know?" If this mark (‽) is accepted by grammarians, printers, and writers, it will be the first punctuation symbol to become part of the printed language since the introduction of the quotation mark in the late seventeenth century. Its inventer is Martin K. Spechter, president of an advertising agency, who makes printing his hobby.*

STRUCTURING LETTERS

It is most important to space and position letters carefully. The margins should frame the body of the letter. Much time can be saved in the long run if a rough draft is made first, especially if the letter is complicated. Upon examining the draft, one can then gauge the margins and set the spacing accordingly.

*How about that, The professional Medical Assistant, November-December 1972, p. 22.

In typing forms, it is well to position the information attractively. Do not bunch the typing in one corner of the form. It is a good practice to maintain a file of various routine sample letters and forms. This will preclude the task of having to compose and originate new letters for similar situations.

Immaculate correspondence is an absolute necessity. Type only on a clean machine using good ribbon.

Be sure to catch careless mistakes that result from a slip of the finger. Remember that a favorable letter creates a favorable impression, but one minor error stands out and ruins the whole effect. In making corrections, make sure they are done so that they cannot be detected. If it is impossible to make a perfect correction, the letter should be typed over again. A secretary should never attempt to make any corrections in pencil or ink.

Those errors arising from carelessness can be eliminated completely by simply getting into the habit of taking time to proofread a piece of correspondence before mailing it. Keeping in mind that nearly every piece of correspondence is essentially an advertisement, do not settle for anything less than perfection. Meticulous correspondence conveys to the reader the impression that the physician and the staff are careful, intelligent, and efficient and that they care enough to pay attention to details.

In large practices and groups where the volume of repetitious work is high the introduction of a Magnetic Tape Selectric Typewriter (MT/ST) such as that made by IBM can have a beneficial impact on the quality of correspondence. Some offices claim that the magnetic tape system has enabled them to increase their volume of correspondence by two thirds and in an error-free manner. The machine allows the operator to type at full speed, proofreading a rough draft, backspacing and typing over errors all at once. By typing over unwanted words, the magnetic tape is automatically corrected.

A large portion of a physician's professional correspondence is conducted with other physicians and invariably concerns the treatment and care rendered to patients. When one physician refers a patient to another physician for further treatment, a letter of referral is transmitted, setting forth the reasons for referral and the service the doctor is expected to render. Reports relative to examinations and findings are expected from consulting physicians in addition to progress reports. One of the most important secretarial duties of the medical assistant is the processing of this type of professional correspondence.

When letters are to be written to other physicians or to other individuals who hold a professional title, it is generally customary to address them by name even though they may not be personally acquainted with the writer, for example, "Dear Doctor Smith," or "Dear Professor Smith." This procedure is in contrast to the more commercial use of "Dear Sir," which is usually reserved for business correspondence. In letters where the salutation contains the name of a specific person, the complimentary close should always be signed, "Sincerely yours," or "Very sincerely yours." However, "Truly yours," and "Very truly yours," should only be used with the commercial salutation, "Dear Sir." The essential elements of both the professional and friendly letter as well as the business letter are illustrated in Figs. 10-1 and 10-2. Note that streets, states, and so on should never be abbreviated in the inside address.

Professional correspondence requires that the responsible secretary be careful to spell all names correctly, verify first names and initials, and be certain of an individual's exact title and his correct address. It is usually good practice not to abbreviate parts of the salutation or address in professional correspondence. Accordingly, all titles and addresses should be stated in full. Obviously the courtesy titles of Mr., Mrs., Miss, or Ms. should always be used in the absence of any professional title.

Nothing is more repugnant to the reader than a poorly positioned letter. The person

23 Fremont Street
Dumond, South Dakota *Heading*
May 6, 1964 *(Except for data, used only in absence of a letterhead.)*

Inside address Morton Manufacturing Co. Inc.
148 W. Main Street
Charlton, Oklahoma

Salutation Gentlemen:

Body Recently I heard that ____________

I am planning to ________________

Will you please ________________

Yours truly *Complimentary close*

(s) James Gregory *Signature*

JAMES GREGORY

Fig. 10-1. Business letter.

designated to handle the physician's correspondence must be careful to construct only attractively arranged letters. This implies that the date, salutation, and complimentary close will be properly situated with adequate room left on each side for margins.

In order to produce a well-balanced letter one must space properly. For more specific information concerning the mechanics of setting up letters and spacing, consult any secretarial manual or typing book. When typing professional or business letters single spacing should be used except for very short letters. A double space should be left between paragraphs in single-spaced letters. If a letter is longer than one page, blank sheets of paper may be used for additional pages. It is mandatory that carbon copies of all correspondence be made and that at least one copy be kept in the file. If the secretary is not certain of some aspect of her shorthand or transcription, she should not hesitate to check with the doctor to make sure of his intended meaning. Every piece of correspondence should be carefully proofread before being placed in the mail or on the doctor's desk for his signature.

The most important rule to follow in typing envelopes is to make sure the address is legible and placed attractively. The Postal Service encourages the double-spacing of envelope addresses, and the general rule is that three-line addresses be double-spaced and four-line addresses be single-spaced. Any special postal instructions (such as "Special Delivery") should be located below the stamps.

There is no steadfast rule governing where to begin typing the address on an envelope, and most experienced secretaries rely upon their own judgment. However, as a rule of thumb, about four inches from the left edge of a No. 10 envelope is approximately the correct place to begin a three- or four-line address. This means about thirteen spaces down from the top of the same envelope. Proper spacing can be determined by measuring the envelope and keeping in mind that both elite and pica type have six single-space lines to a vertical inch. Pica

Date

Charles Smith, M.D.
145 N. Robertson Boulevard
Inside address Beverly Hills, California

Salutation Dear Doctor Smith:

Body In the absence of Dr. Jones, I ____________________

Sincerely yours, *Complimentary close*
(s) Helen Wilson *Signature*
Secretary to Dr. Jones

Fig. 10-2. Professional letter.

face type permits ten characters to the horizontal inch, and elite type permits twelve characters to an inch. In many instances professional offices prefer the smaller elite type for professional correspondence rather than the larger pica type generally used in business.

CARE OF THE TYPEWRITER

If absolute perfection is the goal in turning out professional correspondence it cannot be accomplished with a faulty typewriter. It should be the responsibility of the doctor's assistant or whoever uses the machine to make certain that it is kept in good working order. A typewriter is as important to a medical secretary as a piano is to a pianist, a violin to a violinist, or brushes to a painter. The secretary must be certain that everything is being done to obtain the best results from a typewriter. The machine's ribbon should be neither too heavily inked so that correspondence takes on a smudgy appearance, nor should it be allowed to become worn, resulting in faded-looking type.

A typewriter must be cleaned gently and properly in order to avoid damage. Several typewriter companies have released a list of common mistakes made by secretaries in caring for their machines. Here is a list of things to avoid.

1. Blowing dirt and eraser crumbs away (They may fly where you least want them: into the mechanism.)
2. Brushing dirt from one section to another, where it may do more harm than before
3. Using pins to pry ink out of the typeface (This is an easy way to chip the metal.)
4. Trying to clean the slots between the type bars (This is a job that requires the serviceman's special tools.)
5. Oiling dirty parts of the machine
6. Cleaning with flimsy tissue or paper towels that leave bits of themselves inside the machine
7. Rubbing the outside with detergents or abrasives, which can mar the finish
8. Cleaning the translucent windows with strong solutions (The windows may become opaque.)

If the assistant has any questions about the functioning of the machine, she should immediately check wtih a repairman. He will be only too happy to familiarize her with the machine and recommend the kind of cleaning that will keep the machine in good repair. The following checklist is designed to serve as a guide for those interested in developing good typing habits.

1. The typewriter should be dusted each morning with a soft cloth. Harsh abrasives should not be used. For a more thorough cleaning, a slightly dampened cloth usually suffices.
2. The machine should always be covered when not in use. This will keep the machine cleaner and prevent the accumulation of dust particles that clog the moving parts.
3. Oil sparingly; use only a few drops at a time on the carriage rails only. A regular program of maintenance should be conducted by a serviceman.
4. The type should be cleaned as often as is necessary to ensure clear and uniform letters. A good-quality brush and type-cleaning fluid should be used. When time is a factor, quick cleaning of type can be accomplished by placing blank paper into the machine, setting it for cutting stencils, and striking each key several times. This method helps remove excess ink and grime from the keys.
5. Keep the machine's platen protected. Never type on single sheets of lightweight paper. If one desires to use lightweight paper, it should be backed up with heavier bond to protect the platen from the direct impact of sharp keys. If the platen becomes pitted, the type may become uneven and spotty.
6. Move the carriage to the extreme right or left when erasing in order to prevent shavings from clogging moving parts. Only a typewriter eraser should be used for making corrections.

7. Change the typewriter ribbon as soon as it appears worn.
8. Do not forget to turn off electric typewriters at night. This is a common cause of problems.
9. Remember that good posture is important for good typing.
10. Concentrate on the material to be typed and try to maintain a definite rhythm.
11. Make use of every mechanical aid the machine offers.
12. Keep a list of questions or slight irregularities in the machine for the repairman to take care of on the next visit. In this way minor details will not go uncorrected.

OFFICE MACHINES

Many physicians' offices are now using dictating equipment for processing correspondence and completing medical records. The new electronic dictating machines offer high fidelity recording, are easy to operate, and come in a variety of models to meet the needs of the individual physician. The following kinds of machines are available: (1) machines that the doctor can telephone into from home or office; (2) tank-type machines with the transcribing unit located in a remote area with direct input from one or a multiple number of dictating stations throughout a building; (3) desk-top machines for the doctor and the medical assistant, and (4) portable dictating units that the physician can use for recording a meeting or for dictating away from the office.

The many improvements in dictating equipment over the past few years have tended to make the dictating machine an accepted piece of standard office equipment similar to the typewriter and the adding machine. This new equipment offers advantages for the transcriber as well as the dictator. Magnetic recording on tapes, belts, or discs allows the dictator to correct his own errors so that the secretary does not have to search ahead for the corrections and back the machine to the proper place for insertion. Machines using recording tape package it in small, easily handled cassettes that can record 30, 45, or 60 minutes on a side and can be turned over to record the same amount on the other side.

With the tank-type units there is no physical transfer of the recorded medium from the dictator to the transcriber. The secretary-transcriber does not have to touch the transcribing medium. Only the foot pedal and manual controls on the transcribing unit are used and the rest of the operation is automatic.

There is an increasing use of portable cassette recorders for recording medical programs at conventions and conferences. Most of the cassettes are of a standard size that will play back through the regular office transcribing unit if the physician wishes to have this material typed.

The medical assistant can quickly learn to use dictating equipment. It offers the time-saving advantage of not having to take shorthand notes while the physician is dictating. Other jobs can be done while the physician is dictating and time can be budgeted for the transcribing.

HELPING WITH MANUSCRIPTS

There are many physicians who frequently write for publication. Others engage in writing only occasionally, such as when they wish to describe the results of a study or to deliver a paper. Regardless of the occasion or purpose, it may become the task of the medical assistant to assist in gathering the data, typing the material, and proofreading the draft.

The first procedure to be followed is the gathering of data concerning relevant publications. It is important for the physician to know what has been previously accomplished in his subject field or related fields. In order to be of assistance to the physician and be able to furnish him with summaries or abstracts of the pertinent literature in the field, the doctor's assistant should be familiar with the library card catalog system.

The assistant who enjoys this phase of the work will want to learn all possible about the employer's practice or specialty. Whenever there is a spare moment, medical literature in the office should be studied so that a better understanding of the field can be developed. Moreover, the medical assistant should become familiar with the library facilities in the vicinity, for they often contain many useful publications.

Nearly every medical library contains two excellent sources of information concerning medical publications: the *Index-Catalogue of the Library of the Surgeon General's Office,* which lists publications that have appeared in the past, and the *Cumulated Index Medicus,* which lists the more recent articles published in current medical journals. The latter is published by the National Library of Medicine, Bethesda, Maryland.

If the physician-author is confident that the assistant possesses a good command of medical terminology and is able to analyze material and express her thoughts well in writing, he may enlist her help in actually reviewing the current literature available. Gathering data is a most time-consuming job, and if the physician is blessed with a capable assistant, she can save him a great deal of legwork and valuable time.

When an assistant is asked to review current medical literature, first an abstract, which consists of a brief summary of the main points and conclusions drawn by the author, of each publication is made. One who is familiar with the physician's area of interest is in a better position to select only pertinent material. Actually, there are various journals devoted solely to the publication of abstracts. Abstracts of this nature are usually very brief, but they can be a real timesaver to the trained research worker who is capable of reviewing such an abstract and judging whether enough information has been obtained or whether it is necessary to look up the original articles.

In taking notes on library material or making abstracts, the assistant should be sure to make up an index card for each book or periodical examined. Each index card should contain: the author's full name, the title of the abstract or publication examined, the name of the publication in which it appeared, the date, and the appropriate page numbers. This information is needed in case it is necessary to find the particular material again. If the physician is writing a paper for publication that requires footnotes and a bibliography, the name of the publisher and the place and date of publication of any material that is to be included will also be needed.

The physician will probably want to revise the paper several times before the final copy. In order to avoid the danger of mixing up the various drafts, it is a good idea to use ribbons of various colors for each copy. The mechanics of producing the final copy of any paper or manuscript are governed by its intended use. If the paper is to be read or used as a basis for a lecture, the type should be especially large and clear. Some typewriters can be equipped with magnatype, which is a very large type designed for work that is to be delivered orally.

On the other hand, if the draft is to be published in a journal or other publication, it will usually be necessary to put it in manuscript form prior to submission. Most publishers furnish their authors with specific instructions for preparing manuscripts. Each publishing house may have its own particular requirements for form and style. Nevertheless, there are a few general fundamentals that can be applied in the majority of cases.

1. Always use 8½ by 11 inch white paper of good bond and, of course, type on only one side of the page.
2. Double-space the content material and leave consistent margins on both sides.
3. Place the author's name, the title of the manuscript, and the number on the back of each photograph or illustration to be included.
4. Every manuscript should be proofread several times; check for clarity of meaning, spelling, grammar, and other mechanics before submitting it for publication.

5. Regardless of the system of numbering pages chosen, it should remain consistent throughout the manuscript.

Review questions

1. Explain why it is necessary for a physician's correspondence to be neat and free from errors.
2. Why is the poor speller handicapped?
3. Is there any relation between a good vocabulary and success. Explain.
4. What is the function of punctuation?
5. What advantages does an MT/ST typewriter offer?
6. List the essential parts of a professional letter.
7. Name ten good typing habits.
8. Why is it so important for the assistant who assists in manuscript preparation to be familiar with the physician's field of interest?

Suggested readings

Anderson, R. I., and others: Word finder, ed. 3, Englewood Cliffs, N. J., 1969, Prentice-Hall, Inc.

Doris, L., and Miller, B. M.: Complete secretary's handbook, ed. 3, Englewood Cliffs, N. J., 1970, Prentice-Hall, Inc.

Himstreet, W. C., and Baty, W. M.: Business communications, ed. 4, Belmont, Cal., 1972, Wadsworth Publishing Co., Inc.

Leslie, L. A.: 20,000 words, ed. 6, New York, 1972, McGraw-Hill Book Co.

Shaw, H.: Spell it right, New York, 1965, Barnes & Noble, Inc.

chapter 11

Processing mail

Everyone's cooperation is necessary to achieve maximum efficiency in the physician's office. The size and nature of the practice determine the number of office employees. Each employee is hired to fulfill a definite need and is delegated specific functions to perform. Regardless of the number of employees in the office, it behooves the physician to see to it that each worker becomes familiar with the duties of other workers. Thus, in case an emergency situation arises, illness strikes, or vacation time rolls around, each employee will be capable of filling in temporarily in the absence of another. This system makes it possible for the normal activity of the physician's practice to be carried on without interruption.

INCOMING MAIL

Although the function of handling the mail belongs to the office secretary or receptionist, all other employees in a small office situation should be able to perform the required procedures in her absence. In order to minimize the amount of time spent in handling incoming mail, the secretary should adopt an effective system for dealing with it. Most outsiders would be quite surprised at the amount of mail that arrives in a physician's office each day.

Before any of the incoming mail is opened, it should be sorted as far as possible into two general categories: material requiring immediate attention and material that can wait. The mail may be further sorted and classified into: newspapers and periodicals; advertisements; bills; returned statements containing patient remittances; and, finally, correspondence.

In sorting newspapers and periodicals, select those that the physician likes to read or those that contain articles of interest. These may be placed on the physician's desk to read at leisure. Other newspapers and periodicals of special interest may be placed in the waiting room. In fact, it may be a better procedure to first decide what belongs in the wastebasket and, after discarding extraneous material, go through the remaining items. If the physician is being charged for an unwanted periodical that is of no interest to anyone in the office, the secretary should cancel the subscription.

Glossary

discretion cautious and correct judgment; freedom in the exercise of judgment

inadvertent done without consideration; an effect of inattention; an oversight

invoice a list sent to a purchaser containing the items and charges of merchandise

periodicals pertaining to publications appearing at regular intervals; not generally applied to daily newspapers

Advertisements should not be thrown away until they are thoroughly examined. The assistant must exercise discretion in determining which ones may be of some interest to the physician. Most matters can be expedited by having an established routine to follow.

A physician's mail is usually saturated with a great deal of descriptive information concerning pharmaceutical products. A great deal of the advertising done by the various pharmaceutical houses and drug manufacturers consists of the published results of research and claims concerning their products. They frequently send physicians reprints of articles describing their products that have appeared in medical journals. Much of this kind of information is helpful. The greater part of the advertising matter received in the office each day, however, will be of little value. A good assistant can conserve the physician's time by learning what samples and publications are worthwhile. Offers of samples for which a written request is required should be brought to the physician's attention.

Completed checks, together with envelopes and invoices, should all be clipped together and placed on the physician's desk for signature. The secretary or person responsible should make sure that the necessary information is recorded on the checkbook stubs and later posted to the accounting records. After the checks have been signed and placed in the outgoing mail, the invoices must be filed and retained for tax purposes.

A letter opener should be used to slit open all envelopes neatly. If an envelope is addressed to the physician and marked "Personal," it should not be opened by the secretary unless permission has been granted. Should the secretary inadvertently open personal mail it is a nice gesture to write, "Opened by mistake," on the envelope and sign initials. In any event, no secretary should arbitrarily open all correspondence without first discussing the matter with the employer. All envelopes should be thoroughly checked for enclosures before being discarded lest a patient's remittance be thrown away by mistake.

The important thing to remember when receiving payments from patients is to record receipt of the payments on the patient's ledger cards and post to other appropriate records. There is no need for the physician to examine remittances as long as patient records are kept up to date.

The assistant should strive to have the doctor's mail on his desk before he arrives, if possible. The mail should be arranged in a hierachy of importance with personal and professional correspondence on top and periodicals, newspapers, and any advertisements arranged in their order of importance. In this way the doctor can glance through the mail before the first patient arrives or between appointments if the schedule permits. If the assistant has already replied to some of the incoming correspondence the physician should be informed by a notation to this effect. Undoubtedly, after the physician goes through the mail additional correspondence will be designated for the assistant to handle. Many offices maintain a practice of stamping a date on all incoming matter for future verification.

OUTGOING MAIL

In the previous chapter certain fundamental principles regarding the structuring of letters and correspondence were discussed. At this point we are ready to trace the progress of a letter after it has been typed. When placing letters on the physician's desk for signature, the experienced assistant separates those letters that were dictated from those that were composed by someone else for signature.

The usual procedure for returning typed letters for signature is to remove the carbon copy and file it in the appropriate place, inserting the addressed side of the envelope over the original letter and any enclosures. However, some administrators object to the envelopes being clipped to the original letter. Some assistants find it faster to provide only letters for signature without the envelopes. The envelopes can be addressed quickly from the carbon copies (if they are not already filed) or after the signed letters are returned to the assistant.

The assistant brings the signed mail back for assembling and actual mailing. Each letter should be checked for signature and enclosure (where applicable). The envelope address should correspond with the inside address.

For safety reasons the Postal Service objects to pins or metal clips used to fasten enclosures together. When it is necessary to use enclosures they should be fastened to a letter with staples.

When the material to be enclosed is approximately the size of an accompanying letter (8½ by 11 inches), there is usually no problem. However, when enclosures are larger than the letter to be mailed, a decision has to be made. Such enclosures might include any number of items such as pamphlets, catalogs, and x-ray negatives—any printed material too large to fit neatly into an ordinary size commercial envelope. Such material is generally mailed in larger manila envelopes separately.

The heaviest volume of outgoing mail occurs at the end or the beginning of the month when patients' statements and bills are mailed out. When there are large numbers of envelopes to be sealed and stamped, approaching the problem with a little organization greatly reduces the burden. After the envelopes have been addressed and stuffed, place them face down with flaps upward. With a wet sponge moisten all gummed surfaces with a few long sweeps. The flaps can then be turned back for quick sealing.

Having a postage machine greatly reduces the time spent in stamping envelopes and precludes frequent trips to the post office to purchase stamps. In operating a postage machine, one merely sets the meter for the proper class of mail and then proceeds to feed envelopes into the machine for stamping. In the absence of such a machine, the secretary should purchase stamps in rolls of sufficient quantity. The envelopes can then be moistened with a damp sponge and the stamps attached quickly from the roll.

An efficient assistant will see to it that a record is kept or that a copy is made of all outgoing correspondence, especially where medicolegal forms are concerned. This provides the physician with positive proof as to any exact words in the event that they are later challenged.

WHEN THE PHYSICIAN IS AWAY

The manner in which the assistant handles the mail in the physician's absence depends upon his personal preference. The physician and the assistant should reach an agreement as to the handling of correspondence in his absence. Such an arrangement could very easily be applied to all occasions when the physician is absent from the office for any prolonged period of time. He will feel much more secure in knowing that everything is being adequately taken care of while he is gone.

Regardless of whether the physician is on a business trip or vacationing, his assistant should always have a copy of his itinerary or at least know how to contact him. This is particularly important if the doctor wants important mail forwarded to him or expects weekly reports from his assistant about the office. In either case, the assistant should check to find out how long it takes for mail to reach each destination on the itinerary and allot sufficient time.

If the physician is to be away from the office for an extended period of time, it is the responsibility of the assistant to write periodically to keep him informed of important happenings. On the other hand, if the doctor specifically requests that a weekly report be forwarded to him, the assistant should ask the physician to outline the type of information desired in the report. This will facilitate composing the report and ensure that only the important details are included.

Normally, letters requiring the physician's

attention can be delayed. The assistant, however, should make an effort to reply immediately to all correspondence that requires a reply. It is considered discourteous to neglect or completely ignore such communications. A brief note acknowledging receipt of the letter and explaining that the physician is away but that the matter will be taken care of as soon as possible is usually sufficient. Much of the routine correspondence can be disposed of by an experienced assistant.

The physician may make a practice of telephoning the office each day. If this is the case, the assistant should get into the habit of classifying information into matters related to the office and matters outside the operation of the office. It is often helpful for the assistant to jot down explanatory notes on each letter in order to facilitate a quick report to the physician. The physician should be telephoned or cabled about any urgent matters that require immediate decision or approval.

Telegrams and cable messages can be transmitted over the telephone and charged to the physician's office number. Since charges are based on the numbers of words used, the messages should be clear and concise. If the information to be conveyed is lengthy and involved, it is probably more prudent to write an airmail letter.

When the assistant has agreed to forward packets of important mail to the physician, each packet should be numbered consecutively. This furnishes a safeguard or a check that all the mail has been received.

Accumulated mail can be separated into various categories to await the doctor's return. For instance, all correspondence necessitating the physician's signature could be placed in one folder and marked accordingly. Another folder might contain correspondence for the physician to read, and another might include reports and miscellaneous items, such as advertisements and periodicals.

MAILING EFFICIENTLY

On July 1, 1971, the new United States Postal Service was created by Act of Congress. As the name implies, service to the customer is supposed to be basic to its founding principles. A new booklet published by the Postal Service describes how to use the mail most effectively, including ways to send letters and parcels with maximum speed and security. A free copy may be obtained from any local post office or by writing to the Consumer Advocate, U. S. Postal Service, Washington, D.C. 20260. Simply ask for *Consumer's Guide to Postal Services and Products*. This will provide handy office reference for any medical assistant who handles mail.

The assistant who possesses a working knowledge of when and how to utilize the various types of postal service can occasionally save the physician-employer money. Savings are possible especially if the assistant is familiar with the uses and limitations of the various classes of mail.

Review questions

1. Why is it a good practice to acquaint all office personnel with the procedure for handling mail?
2. What is the first task to perform when processing incoming mail?
3. How should typed correspondence requiring the physician's signature be arranged?
4. Why should the physician's assistant keep a copy of an itinerary?

Suggested readings

Doris, L., and Miller, B. M.: Complete secretary's handbook, ed. 3, Englewood Cliffs, N. J., 1970, Prentice-Hall, Inc.

Hutchinson, L. I.: Standard handbook for secretaries, ed. 8, New York, 1969, McGraw-Hill Book Co.

chapter 12

The appointment system

SCHEDULING APPOINTMENTS

The appointment system is fundamental to the physician's practice. It is one of the most important aspects of public relations. The consensus of several recent studies indicates that patients leave the care of physicians not because of high fees or failure to cure but rather because of the excessive amount of time spent in the office waiting to see the doctor. This is public relations at its worst. Patients with appointments resent having to wait an hour or more before being seen. Not only does this waste the patient's valuable time and arouse his hostility, but it sometimes makes communication between physician and patient more difficult.

Unfortunately, this situation is characteristic of too many offices. If the appointment schedule cannot be made to function so that long delays and backlogs are the exception rather than the rule, then perhaps the appointment schedule should be discarded and patients seen on a first-come, first-to-be-seen basis. This system is used by many small-town general practitioners whereby the physician has fixed office hours each day and patients are seen according to the order in which they arrive.

Experience and a thorough knowledge of the physician's practice are important assets to the medical assistant responsible for scheduling appointments. There are several basic guidelines which, if followed, can help to stabilize the appointment schedule.

All appointments should be made carefully with a sufficient amount of time allotted for each patient. All appointments made should be written down in ink, for the appointment book is regarded as a legal record. It is important that this book be kept as accurately as possible. It will show patients who have made appointments, patients who have made appointments and not kept them, and patients who made appointments and then canceled them. This can be very important in a medicolegal case, particularly if a patient declares that he was unable to get an appointment with the physician. The physician has the appointment book to verify that an appointment was made but that the patient did not come or canceled his appointment. If a patient cancels one appointment and makes one for a later date, this information should also be written in beside the canceled appointment. Patients given appointments where cancellations have been made may have their

---

Glossary

EDP electronic data processing
E.R. emergency room of hospital
preoperative before or prior to a surgical operation
vexation the act of provoking anger or displeasure through irritations

names written in above, below, or beside the name of the patient who canceled. The canceled appointment should have a line drawn through it in ink together with explanatory information as to when and why it was canceled. If another appointment was made, its time should also be noted.

With the increased potential of legal actions that threaten the practitioner today, it is most important that the appointment book be kept accurately and that any changes made be shown clearly. Similar information should also be reflected in the patient's record.

The assistant must calculate, on the basis of the best information available, the time that each individual patient may require. Familiarity with the physician's practice and patients' conditions is essential. The assistant should also know the nature of the treatment, consultation, or examination to be performed.

Although waiting cannot be completely eliminated, good public relations dictates that it be kept to a minimum. Whenever it is found that there is overlapping in appointments and the schedule does not run smoothly, a free period or buffer time of approximately 20 to 30 minutes each day should be provided for during which no appointments are scheduled. The assistant uses discretion in deciding whether it is necessary to allow this open period both in the morning and in the afternoon. In any event, this allows for catching up, particularly when delays or emergencies are anticipated. The appointment book should be marked accordingly.

Emergency cases always take precedence over waiting patients. Experience has demonstrated that most patients are understanding of these matters and usually very cooperative. When emergencies occur, waiting patients are entitled to an explanation as to the reason for any delay.

Regardless of the type used, an appointment book is an absolute necessity for the maintenance of an efficient appointment system. In some offices a daily log (Fig. 12-1) is used, which serves as a combination daybook or receipt book as well as an appointment book. In other offices a separate appointment book is maintained. In any case, an appointment book should contain a separate page for each day and provide space for at least the following information: date, time, name of patient, and service to be rendered.

In an office where patients are scheduled throughout the day for treatments, sufficient time must be allotted for attending to each patient. In a dermatologist's office, for instance, the physician can consult with one patient while another patient is receiving treatment and while yet another patient is being prepared for an examination. The complexity of close scheduling is governed by the nature of the physician's practice. An efficiently run appointment system enables the physician to make the best possible use of professional time. Conflicting appointments should seldom occur, provided the assistant exercises care in consulting the appointment book in order to make certain that the time is available before making an appointment.

When making appointments, the assistant should give consideration to the following guidelines.

1. The assistant should be sure to have the name of the patient spelled correctly—first name, last name, and middle initial, if any. It is also important to secure the home address, telephone number, business address, and business telephone number of each patient. This information should be kept readily accessible in case it is necessary to contact the patient ahead of time.
2. Appointments should be made for the first available time that is convenient for the patient.
3. The patient must distinctly understand the date and time of the appointment. Particulars should be repeated to the patient at least once, and he should be given a card as a further reminder.
4. It is helpful to make a notation some-

Monday · March 7

HOUR		NAME OF PATIENT	SERVICE RENDERED	CHARGE	CASH	REC'D ON ACCOUNT	√
	1	Arnold Wing	on acct.			30 00	✓
	2	Lester Remick	" "			5 00	✓
9:00	3	Mrs. Roger Curry	emergency home visit		10 00		✓
	4	(936 So. Elm)					
9:30	5	Mrs. Mary Feathers	set fracture	50 00			✓
10:00	6	Charles Bird	hospital	10 00			✓
10:15	7	Mrs. Cecil Dean	"	5 00			✓
10:30	8	Betty Witt	"	5 00			✓
11:30	9	John Nyberg	home - Rx	10 00			✓
11:45	10	M. C. Kabel	"	7 00			✓
1:30	11	Stan Hinton	office cons.		5 00		✓
1:50	12	Helen Shelby	" "	5 00		15 00	✓
2:00	13	Vern McBride	dressed arm	5 00			✓
2:30	14	Russell Steffy	change dressing	5 00			✓
2:50	15	Emma Finch	exam	5 00		9 00	✓
3:20	16	Gordon Bishop	exam - Rx		6 00		✓
3:50	17	Olive Smyth	office cons.	5 00			✓
4:00	18	Ella Loftis	treatment		5 00		✓
4:10	19	Luella Young	"	4 00			✓
4:25	20	Norm Fields	exam - Rx	7 00			✓
4:45	21	Marcia Austin	treatment	5 00			✓
5:00	22	M. V. Reynolds	"	5 00			✓
5:15	23	Fred Mattern	exam - inoc.	7 00			✓
7:15	24	Mrs. D. Steele	home - Rx	7 00			✓
	25						
	26						
	27						
	28						
	29						
	30						
	31						
	32						
	33						
	34						
	35						
	36						
	37						
	38						
	39						
	40						
		CARRY TOTALS FORWARD TO **BUSINESS SUMMARY**	TOTALS	147 00	26 00	59 00	

FORM 201 COLWELL CO., CHAMPAIGN, ILL.

Fig. 12-1. Daily log-appointment sheet. (Courtesy The Colwell Company, Champaign, Illinois.)

where in the patient's records whether he has a particular time preference.

5. Whenever possible the patient should be offered a choice of appointment times.
6. If a patient's request for a particular appointment time is not acceptable, he is entitled to an explanation and should be offered another convenient time.
7. The assistant should never trust a confirmed appointment to memory but record it immediately in the appointment book.
8. Tactful questioning of the patient should reveal who referred the patient, whether a physician or another patient. It is a matter of good public relations to make a notation as to the reference source in

the appointment book or on the patient's ledger in red. This could then serve as a reminder to send the referring doctor or patient a letter of appreciation.

9. If a patient calls and cancels his appointment, the special notation "Canceled" should be entered in the book next to his name. On the other hand, if a scheduled patient does not show up for an appointment and does not notify the office, the special notation "Failed" should be made next to his name. Some physicians have a policy of charging patients for not canceling their appointments.
10. More time should be allotted for a new patient, since the doctor will usually want to examine the patient and take his medical history.
11. Where special treatments can be anticipated they should be prepared for ahead of time. Not only does this save time, but it also speeds up the appointment schedule.
12. Patients' charts should be pulled from the files, preferably the night before, and placed in order corresponding to the day's appointment schedule.
13. The appointment book should contain all appointments the physician may have away from the office and telephone numbers where he can be reached. Even when the physician is attending meetings and conferences the appointment book should be so marked.

Most offices make use of what is known as a charge slip (Fig. 12-2), regardless of what bookkeeping system is used. The lone exception to this rule would be those offices that subscribe to an EDP system. The charge slip, a form clipped to each patient's chart, provides a record of the services rendered to a patient during a particular visit. The charge slip contains the patient's name, the date, and a list of the treatments commonly rendered. After seeing the patient the physician merely checks the appropriate treatment and indicates at the bottom of the slip whether the patient should be seen again and approximately when. The assistant computes charges and posts to the patient's ledger sheet from the charge slip. If necessary another appointment is made for the patient before he leaves the office. This system frees the physician to see other patients immediately since time is then not taken out to communicate information to the assistant verbally after each patient.

Date________________

NAME____________________________

CONSULTATION	**LABORATORY**
O.V., INJ., C.Q.	CULT. & SCR.
SP. INJ. 1	SMEAR
2	URINALYSIS
GRENZ., X-RAY	CBC
SP. X-RAY	SER.
SURGERY	PBI
POST-OP.	BL. SUGAR
MISC.	CHOLEST.
1	PATH.
2	SKIN TEST
3	OTHER
4	

HAIR COUNT

RETURN: M T W Th F S

1 2 3 4 Weeks

1 2 3 4 Months

DISCHARGE

Fig. 12-2. Charge slip.

If the physician wishes to see a patient again for further treatment, it is a good policy to make the next appointment before the patient leaves the office. The assistant should be able to suggest several alternative times to the patient. Repeating the date and time for the new appointment is not sufficient in itself—most patients are apt to forget the details. Appointment cards (Fig. 12-3) are helpful in providing the patient with a written reminder of his next appoint-

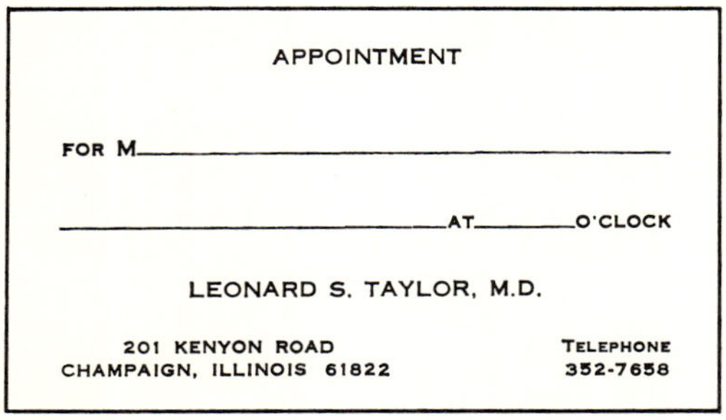
APPOINTMENT

FOR M____________________

________________AT________O'CLOCK

LEONARD S. TAYLOR, M.D.

201 KENYON ROAD
CHAMPAIGN, ILLINOIS 61822

TELEPHONE
352-7658

Fig. 12-3. Appointment card.

ment. All appointments should be recorded first in the appointment book before the appointment card is made out as a safeguard against scheduling two patients for the same time. Where time permits, some offices make a habit of calling patients the day before their scheduled appointments as an added reminder. This policy ensures the physician of a full schedule of patients each day.

It is not enough that there are always emergencies and delays to jam the appointment schedule, but there is often an additional problem for the assistant to cope with: family visits, which are sometimes referred to as piggyback appointments. Most assistants make it a practice to leave some time open in the schedule for unexpected patients, but this allotted time usually constitutes only a small portion of the fixed office hours. The mother who makes a single appointment and then shows up with two or three children presents a special problem.

In most situations of this nature the physician may see the children when it occurs the first time, but the mother should be politely reminded that all office calls are by appointment only and that in the future she should inform the office if she intends to bring the children for the doctor to examine. If the same situation occurs a second time, the mother should be told that the physician is booked solid and unless her children are emergency cases or seriously ill, it is impossible to see them. At this juncture the assistant might suggest making separate appointments for the children.

The medical assistant usually discovers through experience that one of the most important functions is that of educating patients as to the manner in which the physician's practice is conducted. Patients must be made to realize that office policies are established for the convenience of all the physician's patients. Educating patients requires polite firmness tempered by tact and diplomacy. An adequate explanation of the reasons for the existence of certain office policies generally satisfies the persistent patient. In acquainting patients with the policies of the office, the assistant will want to make patients feel that they are being spared as much inconvenience as possible.

CANCELED APPOINTMENTS

Since professional people place a high premium upon their time, a canceled appointment, or worse yet a failed appointment, is a source of vexation. The physician's time is valuable and must be fully utilized; otherwise it can result in a significant loss of income. Thus the appointment schedule is important not only from a public relations standpoint but also financially.

Actually, most appointments are broken for trivial reasons. It should be pointed out to the patient who frequently requests a cancellation that the physician's care is predicated on the basis of regular treatment and that if a regular schedule of visits is not maintained as directed, further harm or injury could result.

If the assistant is not able to persuade a patient to keep a scheduled appointment, another appointment should be immediately made. The appointment book should be marked accordingly and the available time offered to another patient. The responsible assistant sets about to secure another patient to fill this gap in the schedule. Invariably there is some patient who was given an appointment for a much later date or time than he originally requested. This patient should be contacted and offered the time that has now become available. Usually the patient will be pleased and the assistant's problem is solved to the mutual satisfaction of all concerned.

The assistant should try to schedule latecomers and those who frequently break appointments at the end of the day. Then, if they do not appear the physician can leave early, and no harm is done to the appointment schedule.

SPECIAL SITUATIONS

There will be occasions when it will be necessary for the physician to cancel an appointment, as there are times when the physician may be detained because of an emergency. If the physician knows approximately how long the delay will be the assistant should immediately explain the reason for the delay to any waiting patients. If the delay is to be a relatively long one, new appointments should be offered to each patient who does not wish to wait.

When the physician is delayed by an emergency and unable to keep office hours on a particular day, it may not be possible to notify all the scheduled patients ahead of time. The circumstances will have to be explained to those patients who were not contacted and arrive at the office, and new appointments should be made for them. If a patient cannot be contacted by telephone, perhaps one of the best ways to cancel the appointment for the doctor is by telegram. Granted it may be more costly than the telephone, but the small additional expense involved may be more than justified by the goodwill it begets. A telegram to a patient proves to him conclusively that the physician is concerned and interested in preventing him from making an unnecessary trip.

When another physician enters the office, by himself or accompanying another patient, and requests to see the doctor he should be immediately escorted into the consultation room, provided the doctor is not busy with a patient at the time. If the doctor is busy with a patient the visiting physician should be escorted in as soon at that patient leaves. A physician is not going to take up the doctor's time unnecessarily if he knows that the waiting room is crowded with patients. A doctor who is a patient is usually requested to enter the office by the back entrance so not to be seen by patients in the waiting room. He should be immediately escorted into a treatment room.

Very few physicians make house calls as a regular part of their practice. Practically all physicians, however, especially those affiliated with hospitals, make daily visits to the hospital to visit patients under their care. Hospital visits are generally made during fixed hours, and during this time the physician can be easily reached by the office. It may be somewhat more difficult but certainly not impossible for the assistant to reach him when he is not at the hospital. The appointment book should reflect all of the physician's out-of-office appointments.

It probably will not be necessary for every patient to see the physician on every visit. Some patients may be coming for treatments and services that can be administered by the medical assistant or office nurse. Such instances should be noted in the appointment book, and other patients may be scheduled to see the physician. When the physician is not in the office is an excellent time for scheduling routine treatments.

PATIENT REFERRAL

If a patient develops a condition or requires an examination that is not within the scope of the physician's practice, the patient is usually referred to the appropriate specialist. Patients may be referred to another doctor in two ways: by telephone and by letter. If time is an important factor, the telephone should be the initial form of contact, with confirmation by letter. When referring a patient by telephone, the assistant should transmit the following information:

1. Name of the patient, address, and telephone number
2. Condition for which the patient is being referred

3. Treatment rendered to patient thus far, if any (This is very important.)

The telephone conversation should always be followed up with a confirming letter repeating much the same information but also containing a detailed reason or explanation for the referral and any other pertinent data.

A physician referring a patient to a specialist expects and is entitled to a report back from that specialist. The assistant employed by the specialist must have some quick means of identifying the charts of those patients who have been referred by other physicians. An identifying sticker of some sort might be helpful as a reminder that a letter or telephone call is necessary upon completion of the initial visit. Further information should be relayed to the referring physician as treatment progresses.

APPOINTMENTS FOR HOSPITALIZATION

While the exact procedure for admission to hospitals varies somewhat from hospital to hospital, fundamentally the procedure is the same. Most hospitals require the following information about patients.

1. Medical history—hospitals usually supply physicians with the necessary forms (case history).
2. Personal and financial history—these are sometimes filled out at the hospital; sometimes hospitals supply the physician with forms.
3. Working history—the physician must supply the hospital with the admitting diagnosis or operation to be performed, if any.

Emergency admissions are generally handled by the E.R. (emergency room). It is not necessary to call either surgery or the admitting office, but instead the assistant should call the emergency room and tell the nurse the type of emergency to be admitted, the patient's name, the specific orders or tests requested by the physician, and when the physician will be there. Arrangements for admission or surgery are then handled by the E.R.

On an elective hospital admission the patient or his parents may designate the type of room desired. If the physician has given the patient certain instructions for preoperative care, the assistant should type them out for the patient as a reminder. It is ideal if the medical assistant is able to brief the patient as to the rules of the hospital, especially as to visiting hours and what he may bring with him.

TELEPHONE CALLS

When the telephone rings, it should be picked up at once by the doctor's assistant. It should not be allowed to ring and ring while the assistant completes some bookkeeping or other duties. The caller tends to become more and more impatient and difficult to handle with each ring.

It is an act of courtesy to allow the caller to hang up the phone first when a conversation is finished. The assistant should not hang up abruptly as if happy to be rid of the caller.

Managing the physician's telephone is one of the most important functions of the medical secretary. Every time she lifts the telephone receiver she is performing a public relations job, and is creating an image or an impression of the physician's office in the minds of patients through her telephone technique. Handling the telephone in a physician's office offers the medical assistant a real challenge. The medical assistant must know when to be firm or flexible; must be tactful and diplomatic; and must possess a good deal of practical medical knowledge.

Here are several suggestions for improving efficiency in handling the telephone.

1. All telephone calls should be answered promptly.
2. The assistant should have a low-pitched voice that is pleasant in tone.
3. If it is necessary for the assistant to leave the desk for any length of time it should be arranged for someone else to take calls.
4. A pad and pencil should be kept handy to record all calls. Sometimes it is a good

idea to maintain a telephone pad or log in duplicate.

5. All calls must be screened and as many as possible should be handled by the assistant.

In obtaining the reason for the call the assistant might inquire, "May I help you? Do you wish to make an appointment? The doctor is busy with a patient at the moment. Perhaps I can take a message." If a request is involved, it should be attended to at once. In asking a caller to wait, the best procedure to follow is to say, "Will you please hold on for a moment?" When returning to the line, say, "Thank you for waiting." If information is required to complete the call, the assistant should get the correct telephone number and promise to call back. Callers should not be interrupted needlessly; there is nothing more aggravating to a patient. The assistant must listen attentively, secure all the information, and then proceed to handle the matter from there. It is an act of courtesy to complete all conversations with "Thank you and good-bye," in a pleasant manner. Replace the receiver gently.

Dealing with the stubborn caller presents a somewhat more difficult problem. When the assistant encounters a caller who refuses to give his name, he should be told that the doctor cannot be disturbed unless he gives his name and the reason for his call. If the nature of his business is legitimate he should have no reason to be secretive. Should the caller absolutely refuse to give his name, the assistant might respond by saying, "May I suggest that you write to the doctor and mark your letter 'Personal'? I'll be happy to see to it that the doctor gets it at once." In the event that the caller is a physician, the usual procedure is to connect the two immediately and let the doctor handle the situation.

In the capacity as a screener of telephone calls, the medical assistant bears a great deal of responsibility and must learn to recognize the real emergency calls and those that sound like emergencies but really are not. Almost daily there are calls from overly anxious parents and relatives when there actually is no cause for alarm. Such calls provide the medical assistant with an opportunity to exercise good judgment. The ability to make a decision, of course, presupposes a certain familiarity with symptoms. Nevertheless, it is not the function of the assistant to diagnose over the telephone. There is an obligation only to distinguish the real emergencies from the not-so-real, gather all the information possible, and calm the caller.

After securing basic information, the assistant should begin to ask more specific questions. Many less experienced medical assistants find it helpful for easy reference to keep an outline of basic questions to ask. The more panicky a caller is, the greater the effort the assistant must make to keep the response even and the tone reassuring. Care must be taken to avoid making upsetting remarks.

The key to effective telephone control lies in developing a definite system for channeling calls. The general practice is to funnel calls for appointments directly to the receptionist for prompt action, while true emergency calls are immediately handled by the physician. Another procedure that has proved effective in some offices is the maintenance of a telephone log. Such a log can be set up by drawing six columns on a single loose leaf page—for the patient's name, his telephone number, his doctor's name (if this applies), the time of the call, the disposition of the call, and a notation as to whether or not an appointment was made. The great majority of the calls can be handled by well-trained office personnel who screen the calls to offer minor illness counseling, well-child counseling, and further referrals to physicians.

Another way to ease the problem is to schedule regular blocks of time in the late morning and late afternoon for the return of accumulated calls. The assistant might tell nonemergency callers: "The doctor will call you back between 11:45 and 12:15.

Will you be home then?" If the physician becomes unavoidably tied up, the assistant returns the call, explains the situation, and reschedules the call-back.

To cover his practice around the clock the physician probably will want to subscribe to some form of telephone answering service. Such services answer all calls after office hours via a special outside switchboard. When the physician leaves his office, he contacts the answering service and asks them to take all his calls indicating where he can be reached in an emergency. The answering service records information on all calls and relays messages to the physician.

There are various kinds of telephone answering systems, some commercially operated, others are even run by medical societies. The reliability of an answering service should be checked before subscribing to it.

Special equipment is also available in areas where no answering services exist. A recording device can be secured and attached to the office telephone, which automatically answers and notifies the caller that the doctor is out. A recorded voice invites callers to leave a message or, the physician may record a message that is dictated into the machine before he leaves that is relayed mechanically to all callers. Some physicians in isolated areas prefer installing radio equipment or mobile telephone systems in their cars so that messages can be transmitted to them while they are in transit.

In most cities, services are available that page a physician with a tone signal from a small pocket receiver he carries on his person. The signal sounds to notify him to call his home or office for messages. All of these devices are part of an effort to make sure a patient can reach his doctor or secure a substitute medical service in an emergency.

Formal medical society emergency programs utilizing various telephone answering system arrangements are being implemented in many parts of the nation. Under these programs the medical society either locates the patient's own doctor or puts him in touch with another physician serving on emergency call.

One of the most difficult problems for the medical assistant to deal with is patients who try to use the telephone to obtain free medical advice. Such patients accept the fact that an office visit costs money, but may feel that medical care by telephone should be free. Many times these callers insist on speaking directly to the physician despite the fact that he may be busy with a patient in the examining room or in consultation. Excluding legitimate emergency calls, these calls can prove to be a waste of time if the physician is good-natured and feels he must come to the telephone. Meanwhile, the appointment schedule is disrupted.

If the assistant perceives that such callers are taking unfair advantage of the physician's good nature and sense of dedication, it is up to her to step in and correct the situation.

Whenever feasible, patients calling for medical advice should be encouraged to make an appointment. However, in advising such patients to make appointments the assistant must exercise tact and understanding so that no impression is conveyed that the physician only wants them to visit the office so they can be charged.

Some offices make it a rule to charge those patients who habitually call and seek medical advice over the telephone. Where an unusual amount of the physician's time is consumed in listening to long-winded descriptions of patients ailments, a charge is sometimes levied by sending the patient a statement marked "Telephone Consultation Charge."

The conscientious assistant who is truly interested in doing a good job will, without having to be told, limit any personal telephone calls. Where such calls are absolutely necessary they should be kept brief and to the point; visiting over the office telephone is taboo.

Placing outside calls

It is always wise for the assistant when placing calls to plan ahead by collecting and organizing her thoughts. If the message to be transmitted is long and complicated, it may be helpful to have an outline of the points to be covered as the conversation progresses. Also, it may be necessary to gather records and other reference sources before making the call. Every assistant will find that it saves time to maintain near her desk a list of numbers that she calls frequently.

According to the telephone company, area codes are the key to faster long-distance service. The United States and Canada are divided into more than 120 telephone areas, each identified by a three-digit area code. These area codes should be used to facilitate calls from one area to another. Direct Distance Dialing (DDD) is the fast and convenient way to make station-to-station long-distance calls. When making a DDD call, if the area code of the number to be called is the same as the area code of the caller's telephone, usually only the telephone number need be dialed and it is not necessary to also dial the area code. However, if the area code of the called number is different from the area code of the caller's number, then both the area code and the telephone number must be dialed. The telephone numbers that can be dialed directly must have seven numerals or two letters and five numerals. When accepting a person-to-person long-distance call, the assistant should always be careful to note the operator's number, the city and state, the caller's telephone number, the name of the party, and/or the extension number (if given).

For the sake of clarification, a station-to-station call is made when the caller is willing to talk to anyone who answers the telephone at the other end of the line. On the other hand, a person-to-person call is made when the caller is interested in speaking to one specific individual and asks the operator to connect him with a named person, his department, or particular extension. The initial 3-minute period rates for person-to-person calls are somewhat higher than those for station-to-station calls. The caller should place a person-to-person call only when calling a person he knows is difficult to locate. In many instances the time expended in trying to get the right individual to the telephone may make the cost of a station-to-station call higher than the cost of a person-to-person call. Therefore in such cases it is sometimes cheaper and more economical in the long run to place a person-to-person call. The assistant should keep a record of all outgoing long-distance calls so that the monthly telephone bill can easily be reconciled and the various charges allocated.

A collect call may be made if the person or firm being called agrees to pay the charge. If one wishes to make a collect call, he should inform the operator before the call is actually placed.

It is possible to make local and long-distance calls to automobiles, trucks, and boats equipped for mobile telephone service. One should merely ask the operator for the Mobile Service Operator or the Marine Operator.

Station-to-station calls (long-distance) may be made, without a separate charge for each call, to those customers who subscribe to Wide Area Telephone Service (WATS). This service is offered to customers calling from specific locations. Check with the local operator for the proper code and instructions.

DETAIL MEN

A detail man is a sales representative of a pharmaceutical company and a frequent visitor to physicians' offices. The assistant soon becomes familiar with the various pharmaceutical firms and their representatives. Generally, the detail man does not expect the physician to purchase anything on the spot, but he tries to acquaint the physician with his firm's products, hoping that the doctor will prescribe these products for patients. New drugs and other pharmaceutical products are prescribed daily, and almost all physicians are interested in receiving first-hand information about them, if time permits.

It is easy to distinguish between detail men and magazine salesmen, peddlers, and the like. A detail man always presents his card, is never evasive, and never attempts to get into the physician's office under false pretenses. Accordingly, detail men should be greeted graciously. Unless otherwise instructed, the detail man may be permitted to see the physician at the time of his call, if this is convenient for the doctor. It should be explained to him just how much of the doctor's time he may have and the doctor should be reminded when the time is up. The physician is then in a position to close the interview or to prolong it.

If it is not convenient for the physician to see the detail man at the time of his call, he is entitled to an explanation. The assistant should request that he call again when the physician has time for him, preferably after office hours. It is to the advantage of the detail man to talk to a physician who is not distracted or pressed for time.

Regardless of the method selected, a definite system for handling detail men should be established and adhered to as closely as possible. It is the assistant's function to see to it that both he and the physician do not misuse each other's time. The detail man's time is also valuable—being knowledgeable in his field, he renders a valuable educational service. Therefore his goodwill should be cultivated by calling him ahead of time if the physician is unable to keep a scheduled appointment.

SUMMARY OF IMPORTANT RULES

The following summary contains some of the more important items involved in administering the physician's appointment schedule.

1. Make sure you have the correct name of patient and his telephone number when he calls.
2. Keep a record of all calls. Make a copy for the physician.
3. If a patient calls to cancel an appointment, be sure to note this on the appointment book so that the time is made available for another.
4. If the physician has to cancel an appointment, call the patient or mail a note and suggest a new time.
5. During office hours patients should be taken according to an appointment schedule. If one is late, explain that he must wait for an open time or give him a new appointment and stress the importance of being on time.
6. Before a patient leaves the office, arrange his next appointment. In some cases the physician may make it and tell the assistant later. If he fails to mention a second appointment check to be sure he hasn't forgotten to tell you.
7. Protect the physician from unnecessary interruptions.
8. Remind the physician of outside appointments in plenty of time to keep them. Be sure that the appointment schedule has allotted the time for outside appointments.
9. Check with the doctor for any house calls that may have been made.
10. Be prepared with procedures for handling emergency calls. Remain calm. Be helpful.

Review questions

1. What can be done in an office where patients are always forced to wait an hour or more before seeing the physician?
2. How should telephone calls and visits by other physicians be handled?
3. Construct a hypothetical conversation you would have with a caller who refused to give his name or state the purpose of his call.
4. Describe the procedures to be followed when a patient calls to cancel his appointment.
5. If it is known that the physician will be busy all afternoon with an emergency operation, what happens to the appointment schedule?
6. An excited mother calls and complains that her child is running a high temperature. How would you handle this situation?

7. Explain what is meant by DDD.
8. Why should the assistant strive to cultivate the goodwill of the detail man?

Suggested readings

American Medical Association: The business side of medical practice: Chicago, 1973, The Association.

Dallas, R. J., and Thompson, J. M.: Clerical and secretarial systems for the office, Englewood Cliffs, N. J., 1974, Prentice-Hall, Inc.

Doris, L., and Miller, B. M.: Complete secretary's handbook, ed. 3, Englewood Cliffs, N. J., 1970, Prentice-Hall, Inc.

chapter 13

Patients' records

In addition to many other duties, the medical assistant is responsible for the management and maintenance of up-to-date patient records. The main purpose of keeping accurate and complete medical records is to assist in giving the best possible care and treatment to the patient; records are perhaps the best measure of the actual quality of care being rendered. An incidental purpose is their value in defending malpractice suits. Entries in medical records should be written in a clear and legible manner, and summaries should always be signed by the attending physician.

Case histories should be neatly typed, updated, and filed where they can be easily retrieved. When requested to record parts of a patient's case history, the medical assistant should follow the outline provided by the physician. The medical indexing and filing system should be simple enough to assure maximum efficiency.

There will always be a continuous flow of paper work in conjunction with patients' private insurance, veterans' claims, workmen's compensation, and government-financed insurance programs. This work should be accomplished as quickly as possible and, of course, very accurately.

There undoubtedly will be times when, for various reasons, the medical assistant will fall far behind in some duty—transcribing dictation, for example—and could use some help in catching up, but the office simply has neither the equipment nor the space to accommodate another person. At this juncture, there is a great temptation to send out some of the work to a typing firm. This is usually not a good idea unless there is some mechanism for checking the integrity of its employees, as the physician might be violating patients' confidences by sending records out to strangers. Also, there is always the possibility of losing materials when they are allowed out of the office. The medical assistant may have to put in some overtime to reduce the backlogged dictation, or perhaps the doctor could solicit the help of a medical secretary from one of the hospitals where he maintains staff privileges.

The type of medical record varies depending upon the physician's specialty. For example, the general practitioner and internist will keep more detailed records than the dermatologist or radiologist, who may see a patient only on a referral basis. In offices where detailed histories are not necessary, various forms can be used to record vital information such as the patient's name and address, chief complaint, onset and course of the condition, and findings of physical examinations and laboratory tests as well

Glossary

acumen keenness of perception

diagnosis recognition of disease determined by symptoms alone

malpractice wrong or injurious treatment

as diagnosis and treatment. Forms designed for various specialties can be obtained, though some physicians prefer to draw up their own forms and have them printed to order. Some physicians do not use a printed form but develop an outline for taking case histories. The information secured from patients is later typed on regular paper and filed.

Today the trend is toward a more structured type of medical record, one that not only elicits a great deal of background information from a patient but a problem history as well. What is called the "problem-oriented medical record" is gaining wider acceptance. This is a system for logically organizing the information a physician obtains about a patient and analyzing it in relation to specific patient problems. Then on the basis of this structured data a physician works out an initial plan for dealing with each specific problem noting progress toward solving each problem as treatment progresses.

Problem-oriented medical records are helping to make significant changes in medical care delivery. This type of record makes it possible for physicians to remember important medical aspects about a patient at a glance; it organizes the physician's thoughts and views each patient as a totality. The physician cannot help but recognize that the patient who complains of a backache, headache, and insomina is suffering from something more profound.

A medication list comprises a part of each record and serves to alert the physician about drug interactions or dangerous side effects. With this new record system, the office staff actually becomes part of the health care team. Medical assistants and nurses can have access to the record in terms of data input. The problem-oriented record is also designed to allow the physician more time to talk with patients rather than having to leaf through charts for test results and other information.

Self-administered medical histories also are being utilized by many physicians, medical groups, and clinics. These are medical histories that the patient himself completes in any number of ways. He may answer it by writing or marking the questionnaire, sorting a set of cards, typing his answers on a special typewriter or even by activating a computer terminal on which questions are flashed. At the moment, no one history-taking system will solve the problem for every physician. However, many experts predict that some kind of self-administered medical questionnaires will be used in nearly every physician's office, clinic, and hospital within ten years. The ultimate effect, hopefully, will be improved patient care through more comprehensive review in recording of patient problems.

Medical records belong to the physician not the patient. They are his own notes. Such information or laboratory reports should be transferred only to physicians to whom patients are referred. Some physicians, however, give patients copies of certain records so that they can maintain a personal health record. This is done to encourage continuous attention to good health. The AMA now provides a family health record booklet and a health identification card in quantity for a nominal charge to physicians for distribution to their patients.

THE DAILY RECORD SHEET

Some type of record form must be used on which each day's occurrences can be itemized. In order to correlate the day's activities so that an accurate statement of the number of patients seen, the amount of money collected or charged, and the amount of money disbursed will be apparent at a glance, a daily record sheet should be scrupulously kept. On this sheet should be listed the following: the name of every patient seen (whether at the office or at home), a brief account of the treatment rendered, the charges incurred, and the manner of payment (whether by cash, by check, or if charged). Payments received through the mail must also be indicated. A bound book may be used for this purpose, but a looseleaf notebook is less cumbersome, more economical, and generally neater. Inasmuch as the purpose of this sheet is to present, in as nearly complete fashion as possible, what transpired during the day so that the busy physician or assistant can forego making entries on individual patient's accounts until a more convenient time, it should be detailed and yet not too involved.

The data thus collected should be an accurate professional and financial record that can be used in connection with the bookkeeping system being maintained. The physi-

Saturday May 23

HOUR	NAME OF PATIENT	SERVICE RENDERED	CHARGE	CASH	REC'D ON ACCOUNT	√
	1					
	2					
	3					
	4					
	5					
	6					
	7					
	8					
	9					
	10					
	11					
	12					
	13					
	14					
	15					
	16					
	17					
	18					
	19					
	20					
	21					
	22					
	23					
	24					
	25					
	26					
	27					
	28					
	29					
	30					
	31					
	32					
	33					
	34					
	35					
	36					
	37					
	38					
	39					
	40					
CARRY TOTALS FORWARD TO **BUSINESS SUMMARY**		TOTALS				

FORM 4201-63 COLWELL CO., CHAMPAIGN, ILL.

Fig. 13-1. Daily record sheet. (Courtesy The Colwell Company, Champaign, Illinois.)

cian can form a personal code of abbreviations for daily procedures so that only one line per entry will be necessary. There are many types of books available for this purpose. The most popular ones are one made by the Colwell Company called The Daily Log and one made by the Histacount Company, both of which can be purchased from your surgical or medical supply dealer (Fig. 13-1).

If each patient's name is entered upon this daily sheet immediately upon his arrival at the office or upon the physician's return from a house call or the hospital, charges to be entered on monthly bills will not be overlooked. The medical assistant can later transfer the financial details to the patient's record card and, if necessary, to the charge account record. In some busy offices an automatic clock stamp imprints not only the date of the visit but also the hour on a small slip of paper on which the patient's name has been entered. This slip, which is forwarded to the physician upon the patient's arrival, is a very efficient record and an effective means of avoiding controversies. The anxious patient who is sure he has waited for an hour for the physician can readily see from the entry slip that in reality he has indeed not waited that long. Should some dispute arise as to the number of visits made or the accuracy of the bill rendered, reference to the record sheet of the date in question serves as conclusive evidence.

STATISTICAL DATA

When a new patient enters the office the medical assistant should first obtain the essential identifying data from the patient, recording it on the appropriate form, and allowing the physician to complete the medical aspects of the patient's history if it is desired. This information can be recorded on a form such as that in Fig. 13-2. These data are often called vital statistics and constitute an important part of the case history and record of the patient. They include at least the date of the visit, name of the patient, home address, occupation, business address, home telephone, business telephone, age, sex, marital status, and the responsible party. Another important question to ask the patient is who referred him. This is a very important question insofar as it relates to public relations in the office. Anyone who refers a patient should always receive a note of thanks from the office (it need not be signed by the physician) indicating that the patient has come to the office and is being properly cared for.

In the event that the physician is a consultant to whom a case has been referred by another doctor, it is most important that a note be sent advising him that the patient has presented himself for examination and treatment. The assistant may sign this note

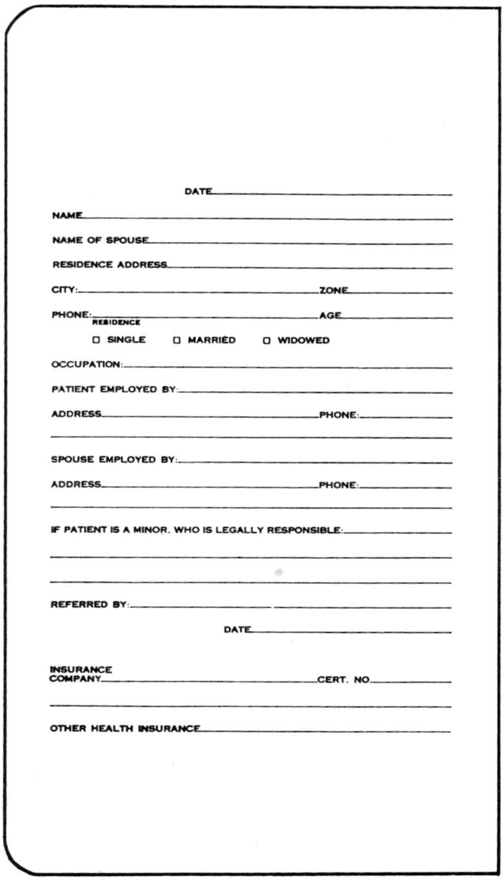
DATE

NAME

NAME OF SPOUSE

RESIDENCE ADDRESS

CITY: ZONE

PHONE: RESIDENCE AGE

☐ SINGLE ☐ MARRIED ☐ WIDOWED

OCCUPATION:

PATIENT EMPLOYED BY:

ADDRESS PHONE:

SPOUSE EMPLOYED BY:

ADDRESS PHONE:

IF PATIENT IS A MINOR, WHO IS LEGALLY RESPONSIBLE:

REFERRED BY:

DATE

INSURANCE COMPANY CERT. NO.

OTHER HEALTH INSURANCE

Fig. 13-2. Statistical data sheet. (Courtesy Pacific Business Forms, Santa Monica, California.)

of thanks, without requesting the physician to do so. However, in this case it is necessary to send a second report to the referring doctor as soon as the attending physician has completed diagnosis and examination of the patient. This is a matter of courtesy to the referring physician and should always be observed.

ELEMENTS OF A MEDICAL HISTORY

In addition to compiling the vital statistics (general information) about a patient, the rest of the case history develops into a more involved questioning. Usually the next question is in reference to the patient's chief complaint. Then the history of the present illness is usually investigated

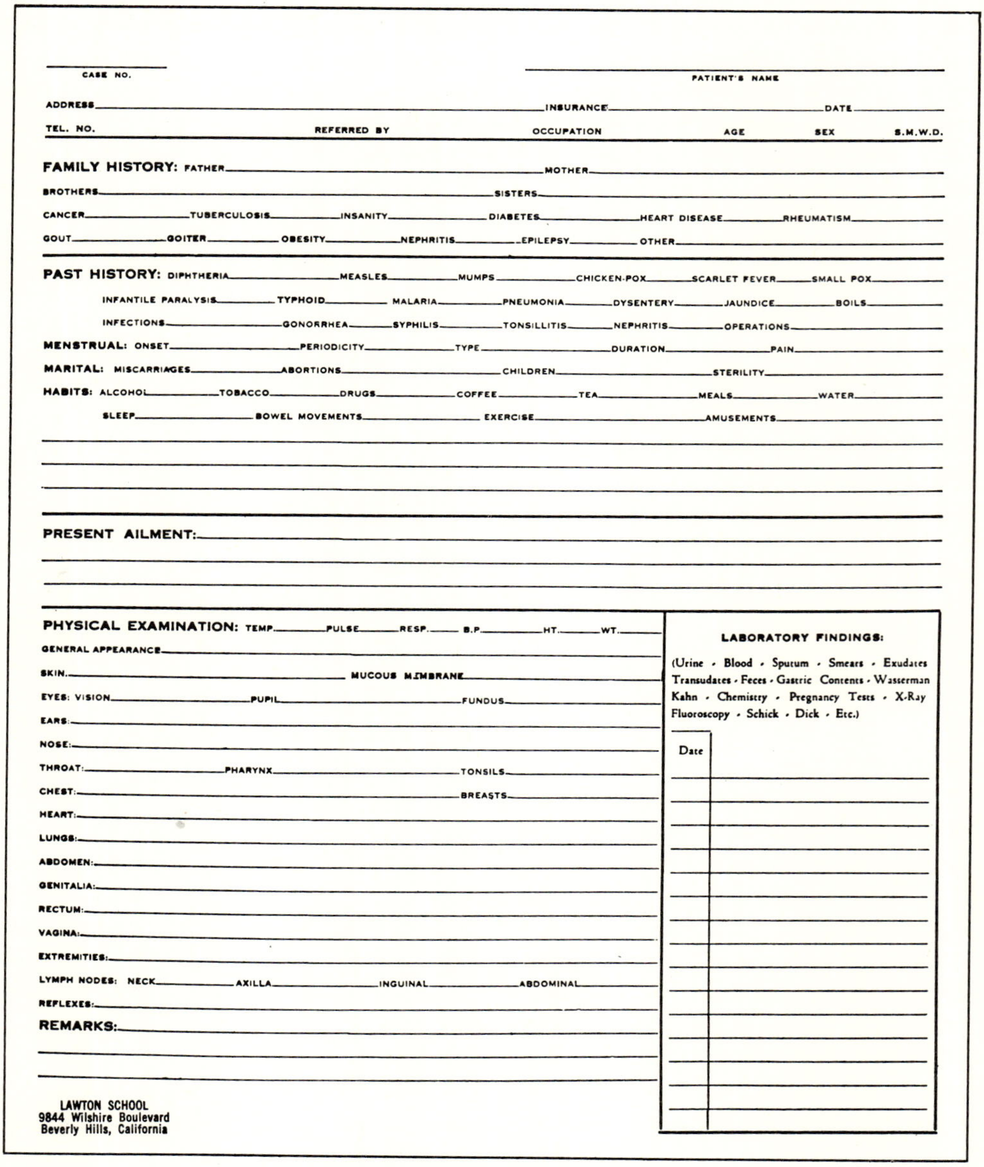

CASE NO.
PATIENT'S NAME
ADDRESS ___ INSURANCE ___ DATE ___
TEL. NO. REFERRED BY OCCUPATION AGE SEX S.M.W.D.

FAMILY HISTORY: FATHER ___ MOTHER ___
BROTHERS ___ SISTERS ___
CANCER ___ TUBERCULOSIS ___ INSANITY ___ DIABETES ___ HEART DISEASE ___ RHEUMATISM ___
GOUT ___ GOITER ___ OBESITY ___ NEPHRITIS ___ EPILEPSY ___ OTHER ___

PAST HISTORY: DIPHTHERIA ___ MEASLES ___ MUMPS ___ CHICKEN-POX ___ SCARLET FEVER ___ SMALL POX ___
INFANTILE PARALYSIS ___ TYPHOID ___ MALARIA ___ PNEUMONIA ___ DYSENTERY ___ JAUNDICE ___ BOILS ___
INFECTIONS ___ GONORRHEA ___ SYPHILIS ___ TONSILLITIS ___ NEPHRITIS ___ OPERATIONS ___
MENSTRUAL: ONSET ___ PERIODICITY ___ TYPE ___ DURATION ___ PAIN ___
MARITAL: MISCARRIAGES ___ ABORTIONS ___ CHILDREN ___ STERILITY ___
HABITS: ALCOHOL ___ TOBACCO ___ DRUGS ___ COFFEE ___ TEA ___ MEALS ___ WATER ___
SLEEP ___ BOWEL MOVEMENTS ___ EXERCISE ___ AMUSEMENTS ___

PRESENT AILMENT: ___

PHYSICAL EXAMINATION: TEMP ___ PULSE ___ RESP. ___ B.P. ___ HT. ___ WT. ___
GENERAL APPEARANCE ___
SKIN ___ MUCOUS MEMBRANE ___
EYES: VISION ___ PUPIL ___ FUNDUS ___
EARS: ___
NOSE: ___
THROAT: ___ PHARYNX ___ TONSILS ___
CHEST: ___ BREASTS ___
HEART: ___
LUNGS: ___
ABDOMEN: ___
GENITALIA: ___
RECTUM: ___
VAGINA: ___
EXTREMITIES: ___
LYMPH NODES: NECK ___ AXILLA ___ INGUINAL ___ ABDOMINAL ___
REFLEXES: ___
REMARKS: ___

LABORATORY FINDINGS:
(Urine · Blood · Sputum · Smears · Exudates Transudates · Feces · Gastric Contents · Wasserman Kahn · Chemistry · Pregnancy Tests · X-Ray Fluoroscopy · Schick · Dick · Etc.)
Date

LAWTON SCHOOL
9844 Wilshire Boulevard
Beverly Hills, California

Fig. 13-3. Medical history sheet (printed form).

thoroughly, the past history is evaluated by the physician, and finally the family history is recorded (Fig. 13-3).

After the history has been completed, the usual procedure is for the patient to have a physical examination by the physician; for this the patient should be taken into a treatment room and asked to disrobe as much as necessary for the type of examination involved. Very often assistants are asked to take a blood count or blood differential, complete a urinalysis, and take the blood pressure, temperature, pulse, respiration, and weight of the patient. Laboratory and x-ray examinations and special examinations such as electrocardiograms may also be ordered. When the results are available, the physician is ready to evaluate the findings, complete the diagnosis, and prescribe the patient's plan of treatment.

If the assistant does some of the questioning in gathering information about the patient's present complaints and past history, any questions of a delicate and personal nature should be omitted. This first copy of the history is then expanded and edited by the physician and later is typed as the finished product on the card or form selected for use by the office record system. This is preferable to the immediate typing of the history, since it eliminates the possibility of error or omission and necessity for erasures, which spoil the neatness of the record and give a poor impression should it ever be necessary to produce it in court.

During the process of obtaining the patient's past history and current ills, the physician is afforded an excellent opportunity to observe the individual and to arrive at some opinion as to the nature of his problem. The patient can relax and begin to feel at ease. In a sense, taking a case history is somewhat similar to collecting evidence and examining a witness. Should the patient be interpreting his symptoms fancifully, the examiner must have sufficient acumen to disassociate the patient's elaborations from the facts.

In taking a patient's medical history, there are several aspects that directly influence the specific type and number of questions asked by the doctor or assistant. The first is to inquire about past medical records or family illnesses, which will aid in arriving at the correct diagnosis. Symptoms and facts of previous illnesses, perhaps casually noted, often prove of great significance at a later date. Occasionally these facts prove of immediate use when a patient is to be referred to another physician.

The citation of relevant facts, even though negative, is important, for it is by no means unusual to have patients claim some loss or impediment following an operation; examination of the records often reveals that the complaint was present before the operation. Patients' medical records must be as complete as possible for the various reasons already mentioned, and especially as a safeguard for the physician. It is conceivable that the physician may be called as a witness on behalf of a patient or as an expert witness on one side or another of a case. In some instances he may need a medical record for citation in his own defense against a suit for malpractice or for presentation in court supporting collection of his fee.

TYPES OF CASE RECORDS

There are many types of printed forms available for taking case histories, devised either by commercial stationers or by physicians themselves. Printing houses produce forms designed for different specialists, and these are available through medical or surgical supply houses (Figs. 13-4 and 13-5). A report on a variety of medical history forms and systems can also be purchased from Medical Computer Services Association, 1116 Summit, Seattle, Washington 98101.

Such forms, it is true, save a considerable amount of writing and give the assurance that no question of importance will be omitted. They are usually carefully thought out in both content and arrangement, but their great disadvantage is the fact that it is hardly possible to figure out in advance the

FORM 8041 CLINICAL DATA GENERAL

NAME AGE SEX S M D W

ADDRESS PHONE DATE

SPONSOR ADDRESS

OCCUPATION REF BY ACKN

Fig. 13-4. Medical history sheet (blank form). (Courtesy The Colwell Company, Champaign, Illinois.)

amount of space that will be required for each aspect of a medical history. While the information as to address, telephone number, and so on is uniform, the past history of one patient may require several more lines than are allotted to it on the forms; in another case, it may be the present symptoms that require considerable amplification.

In some instances, a blank card or sheet of paper is often just as convenient as a commercially printed form, provided it is arranged properly. A list of the essential

FORM 524

LABORATORY FINDINGS

NAME | AGE | SEX | S M D W

ADDRESS | PHONE | OCCUPATION

PREPARED FOR | REF BY | DATE

URINE				BLOOD				REMARKS
DATE				DATE				
24 HRS AMOUNT				HEMOGLOB				
COLOR				C I				
APPEARANCE				R B C				
REACTION				W B C				
SP GRAVITY				POLY				
TOTAL SOLIDS				LG LYMPH				
UREA				SM LYMPH				
ALBUMEN				MONO				
SUGAR				TRANS				
INDICAN				EOSIN				
DIACETIC ACID				BASO				
ACETONE				CLOTTING TIME				
BILE				BLEEDING TIME				
CASTS				PARASITES				
BLOOD				GROUP				
PUS				BLOOD WASSERMAN				
EPITHELIUM				KAHN				
CRYSTALS				CULTURE				
MUCUS				CHEMISTRY				
BACTERIA								

SPUTUM

FECES

GASTRIC ANALYSIS | TOTAL ACID | FREE HCL | PEPSIN | BLOOD

MICROSCOPIC

Fig. 13-5. Laboratory sheet. (Courtesy The Colwell Company, Champaign, Illinois.)

questions to be covered in questioning the patient should be kept by the assistant for easy reference. The great convenience of the blank card lies in the fact that no limitations of space will prevent the adequate handling of each aspect of the medical history. Some physicians use a series of rubber stamps depicting various portions of the anatomy; when the diagram has been stamped on the case card, they mark the pathologic area involved. If the headings are sufficiently outstanding, particular items can be quickly located without reading through all other notations.

A system known as Current Procedural Terminology (CPT) is currently receiving considerable attention. CPT is a comprehensive reference listing of terminology and coding for use by physicians in reporting diagnostic and therapeutic procedures. The system includes more than 5,000 medical procedures. Each procedure has its own five-digit code to facilitate recording. CPT reduces the sheer size of the medical record and enables the consulting physician, peer reviewer, nurse, patient, or insurance carrier to look at the patient's record, billing document, or insurance claim form and know precisely what services were rendered.

Patient records are the essence of peer review. Since every physician has a personal style of keeping records, the major problem in review has been the misunderstanding or misinterpretation of what a physician has done for the patient. Now that peer review is on the way to becoming nationwide with passage of PSRO legislation, a uniform system of record keeping is sorely needed and CPT has been developed in part to meet this need. The CPT system, which was first published in book form in 1966, has evolved from efforts made by the AMA to arrive at a universally accepted system of terminology classification and coding. The third edition of the CPT manual, *Physician's Current Procedural Terminology,* is now available through the AMA.*

*From Gordon, B. L.: CPT, Prism, Chicago, 1973, American Medical Association, pp. 26-27.

RECORD INDEXING AND FILING

Medical records should be filed where they are easily accessible with all information pertaining to each patient organized in an individual folder bearing his name. Some physicians microfilm medical records for easier storage. In any event, it is advisable to investigate and compare the cost of standard filing cabinets of fireproof design. Filing space should be considered in terms of estimated practice growth over a period of approximately ten years. It is wise to tighten the filing system periodically by weeding out "dead" material and storing it elsewhere.

A review of the basic filing systems may now be useful. There are four basic filing systems used in the physician's office.

1. *Alphabetic.* Materials are arranged in the same sequence as letters of the alphabet. The advantages of this system are provision of miscellaneous paper, simplicity of guide and folder arrangement, and no need for a reference index. The only perceptible disadvantages might be the possibility of filing errors through lack of definite indexing control and the congestion that might occur under common names.
2. *Numeric.* Materials are categorized by number. This system requires an alphabetical cross-reference list. This system possesses the advantages of accuracy, unlimited expansion, and opportunity for permanent and liberal cross-reference. The inherent disadvantages are indirect filing and reference, unsatisfactory provision for miscellaneous papers, and no provision for eliminating "dead" material.
3. *Geographic.* Materials are arranged alphabetically according to locale of patients. This has the advantages of direct filing and reference, provision for miscellaneous material, and provision for grouping patients by location. The only disadvantages of this system are the possibility of error in sorting papers and the necessity of knowing location as well as name.
4. *Diagnostic.* Materials are classified alphabetically according to disease content. This system usually requires cross-filing. The advantages of the system are provision for grouping of papers by topics and unlimited expansion. The disadvantages are the difficulty in classifying papers for filing, the need for liberal cross-referencing, unsatisfactory provision for miscellaneous papers, and the need for occasional reference to index to determine subject.

The aforementioned systems are quite flexible in that they can be combined, or different systems may be used for different sets of files. If you decide that you'll really have to dig in and make some changes in your filing system, you may want to review the particular system (or systems) you're going to use. You might also bring yourself up-to-date on the latest filing equipment and material. Your local office supply company can furnish you with information about this.

The best method of filing will vary from office to office. Experience has demonstrated that there is much less confusion and less chance of misfiled papers in those offices that use the numeric system. This is one of the reasons this system is used in hospitals. Numbers are much harder to lose and misfile than are letters. Names are easily misspelled and misplaced. Too many people have names that are alike or similar, which creates a great problem in filing the numerous papers that must be placed in patients' folders. Perhaps the biggest single advantage of numeric filing is that of accuracy. Numeric systems are becoming increasingly popular because of their demonstrated efficiency and rapid retrieval capability. The numeric system eliminates having to plow through perhaps twenty files with the name Smith in order to locate the file of Mary Smith.

The diagnostic index is especially valuable when the physician is engaged in research or in the assembling of medical statistics. For the general practitioner, who places most emphasis on the efficient handling of his practice, it is unduly complex.

Color coding in filing has also come into widespread use in the medical office. Color coding possesses the advantages of immediate visual recognition. No system is absolutely foolproof, however, especially when its accuracy depends upon human beings.

To make active cases readily available, case histories should be segregated into three separate drawers of a filing cabinet, labeled as follows: (1) the active file, holding the records of those patients under care at the time, (2) the open file, holding the records of those who visit the doctor at infrequent intervals or those whose accounts have for some reason not been fully settled, and (3) the closed file, containing records of old cases and of discharged patients. The segregation of the records of active patients precludes the long search and makes their histories immediately accessible for frequent use. If a former patient visits the office with a revival of an old ailment or a totally new one, his record can easily be transferred from the closed file to the active one.

Naturally, this system may need to be modified to conform with the physician's type of practice. Some physicians, usually specialists, have practices consisting largely of patients referred to them by other physicians, who are seen for one specific ailment and then perhaps never seen again. In general practice, however, where the physician has a following of his own and where he deals with all kinds of ailments, the same patient will generally be seen fairly frequently for a variety of complaints.

FILING OF ADDITIONAL DATA

Frequently additional data regarding patients, such as x-ray pictures, laboratory reports, or correspondence about his case, accumulates in the file. Some physicians arrange such information separately in the file, while others clip it to the case histories and keep it in some form of a folder. Although the accumulation of all data regarding a case in one place is extremely convenient in certain instances, this procedure proves cumbersome when it is necessary to record a patient's office visit or examine a case history. At such times the x-ray pictures or laboratory reports become unwieldly. X-ray films, moreover, are usually too large for regular-size folders; it is therefore better to keep them filed in a separate compartment, each marked with a number that is also listed on the patient's card, thus creating a cross-reference.

Here are a few basic tips for organizing your files.

1. Always file papers behind division guides.
2. As a general practice, use a dividing guide about every six to eight folders.
3. Start an individual folder on any subject in miscellaneous files when you have five or six pieces of material for it.
4. Arrange correspondence in individual folders chronologically, with most recent material in front of holder.
5. Place material in folder so that everything is face up and right side up.
6. Remove clips and pins before filing papers.

Regardless of how efficiently your files are set up, they can't give you good service for long unless you keep them in good order. Always remove outdated material periodically; transfer old files at regular intervals; keep your files neat; and don't leave any papers dangling over the edges of folders. It is also an excellent idea to maintain a check-out system, particularly if there are a number of people using the files. Note who took what and when. This procedure will save a great deal of time trying to track down missing material later.

FINANCIAL RECORDS

The daily sheet or log is the basis for recording all transactions. From the information listed thereon, recording of payments and charges should be made on patients' cards. When credit is extended, however, the mere notation of this fact in the patient's folder is insufficient for collection purposes, since charges will be scat-

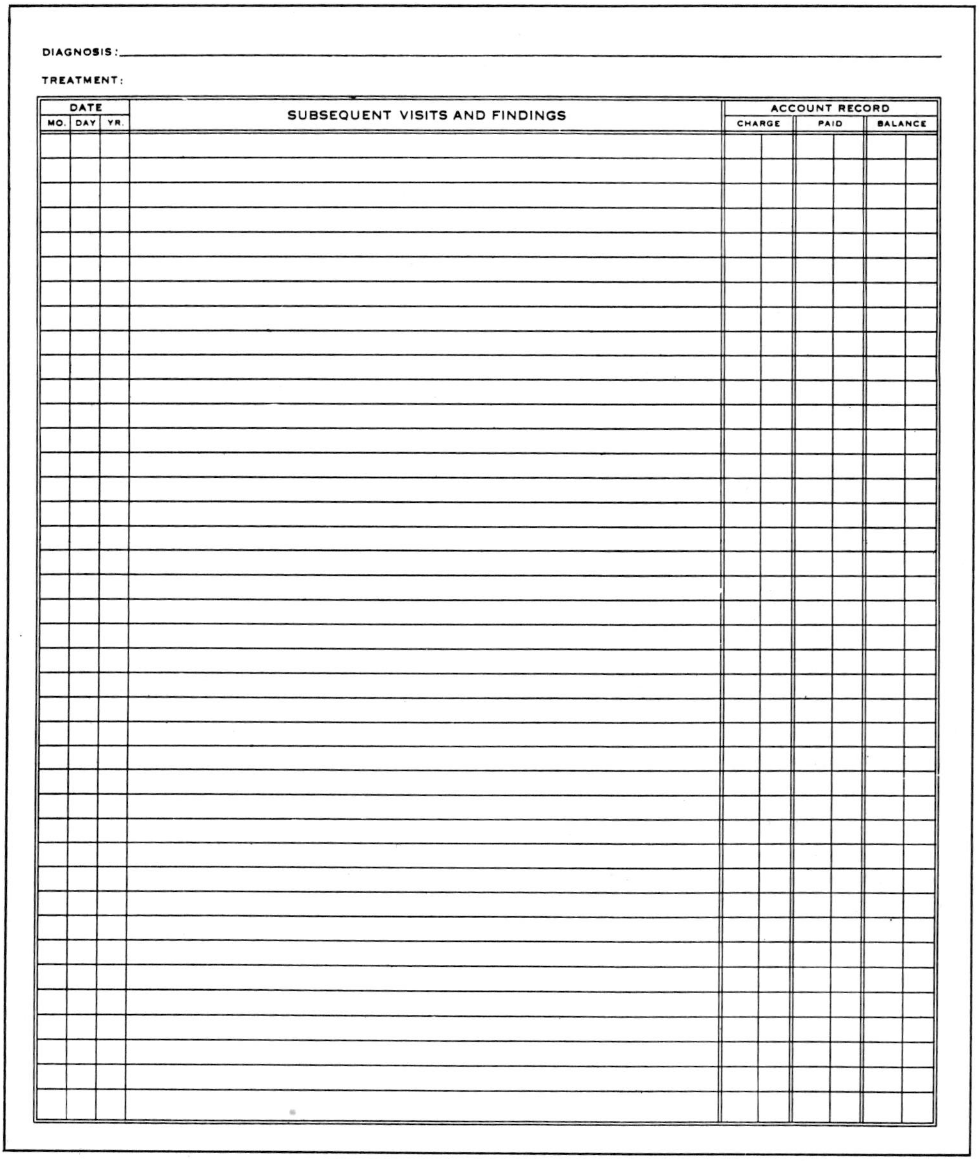

DIAGNOSIS:

TREATMENT:

DATE			SUBSEQUENT VISITS AND FINDINGS	ACCOUNT RECORD		
MO.	DAY	YR.		CHARGE	PAID	BALANCE

Fig. 13-6. Patient ledger card.

tered intermittently throughout the files. Such a situation would most certainly impede the process of maintaining accurate financial accounts and sending out up-to-date bills to patients. What is needed is a system whereby all of the charges recorded against a patient can be gathered in one central place for ease of billing.

A simple and effective means of making outstanding balances readily apparent is the use of a visible card record, such as the type now so widely popularized as a bookkeeping instrument (Fig. 13-6). When a charge is made against a new patient, a card is immediately made out in the individual's name. All further charges and receipts are recorded under the appropriate heading. On the first of each month, the balance can be easily computed, and bills sent to every patient for whom there is a card in the visible index. As soon as the balance is completely paid, the card is placed in the closed file. By virtue of its simplicity, a bookkeeping system of this sort is an effective check on unpaid bills, and if accurately kept up-to-date, it can earn its way by preventing even one or two charges from being overlooked.

Although it may appear to be simpler to record both medical and financial information on only one card to save extra handling, the possibilities of losing records, and the added inconvenience when the physician and the assistant compete for the one record at billing time are factors that argue against a one-card record system.

The possibility of error is lessened by the fact that each charge or payment is listed first on the daily sheet, then on the patient's ledger card. When a bill is mailed at the beginning of the month, this fact can be noted on the ledger card in red ink. Repetition of this red ink notation enables the assistant to see at a glance the age of the bill in question.

Some physicians, rather than keeping a separate ledger card for each individual patient, use a family ledger system containing sheets headed with the name of the individual responsible for the family medical bills. On these sheets debits and credits are made in the usual bookkeeping fashion. For additional information concerning fees and methods of collection, see Chapter 16.

Review questions

1. Why is the daily record sheet or log so essential in the physician's office?
2. Which system of filing is probably the most accurate and least confusing? Why?
3. Name the component parts of a medical case record.
4. What system is most often used for keeping patients' financial accounts accurate and updated?

Suggested readings

Alcazar, C. C.: Medical typist's guide for histories and physicals, ed. 2, Flushing, N. Y., 1974, Medical Examination Publishing Co., Inc.

Bassett, E. D., et al.: Business filing and records control, ed. 3, Cincinnati, 1963, South-Western Publishing Co.

Goldfinger, S. E.: The problem-oriented medical record: a critique from a believer, N. Engl. J. Med. **288**:606-608, March 22, 1973.

Raus, E. E., and Raus, M. M.: Manual of history-taking, physical examinations and record-keeping, Philadelphia, 1974, J. B. Lippincott Co.

Siegfried, W.: Typing medical forms, New York, 1969, McGraw-Hill Book Co.

Weed, L. L.: Problem-oriented medical record described, Medical Opinion **2**:22-27, Feb., 1973.

chapter 14
Private health insurance

The value and success of insurance are based upon the premise that man is essentially improvident; that is, if left on his own he will not provide for future contingencies. While most people recognize the necessity, in principle, of having insurance to protect themselves against the insecurities of life, the vast majority have adopted a more or less indifferent attitude regarding insurance, looking upon it as a necessary evil. Many policyholders never take the time to read their policies to determine the extent of their coverage and liability. This is a rather unfortunate situation, since it is only by scrutinizing insurance policies that one discovers which policy furnishes the greatest amount of protection for the least possible cost. Since the medical assistant encounters few patients who are thoroughly familiar with the nature of their coverage under the various health insurance plans, a twofold obligation is created. On one hand, patients expect help in the interpretation of their respective insurance plans. On the other hand, the greatest part of a physician's income is derived from these so-called "third-party payers," thereby making the connection between health insurance and physician income closely intertwined. Hence, the more knowledgeable the medical assistant

Glossary

assignment the signed transfer of the benefits of a policy by an insured person to a third party

Blue Cross an independent, nonprofit membership corporation providing protection primarily against the costs of hospital care

Blue Shield an independent, nonprofit membership association providing protection primarily against the costs of professional services and other items of medical care

carrier a large insurance company

coinsurance a policy provision, frequently found in major medical insurance, by which both the insured person and the insurer share in a specified ratio the hospital and medical expenses resulting from an illness or injury

coverage the risks assumed by an insurance carrier; the extent of insurance benefits

deductible a term used, mainly in major medical insurance plans, referring to that position of covered hospital and medical charges which an insured person must pay before his policy's benefits begin

fiscal intermediary a representative of another in matters of finance

group insurance a policy protecting a specified minimum number of persons usually having the same employer

improvident lacking in foresight; not careful in providing for the future

indemnity a benefit paid by an insurer for a loss insured under a policy

major medical expense insurance policies especially designed to help offset heavy medical expenses resulting from catastrophic or prolonged illness or injury

premium the amount of money paid for insurance coverage

prepayment medical insurance benefits paid for in advance, generally through monthly premiums

service benefits an insurance benefit which pays in full the actual costs of specific hospital or medical care services

subscriber usually refers to one who belongs to a group plan; a beneficiary

third party payer the party (usually insurance carrier, plan, etc.) besides the physician and the patient that intervenes to pay hospital and medical bills becomes concerning all forms of third party reimbursement and the processing of claims, the greater the doctor's income is likely to be. The medical assistant who is capable of efficiently coping with the various health plans and their claim forms is seldom out of a job.

BACKGROUND

In the post–World War II period, three powerful stimuli interacted to provide modern health insurance with its strongest impetus. The first of these was a decision of the United States Supreme Court, which held that fringe benefits—including health insurance—were a legitimate part of the bargaining process wherein labor negotiated its contracts with management. Second was the sharply escalating costs for care, which motivated the public to find a way to protect itself against the expense. The third force was the continuing improvement of health insurance itself, through the introduction and the broadening of coverage.

The emergence of the nation from a depression economy to the beginnings of an affluent society also brought the introduction of the broadest form of health insurance devised to date—major medical expense insurance. From its start as an executive coverage, major medical insurance grew rapidly in response to the family's need for protection against serious and prolonged illness in an age characterized by swiftly rising hospital, surgical, and medical costs.

Major medical insurance encompasses virtually all types of medical expense—both in and out of hospital—as prescribed by a physician. In general, it includes hospital care and special hospital services, such as drugs, operating room and anesthesia, surgery and other physician care, nursing, special medications, diagnostic services, appliances, and certain types of dental care.

The general trend of health insurance has been not only to provide protection against a wider spectrum of health care services, but also toward coverages that were broadened to reflect changes in the economic environment. Among the newer forms of coverage, one that is currently experiencing an upsurge is dental care. Dental care coverage is generally available today through group insurance programs offered by dental society–sponsored insurance companies (dental service corporation) and Blue Cross and Blue Shield. The two main deterrents that retarded pioneering efforts in dental insurance were the feasibility of insuring dental care and the question regarding the demand for the coverage. Other significant trends in health insurance coverage include nursing homes, mental illness, alcoholism, and out-of-hospital drugs.

In its embryonic stage, the primary emphasis of the health insurance policy was directed toward replacement of income rather than providing hospital or surgical benefits. The early insurance company policy insured the policyholder against loss of earned income due to a limited number of diseases, including typhus, typhoid, scarlet fever, smallpox, diphtheria, diabetes, and a few others.

By 1960 about 72% of the civilian population in the United States were reported to have some protection against hospital expenses. An estimated 66% had some surgical coverage, 47% some regular medical coverage, and 12% major medical coverage. At the end of 1968, over 169 million Americans were protected by one or more forms of private health insurance. This total represented 85% of the civilian resident population. A recent survey conducted by the Health Insurance Institute shows that only 10% of Americans under age 65 have no protection at all against the often ruinous costs of serious illness. The federal government's National Center for Health Statistics suggests that this number is greatly underestimated and that perhaps some 20 million persons may not have insurance protection.

It is interesting to note that, despite the degree of voluntary health insurance coverage, the consumers of medical care still pay about 60% of the cost of the services delivered. According to a Social Security Administration study, though 43% of the population had private coverage of home and office care at the beginning of 1969, the insurance had little effect in reducing the patients' direct payments to physicians. The reason: much of the insurance was tied to deductibles and other limitations and therefore covered little of patient costs.

Health insurance premiums have been rising steadily now for the past five or six years not merely because of expanded benefits and greater coverage, but chiefly because of the inflationary rise in the cost of medical care. Total spending for health care in the United States during fiscal 1973 reached an estimated 94.1 billion representing an 11% increase over the previous year—the lowest in several years. The Social Security Administration calculates that the nation's health outlays during fiscal 1973 remained at the 1972 proportion of the gross national product, 7.7%. Per capita expenditures amounted to about $441, an increase of $41 over fiscal 1972. The per capita figure only five years ago, in fiscal 1969, was estimated at $292.

Broadly speaking, there are three major categories of health insurance: (1) provider-sponsored plans, (2) commercial or indemnity plans, and (3) public (government) medical care programs. This chapter is chiefly concerned with a comparison of the first two categories. Public medical care programs will be discussed in more detail in a subsequent chapter.

The five major forms of health insurance coverage are: hospital expense, surgical expense, regular medical expense, major medical expense, and disability income protection. The first four help insured persons pay hospital and doctor bills and the cost of other medical care needs. The latter provides a disabled individual with a guaranteed income.

PROVIDER-SPONSORED PLANS

Provider-sponsored health insurance refers to those plans that were founded, promoted, and developed by actual providers of medical care—hospitals and physicians. Provider-sponsored plans are commonly known as service plans; they differ somewhat from the indemnity plans, which operate strictly on the insurance principle, reimbursing the insured with stipulated sums of money to be applied against expenditures for the insured risks. A service plan, in theory, assures its members certain units of necessary medical services, such as a day of hospital care or a special surgical procedure. Benefits are usually provided through contractural agreements between the insured plan and participating physicians, hospitals, and other providers of care. Blue Cross and Blue Shield exemplify service plans of an indirect type, for they reimburse those who provide the service to the patient. Direct-service plans like Health Insurance Plan (HIP), Ross Loos, the Kaiser Plan, and other well-known, so-called independent types combine the functions of both insurance carrier and provider of services. Their most distinguishing feature is that they furnish the insured services directly through their own hospitals and/or affiliated professional staffs.

The commercial or indemnity insurance companies negotiate agreements between themselves and the individual subscriber. Since indemnity companies are corporately owned, they operate on the profit motive, while service plans are nonprofit and should be able to provide greater benefits for less money.

Service plans offer enrollment to both individuals and groups. Generally speaking, the individual who obtains membership in a plan as part of a group is assessed a smaller premium and receives more extensive coverage than the individual subscriber. In fact, the larger the group the greater the amount of benefits that accrue to each group member.

All service plans are based on the well-established philosophy of prepayment, which permits the individual family to budget expenses for medical care. It is practically the only way that people of moderate income can cope with the increasing costs of modern medicine. Medical services far beyond the financial ability of the average family can be provided as needed when the costs are met through periodic payments by many families. This is possible because some persons require a great deal of treatment during a given period of time, while others require a minimum of medical care. This is known as spreading the risk. Winston Churchill once referred to health insurance as "The magic of averages applied to the rescue of millions."

For the sake of our discussion, service plans may be subdivided into three categories on the basis of the method of reimbursement to the providers of service, principally physicians; (1) fee for service, (2) capitation, and (3) salary. There are no fine lines of distinction among these categories; instead there exists a good deal of overlapping.

Fees for service type plans (Blue Shield and Blue Cross) pay the providers of care (physicians) for each service rendered to a member patient. Such plans, as distinguished from indemnity types, which pay benefits in fixed dollar amounts, are designed to cover the major portion of the actual cost of treatment. Health insurance plans embracing the principle of fee for service also impose small coinsurance and/or deductible charges in their contracts. The deductible provides that the carrier (plan) pays only that portion of the total cost of covered expenses for an insured individual that exceeds the specified deductible amount. In other words, the patient pays the first $50.00 or the first $100.00 of the bill. The coinsurance feature provides that, in addition to the deductible, the insured patient will pay an agreed portion of the remaining amount, usually 20%.

The second category into which service plans fall is capitation. A capitation fee is a per person charge made by a provider of service or group of providers for services to be provided to individuals or groups for a specified period of time. This average charge is usually based on the total number eligible to use the service but also be based on the number actually using the plan. Under capitation, enrollment consists namely of large groups of employees, particularly employees from large industrial firms. Members receive extensive medical care generally without having to pay any additional charges over their premiums. The cost of premiums may be shared partially by the employer and partially by the employee through payroll deductions, or the cost may be absorbed completely by the employer as a fringe benefit. The most distinguishing characteristic of capitation is the fact that funds collected from the various member groups pay the providers a fixed fee per patient per month regardless of the services rendered or the number of times a patient visits the physician.

The mechanics of the capitation type of plan differ from the fee for service type in that the physicians who contract with employer-employee groups have joined together to establish group practice organizations that generally include most of the medical specialties. For the convenience of their patients, they may be located in an area of close proximity; often the physicians occupy their own building. Patients are free to choose a family physician from among the general practitioners in the group. Participating physicians may treat private or nonmember patients as well. This provision differentiates capitation-type contracts from the closed panel plans, which do not permit member physicians to treat nonmember patients. Under a capitation arrangement, billing is simplified for the medical assistant, who merely submits to the central office of the organization a monthly report as to the number of different patients seen by the physician or physicians.

The final category under which service plans operate is the salary method. Under this type, physicians form their own groups, consisting of general practitioners and specialists. Subscribing members are assessed monthly dues, depending upon the extent of their family coverage, for which they receive practically complete comprehensive medical care by all the physicians comprising the group. Physicians contract with the plan to devote their entire practice to the exclusive care of plan member patients. Private patients are not accepted for treatment. Such contracts are restrictive to some degree by the choice of physicians available to the insured person, since he must choose from among members of the group and also use the facilities provided by the plan to receive treatment.

Matters pertaining to the collection of dues and payments from patients are handled by a centralized administrative office. Patients' records are also maintained in a central file generally under the supervision of a qualified medical records librarian. The functions of a medical assistant employed by a closed panel group plan might consist of scheduling appointments, handling correspondence, taking and transcribing dictation, and typing case histories.

Closed panel contracts are held by large and small physician groups alike and are scattered throughout the country. By far the largest of such groups is the Kaiser Foundation Health Plan.

BLUE CROSS–BLUE SHIELD

The medical assistant usually will have more contact with Blue Cross and Blue Shield plans, or combinations of both, than any other single plan because these two plans cover more subscribers. Thus some brief mention of the general structure, operation, and special features of each is warranted.

The Blue Cross concept was a product of the economic distress of the nation's hospitals when the Great Depression of the 1930s left them with empty beds and unpaid bills. The national movement was sparked by Justin Ford Kimball, executive vice-president of Baylor University, who, in 1929, worked out a plan under which Dallas schoolteachers were to be provided twenty-one days of hospitalization in a semi-private room at the University Hospital for a prepayment of 50 cents a month. The Baylor plan was an immediate success. A group of hospitals in Sacramento, California, joined together in organizing a communitywide prepayment plan. Similar plans began to spring up elsewhere. Today there are some seventy-four Blue Cross Plans in the United States. Each Blue Cross Plan has a board of directors, whose members serve without pay, comprised of prominent members of the industrial, labor, and general communities, as well as leading members of the health professions. Blue Cross Plans cover the entire nation and provide hospital protection to an estimated one of every three Americans.

In 1964, for the Blue Cross system as a whole, 4.6% of subscriber income was used for operating expenses. The remainder was paid out for hospital care benefits. Moreover, Blue Cross Plans have contracts with 6,471 hospitals (approximately 96% of the nation's registered hospitals) and make special provisions for emergency coverage in others. The Blue Cross Association was organized in 1948 and serves as spokesman for the various member plans on matters of national or regional concern. The American Hospital Association has played a major role in the development of Blue Cross.

Blue Cross plans are autonomous nonprofit corporations usually established under special state legislation. The various state legislatures have adopted "enabling acts" that legally differentiate nonprofit hospital service plans from insurance companies, and exempt them from the incorporation and reserve requirements imposed on insurance companies and from taxes on earned income. Consequently, Blue Cross has no stockholders and pays no dividends.

Blue Cross contracts with it members to provide protection in terms of actual hospital service. Through "service benefits," Blue Cross pays for the care each hospitalized member needs less any deductibles and coinsurance (20% paid by subscribers).

No maximum dollar amount is set. Benefits are designed to cover both short-term, nonacute stays and longer, more serious hospitalizations that may require special medications and use of costly equipment. This method of providing benefits is in contrast to the indemnity method, which provides specific per diem payments for hospital care. Also, unlikely indemnity plans, an individual record of each covered member is maintained at the Blue Cross central office.

Most patients are not aware that certain kinds of treatment require a waiting period before coverage under a plan becomes effective. For instance, most plans provide for a six-month waiting period from the date coverage began before the subscriber is eligible for benefits for a tonsillectomy or an adenoidectomy. A nine- to ten-month waiting period is usually required for the treatment of any condition that existed prior to the effective date of the contract. Any other pertinent information that would help the assistant to bill accurately should be recorded on the patient's ledger.

Like Blue Cross, the first Blue Shield organizations were born of the Depression and the need of doctors to protect their incomes. Blue Shield plans are also nonprofit and have sought to differentiate themselves from commercial insurance company operations. Like Blue Cross, Blue Shield plans are local or statewide autonomous corporations, usually organized under special state "enabling acts" intended primarily to exempt them from the insurance laws.

The thinking that eventually led to the founding of the first statewide, doctor-sponsored prepaid medical care plan, California Physicians' Service (CPS), was stimulated by Dr. Ray Lyman Wilbur. When the Committee on the Cost of Medical Care was formed in 1927, Dr. Wilbur was named chairman. After five years of intensive study by its fifty members, a final report was published in 1932. Included among its specific recommendations was the establishment by the medical profession of a voluntary health security plan on a group, prepayment basis.

As a result, California Physicians' Service was incorporated as a nonprofit medical service organization in 1939. Michigan Medical Service was organized the same year. Both started out as comprehensive service-benefit plans, but soon encountered unexpectedly high utilization, ran into serious financial difficulty, and were forced to abandon comprehensive service contracts in favor of income ceilings and limited benefits. In 1943 the American Medical Association endorsed the principle of medical service plans by establishing the Council on Medical Service, which formulated a set of approval standards later adopted by the AMA's house of delegates.

The National Association of Blue Shield plans now boasts a membership of some seventy-one plans, providing protection for more than 83 million people. Blue Shield plans cover over 40% of the United States population. The Association, with headquarters in Chicago, serves as a clearing house for data collection, suggestions, and information from all Blue Shield member plans.

Blue Shield generally offers benefit payments based on the cost of covered services rendered to the patient, rather than on flat indemnity (fixed amount) allowances. Payments are made directly to participating physicians. For families whose income is less than a level stipulated in the particular contract, physician members agree to accept Blue Shield established fees as payment in full. For those above the stated income level, the doctor may opt to make an additional charge, which might constitute the difference between his usual fee and the Blue Shield fee. Blue Shield also offers programs that pay the physician his usual and customary fee. Thus service-type or indemnity programs or combinations of the two are available from Blue Shield to suit the needs or wishes of the group and the individual.

Eligibility requirements under Blue Shield are generally similar to those of Blue Cross. Practically all plans permit nongroup enrollment, although group coverage is emphasized. The minimum size of a group is generally four or five, with participation requirements varying from 100% for the smaller groups down to 60% for the larger.

As in Blue Cross, the enrolled Blue Shield member can usually keep his coverage regardless of age or type of policy. All plans now permit group retirees to convert to individual policies, usually without substantial change of benefits and only a small increase in premiums. Most plans permitting nongroup enrollment require health statements and/or physical examinations as evidence of insurability.

The typical Blue Shield contract provides rate schedules for surgical care (in the physician's office as well as in the hospital), obstetrical care, and in-hospital care by the physician. These schedules specify allowances—generally maximum allowances—for customary procedures.

A recent survey of Blue Shield plans indicated that sixty-two of the seventy-one member plans now provide catastrophic–major medical coverage up to $250,000 to groups of five or more. The remaining nine plans are in the process of making the benefit available. The marketing of a $250,000 catastrophic–major medical program without coinsurance and deductibles is the first phase of a far reaching catastrophic benefit program being implemented by Blue Shield.

Under Blue Shield's reciprocity plan, physicians treating out-of-area patients can bill their own Blue Shield plan directly for covered services. For noncovered services, or for subscribers not covered by a reciprocity contract, the physician must bill patients directly, often having to wait for payment until the patient is reimbursed by his own home-state plan. Negotiations between Blue Shield and the United Auto Workers and several other labor unions will soon result in 2.5 million subscribers being covered by reciprocity. Blue Shield will soon have approximately 10 million of its 80 million subscribers covered under its reciprocity program.

Physicians treating reciprocity patients should submit claims directly to their own plans with their other regular claims. The number contained in the reciprocity symbol on the patient's Blue Shield card should be included on the claim form.

In most cases, Blue Cross coverage and Blue Shield coverage complement each other, with Blue Cross coverage addressing itself primarily to hospital inpatient costs and Blue Shield concentrating on physicians' services, both in and out of the hospital. However, there are several states in which Blue Cross and Blue Shield plans are competitive—each sells the other's product and offers the same coverage.

It is interesting to note that, despite the Medicare program, over 10 million persons, or 53% of the total population age 65 and over, still hold private health insurance policies to supplement coverage under Medicare. Both Blue Cross and Blue Shield offer plans for those over age 65 that help pay the bills Medicare misses. For example, Blue Cross provides supplementary benefits to Medicare through its "Companion Care." Blue Shield's "Major Medicare" plan works to fill in the gaps of the Medicare program (both Parts A and B) as well as certain other items. One interesting feature of Major Medicare is that it covers subscribers anywhere in the world, whereas regular federal Medicare benefits are generally available only to program beneficiaries within the United States.

AVOIDING DIFFICULTIES WITH SERVICE PLANS

Coping with the complexities of the various prepaid plans has proved to be quite a headache to many offices. Different forms and billing procedures are characteristic of each plan. Insurance paper work can become almost a full-time duty for any medical assistant.

In offices experiencing insurance problems it was found that scarcely a day passes that some minor mistake does not evolve into a major one. Assistants find themselves constantly billing patients directly who are covered by insurance and failing to bill others who are not covered. Naturally, a great deal of time is wasted answering requests from insurance plans for further information. These assistants often neglect to report services for which the physician should have been paid, thereby snarling the bookkeeping and resulting in lost revenue for the physician.

Many of these difficulties can be avoided if the physician and the assistant work out an effective routine that minimizes friction and at the same time cuts down paper work. To begin with, the physician and the assistant should make an intensive study of their insurance problems in an attempt to review the main kinds of problems plaguing them. Reading the manuals and literature issued by the various plans helps to clarify many points. As a result, one soon becomes familiar with the types of care provided and not provided by each plan. The medical assistant is then able to distinguish between the different kinds of contracts and their fee schedules. In this way the meaning of each item that must be completed on the claim forms becomes much clearer.

With this background of knowledge an assistant is prepared to follow a sound routine in dealing with member patients. On the patient's first visit to the office he is asked whether he is enrolled in a plan. It should be as automatic to obtain this information as it is to secure the patient's name and address. If the patient is covered, the contract number printed on his plan's identification card is recorded. If he is not sure whether he is covered (and some patients are not), he should find out and bring his card on his next visit. In this way the awkwardness that can result from leaving it up to the patient to reveal at some later date whether he is insured is avoided.

A situation that helps to illustrate this predicament occurred several years ago. A physician performed an appendectomy on a man who agreed to the fee without question but then ignored the physician's bills. Some months later when the secretary phoned him he announced blithely, "Oh, I belong to Blue Shield." At that late date the office had to initiate the process of filing the physician's claim. Aside from the fruitless billing and the delay in this case, the physician had set the fee without knowing the real circumstances involved. As a result, he had asked one fee of the patient, but received a different one from the plan.

During the first visit it is customary for the medical assistant to obtain an idea of the subscriber patient's income. In this way the physician knows in advance and without undue embarrassment whether or not he must accept the plan's scheduled fee as payment in full for his services when this is applicable. Since some patients are likely to take offense at being asked directly how much they earn, the assistant uses a more tactful approach. To find out whether a person is entitled to full-service benefits, she inquires, "You plan classifies its subscribers into groups: those with incomes under a certain amount and those with incomes over a certain amount each year. I must record this information so that you'll get all the benefits to which you are entitled. Would you mind telling me whether your annual income is under or over this amount?" Before treatment is begun, the medical assistant should attempt to brief the patient on just what kind of coverage he actually has. This prevents misunderstanding and possible resentment later.

Suppose that the physican plans to remove a patient's gallbladder. Suppose also that the patient has a Blue Shield contract covering only physician's services in the hospital. The medical assistant explains to the patient that Blue Shield will take care of the surgical fee and that he will be billed only for such preoperative and postoperative care as he may need at home. If he is a member of Blue Cross, the extent of his coverage is pointed out. Occasionally, of course, the medical assistant may be puzzled about a patient's coverage. Some people, for instance, have overlapping Blue Shield and idemnity insurance. Others may need operations that their contracts apparently do not specify. In such an event, the assistant takes no chances but phones or writes a note to the plan for guidance. If the case is complicated, it could even be requested that a plan's representative call.

In processing claims to the plans, the medical assistant sees to it that every item on the various forms is answered. Aware that payment to the office will be held up unless the plan receives everything it wants to know, particular care is used to complete all of the following items.

ATTENDING PHYSICIAN'S STATEMENT – HEALTH INSURANCE CLAIM – GROUP OR INDIVIDUAL COMB-1 (1964)

Spaced for Typewriter -- Marks for Tabulator Appear on this Line

PATIENT'S NAME AND ADDRESS | AGE

INSURED'S NAME IF PATIENT IS A DEPENDENT

IF GROUP INSURANCE GIVE NAME OF POLICYHOLDER *(i.e., Employer, Union or Association through whom insured)* | POLICY NUMBER

(1A) NATURE OF SICKNESS OR INJURY *(Describe Complications if any)*

(B) IS CONDITION DUE TO INJURY OR SICKNESS ARISING OUT OF PATIENT'S EMPLOYMENT? IF "YES" EXPLAIN — YES ☐ NO ☐

(C) IS CONDITION DUE TO PREGNANCY? IF "YES" WHAT WAS APPROXIMATE DATE OF COMMENCEMENT OF PREGNANCY? — YES ☐ NO ☐ DATE 19

(2A) WHEN DID SYMPTOMS FIRST APPEAR OR ACCIDENT HAPPEN? — DATE..............19....

(B) WHEN DID PATIENT FIRST CONSULT YOU FOR THIS CONDITION? — DATE..............19....

(C) HAS PATIENT EVER HAD SAME OR SIMILAR CONDITION? IF "YES" STATE WHEN AND DESCRIBE — YES ☐ NO ☐

(3) DESCRIBE ANY OTHER DISEASE OR INFIRMITY AFFECTING PRESENT CONDITION

(4A) NATURE OF SURGICAL OR OBSTETRICAL PROCEDURE, IF ANY *(Describe Fully)*

(B) CHARGE TO PATIENT FOR THIS PROCEDURE INCLUDING POST-OPERATIVE CARE — $............ DATE PERFORMED..............19....

(C) WHERE PERFORMED — IF IN HOSPITAL INPATIENT ☐ OUTPATIENT ☐

(5) GIVE DATES OF OTHER MEDICAL (NON-SURGICAL) TREATMENT, IF ANY — CHARGE PER CALL

OFFICE.............. $.........

HOME.............. $.........

HOSPITAL.............. $.........

NURSING HOME.............. $.........

TOTAL (NON-SURGICAL) CHARGES $

(6) WHAT OTHER SERVICES, IF ANY, DID YOU PROVIDE PATIENT? (ITEMIZE, GIVING DATES AND FEES)

(7) WERE REGISTERED PRIVATE DUTY NURSE (R.N.) SERVICES NECESSARY? — YES ☐ NO ☐

(8) IS PATIENT STILL UNDER YOUR CARE FOR THIS CONDITION? IF "NO" GIVE DATE YOUR SERVICES TERMINATED — YES ☐ NO ☐ DATE 19

(9A) HOW LONG WAS OR WILL PATIENT BE CONTINUOUSLY TOTALLY DISABLED *(Unable to work)*? — FROM..........19... THROUGH..........19...

(B) HOW LONG WAS OR WILL PATIENT BE PARTIALLY DISABLED? — FROM..........19... THROUGH..........19...

(C) DID TREATMENT REQUIRE HOUSE CONFINEMENT? IF "YES" GIVE DATES — YES ☐ NO ☐ FROM..........19... THROUGH..........19...

(10) TO YOUR KNOWLEDGE DOES PATIENT HAVE OTHER HEALTH INSURANCE OR HEALTH PLAN COVERAGE? IF "YES" IDENTIFY — YES ☐ NO ☐

REMARKS

HEALTH INSURANCE COUNCIL

DATE | SIGNATURE (ATTENDING PHYSICIAN) | DEGREE | TELEPHONE

STREET ADDRESS | CITY OR TOWN | STATE OR PROVINCE | ZIP CODE

AUTHORIZATION TO PAY: I,..............(NAME OF INSURED)..............HEREBY AUTHORIZE..............(NAME OF COMPANY)..............TO PAY DIRECTLY

TO..............(NAME OF PHYSICIAN).............. THE SURGICAL AND/OR MEDICAL BENEFITS, IF ANY, OTHERWISE PAYABLE TO ME FOR HIS SERVICES AS DESCRIBED ABOVE, BUT NOT TO EXCEED THE CHARGES FOR THESE SERVICES. I UNDERSTAND THAT I AM FINANCIALLY RESPONSIBLE FOR THE CHARGES NOT PAID BY MY INSURANCE.

DATE..............19.... SIGNED (INSURED PERSON)..............

MEMORANDUM REGARDING DISPOSITION OF THIS FORM ON REVERSE SIDE — Approved by Council on Medical Service, AMA Feb. 1964

Fig. 14-1. Attending physician's statement–release form. (Courtesy Health Insurance Council.)

1. Diagnosis
2. Description of preexisting conditions
3. Admission and discharge dates
4. Dates of the physician's services
5. The physician's name, precisely as used on letterheads

The form should also be double checked to make sure that all the information is typed legibly, the patient's name is spelled correctly, the policy number is accurate, and the service provided is covered under the patient's contract.

Most important of all, of course, is the required explanation of services rendered. This information is obtained either directly from the physician or from the patient's record. The assistant realizes that a vague, nonspecific description of an operation may bring only the minimum fee, whereas an amount more than that may legitimately be due. If the surgical procedures necessitated by the case were numerous or complex, the report should so indicate.

In other words, in filling out claim forms, the assistant should not scribble "Hysterectomy" and let it go at that. "Total hysterectomy" or "Subtotal hysterectomy" should be written with a full account of just which organs were removed. In the same way, a benign and a malignant tumor is distinguished, and its size given, the extent of the incision, and so on. All reports are submitted as soon as services have been rendered, and it is noted on the records that this has been done. Then no risk is run of turning in a duplicate report by mistake.

Standard billing forms, sometimes called Attending Physician's Statements (Fig. 14-1), are accepted by all insurance companies. Their use simplifies the work of the medical assistant. It does not, however, completely eliminate the use of insurance company forms. If you use the standard form for group insurance, it is still necessary in most instances to have the patient sign the specific company form to which the medical assistant would attach the standard statement when completed. Both forms would then be mailed to the employer or the insurance carrier.

The impact of Medicare and Medicaid has contributed significantly to the growth of mechanization in the health care field. The government recognized at the outset that it did not possess the necessary expertise, experience, and medical claims processing equipment to mount such a program and therefore requested Blue Shield to assist in Part B claims processing for Medicare.

Blue Shield plans are continuing to explore both subscriber and physician needs and are increasing computer capabilities for faster claims processing, improved information, greater accuracy, and more simplified reporting. Reductions in the processing time of claims have been accomplished not only through data processing but also through staff increases, improved training of staff, and simplifications in procedures.

The role of the medical assistant has not been overlooked in Blue Shield's efforts to minimize claims processing problems. Most Blue Shield plans throughout the country assign specific representatives from their professional relations departments to serve as the official liaison between the physician's office and the plan. In addition to providing assistance to the individual medical assistant through office visits, educational meetings, printed materials, and newsletters, Blue Shield professional relations departments also work closely with local chapters of the American Association of Medical Assistants.

COMMERCIAL OR INDEMNITY PLANS

The second major category or source of medical insurance is the health and accident policies written by the numerous commercial insurance companies that incorporate the traditional insurance approach. The most important distinguishing characteristic of an indemnity company is that its contracts represent an agreement between the company and the insured. This type of insurance provides for the payment of a fixed indemnity for various injuries and treatments with the intention of placing the insured in a position similar to that as if the loss had never occurred. Obviously, the greater the amount of indemnity or benefits, the higher the premium. Unlike service plans, payments are generally made directly to the insured person and not to the provider of care unless the patient authorized an assignment.

The medical assistant bills the patient for the entire amount of the physician's fee. The patient is obliged to pay the physician's bill and file a claim for compensation from his insurance company according to the provisions of his policy. The attending physician is normally requested to later complete a report for the insurance company stating the amount of the fee and nature of the services rendered the patient.

Some patients tend to put off paying the physician's bill until they receive reimbursement from their insurance companies. This can often mean a matter of months before the claim is finally processed; meanwhile the physician has to wait for his money. The best way of preventing this situation from arising and to protect the physician's interests is to obtain an assignment of rights from the patient. Preferably this should be done prior to administering treatment. To accomplish this objective the patient merely signs a release form or notice of assignment form authorizing and directing his insurance company to render direct payment to the attending physician. The Health Insurance Council developed and standardized an all-purpose form that serves as a combination attending physician's statement and a release form or assignment of rights form (Fig. 14-1). This form has received the approval of the Council on Medical Service of the American Medical Association and is uniform throughout most of the United States. Almost every major insurance company accepts this form for all types of health insurance claims filed on behalf of their policyholders; the form is adaptable to electronic data processing. The form may be used for almost all insurance claims except possibly for Blue Shield and Workmen's Compensation. Samples may be obtained from the Health Insurance Council, 750 Third Avenue, New York, N. Y. 10017.

More recently, to ease medical office paperwork, an American Medical Association–sponsored study group has developed a computer-adaptable uniform health insurance claims form (Fig. 14-2), which it hopes all physicians, insurance companies, and fiscal intermediaries will adopt. Claims forms (in single, multi-pact, or continuous form for computer use) and a brochure describing their use can be obtained directly from the AMA.

Among other things, the new form is expected to expedite the work of physicians participating in Professional Standard Review Organizations. The task force on data collection, processing, and storage of the AMA's Advisory Committee on PSRO has endorsed it as an initial screening form for PSRO review. Development of this form represents an expansion of activities that have been carried on for many years by the AMA and the Health Insurance Council, whose 320 member companies write 90% of the commercial health insurance business.

It is estimated that the medical assistant will spend 10% to 15% less time in completing the newly structured forms than with previous ones. Blue Shield and the government-sponsored programs (Medicare, Medicaid, Champus) are withholding final approval pending completion of a series of feasibility tests.

Disability income insurance is another form of indemnity insurance. Loss of income protection is designed to provide wage earners with regular weekly or monthly cash payments in the event that wages are cut off as a result of accident or illness. This coverage may be in the form of short-term or long-term protection. Short-term policies are those with maximum benefit periods up to two years; long-term plans have benefit periods greater than two years.

In addition to serving subscriber members, both Blue Cross and Blue Shield administer several government sponsored medical service programs including Medicare, Medicaid, and the Federal Military Dependents Medical Program by functioning as

HEALTH INSURANCE
CLAIM FORM

Read instructions on back before completing form

TYPE OR PRINT ☐ MEDICARE ☐ MEDICAID ☐ CHAMPUS ☐ OTHER

PATIENT & INSURED (SUBSCRIBER) INFORMATION

1. Patient's name *(First name, middle initial, last name)*	2. Patient's sex ☐ Male ☐ Female	3. Insured's Identifying No. *(Include any letters)*
4. Patient's address *(Street, city, state, ZIP code)*		5. Insured's Group No. *(or Group Name)*
6. If patient has other health insurance, health plan or state assistance, enter its Name, Address and Policy or Medical Assistance Number		
7. Was illness or injury connected with patient's employment? ☐ No	☐ Yes	☐ Unknown
8. Patient's or authorized person's signature *(Read back before signing)* I authorize the release of any medical information necessary to process this claim. SIGNED	9. Date signed	10. Patient's date of birth
11. Patient's relationship to insured: ☐ Self ☐ Spouse	☐ Child	☐ Other
12. Insured's **name** *(First name, middle initial, last name)* **Address** *(Street, city, state, ZIP code)*	13. I authorize payment of medical benefits to undersigned physician or supplier for service described below. **SIGNED** *(Insured or Authorized Person)*	

PHYSICIAN OR SUPPLIER INFORMATION

14. DATE — ILLNESS (DATE OF FIRST SYMPTOMS), INJURY (DATE OF ACCIDENT), PREGNANCY (DATE OF LMP)	15. DATE FIRST CONSULTED YOU FOR THIS CONDITION	16. HAS PATIENT EVER HAD SAME OR SIMILAR SYMPTOMS? ☐ NO ☐ YES
17. DATE PATIENT SHOULD BE ABLE TO RETURN TO WORK — 18. DATES OF PATIENT'S DISABILITY	TOTAL DISABILITY: FROM DATE, THROUGH DATE	PARTIAL DISABILITY: FROM DATE, THROUGH DATE
19. NAME OF REFERRING PHYSICIAN	20. FOR SERVICES RELATED TO HOSPITALIZATION GIVE HOSPITALIZATION DATES	DATE ADMITTED — DATE DISCHARGED
21. NAME & ADDRESS OF FACILITY WHERE SERVICES RENDERED *(If other than home or office)*		
22. DIAGNOSIS OR NATURE OF ILLNESS OR INJURY REQUIRING SERVICES OR SUPPLIES (RELATE DIAGNOSIS TO PROCEDURE BY REFERENCE TO NUMBERS 1, 2, 3, ETC. IN COLUMN D) 1. 2. 3.		

23. A DATE OF EACH SERVICE	B PLACE OF SERVICE *See codes below	C PROCEDURE CODE	C DESCRIBE SURGICAL OR MEDICAL PROCEDURES AND OTHER SERVICES OR SUPPLIES FURNISHED FOR EACH DATE GIVEN (EXPLAIN UNUSUAL SERVICES)	D DX NO	E CHARGES *(Explain unusual circumstances in Column C)*	F LEAVE BLANK

24. PHYSICIAN'S OR SUPPLIER'S NAME, ADDRESS, ZIP CODE & TELEPHONE NO.	25. SOCIAL SECURITY NO.	28. TOTAL CHARGES
	26. EMPLOYER I.D. NO.	29. AMOUNT PAID
	27. OTHER IDENTIFYING NO.	30. BALANCE DUE

31. ACCEPT ASSIGNMENT *(See back)* ☐ YES ☐ NO	32. SIGNATURE OF PHYSICIAN OR SUPPLIER *(Read back before signing)* SIGN HERE	33. DATE SIGNED	34. YOUR PATIENT'S ACCOUNT NO.

*PLACE OF SERVICE CODES

1–(IH) –INPATIENT HOSPITAL
2–(OH)–OUTPATIENT HOSPITAL
3–(O) –DOCTOR'S OFFICE
4–(H)–PATIENT'S HOME
5– DAY CARE FACILITY (PSY)
6– NIGHT CARE FACILITY (PSY)
7–(NH) –NURSING HOME
8–(SNF)–SKILLED NURSING FACILITY
9– AMBULANCE
O–(OL)–OTHER LOCATIONS
A–(IL) –INDEPENDENT LABORATORY
B– OTHER MEDICAL/SURGICAL FACILITY

APPROVED BY AMA COUNCIL ON MEDICAL SERVICE 10-73

Fig. 14-2. Health insurance claim form. (Courtesy the American Medical Association.)

fiscal agents. Each of these programs is discussed in Chapter 15.

Review questions

1. Why should the medical secretary be well acquainted with the various health insurance plans and the benefits they provide?
2. What is meant by prepaid medical care?
3. Compare the basic differences between service plans and indemnity plans.
4. Name and describe the principal methods of reimbursing providers (physicians) of medical care.
5. What is meant by the salary method plan and how does it differ from other service plans?
6. What precipitated the growth of Blue Cross?
7. How are Blue Cross and Blue Shield similar? How do they differ?
8. Describe the relationship between Blue Cross–Blue Shield and the federal government.
9. What is the "assignment" method?
10. Why is it important to be meticulous in completing insurance claim forms? What is a good source of help for the medical assistant in processing insurance claims?

Suggested readings

Harris, S. E.: The economics of American medicine, New York, 1964, The Macmillan Co.

Somers, H. M., and Somers, A. R.: Doctors, patients and health insurance, Washington, D. C., 1961, The George Banta Company, Inc.

1969 Source Book of Health Insurance Data: Health Insurance Institute, New York.

chapter 15
The role of government in health

The idea that the government should share some of the responsibility for health care has a long history, going back at least to the Greek city-states, where citizens enjoyed the ministrations of tax-supported public physicians. Even the principle of compulsory participation is not new. In 1798 the United States government set up a Marine Hospital Service (forerunner of the Public Health Service) and required the owners of merchant ships to contribute to a sickness fund the amount of 20 cents a month for each seaman under their employ. During the nineteenth century, as the industrial revolution gathered momentum, a number of labor unions and individual employers required that their workers join relief funds, many of which eventually came under government regulations.

Ironically, the first broad-gauged compulsory health insurance law was enacted in the state of Prussia in 1854, 29 years before Germany was united under Bismarck. The chancellor was thus able to draw upon this precedent in 1883, when he persuaded the German government to extend compulsory health insurance to workers throughout the German nation.

Medical and scientific progress has created some rather complex problems. Important among them is the fact that the public's expectation for health has been raised to a high degree. Moreover, the services offered and available and those that are expected are far more complicated to deliver than those of a generation ago, for our resources are spread very thin. Virtually every thoughtful analyst of today's medical world must acknowledge that there exists a serious gap between scientific capability and medical performance. How can our medical care system meet a rising demand for more

---

Glossary

antedate to precede in time; come before in date

beneficiary a person or persons designated to receive a specified cash payment or receive a group of services upon illness or injury

benefit period a period of time for measuring use of Medicare hospital insurance benefits: A benefit-period begins when a program beneficiary first enters a hospital and ends as soon as he has not been a bed patient in any hospital (or facility that mainly provides skilled nursing care) for 60 consecutive days. After that, a new benefit period begins the next time he enters a hospital.

claim a demand to the insurer by the insured person for the payment of benefits under a policy

disability a condition which renders an insured person incapable of performing one or more duties of his regular occupation

indigent a poor or needy person

liability a debt; an amount which is owed, whether payable in money, other property, or services

Medicare a system of hospital insurance and supplementary medical insurance for the aged created by the 1965 Amendments to the Social Security Act and operated under provisions of the Act

remunerative paying an equivalent for any service or loss

time limit the period of time in which a notice of claim or proof of a loss must be filed

traumatic pertaining to a condition caused by a wound, injury, or shock complex services with limited resources at its disposal? In response to this question, government, especially the federal government, continues to assume a wider role in health.

According to a Social Security Administration report, the nation's health care bill was $94.1 billion in fiscal 1973, up 11% from a year earlier but this constituted the lowest advance in several years. On a per-person basis, health spending averaged $441. Direct out-of-pocket payments averaged $132, or $9 more than a year earlier. Third parties paid an estimated 65% of personal health bills, with the government share 38% and that of private health insurance 27%. Public funds now pay nearly half of the hospital care bill, while private funds still pay the bulk of the bill for physicians' services.

A physician swamped with insurance forms may find it hard to believe, but a great number of patients still pay their doctor bills directly. Cash and personal checks represent the largest single block of income for physicians despite the growing involvement of third party payers in recent years.

The role of government in health is broader and deeper than the mere contribution of dollars. The limitations of space will not allow a detailed discussion of the various activities of government in health. However, it is an acknowledged fact that the government exercises a positive and formidable influence on the health care system through its involvement in the following broad areas.

1. Direct provision of medical care for federal beneficiaries
2. Purchase of private medical care for certain categories of beneficiaries (Medicare, Medicaid, etc.)
3. Development of resources—manpower (physicians), etc.
4. Regulation and supervision—setting and enforcing standards for compliance
5. Consultation and coordination
6. Planning and research

The Public Health Service, a component of the Department of Health, Education, and Welfare, is the principal and largest agency of the federal government specifically responsible for protecting and improving the health of the American people. In accomplishing this mission the Service works closely with state and local agencies, with other agencies of the Department of HEW, and with the federal government. It also works with many professional, voluntary, civic, and special interest groups. Some of the functions assigned to the Public Health Service include the following.

1. To provide leadership and direction in health at the national level
2. To provide contributions to the advancement of health knowledge through research
3. To contribute to the improvement and extension of community and personal health services
4. To help promote and maintain a healthier environment for everyone
5. To enlarge and improve manpower resources for health purposes
6. To increase the number and improve the conditions of health facilities
7. To furnish direct health and medical services for its legal beneficiaries and for special groups in the population
8. To work with other national and international agencies in the solution of international health problems
9. To participate with other agencies of the federal government in discharging their various health functions
10. To collect, evaluate, and present statistical data and other intelligence information concerning the health status of the nation
11. To provide library services in order to advance communication in medicine and the health-related sciences
12. To provide information on health and well-being to the health professions, health agencies, and the general public

In the course of discharging these responsibilities, the Public Health Service plays a leading role in America's quest for better health. It provides the citizenry with a comprehensive view of national health problems as a basis for decision and also helps formulate policies by which appropriate action can be taken. Since the Service has a limited supply of manpower, many of the functions described in the preceding list must be accomplished under contracts with private agencies and individuals throughout the country. However, the sharing of responsibility for health is the very thing that is encouraged by the Public Health Service.

WORKMEN'S COMPENSATION

Every state possesses its own individual Workmen's Compensation Law, and the basic purpose of each law is the same: to guarantee that an employee who is injured in the course of his employment will have an adequate means of support during the period he is unable to work. According to the law, employees injured on the job are indemnified, and their medical bills are paid for regardless of whether the injury sustained resulted from carelessness or was purely accidental. Furthermore, the Workmen's Compensation Law generally provides medical care and sickness benefits for those workers who incur an illness in connection with their occupation. For example, coal miners are prone to contract respiratory ailments after many years of working in mine shafts.

An industrial injury refers to any injury or disease, including damage to artificial limbs, dentures, and medical braces, that occurs while the employee is performing a service for his employer and that is the result of his working conditions. The law further provides that the employer be notified immediately when an employee is injured. It then becomes the employer's responsibility to provide temporary medical treatment and report the injury to the appropriate insurance company and proper governmental agency. Most large firms employ their own medical personnel who are authorized to administer first aid but who are not permitted to render further treatment. In order to protect themselves against losses for medical expenditures, employers contract with insurance carriers who agree to assume the risk and pay for the medical care of an injured employee. Each state varies somewhat but the administration of the Workmen's Compensation Law in the respective states usually comes under the jurisdiction of a department of Industrial Relations or a Workmen's Compensation Appeals Board, as is the case in California. A physician who elects to treat workmen's compensation cases is required to register with the appropriate state body and is usually limited to the practice of a particular speciality. Each state has its own fee schedule of allowances that determines the amount the physician may charge. The fee schedule is prepared by the regulatory authority in each state and registered physicians generally agree to accept the established fee as payment in full for their services. The employer's insurance carrier pays the physician directly, and the physician understands that he may not bill the patient for treatment authorized by the insurance carrier. However, if the insurance carrier does not accept the case and denies that it is liable for the costs of medical care, then the patient is billed directly by the physician. In this instance, the patient would be notified that his injury or occupational illness is not accepted as being related to his employment.

Some of the knottiest problems of workmen's compensation are related to the determination of liability—that is, determining if the injury or disease "arose out of, or in the course of, employment," and determining the extent of disability, the degree to which the injury or disease has affected the claimant's ability to engage in remunerative work or hampered his physical or mental functioning. These questions can be especially preplexing in those cases in which the impairment and consequent disability result not from traumatic injury, but from disease, since causality in both the medical and legal senses is far more complex in the case of disease than it is in the case of traumatic injury.

Some employers are large enough and have the financial backing to become self-insured. In other words, they agree to assume the risk and post a bond for a fixed amount set by the regulatory authority in their states. In cases where an employee experiences an injury or occupational disease, the company for which the employee

FILL OUT AND FORWARD 1 COPY IMMEDIATELY AFTER FIRST SEEING PATIENT

DOCTOR'S FIRST REPORT OF WORK INJURY

STATE OF CALIFORNIA

STATE COMPENSATION INSURANCE FUND

P. O. BOX 2134. LOS ANGELES 90054

ALSO, Immediately after first examination mail one copy directly to the Division of Labor Statistics and Research, P. O. Box 965, San Francisco 94101.

Failure to file a report with the Division is a misdemeanor. (Labor Code, Sections 6407-6413.)

Answer all questions fully.

Do not write in this space

1. EMPLOYER ______
2. Address (No., St. & City) ______
3. Business (Manufacturing shoes, building construction, retailing men's clothes, etc.) ______

SOCIAL SECURITY NO. ______

4. EMPLOYEE (First name, middle initial, last name) ______
5. Address (No., St. & City) ______
6. Occupation ______ Age ______ Sex ______
7. Date injured ______ Hour ______ M Date last worked ______
8. Injured at (No., St. & City) ______ County ______
9. Date of your first examination ______ Hour ______ M Who engaged your services? ______
10. Name other doctors who treated employee for this injury ______

11. ACCIDENT OR EXPOSURE: Did employee notify employer of this injury? ______ Employee's statement of cause of injury or illness:

12. NATURE AND EXTENT OF INJURY OR DISEASE (Include all objective findings, subjective complaints, and diagnoses. If occupational disease state date of onset, occupational history, and exposures.)

13. X-rays: By whom taken? (State if none) ______
Findings:

14. Treatment:

15. Kind of case (Office, home, or hospital) ______ If hospitalized, date ______ Estimated stay ______
Name and address of hospital ______
16. Further treatment (Estimated frequency and duration) ______
17. Estimated period of disability for: Regular work ______ Modified work ______
18. Describe any permanent disability or disfigurement expected (State if none) ______

19. If death ensued, give date

20. REMARKS (Note any pre-existing injuries or diseases, need for special examination or laboratory tests, other pertinent information.)

N. B.—ONLY UNDER EXCEPTIONAL CIRCUMSTANCES WILL A HERNIA BE CONSIDERED DISABLING PRIOR TO OPERATION. THE INJURED SHOULD BE ADVISED TO CONTINUE WORK, IF POSSIBLE, UNTIL NOTIFIED THAT HIS CLAIM IS ACCEPTED.

Name ______ (Type or print) Degree ______ [PERSONAL SIGNATURE OF DOCTOR] ______

Date of report ______ Address (No., St. & City) ______ Tel. No. ______

FORM 10-LA *Use reverse side if more space required* 21762-218 5-64 500M

Fig. 15-1. Doctor's first report (Workmen's Compensation).

works is then obligated to pay the costs of the employee's medical treatment and disability payment. However, if the injured employee fails to report an injury within a specified period of time or does not accept medical attention offered, he may forfeit his right to benefits.

When treating a workmen's compensation patient for the first time, the physician must submit a report describing the nature of the treatment rendered together with an itemized bill. This form (Fig. 15-1) is made out in quadruplicate and copies are submitted to: (1) the employer of the injured, (2) the insurance carrier, and (3) the Workmen's Compensation Board or appropriate regulatory body. The fourth copy should be retained by the physician for office files. Special forms are generally available through the appropriate government office or the local county medical society. Time is of the essence in submitting accident reports. Some states even maintain an established time limit (often 48 hours).

The assistant whose physician-employer accepts and treats workmen's compensation patients should take the initiative to become acquainted with the requirements of the law in the state. Despite the fact that the physician maintains a regular practice in addition to workmen's compensation cases, the medical assistant spends a good portion of time typing the necessary reports for these patients. It is recommended in some offices that the records of workmen's compensation patients be filed separately from other patients. This, of course, will depend upon the type of filing system and other office procedures used in each individual medical office.

Most employers are required by state law to carry workmen's compensation insurance. Generally they pay an estimated premium in advance; then, at the end of the year, they pay an additional premium (or receive credit for overpayment) based on an audit of the payroll for the year. The rate of the insurance premium varies with the risk involved and the nature of the work performed. Therefore employees are classified according to the kind of work they do.

HEALTH INSURANCE FOR THE AGED (TITLE XVIII, MEDICARE)

Health insurance for the aged, popularly known as Medicare, has had a broad impact on the living patterns of Americans, young and old. The legislation, which provides low-cost hospitalization and medical insurance for the nation's elderly, directly aids nearly one tenth of the population. Millions of younger people also benefit indirectly by being relieved of heavy financial responsibility when an aged member of the family encounters major health expenses.

Though the program is relatively new, the idea of government health insurance antedated Medicare by many years. The gradual evolution of this concept throughout most of this century provides an excellent case history illustrating how major social policy decisions in the United States are refined and shaped through the legislative process. From 1935, when the first health insurance bill was introduced in Congress, to 1965, when Medicare was passed, an entire generation of Americans acted and reacted to the various proposals. Through this process a program eventually emerged that proved acceptable to a majority of the public and congressional lawmakers.

The problem of providing adequate coverage for the aged has attracted more public attention than any other current issue in health insurance. The medical needs of older persons and their utilization of health services are obviously far greater than the rest of the population, but their financial resources for meeting such needs are smaller, and they have far less access to the financial advantages of private group insurance coverage.

There are approximately 20 million persons aged 65 years and over. They have far higher rates of physical impairment, morbidity, and medical care utilization than younger persons. The aged experience nearly three times as many days of "restricted activity" per year, and spend nearly two and one-half times as many days in short-term hospitals.

The Social Security Amendments adopted by Congress in 1965 provided for a program of medical care for the aged. Added to the original Social Security Act (1935) as Title XVIII, Medicare provides two separate but complementary health plans for meeting the national problem of adequate medical care for the aged. The basic hospital plan consists of contributory insurance protection for aged people against the costs of hospital and related care. The plan applies to all people aged 65 years and over who are eligible for monthly Social Security or railroad retirement benefits. The same protection extends also to other aged people who are not Social Security or railroad retirement beneficiaries, so that almost everyone can look forward to having protection under one or both parts of Medicare when he reaches 65.

Begun in July, 1966, as part of the Social Security system, the plan is financed through a special earnings tax paid by employers, employees, and the self-employed. The hospital insurance tax contributions go into a trust fund kept entirely separate from other funds of the system. The cost of benefits for aged people not insured under the railroad retirement system or Social Security system is paid out of general funds of the treasury. The Social Security tax rate for the hospital insurance program is presently 0.9%. It is scheduled to increase to 1.1% in 1978.

The basic plan of hospital insurance referred to as Part A covers the following broad categories of service. (1) Up to 90 days of hospital care for each benefit period, with the patient currently paying a deductible amount of $92.00 for the first 60 days plus a coinsurance charge of $23.00 a day for the sixty-first through the ninetieth days. Medicare pays all other charges. Inpatient psychiatric hospital services are covered, with a lifetime limit of 190 days. Inpatient tuberculosis hospital services are also included, and the cost of any blood after the first three pints furnished to a patient during a given illness. (2) Up to 100 days of extended care services in a certified skilled nursing facility after three or more days of hospitalization, with a coinsurance payment by the beneficiary of $11.50 per day for each day of extended care beyond the twentieth day. (3) Home health services (such as a visiting nurse) for up to 100 visits to a homebound patient following discharge from a hospital (after at least a three-day stay) or an extended care facility.

Major changes in program eligibility and coverage have come about as a result of the 1972 amendments to the Medicare law that were contained in legislation known as Public Law 92-603. For the first time, Medicare's hospital insurance (Part A) and medical insurance (Part B) are now available to certain categories of people under 65 who are disabled. The law also broadened coverage to include a wider range of health care services. There were other changes included in the 1972 amendments designed to improve the administration of Medicare—changes designed to find better ways of delivering medical care, to help control rising program costs, and to make overall operation of the program more efficient and equitable.

The 1972 amendments extended Medicare coverage to individuals under age 65 who require hemodialysis or renal transplantation for chronic renal disease and who are currently or fully insured, or entitled to monthly Social Security benefits, or are the spouses or dependent children of such insured or entitled individuals.

Another significant change brought about by the 1972 amendments relates to people who may not have worked long enough under Social Security to be eligible for hospital insurance under Medicare when they reach 65. They are now able to buy this protection on a voluntary basis. If they choose to enroll for hospital insurance they pay a monthly hospital insurance premium.

A problem that continues to plague the program and contributes to higher program costs is the fact that many beneficiaries assume that they are automatically entitled to the maximum number of benefit days and services. This assumption has led to a great deal of confusion and disappointment. Actually, entitlement to benefits is based solely upon medical necessity and certification by the attending physician.

Prior to adoption of the 1972 amendments, determinations as to whether a beneficiary required the level of skilled care necessary to qualify for posthospital extended care or home health care generally could not be made until sometime after the services were rendered. If the services were found not to be covered the beneficiary was faced with an unexpected large bill. Beginning in 1973 the program began authorizing "periods of presumed coverage"—limited lengths of stays in skilled nursing facilities or numbers of posthospital home health visits—for designated medical conditions during which a patient is presumed to be eligible for benefits.

Since 1973 the medical insurance part of Medicare (Part B) is no longer voluntary. Everyone who becomes eligible for hospital insurance is automatically covered by medical insurance unless they refuse the protection. The automatic enrollment also applies to those newly eligible for Medicare because they are disabled. Those enrolled in medical insurance pay a monthly premium to help defray part of the cost of the coverage. The current (1975) premium of $6.30 per month covers half the cost of medical insurance protection—the federal government contributes the other half. The monthly premium has increased steadily from the outset of the program and is subject to further increases with rises in the cost of medical care. Furthermore the law requires that the medical insurance premium rate be reviewed annually in order that the full costs of the program continue to be met.

Medical insurance premiums are automatically deducted from monthly checks for those who receive Social Security benefits, railroad retirement benefits, or a civil service annuity. Those who do not receive any of these monthly checks pay their premiums directly to the Social Security Administration.

Medical insurance pays 80% of the reasonable charges after a deductible of $60.00 (1975) during a calendar year for the following general services: (1) physicians' and surgeon's services, whether furnished in the hospital, clinic, office, home, or elsewhere; (2) home health services (with no requirement of prior hospitalization) for up to 100 visits during each calendar year (instead of paying only 80% of the reasonable cost for home health care covered under medical insurance, Medicare now pays 100% of the reasonable cost of such covered care after the annual $60.00 deductible is satisfied); (3) outpatient hospital services; (4) medical services and supplies; and (5) outpatient physical therapy and other health care services.

Overall responsibility for administration of the Medicare program rests with the Secretary of Health, Education, and Welfare. To the extent possible, the Secretary contracts with state agencies and fiscal intermediaries (insurance carriers) to carry out the major administrative functions such as determining rates of payments under the program, holding and disbursing funds for benefit payments, determining compliance, assisting in the application of safeguards against unnecessary use (utilization review), and assuring that payment for a service is made on a reasonable cost basis.

Within the Department of Health, Education, and Welfare, specific responsibility for the operational aspects of the program have been delegated to the Social Security Administration's Bureau of Health Insurance. In carrying out its various responsibilities the Bureau of Health Insurance works very closely with the Public Health Service, which has the principal responsibility for providing consultation on the professional aspects of the program. A Health Insurance Benefits Advisory Council advises the Secretary on general policy matters in the administration of the program.

REQUEST FOR MEDICARE PAYMENT

Form Approved OMB No. 72-R0730

MEDICAL INSURANCE BENEFITS—SOCIAL SECURITY ACT (See Instructions on Back—**Type or Print Information**)

NOTICE—Anyone who misrepresents or falsifies essential information requested by this form may upon conviction be subject to fine and imprisonment under Federal Law.

PART I—PATIENT TO FILL IN ITEMS 1 THROUGH 6 ONLY

When completed, send this form to:

Copy from YOUR OWN HEALTH INSURANCE CARD *(See example on back)*

1 Name of patient (First name, Middle initial, Last name)

2 Health insurance claim number *(Include all letters)* ☐ Male ☐ Female

3 Patient's mailing address | City, State, ZIP code | Telephone Number

4 Describe the illness or injury for which you received treatment *(Always fill in this item if your doctor does not complete Part II below)*

Was your illness or injury connected with your employment? ☐ Yes ☐ No

5 If you have other health insurance or if your State medical assistance agency will pay part of your medical expenses and you want information about this claim released to the insurance company or State agency upon its request, give the following information.

Insuring organization or State agency name and address | Policy or Medical Assistance Number

6 I authorize any holder of medical or other information about me to release to the Social Security Administration or its intermediaries or carriers any information needed for this or a related Medicare claim. I permit a copy of this authorization to be used in place of the original, and request payment of medical insurance benefits either to myself or to the party who accepts assignment below.

Signature of patient *(See instructions on reverse where patient is unable to sign)* | Date signed

SIGN HERE ➧

PART II—PHYSICIAN OR SUPPLIER TO FILL IN 7 THROUGH 14

A

7 A. Date of each service	B. Place of service (*See Codes below)	C. Fully describe surgical or medical procedures and other services or supplies furnished for each date given	D. Nature of illness or injury requiring services or supplies	E. Charges (If related to unusual circumstances explain in 7C)	Leave Blank
				$	

8 Name and address of physician or supplier *(Number and street, city, State, ZIP code)*

Telephone No.

Physician or supplier code

9 Total charges $

10 Amount paid $

11 Any unpaid balance due $

12 Assignment of patient's bill ➧ ☐ I accept assignment *(See reverse)* ☐ I do not accept assignment.

13 Show name and address of facility where services were performed *(If other than home or office visits)*

14 Signature of physician or supplier *(A physician's signature certifies that physician's services were personally rendered by him or under his personal direction)* ➧ | Date signed

*O—Doctor's Office; IL—Independent Laboratory; H—Patient's Home *(If portable X-ray services, identify the supplier)*; IH—Inpatient Hospital; ECF—Extended Care Facility; OH—Outpatient Hospital; OL—Other Locations; NH—Nursing Home

FORM **SSA-1490** (8-72)

Department of Health, Education, and Welfare
Social Security Administration

Fig. 15-2. Medicare Claim Form SSA-1490.

HOW TO FILL OUT YOUR MEDICARE FORM

There are two ways that Medicare can help pay your doctor bills

One way is for Medicare to pay your doctor.—If you and your doctor agree, Medicare will pay him directly. This is the assignment method. You do not submit any claim; the doctor does. All you do is fill out Part I of this form and leave it with your doctor. Under this method the doctor agrees to accept the charge determination of the Medicare carrier as the full charge; you are responsible for the deductible and coinsurance. Please read Your Medicare Handbook to help you understand about the deductible and coinsurance. (Because Medicare has special payment arrangements with group practice prepayment plans these plans handle all claims for covered services they furnish to their members.)

The other way is for Medicare to pay you.—Medicare can also pay you directly—before or after you have paid your doctor. If you submit the claim yourself, fill out Part I and ask your doctor to fill out Part II. If you have an itemized bill from him, you may submit it rather than have him complete Part II. (This form, with Part I completed by you, may be used to send in several itemized bills from different doctors and suppliers.) Bills should show who furnished the services, **the patient's name and number,** dates of services, where the services were furnished, a description of the services, and charges for each separate service. It is helpful if the diagnosis is also shown. Then mail itemized bills and this form to the address shown in the upper left-hand corner. If no address is shown there, use the address listed in Your Medicare Handbook—or get advice from any social security office.

SOME THINGS TO NOTE IN FILLING OUT PART I
(Your doctor will fill out Part II.)

1 & **2** Copy the name and number and indicate your sex exactly as shown on your health insurance card. Include the letters at the end of the number.

3 Enter your mailing address and telephone number, if any.

4 Describe your illness or injury. Be sure to check one of the two boxes.

5 If you have other health insurance or expect a welfare agency to pay part of the expenses, complete item 5.

6 Be sure to sign your name. If you cannot write your name, sign by mark (X), and have a witness sign his name and enter his address on this line.

If the claim is filed for the patient by another person he should enter the patient's name and write "By," sign his own name and address in this space, show his relationship to the patient, and why the patient cannot sign. (If the patient has died, the survivor should contact any social security office for information on what to do.)

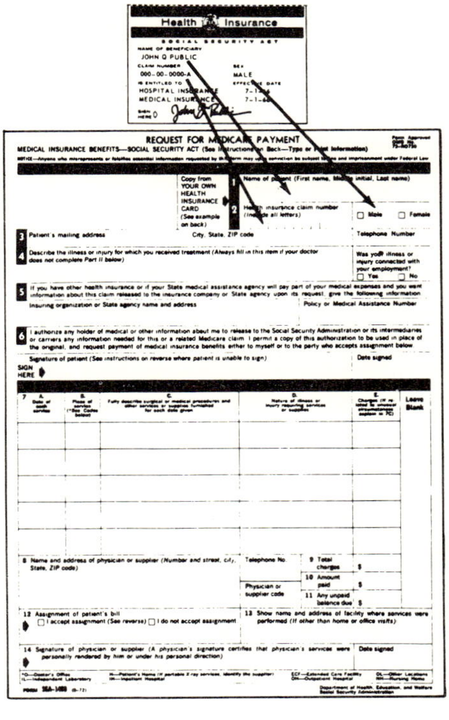

B

IMPORTANT NOTES FOR PHYSICIANS AND SUPPLIERS

Item 12: In assigned cases the patient is responsible only for the deductible, coinsurance, and non-covered services. Coinsurance and the deductible are based upon the charge determination of the carrier if this is less than the charge submitted.
This form may also be used by a supplier, or by the patient to claim reimbursement for charges by a supplier for services such as the use of an ambulance or medical appliances.

If the physician or supplier does not want Part II information released to the organization named in item 5, he should write "No further release" in item 7C following the description of services.

Each Medicare beneficiary receives a red, white, and blue identification card once his eligibility has been established. A covered patient should be prepared to show his card to the medical assistant when he visits the physician's office.

There are two ways that Medicare can help pay doctor bills. One way is for Medicare to pay the physician directly. This is known as the assignment method. The patient completes Part I of Form SSA-1490, shown in Fig. 15-2, *A*, and leaves it with his physician. Under this method the physician agrees to accept the charge determined by Medicare as the full charge; the patient remains responsible for the deductible and the coinsurance. The other way is for Medicare to pay the patient directly, before or after he has paid the physician. The patient may submit the claim himself by filling out Part I and asking his physician to complete Part II (Fig. 15-2, *B*). If the patient has an itemized bill from the physician, he may submit it rather than have the physician complete Part II. This form, with Part I completed by the patient, may be used to send in several itemized bills from different physicians and suppliers. Bills should show who furnished the services, the patient's name and claim number, dates of services, where the services were furnished, a description of the services, and charges for each separate service. It is helpful if the diagnosis is also shown. The itemized bills along with completed form SSA-1490 can then be mailed to the address shown in the upper left-hand corner of Block A. If no address is stamped there, one can consult his Medicare Handbook or obtain advice from the nearest Social Security district office.

A recent Michigan Blue Shield study of Medicare claims found that 80% of the forms that caused delay in payment involved missing or incomplete information. More than half the errors on claims from physicians were ascribed to missing or invalid Medicare Health Insurance claim numbers, more than 12% involved a failure to include an adequate beneficiary's address, and 10% evidenced a failure to describe sufficiently the treatment rendered. The medical assistant must be careful to avoid these errors and must also be conscious of the fact that, under the law, there are certain time limits for submitting claims.

MEDICAL ASSISTANCE PROGRAM (TITLE XIX, MEDICAID)

In order to provide a more effective program of medical care for needy persons, Title XIX (often referred to as Medicaid) was added to the Social Security Amendments of 1965, establishing a single and separate medical care program, which improves and expands various provisions for the needy previously covered under five different titles of the original Social Security Act. Title XIX extends the advantages of an expanded medical assistance program not only to the needy aged (those over 65) but also to people receiving cash assistance under the programs of aid to families with dependent children, to the blind, to the permanently and totally disabled, and to people who would qualify under these programs if their needs were sufficiently great. Title XIX seeks to do for children and adults in low-income families what Medicare does for all people over 65. Under Title XIX states receive substantially more federal funds than they received under programs that paid for the medical care of public assistance recipients.

A significant feature of the Medicaid program is that all public assistance groups are entitled to care that is equal in amount, duration, and scope. Whatever is provided for one public assistance group—for example, the aged—must also be provided for others: the blind, the disabled, and families with dependent children. Medical assistance in the form of direct payments to suppliers of medical care and services is provided by the states, with federal financial participation.

To obtain federal funds a state's program must be approved by the Secretary of HEW as meeting the requirements of the Social Security Act. The federal share of state assistance costs is based on a formula, which includes each state's average monthly payment (including medical costs) multiplied by the number of recipients in each program. The Social Security Act fixes limitations on the amount of payments to be shared, and sets the ratio of federal contributions. The states may make higher payments to its beneficiaries by using state or local monies or both.

The federal share of medical assistance expenditures under the program varies in relation to a state's per capita income with no maximum on the amount of such expenditures in which there would be sharing. The federal government contributes from 50% (to the wealthiest states) to approximately 81% (to the state with the lowest per capita income) of medical care costs for medically needy and low-income people who are aged, blind, disabled, or members of families with dependent children. In addition, some states with more ambitious plans pay medical bills for low-income persons not aged, blind, disabled, or members of families with dependent children.

A person usually applies for medical assistance at a local public welfare office. The Social Security Act requires the state to give an individual the opportunity to apply for assistance under any one of the programs and to provide assistance with reasonable promptness to all eligible persons. The state, through its local public welfare office, determines individual eligibility.

Since July 1, 1967, a state's Medicaid program, at a minimum, has been required to include at least five basic services—inpatient hospital care, outpatient hospital care, physicians' services, skilled nursing home care, and laboratory and x-ray services. The 1972 amendments to the Social Security Act added two significant requirements. Family planning services for at least the categorically needy are now mandatory under Medicaid. Another new section imposes a financial penalty upon states for failure to implement child health with periodic screening, diagnosis, and treatment services. Naturally there are individual state differences in providing these services, but all states must administer their programs within broad federal guidelines. States can at their option include a wide range of other medical services, such as dental services, prescribed drugs, eyeglasses (prescribed by a physician skilled in the diseases of the eye, or by an optometrist, whichever the patient may elect), dentures, and prosthetic devices.

A state must also establish and maintain standards for institutions providing medical care. The Secretary of the Department of Health, Education, and Welfare is authorized to establish standards relating to protection against fire and other hazards to health and safety.

The states are required to use professional medical personnel and supporting staff in the administration of the program, with 75% reimbursement of the cost for training as well as compensation of such personnel, by the federal government. The medical care unit (state health agency) operating the program in each state must also make cooperative arrangements with health and vocational rehabilitation agencies, and establish other standards and methods designed to assure quality.

The state, in determining eligibility and the medical assistance to be provided, must pay the deductibles and coinsurance imposed under the Medicare program for those who are aged 65 and poor. In other words, Medicaid can pay what Medicare does not pay for people who are eligible for both programs.

Comparatively speaking, Medicaid is not an insurance program like Medicare, but is rather an assistance program. Unlike Medicare, Medicaid is a state-administered program, which operates under federal guidelines. It is financed from federal, state, and local taxes rather than from employer-employee contributed funds. In other words, Medicaid is basically a federal-state partnership, with each state able to design its own plan or program consistent with established federal guidelines.

There are presently approximately thirty-one state and territorial Medicaid programs covering both people who are eligible for public assistance (cash payments) and certain other lower income categories. There are an additional twenty-two Medicaid programs in effect that cover *only* people who are eligible for public assistance.

The Social and Rehabilitation Service in the Department of Health, Education, and Welfare is responsible for the operational aspects of the Medicaid program at the federal level. Individuals who are not sure whether they are entitled to benefits under the program should be directed to contact their nearest local welfare office.

PROFESSIONAL STANDARD REVIEW ORGANIZATIONS (PSROs)

The 1972 amendments to the Social Security Act provide for a new system of peer review to be performed by organizations called Professional Standard Review Organizations (PSROs). All health services for which payment may be made under the Social Security Act, including services provided under Medicare and Medicaid, will be subject to PSRO review.

The Secretary of HEW was directed by law to divide the nation into appropriate PSRO areas by no later than January 1, 1974, which has been accomplished. The Secretary is now in the process of carrying out the intent of the legislation by entering into conditional agreements with organizations that qualify as PSROs. These conditional agreements cannot exceed two years, during which the PSROs will develop and begin their review activities.

A PSRO must be a nonprofit professional association composed of licensed doctors of medicine or osteopathy engaged in the practice of medicine or surgery in the area serviced by the organization. The membership must be open to all physicians on a voluntary basis. Each area generally will contain a minimum of 300 practicing physicians and in most situations, many more. In smaller or more sparsely populated areas an entire state may be designated a PSRO area.

To assure that applicant organizations are truly representative, the Secretary is required to poll the practicing physicians in an area, at the request of 10% or more of such physicians, as to whether or not an organization represents them. If more than 50% of physicians responding to the poll indicate the organization is not representative, the Secretary cannot enter into an agreement with that organization.

Physician organizations (usually medical societies) are free to undertake or decline the responsibilities of organizing a PSRO. Should they decline, the Secretary can, after January 1, 1976, seek alternative applicants from among other organizations, that is, state and local health departments, medical schools, insurance carriers, fiscal intermediaries, and other health insurers. In no case, however, can any organization be designated as a PSRO that does not have professional medical competence, since decisions with respect to the conduct or provision of care by a physician must be made by qualified physicians.

PSROs will be required to review, on a regular basis, the patterns of services delivered to beneficiaries of federally supported programs by health care institutions as well as to evaluate the necessity, quality, and appropriateness of services for which payment is made under such programs. Where effective utilization review committees already exist a PSRO may utilize their services.

The concept of peer review is not new. Physicians have been evaluating other practicing physicians for many years on a voluntary basis and most qualified physicians have been subjected to peer review in one form or another during their professional careers. It is therefore surprising that no other topic has prompted as much intense debate within the medical community as has PSRO.

Many physicians view PSROs as an attempt on the part of the federal government to control and destroy the private practice of medicine through regulation. They regard PSRO as a needless and unwarranted incursion by government into the practice of medicine that threatens the sanctity of the doctor-patient relationship and the confidentiality of medical records.

On the other hand, the nation's first PSRO contract was awarded in June, 1974 to a subsidiary of the Utah Professional Review Organization, one of the original medical society–sponsored PSRO prototypes. The Utah PSRO, the first of more than 100 awarded start-up funds during 1974, received $951,495 over an 18-month period. The Utah PSRO will monitor the quality and necessity of hospital care provided to beneficiaries of Medicare and Medicaid in Utah and is operated by practicing physicians. The Utah prototype had been in operation for almost three years under the auspices of the local medical society prior to qualifying as a PSRO.

The American Medical Association has cooperated with the government since enactment of the legislation in order to exert a positive influence on the structure and direction of PSROs. At its June, 1975 Annual Meeting, the Association's House of Delegates reexamined its present policy regarding PSROs and instructed the Board of Trustees to continue to direct its efforts to achieve constructive amendments to the PSRO law and to ensure appropriate regulations and directives. Particular effort is being directed at amending those sections of the law that present potential dangers in the areas of confidentiality, malpractice, development of norms, quality of care, and the authority of the Secretary of HEW.

The House further directed that the Association should continue its efforts to achieve legislation that allows the profession to perform peer review in accordance with the profession's philosophy and the best interests of the patient. At the same time those individual state associations that elect nonparticipation shall not be precluded from such a position by AMA's policy statement, but will be urged to develop effective non-PSRO peer review programs that embody the principles endorsed by the profession as constructive alternatives to PSRO. In the event that an evaluation of the PSRO program reveals that it does, in fact, adversely affect the quality of patient care, or conflict with Association policy, the Board of Trustees is instructed to use all legal and legislative means to rectify these shortcomings.

Guidelines and norms of care will be adapted and interpreted locally by the various PSROs. There will be no nationally prescribed set of standards that will be applied to all cases.

To provide the national sets of norms and criteria that are required by the law, HEW turned to the American Medical Association. The AMA has signed a contract with HEW to develop model sets of criteria for screening the appropriateness, necessity, and quality of medical services in hospitals. Under terms of the contract, the AMA will coordinate preparation of the sets of norms and criteria, which will be prepared by the national medical specialty societies.

It has been the AMA's consistent position that medical criteria development must be a function of the individual specialty societies and must be coordinated nationally, with the completed criteria made available to all physician groups for adaptation and use at the local level. Recognizing that the law required someone to develop such criteria, the AMA entered into negotiations for the contract.

CIVILIAN HEALTH AND MEDICAL PROGRAM OF THE UNIFORMED SERVICES (CHAMPUS)

The Dependents' Medical Care Act of 1956 opened the door to civilian inpatient and limited outpatient medical care for dependents of Armed Forces active duty personnel when such care was not available in service facilities. Legislation (Public Law 89-614) signed by the President on September 30, 1966, authorized an expanded program of civilian inpatient and outpatient care. The original Dependent's Medical Care Act applied only to dependents of active duty personnel and was essentially a program for short-term hospitalization in civilian facilities. The 1966 law for the first time extended civilian medical care for retired members of the Uniformed Services and their dependents, and dependents of deceased active duty and deceased retired members.

Within the United States, Puerto Rico, Canada, and Mexico the program is administered by the Executive Director, Office for the Civilian Health and Medical Program of the Uniformed Services (OCHAMPUS), Denver, Colorado. Administration elsewhere in the world is the responsibility of designated major overseas commanders. The program applies to all of the Uniformed Services: Army, Navy, Air Force, Marine Corps, Coast Guard, and Commissioned Corps of the Public Health Service and of the Environmental Science Services Administration (formerly the Coast and Geodetic Survey).

All beneficiaries, other than dependents of active duty personnel, who at age 65 become entitled to Medicare lose their eligibility for CHAMPUS benefits. This is true whether or not they are in fact enrolled in the Medicare program. This includes loss of CHAMPUS benefits outside the United States.

Loss of eligibility for CHAMPUS benefits is automatic at age 65 unless the retired member or dependent has a Notice of Disallowance from the Social Security Administration showing that he has filed with Social Security for hospital Medicare benefits and has been proved ineligible Therefore it is particularly important for CHAMPUS beneficiaries to apply for Medicare at a Social Security office about three months before reaching age 65. If this action is taken, a determination of entitlement under Social Security can be made before eligibility for CHAMPUS benefits would otherwise end. However, a person does not lose authorization for care in Uniformed Services (military) facilities because of entitlement to Medicare. As proof of eligibility for medical care from both civilian and Uniformed Services sources, a beneficiary must present a valid Uniformed Services identification card. This is the only identification needed. The identification card for all dependents of active duty, retired, and deceased personnel is DD Form 1173, Uniformed Services Identification and Privilege Card.

Except for emergencies, nonavailability statements are needed by active duty dependents residing with their sponsors when applying for civilian hospitalization in the United States and Puerto Rico. Regulations require these dependents to use Uniformed Services hospitals, when available, for hospitalization. These statements, which are used only for immediate needs, are issued to dependents at Uniformed Services facilities when the required inpatient care cannot be provided at a nearby Uniformed Services medical facility. A nonavailability statement may be issued on a retroactive basis to cover civilian inpatient care already begun or completed under extenuating circumstances.

Under the CHAMPUS cost-sharing plan the government pays a share of the reasonable charges for authorized health benefits. In determining if a charge is reasonable, the customary charges made by the physician and the prevailing charges of other physicians in the community for similar services are considered.

Spouses and children of active duty members are covered by a cost-sharing plan different from that covering all other beneficiaries. For authorized inpatient care the patient must pay the first \$25.00 of the hospital charge or \$1.75 a day, whichever is greater. The government pays the remainder of the reasonable hospital charge and the reasonable fees of professional personnel. For authorized outpatient care (for example, visits to the doctor's office or a clinic) a deductible (the first \$50.00) must be paid by the beneficiary each fiscal year (July 1 through June 30). When a claim for authorized care is submitted for two or more beneficiaries of a family, the deductible is $100.00 each fiscal year. After the deductible has been satisfied, the government pays 80% of the remaining reasonable charges for authorized outpatient care.

Retirees, their dependents, and dependents of deceased active duty and deceased retired personnel are covered by the following cost-sharing plan: for authorized inpatient care the government will pay 75% of the reasonable charges of the hospital and professional personnel. For authorized outpatient care a deductible must be paid by the beneficiary each fiscal year. When a claim for authorized care is submitted for only one beneficiary the deductible is $50.00. When claims for authorized care are submitted for two or more beneficiaries of a family, the deductible is $100.00. After the deductible has been paid the government pays 75% of the remaining reasonable charges for authorized outpatient care.

A special program of civilian health services training and rehabilitation is available for the seriously physically handicapped and moderately or severely mentally retarded spouses and children of members of the uniformed services who are serving on active duty. The following are authorized services (but service is not limited to these).

Diagnosis
Inpatient, outpatient, and home care
Surgery and medical care
Dental care, including orthodontia needed to correct handicapping conditions
Special optical devices
Purchase or rental of durable equipment such as a wheelchair, iron lung, hospital bed, and similar items
Training, rehabilitation, and special education
Institutional residential care in private nonprofit and in public institutions and facilities operated by federal, state, county, or local governments
Transportation to and from facilities in which the dependent is to receive or has received institutional care

To qualify for benefits under the Program for the Handicapped, public facilities must be used to the extent they are available and adequate. For services in other than a public facility in the United States or Puerto Rico, to be covered under the program the sponsor or other responsible family member must obtain a statement from a public official that the services are not available in public facilities. The statement must be attached to the claim for services provided by the private facility. Institutional (residential) care in private facilities operated for profit may not be paid for by CHAMPUS.

To obtain benefits under the Program for the Handicapped, the sponsor or other responsible family member must send a request for acceptance of the dependent under the program to:

Executive Director
Office for the Civilian Health and Medical Program of the Uniformed Services
Denver, Colorado 80240

Participation in CHAMPUS is entirely voluntary for the physician or any other provider of medical care. A physician participates in CHAMPUS when he provides authorized services and submits a CHAMPUS claim. The claim form the physician signs contains a certification to the effect that the allowable payments under CHAMPUS will be accepted as payment in full for the services listed on the form.

A claim for reimbursement of the government's share of allowable charges for either inpatient or outpatient care may be filed by completing the first thirteen items of DA Form 1863-2 (Fig. 15-3), attaching thereto itemized receipted bills, and forwarding the form with the supporting itemized bills to the fiscal agent of the state in which the care was obtained. A different form (DA 1863-3) is used for filing claims under the Handicapped Program.

Claims for payment are submitted to civilian agencies under contract with the govern-

CHAMPUS

SERVICES AND/OR SUPPLIES PROVIDED BY CIVILIAN SOURCES (EXCEPT HOSPITALS)

CIVILIAN HEALTH AND MEDICAL PROGRAM OF THE UNIFORMED SERVICES (CHAMPUS)
For use of this form, see AR 40-121; the proponent agency is the Office of The Surgeon General.

SEE INSTRUCTIONS ON REVERSE

SECTION I *(To be completed by patient or other responsible family member. Please print or type)*

PATIENT DATA

1. NAME *(last, first, middle initial)*
2. DATE OF BIRTH
3. ADDRESS *(Include Zip Code)*
4. PATIENT IS A *(Check one)*
☐ (1) SPOUSE ☐ (2) DAUGHTER ☐ (3) SON ☐ (4) RETIREE
5. IDENTIFICATION CARD *(DD Form 1173, DD Form 2 or PHS Form 1866-3)*
CARD NO.

	MONTH	DAY	YEAR
EFFECTIVE DATE			
EXPIRATION DATE			

6. BASIS FOR CARE – ACTIVE DUTY DEPENDENTS ONLY *(Check one)*
☐ (1) RESIDING APART FROM SPONSOR ☐ (2) RESIDING WITH SPONSOR DD FORM 1251 ATTACHED ☐ (3) OUTPATIENT
☐ (4) OTHER *(Specify)*

SERVICE MEMBER DATA

7. NAME OF SPONSOR. *(last, first, middle initial)*
8a. SERVICE NUMBER
8b. SOCIAL SECURITY ACCOUNT NUMBER
9. GRADE
10. ORGANIZATION AND DUTY STATION *(Home Port for Ships) (Address for Retired)*
11. SPONSOR'S OR RETIREE'S BRANCH OF SERVICE
☐ (1) USA ☐ (2) USAF ☐ (3) USMC ☐ (4) USN
☐ (5) USCG ☐ (6) USPHS ☐ (7) ESSA
12. STATUS
☐ (1) ACTIVE DUTY ☐ (2) RETIRED ☐ (3) DECEASED

13. CERTIFICATION

I certify to the best of my knowledge and belief the above information in Section I is correct. To the extent that I have authority to do so I hereby authorize the release of medical records in this case to both the contractor and the Government.

If a RETIRED MEMBER or dependent of a retired or deceased member, I certify that to the best of my knowledge and belief, that
(Check appropriate box) *(Delete portion in parenthesis not applicable)*

☐ (I am not) (the patient is not) enrolled (neither is sponsor) in any other insurance, medical service, or health plan provided by law or through employment.

☐ (I am) (the patient is) enrolled (so is sponsor) in another insurance, medical service, or health plan provided by law or through employment; however the particular benefits claimed on this form are not payable under the other plan.

Name (print or type) (Relationship to Patient) Date Signature

SECTION II *(To be completed by Source of Care)*

14. NAME AND ADDRESS OF SOURCE OF CARE *(Include Zip Code)*
a. SOURCE OF CARE LOCATION CODE
b. PROVIDER OF SERVICES
☐ (1) ATTENDING PHYSICIAN
☐ (2) OTHER *(Specify)*
c. PATIENT STATUS
☐ (1) INPATIENT
☐ (2) OUTPATIENT

15. NAME AND TITLE OF INDIVIDUAL ORDERING CARE

16. INCLUSIVE DATES OF CARE

	MONTH	DAY	YEAR		MONTH	DAY	YEAR
FROM				TO			

17. DIAGNOSIS *(Use standard nomenclature)*
(Check when applicable) ☐ *services were necessary for treatment of a bonafide medical emergency*
a. INTL STAT CODE
b. 12 BREAK CODE

18. RELATED HOSPITALIZATION *(If applicable)*
FROM TO

19. ENTER ESTIMATED OR ACTUAL DATE OF DELIVERY IN MATERNITY CASES. LIST BY DATE SURGICAL OPERATIONS AND/OR CARE FURNISHED INCLUDING VISITS FOR WHICH SEPARATE CHARGES ARE CLAIMED *(Type or print)* *(Attach additional sheets if required)*

DATE(S) OF SERVICE	a. ITEM OR DESCRIPTION OF SERVICE	b. CHARGES	c. PROCEDURE CODE
		$	
	d. TOTAL CHARGES THIS STATEMENT FOR CARE AUTHORIZED	$	
	e. (PAID BY) OR (DUE FROM) PATIENT *(Cross out one)*	$	
	f. DUE FROM GOVERNMENT TO SOURCE OF CARE	$	
	g. DUE PATIENT OR SPONSOR, REIMBURSEMENT	$	

20. CERTIFICATION BY SOURCE OF CARE

I certify that the services and / or supplies listed hereon were performed or authorized by the attending physician, dentist or other professional personnel in charge, that payment due from the Government has not been received, and that, except for the amount payable by the patient in accordance with the terms of the Civilian Health and Medical Program of the Uniformed Services, the amount paid by the Government will be accepted as payment in full for the authorized services and / or supplies listed hereon.

I further certify that I am not an intern, resident or otherwise in training status for which I am receiving compensation for services listed on this claim.

Name (print or type) Title Date Signature

The persons signing this form are advised that the willful making of a false or fraudulent statement herein renders them liable to prosecution under applicable Federal Laws.

DA FORM 1 JUN 67 1863-2 (Civilian Sources) REPLACES DA FORM 1863-2, 1 SEP 61, WHICH IS OBSOLETE. Form Approved Comptroller General, U. S., 22 Sep 67

1

Fig. 15-3. CHAMPUS Claim Form DA-1863-2.

ment to serve as fiscal agents for the program. In determining if a charge is reasonable, the fiscal agent takes into account the customary charges made by the physician, and the prevailing charges of other physicians in the community for similar services. If the care furnished involves unusual circumstances and professional effort, this also is taken into account. Similar procedures are used to determine reasonable charges for services allied to medicine. Hospital charges are determined to be reasonable when they are the customary charges of that hospital. A charge determined to be reasonable is allowable under CHAMPUS.

Delays in CHAMPUS claim payments can be avoided by submitting claims on a regular basis after the annual deductible charge has been met. One need not wait until the end of the fiscal year.

The social security number (SSN) of the sponsor must be included on all applications for CHAMPUS benefits. A digital system based on the sponsor's SSN will soon be operational, and applications for benefits received without an SSN will be returned without action.

Detailed information on medical care from civilian sources under the Uniformed Services Health Benefits Program may be obtained from one of the following sources.

The medical facility of any military installation

Executive Director, OCHAMPUS, Denver, Colorado 80240

The Surgeon General of the appropriate military service

A new Veterans Administration Program, Civilian Health and Medical Program–Veterans Administration, will provide medical care for widows and children of veterans who died of service-connected disabilities after leaving military service and for dependents of veterans who have service-connected total and permanent disabilities. Until legislation was passed last year, the VA was not authorized to provide care for anyone except veterans. CHAMPVA will pay 75% of the reasonable costs of hospital care and 75% of remaining costs in any calendar year after the patient has paid the first $50. Care is provided at non-VA hospitals at VA expense. It closely parallels the CHAMPUS program for dependents and survivors of military retirees.

TRENDS IN MEDICAL CARE

Expansion of private and public financing of medical services has created a demand far in excess of the capacity of our health system to respond. This situation has resulted in an inflationary spiral in medical costs causing significant increases in government health expenditures without a proportionate return, raising private health insurance premiums, and reducing the purchasing power of the health dollar.

Many critics of our present system of medical care contend that we have no system at all, that medical care is very much fragmented and that radical changes are needed. Although the situation has been grossly exaggerated there is no doubt that the overspecialization of medical practice has resulted in some fragmentation of the patient. The task of putting the patient together again, of reconstructing the whole man, is an essential next step in the progress of medical practice. The numerous approaches suggested to meet this need include:

1. Upgrading the general practitioner
2. Replacing the general practitioner with a better-trained type of personal family physician (for example, the internist, family practitioner, and pediatrician
3. Training all physicians in the philosophy and techniques of comprehensive care
4. Promoting an organized institutionally oriented environment that will facilitate a coordinated approach with emphasis on multispecialty group practice using shared ancillary services and based on the principle of prepayment

Much of today's activity is focused on the latter approach.

Congress passed and President Nixon signed a Health Maintenance Organization

(HMO) bill during the last days of 1973. An HMO is usually interpreted to mean an organized system of medical care that provides a wide range of health maintenance and treatment services to an enrolled population in return for the prepayment of a fixed monthly premium.

Before passage of this law, the Department of Health, Education, and Welfare had spent $30 million for planning and development of HMOs. Seed money went to seventy-nine organizations. As of January, 1975, there were 137 HMOs serving an enrollment of about 6.5 million people.

It is an undisputed fact that the prototype for the HMO is the Kaiser-Permanente plan established by Henry J. Kaiser when he built a magnesium plant in a then-wilderness area in California during World War II. The plant was financed with a $30 million loan from the Reconstruction Finance Corporation (RFC), a government agency, and provided comprehensive medical services for workers not only on the job but off the job as well, and for their families. These comprehensive services were provided principally because no other medical services were available in this remote area.

Under the new HMO law, required basic services, which must be prepaid, include: physicians' services, hospital services and emergency services; mental health services (a minimum of 20 visits must be covered); medical treatment and referral services for drug abuse and alcoholism; laboratory services; home health services; and preventive services, family planning, and preventive dental care and eye examinations for children. Estimated cost of the mandatory basic benefit package for an HMO was put at $70 a month per family plus nominal copayments.

Few existing prepaid group plans or other HMO-like arrangements fully qualify today as HMOs under the law's definition, according to HEW officials, because they provide significantly fewer benefits than the law requires. It is predicted that many groups will apply for certification to secure financial aid or to qualify for the employer-option rule. A significant provision requires employers of more than twenty-five people to offer the HMO as an option where an HMO is available in an area. The Health Services Administration (under HEW), parent structure for the HMO program, points out that the employer does not have to pay more for the HMO coverage than he may pay for other types of coverage. Thus employees opting for the HMO will probably have to pay out of their own pockets if the HMO premium is higher.

Optional supplemental services are also provided for in the law. These may be either fee for service or prepaid, and include: intermediate and long-term care; dental and eye care and mental health services not included in the basic package; long-term physical medicine and rehabilitative services; prescription drugs. The estimated cost of these supplemental services is $38 to $42 per family per month, plus "copayment," making the total monthly tab for a worker around $110. Because of the high cost of the optional supplemental services, it is assumed that if an HMO offers them at all they will be on a fee for service basis.

Copayment allows the HMO to charge the patient a nominal sum each time he receives a service—but no more than 20% of the total cost. The routine office visit is one of the services for which copayment is most likely, but the typical insurance policy does not cover office visits at all.

The compromise HMO bill, enacted at the end of 1973, authorized $325 million over a five-year period to help set up some 100 health maintenance organizations. The bill contains a provision preempting state laws in some states that prohibit the corporate practice of medicine. PSROs will be used to monitor care provided under the HMO program along with Medicare, Medicaid, and any national health insurance program that may be forthcoming.

The HMO Act of 1973 is actually relatively mild compared with the previous legislation submitted. In 1972 Senator Kennedy's $5.2 billion HMO bill was passed by the Senate but then died in committee in the House.

The final HMO package is the start of a significant federal experiment in structuring the delivery of medical care. Predictions on the results of the program vary, of course, with considerable concern expressed that a crucial stage will be reached when the government-sponsored HMOs run into trouble and turn to the government for help in bailing them out. Congress will have to decide whether to subsidize such HMOs, despite the clear intent of the present law to avoid such an outcome.

Almost any discussion of health costs necessarily includes some mention of prospects for adoption of a national health insurance program. A growing number of people of all political persuasions regard some sort of universal comprehensive coverage as not only desirable but inevitable. *Business Week* magazine, in an article devoted to medical care, forecasted that Congress will put tougher cost and quality controls in any national health insurance program than it did in Medicare. The extent of the controls will largely depend upon what is happening to medical costs as the fight over such a program comes to a climax.

There are a number of bills for National Health Insurance (NHI) in the Congressional hopper and all of them will increase, to a varying degree ($1 billion to $90 billion), the overall cost of medical care. Much of the discussion centers on those fundamental principles that should underlie a wise use of federal tax dollars in subsidizing elements of medical service. Also, much of the drive for National Health Insurance legislation arises from an allegation of crisis in health care. This charge can be challenged by the fact that more people are receiving more and better medical care from more and better trained physicians in more and better equipped facilities than ever before in history. This is true despite the fact that there are many medically underserved areas throughout the country largely due to the acknowledged maldistribution of physicians. It has further been recently established that the public, as its opinion has been judged in various polls, does not perceive medical service to be a major problem area.

Most medical observers agree that there are significant gaps in our present system of health insurance that require closing, especially in terms of catastrophic coverage. But the key question is can an NHI program be built around the present system of private health insurance capitalizing on the best of private financing mechanisms. Can needed improvements be made without exhorbitant increased government spending and disruptive legislation?

The American Medical Association has had its own specific proposal for a financing mechanism introduced in Congress embodied in what is called the Comprehensive Health Care Insurance Act of 1975 (HR 6222). This bill would establish a program of comprehensive medical, hospital, and dental care and require that employers make insurance available to each employee and his family as protection against the cost of ordinary and catastrophic illness. The program would further provide for the federal financing of insurance for persons of low income, in whole or in part according to ability to pay. The availability of insurance would be assured to all persons regardless of medical history and on a guaranteed renewable basis.

In 1974, prior to Nixon's resignation, his administration sent Congress a sweeping national health insurance proposal aimed at making a comprehensive health insurance policy available to all, regardless of income. To carry out the program, the Administration proposed a far-reaching set of recommendations that would have a great impact on the private health insurance system and that would cost business an extra $20 billion and add some $7 billion to federal and state taxes. In addition, the plan includes a provision for continuation of the new and controversial controls on medical care delivery, that is, PSROs.

More ambitious and costly proposals have been introduced in Congress, such as that of the Committee for National Health Insurance with the backing of organized labor and a compromise NHI measure sponsored by Wilbur Mills and Senator Edward Kennedy. Both of these proposals were dedicated to restructuring the present system of delivering and financing medical care.

Senators Russell Long and Abraham Ribicoff also submitted an NHI bill during the 1974 session that favored the incremental approach emphasizing catastrophic coverage only for all using the Social Security system. According to Senator Ribicoff, a former HEW Secretary, we do not possess the administrative capacity to administer and pay claims for over 200 million Americans dealing with over 7,000 hospitals and 360,000 physicians.

Additional NHI bills sponsored by the American Hospital Association and the health insurance industry have been introduced along with a number of other lesser known proposals. There is no sign of a consensus in Congress on the crucial NHI questions. Despite widespread agreement on benefits, lawmakers are far apart on financing and administration. No strong body of support has begun to form yet around any single measure that could make it a "favorite choice" although the AMA's NHI proposal has more individual Congressional sponsors than any other single bill.

Since 1965 the federal-state Medicaid program has attempted to provide medical care for indigents. Because the benefits have been uneven from state to state, most national health insurance bills would scrap Medicaid and substitute a federal program to pay for medical care for the indigent.

There are a number of basic questions that the Congress must resolve before determining what type of national health insurance should be enacted. Among them are:

1. *Public responsibility or private responsibility.* Is it the role of the government to care for all of the people regardless of their need? Should people be responsible for paying for their own health care in any way they can? Or should government assume the role of helping each citizen pay for his health care costs to the degree that he requires that help?
2. *Universal or categorical coverage.* Should all people be covered by the federal plan or just those with special problems, such as the poor, the aged, or the chronically ill?
3. *Continuous or episodic coverage.* Should the federal government pay most medical bills or only those that are "catastrophic" in their dollar amount?
4. *Compulsory or voluntary.* Would participation be mandatory through use of a payroll tax (plus general revenues for the nonemployed) or should financing be through a partnership between federal government, state government, employer, and/or employee?
5. *Financing.* Should the federal cost be paid through a payroll tax, general revenues, or tax credits? What balance would there be between federal revenues and private expenses? What would be the role of existing employer-employee health insurance agreements?
6. *Federal or private administration.* Should control of the health insurance plan be vested exclusively with the federal government (Social Security Administration or some similar agency) or should the federal role be confined to paying for insurance or health care for the appropriate persons or categories?
7. *Reimbursement pattern.* For institutional care, should payment be on a schedule basis, retroactive, or prospective? For noninstitutional providers, would the Medicare/Medicaid procedures of "usual, customary, and reasonable" fees (UCR) be used or would there be federal or locally imposed fee schedules?

Review questions

1. Why is government participation and responsibility in health care not a new concept?
2. What is the chief function of the Public Health Service? Name five specific functions.
3. What is the nature of the problem in determining liability under Workmen's Compensation?
4. How does a company become self-insured?
5. Describe the basic differences between Medicare and Medicaid.
6. Why did Congress single out those over age 65 for a national program of health insurance?
7. Distinguish between Part A and Part B of Medicare.
8. How is the Medicare Program financed? How is it administered?
9. What is a PSRO and describe some of its features?
10. Why is it important for CHAMPUS beneficiaries to register for Medicare when reaching age 65?
11. What is a nonavailability statement and when is it required?
12. Describe an HMO and the impact it will have on employees.

Suggested readings

Hanlon, J. J.: Principles of public health administration, ed. 5, St. Louis, 1969, The C. V. Mosby Co.

U. S. Department of Health, Education, and Welfare: The Public Health Service today, Washington, D. C., 1964, Public Health Service Publication No. 165.

U. S. Department of Health, Education, and Welfare: The Evolution of Medicare—from ideas to law, 1969, Office of Research and Statistics Research Report No. 29, Social Security Administration, Baltimore, Maryland 21235.

U. S. Department of Health, Education, and Welfare: Your Medicare handbook, February, 1973, Social Security Administration, Baltimore, Maryland 21235.

U. S. Department of Health, Education, and Welfare: 1972 Amendments Medicare Chart Booklet, February, 1973, Social Security Administration, Baltimore, Maryland 21235.

chapter 16

Medical office economics

Managing the financial side of the physician's practice is one of the most important duties of the medical assistant, particularly in those offices where a full-time bookkeeper may not be in attendance. Assuming such responsibility presupposes a knowledge of the physician's fees, how to negotiate fees with patients, the handling of cash payments, and, of course, making out statements.

Physicians traditionally dislike discussing financial matters directly with patients. Many physicians encourage and expect their assistants to make the financial arrangements, that is, to name the amount of the fee and to arrange the manner of payment with the patient. The method to be followed, however, depends exclusively on the wishes of the physician and will be largely determined by the type of practice.

All physicians should maintain a fixed schedule of fees for the various services rendered. Neither the physician nor the assistant should be embarrassed or reluctant to quote fees. Actually, discussing them in advance with patients often precludes confusion and future misunderstandings. The patient who makes his initial contact with a medical office by telephone and inquires about fees should receive a reply that has been previously approved by the physician. A fee schedule should be kept handy for easy reference.

When a patient understands what he is paying for and is satisfied with the services he received, the physician rarely has difficulty in obtaining the fee. The American public is conditioned to itemized bills, regular billing, and budget plans for paying for goods and services. People expect physicians to adopt the same business principles in handling medical fees.

When receiving a new patient, it is most important to find out tactfully how the patient wishes to pay for his medical treatment. If the doctor is a participating member of any prepayment plan's panel of physicians or other medical plan and accepts member patients, the assistant should seize the initiative and be familiar with the rules

Glossary

delinquent something that is due and unpaid; overdue

executor a person named in a will to carry out the provisions of the will; usually an attorney

ledger a chronologic history of a patient's financial record

protracted lengthened; extended over a long period of time

terse brief and to the point

transient not settled, established, or permanent; staying for a short time and regulations pertaining to the plan. For instance, if a patient possesses medical coverage with an indemnity company, he is billed directly for the doctor's regular fee and is obligated to remit to the doctor, claiming reimbursement from his insurance company later. It is customary, however, for the attending physician to fill out for the patient's insurance company a form that describes the nature and extent of the treatment given.

The time-honored obligation of the physicians to give free treatment to their colleagues and their immediate families has been updated in two significant ways. The American Medical Association's current interpretation of the Principles of Medical Ethics permits physicians (1) to accept insurance benefits and (2) to charge adjusted fees if "called upon to render services with such frequency as to involve a significant amount of his professional time, or in cases of long-term extended treatment."

Acceptance of insurance benefits as payment in full has become customary with at least two out of five physicians, but few physicians, other than perhaps psychiatrists, follow the alternative of discounting fees for colleagues. These are among some of the facts uncovered by the most recent *Medical Economics* continuing survey.* Overall, 96% of the physicians included in the survey offer some form of professional courtesy to fellow practitioners compared with a 93% figure discovered in a similar 1962 survey. Although colleagues and their families are still receiving a full measure of professional courtesy, doctors are tightening up on the fee discounts they used to extend to many nonphysicians.

Although physicians are not ethically bound to extend professional courtesy to their own relatives, four out of five do so. Free care, rather than reduced fees or acceptance of insurance benefits as full payment is more often the rule here than with colleagues and their families.

Professional courtesy for medical assistants, which often includes payment by the employing physician of all or part of their health insurance premiums, is almost a universal practice. Surgeons are more inclined to accept third party payments as full settlement for services to their employees. Where such coverage is lacking, free care is slightly more widespread among older practitioners than among younger ones. The relatively few doctors who may bill their uninsured assistants at all generally show a preference for charging half the standard fee.

The same *Medical Economics* survey shows that nurses obtain professional courtesy from two thirds of the polled physicians, dentists from about half of them, and pharmacists from about one third. Reduced fees are the form of courtesy most commonly offered to such allied medical workers with the most common discount being 20% to 25%.

BILLING PROCEDURES

Patients' accounts must be carefully and accurately maintained if the doctor is to collect the correct fee for his services. A record must be kept of each office visit and of all extra services and supplies such as x-ray films, laboratory work, medications, special dressings, and so on. This means entering all charges incurred and payments made by patients and keeping all patients' accounts up-to-date. The conscientious assistant will make time at the end of each day to post all charges from her daybook (appointment book) or daily log to patients' ledgers. It is better to perform this task at the end of each working day rather than put it off, so that important details will not be forgotten.

The goodwill or ill will of patients often depends upon proper billing and collecting of fees. Specific responsibility of both the doctor and his assistant in the handling of medical bills should be clearly defined after

*From Owens, A: See how professional courtesy is changing, Medical Economics, February 4, 1974, pp. 79-84.

a thorough discussion of the various aspects of the procedure. To do the best public relations job for the physician, here are some suggestions that may help you handle touchy fee problems.

1. If he has not already done so, suggest that the physician post the American Medical Association plaque that encourages fee discussions.
2. Send statements regularly.
3. Itemize all statements.
4. Get to know the patients so you can help the physician evaluate their ability to pay.
5. Keep accurate financial records; avoid billing mistakes.
6. Send reminders when bills are past due, but never send threatening letters until absolutely necessary. Threatening letters will be discussed later in this chapter.
7. Familiarize yourself with the physician's wishes and practices in regard to fees so that you can answer simple questions about medical bills.

It is advisable to encourage patients to discuss payments before they leave the office. Some patients prefer to pay by cash after each visit. Some physicians even give patients a billfold-size record card showing charges and payments. This serves as a permanent medical financial record.

A supply of small bills should be kept on hand in order to make change for patients who prefer paying by cash. It is therefore necessary to maintain a receipt book with carbon slips for duplicate office copies, which suffice as a permanent record of payment. Patients who pay by cash should be reminded to keep their receipts for income tax purposes. The assistant must not forget to post daily from the receipt book to the various patients' ledgers and to include such payments in the summary of receipts for each day.

It is unwise to cash checks or make change for large bills if they are offered by patients about whom little is known. This applies especially to new or transient patients. Transient patients who are paying their bills by check should usually not be offended if they are requested to furnish further identification, such as a driver's license.

Occasional disputes with patients over fees are bound to crop up in any practice. Some physicians cope with these situations by offering such patients the option of paying less than standard fees. Patients are given a special form inviting them to decide how much they wish to pay and writing the amount on the statement. The form usually suggests a 25% reduction but explains that a larger or smaller reduction, or regular partial payments, also would be acceptable.

The majority of patients prefer to be billed by mail. Statements should be mailed to patients near the end of every month. Itemized statements indicating specific services rendered and fees charged are desirable. Itemized bills are more efficient in that they save a good deal of time from being consumed by telephone inquiries from patients wishing to have charges explained to them.

Many of those firms engaged in selling professional business forms and record-keeping systems offer a ledger card (Fig. 16-1) that serves a twofold purpose. This popular form functions as a combination patient's ledger and itemized statement. The patient's ledger is coded as to professional services and contains provisions for recording charges incurred on a particular day, amounts paid on account, and a column for showing the patient's latest outstanding balance. It is imperative that the assistant post to this type of ledger daily and keep it up to date. At the end of the month the assistant merely makes a copy of each patient's ledger, using a copying machine, and mails an itemized statement to each patient. This system eliminates the more time-consuming task of typing a separate statement for each patient.

Some patients may request a statement as soon as their treatment is completed. Bills should be mailed out to these patients

STATEMENT

LEONARD S. TAYLOR, D.D.S.
2100 WEST PARK AVENUE
CHAMPAIGN, ILLINOIS 61822

TELEPHONE 367-6671

DATE	PROFESSIONAL SERVICE	CHARGE	PAID	BALANCE

PAY LAST AMOUNT IN THIS COLUMN

O—OFFICE CALL
X—X-RAYS
E—EXTRACTION
P—PROPHYLAXIS
S—SEDATIVE TREATMENT
SR—SILVER RESTORATION
GR—GOLD RESTORATION
PR—PORCELAIN RESTORATION
OS—ORAL SURGERY
CB—CROWN OR BRIDGE SERVICE
DS—DENTURE SERVICE
GT—GINGIVAL TREATMENT
CA—CORRECTIVE APPLIANCE
RP—REPARATIVE PROCEDURE
PA—PREPARATORY APPOINTMENT

Fig. 16-1. Ledger-statement for photocopy billing. (Courtesy The Colwell Company, Champaign, Illinois.)

immediately rather than be held until the end of the month. In cases where a protracted series of treatments is involved and the assistant is aware that there will be a large fee, it should be suggested to the patient that he pay a fixed amount each week. Not only does this ease the burden on the patient, but it also ensures that the physician will realize at least a portion of the fee rather than having to wait perhaps months before receiving payment.

While it is absolutely essential to bill patients correctly, it is equally as important to bill the right person. Most of the time there is no problem; the person whom the physician treats receives the bill. If there is no third party involved, an implied contract exists between the doctor and the patient. In any case, however, the agreement is based on the law of contracts and even if given orally is still binding.

A third party may be a company that employs an injured employee, a health insurance plan, or an adult individual. From a billing standpoint it is important for an assistant to understand who can act as the third person in a contract with a physician.

The physician must show an express or implied contract to hold anyone other than the patient legally liable for his fees. However, it is of little value to have only verbal promises in the absence of friendly witnesses; otherwise it becomes the word of one person against that of another.

Third party responsibility exists where a married woman receiving treatment from a physician requests that the bill be forwarded to her husband. She is perfectly justified in making such a request since her husband is legally liable for her debts.

The teenager who goes by himself to the doctor's office for treatment offers another typical illustration. His parents or legal guardians are responsible for the fee even though treatment may be performed without their knowledge. The only exception to this rule is the teenager who is self-supporting and not living at home.

A parent engages the services of a physician for an adult child. The parents are responsible for the fee if the child lives under the same roof and is not self-supporting. On the other hand, when an adult child requests the services of a physician for a parent living under the same roof, it's the responsibility of the adult child requesting the services to pay the bill. In neither instance is the parent liable for the fee even though he is an adult. The law holds the adult who requests the physician's services as being liable, and hence a contract exists between the physician and the third party.

Generally, in order for a physician to hold a third party liable and be able to recover his fee, it is necessary to make an express contract containing the word "accepted" and obtain the signature of the third party. The relationship of the patient to the third party is not sufficient in itself to establish the responsibility of a third party. The facts in the situation must tend to substantiate third party responsibility.

For the most part, the assistant can assume that the patient treated by the physician is responsible for his fee, especially when he is an adult. The fact that a patient is brought to a physician's office in an unconscious state, not having had an opportunity to request treatment, does not alter his financial responsibility.

The medical assistant must be mindful of these exceptions and remain alert to situations where a patient is treated at the request of a third person. The name and address of any third party should be obtained so that he can be billed if necessary.

A bill to an estate must generally be submitted within a specified period of time after the death of the patient. It should be itemized in full and forwarded to the executor by registered mail requesting a return receipt. Suits may be filed against estates even if the bill for services is not sanctioned by the executor. However, they are usually very difficult to collect, and unless their payment is sanctioned by competent legal advice, it is of doubtful value to sue.

It can be very frustrating to a conscientious assistant who, through no fault of her own, is prevented from doing an efficient job of billing because all the facts were not supplied. It is not uncommon for some physicians who make frequent house calls after hours to forget to relate the details of these calls to their assistant. This creates problems in that some patients may never be billed for house calls; nor will there be any notation of these calls in the patient's record.

Most physicians mean well but are usually too busy or preoccupied with medical matters to give much attention to details. Although there are many solutions to the problem, the assistant who wishes to make things easier should begin by first making detailed work simple for the physician.

One suggestion might include use of an index card with the following typed headings: "Patient's name," "Date visited," "Address," "Fee," "Date billed," and "Date paid." The entire card might be headed "Doctor's house calls for the month." This card, clipped to a piece of cardboard to keep it firm, should be placed in the physician's bag. Hopefully, the physician will notice the card and be reminded to fill in the necessary information. At the end of the month or sooner the assistant removes the card from the doctor's bag for billing and replaces it with a new card for the succeeding period. When billing is completed the card should be filed as a permanent record.

Some offices have attempted to solve the problem of not reporting all details by having the physician complete all prescription blanks in duplicate. The carbon copies are retained in the pad and can be referred to the assistant when the doctor's bag is checked. The assistant then shows each copy to the doctor and inquires whether or not the call was paid for. Through a process of associating a patient's name with the medication administered the physician is better able to remember the call and the charge.

Some physicians have gone so far as to include with their statements prestamped return envelopes. Often, however, this is a waste of money since slow payers probably throw away the first two or three bills anyway. Management consultants sometimes recommend having a postal permit stamped on all return envelopes so that the sender pays only for those sent back to him. Others advise enclosing preaddressed but not postpaid envelopes on the assumption that it is the ready envelope and not the postage that provides the incentive for prompt payment.

Some solo practitioners and groups have discontinued sending out their statements. At the end of an office visit, the assistant informs each patient of the amount of his current balance and asks if he would like to pay it then and there. If the patient indicates he would prefer to have a bill sent to his home the assistant informs him that the office is no longer sending out statements. The assistant gives him a preprinted envelope with the doctor's name and address and requests the patient to enclose his payment and mail it to the office. If the patient uses the envelope to pay the bill, the office saves the substantial amount of time and expense ordinarily involved in sending out monthly statements. Should payment not be received after two months has elapsed, the office will send a statement followed by a series of collection reminders.

It is difficult to separate billing procedures from the collecting process since the latter is very much dependent upon an efficient billing system. Most management consultants recommend billing patients at least once a month and emphasize sending notices out before the first of the month. It often makes a big difference in the physician's rate of collections if the bill arrives early enough to compete with the patient's other bills for payment rather than later after the patient has exhausted the balance in his checkbook.

There are two schools of thought on collection, totally opposed to one another. One of them advocates no collections at all and the other one is very strong on collection efforts. In the medical field, the "no-collection efforts" position occupies a prominent place. Some physicians theorize that, if patients have accounts that are actively followed up or turned over to a collection agency, they will not get any referrals from these patients. Generally, this is no great loss since experience has shown that the people such patients might refer will not pay promptly, either.

There is a growing trend toward the use of bookkeeping and billing services to help physicians with accounts receivable management problems. Some of the services do the complete operation for the doctor outside of the office. Others make available the use of outside electronic data processing equipment for procedures that can be automated but keep the program largely in the doctor's office, using his medical assistants and under his supervision.

Some accounts receivable management services have been providing satisfactory service to physician clients for the past thirty-five years. Others are relatively new and untried. No blanket rule can be used for judging these services. Rather, cash service must be evaluated in terms of its need and effectiveness in the individual physician's office. In general, such services are designed to provide modern and efficient billing and bookkeeping procedures in order to reduce the business expense of the medical office and to save time for the physician and medical assistants. Management consultants say it is rare, however, for a solo practitioner to justify the expenditure for an automated system. On the other hand, a practice with three or four men or larger group might find it a sound investment.

While credit cards constitute an innovation in our economic system, their recent proliferation has created problems for everyone. A new form of card, the so-called bank card, has been widely introduced. Bank cards are issued at no cost to the cardholder and are generally acceptable at many more places than conventional credit cards. As these bank cards have come into widespread use throughout the country, physicians have naturally wondered whether they may ethically use bank cards as a form of payment for professional services. Some medical societies have sanctioned physician participation; others have not.

The Judicial Council of the AMA has expressed the opinion that physician participation in bank card programs is not unethical per se. It is of the opinion that physicians may ethically accept bank cards for the payment of current medical bills in lieu of cash or check, that is, as a medium of exchange. However, although patients may not be denied the right to determine matters of their personal budgeting, physicians must not encourage the use of this financing method if in operation it might compromise the ideals of the medical profession or add to the financial burden of patients. Consequently, the Judicial Council and the Council on Medical Service of the AMA have jointly agreed that any proposed plan for financing medical care or parts of medical care should be judged by the individual physician in the light of whether or not it might "result in advertising or solicitation of patients by physicians, profit to physicians for other than professional services, exploitation of the patient, or unnecessary increase in the cost of medical care."

With medical payments lagging far behind in the race for the consumer credit dollar, the relationship that exists between medical and retail credit is vital to the foundation of a proper attitude toward medical credit. It is important because it gives the medical assistant the confidence to approach a new patient and request credit information—the same type of credit information consumers customarily give when making application for a retail account. The proper attitude is necessary in a consideration of medical credit, but in order to collect accounts receivables in the shortest time with the least effort, the medical assistant and employer(s) should define what credit policies will be used. Once these policies are established they should be written down and followed. As a matter of fact, it might be wise to post them in a place where patients can easily see them. Once patients know what is expected of them, they may be less inclined to put the physician's bill at the bottom of the pile.

COLLECTING ACCOUNTS

No other secretary possesses such a uniquely complex job as does the medical assistant who without creating embarrassment or ill will must face the duty of collecting overdue bills. It is the assistant's duty to remind the physician of delinquent accounts and to discuss with him preferred methods of collection. And it must be certain that adequate information has been recorded on patients' records to assure accurate collection notices. Generally speaking, accounts that are delinquent for more than three months should be actively followed up.

Normally, a medical assistant, through the experience of trial and error, works out a successful approach for collecting fees. Developing a system of prompt and regular follow-up increases the percentage of collections and enhances the physician's income. The assistant should not permit an account to become three months delinquent before making an initial follow-up. The value of the doctor's services fades as the weeks pass. New illnesses may intervene; the patient may lose his job or move. The longer a bill remains outstanding, the more difficult it becomes to collect, and the less the chances are that it will be paid in full.

Almost all states possess statutes of limitations that apply to civil as well as criminal matters. According to the civil statute of limitations, if after a certain period of time has lapsed a physician still has not collected his bill, it becomes outlawed or legally uncollectible, and he has no further claim. The time element varies from state to state. In California, for example, the statute of limitations in civil matters is applicable after four years.

As a medical assistant you should be aware of several major federal laws which affect all retail credit in the United States. These regulations provide legal guidelines governing the actions of opening or collection of accounts. An understanding of these laws is of vital importance not only because you are bound by law to adhere to these regulations, but also because they help facilitate better patient relations.

Such laws include: the Federal Trade Commission's Guides Against Debt Collection Deception, the Federal Communications Commission's Public Notice on Use of Telephone for Debt Collection Purposes, the Truth-in-Lending Provision (Regulation Z of the Consumer Protection Act of 1968) and the Fair Credit Reporting Act (Title V of the Consumer Protection Act of 1968).

Perhaps the most significant of the above laws from the standpoint of the medical assistant is the Truth-in-Lending provision, better known as Regulation Z of the 1968 Consumer Protection Act. It deals with the collection of patients' payments. Regulation Z requires a written agreement when credit is extended beyond four scheduled installments, even though no interest charges are involved.

The Federal Trade Commission has developed a disclosure form that it recommends be used (Fig. 15-2).* You will notice that the fee advance payment, unpaid balance, and amount to be financed are listed. Along with provision for the finance charge (none), space is included for the total number of payments, deferred payment price, and annual percentage rate. This type of form presented to the patient listing essential information concerning the installment payments satisfies the requirements of Regulation Z.

There is a great deal of truth in the theory that people pay their doctor's bill last. It is the assistant's job to put patients in a "paying frame of mind," so to speak. The problem, however, is how to perform this task gracefully.

The most desirable procedure, of course, is to put the patient in the proper mood before the physician even sees him, and then encourage him to pay his bill at the end of the month. In trying to achieve this goal, the assistant must devise a plan of action and endeavor to operate within the framework of its objectives.

In all probability, when a patient first comes to the office, he will be asked to fill out a personal data form. It is suggested that the physician's billing policy be placed on the form for the patient to read at that

*From Blair, V.: You and the law, The Professional Medical Assistant **6**:10-11, September-October 1973.

time. Before and after he completes the form, the assistant can offer to answer any questions. Then, should any misunderstanding arise, it can be clarified immediately.

It is wise to mail out statements around the twenty-eighth day of the month so that they reach the patient before his other bills. Hopefully, he may decide to pay the physician before he pays the others. In the event that payment is not received by the middle of the next month some offices (with the doctor's approval) prefer to send a second statement at that time. This practice is predicated on the fact that there are many individuals who automatically ignore bills the first time around.

A physician should not be embarrassed about following up on bills that are justly owed him. An intelligent, efficient medical assistant can handle most of the collection aspects, often simply by telephone, cleaning up many misunderstandings about charges and serving as a goodwill ambassador.

When a statement has been sent and no payment received, what is the next collection step? Send another statement with a courteous request for payment. You may want to write "An early settlement will be appreciated," across the bottom of the bill. If this fails, write a personal letter accompanying the next bill, asking as cordially as possible the reason for nonpayment. Suggest that perhaps a part of the bill can be paid and arrangements worked out to pay a little at a time. Always encourage the patient to drop in at the office to discuss his reasons for nonpayment or to write a letter to the physician explaining the circumstances.

If no results are obtained after these attempts, the assistant, with the doctor's sanction, might telephone the patient. The patient can then be pinned down as to the date he expects to pay and be informed in a diplomatic manner that this information will be recorded on his records. At this time the assistant might inquire as to whether or not the patient is receiving the doctor's bills and request him to verify his address for the office records. This method places the patient in a position where he must reply in some way. Problems with overdue bills are often solved at this point, for when patients are made aware of their bills, most are willing to make arrangements to pay.

Some management consultants believe that the most effective instrument for collecting overdue accounts is a telephone in the hands of a skilled person using the right techniques. The first rule is, of course, not to wait too long to follow up. Many physicians erroneously assume that the slow-paying patient appreciates their willingness to wait indefinitely for payment. In general, it is good practice to begin the collection process three months after the patient has received his first bill or after he has received at least two follow-up statements. At this point the entire amount should be asked for. If there is to be any discussion of partial payments, it should be the patient who initiates it. Asking for the full amount at the outset generally increases the debtor's partial payment offer. The assistant must be careful not to be drawn into a prolonged discussion of the patient's troubles.

It is important psychologically to keep the patient off balance and on the defensive during the telephone contact. The assistant should not be content to hang up after a general promise has been made by the patient to do something about the account but should have a promise from the patient of exactly how much will be paid and when. Throughout such a conversation the assistant should remain polite but firm.

The average medical assistant cannot be expected to be capable of dealing with an experienced "deadbeat." Moreover, there is no need to worry about the alienation of this patient since he has already alienated himself. The only possible success to be achieved from a call of this type would result from the "deadbeat's" fear of legal action. In any event, the assistant should not be too quick to hang up at the first note of rudeness, for at the outset some embarrassment makes otherwise good patients hostile, until reason catches up with them.

In summary, then, "deadbeat" and hardship cases require no particular skill on the part of the collection caller, but for slow-paying accounts the chief requirement is that the assistant be polite but firmly persistent in reaching an agreement for payment. A good rule of thumb is to regard as token any sum less than 20% of the total balance. It is better to receive no promise of payment than one so small as to be meaningless. According to some experts, if a token payment is received in the office unsolicited or in disregard of its rejection by the collection caller, it should in most cases be returned. This may seem a rather strange thing to do, but acceptance of a token payment usually hinders achievement of the ultimate goal, which is collection of the entire balance. A token payment, when accepted, tends to set a limitation on the size of future payments, and it also delays the taking of effective collection action. It may be a token of goodwill and honest intentions, but more often it is a bid for more time. Also, a token payment is sometimes so small as to be hardly worth the bookkeeping costs of its collection and entry.

Should the patient still not remit payment by the time arranged, the assistant must adopt a firmer attitude. It might be a good idea, with the physician's approval, to initiate a series of collection letters. An attempt should be made to make each letter a personal one. Form letters, especially duplicated ones, should be avoided, for people tend to ignore what looks routine.

The older an account becomes the less likely it will be paid. Accounts over a year old seldom return more than 45 cents on the dollar—those two years old, 23 cents. After three years the return drops to about 15 cents on the dollar and, after five years it wouldn't buy a postage stamp. Collections therefore should be pursued vigorously while accounts are "fresh."

The statistics compiled by various associations show that professional men in the United States lose 296 million dollars each year in uncollectible accounts. This is nearly one million dollars for every business day of the year. These figures also show that only 2% of a physician's income is derived from collection agencies or attorneys. This means that 98 cents out of every dollar that the average physician collects must be secured through his own efforts.

The rate of collections is very much dependent upon the status of the economy. When business recessions occur, there will usually be a drop in collections resulting from layoffs, especially in urban areas; this is to be expected. During such periods it is advisable for medical assistants to present bills to patients before they leave the office, giving them an opportunity to pay them. In real hardship cases consultants advise allowing payments in no more than four installments.

Collection letters

Though "deadbeats" infest every doctor's accounts receivable, many of the dollars he writes off each year could be his with the right collection letter. Collecting by letter is the same as collecting in person. If the medical assistant made the first collection call on a patient in person, the conversation would not be opened by a threat to sue. In a face-to-face situation the visit would be a friendly one and, hopefully, a schedule of payments that was mutually satisfactory would be arranged. Such a method enables the physician to retain the goodwill of the patient. A letter must use the same method to be successful.

If an office has not been using a systematic collection to follow-up in the past, it should be careful to use only persuasive letters when first initiating a planned system of follow-ups, irrespective of the age of the account. If an account has received only monthly statements, even if the account is a year old, one should never begin with threatening letters. The account should be handled the same way it would be if it were only 90 days old. When starting to collect a ledger full of accounts of various ages, each account should be sent a friendly, persuasive collection letter each month for five consecutive months. Persuasive letters generally bring payments from at least 80% of those patients who have any intention of remitting.

Usually the patients who pay promptly will take care of their accounts within 90 days if they are merely sent monthly statements. A year-old account is much harder to collect than an account 90 days old. The problem is to keep the 90-day account from becoming old. Collection letters sent to accounts that are from three to seven months old will bring in much more money than collection letters sent to accounts a year or more old. Therefore it is recommended that the assistant send a "friendly persuasion" collection letter each month to all accounts that are three to seven months old. Threatening language of any kind should be omitted. This approach is designed to appeal to the patient's sense of fairness.

Experience has demonstrated that it is unwise to start collecting old accounts by sending threatening letters. Although it is agreed that this is what we sometimes feel like doing, it does not bring the desired results. The goodwill of the patient is a physician's greatest asset. The secret of successful professional collections is not to permit accounts to become delinquent. Persistence, patience, and courtesy reap the best results.

Every physician has a few bills which may be a year or more old but which he knows will be collected. If it is a large bill, he may be receiving small but regular payments each month. However, the doctor knows it will eventually be paid because the patient has kept in touch with the office and has demonstrated a sincere effort to pay.

With patients who are making a sincere effort to pay, irrespective of age of the account, only persuasion should be used because threats will generally do more harm than good at this point. The assistant should continue to use persuasion to keep such patients in the habit of paying as soon as they are able.

Patients must be convinced that they should pay the physician something after their more immediate bills are paid. It is only human to take the path of least resistance to pay nothing until other priority debts are satisfied. Most patients will do this unless they are sent friendly collection letters regularly every month as soon as the bill becomes past due.

If the assistant writes a collection letter one month and then skips two or three months, chances are that most patients will not pay any attention to these occasional letters. It is recommended that to every monthly statement, starting with the third month, a persuasive collection letter be attached. A sound collection system will not permit inconsistent follow-ups. Patients must be convinced from the outset that the physician's bill is important and that payment is expected within a reasonable period of time.

In summary, five persuasion letters should be used for delinquent accounts, starting with the third month. Persuasion letters are sent once a month. If a patient makes no effort to pay something on account or does not show the courtesy of a reply, the assistant should follow with three threatening letters. The threatening letters should be sent twice a month. Sending threatening letters twice a month should convince a patient that the physician expects action.

The assistant will find it very helpful to make a notation on the patient's ledger card, indicating the date and the number of each collection letter sent. A glance at a patient's file will tell exactly what has been sent to a patient.

It is well for the assistant to become familiar with patients' paydays or other income dates. This information should be recorded on their ledgers. Like monthly statements, collection letters will not be effective if they arrive after the paycheck is spent; the collection letters should be timed so that they arrive the same day or preferably the day before the patient receives his paycheck.

Collection agencies

If all collection efforts prove ineffectual, the last resort is, of course, a collection agency. It is the duty of the physician to select carefully the collection service he believes will handle his accounts in the most nearly correct manner, taking into consideration medical ethics and the public relations factors in bill collecting. Money collected on bad accounts through the tactics of unscrupulous and hard-boiled collection agencies is a poor offset against a loss of goodwill for the individual doctor and the profession.

Medical collections require a different approach than do collections in other businesses. This is precisely why selection of a reputable agency is the physician's first consideration. It is usually best to select a local agency with a good reputation in the community and avoid out-of-state or mailorder-type agencies. The local medical society, chamber of commerce, or Better Business Bureau are generally in a position to offer a recommendation.

Some offices have found use of promissory notes to be effective. If the patient appears to constitute a collection problem, he might be persuaded to come in and sign a note for the entire amount of the account. Then, if the account is later turned over to a collection agency, the note will strengthen the hand of the agency. The agency can sue on the promissory note itself, rather than for the reasonable value of the services rendered by the physician.

Other methods of collecting

The physician is sometimes faced with the decision as to whether to turn an account over to a collection agency or to an attorney. Most physicians are reluctant to take a delinquent account to small claims court because of the time involved and the unfavorable publicity connected with such appearances. Placing an account in the hands of an attorney is more justifiable when the amount of money owed is quite large.

Suing to collect a bill is a drastic step that sometimes is offset by the resultant ill will it creates. A vengeful patient—justly or unjustly—may sometimes file a malpractice suit countering the doctor's collection suit. Consequently, many physicians delay any legal actions until after the statute of limitations determining the extent of time during which a malpractice action can be filed expires. The period varies from state to state.

In reaching a final decision, a number of factors should be weighed. Points to consider are the clear rights of the claim, the patient's ability to pay, exhaustion of other collection means, and justification of the amount by comparison with the fees for similar services locally. In all collection efforts, a balance of humanitarianism and firmness appear to achieve the best results.

The physician must be careful in terminating the medical care of "deadbeat" patients. Lack of payment itself does not justify the abrupt, unilateral termination of the doctor-patient relationship. Instead of simply putting a flagrant "deadbeat" off on appointments, he should be given written notice of the physician's intention to withdraw services following completion of any ongoing treatment. This notice should make reference to his unwillingness to abide by the doctor's financial policies and thereby serves to absolve the physician of an abandonment charge.

A problem that is becoming more significant is the physician with a busy office practice and an equally busy hospital practice. With efficient help the office generally runs smoothly; it is the hospital portion of the practice that is disruptive and often creates the problem. Some physicians claim they have eliminated the problem by hiring an additional assistant to accompany them on hospital rounds. In addition to recording progress notes on patients' charts and running errands throughout the hospital, the hospital assistant saves time when the

John Doe, MD
10 Main Street
Washington, DC

____
(patient's name)

____

____
(patient's address)

1.	Cash price (medical fee)	$500
	Less: cash down payment (advance payment)	$100
2.	Unpaid balance of cash price	$400
3.	Amount financed	$400
4.	**Finance charge**	**none**
5.	Total of payment (3&4)	$400
6.	Deferred payment price (1&4)	$500
7.	**Annual percentage rate**	**none**

(the above are sample figures)

The "total payment" shown above is payable to Dr. John Doe at the address shown above in 10 monthly installments of $40.00, the first installment being payable __________, 19___, and all subsequent installments are due on the same day of each consecutive month until paid in full.

__________ (date) __________ (patient's signature)

Fig. 16-2. Disclosure form.

patient is discharged. The assistant instructs the patient in how to fill out the Blue Shield or Medicare forms, frequently holding lengthy bedside discussions. Back at the office the hospital assistant records all the information and mails an appointment reminder to the patient for follow-up care. The assistant is also often given complete charge of following up on all insurance claims and billing for hospital patients.

Physicians claim that this system permits them to spend time with their patients and not with their paper work. It even gets them home at a more reasonable hour and gives them peace of mind in knowing that the office is not stacked with incomplete patients' records. Not to be overlooked is a much-improved collection ratio, which more than compensates for the added payroll expense.

SAMPLE LETTERS

The letters in Figs. 16-2 to 16-5 are printed only to illustrate the variance in tone of the letters previously mentioned. Each assistant should be resourceful enough to compose her own or at least modify existing ones to suit the circumstances.

Persuasion letter

Dear ________________________________:

I am sure you dislike receiving reminder letters, and I am not at all fond of writing them. A remittance this week would save us both a lot of bother. Your account dates back several months.

Will you please give this your attention and send your remittance before the end of the month? This will avoid the necessity of sending you another statement.

Sincerely yours,

Fig. 16-3

Threatening letter (collection agency)

Dear ______________________________.

Your past due account has become an administrative problem to this office. It costs the doctor money to send out monthly statements and to keep an account in the office.

Therefore, unless payment is made immediately, we can no longer continue to handle the account. We will be forced to turn it over to an agency. We very much dislike having to do this to a patient, for it can only jeopardize his credit rating.

Truly yours,

Fig. 16-4

Threatening letter (attorney)

Dear ______________________________:

Despite the fact that we have sent you numerous statements and letters regarding your long past due account, you have neither sent your remittance nor set forth any reasons why you are withholding payment.

You have been given every opportunity to work out convenient payment arrangements. You give us no choice but to place your account in the hands of an attorney.

We heartily dislike the idea of bringing upon you the undesirable publicity and cost of a lawsuit. No person can afford to have judgment and costs rendered against him. Therefore, in justice to the doctor and to yourself, it behooves you to settle your account within ten days.

Yours truly,

Fig. 16-5

SUMMARY OF MEDICAL OFFICE ECONOMICS

In the role as a collector of accounts the medical assistant should consider the following points.

1. The patient always deserves the benefit of any doubt that may exist in regard to his intentions.
2. The physician's office should display a sincere interest in working out the payment schedule for patients that is easiest for them. Besides simply trying to collect fees, the assistant should express a willingness to help. There are always a few patients who may be too embarrassed to return to a physician's office knowing that their bill is past due. In some cases such patients may be depriving themselves of adequate medical treatment. By understanding their financial problems and working out convenient methods of payment, the assistant paves the way for them to return with a free conscience. Paying something regularly, regardless of the amount, soon gets a bill paid.
3. Letters should be kept friendly for the

most part. Persuasion is much more effective than force. If time permits, collection notices should be typed separately and attached to the patient's statement rather than be typed on the statement itself.

4. As the tone of collection letters becomes sterner, the words should become more terse and the letters shorter.
5. Patients should be put in the habit of paying. Many of them are ready to leave a check on their first visit to the doctor's office. The assistant should be familiar with the physician's fees, be able to justify them, and be prepared to work out a payment plan. It should never be assumed that the patient's insurance company will take care of all fees; his coverage may be incomplete or inapplicable, and there are usually deductibles involved.
6. The assistant should try to get out-of-town patients as well as transient patients to make a payment before leaving the office. Credit information can often be obtained diplomatically as part of the regular personal data form. Provision can be made for securing local references, referrals, driver's license number, and insurance and credit card numbers—anything that will help to check on a patient if necessary.

Review questions

1. How has the concept of professional courtesy changed in recent years?
2. Explain why record keeping and billing are so closely related.
3. How should you deal with patients who prefer to pay cash for their medical bills?
4. List several instances where someone other than the patient treated might be responsible for the physician's fee.
5. How would you deal with a physician who continually forgets to inform you about out-of-office calls?
6. Is it ethical for physicians to accept bank credit cards for payment of medical fees?
7. Why is it important to follow up delinquent accounts immediately?
8. What is meant by the statute of limitations, and how does it concern the medical assistant?
9. What is Regulation Z and how does it affect billing procedures?
10. Why is it a good practice to mail statements before the end of the month?
11. Some collection experts recommend returning token payments to patients. What is the reasoning behind such advice?
12. Why must a physician be careful in choosing a collection agency?

Suggested readings

The American Medical Association: The business side of medical practice, Chicago, 1973, The Association.

Freeman, M. H., et al.: Gregg bookkeeping and accounting, ed. 3, New York, 1963, McGraw-Hill Book Co.

chapter 17

Medical office bookkeeping

WHY KEEP RECORDS?

An analysis of recent statistics pertaining to the causes of business failures in the retailing and service trades reveals that a heavy preponderance of these failures stemmed from one particular cause: the owners' inability to avoid certain conditions that adequate bookkeeping records would have exposed in time to take early corrective action. Generally speaking, it is practically impossible to negotiate a bank loan without properly prepared financial statements. Bankers and other granters of credit need to study balance sheets and income statements before deciding whether or not to extend credit. In many cases, audited financial statements are required, and the record keeping system used must be able to provide the basis for these statements. A physician, like any businessman, must be able to evaluate his own financial situation at any given time by checking his records.

The importance of record keeping is further substantiated by the fact that a number of publishing firms and trade associations have, over the years, conducted a successful business in supplying simple one-book systems with instructions and forms designed for specific kinds of businesses and professions. A physician, for instance, sometimes finds it to his advantage to have a bookkeeping system adapted to his particular needs and requirements.

The physician must maintain accurate records for several other obvious reasons.

1. He must be able to judge whether his income is sufficient to cover his expenses and provide a reasonable profit.
2. Records provide the data needed to prepare or substantiate tax returns.
3. Records enable the physician to check or trace payments made to him and by him.
4. Records preserve the financial data of the physician's practice for future needs and reference.
5. The Internal Revenue Service requires that bills and records be kept for at least three years.

Ordinarily, the statute of limitations as applied to an income tax return expires three years after the return is due to be filed. However, there are some reasons why

---

Glossary

assets entries on a balance sheet that express in terms of money the value of the tangible things or intangible rights that constitute the resources of a business or practice as of a given date

credit the entry of money paid on account; the right-hand side of an account

cumulative increasing or growing in amount or value

debit an entry of something owed in an account; the left-hand side of an account

disbursement the act of paying out; expenditure

footing an accounting term meaning the addition of a column of figures to obtain a total

journalizing to keep or make entries in a journal

liabilities the debts or other financial obligations of a business for money, goods services, etc., received

posting the transferring of an entry from journal to ledger

proprietorship synonymous with ownership; usually a business

reimburse to pay back; to refund

the taxpayer should retain his records indefinitely. Sometimes legislation is enacted that provides relief for taxpayers if they can establish facts that can only be proved by records of transactions from prior years.

Records are required so that an individual can determine his correct tax liability. To substantiate items appearing on an income tax return, one must maintain permanent records that clearly indicate income, deductions, and credits; inventories; employees' names, addresses, and social security numbers; and sales or rentals of items subject to excise taxes.

Proper disposal of records is an integral part of the record keeping process. The shredding of records is the organized way of disposal. There are a number of companies that specialize in making available a record retention timetable that describes retention periods allowed by government authorities as well as the appropriate way to dispose of records safely without loss or worry.

KINDS OF RECORDS

The kinds of records a practice should maintain are not specified by the law. However, regardless of the system of bookkeeping selected, the books must be permanent and contain a systematic record that will accurately and clearly reflect income, deductions, credits, and other matters that must be reported in an income tax return. Memorandums or sketchy records that merely approximate income, deductions, or other pertinent items affecting one's tax liability are not considered adequate for compliance with the law.

The physician is required to keep available at all times the books and records of his practice for inspection by Internal Revenue officials. These records must be retained as long as their contents may become material in the administration of any Internal Revenue law.

A recent survey of physicians' tax advisers reveals the single most important problem to be income reporting. The Internal Revenue Service judges income by especially severe criteria. If one does not have the exact figures on his deductions, he can take a chance and estimate them because there exists a gray area between exaggeration and fraud. But when it comes to income there is no such thing as a gray area. If one fails to report all of it, he is open to a charge of fraud. The point to be made here is that any mistake on reporting income can lead to a suspicion of wrongdoing, and agents are likely to follow up such leads by making an audit more difficult. Examining agents know that physicians traditionally have trouble reporting their incomes accurately.

The physician is responsible for making sure that all practice-connected receipts are reported as income. Checking bank deposits against receipts is not a bad starting point, but this method has shortcomings if one uncritically accepts the deposits as the basis of one's receipts, rather than using the figures from the daily log. For one thing, if the physician borrowed any money during the year and deposited the proceeds of the loan in his professional account, his total deposits will be artificially inflated. He may also inflate deposits with the proceeds of stock sales or dividend and interest payments. Perhaps the only accurate way to compute all practice-connected income is to check the daily logs for each week and each month against patients' ledgers.

According to recent surveys, it is apparent that many physicians with elaborate systems for keeping track of practice income have trouble tracking down and reporting outside income. The fees doctors receive from such professional activities as speaking or writing are a frequent source of tax trouble, the Internal Revenue Service reports. Investment income constitutes another problem area.

The physician's books should be set up in accordance with the method of accounting selected. After determining the period that constitutes the doctor's tax year, the doctor's accountant will normally arrange the books to coincide with this 12-month period. If the books or records are judged to be inadequate under these circumstances, the physician may be required to use the calendar year for federal tax purposes.

Whenever possible, all disbursements should be made by check so that expenses may be well documented. Checks should not be made payable to cash or to oneself unless they are drawn for personal reasons. If it is necessary to make a check payable to cash or to oneself in order to pay a professional expense in cash, a receipt for the cash payment should be made a part of the records. If the physician, for instance, cannot obtain a receipt for a cash payment, he should see to it that an adequate explanation is placed in the records at the time such payment is made.

Accounts must be properly classified, and all expenditures should be posted to the correct account. Like matter should be grouped under appropriate headings such as purchases, rent, repairs, supplies, and so on. Accounts listed as assets should reflect detailed information such as the dates of acquisition, cost, depreciation, depletion, and any other item that affects the basis of such property.

Invoices and paid bills should not be filed together without regard to date or the types of items involved. One method is to have an alphabetical index by subject for each year. Invoices for purchases, rent, repairs, supplies, and so on would be filed separately according to subject. This makes it easy for examination at the end of each fiscal year and to determine the various amounts of monies spent in each of these categories. In addition, physicians often may wish to reorder a specific supply or instrument that had been purchased several years before. By checking back through the subject file, it is easy to ascertain from what company the supply or instrument was obtained and what the initial cost was.

There are many excellent simplified bookkeeping systems on the market today that are designed specifically for physicians. They are not an absolute necessity, for the doctor can get along without a purchased system if he is willing to pay for the services of a regular bookkeeper. The single most important advantage of a bookkeeping system is that it brings all phases of bookkeeping together and combines them into a single volume.

Some medical practice consultants strongly recommend that physicians use a "write-it-once" type of bookkeeping. Such a system, as opposed to a "write-it-twice" system, guarantees current postings and facilitates the simultaneous posting of daybook and patients' ledger cards, they contend.

Machine posting is one of three basic ways to accomplish write-it-once bookkeeping. It requires the use of a bookkeeping machine, however. Using a source document such as a charge slip, the medical assistant can, in a single operation, post a transaction to the ledger card and also make out the patient's bill ready for mailing. At closing time, the machine totals the day's charges and payments received at the touch of a key, giving the needed data. The arithmetic required to arrive at each ledger card's new balance is done by the machine. At billing time, the assistant mails out all statements that show outstanding balances. There are also machines available that will list and total charges and payments for different kinds of services for the physician who wants to know how much of his income comes from office visits, how much from hospital visits, how much from diagnostic tests, and so on.

Pegboard posting is another write-it-once bookkeeping system consisting of nothing more than a clipboard fitted with pegs down one edge rather than a spring clip at the top. The pegs hold the forms used by the system and maintain them in proper alignment. The three basic forms comprising the system are a daybook sheet, a patient ledger card, and a charge slip. The charge slip tells more than the fee that is due—it also serves as a receipt for the patient's next appointment. To do her posting the assistant uses a ballpoint pen or hard black pencil. She computes a new balance and arrives at her daily totals with the aid of an adding machine. For monthly statements she can use a pen, a typewriter, or an office copier. The chief advantage of this system is that the patient receives his first bill while he is in the office, and his ledger card is posted in his presence. There is no time lag and no accumulation of postings, which frequently cause billing mistakes.

A third way to accomplish write-it-once bookkeeping is computer billing, which requires the sophisticated services of a data processing firm. This will be discussed in more detail in Chapter 18.

A physician's bookkeeping system need not be complicated and as a matter of fact some of the most efficient systems are the simplest ones. The physician's choice of any one of these systems should be based on the volume of the monthly billings and the capabilities of the office staff to cope with the complexities of the system. Also, each system has certain advantages as well as disadvantages when related to a particular type of practice.

Regardless of the bookkeeping system or method chosen by the physician, it should be relatively easy to maintain. Any system must be able to generate the following basic information:

1. A record of daily income (money actually collected) and expenses.
2. A record of the amount of fees charged to patients' accounts each day (but not necessarily collected). The physician's books, as are those of most professional men, are usually kept on a cash basis. In other words, the physician's taxable income consists of only cash receipts. Outstanding patient charges are not considered as income or figured as such until actually received. In professional bookkeeping, therefore, there is no need for a separate accounts receivable control.
3. The total annual income.
4. The total annual expenses. Taxes are paid only on net income, which consists of collected income after expenses are deducted.

No one system will meet the needs of every physician, but every good one includes the following basic elements.

1. A daily log or appointment book. Many daily logs for physicians also contain a provision for recording daily receipts.
2. A combined journal indicating all income and disbursements made during a monthly period. Daily disbursements may be recorded according to check number, to whom issued, and the appropriate account charged or debited. For those expenses that occur frequently, special columns are established and headed with the appropriate description.
3. A patient's ledger upon which patients' charges are entered, payments made are recorded, and outstanding balances posted (Fig. 17-1). The ledger serves as a chronologic history of a patient's account. Patient ledgers should be kept separate from patients' folders, and a ledger should be maintained for each patient. If the ledger is brought up to date each day, it reflects a current picture of the patient's account.
4. A general (permanent) ledger, which is a chart containing all of the physician's accounts. From the information provided in the general ledger it is a simple matter to compute a summary of the physician's assets, liabilities, income, and expenses.
5. Individual employee earning records. A separate payroll sheet, also known as a compensation record, must be maintained for each employee. The employee's earning record (Fig. 17-2) contains the necessary information on each employee such as his social security number, his home address, and the number of exemptions he claims. Each time the employee is paid it must be recorded on his payroll record sheet. The gross salary earned, net salary paid, income tax withheld, social security tax deducted, and state unem-

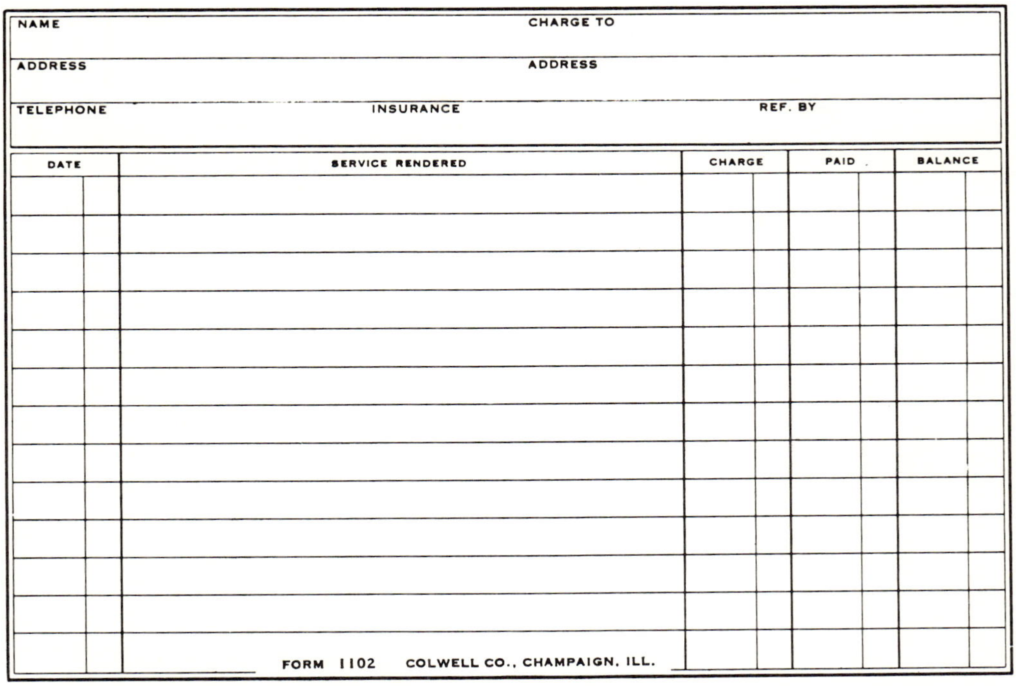

NAME CHARGE TO

ADDRESS ADDRESS

TELEPHONE INSURANCE REF. BY

DATE	SERVICE RENDERED	CHARGE	PAID	BALANCE

FORM 1102 COLWELL CO., CHAMPAIGN, ILL.

Fig. 17-1. Patient's ledger card. (Courtesy The Colwell Company, Champaign, Illinois.)

ployment tax deducted (where applicable) must be posted to the individual's compensation record each pay period. Each compensation record can be used for the entire year, and quarterly totals can be easily figured for use in completing the quarterly report to the government.

6. Petty cash account (to be described later in this chapter).
7. Trial balance sheets, which are used for running a trial balance of the general ledger of accounts as of the end of each month. The trial balance sheet (Fig. 17-3) may be used to list each account according to whether it is a debit or a credit. After the balances of all the accounts have been posted, the two columns are footed or totaled; these totals must equal one another in order to achieve a balance of accounts, thereby verifying the equality of debits and credits.

BOOKKEEPING FUNDAMENTALS

A method of accounting is a set of rules under which the accountant ascertains when and how to record income and expenses in the physician's books. It also includes instructions in preparing the profit and loss statement for the physician's accounting period. If the physician employs a professional management consultant, his firm may install its record keeping system in your office or provide guidance in the selection of a suitable system.

Consistency is most important, for whoever is responsible for computing the physician's taxable income must do so in accordance with the method regularly used in keeping the books, provided that method clearly reflects the physician's income. "Any method of accounting which reflects the consistent application of generally accepted accounting principles in a business or profession and in accordance with accepted conditions

NAME　　　　EMPL. NO.　　　　SOC. SEC. NO.

ADDRESS　　　　WITHHOLDING EXEMPTIONS

DATE OF BIRTH

	DATE		HOURS WORKED		RATE PER HOUR	E A R N I N G S			CUMULATIVE TOTAL	D E D U C T I O N S		
	PER. ENDED	PAID	TOT. HRS.	O. T. HRS.		REGULAR AMOUNT		TOTAL AMOUNT		F. I. C. A.	INCOME TAX WITHHELD	OTHER

Fig. 17-2. Employee's earnings record.

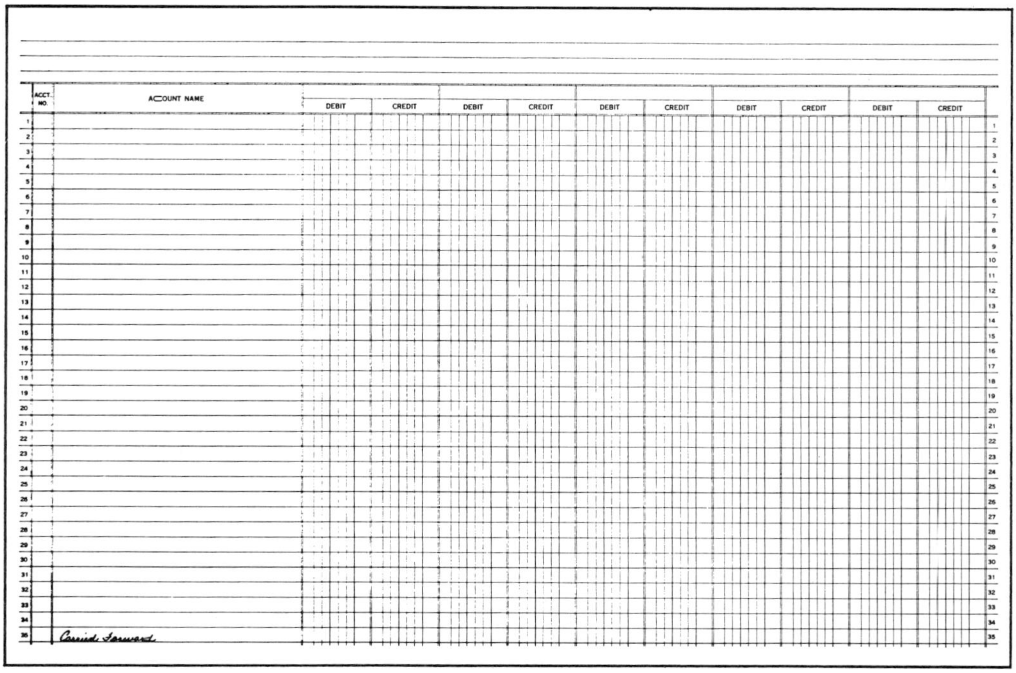

Fig. 17-3. Trial balance worksheet.

or practices in such a business or profession will ordinarily be regarded as clearly reflecting income."* A particular method of accounting does not clearly reflect income unless all items of gross income and deductions are treated consistently from year to year.

No one particular method of accounting is prescribed for all taxpayers. Each taxpayer, be he individual or corporate, is required to adopt such forms and systems of accounting that are in his judgment best suited to his purpose and that will enable him to make a tax return reflecting true income. In order to accomplish this, it is necessary, in addition to permanent records of account, to maintain additional records and data (receipts, vouchers, and so on) as may be required to substantiate entries made on the books and on tax returns.

*From U. S. Treasury Department: Tax guide for small business, Internal Revenue Service Report No. 334, Washington, D. C., 1965, Government Printing Office, p. 14.

The physician's financial status is reported in a formal report called a balance sheet. The accounts are classified under the following divisions: assets, liabilities, proprietorship or equity, income, and expense. The balance sheet may be described as a statement showing the financial condition of a practice or business on a given date. Much like other formal accounting statements, the balance sheet provides answers to who, what, and when.

The word balance in the term balance sheet has a rather special meaning. It serves to emphasize that the sum of the figures on the left equals the sum of the figures on the right. In accounting terminology, assets are equal to the sum of the liabilities plus the proprietorship. Expressed in equation form:

$$\text{Assets} = \text{Liabilities} + \text{Proprietorship (Owner's Equity)}$$

This relationship is called the fundamental equation in accounting.

Most businesses use what is known as a double entry system. This practice involves recording both effects of a transaction in order to present a more complete picture. Entries made on the left side of the ledger are called debits, and entries recorded on the right side are called credits. While it is difficult to arrive at specific definitions of the terms debit and credit, a debit is best described as something owed on account, and a credit is something paid on account. Professional men usually maintain their books on a cash basis, and also use only a double entry system in recording transactions.

A general ledger usually consists of a book of accounts with a separate sheet for each individual account. The bookkeeper posts monthly totals from the daily journal (daily record) to the general ledger, and as such it constitutes a record of final entry and the master reference book for the entire bookkeeping system. On the other hand, the daily journal is commonly known as a book of original entry. This process of transferring data from one record to another record (the daily journal to the general ledger) is known as posting. A check mark placed beside a transaction serves as a reminder that the details of the transaction have been posted to the appropriate account or record. The check mark is merely a precautionary measure to guard against posting the same entry twice or not at all.

The process of recording all the details of a transaction in the daily journal before an entry is made in the general ledger is known as journalizing. By following this process, the bookkeeper is assured of having all the data in one place before any details are forgotten.

In working with numbers and placing figures in their proper location on accounting sheets, experienced bookkeepers and accountants record digits in columns, working from right to left and beginning with cents. Also, in posting to accounting records, it is not necessary to include dollar signs, for it is assumed that money is involved.

A situation often arises where it is necessary to record a debit transaction, and no debit column has been established in the daily journal for that particular account. The best alternative solution is to post the amount involved with a circle around it under the appropriate account in the credit column. Placing a circle around a figure indicates to the bookkeeper that it is to be subtracted from the column total or cumulative total to that point.

One of the first actions of an accountant employed by the physician would be to make a thorough study of the physician's practice in order to develop an appropriate chart of accounts. This provides a starting point for the design of a suitable journal that will be compatible with the doctor's practice. Special columns can be justified in the daily journal (combined journal) only for those accounts that are likely to be used a great deal in recording routine transactions. This journal is ideally adaptable to record the transactions of a professional man, especially a physician.

The medical assistant who takes care of the physician's bookkeeping is certainly not expected to possess as much financial knowledge as an accountant. Indeed, this is precisely the reason most physicians entrust the confidential details of their finances to those with the proper training and background. Nevertheless, the assistant who is curious and makes a special effort to become familiar with some of the more important concepts of accounting will do a more efficient job of record keeping. Terms such as current assets, fixed assets, current liabilities, and long-term liabilities represent concepts the assistant-bookkeeper frequently encounters and with which she should become familiar.

Current assets are those assets that will usually be converted into cash or consumed during the operation of a business cycle or within a relatively short period of time. Fixed assets consist of a piece of land or the building owned by a business. In other words, fixed assets are long-lived property that is used permanently in the conduct of a business operation. The physician's major medical equipment such as x-ray machine, electrocardiogram machine, and examining table are fixed assets. Current liabilities are obligations that mature within a relatively short period of time. Usually they must be paid within one year or paid out of the current assets of a business realized over a normal operating cycle. Long-term liabilities are those debts of a business that are not due for more than a year in the future. The mortgage on a building is considered a long-term liability.

The physician should maintain accurate records on personal affairs as well. Such records include his property ledger in which he enters information about his personal property, real estate, securities, professional travel, and other tax deductible expenses and honoraria, and so forth. He will also want to set up separate files for listing his insurance and other personal financial information.

He must maintain bank accounts and it is much simpler to keep separate accounts for his practice and his personal affairs. All deposits from fees and all withdrawals for professional expenditures should be handled through his professional account. Ideally, a deposit should be made daily for each day's receipts with the deposit slip made up from the information on the day sheet.

PETTY CASH FUND

Practically every office maintains a petty cash fund. This fund eliminates the necessity of writing numerous checks for the disbursement of small amounts of money. From time to time (usually monthly) the money expended from the petty cash fund is replaced by writing a check for the exact amount and cashing it. At the time the fund is reimbursed, the petty cash vouchers and receipts are analyzed to determine the amount and kind of each expense. This is done so that the appropriate accounts can be charged or debited.

Petty cash is normally used for such incidental expenses as tips, stamps, coffee, newspapers, cards, cleaning supplies, cigarettes, ink, and pencils. In other words, the petty cash fund is established for items that are too small to justify being taken through the entire bookkeeping cycle. The assistant must exercise discretion in dispensing funds from petty cash. Major expense items should be paid for by check; otherwise the petty cash fund becomes depleted too rapidly.

To initiate a petty cash fund, a check is drawn and made out to petty cash for an amount sufficient to cover approximately one month's incidental expenses. The average medical office petty cash fund ranges anywhere from $10 to $50. Some offices require a larger amount, depending upon their needs. The amount of the check is entered in the daily journal as an expense or disbursement for that particular day. The check itself is usually taken to the bank to be cashed along with the regular deposit for the day.

To facilitate the work of the bank teller and save time, the assistant should attach a separate sheet of paper to the check indicating the currency breakdown desired in dollar bills, quarters, dimes, nickles, and pennies. If the amount of the check is $10, a practical breakdown might consist of four dollar bills, 18 quarters, 5 dimes, 10 nickles, and 50 pennies—a total of $10.

All monies spent from the petty cash fund are immediately recorded in a special expense book or listed on some type of petty cash expense sheet that actually describes the expense. Whenever possible the assistant should try to obtain receipts or vouchers for expenditures.

Petty cash currency is generally placed in a small cashbox, and the special expense book or sheet should be small enough to fit inside. At the end of the month or whenever the fund becomes depleted, the expenses are totaled from the expense book and a check is written for this amount. For example, if an office maintains a monthly petty cash fund of $10 and the expenses from petty cash for a monthly period total $8.45, the amount remaining in the cash box should be $1.55. By drawing a check for $8.45, cashing it, and adding the currency to the cash on hand, the original balance of $10 is replaced. At any time, the amount of cash on hand plus the total of expenses should equal the original amount.

PRACTICE MANAGEMENT

The role of the accountant or management consultant in business and industry is an increasingly important one. Not only does he provide the necessary information through recording and reporting, but the accountant also assists management in the interpretation of financial reports. Moreover, accountants are often called upon to render advice concerning special problems and to offer guidance in the financial planning of future operations. In most cases the medical assistant works in close conjunction with an accountant-consultant who is retained by the physician to advise him on financial matters, make out various government reports, and prepare annual income tax returns. The assistant should feel free to contact the accountant's office when seeking information or searching for solutions to record-keeping problems.

The many complexities that comprise medical office practice today have increased the ranks of those who specialize in giving business help to physicians from about 150 in 1959 to well over 500. More and more physicians are becoming aware of the management consultant and wondering whether he could make their offices run more smoothly and profitably. Whatever the cause and effect, surveys indicate that physicians who use management consultants tend to be in the higher income brackets.

The following is a list of the problems most management consultants are capable of dealing with:

- Income on expenses
- Double-entry ledger bookkeeping
- Billing (not billing service)
- Fees, taxes, insurance
- Medical records
- Business records
- Financial analysis
- Collections (not collection agency service)
- Patient relations
- Office systems and procedures
- Employee recruitment and compensation
- Medical buildings
- Physician recruitment
- Professional corporations
- Semiretirement and retirement
- Legislation affecting practice
- Investments
- HMOs, foundations, prepaid plans
- Office layout, equipment, furnishings
- Practice expansion
- Partnerships
- Professional relations
- Closing of practices
- Pension and profit sharing plans
- Estate planning and wills
- Emergency room practice

Matching up consultants and physicians is a problem that the Society of Professional Business Consultants recognizes and is trying to correct. A physician needs more than a glorified accounting service, which in itself indicates that there is more to practice management than hiring an accountant-consultant. A physician should have some idea as to what services he wants and then make sure he obtains a consultant who can furnish them. A consultant cannot, however, manage all aspects of the doctor's practice for him. There have been situations where the doctor, after hiring a consultant, became so absorbed in patient care activities he was oblivious to the fact that his office staff while getting along well with patients were making an absolute mess of the office records. At the same time, his management consultant concentrated on accounting chores only and neglected practice management.

There are certain precautions that every physician should take to keep his finger on the pulse of the business side of his practice, even if he has no professional adviser at all. A lack of time is no excuse since by setting aside as little as ten minutes a day a physician can make checks that will enable him to avoid serious record-keeping problems. The following are a few simple ones that should be made regularly.

1. Check a few entries on the daysheet or daily log against postings on patients' ledger cards to be sure that charges and payments are being recorded.
2. Look at each deposit slip before the deposit goes to the bank, and check the

cash total on the day sheet against the deposit on the deposit slip.

3. Flip through a few statements just before they are mailed, to check for general appearance, itemization, full listing of charges, payment balances, and exceptionally large balances that should be brought to patients' attention.
4. Jot down a few patient services as they are rendered and later check these services to make sure they were recorded in the daily log and patients' ledger cards.

In addition, management consultant firms recommend that physicians confer occasionally with their assistants to find out how they spend their time, what problems they have, and where they file important records. Some consultants even recommend that physicians periodically hire temporary outside help as a means of uncovering irregularities in office procedures. The need for such drastic measures is greatly reduced if there exists a good dialogue between the physician, the office staff, and the practice management consultant.

Review questions

1. List at least three good reasons every physician's office must keep adequate records.
2. What is the advantage of a bookkeeping system?
3. Although the law does not specifically recommend any particular record system, it does insist upon one requirement. What is this requirement that should be characteristic of record keeping systems?
4. If you were asked by the doctor to set up a bookkeeping system for his new office, what basic information would you expect it to provide?
5. What is a general ledger?
6. Define the following double entry system and fundamental equation.
7. Explain the significance of placing a circle around a figure in a credit column.
8. What is the purpose of maintaining a petty cash fund?
9. Name at least eight items for which you would dispense petty cash funds.
10. Explain the procedure for replenishing the petty cash fund.
11. How can the physician's accountant help the medical assistant?

Suggested readings

Freeman, M. H., et al.: Gregg bookkeeping and accounting, ed. 3, New York, 1963, McGraw-Hill Book Co.

The American Medical Association: The business side of medical practice, Chicago, 1973, The Association.

U. S. Treasury Department: Tax guide for small business, Internal Revenue Service Report No. 334, Washington, D. C., 1965, Government Printing Office.

chapter 18
Banking activities

CHECKS

Most people are inclined to think that checks are a relatively new convenience. Actually, the use of checks is an old practice. Clay tablets representing checks that date back to the ninth century have been unearthed by archeologists. Some African tribesmen used giraffe tails for financial transactions. King Edward I of England, who reigned from 1272 to 1307, used checks in payment for purchases he had made. Checks were introduced in Italy in the fifteenth century. However, they were not used widely as a medium of exchange in Europe until the 1800s.

A check (Fig. 18-1) is a written order for the payment of money through a bank. Anyone who has sufficient funds in a checking account at a bank may write a check directing the bank to pay a specified sum to a specifically named individual or to the bearer. The person who receives payment is called the payee. The person drawing the check is known as the originator or maker. Checks are used by both business firms and individuals. The medical assistant collects and processes checks received in payment for the physician's services. She also writes checks to pay his professional expenses. The use of checks makes it possible to exchange large sums without keeping like quantities of cash or currency on hand. In addition to the advantage of safety, the use of checks simplifies the task of balancing receipts and disbursements.

The signature on a check should always be written exactly like the original specimen on file at the bank. When a person opens a checking account, he signs his name on a card. The bank later compares this signature with the signature on the drawn checks to be sure they match. It is also important that a check be endorsed exactly the way it is made out to the payee.

Although checks are ordinarily written on a special form provided by the bank, any clear statement to pay, properly signed, may be legally accepted for payment by a bank. In fact, the check forms of one bank may be substituted for another by crossing out

---

Glossary

check a written order for the payment of money through a bank

depositor one who places funds with a bank for his own account, subject to withdrawal on his order

EDP abbreviation for electronic data processing

endorsement the signature of the payee or other holder placed on the back of the check or other commercial paper for the purpose of transferring ownership

overdraft the act of overdrawing a bank account

payee the person or firm to whom a check is payable

postdated refers to a check bearing a future date; one that has not yet matured and is therefore not negotiable

recapitulate to repeat the principal points of some treatise; to sum up

reconciliation the process by which the balance shown in a checkbook and the balance shown in the bank's statement are checked against one another and the difference accounted for

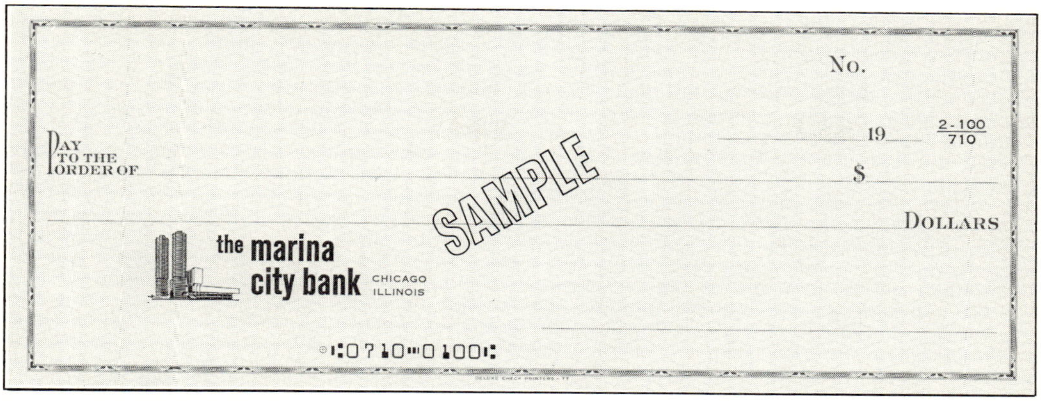

Fig. 18-1. Commercial check. (Courtesy Marina City Bank, Chicago, Illinois.)

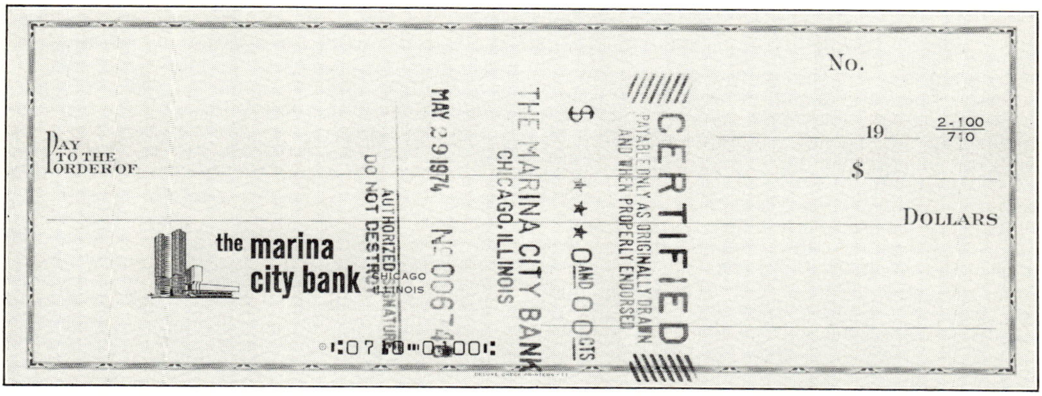

Fig. 18-2. Certified check. (Courtesy Marina City Bank, Chicago, Illinois.)

the name of the bank on the check and writing in the new name along with the other pertinent information. This practice is frowned upon by the banks and should be avoided since the depositor may in the absence of a format forget to record all the details of the payment. The making of a check with the words "Pay to cash" or "Bearer" is not advisable. These words make the check payable to anyone holding the check. If the check is lost, anyone who finds it may cash it.

A check generally possesses three functions: (1) the payee may obtain cash for it, (2) it may be transferred or assigned to another person, or (3) it may be deposited to one's own bank account.

If one wishes to cash a check, he merely signs his name on the back across the left end of the check. This is called endorsement in blank. However, if such a check is lost, there is a chance that anyone finding it may cash it since it is already endorsed. Therefore, the payee should refrain from endorsing a check until he is ready to deposit it or cash it at the bank. All checks received from patients should be readied for deposit. Practically every office maintains a rubber stamp to facilitate the deposit of checks and save the doctor from having to endorse each one individually. Such a stamp usually reads "Deposit to the account of Dr. ...."

A payee may transfer a check to another person by simply writing: "Pay to the order of (name)," above his own endorsement. The person to whom the check is endorsed becomes the new payee and must then add his signature before the check can be cashed. It is important that the payee endorse his name exactly as it appears on the face of the check. If the spelling is not correct, the proper spelling may be given below the endorsement.

There are certain creditors and governmental agencies who will not accept a personal check as payment. Often they require a certified check or a cashier's check. A certified check (Fig. 18-2) or a cashier's check is sometimes required for the payment of special fees. For example, the U. S. Treasury Department requires either a certified check or a cashier's check for payment of the fee for the annual renewal of a physician's narcotics license. Moving companies, for obvious reasons, often request a certified check or even a cashier's check.

Cashier's checks and certified checks accomplish a similar purpose; they both guarantee to the payee that the depositor possesses sufficient funds in his account to cover the amount of the check. Such checks are accepted as readily as cash since there is no chance that the checks will be returned. The bank upon which the checks are drawn actually assumes responsibility for their payment.

There is, however, a slight difference between the certified check and the cashier's check. A certified check is written for the required amount on the depositor's personal check form. This check must then be taken to the bank and stamped "Certified" by the bank. At this time the necessary funds may be transferred from the depositor's account to the bank's own account or held out and placed in the bank's neutral account for future payment. A number of banks levy a small service charge for both certified checks and cashier's checks, especially when funds are to be withdrawn from a checking account. Most banks, however, do not make a charge for such checks when the money is to be withdrawn from a savings account. Perhaps banks feel that the goodwill of the depositor is more important.

On the other hand, a check written on the bank's form and made payable out of its own account is known as a cashier's check. Normally, before drawing such a check, the teller first debits the depositor's account the amount indicated and transfers the funds to the bank's own account, thus ensuring payment. The cashier's check is more frequently used to withdraw funds from a savings account than from a checking account.

Other types of checks include the counter check and the limited check. A counter check may be written by the physician to draw funds from his own checking account. This kind of check serves as a record of cash withdrawn from the account when his checkbook is not available. The form upon which the check may be written is generally provided by the bank.

A so-called limited check may not be made out for more than a certain amount. A statement may appear on the check specifying the maximum amount and indicating that the check is void if written for more than that amount. This type of check is often used for payroll and insurance payments.

Money orders also fall into the category of checks. A money order is a type of check purchased for a particular fee. Actually, there are three different kinds of money orders. Express money orders are purchased from and drawn on the American Express and Railway Express companies. Postal money orders are bought from and drawn upon the U. S. Post Office. This is the type most frequently used and most familiar to everyone. Finally, there are bank money orders, which are purchased from and drawn upon a particular bank. Money orders are somewhat similar to cashier's checks and certified checks in that payment is guaranteed.

A traveler's check is a check designed specifically for the traveler who is unable to use his personal check because it probably will not be accepted in a city where he is not known. Moreover, the traveler is always advised not to carry a large amount of cash on his person. When traveler's checks are purchased a small fee is charged for the service. Currently American Express traveler's checks cost $1 for each $100 purchased. Cooke's traveler's checks cost the same.

The purchaser is required to sign his name on the face of the check in the presence of a bank official or some other authorized witness. When cashing the check, the purchaser again signs his name in the presence of the person cashing the check. In this way the individual cashing the check can compare the two signatures to be sure that the endorsement is legitimate. Only one endorsement is permitted on traveler's checks. Like certified checks, cashier's checks, and money orders, traveler's checks guarantee payment and are used in lieu of cash.

If the physician makes a trip and purchases traveler's checks to use for expenses, an office record of the check numbers should be made. In case the checks are lost or stolen, if the numbers can be furnished to the source of purchase, replacement is guaranteed.

All outgoing checks should be submitted to the physician for signature. The only exception to this practice occurs when the physician grants power of attorney to someone else, perhaps the assistant. By filling out a form for the bank the physician can make arrangements to permit another person to sign checks for any single account. This might be necessary when the phyisican is to be away from the office for a prolonged period of time.

Stopping payment on a lost check or a check the originator no longer wishes to pay is accomplished by notifying the bank, hopefully before the check is presented for payment by the payee. This is usually done by calling the bank and instructing them to stop payment on that particular check, giving the number, the date, the name of the payee, the amount of the check, and the account number. A telephone call is not always sufficient by itself; it usually must

Account No. ______ Name ______ No.

Please refuse to pay Check No. ______ Amount ______

Payable to ______ Dated ______

I agree to hold you harmless for all expenses and costs incurred by you on account of refusing payment of said check and agree not to hold you liable on account of payment contrary to this request if same occurs through inadvertence, accident, or oversight. And it is understood that this order will automatically expire at such time as established by banking regulations, unless renewed in writing.

Signed ______

Received by ______ Date Rec'd. ______ Time ______ How Received. ______

Duplicate ______ Dated ______ No. ______ Marked Duplicate ______

Reason for stop payment is ______

Telephone ______ Address ______

RELEASE: Please release Stop Payment on the above check.

THE MARINA CITY BANK
300 N. STATE STREET
CHICAGO, ILLINOIS

Signed ______

Fig. 18-3. Stop payment notice. (Courtesy Marina City Bank, Chicago, Illinois.)

be confirmed in writing. Some banks even require a personal appearance by the depositor. Should the Stop Payment Notice (Fig. 18-3) issued by the bank be dated and confirmed prior to the time the check reaches the bank for payment out of the depositor's account, and the bank slips up and cashes it anyway, the depositor is entitled to damages. These usually amount to the sum wrongfully paid out by the bank. Businesses and professional men must be extremely careful about cashing checks. For instance, if the Stop Payment Notice is in effect before the check reaches the bank for payment, and the bank does not slip up and honor the check, the originator of the check is not completely freed from all responsibility. The innocent third party who cashed the check for the payee may claim to have done so in good faith and seek to negotiate with the originator of the check for reimbursement. The bank should also be notified in case a check is lost or misplaced. A second replacing check may be issued and marked "Duplicate." Remember that a check that is more than six months old is referred to as a "stale" check and a bank is not required to honor it.

The originator of a check must fill it in with care to prevent alterations or tampering. If he does so, the bank is held responsible for payment as indicated by the depositor. But the depositor may lose this protection if he carelessly leaves blank spaces in which additional figures could be inserted. A bank is not liable for any loss incurred through a tampered check made possible by the writer's negligence. This is precisely why the prudent check writer draws lines through all blank spaces and leaves no room for alterations.

Most offices that write numerous checks maintain a machine known as a check protector, which usually precludes tampering. Such a machine perforates the check with the amount to be paid, thereby enabling banks to process the checks with greater accuracy. The magnetic characters or numbers printed on the check usually identify the person drawing the check and the bank on which it is drawn.

CHECKING ACCOUNTS

A checking account provides a complete and permanent record of all sums of money deposited in a bank and a record of all expenses paid. It simplifies bookkeeping considerably.

There are many variations among checking accounts, depending upon the individual bank. Basically there are three general types: (1) ordinary checking account, (2) special checking account, and (3) business or commercial checking account.

With an ordinary or individual checking account, the depositor purchases three or four books of checks for a nominal sum. Each checkbook usually contains at least 25 checks. The bank debits the depositor's account with a handling charge for each check issued and paid from the depositor's account. The depositor must be very careful to deduct from the balance in his checkbook the fee for each check written in order to avoid embarrassing and costly overdrafts.

For a special checking account, the bank makes a flat monthly charge for the handling of the account, and the cost of checkbooks is paid by the depositor. The depositor is permitted to write an agreed number of checks (usually 20) each month, and there is no charge for each individual check. This type of checking account is most appealing to an individual who writes a fixed number of checks each month.

In the case of the business or commercial checking account, a large quantity of checks is purchased or, in some cases, furnished by banks to large depositors free of charge. If a depositor maintains an agreed upon balance in his account at all times there may be no charge at all. On the other hand, if the balance in the account falls below the agreed upon amount, a service charge is sometimes levied by the bank. The professional man's checkbook usually contains approximately 300 checks.

Some banks offer checking accounts containing elements of all three of the previously described. There seems to be a trend for new banks, anxious to become established and grow in size, to offer regular checking accounts that are service free and require no minimum balance.

The most important advantage of an efficient procedure for recording cash receipts is that the funds reach the bank sooner preferably on the date received. Cash receipts should not be kept on the premises. Not only are they safer in the bank, but as deposits they constitute funds available to pay bills owed by the depositor.

Practices of individual banks vary in identifying the checks to be deposited. In making out a deposit slip (Fig. 18-4) the medical assistant fills in the date, the physician's name and address, and the account number. Cash amounts are listed in the space adjacent to the heading "Coin" or "Currency." The currency should be sorted according to denomination and totaled; that is, all dollar bills together, all five-dollar bills together, and so on. In this way the teller can count the money rapidly. Each check to be deposited is listed separately on the deposit slip, and the total sum of all checks and cash is listed on the bottom line. Checks are identified by the number assigned individual banks by the American Banking Association. This is often referred

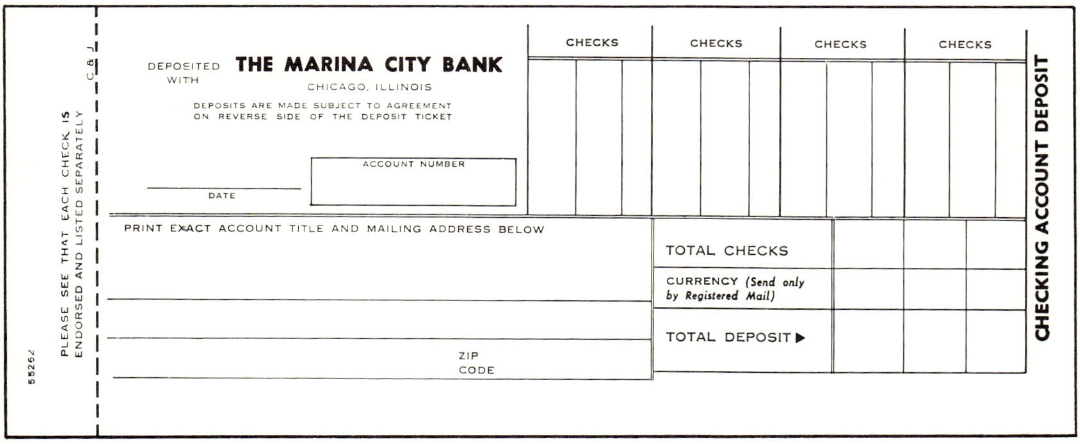

Fig. 18-4. Deposit slip. (Courtesy Marina City Bank, Chicago, Illinois.)

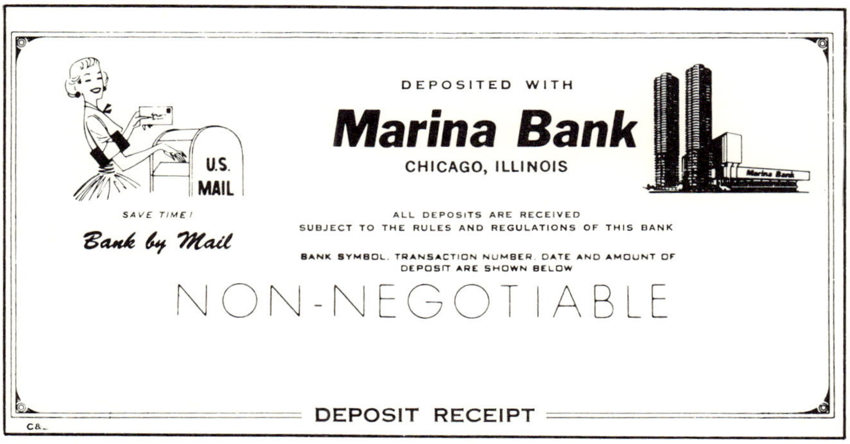

Fig. 18-5. Deposit receipt slip. (Courtesy Marina City Bank, Chicago, Illinois.)

to as the A.B.A. number. Once the deposit slip is completed and totaled, the day's receipts should be sent to the bank. A receipt (Fig. 18-5) is usually obtained from the bank as evidence that the funds were deposited. This receipt should be filed or attached to the duplicate copy of the deposit slip for future reference. After a deposit has been made the amount is entered in the checkbook and added to the previous balance.

Most banks issue their professional depositors a bank deposit book containing blank deposit slips and blank sheets for duplicate copies. Some banks issue a triple deposit slip, keeping two for their own records and returning the carbon copy to the depositor. These slips should also be filed and can be used monthly to reconcile deposits with bank statements.

Before checks are deposited they should be examined to make sure they have been properly made out with reference to date, amounts, and signature. Each check should also be examined on the back side for an endorsement or stamp. Checks bearing future dates (postdated) are generally not acceptable by banks for deposit and are often returned to a depositor with a bill for a service charge. It is encumbent upon the assistant to keep track of the physician's bank balance and never to issue checks for sums greater than are on deposit above the minimum balance required by the bank if this is applicable.

BASIC RULES FOR HANDLING MONIES

When accepting a personal check, the assistant must always be aware that a check drawn on a special account is more likely to be returned than a check drawn against a regular account. If the patient has failed to balance his records carefully, his account may not possess sufficient funds to cover the check. There is also the chance that he may not have waited three banking days, as recommended by banks, before writing a check on his last deposit. There are many occasions where a check written under such circumstances will be returned unpaid to the physician's office marked "Uncollected funds." This presents bookkeeping problems and means that the check must be redeposited and again presented for payment.

The medical assistant is usually safe in accepting checks from known patients. In addition, there is little or no risk in accepting any of the guaranteed-payment checks such as certified checks and cashier's checks. Bank authorities usually recommend that when accepting personal checks it is good practice to request proper identification since there is always an element of risk involved in accepting personal checks from new or transient patients.

The following list of reminders recapitulates some of the more important rules for handling monies.

1. Checks that arrive in the mail or those handed to the medical assistant by patients should immediately be endorsed on the back with a rubber stamp reading, "Deposit to the account of (doctor's name), M.D."
2. Each check received for payment should be examined before being included in the bank deposit to make sure it is properly endorsed. It also should be checked to make sure it is properly made out.
3. When a check is drawn to pay a bill, the stub or receipt should always be filled out before completing the check in order to avoid the possibility of sending off the check and forgetting the details. If someone demands a check in advance of providing a service or a product, it is wise to add the additional endorsement: "Good only on satisfactory completion of (such-and-such a service or provision of such-and-such a product)."

   Checks received marked "Payment in full" must be handled carefully especially when there is some dispute over the amount of the bill. If there is a disagreement as to the amount, by signing and cashing a check marked

"Payment in full," the depositor forfeits his right to collect any additional money. The best way to proceed is probably to return the check to the originator and insist on full payment. Checks can present collection problems, unless you have a definite system or guidelines for dealing with them.

4. Figures on checks should be written close to the dollar sign, and the words should start at the beginning of the line to guard against any alteration, which could be made by placing another figure or word before the correct amount.
5. On the line provided for writing the amount of a check in words, the cents are usually expressed in fractions, that is, fifty cents would be written 50/100, or if the amount is for even dollars, no/100 would be added. When a check is made out for less than one dollar, the entry should read, "only fifty cents" or "only seventy-five cents," with the amount written out in words.
6. There must be a minimum of corrections or erasures on a check, or it will not be accepted by the bank. If a gross mistake has been made, the check should be destroyed, the check stub marked "Void," and the next check used. If it is necessary to keep checks in number sequence, it is permissible to write a new check using the same number.
7. Checks made out to "Cash" or "Bearer" must be handled with care, and such checks for large amounts should not be sent through the mail. In the event that such checks become lost, anyone who finds them can cash them.
8. Checks must not be dated ahead of time. Banks will not pay out funds or accept for deposit checks bearing future dates. Legally, a postdated check is considered a loan rather than payment for anything until it matures.
9. A check drawn in excess of money in an account will cause an overdraft. The check will, of course, not be paid by the bank when presented but returned to the depositor. A charge, sometimes as much as $5, is usually levied by the bank for this. Overdrawing an account is considered negligence and is generally not legally punishable (except in a few states). However, if the practice becomes habitual, the depositor is considered a poor credit risk by the bank, thus jeopardizing his overall credit rating.
10. After paying a bill by cash a check made out to cash should be drawn on the physician's professional account and placed with the day's receipts to replace the cash paid out. If this procedure is followed, bank deposits will nearly always equal the day's income.
11. Cash receipts should always be placed in a locked cashbox containing small bills and coins for making change prior to being deposited at the bank.
12. Money (cash or check) should be deposited in the bank every day or every other day, depending upon the amount involved.
13. All additions and subtractions accomplished in computing cumulative totals must be done very accurately so that the physician knows exactly how much he has in the bank at any particular time.

RECONCILING BANK STATEMENTS

On the last day of the month (sometimes every three months), the bank sends each depositor a statement (Fig. 18-6) that shows all deposits made, any charges incurred for services the bank has rendered, and each check cleared for payment during that month, together with all the canceled checks that have been paid out of the depositor's account. It is then the task of the depositor to reconcile the bank statement with his checkbook. If the amount shown on the bank statement is exactly the same amount shown in the cash account or checkbook, the depositor needs no further assur-

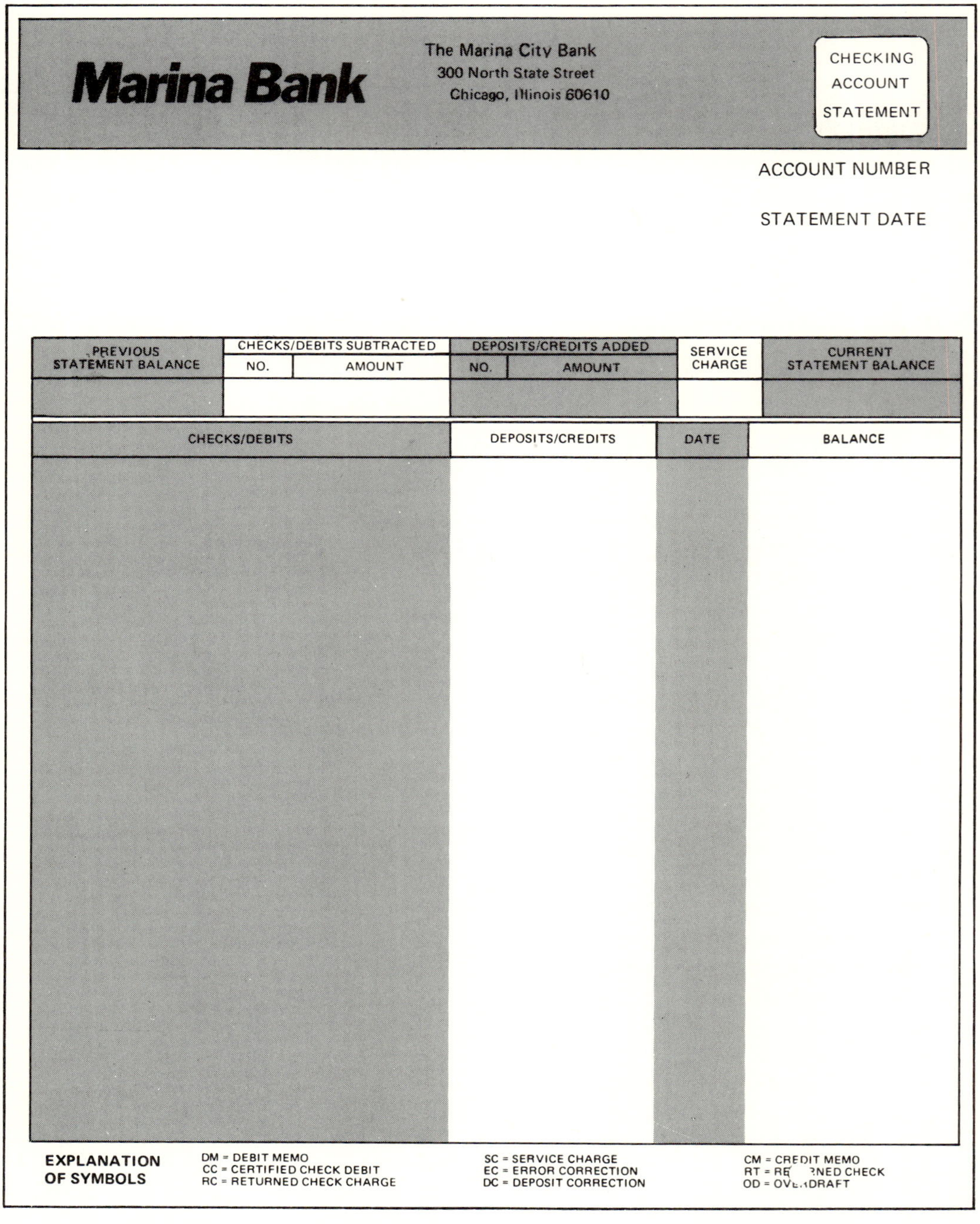

Marina Bank

The Marina City Bank
300 North State Street
Chicago, Illinois 60610

CHECKING ACCOUNT STATEMENT

ACCOUNT NUMBER

STATEMENT DATE

PREVIOUS STATEMENT BALANCE	CHECKS/DEBITS SUBTRACTED		DEPOSITS/CREDITS ADDED		SERVICE CHARGE	CURRENT STATEMENT BALANCE
	NO.	AMOUNT	NO.	AMOUNT		

CHECKS/DEBITS	DEPOSITS/CREDITS	DATE	BALANCE

EXPLANATION OF SYMBOLS

DM = DEBIT MEMO
CC = CERTIFIED CHECK DEBIT
RC = RETURNED CHECK CHARGE
SC = SERVICE CHARGE
EC = ERROR CORRECTION
DC = DEPOSIT CORRECTION
CM = CREDIT MEMO
RT = RETURNED CHECK
OD = OVERDRAFT

Fig. 18-6. Bank statement. (Courtesy Marina City Bank, Chicago, Illinois.)

ance of the correctness of his records for his cash balance. There is nothing to reconcile.

In nearly all cases, however, there will be a difference between the amount shown on the bank's monthly statement and the balance shown in the depositor's checkbook. Moreover, the amount shown on the bank's statement will generally be greater than that shown in the depositor's checkbook. The function of reconciling is to determine why this discrepancy exists. Many banks provide a reconciliation statement on the reverse side of the bank statement. Once completed, this reconciliation statement becomes a formal record of the fact that the variance in the cash balance has been fully accounted for and investigated. Reconciliation is accomplished by making the last amount shown in the checkbook agree with the bank statement.

There are several reasons why the balance in the depositor's checkbook is usually less than that shown in the bank statement. However, the most obvious explanation for the difference is the fact that some checks have not as yet reached the bank for payment but nevertheless have been deducted by the depositor from his checkbook balance. A number of other possibilities that might account for the difference between the two records are the following.

1. The bank has deducted service charges or other items that have not been reflected in the depositor's records.
2. The bank has credited or debited the depositor's account for special collection items that have not been recorded in the depositor's records.
3. A bank deposit has been entered in the checkbook that did not reach the bank in time to be included in the statement for the current month. This is called a deposit in transit or an uncredited deposit. Such an occurrence happens frequently, making the checkbook balance larger.
4. Some checks from previous months that did not appear before may have since cleared and are shown on the current statement.

There are a number of different procedures to be followed in the process of reconciliation. Perhaps the simplest procedure for reconciling the monthly bank statement with the checkbook balance is the following.

1. Arrange in numerical order according to check number all the canceled checks that have been returned with the bank's statement, lowest number on top.
2. Beginning with the first number, compare the check with the corresponding stub in the checkbook and place a checkmark on the stub with a colored pencil (preferably red) to show that the check and stub agree.
3. Whenever you come to a stub for which there is no canceled check, this means that the check has not yet been presented for payment. It is called an outstanding check. The amount has been subtracted by the depositor from his checkbook balance, but the money is still in the account. The balance on the bank's monthly statement will therefore be greater than that in the checkbook for this reason alone. When a check is determined to be outstanding, do not mark the stub. When the entire month's stubs and checks have been listed, total the list of outstanding checks.
4. If any service charges are included on the bank's statement, make them the last entry in the checkbook for that month and subtract them from the balance shown in the checkbook. These service charges were not accounted for during the month because the depositor was unaware of them.
5. Add the new balance in the checkbook to the total of checks outstanding. The amount should equal the balance shown on the bank's monthly statement, and the process is completed.

Perfect bookkeeping demands that all checks and cash received be deposited in the bank and that all disbursements (except petty cash) be made by check. Normally, most medical offices make deposits about twice weekly, and this is usually sufficient, except during peak periods, which usually warrant daily deposits.

ELECTRONIC DATA PROCESSING

The effects of electronic data processing (EDP) have been quite pervasive. Few industries have remained unaffected by the efficiency of automation. The last few years have witnessed a significant increase in the application of EDP to medicine.

It is not inconceivable that within a few short years computers will be managing the financial aspects of most businesses. Many physicians throughout the country are already utilizing an automated billing service. Computers can also be programmed to take dictation, write letters, and read incoming mail, among other things.

The computer was first introduced into medicine primarily for accounting and bookkeeping purposes. Today it is capable of generating a great deal of valuable financial information for a physician that enables him to manage his practice more efficiently. However, if an automated service produces voluminous and complex financial data, in addition to producing statements, that a physician does not understand or use in planning, the investment may be questionable. For the most part, physicians using computer billing services must depend upon EDP centers for generation of statements and reports although minicomputers are becoming more available for placement in physicians' offices.

A number of banks as well as independent computer service bureaus have entered the field and are competing to obtain subscribers to their own particular systems. Some computer service bureaus currently offering EDP services to physicians include: Medibilling Inc., Akron, Ohio; Systemedics, Princeton, New Jersey; Midwest Business Information Systems, Chicago, Illinois; Computer Servicenters, Inc., Birmingham, Alabama.

Among some of the prominent banks offering EDP services are the United California Bank of Arcadia and San Francisco, California; the Northern Trust Company Bank of Chicago, Illinois; the Bank of America, San Francisco, California; First National City Bank, New York, New York, to name only a few.

In order to assess the various types of services currently being provided to physicians by data processing service organizations, a survey of these organizations was recently undertaken by the American Medical Association in cooperation with the Association of Data Processing Service Organizations, Inc. The response to this survey indicates that the principal emphasis of the firms surveyed is in the administrative (for example, accounts receivable, billing) systems support area. To some extent, data processing organizations have historically provided the latter type of support to all users, and the survey results reflect this traditional orientation. Survey results further indicate that, in general, the data processing service organization is not inclined to provide clinical EDP support services. This probably reflects reluctance to engage in costly developmental activity without substantial indications of medical market need or acceptance.

Essentially, data processing service organizations appear to offer a viable alternative to physicians interested in automating segments of their administrative activities. Physicians seeking clinical EDP support (for example, ECG analysis) will probably continue to experience difficulty in obtaining these services from the data processing service organization until such time as the need for those services is more firmly established in the market place.

Each physician must decide whether or not automated billing will enhance the practice. Each system can be adapted to a particular specialty. Probably the most important single advantage of such systems is that they free the assistant from spending a large portion of time with billing and record keeping, thereby enabling more time to be devoted to assisting the physician and patients. Another major reason for switching to a computer billing system is an improved collection ratio. Some champions of computer billing indicate that their collection ratios improved by as much as 25% following conversion.

The bank-sponsored EDP systems currently being offered to physicians across the country are quite similar. Typical among these systems is the Medac system. This system utilizes IBM computers and telephone transmission units for complete, individualized medical bookkeeping, including patient billing and a collection system.

Once the physician makes the decision to subscribe to the system, the bank's Medac representatives visit the physician's office and quickly photograph current financial records, particularly patients' ledgers. This information is analyzed by the bank, and a system is individually tailored to meet the needs of the physician's practice. All services performed by the physician must be given a coded numerical equivalent, making translation to the bank's computer possible. The computer interprets the service codes in accordance with wording assigned by the physician.

The bank provides the physician with a keypunch ledger card and a file card for each patient. The patient's name, address, and number are imprinted on the card. The file card is used for the master file, and space is provided in which information such as insurance company and policy number is written. The keypunch ledger card is used by the assistant to record information to be transmitted to the bank.

When a patient comes in for treatment, his ledger card is removed from the file. The card serves as a charge slip and is attached to the medical history file and sent to the treatment room with the patient.

After the patient's visit is completed, the physician or his aide merely fills in the service code identifying the kind of treatment rendered and notes the charge. Balances may be carried forward if the physician so desires. The card is then returned to the receptionist's desk.

The patient's ledger card, used as a charge slip, serves a twofold purpose: (1) it saves recopying charges onto the ledger card and thus eliminates one area of possible error and (2) it gives the physician a look at the patient's financial account at the time of treatment. In some cases, payment may be psychologically stimulated by the fact that the patient is aware the physician sees his ledger card with a history of charges and payments each time treatment is rendered.

Each day the medical assistant transmits patients' charges and payments received to the computer at the bank's Medac center. This is done on an electronic transmitter connected to the receptionist's telephone. The medical assistant dials the Medac center and inserts the patient's ledger card into the data transmitter, which immediately identifies the transmitting physician's office.

Variable data such as the date, the patient's name, the service code, and amount of the charge or payment are entered on the transmitter's keyboard. Electronic error-detecting devices signal the assistant if an erroneous transmission is made. According to the system's representatives, the transmission of sixty records can be accomplished in approximately 15 minutes.

Cash disbursements and payroll records are entered on a different type of punch card, but transmission remains the same. Each day's transmissions are computer printed in journal form and mailed to the physician. The journal provides a chronologic day sheet of each cash and charge transaction with daily totals. It further provides a means of maintaining a continuing audit of each day's transmissions.

At the end of each month the Medac system prepares itemized statements in duplicate. The original statement is mailed by Medac directly to the patient in a special double-window envelope to assure complete accuracy in mailing. The duplicate copy is sent to the doctor.

A listing of all outstanding balances is prepared at the end of each statement run. An age listing groups the individual accounts according to the length of time each charge has been outstanding. This Accounts Receivable Aging Report provides a breakdown by patient as to current, 30 days, 60 days, 90 days, 120 days, and over 120 days. The physician can quickly determine those delinquent accounts for which additional col-

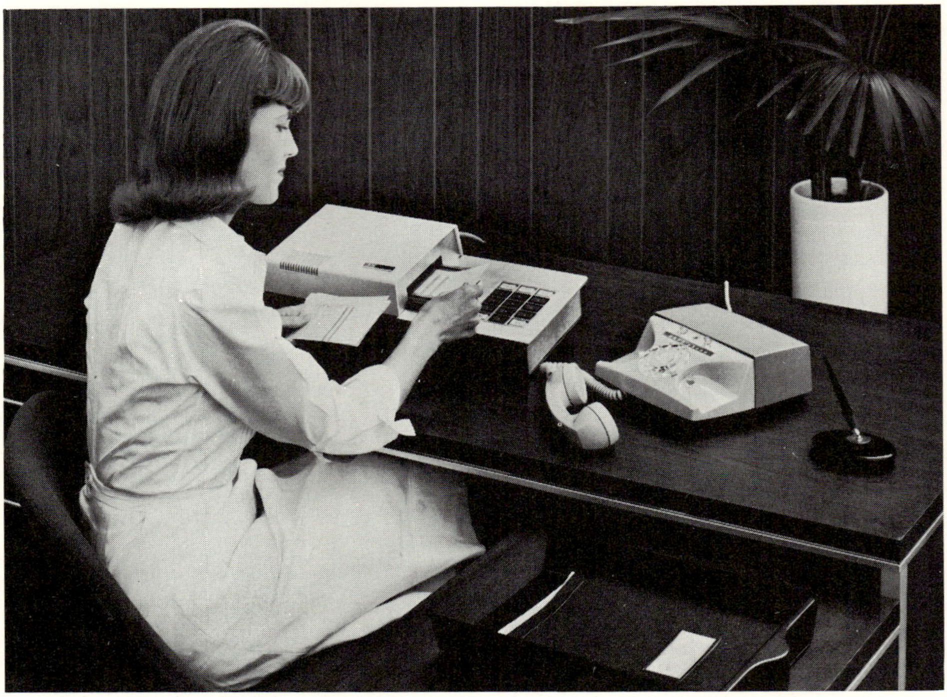

Fig. 18-7. Medac telephone transmission unit. (Courtesy United California Bank, Los Angeles, California.)

lection procedures should be instituted.

By combining the cash disbursements portion of the service with the patient billing service, the physician is provided with a complete double entry system of bookkeeping. The records produced by the system furnish information required for income tax returns, federal and state employee income tax withholding reports, state and federal unemployment tax reports, and federal social security reports.

The advantages of a fully automated accounting system to a group practice situation are obvious. The advantages enumerated by the sponsor of the service may not be so apparent to the individual physician who must, after careful analysis of the practice, be able to justify its cost.

In weighing computer billing costs, the first factor to be considered is the number of monthly statements to be prepared. There is usually a price break for a large-volume practice.

Computer-prepared health insurance claim forms can be especially useful to orthopedic and other practices with a heavy volume of insurance work—particularly where much of the coverage is with commercial carriers. Most of the commercial or indemnity companies appear willing to accept the computerized forms, but to date cooperation from Blue Cross, Blue Shield, and other governmental third parties has been sporadic.

Most experts tend to agree that the computer will probably not make any further significant inroads to the average physician's practice as long as it is used primarily as a very sophisticated and expensive bookkeeping machine. When a computer system is developed to the point of providing as a package data-bank information, patient care services, and billing, it will definitely have a great impact on office-based practice.

A rather diverse EDP market for the medical computer field is envisioned for the balance of the 1970s ranging from billing, administration, and specialized services to facilities and management of larger clinics and hospitals. One area of growing interest is in the development of information that will enable physicians and clinics to evaluate their own performance. Analysis of performance by peer groups (PSRO) within their own state or county will undoubtedly be one of the requirements of a national health insurance system.

Review questions

1. What are the advantages of using checks?
2. Describe the functions of a check.
3. What is the purpose of the certified check, and how does it differ from the cashier's check?
4. What is a limited check and when would it be used?
5. What are the advantages of traveler's checks?
6. Name and describe the various types of checking accounts.
7. All checks readied for deposit must be listed according to their A.B.A. number. What is the significance of this number?
8. Why is a postdated check not negotiable?
9. Define outstanding check and canceled check.
10. What is meant by reconciling? List several possibilities that might account for the difference between the two records.
11. In determining whether or not to convert to an automated system of accounting, what must the doctor consider?
12. Discuss some of the advantages of a computerized billing system.

Suggested readings

Doris, L., and Miller, B. M.: Complete secretary's handbook, ed. 3, Englewood Cliffs, N. J., 1970, Prentice-Hall, Inc.

Van Voorhis, R. H., and others: College accounting theory and practice, part I, New York, 1963, McGraw-Hill Book Co.

chapter 19
Payroll deductions

INCOME TAX

It is interesting to note that the federal government derives more than half of its revenue from the personal income tax. Congress derives its authority to levy a tax upon individual incomes from the sixteenth amendment to the Constitution, passed in 1913. Every person who has an income of over $750 per year or whose net earnings from self-employment are $400 or more, regardless of source, must file an income tax return, except those who are 65 or over; they must file if they had income of $2,800 or more. This refers to all earned income other than Social Security retirement benefits, which are not taxable.

Employers will generally find it convenient to determine the amount of income tax required to be withheld from employee salaries from the wage-bracket tables appearing in Circular E of the *Employer's Tax Guide*. Tables are provided for weekly, biweekly, semimonthly, monthly, and daily or miscellaneous payroll periods. A copy of the guide is furnished to each employer by the Internal Revenue Service each year.

Taxable income includes almost all items of income minus the various deductions and exemptions allowed by law. The amount of income tax one must pay is dependent upon three main factors: (1) the amount of income, (2) the number of dependents claimed, and (3) the tax rate established by Congress.

The present individual income tax system is a progressive one and would appear to be somewhat inequitable at first glance; the greater the individual's income, the greater the percentage of taxes that must be paid. This is often referred to as one's tax bracket. It must be pointed out, however, that individual income tax is computed on the basis of one's net taxable income and not gross income. The number and amount of one's deductions considerably lower the income to be taxed. In fact, some people in the higher income brackets frequently invest in business enterprises that they know to be in the red and losing money simply because such a loss will tend to lower their overall taxable income, placing them in a lower tax category. These enterprises are commonly referred to as tax shelters.

In order to properly comply with the federal income tax system and provide adequate records, the physician is obliged to

---

Glossary

deductions monies withheld from employee earnings

exemptions the number of legitimate dependents one may claim for income tax purposes

F.I.C.A. stands for Federal Insurance Contributions Act; deductions for Social Security taxes are listed on employee paychecks as F.I.C.A.

F.U.T.A. stands for Federal Unemployment Tax Act; each employer of four or more employees must pay an annual federal unemployment tax

revenue the income of a government

wage base the maximum amount of wages earned upon which certain taxes are levied; the maximum amount of wages that can count for F.I.C.A. on unemployment taxes maintain on file the following employee information: name of employee, address of employee, date employment commenced, number of exemptions claimed by employee, gross salary earned, income tax withheld or deducted, Social Security tax deducted, unemployment insurance (if any), and net salary earned or paid.

At the beginning of each year or when a new employee is hired, an Individual Earnings Record (sometimes called a compensation record) is made out for each employee. This record should contain provisions for recording all of the aforementioned employee data plus any other information that may be pertinent.

The income tax due from an employee earning a salary or wages must be withheld along with the Social Security taxes (F.I.C.A.) by the employer and paid to the government periodically. At the end of the year, the individual employee files his tax return, computes his tax, and either pays the balance of tax due or receives a refund for any overpayment.

For purposes of income tax withholding, employers are required to allow exemptions to each employee on the basis of a withholding exemption certificate signed by the employee. In general, the number of withholding exemptions corresponds with the exemptions to which an employee will be entitled in computing his annual income tax return.

Prior to commencing employment each new employee should be requested to complete a Withholding Exemption Certificate (Fig. 19-1). A completed certificate (Form W-4) must include the employee's name, address, Social Security number, and the number of exemptions claimed. Both completed and blank copies of this form must be kept on file by an employer.

A person is ordinarily entitled to one personal exemption, one for a spouse (unless the spouse also works and claims a personal exemption), and one for each legitimate dependent. The claimant must be certain that each dependent claimed meets all the criteria to qualify as a dependent. Information may be secured from the local Internal Revenue Service office or by consulting any federal tax guide.

Prior to December 1 of each year, the employer should routinely request employees to file new exemption certificates for the succeeding year to allow for any possible changes in their exemption status since the filing of their latest certificates. If a worker fails to file a W-4 certificate, the employer

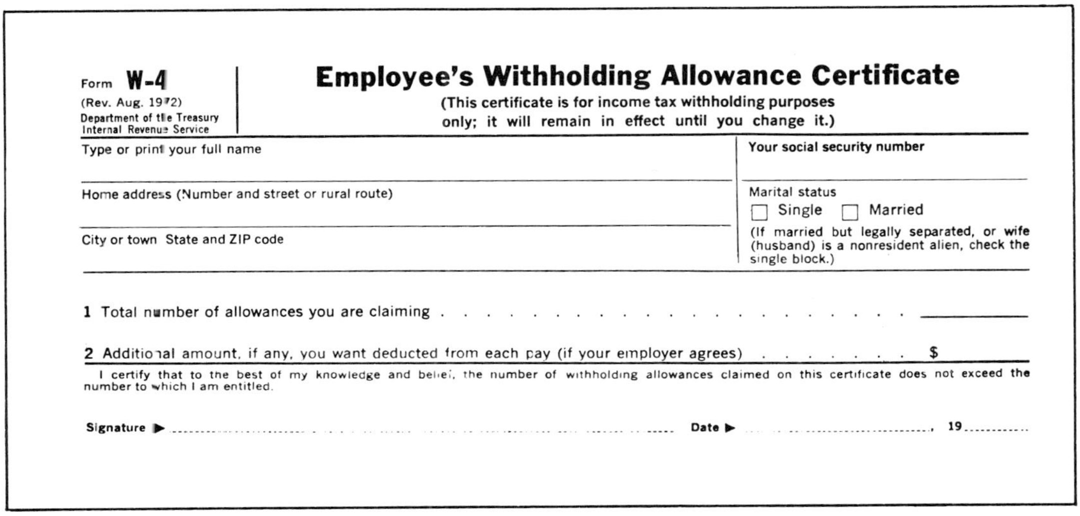
Form **W-4**
(Rev. Aug. 1972)
Department of the Treasury
Internal Revenue Service

Employee's Withholding Allowance Certificate

(This certificate is for income tax withholding purposes only; it will remain in effect until you change it.)

Type or print your full name | **Your social security number**

Home address (Number and street or rural route) | Marital status ☐ Single ☐ Married

City or town State and ZIP code | (If married but legally separated, or wife (husband) is a nonresident alien, check the single block.)

1 Total number of allowances you are claiming . . . . ________

2 Additional amount, if any, you want deducted from each pay (if your employer agrees) . . . . $

I certify that to the best of my knowledge and belief, the number of withholding allowances claimed on this certificate does not exceed the number to which I am entitled.

Signature ▶ ________________ **Date ▶** ________________, 19____

Fig. 19-1. Employee's withholding allowance certificate.

must withhold tax from his wages as though he had no exemptions. When the number of his allowable exemptions decreases, the employee must file a new W-4 certificate with his employer within ten days. Likewise, if the number of his exemptions increases, the employee may file an amended W-4 certificate.

In many states, income tax, unemployment tax, and disability (sickness) taxes must also be deducted from employees' wages. The amounts to be deducted are determined by applying the specified rates to taxable wages as determined by the laws of the respective states.

Many other kinds of deductions, not required by law, may be made from the pay of an employee by agreement or contract between the employee and the employer. For instance, a specified deduction from the pay of the employee may be made each month or each payroll period for group life insurance or group health insurance. Regardless of the nature of the voluntary deduction, it always requires the written authorization of the employee.

Individual payroll checks are written for each employee. The appropriate check information must be entered by the person responsible in a daily journal or disbursements record. Gross pay and deductions are usually shown on a detachable stub of the paycheck for the employee's own information, but the check is drawn for the net pay. The same withholding information must be recorded on the stub remaining in the employer's checkbook. Payroll checks are commonly drawn on the physician's regular professional bank account, although a separate payroll bank account may be established at the physician's discretion.

After the responsible individual has verified the accuracy of the payroll and all pertinent withholding data have been posted to each employee's compensation record, a permanent entry may be made in the general ledger accounts. Gross salary earned by each employee must be charged and debited to the appropriate expense account. Separate liability accounts should be established in the general ledger for each type of deduction. When employees are paid and the various deductions are withheld, they are recorded in these liability accounts as credits. When funds are paid out of these accounts to federal and state governments they are later recorded as debits.

SOCIAL SECURITY TAX

In 1935 the Federal Social Security Act was passed. The Federal Social Security Act, or to be more precise, the Federal Insurance Contributions Act (F.I.C.A.) consists of the old-age, survivors, and disability insurance programs. These three basic types of benefits payable under the federal social insurance system are financed by taxes based on workers' earnings. Employees and employers share the F.I.C.A. tax equally. Self-employed individuals pay the tax at a slightly lower rate than the combined rate for an employee and his employer.

Practically all employed persons have F.I.C.A. taxes deducted from their wages automatically each pay period. The employer must send all such monies withheld from employees' wages, along with an equal amount as his own share of the tax, to the District Director of Internal Revenue or the Federal Deposit window of the bank where he maintains an account. Each employer is required by law to deduct and withhold Social Security taxes from the salaries and wages of his employees. No withholding exemptions are allowed for Social Security taxes. The employer is liable for the payment of such tax whether or not he collects it from his employees. However, since 1951 employers in nonprofit institutions have been exempt from participating in the Social Security program unless two thirds of their employees choose to do so. Nonprofit hospitals offer a good example.

The correct Social Security tax to be deducted may be computed on the percentage basis by multiplying the employee's gross salary for any payroll period by the current tax rate. Also, a convenient reference table that shows the amount to be withheld may be found in the *Employer's Tax Guide*.

If one is self-employed and his net earnings are $400 or more in any given year, he must report his earnings and pay Social Security self-employment tax (currently 7.9%) each year at the time he files his individual income tax return. Even if one is not required to pay any income tax, he must file an income tax return and pay any Social Security self-employment tax due. According to the Internal Revenue Service, all individuals engaged in a trade, business, or the pursuit of a profession in any capacity other than as employees are subject to the self-employment tax.

The wages earned by employees and the income of the self-employed are entered on each individual's permanent record maintained by the Social Security Administration. This record is used to determine a person's eligibility for retirement benefits and to compute the amount he will receive. Full retirement benefits may be claimed by insured male workers after retirement at age 65. Male workers who wish to retire sooner may retire at age 62 with reduced benefits. Female workers may retire with full benefits at age 62.

In accordance with the Federal Insurance Contributions Act, taxes are levied on both the employer and employee at the present rate of 5.85%. The employer contributes 5.85% to match the employee's contribution of 5.85%, for a total of 11.7%. The wage base or the maximum amount of earnings that can count for Social Security and upon which taxes are paid is presently (1975) $14,100. Wages paid to an employee in excess of $14,100 are referred to as tax-exempt wages. When an employee earns $14,100 in any one year, his F.I.C.A. deductions are discontinued at that point for the balance of the year. Social Security (F.I.C.A.) deductions are resumed in the first pay period of the new year.

On the present maximum wage base of $14,100, the tax in any one year on each employee and employer is $824.25. It is interesting to note, however, that today more than one in four workers earns more than $14,100 annually. Hence, more than one in four workers gets a break on Social Security taxes. In fact, the higher the earned income goes, the lower the effective percentage payroll tax for Social Security. This particular tax is therefore regressive, unlike, for example the individual income tax for which rates become higher and higher as income increases.

The Social Security tax has risen faster than any other tax since World War II. Total contributions to the fund in 1975 are expected to exceed $60 billion.

As previously mentioned, there are three basic types of benefits payable under the federal social insurance system of Social Security: old-age, survivors, and disability insurance benefits. To obtain monthly payments for oneself and one's family, or for one's survivors to receive payments in case of death, one must first have credit for a certain amount of work under Social Security. A claimant may have earned Social Security credit by working in employment covered by the law at any time after 1936 and in self-employment covered by the law after 1950.

Social Security credits are called quarters of coverage. In general, this means a three-month period in which wages of $50 or more are paid. A self-employed person gets four quarters of coverage for a year in which his net earnings are $400 or more.

Credit for four quarters, earned at any time, is equal to credit for one year of work under Social Security. A person never needs more than 40 quarters but he must have at least six quarters to qualify. If a person should stop working under Social Security before he has earned sufficient credit to become insured, no benefits will be payable. If an individual should later return to work covered by Social Security, regardless of his age, both his past earnings and any additional earnings are combined in determining whether he qualifies for benefits. To be "fully insured" does not mean that a person receives the highest monthly benefit. It only means that he is eligible for benefits when he retires or his survivors can receive benefits when he dies. Maximum benefits are based on an individual's highest average monthly earnings during any ten-year period of his working life.

The more regularly one works under Social Security and the higher his earnings, the greater will be his monthly retirement benefits. The amount of old-age payments also depends on whether a male beneficiary applies for them at age 65 or decides to apply for them earlier at age 62. Monthly payments will be lower (80% of primary insurance amount) for males if they choose to receive benefits before age 65.

If a person becomes disabled before age 65, he may qualify for monthly disability benefits, and certain members of his family may also be paid monthly benefits. To be found disabled under the Social Security law, one must have a condition so severe that, in the words of the law, "it makes him unable to engage in any substantial gainful activity." If an employee is unable to pursue his regular work but can do other substantial gainful work, he cannot qualify under these disability provisions. The nature of one's disability must be the kind of physical or mental condition that will show up in a medical examination or test; it must have lasted or be expected to continue for at least 12 months. Payment of benefits begins after the five-month waiting period.

In addition, a survivor's lump sum death payment may be made to the widow or widower who was living in the same household with the worker at the time of death; otherwise the payment can go to pay the worker's burial expenses. The lump sum benefit is figured at three times the amount of the decedent's monthly retirement benefits, but it is not to exceed a specified amount (that is, 80% of an individual's average monthly earnings before he became disabled).

A retired person may earn up to a maximum of $2,520 or less in any one year without losing any of his Social Security benefit payments. If he earns more than $2,520 in a year, one dollar of his benefits may be withheld for each two dollars he earns. Moreover, Social Security (F.I.C.A.) taxes must be paid by workers over age 65 on all income up to $14,100.

Regardless of an individual's total earnings for a year, benefits will be payable for any month in which he neither earns wages nor performs substantial services in self-employment for more than $200. This provision furnishes the retired individual with a convenient loophole, so to speak. Conceivably, a retired person could make a great deal of money in one month and only be penalized one month's Social Security benefits. After one reaches age 72, there is no limitation on the amount he may earn. Persons 72 years of age and over receive full Social Security benefits regardless of the amount of their incomes but continue to pay Social Security taxes.

UNEMPLOYMENT TAXES

The Federal Social Security Act, as passed in 1935, consisted of two important segments: the Federal Insurance Contributions Act (F.I.C.A.) that we have already described and the Federal Unemployment Tax Act (F.U.T.A.). The second part of the 1935 act is known as the Federal Unemployment Insurance program. This program is financed jointly by the federal government and the states through taxes levied under the provisions of the act and in conformity with the corresponding state unemployment tax laws. Employers are therefore subject to F.I.C.A. tax and to both federal and state unemployment insurance taxes. The act was primarily designed to encourage the states to establish and maintain unemployment insurance programs.

The original legislation of 1935 provided for a direct tax on the payrolls of certain employers to provide funds for an unemployment insurance program. An employer is not subject to this tax unless during the calendar year he employed four or more individuals on at least one day in each of 20 or more calendar weeks. The 20 weeks need not be consecutive. These requirements apply only to unemployment tax and not to Social Security taxes or the withholding of income taxes. Moreover, the Federal Unemployment Tax is imposed on the employer only and must not be deducted from the wages of employees. The rate of this federal tax is currently 3.28% on the first $4,000 of wages paid by the employer during the calendar year to each of his employees.

Again, it should be pointed out that a physician who employs fewer than four persons in the office is not considered an "employer" and therefore is not subject to the Federal Unemployment Tax. For detailed instructions on how this tax is determined and credit allowed for contributions to state unemployment systems, refer to Circular E of the *Employer's Tax Guide.*

REMITTANCE OF MONEY WITHHELD

If the income tax withheld from employee wages plus the combined employee and employer F.I.C.A. taxes for a given month amount to more than $200, the total must be deposited by the employer on or before the fifteenth day of the following month in a Federal Reserve Bank or any commercial bank authorized to accept such deposits. The deposit should be accompanied by Depository Form (card) 501. Should an employer desire to make monthly deposits of these taxes even if the monthly total is $200 or less, he may do so. If withheld income taxes and Social Security taxes withheld are less than $200 per calendar quarter, employers may remit the taxes with Form 941 (Employer's Quarterly Federal Tax Return). On the other hand, if liability is at least $2,000 per month the employer must make deposits within three banking days after the seventh, fifteenth, twenty-second, and last day of each month.

Therefore, generally near the fifteenth of each month a check is drawn on the physician's professional account for all the income taxes and Social Security taxes withheld or deducted from employees' earnings for the previous month, plus an equal amount of Social Security tax contributed as the physician's share. A check for the total amount owed to the government is made out to the bank where the doctor maintains his account. This check, deposited at the tax window of the bank, must be accompanied by a special form provided by the government, a Federal Depository Receipt (Form 501, Fig. 19-2). Several days later the bank mails the stamped Form 501 Receipt back to the physician or accountant, along with a new blank for the next monthly deposit. It is important that these stamped receipts be retained, for they offer proof that taxes

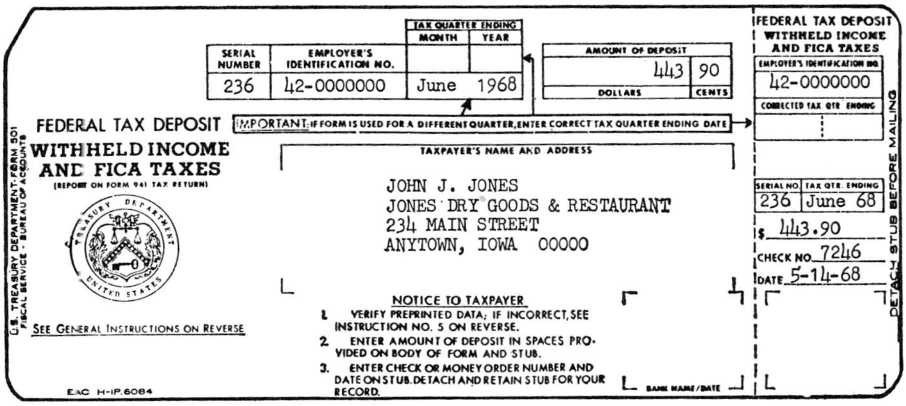

SERIAL NUMBER	EMPLOYER'S IDENTIFICATION NO.	TAX QUARTER ENDING MONTH	YEAR
236	42-0000000	June	1968

AMOUNT OF DEPOSIT DOLLARS	CENTS
443	90

FEDERAL TAX DEPOSIT
WITHHELD INCOME AND FICA TAXES
(REPORT ON FORM 941 TAX RETURN)

IMPORTANT: IF FORM IS USED FOR A DIFFERENT QUARTER, ENTER CORRECT TAX QUARTER ENDING DATE

TAXPAYER'S NAME AND ADDRESS

JOHN J. JONES
JONES DRY GOODS & RESTAURANT
234 MAIN STREET
ANYTOWN, IOWA 00000

U.S. TREASURY DEPARTMENT-FORM 501
FISCAL SERVICE - BUREAU OF ACCOUNTS

SEE GENERAL INSTRUCTIONS ON REVERSE

NOTICE TO TAXPAYER

1. VERIFY PREPRINTED DATA; IF INCORRECT, SEE INSTRUCTION NO. 5 ON REVERSE.
2. ENTER AMOUNT OF DEPOSIT IN SPACES PROVIDED ON BODY OF FORM AND STUB.
3. ENTER CHECK OR MONEY ORDER NUMBER AND DATE ON STUB. DETACH AND RETAIN STUB FOR YOUR RECORD.

BANK NAME/DATE

EAC H-IP.6084

FEDERAL TAX DEPOSIT
WITHHELD INCOME AND FICA TAXES
EMPLOYER'S IDENTIFICATION NO. 42-0000000
CORRECTED TAX QTR ENDING

SERIAL NO.	TAX QTR. ENDING
236	June 68

$ 443.90
CHECK NO. 7246
DATE 5-14-68

DETACH STUB BEFORE MAILING

Fig. 19-2. Federal depository receipt, Form 501.

due in the first two months of the calendar quarter were paid.

During the month following the end of each calendar quarter (April, July, October, and January), the employer must file a quarterly tax return and pay any balance of tax due for the third month of the quarter. Failure to comply warrants a fine. The stamped Federal Depository Receipts (Form 501) for the first two months of the quarter must be filed with Form 941.

At his own option an employer may make a bank deposit of the federal taxes for the third month of the calendar quarter, but he should do so in ample time for the bank to return the validated receipt so that it can be included with his quarterly return on Form 941. Taxes due as shown on Form 941 must accompany the return in the form of validated depository receipts, check, or money order. Both criminal and civil penalties are provided for those employers who willfully fail to file returns and pay taxes due. Similar action may also be taken for willfully filing false or fraudulent returns.

The first step in preparing the quarterly tax return is to complete Schedule A of Form 941 (Quarterly Report of Wages Taxable Under F.I.C.A.). This is a list showing the Social Security number and name of each worker, the amount of total taxable wages paid to him under F.I.C.A. during the quarter, and the state in which the wages were paid.

The actual tax return itself is in the form of a prepunched card. The depository receipts for the payment of taxes in the previous months of the quarter are listed and totaled on Schedule B located on the reverse side of the card. The front side of the form identifies the employer by name and number. The total amount of income tax withheld during the quarter is entered, together with any adjustments for preceding quarters if applicable. The wages subject to F.I.C.A., as shown on Schedule A, are indicated. The total of gross taxable wages paid is multiplied by the combined tax rates for employees and employer (presently 11.7%) to obtain the amount of F.I.C.A. taxes due. The sum of income tax withheld plus the F.I.C.A. taxes equals the total tax due. From this total is deducted the sum of the amounts shown on the depository receipts accompanying the return to determine the net amount payable. The balance due must be sent with the return to the local District Director of Internal Revenue.

Each employer with four or more employees is required to file an Annual Federal Unemployment Tax Return (Form 940) and pay the tax due the federal government for the year by the following January 31 using Federal Tax Deposit Form 508. The information for this return comes partly from the individual earnings records and partly from copies of the state unemployment tax reports that the employer has filed quarterly during the year.

By January 31 of each year or within 30 days after an employee leaves the service of an employer it is the responsibility of the employer to furnish each of his employees a Withholding Tax Statement, Form W-2 (Fig. 19-3). This form contains the employer's name, address, and identification number, as well as the employee's name, address, and Social Security number. Four amounts are indicated: federal income tax withheld, total wages paid, F.I.C.A. tax withheld, and total wages subject to F.I.C.A. tax.

Four copies of Form W-2 must be prepared for each employee. Two copies are furnished to the employee, one of which he must attach to his federal income tax return; he keeps the other for his own records. The employer keeps one for his records and must send one to the government with his Annual Reconciliation of Tax Withheld Report (Form W-3, Fig. 19-4).

Every employer subject to the employment taxes described in this chapter is required to keep all records pertinent to these taxes available for inspection by officers of the Internal Revenue Service if the need should arise. Such records should be kept for a period of at least four years after the

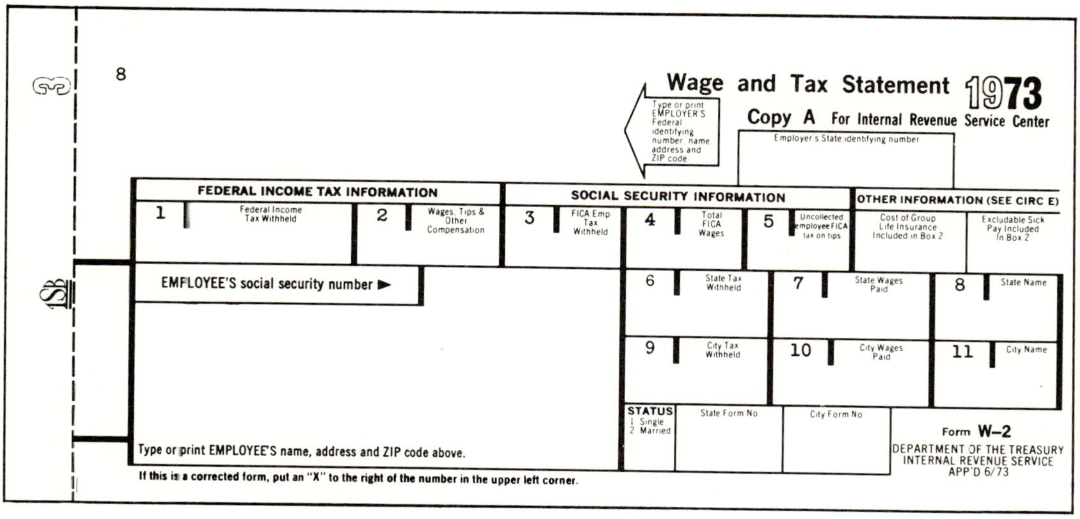
8

Wage and Tax Statement 1973

Type or print EMPLOYER'S Federal identifying number, name, address and ZIP code

Copy A For Internal Revenue Service Center

Employer's State identifying number

FEDERAL INCOME TAX INFORMATION

1 Federal Income Tax Withheld

2 Wages, Tips & Other Compensation

SOCIAL SECURITY INFORMATION

3 FICA Emp Tax Withheld

4 Total FICA Wages

5 Uncollected employee FICA tax on tips

OTHER INFORMATION (SEE CIRC E)

Cost of Group Life Insurance Included in Box 2

Excludable Sick Pay Included In Box 2

EMPLOYEE'S social security number ▶

6 State Tax Withheld

7 State Wages Paid

8 State Name

9 City Tax Withheld

10 City Wages Paid

11 City Name

STATUS 1 Single 2 Married

State Form No

City Form No

Type or print EMPLOYEE'S name, address and ZIP code above.

Form W-2

DEPARTMENT OF THE TREASURY INTERNAL REVENUE SERVICE APP'D 6/73

If this is a corrected form, put an "X" to the right of the number in the upper left corner.

Fig. 19-3. Wage and tax statement, Form W-2.

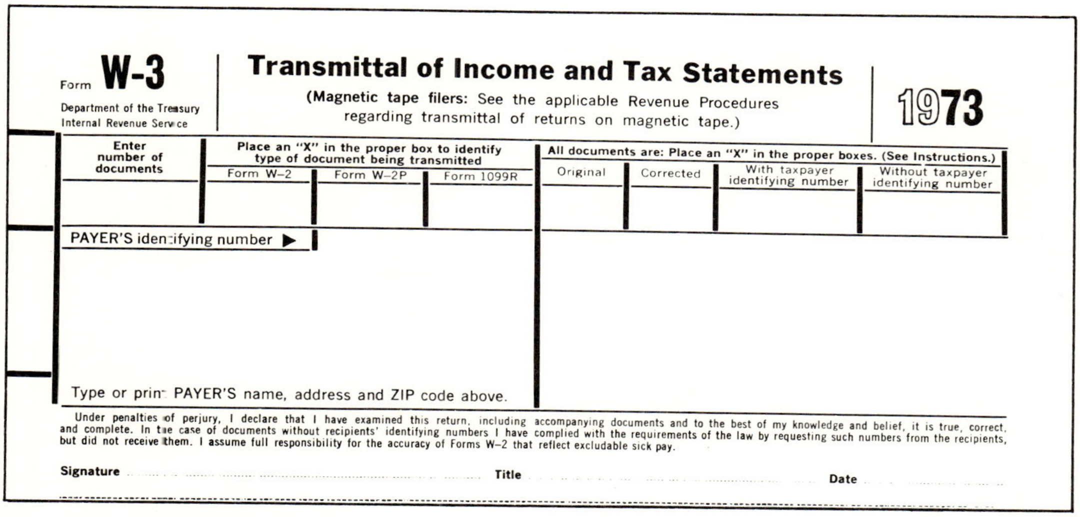
Form W-3

Department of the Treasury Internal Revenue Service

Transmittal of Income and Tax Statements

(Magnetic tape filers: See the applicable Revenue Procedures regarding transmittal of returns on magnetic tape.)

1973

Enter number of documents

Place an "X" in the proper box to identify type of document being transmitted

Form W-2 | Form W-2P | Form 1099R

All documents are: Place an "X" in the proper boxes. (See Instructions.)

Original | Corrected | With taxpayer identifying number | Without taxpayer identifying number

PAYER'S identifying number ▶

Type or print PAYER'S name, address and ZIP code above.

Under penalties of perjury, I declare that I have examined this return, including accompanying documents and to the best of my knowledge and belief, it is true, correct, and complete. In the case of documents without recipients' identifying numbers I have complied with the requirements of the law by requesting such numbers from the recipients, but did not receive them. I assume full responsibility for the accuracy of Forms W-2 that reflect excludable sick pay.

Signature .... Title .... Date ....

Fig. 19-4. Reconciliation of income tax withheld from wages, Form W-3.

date the tax to which they relate becomes due, or the date the tax is paid, whichever is later.

Admittedly, few medical assistants are entrusted with the complex responsibility of preparing the various federal and state employer tax returns and reports. This task is generally reserved for the physician's accountant-consultant, who would be responsible for completing the physician's annual tax return. In the majority of cases the assistant's functions are those of supplying the data necessary for completing the reports, drawing a check for the amounts indicated, and securing the physician's signature. Nevertheless, it is the author's contention that the assistant who possesses a working understanding of these returns and reports is apt to do a more efficient job than one who is totally uninformed about such matters.

KEOGH RETIREMENT PLAN

Income tax authorities estimate that more than 12 million self-employed persons—many of them members of trade and professional associations—are passing up tax savings they could claim every year through a government-approved pension and retirement program.

These experts say that only one person out of every seven or eight who work for themselves are taking advantage of a law that gives the self-employed person some of the same pension benefits offered to employees of big corporations.

Under a law passed in October, 1962, known then as H.R. 10, or more simply as the Keogh Act, operators of small enterprises—or independent professionals such as physicians, dentists, attorneys, architects, nurses, accountants, shopkeepers, and others—are permitted to set aside as much as 15% of their annual income, up to a yearly maximum of $7,500 toward a personal retirement plan.

The money put into such a plan each year is completely free from current federal income taxes. Moreover, the buildup of dividends or interest on the accumulated savings also remains tax free from year to year until the plan matures at retirement. Taxes must be paid only when the individual retires and starts drawing on his investment. By that time, he is likely to be in a lower income tax bracket than he was in his working years; thus the tax bite tends to be softened.

An important provision of the Keogh law from the medical assistant's standpoint requires that an individual who hires one or more other persons to work full time must have those employees also covered by the tax-sheltered retirement plan. In fact, a self-employed business or professional man who has others working for him is entitled to set up a Keogh Plan for himself only if he provides a similar plan for every full-time employee who has been on his payroll for three years.

Despite the obvious tax savings, plus the allure of a retirement nest egg, relatively few individuals who are qualified for Keogh Act benefits have set up their own retirement plans, say revenue officials. James Attwood, Senior Vice President of Equitable Life Assurance Society, who has headed the life insurance industry's Task Force on Pension Legislation, estimates that only 20% of all self-employed professional people, and as few as 5% to 8% of nonprofessionals, are covered by a Keogh Plan.*

During the past few years the Internal Revenue Service has liberalized procedures for setting up a Keogh Plan, and has issued easy-to-understand rules explaining how the plan works. Information and application forms are available at many banks, insurance companies, and investment funds. Internal Revenue Service Publication No. 566 (10-72) contains questions and answers on the Keogh Plan. Also, the American Medical Association administers a Keogh Plan for its members. Further information about the AMA's Members' Retirement Plan may be obtained by contacting the Association directly at 535 N. Dearborn Street, Chicago, Illinois 60610.

Review questions

1. Upon what three factors does the amount of income tax to be deducted from an employee's salary depend?
2. What information is contained on each employee's Compensation Record?
3. What is the function of the W-4 form?
4. Explain what is meant by F.I.C.A.
5. Name three benefits payable under Social Security.
6. Up to what annual salary is Social Security tax deducted from employees' salaries?
7. Dr. Taylor withholds $30.45 in F.I.C.A. taxes from his two employees each month. How much F.I.C.A. tax must Dr. Taylor pay each month?

---

*Your members may benefit by this tax-sheltered retirement plan; Association Management, April 1973, p. 61.

8. How does one qualify for retirement benefits under Social Security?
9. Are there any limits on the earnings of retired workers?
10. Dr. Taylor employes two workers in his office. Is he required to pay F.U.T.A. tax? Explain your answer.
11. Describe the function and importance of the Federal Depository Receipt.
12. How often is it necessary to transmit withheld payroll taxes to the federal government?
13. What is a W-2 form?
14. Of what relevance is the Keogh Plan to the medical assistant?

Suggested readings

Doris, L., and Miller, B. M.: Complete secretary's handbook, ed. 3, Englewood Cliffs, N. J., 1970, Prentice-Hall, Inc.

U. S. Treasury Department: Tax guide for small business, Internal Revenue Service Report No. 334, Washington, D. C., 1965, Government Printing Office.

U. S. Treasury Department: Employer's tax guide, Internal Revenue Service Report No. 15, Circular E, Washington, D. C., 1966, Government Printing Office.

Van Voorhis, R. H., et al.: College accounting theory and practice, part I, New York, 1963, McGraw-Hill Book Co.

chapter 20

Medical office maintenance

CARE OF THE OFFICE

A medical office, more than any other type of office, is expected to be immaculately neat and clean in order to create the proper impression. A distinctive professional office mirrors the quality and integrity of the physician and the staff. Such an office is one that is pleasant to work in as well as pleasant to visit. It provides an atmosphere of noticeable efficiency, cleanliness, and comfort.

The proper maintenance of a physician's suite of rooms requires constant care and attention. The responsibility for seeing that the necessary housekeeping is accomplished usually rests with the medical assistant. There are numerous items of equipment and apparatus that need regular attention. Only the office staff is familiar with these and knows how to handle them. A commercial cleaning service cannot be expected to know how to manage delicate material and actually should not be permitted to do so.

It is sometimes helpful for the medical assistant to know what services, if any, are included in the office rental. This may include certain maintenance services as well as electricity, heating, lighting, and air conditioning. The assistant should see that those services contracted for in the lease are received, but must not be above taking care of minor emergencies when they occur.

Cleaning services are not included in general building maintenance, and in most cases a janitorial service is retained to take care of heavy cleaning. A reliable service will provide its customers with a schedule of their daily, weekly, and monthly cleaning activities. Having such information available, the assistant can better arrange a personal schedule. Where there are several employees in the office, the duties might be divided, each individual being made responsible for one section or area. Furniture, medical equipment, and special items such as mirrors, which require additional care, may not be adequately taken care of by the janitorial service.

Few physicians have the time to worry about the appearance of their offices. A

Glossary

antiquated refers to something that is considered old-fashioned or out-of-date

decor the arrangement of furnishings in a room

depreciation a lessening or lowering in value; a loss figured as part of the cost of doing business

expendable refers to that which can be used up or sacrificed

inventory a detailed list of articles with their estimated value; a detailed list or account

nocturnal active in the night

pharmaceuticals drugs

physician generally assumes that the assistant will display enough initiative to automatically take charge of this aspect, thereby precluding the need for his involvement.

In this capacity, the assistant sees to it that things are done properly. A lack of organization does not help to foster orderliness and cleanliness without also generating confusion. An efficient person knows well ahead of time what is to be done and when it is to be done.

Each patient should be made to feel that he is important. To help convey this impression, the physician's waiting room should be as comfortable, tidy, attractive, and cheerful as possible. The patient's comfort and enjoyment should receive top priority.

The medical assistant should see to it that the furniture is comfortable and adequate. Furniture should be arranged in the most conducive manner for reading, writing, or conversation.

There should be an abundance of good lighting, ventilation, and storage space for coats, hats, overshoes, umbrellas, and so on. The reception room should be bright and cheerful but not overly so. Plants, pictures, and posters often lend a great deal of charm to a simple room. Most doctors subscribe to a number of good magazines than can be temporarily preserved by keeping them in leather-bound covers in the waiting room. Many modern offices contain television sets or relaxing music.

There has been a considerable amount of discussion concerning whether or not patients associate modern surroundings with up-to-date medicine. Actually, the physician's staff represents the more important contribution to the patient's opinion of the doctor. Sympathy and a warm, kindly approach in tone or manner can modify an atmosphere of apprehension and tension, leaving the patient more relaxed and receptive to the physician's consultation and examination.

The majority of patients prefer one simple form of diversion to pass their waiting time —reading. Therefore, the medical assistant should be sure that the publications placed in the waiting room are of a wide variety with suitable reading material for the worried, anxious, or annoyed patient. Professional publications are rarely intended for the patient and should not be permitted to stray into the reception room. Magazines should be carefully selected keeping the readership in mind. Out-of-date magazines should be discarded.

One of the most appropriate magazines available for the physician's waiting room is *Today's Health,* a publication of the American Medical Association designed specifically for the layperson. One purpose of this magazine is to generate good will toward the medical profession through authoritative, easily understood health information and to aid the practicing physician by dispelling myths, warning of health hazards, exposing quackery and fads, encouraging sensible personal care, and eliminating misinformation that can prevent people from seeking sound medical advice. Other magazines of general interest to adults that would be appropriate for the reception room include: *Parents', Reader's Digest, Newsweek, Time,* and *U.S. News and World Report.* Of special interest to women are *Ladies' Home Journal, Good Housekeeping, McCall's,* and *Redbook* while men might enjoy *Argosy, Field and Stream,* and *Sports Illustrated.* Young adults may enjoy *Hot Rod, Seventeen, Glamour, Mademoiselle,* and *Road and Track,* as well as various screen magazines. For children, *Jack and Jill* and *Highlights* are good choices in addition to inexpensive storybooks.

Great numbers of comic books and similar literature do not add to the appearance of an office. Perhaps a few may be selected and saved for children to look at. Many of the more expensive magazines may be kept for a longer period of time until they become ragged.

The consulting room should be kept in the best possible order at all times. Charts should be filed in their proper places and not allowed to accumulate on the physician's desk. Books and bookshelves should be dusted as often as possible.

Flowers add charm to any office. However, indoor plants are more practical and economical. These can be purchased in a wide variety of shapes and sizes and are ideal for adding a feeling of charm and comfort to the office. However, it should be remembered that plants must be cared for and if they begin to look dying or scrawny, should be replaced immediately. Remember, it is depressing to the patient to see old, neglected, worn-out looking plants around him. There are many good books available on the care of indoor plants. It might be wise for the assistant to invest in one of them and refer to it whenever necessary.

HOUSEKEEPING FUNCTIONS

There are some duties that require daily attention and other more time-consuming ones that need only weekly or periodic attention. The following schedules apply in general to most medical offices; they are intended to serve primarily as checklists for reference purposes:

Daily housekeeping functions

1. The physician's office requires special attention. It should be in perfect order at all times. Furniture should be arranged so that the physician's chair faces the door; consultation chairs should always face the physician's desk.
2. The physician's desk and the reception desk require daily attention. Supplies such as scratch paper and paper clips should be replenished when they become low.
3. The entire office, including treatment and reception rooms, must be kept clean and tidy during the course of the working day.
4. If the physician keeps a supply of business cards in the reception room, they should be checked each day to make sure the supply is adequate.
5. All plants should be kept watered and dusted. Plants with shiny leaves should be wiped with a damp cloth.
6. The assistant should check the supply of clean towels, soap, and similar items each day.
7. If patients are permitted to smoke in the waiting rooms, an adequate supply of ashtrays must be provided and emptied regularly. Some offices furnish matches and even cigarettes.
8. Calendars should be turned, pencils sharpened, pens filled, and the supply of stationery checked daily.
9. If possible, the entire office should be aired thoroughly. The thermostat should be regulated to maintain an even temperature of approximately 68 to 70° F.
10. Each morning, examining rooms should be checked for the following: cleansing tissues, soap, and adequate linen (gowns, sheets, and so on).
11. A patient should never be left alone in a treatment room where he may have access to his chart.
12. Everything within reach should be dusted daily; this includes waiting rooms, consultation rooms, treatment rooms, and, of course, the physician's private office.
13. Ashtrays may have to be emptied throughout the working day, but they also should be wiped out once each day.
14. Washbasins should be attended to on a daily basis. Sinks with stains can be cleaned by pouring liquid bleach on a rag and applying it directly to the stain.
15. Light bulbs must be replaced as they burn out. An extra supply of bulbs should always be kept on hand.
16. Gum stuck to surfaces should be removed when discovered, for the longer it remains the more difficult it becomes to remove. Gum may be scraped from surfaces after first using spot remover or placing an ice cube on the gum to soften it.

Weekly housekeeping functions

1. Appropriate reading material should be selected for the reception room. Biased

religious and political publications have no place in a physician's office.

2. Periodical reading matter should be kept up-to-date. This will help preclude many of the worn-out jokes about the antiquated reading material found in doctors' offices.
3. Drug samples should be properly disposed of at regular intervals.
4. Check on supplies at least once a week so that orders can be placed at regular intervals.
5. Counter tops in examining rooms should be cleaned and scrubbed with soap and water each week. Any solutions that need changing can be changed at the same time.
6. A sufficient supply of hangers should be provided for patients' clothing in the examining room.
7. If there is a refrigerator on the premises it should be kept immaculately clean, and it should be defrosted on a regular basis.
8. All storage areas require frequent cleaning. Contaminated material should be well wrapped before being discarded.
9. Fish and their tanks must be cared for where present.
10. Lamps should be dusted unless they are handled by the janitorial service. Parchment should be wiped with a damp cloth and fabric dusted with a wisk broom.
11. Brass should be polished when needed.
12. Upholstery should be cleaned once a week.
13. All bottles should be cleaned weekly, using a damp cloth.
14. All pictures should be cleaned and dusted weekly.
15. Mirrors should be polished and cleaned weekly.
16. Furniture should be polished once every two or three months.
17. An autoclave should be polished with silver cream polish only. One should never use harsh scouring powder on the exterior, although it may be used to clean the inside.

The office must maintain an adequate supply of cleaning materials on hand if proper housekeeping is to be accomplished. Even though most janitorial services supply their own cleaning materials, a duplicate is needed to carry out those chores not included in the service. Some of the necessary items include: rags for damp cleaning, furniture polish, scouring powder, silver cream polish, whisk broom, Brillo pads and steel wool, Lux or Ivory soap, dust mop, ammonia, bleach, Drano, glass cleaner, sponge, and chamois.

MAINTENANCE OF EQUIPMENT

There are two elements to consider in dealing with office equipment: keeping it in good working order and protecting it from damage or theft. Delicate and precision apparatus cannot be expected to perform accurately over an extended period without being given proper and regular care. No physician can settle for less than properly functioning equipment if he hopes to conduct an efficient and profitable practice. In addition to general housekeeping obligations, the medical assistant possesses the added responsibility of maintaining this equipment. This responsibility does not mean repair work but duties more preventive in nature.

In carrying out a program of this sort, there are several points to consider. First, the assistant should devise a schedule, making a list of the dates on which maintenance is due on each piece of equipment. The manufacturer provides maintenance instructions with each piece of equipment, and such information should be carefully filed for future reference. Perhaps most important of all, major equipment repairs should always be left to qualified repairmen. Overzealous amateur tinkering with sensitive equipment can only cause further damage and add to the cost of repairs.

PROTECTION OF THE OFFICE

One of the most serious problems facing physicians today is the protection of their medical equipment and supplies from theft.

Unfortunately, one of the major discords between physicians and their assistants concerns internal dishonesty. Strangely enough, many employees who consider themselves to be basically honest do not hesitate to help themselves to pharmaceuticals, stamps, office supplies, periodicals, and a host of other expendables. However, the threat from outside the office is more immediate and far more dangerous.

It is essential that a physician and the entire staff become crime-conscious, since the best way to deal with crime is to prevent it. It is not too difficult to imagine why a doctor's office is often a burglar's target. The desperation of a narcotics addict, for example, makes him a potentially dangerous criminal against whom a physician must especially guard.

The local police are only too anxious to reduce the incidence of crime. Through cooperation with the authorities and the installation of adequate precautions, a physician can ensure the safety of the office. As a matter of fact, many local police departments through the country have conducted workshops for physicians on the very subject of crime prevention. This dialogue and exchange of ideas between the two parties has resulted in the formulation of the following list of suggested precautions.

1. The physician should feel free to call in the police to check the office. They can often offer valuable advice on where and how to make changes in the physical arrangement of the office.
2. The physician should provide the police with a schedule of office hours so that they can keep an eye on the building when it is empty. Patrolmen can leave messages to let the physician know if anything unusual occurred, for example, a window or door that had been tampered with.
3. The physician should contact the police immediately if anything indicates criminal activity. Trampled bushes or footprints under windows could mean a burglary was planned or attempted.
4. It is always a wise precaution, even for a doctor's office, to install a burglar alarm. The most obvious advantage of an alarm system is, of course, that the thief is usually scared away before he has a chance to steal or damage anything.
5. Adequate night lights are very important. Well-placed external lighting puts the nocturnal burglar at a disadvantage. It is also good practice to keep lights on inside the office. However, if this is done, it is wise to keep blinds and curtains closed.
6. The police recommend leaving a radio turned on in the office at a low volume. According to the police, it is almost impossible for a person prowling outside to tell the difference between soft voices on the radio and live voices engaged in conversation.
7. Drugs and narcotics should always be kept out of sight and under lock and key when not in use. This makes it much more difficult for a potential thief. If the doctor is careless with them, he is practically inviting thievery. Large amounts of narcotics should probably not even be kept in the office.
8. The credentials and references of callers should be checked. Solicitors, agents, and contractors should have permits or should otherwise be able to identify themselves properly. Unidentified visitors could very well be "casing" the office.
9. When installing protective devices, it does not pay to look for bargains; only the most reliable services should be used when installing or changing locks.

Experience can often be a very expensive teacher. It is much easier and cheaper to learn from the mistakes of others. Therefore, anyone presently employed in a physician's office or contemplating future employment should be familiar with precautionary measures. Most physicians will appreciate such concern and diligence.

PURCHASING SUPPLIES

In ordering supplies, perhaps the most important single item to remember is to obtain the most for the physician's money. In addition to other numerous duties, the medical assistant also functions as the doctor's purchasing agent. Most physicians pay very little attention to this phase of their practice so long as there are plenty of supplies on hand. The assistant should see to it that supplies do not run out.

No efficient organization can afford to be constantly running out of supplies. On the other hand, space is not always adequate to house a large inventory, which, moreover, costs money in terms of capital investment. The secret of proper stock maintenance is reaching a happy medium between supply and usage, and it is here that experience plays a major role.

There is no way of telling how much income a physician loses each year without realizing it, simply because the assistant bought too much of the wrong things. The overordering of smaller, expendable items becomes a substantial expense when continued over the course of a year. More importantly, expensive items purchased hastily and in quantity can greatly reduce the physician's overall net income. Therefore it is absolutely necessary for the medical assistant to stick to certain prudent ground rules in purchasing supplies for the office.

Before purchasing a new product, it is generally helpful for the purchaser to make a checklist of questions to aid in the evaluation of a product. Information derived from the following questions can be of some assistance: Is it really needed? Why? In what way is it better than the product now being used? What are its disadvantages?

It is generally a good idea, if time permits, to give salesmen an opportunity to provide the facts. The information gained may often provide valuable ideas that can be utilized in lieu of purchasing the item or items involved. Some ingenuity may be required, but this should not be beyond the capacity of a good assistant.

New instruments should be ordered only with the physician's approval. In purchasing expensive items it pays to be selective and to shop around, since prices sometimes vary even on standard supplies. Also, it does not always hold true that the biggest supply houses are the ones that offer the lowest prices.

When the physician is considering the purchase of a costly item, the assistant can be of great help by prompting some important questions. For instance, the physician may want to inquire into the tax consequences of such a purchase. From a tax standpoint it is often more advantageous to rent or lease than to buy outright. Renting affords the opportunity of carrying the item on the books as a current expense rather than tying up funds in a large capital outlay.

In arriving at a decision it would also be helpful for the physician to know how much annual depreciation is allowed on the new equipment. This information can be readily obtained by calling the doctor's accountant. Another important consideration is the amount of depreciation remaining on the old equipment, if this is relevant. The doctor's accountant can provide advice and answers to both of these questions. In any event, the assistant should obtain in advance a list of quoted prices from the various competing companies.

"A proper inventory is the key to a well-managed program of stock maintenance. It is invaluable in the completion of tax forms; it aids in maintaining a stable financial status in the office; it prevents waste and the accumulation of unnecessary equipment and supplies; it saves time in numerous ways; it helps new personnel to become familiar with the office; and it is essential in the transfer of a practice, if this ever becomes necessary."*

An inventory of standard supplies should

*From Peterson, S.: The dentist and his assistant, ed. 2, St. Louis, 1967, The C. V. Mosby Co., p. 204.

be taken at least once a month. Prior to ordering standard supplies, the assistant should note whether or not a product deteriorates. Replacement dates for antibiotics and other pharmaceuticals must be checked. Only a reasonable supply of items requiring replacement should be kept on hand; otherwise there is the risk that money will be wasted.

The usage factor is another important aspect to consider. In other words, how much of a product does the physician consume during a given period? Furthermore, the product may or may not be a standard one. If it is not, there is a good chance that another manufacturer will introduce something better, and present stocks on hand will be rendered obsolete. The various types of medications, bandages, and certain kinds of supplies are continually being improved and replaced with more advanced types. In light of these developments, the doctor's office should adopt a general policy of purchasing in small quantities.

The medical assistant should assume the responsibility of organizing and maintaining an office inventory if one does not already exist. A complete list of all capital items such as reception room furniture, business office furniture and machines, laboratory equipment, and x-ray equipment should be incorporated into a master inventory. It is good practice to list each capital item of equipment on a separate card, with provision for recording the date the item was purchased, the price, the name of the manufacturer, and the name of the supplier. Provision should also be made for listing any major repair and maintenance checks. The dates and charges for services should also be included. This list is best arranged according to rooms. Filing each inventory card in alphabetical order in an index card file makes for handy reference and the addition of new items.

A separate inventory should be maintained for all instruments used in the physician's practice. Such items are classified as nonexpendable, for they are used over and over again. A card file is probably also the best way to facilitate such an inventory.

An inventory of standard supplies should be taken at least once a month. These materials consist of items classified as expendable because they diminish in quantity, and in most cases cannot be used more than once.*

A notebook system may be more practical than the card file for keeping an inventory of expendable supplies because of the larger number of items involved. A purchasing chart for the entire year can be made in advance. Across the top of the page may be typed the months of the year, while items of supply may be listed down the left of the page according to the order in which they are stored in cabinets and on laboratory and refrigerator shelves. A more graphic effect is achieved by ruling lines down and across the page. Whenever an item is ordered, the quantity and date of the order should be recorded in the appropriate box. The chart then becomes an easy reference of past orders as well as a guide for future ones.

It is advisable to order those items classified as expendable from a running inventory. This will normally include a maximum and a minimum ordering quantity to ensure sufficient storage space and an adequate supply. With the doctor's help, the assistant should determine the actual minimum-maximum ordering quantity for each item. "The maximum limit permits bulk buying for financial savings and convenience, and the minimum limit prevents the stock of an item from being completely depleted. Caution must be exercised in bulk purchases of items with short shelf life, because any savings realized through bulk purchase will be lost if the item deteriorates before it can be used."*

Careful purchasing habits are fundamental to the efficiency of any medical office.

---

*From Peterson, S.: The dentist and his assistant, ed. 2, St. Louis, 1967, The C. V. Mosby Co., pp. 205, 208.

The office that develops and adheres to sound principles in ordering supplies and equipment should rarely run out of supplies, overstock them, or be stuck with obsolete supplies or equipment. The assistant will find the physician more than willing to cooperate with any reasonable system that helps to improve patient care as well as increase net income.

CARE OF THE DOCTOR'S BAG

The doctor's bag is an indispensable traveling companion. The responsibility for packing and checking it rests with the assistant. Time is precious once an emergency call is received, and since the first thing the doctor reaches for is the bag, it must be ready for use at any time.

When cleaning and refilling the doctor's bag the assistant must be careful to include any special diagnostic instruments, test materials, apparatus, medications, and accessories that might be needed. The best way to guarantee that important items will not be forgotten is by performing a daily inspection of the doctor's bag. A checklist of items normally included should be kept at close hand to serve as a reminder when needed.

Before composing such a list, the assistant should always discuss it with the physician to make sure all the required items have been included and ones not wanted omitted. The specific contents of the bag depend upon the nature of the doctor's practice and personal preferences, but many items are also used each day that must be replaced.

A daily inspection might include the following routine.

1. Removing any specimens that may have been taken on house calls, making certain they are properly labeled with the patient's name, the date, and the type of test required.
2. Making sure that any instruments or other nonexpendable materials used are removed and sterilized. A duplicate set of sterilized instruments or disposable materials should always be kept on hand for immediate replacement.
3. Checking the supply of cotton, tongue depressors, microslides for specimens, and alcohol to make sure they are in sufficient supply.
4. Determining what medications have been used and comparing those used against the inventory. The supply should be replenished at once, and the bag should be readied for use.

Part of this routine should include an inspection of the various medications to discover any deteriorated or outdated items. It is also most important to take note that, whenever narcotics are dispensed, it is necessary that the patient's name and address, the date dispensed, the quantity, and the physician's diagnosis be recorded in the office narcotics directory.

An assortment of narcotic drugs is necessary in all medical practices. Narcotics are legally administered by members of the medical profession only, and their use is regulated by the federal government. Once a year the physician must renew his narcotics license and render an inventory of the amount of such drugs in his possession.

Narcotics cannot be legally sold to patients without a physician's prescription, and this prescription cannot be filled after 24 hours has elapsed. The prescription must be written in ink and contain the date, the physician's narcotics registration number, and the patient's name and address. If more than the ordinary amount is prescribed, the condition for which it is given is generally noted on the prescription. Narcotics prescriptions cannot be refilled. All states now require individual prescriptions for barbiturates and certain tranquilizers. In other words, such prescriptions cannot be refilled by a pharmacist without a new prescription written by the physician.

Many physicians now spend considerably less time on the telephone thanks to recent legislation which permits nurses and assistants to telephone prescriptions to pharmacies, providing that physicians confirm such action in writing to the pharmacies. Of course, narcotics prescriptions are excluded from this provision.

The following inventory is a checklist for those basic instruments, accessories, and medications that virtually all physicians carry in their bags. It is hoped that the assistant will use this model as a guide.

Instruments and equipment

Hypodermic syringes and needles (may be disposable)
Scalpel
Dressing forceps
Tourniquet
Illuminated diagnostic set
Aspiration equipment
Stethoscope
Sphygmomanometer
Otoscope
Ophthalmoscope
Hemostats
Tissue forceps
Probe
Scissors
Percussion hammer
Pen-type flashlight
Blood pressure apparatus
Thermometers (oral and rectal)

Accessories

Prescription pad
Fountain pen
Slides
Gauze
Cotton
Adhesive tape
Wooden applicators
Towels
Containers for specimens
Sterile swabs
Safety pins
Tongue depressors
Lubricant (petroleum jelly)
Sterile gloves
Dressings (various sizes)
Bandages (various sizes)

Medications

Narcotics: morphine, codeine
Stimulants: Adrenalin, digitalis, spirits of ammonia
Antibiotics: penicillin, aureomycin, streptomycin, Chloromycetin, Bicillin, sulfonamides
Sedatives: phenobarbital, Demerol, Seconal
Skin sterilizers: alcohol, Merthiolate
Eardrops
Eyedrops

Physicians such as obstetricians and ear, nose, and throat specialists, who provide special treatment, need supplies peculiar to their specialty. The assistant can soon learn these requirements. Supplies should be wrapped in sterile towels and so arranged that all do not become contaminated when only a few are used.

Medications are distributed by the various pharmaceutical houses in different forms: pills, tablets, capsules, injectibles, and so on. Most physicians prefer to carry several different forms of each.

Review questions

1. Describe the responsibility of the medical assistant for office housekeeping.
2. Why is it important for the physician's office to be comfortable and clean?
3. Name five precautions a physician might adopt to prevent the office from being burglarized.
4. How important is an efficient purchasing system?
5. List several ways the physician's income can be increased through efficient purchasing of supplies.
6. What are the advantages of a proper inventory? Describe an effective program for maintaining supplies.
7. Some items are classified as expendable. What are expendable items? Give several examples.
8. List several functions performed by the medical assistant in caring for the doctor's bag.

Suggested readings

Doris, L., and Miller, B. M.: Complete secretary's handbook, ed. 3, Englewood Cliffs, N. J., 1970, Prentice-Hall, Inc.

Peterson, S.: The dentist and his assistant, ed. 3, St. Louis, 1972, The C. V. Mosby Co.

Frederick, P. M., and Kinn, M. E.: Medical office assistant: administrative and clerical, ed. 4, Philadelphia, 1974, W. B. Saunders Co.

part two
Clinical practices

chapter 21

Anatomy and physiology

The study of medicine in all its branches is an important part of a medical assistant's education. It would appear to be true that the mark of a qualified medical assistant would be a knowledge of human anatomy sufficient to give some intelligent appreciation and understanding of medical science. Anyone beginning such a professional career is bound to be overwhelmed by the complexity and multitude of the studies that lie ahead.

This chapter is meant to be a general introduction to anatomy and physiology and must of necessity be brief; it is not offered as a substitute for a textbook on anatomy and physiology, but it is intended to supplement such textbooks, of which there are many excellent ones available.

THE CELLULAR BASIS OF MAN

Before 1838, little was known of the minute structure of the human body. Aristotle's notions of humors and ridiculous superstitions prevailed. In these years, however, Schleiden and Schwann published a description of cell structure that established the fact that all organic bodies were composed of definite units of material called cells, which were arranged in characteristic patterns in different animals and plants. In man the cells are similar to cells in other animals and in plants; in some instances the similarity of form with those of other animals is so great that they appear to be identical.

Cells arise from cells. The origin of the human body is the germ cell (ovum) of

Glossary

acetabulum the rounded cavity of the hipbone that receives the head of the femur

aorta the main artery or blood vessel that distributes blood pumped from the heart

arteriosclerosis degenerative process that produces thickening and hardening of arteries

calcaneus the heel bone or os calcis

carpal pertaining to the bones of the wrist

catheter a tube for evacuating or injecting fluids

epilepsy a neurologic disorder characterized by disturbances of consciousness and/or abnormal convulsive movements

esophagus a musculomembranous canal extending from the pharynx to the stomach

hormone a substance produced by a gland in one part of the body that affects the function of another part of the body

leukocyte white blood corpuscle

meningitis inflammation of the membranes of the brain or spinal cord

plasma the liquid part of the blood and of the lymph

patella the kneecap

pericardium the membranous sac enclosing the heart

periosteum a membrane that invests and nourishes the bone

prostatitis inflammation of the prostate gland

rickets a metabolic disease associated with weakness and deformity of bones

sphygmomanometer an instrument used to measure blood pressure the female that has been fertilized by the germ cell of the male. Thus the fertilized germ cell is a human individual in the one-cell stage of his development. This cell splits into two cells, and these resulting daughter cells into four. This process continues until the developing individual is an intricate mass of many cells.

In the early stages of development the cells are all alike. One looks like another. As development proceeds, however, these cells begin to take on special characteristics and look different from those nearby. This change is called differentiation of the cell. Thus, from cells that are at one stage alike, there arise particular cells known as muscle cells, epithelial cells, connective tissue cells, blood cells, and nerve cells.

This change in structure of the cell is the outward manifestation of profound changes in the functions of the cell. In the stage preceding differentiation, the cells carry on all the processes of life. They take in food, eliminate waste, respond to stimuli, move, and reproduce their kind. Now, with differentiation these functions become highly developed in certain cells. Muscle cells specialize in contraction and hence are foremost in producing movement; nerve cells develop the ability to receive and transmit stimuli and hence play a special part in making the individual aware of his world; the epithelial cells specialize in producing secretions and certain protective functions; and the blood cells engage in transmitting to distant parts the gases necessary for life.

As development proceeds, like cells become organized into masses known as tissues and grouped in arrangements that permit them to carry on effectively their functions. Thus a group of muscle cells form muscle tissue in certain parts; the connective tissue cells mass together in structures known as bones, ligaments, and other supporting structures. This is a disposition and arrangement of cells for highly specialized tasks.

Beyond these simple groupings of like cells in tissue arrangements there are more complex groupings in the body into coordinated organizations known as systems. Thus epithelial cells, connective tissue cells, muscle cells, nerve cells, and blood cells may all coordinate in a mass effort to produce a highly specialized function such as breathing, which is carried on by the respiratory system.

THE SKELETAL SYSTEM

Skeletons of animals vary widely in their design. In some the skeleton is on the outside of the animal, as in the lobster; in others it is enclosed within soft parts, as in man. In some animals the skeleton serves as a protection against enemies (note the remarkable case of the oyster), but in man its function is primarily that of support and movement.

The skeleton is composed of bones and strong bands, called ligaments, that hold the bones together in joints. There are 206 bones in the human body.

In the front view of the skeleton (Fig. 21-1) the spine will be seen as the central axis. From the thoracic section of the spine lead twelve ribs on each side, which swing laterally and forward. The upper seven, terminating in cartilage, completely enclose the thorax as they join the breastbone (sternum). The eighth, ninth, and tenth ribs also end in cartilage and attach to the cartilage of the rib above, thus forming a cartilaginous margin to the lower boundary of the thorax in front. The eleventh and twelfth ribs remain unattached to bone at their forward (anterior) ends, although they are embedded in muscle and other soft parts.

Balanced on top of the first vertebra of the spine is the skull. The skull presents two chief parts: the cranium, which contains the brain, and the face.

The trunk

The bones of the trunk are the vertebrae, the sternum, and the ribs. The backbone of the adult consists of twenty-six sections or vertebrae (Fig. 21-2). Each section is a bony ring with spikes or projections on three sides.

Table 1. Bones

Classification	Name of bone	Single	Paired
Skull	Frontal	1	
	Parietal		2
	Occipital	1	
	Temporal		2
	Sphenoid	1	
	Ethmoid	1	
Face	Nasal		2
	Lacrimal		2
	Maxilla		2
	Turbinate		2
	Zygoma		2
	Palatine		2
	Vomer	1	
	Mandible	1	
Vertebral column	Cervical	7	
	Thoracic	12	
	Lumbar	5	
	Sacrum (5 fused)	1	
	Coccyx (4 fused)	1	
Thorax	Ribs		24
	Sternum	1	
Upper extremity	Clavicle		2
	Scapula		2
	Humerus		2
	Radius		2
	Ulna		2
	Carpus		16
	Metacarpus		10
	Phalanges of hand		28
Lower extremity	Hip (3 fused)		2
	Femur		2
	Patella		2
	Tibia		2
	Fibula		2
	Tarsus		14
	Metatarsus		10
	Phalanges of foot		28
Miscellaneous	Ossicles of ear (3 pairs)		6
	Hyoid	1	
Total		206	

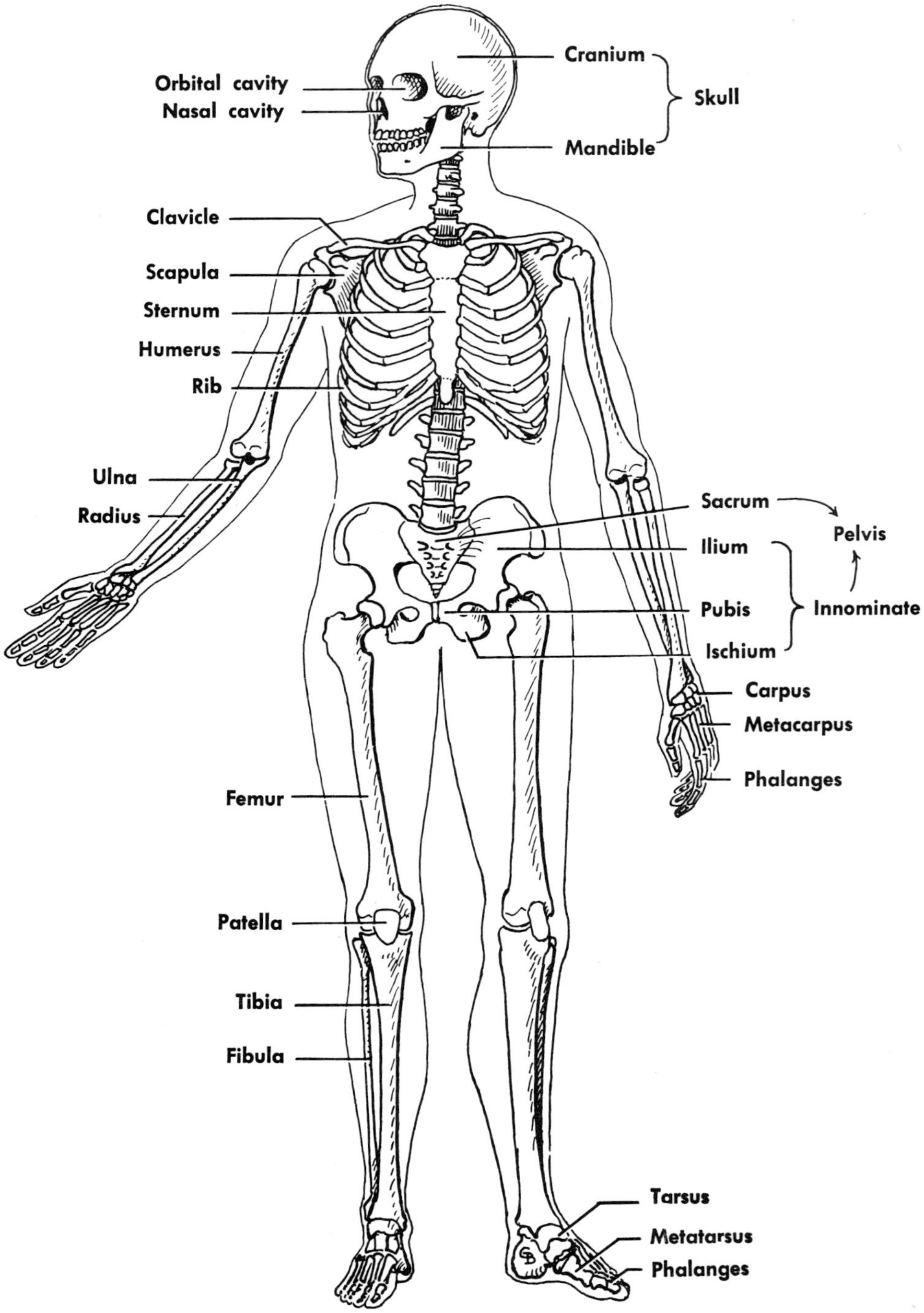

Fig. 21-1. Bones of the adult skeleton.

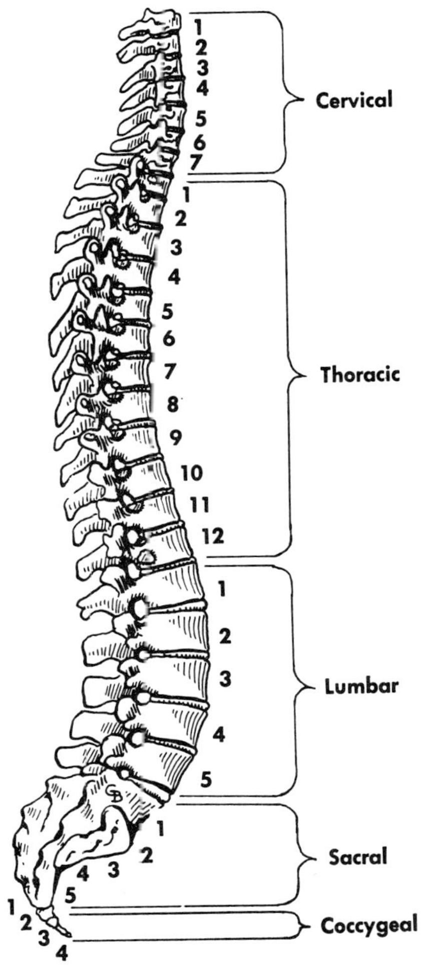

Fig. 21-2. Lateral view of an adult vertebral column, showing the curves and the divisions of the column with reference to the spaces from which the spinal nerves emerge.

They are separated by pads of cartilage, called intervertebral disks. The backbone has four normal curves that sometimes become exaggerated through injury, disease, or poor posture. The vertebrae are divided into groups as follows: the top seven are called the cervical vertebrae, the next twelve are called the thoracic, and the next five the lumbar. The next section, the sacrum, is formed from five vertebrae fused together into one solid bone. The coccyx or tip of the backbone is made up of four small sections and is regarded as one bone. The vertebral column supports the head and trunk; its curves permit a variety of motions, and the pads between the vertebrae ease the jolts of walking or falls.

The spinal cord passes from the brain through the bony rings of the vertebrae, and they serve as a protection for its delicate structure.

The sternum. The front boundary of the upper part of the trunk is called the sternum or breastbone, a flat, narrow bone opposite the upper part of the spine.

The ribs. The ribs form the sides of the chest cavity. They are narrow, flat bones arranged in pairs. There are twelve on each side, and they are attached to the spine at the back, curving around like hoops of a barrel and attached to the sternum in front except for the last two pairs. These are called floating ribs. Thus the spine, sternum, and ribs form what is known as the bony cage around the heart and lungs. The ends of the ribs are composed of cartilage, a substance that resembles bone but that is not as hard as bone. The spaces between the ribs are covered by muscles and are called intercostal spaces.

The pelvis. The lower part of the main bony framework of the body is called the pelvis. It is formed by two large, flat irregular bones that spread outward at the top and narrow down at the lower edges in front. These bones are not completely grown together in the infant, but by the time adulthood is reached they form a single bone. They are joined to the sacrum at the back and are usually referred to as the hipbones. Each bone has a large hollow at the side below the flaring portion for the upper end of the thighbone which fits into this socket. The pelvis of a woman is relatively larger and wider than that of a man. Most of the male organs of reproduction are on the outside of the body. The size and shape of the female pelvis are significant in the birth of a baby. If the pelvis is too small to permit the baby to pass through, an abdominal operation known as a cesarean operation becomes necessary. The pelvis can be measured and x-ray photographs made to determine whether or not it is sufficiently wide to allow the baby's head to pass through.

The upper extremities

Above and in front of the rib cage extending outward on either side at right angles to the breastbone are two long bones known as the clavicles or collarbones. The inner ends are joined to the breastbone and the upper bones of the arm are joined to the outer ends. Opposite these bones at the back are two flat, triangular bones called scapulae or shoulder blades. The single long bone of the upper arm is known as the humerus. The upper end is joined to the collarbone and the lower end to one of the bones of the forearm, forming the elbow joint.

There are two bones in the forearm. The larger, known as the ulna, has two hollows in the upper end. The lower end of the humerus fits into one of these cavities, and the upper end of the other forearm bone fits into the second cavity. The second bone of the forearm, the radius, lies side by side with the ulna but is smaller and shorter. The upper end is connected to the ulna and the lower end to two of the wristbones.

Eight small irregular bones, known as the carpal bones, form the wrist. They are placed in two rows and are so joined together that they allow a small amount of motion. Attached to the bones of the wrist are the five metacarpal bones that form the palm of the hand. These bones are long and slightly curved. Attached to the metacarpal bones are the phalanges or the finger bones. There are three of these bones in each finger and two in the thumb.

The lower extremities

The upper bone of the leg is called the femur, and it is the longest and strongest bone in the body. The upper end of this bone fits into the cavity of the hipbone, the acetabulum. There are two bones in the lower leg; the larger of these bones is known as the tibia or shin bone. It is attached to the lower end of the femur and forms the knee joint. The tibia is much smaller at the lower end, and its inner side ends in the projection of the inner ankle. Lying side by side with the tibia is the fibula. This bone is smaller than the tibia and very slender, and the upper end is attached to the tibia. The pointed lower end forms the outer anklebone. Directly in front of the knee joint lies a small, flat, triangular bone known as the patella. It is commonly called the kneecap and serves as protection for the knee joint and as an attachment for the muscles of the thigh that straighten the leg.

The seven bones of the ankle are called the tarsal bones. They are irregular in shape, and the largest and strongest one is the bone of the heel called the calcaneus. It is the contact between the body weight and the ground. The tarsal bones join the five metatarsal bones or instep bones in such a way as to form two arches, one extending from heel to toe and the other across the foot. These arches sometimes flatten out when supporting muscles become weakened or the body weight is unevenly distributed because of poor posture or improper shoes.

The fourteen bones of the toes, like those of the fingers, are also called phalanges. At times, foot deformities are caused by crowding these bones together into shoes that are too narrow or too short, sometimes resulting in that painful and disfiguring enlargement of the great toe joint called a bunion.

Although the structural plans in the lower and upper extremities are alike, the functional uses are quite different. The hip joint is much less movable than the shoulder; the knee joint moves only forward and backward; and the foot is built strongly to support the body weight, thus lacking the dexterity and suppleness of the hand.

The skeleton is not a dead and static affair. In youth, bones are more readily altered in shape than in mature years. Cells within bones are constantly functioning in response to stresses placed upon them. An example of this occurs when a bone is broken or fractured and healing occurs during the next few weeks. But even in maturity the bone cells are active and are always responsive to the physical and chemical forces that play upon them.

Bones also serve a very important function in making blood cells. The cavities of many bones are filled with spongy tissues, commonly called bone marrow, that produce most of the cells of the blood.

THE MUSCULAR SYSTEM

There are three areas in which different kinds of muscle are found in the body. One is the extensive distribution of muscle masses over the skeleton, providing power for movement and giving form and substance to the extremities. These are the *skeletal* muscles. Another is a special kind of muscle that forms the heart walls. This is *cardiac* muscle. The third, *smooth muscle,* differs from the preceding two. It is found in the eye, the walls of the alimentary canal, blood vessels, various ducts and channels that transmit fluids, and it even comprises the bulk of an organ as in the womb (uterus). Skeletal muscle is sometimes called voluntary because it can contract under voluntary control. Smooth muscle is called involuntary because its contractions are not under voluntary control, and is controlled instead by reflexes and portions of the nervous system below the centers of consciousness. Sometimes skeletal muscle is called striated because it shows parallel markings under the microscope, and smooth muscle is called nonstriated since it lacks these markings.

Skeletal muscles generally attach to bones and commonly to two bones. Skeletal muscles usually produce their effects on parts at some distance from the muscle mass. Thus the power shown in the foot when one runs or rises on the toes is located in the calf of the leg. It is transmitted to the foot through the interposition of a structure called a tendon, which attaches to bones. If the strong movement in the ankle had to be accomplished by muscle masses located there, the ankle would be many times its present size, and the presence of the muscles there would of course limit movement itself.

Bodily line is in part determined by skeletal formation and in part by fat underneath the skin, but bodily line is determined very largely by the size and contour of muscles. Notice, for example, the curves of the arm that reflect underlying muscles, the lateral swelling of the calf, the margins of the trunk, and the crescentic roll of the neck. It is an interesting and important fact that a person's postures are expressions of muscular action.

The second variety of muscle, *cardiac,* forms the wall of the heart. The left ventricle is much thicker than the right. There is a reason for this striking difference. The left ventricle pumps blood over the entire body against a high resistance or pressure. The right ventricle supplies blood a shorter distance to the lungs against a lower resistance or pressure and its walls are therefore not as thick as those of the left ventricle. Most persons appreciate from their own experiences that work of a muscle increases its size and strengthens it. The heart is a muscle and the greater work done by the left side produces a larger muscle than the right. The heart muscle is kept strong by physical activity in precisely the same way that other muscles are maintained in strength.

Smooth muscle, which is not under voluntary control, composes important parts of the walls of all blood vessels except the tiny capillaries. It is found in the walls of all hollow organs or tubes and hence in the whole length of the digestive tract. It forms also the main part of the iris of the eye, and its movements there dilate and constrict the pupil.

It is not as important for a medical assistant to know the names of the muscles as it is to know the kinds of things muscles do. The muscles of the face are used when we laugh or smile or frown. Muscles control the movements of the eyes and open and close the lids. They move the lips and tongue and jaw. Large flat muscles extend like bands along the shoulders and on either side of the backbone. We stimulate the nerves and circulation of blood in these muscles when we rub a back. They furnish support for the abdominal organs and hold the uterus in place. They are indispensable to the breathing process and in moving food along the digestive canal.

THE CIRCULATORY SYSTEM

Circulation in man exhibits several distinctive characteristics. The heart in the thorax hangs from several large vessels and rests on the diaphragm, the muscle that separates the chest from the abdominal cavity.

The vessels lie in protected places. The large vessels of the arm, lying in the armpit, pass on the inner side of the arm. In the lower extremity they are disposed to the center line and at the knee pass behind the joint.

Food materials and oxygen are necessary to all parts of the body. Waste materials must be carried to the organs through which our bodies rid themselves of waste. These two functions are performed by means of the blood itself, the blood vessels, and the heart. The circulatory system fulfills these needs, and in addition to circulating blood it carries hormones, enzymes, and other substances to all parts of the body.

THE BLOOD

The amount of blood in the body of an adult varies with weight. If one weighs 132 pounds, the amount will be about four quarts. The color varies from bright to dark red, depending upon the amount of oxygen present. It is half cells and half liquid, although it appears all liquid until it comes in contact with the air. The liquid part is known as the plasma; it is light yellow in color, transparent, and almost entirely water. Dissolved in this liquid are food materials, carbon dioxide, salt, and waste materials. The blood picks up waste materials from all parts of the body. It also contains those substances made by the endocrine glands called the hormones and certain other substances that aid in body resistance. There are three kinds of cells or corpuscles in the blood.

The red cells are the most numerous and get their color from an iron compound called hemoglobin. Hemoglobin combines with the oxygen breathed into the lungs and the red cells are a bright or darker red, depending upon the amount of oxygen they have absorbed. The red cells are made in the marrow of the bones, are released into the bloodstream and live for about four months. The white cells, which are formed in the bone marrow and also in the lymph nodes, are larger than the red cells but fewer in number. There is about one white cell to every 600 or 700 red cells. They can move through the walls of the blood vessels and are the body's greatest protection against infection. When infectious organisms enter the body, these white cells move in great numbers and surround and destroy the invading organisms. The pus in wounds is composed of dead and living white cells. In addition to red and white cells, the blood contains small cells called platelets. These cells, also called thrombocytes, are important in the process of blood clot formation.

When blood vessels are injured, the blood is exposed to substances that cause it to clot. The clots act as a plug or cork at the end of cut vessels, and the bleeding stops. There is a normal time for the clotting of blood and if the blood does not clot within that time there may be a deficiency of either platelets or one of the other factors responsible for clotting. A deficiency of any one of these clotting factors is responsible for hemophilia, a disease characterized by an increased tendency toward bleeding.

Loss of large amounts of blood is called hemorrhage. Hemorrhage may also be caused by many conditions. There may be a decreased number or altered function of platelets when the clot will form but it will not retract. Again the capillaries may be weak and hemorrhage result. Many infections, allergies, and certain diseases may be the cause of these conditions.

A thrombus is a blood clot within the walls of a blood vessel. If a thrombus becomes loosened from the blood vessel it is called an *embolus*. A loosened blood clot may block circulation at some vital point and cause death.

Anemia is a condition characterized by an insufficient concentration of hemoglobin, which carries oxygen in the blood or a reduction of the number of red blood cells. Often both situations exist. The number of blood cells and the amount of hemoglobin can be estimated in the laboratory. The red cells are called erythrocytes and usually number 4,500,000 to 5,000,000 per cubic millimeter. The white cells are called leukocytes and usually number between 5,000 and 9,000 per cubic millimeter. The term leukocytosis is applied to the condition in which there are more than this number present, as in the presence of infections.

The blood vessels. The blood is carried through the body in a network of tubes of various sizes called arteries, veins, and capillaries. The arteries carry the blood away from the heart through the aorta, the largest artery, and its branches. The aorta resembles a large tube and divides into smaller tubes to carry the blood to all parts of the body. The walls of the arteries are very elastic. The smallest division of the arteries joins a network of very tiny tubes called capillaries, which bring the blood to similar divisions of the veins, the blood vessels that bring the blood back to the heart. The blood is emptied into the heart by two large veins known as the superior and inferior vena cava, so called because one brings the blood from the upper part of the body and the other from the lower. These two large veins, like the aorta, divide into many branches. Many of them contain little flaps or folds called valves, which prevent the blood from flowing back into the capillaries.

The heart pumps the blood through the blood vessels. We can feel the force of the heart contraction over certain arteries that lie fairly close to the skin. By putting the finger over these arteries we can feel the wave of pressure caused by each heartbeat. Counting the number of waves for a minute is called taking the pulse. Pulse is usually counted on the wrist, the side of the neck, or the temple because these arteries are easily accessible. As the arteries become older their walls are harder and less elastic and a condition that is popularly called hardening of the arteries (arteriosclerosis) sometimes develops. The pressure within arteries is called the blood pressure and is higher in adults than in children. Weight, exercise, and emotional disturbances influence blood pressure. Pressure greatly above or below normal for any age has great medical significance. It can be measured by an apparatus known as the sphygmomanometer, and this measurement should always be included in any complete physical examination.

The heart. The heart is a hollow muscular organ that pumps blood through the body. It is located in the left lower part of the chest cavity and is divided into two sides, the left and the right. Each of these sides is divided into two chambers. Blood is brought from the upper and lower parts of the body by the superior and inferior vena cava and emptied into the right atrium, which is the upper right chamber, and then passes into the right ventricle, which is the lower right chamber (Fig. 21-3). The opening between these chambers is provided with flaps that create a valve (the tricuspid valve) that prevents blood from flowing backwards. As the heart contracts, it pumps blood from the right ventricle into the pulmonary artery to the lungs where the blood is mixed with oxygen that is brought into them from the air. The blood in the right side of the heart is bluish in color, having left most of its oxygen in the cells of the body. Picking up

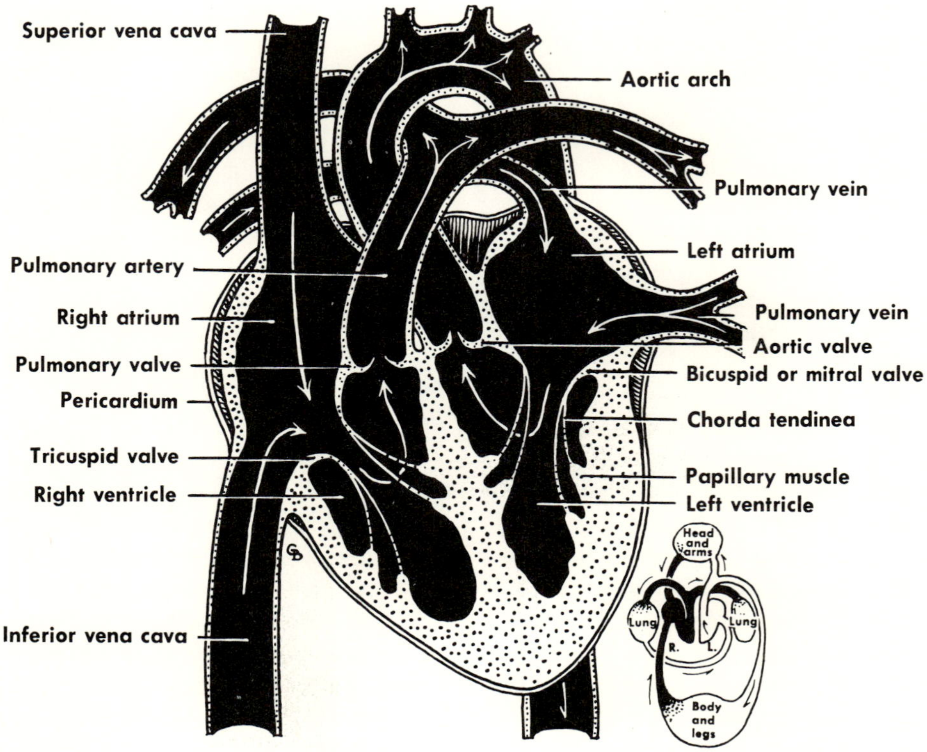

Fig. 21-3. Direction of the blood flow within the heart.

oxygen in the lungs, the blood again becomes red and flows back to the heart through the pulmonary vein into the left atrium, the upper chamber on the left side of the heart. On the left side of the heart, between the left atrium and the left ventricle, there is another set of flaps that form a valve (the mitral valve) that keeps the blood from flowing backward. Blood passes into the left ventricle and is then pumped out through the aorta into the body. Blood is kept from flowing backward from the aorta to the ventricle by the aortic valve. Failure of any of the valves of the heart may cause the heart to pump inefficiently and lead to heart failure.

In addition to proper functioning of the valves, in order to pump efficiently the heart needs a continuous supply of blood to provide oxygen and nutrients, which it gets from two arteries, the coronary arteries, that arise from the aorta just beyond the aortic valve.

The heart is enclosed in a thin sac called the pericardium. The muscular part of the heart is called the myocardium; the inner lining of the heart, the endocardium. Pericarditis, myocarditis, and endocarditis are forms of heart disease caused by the infection or inflammation of these structures.

If the coronary arteries become severely narrowed, insufficient blood reaches the heart muscle. Narrowing and occlusion of these arteries because of deposition of fatty substances is called coronary artery disease and is a leading cause of death throughout the world.

When insufficient quantities of blood reach the heart muscles, severe chest pain, called angina pectoris, may result. Individuals suffering from this condition are said to have coronary insufficiency. If the supply is seriously impaired some of the heart muscle may actually die. This is called a heart attack or a myocardial infarction. It was formerly thought that most individuals with a heart attack had a clot or thrombus in their coronary arteries, but it is now known that most cases of heart attack do not involve a clot in the coronary arteries and the term coronary thrombosis is no longer used.

THE NERVOUS SYSTEM

Many persons who try to study anatomy and physiology fail to comprehend the nervous system; yet it is simple if one omits the complex details.

Consider an animal much simpler than man. The amoeba is a single cell of protoplasm, the substance of which cells in all animals are composed, and has no nervous system; nevertheless the protoplasm of the amoeba shows the qualities that characterize all nervous organizations. It shows excitability, conductivity, and integration. This means that the amoeba shows a change in its behavior when stimulated (excitability), that this change is conducted to other parts of the cell (conductivity), and that the organism responds with reference to the excitation (integration). Thus, if a needle pricks the amoeba it is excited, the stimulus is conducted throughout the cell, and the protoplasm shows an integrated action by withdrawing from the offending needle.

In animals with nervous systems this typical behavior of excitability, conduction, and integration can be further illustrated. In some of the wormlike animals with a head end, the real beginning of a nervous system may be observed. The three qualities remain as characteristic as in the behavior of the nervous system, but now there are parts that are prominently identified with each quality. Excitability is enlarged and becomes more selective by means of sense organs called receptors. Conduction is facilitated by pathways called nerves, over which the excitation can pass. Integration operates through a central clearinghouse to which excitations from several areas may be sorted out and responses made with reference to particular excitations.

Integration becomes increasingly more marked in high forms, and the various centers are connected. The center located in the head of the animal usually receives more excitation than the others because of the more varied environmental situations met by the head of the animal, and this center grows larger and dominates the others.

This brief sketch of the nervous system in lower forms gives the pattern of the complex organization in man. The receptors are the far-flung sensory mechanisms in which sight, hearing, taste, smell, and touch are so well known. The pathways are reproduced a countless number of times in the nerves. The head ganglion becomes the brain, and the separate centers are fused in the coordinated structure of the spinal cord. It should be remembered that conduction pathways (nerves) lead also from centers to muscles and glands that can translate into action and myriad messages coming into the cord and brain.

Thus this tremendously complex structure of brain, cord, and nerves is reduced to simple terms by understanding the unit of behavior observed in simple forms of life. One may, however, examine with more detail the parts of the mechanism, but regardless of the elaborations that occur in the structure, the simple pattern persists. There are excitation, conduction, and integration; the latter is usually manifested in a response in gland or muscle.

Excitation operates through the function of specialized cells arranged to form structures that pick up particular messages from the environment. The papillae of the tongue are taste receptors. The ending of the auditory nerve is an elaborate receptor for picking up sound vibrations transmitted to the inner ear. The eye is one of the most highly developed of the sensory receptors with numerous parts that direct light rays upon the retina in which are filaments of the optic nerve. Touch receptors are in the skin. These are the more obvious receptors, but in addition to these of the external environment there are sense organs that pour into central stations messages of excitation from internal parts. It may be said then that from the environment and from the organism itself constantly arise excitations that bring to central stations a vast amount of information regarding the surrounding world and the state of the organism itself.

The conduction pathways or nerves pass to and from the cord and brain. The structure known as a nerve is composed of fibers that are extensions of nerve cells in the cord, brain, or masses outside the cord known as ganglia. Some of these fibers are carrying impulses toward and some away from the cord or brain. The former are known as afferent nerves and the latter as efferent nerves. The cell bodies of efferent nerves are in the cord or brain, and those of afferent nerves are in the ganglia or brain.

The spinal cord extends down through the length of the thoracic vertebrae. Messages come through the nerves of the body to the spinal cord and through to the brain. The brain in turn sends messages through the cord to the nerves, which go out to all parts of the body. The spinal cord is covered by extensions of the three membranes covering the brain, and the space between the two inner membranes is filled with the same clear fluid (cerebrospinal fluid or CSF).

When nerve pathways are interrupted, the nerve fibers separated from the cell body degenerate. Destruction of the cell body also results in degeneration of the pathway. This explains what happens in various types of paralysis—an injury to the pathway that severs a nerve, as when a nerve to the arm is cut, causes loss of function of the nerve beyond the cut end and paralysis results.

The brain is a highly developed center. It serves to integrate messages received from both the external and internal environment. Some of these messages are handled automatically by centers in the cord, as some reflexes are, and never reach the brain for decision. The brain weighs about three pounds in the adult, and actual growth stops at about the twentieth year.

The brain is a sensitive structure and the bones of the skull serve as a protection against injury. It is covered by three membranes. The first is located next to the skull; the second is next to the brain and is filled with blood vessels; and the third is located between the first and second membranes. There are spaces between these membranes and between the two inner membranes that are filled with a clear fluid that acts as a cushion. The outer surface of the brain is made up of a substance called *gray matter* and is filled with nerve cells that connect with nerves going out from and coming into the brain. The inside of the brain is composed of *white matter* filled with nerve fibers that communicate with the nerve cells in the gray matter.

The front part of the brain, the cerebrum, is its largest part and contains the control centers for the special senses of seeing, hearing, smelling, and tasting. It also controls speaking, learning, thinking, and remembering. It sets in motion many acts we do voluntarily as well as those we have done so often that they take place almost without our thinking about them, such as passing urine and feces and laughing or crying. The back part of the brain is known as the cerebellum and controls the action of the muscles to keep them working together; it has a direct connection with the cerebrum through many tiny nerve threads. The connection between the brain and the spinal cord is through the spinal bulb or the medulla. The medulla is beneath the cerebellum, and its lower end is a part of the spinal cord. It controls the breathing and the action of the heart and blood vessels.

We have been describing the central nervous system. There is another nervous system, the autonomic, that is probably older, but in some respects less well known. It is composed of ganglia lying outside the cord with nerves connecting with viscera and various glands. The functions of this part of the nervous system relate to breathing, nutrition, and excretion. The autonomic system operates without voluntary control and can function independent of the cerebrum, although it is frequently influenced by cerebral function. Fear, for example, may stop digestion, cause evacuation of bowels, accelerate the heart, and contract numerous structures.

THE DIGESTIVE SYSTEM

In simple terms the digestive system (Fig. 21-4) is like a conveyor belt along which articles are moved and to which articles are added from time to time and likewise removed. Of course, this analogy is very rough. Rather food is propelled through the tubes by coordinated contraction of the muscular wall of the intestines.

Food is taken into *the mouth* where it is chewed by the teeth and mixed with saliva from the salivary glands. The tongue, which is also the chief organ of taste, moves the food in the mouth, and the stimulation of the taste buds on the tongue increases the flow of saliva. This is the next step toward getting the food ready for body use because a substance in the saliva changes starch into sugar. As we swallow, muscles raise the pharynx to receive the food, and as the muscles relax they push the food into the esophagus.

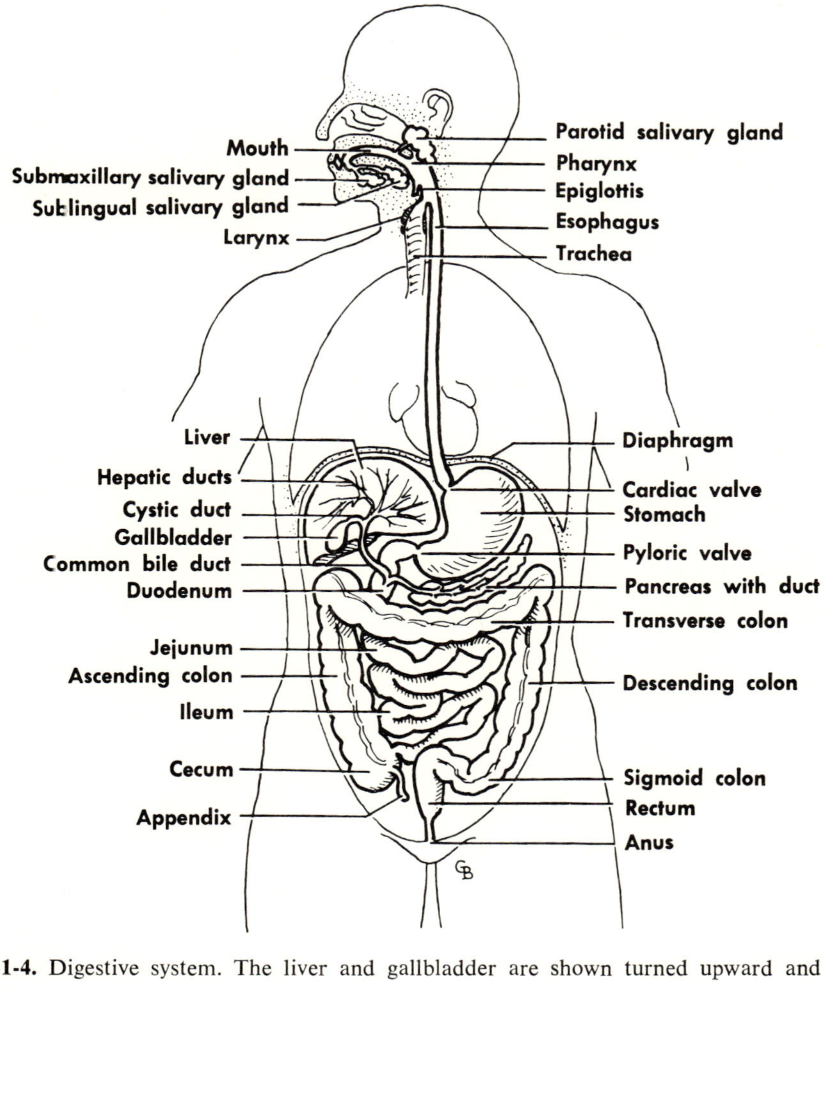

Fig. 21-4. Digestive system. The liver and gallbladder are shown turned upward and to the right.

The teeth also aid in digestion by grinding food into a readily digestible form. The teeth are set in sockets in the upper and lower jawbones. The root is that portion of the tooth extending into the bony socket (Fig. 21-5). The crown extends above the gum, and the neck is the slightly narrowed part between the crown and the root. A tooth is composed of dentin and contains a central cavity that encloses the pulp, blood vessels, and nerves. Enamel protects the crown and cement covers the root. Dentin, enamel, and cement are harder than bone. The front and side teeth are shaped for biting and cutting, and the back teeth are shaped for grinding. The first set of 20 teeth is temporary and later is replaced by the 32 permanent teeth. The last upper and lower teeth on each side of the mouth are the so-called wisdom teeth and often do not appear before the twenty-fifth year. If they are crowded for space, then they become troublesome and painful.

The *esophagus* is a tube about nine inches long; it is just behind the trachea and connects the pharynx and stomach. *The stomach* resembles a collapsible sac and is very muscular, which enables it to enlarge and contract freely. It moves the food toward the small intestine and churns it vigorously. The gastric juices mix with the food and start to break down the food into a form that the

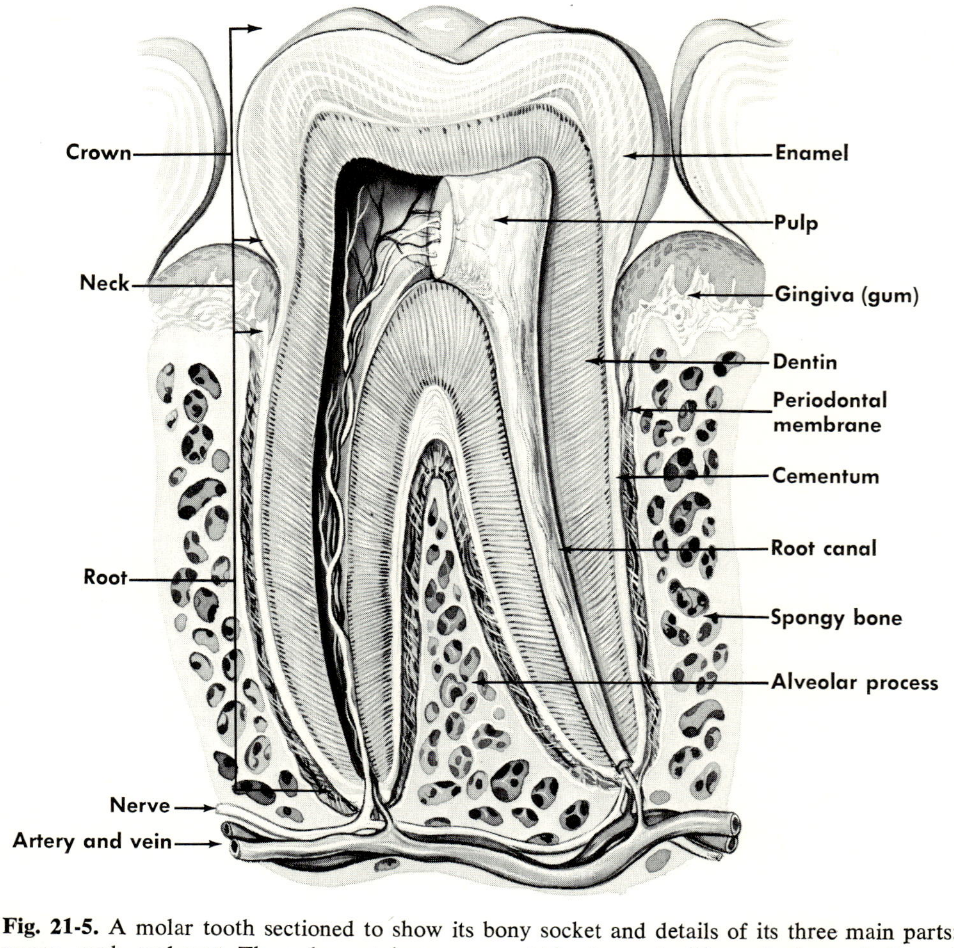

Fig. 21-5. A molar tooth sectioned to show its bony socket and details of its three main parts: crown, neck, and root. The pulp contains nerves and blood vessels. (From Anthony, C. P., and Kolthoff, N. J.: Textbook of anatomy and physiology, ed. 9, St. Louis, 1975, The C. V. Mosby Co.)

intestines can later absorb. This process is called digestion. Food may remain in the stomach a few minutes or several hours until it is partially liquefied. It passes in small amounts through the opening at the lower end of the stomach into the intestines.

The greatest amount of digestion occurs in the *small intestine.* It contains a digestive juice that comes from its walls. It contains bile from the liver and pancreatic juice from the pancreas. Through the action of these juices, digestion is carried still farther. The small intestine, which is about twenty feet long, grows narrower toward the lower end, and its lining is thrown into many folds covered with tiny fingerlike projections filled with capillaries. These capillaries take up the food material that is ready for use so that it can be carried to all parts of the body. The divisions of the small intestine are the duodenum, the jejunum, and the ileum. The material that has not yet been digested passes on to the large intestine, which is wider than the small intestine, about five feet long, and divided into the cecum, the colon, and the rectum.

The appendix is attached to the cecum. It is of no known importance in man except as a cause of inflammation or appendicitis. The colon is a major site of reabsorption of fluids that have passed from the small intestines. The lower part of the large intestines, the rectum, ends in a tube about one and one-half inches long. Its outer opening, known as the anus, is kept closed by means of two round, tight muscles. Solid, nonabsorbable wastes pass into and through the large intestine and accumulate in a bulky mass in the rectum. This mass presses upon the muscles in the anus and they expand to permit defecation. Feces remaining in the rectum for any length of time may become hard and dry and are difficult to expel, a condition called fecal impaction.

Food is moved through the intestines in a wavelike motion by contractions of the tiny muscles in the intestinal walls. We call this movement peristalsis, and it usually takes over five hours for food to pass through the small intestine. Through the use of x-ray films it is possible to discover whether or not food is going through the food canal normally and to locate growths in the stomach or intestines that interfere with its progress. Inflamed and irritated areas sometimes develop on the inside of the stomach and the intestine. These areas of irritation, called ulcers, are localized and cause erosion of the surface of the stomach or duodenum.

The liver, which lies beneath the diaphragm and is the largest gland in the body, produces bile, a digestive juice that helps in the emulsification of fats and assists in their digestion. An extra amount of bile is stored in the small sac known as the gallbladder, which is connected with the small intestines by a narrow tube. It is very common, especially in women, for stones to form in the gallbladder. This is known as cholelithiasis. The liver is a major storage space for sugar in the form of glycogen as well as the body's major site for the synthesis of protein. The liver also helps to modify a large number of drugs and other substances naturally occurring in the body into a form that can be easily excreted by the kidneys.

The pancreas is situated behind the stomach. The pancreatic juice, which is delivered to the intestines, aids in the digestion of food. The pancreas also secretes insulin into the blood. Lack of insulin results in diabetes mellitus, a condition characterized by abnormally high blood sugar. An insufficient production of pancreatic juice causes an inability to absorb nutrients and results in severe malnutrition.

THE RESPIRATORY SYSTEM

Respiration is a process in which oxygen, a gas needed by body cells, is made available for them and the waste gas, carbon dioxide, is removed from the blood. The lungs and circulation cooperate in this function. Air is drawn into the lungs, which is called inspiration, and expelled from the lungs, which is called expiration. Oxygen in the inhaled air passes into the blood from the air sacs in the lungs and is carried to the body cells. Carbon dioxide passes into the blood from the body cells, is carried to the air sacs in the lungs, and leaves the body in the exhaled air. The organs of respiration are the nose, the pharynx, the larynx, the trachea, the bronchi, and the lungs. The first five serve as passageways to and from the lungs. They warm and moisten the air and catch particles of dust and dirt.

The nose is formed by bone and cartilage and is divided into two cavities by a cartilaginous partition called the septum. The nasal cavities open into the upper part of the throat and at the upper end contain the openings to the sinuses and tear ducts. Three small bones, the turbinates, project into each nasal cavity. The nasal cavities are lined with mucous membrane and filled with small blood vessels. Tiny hairs at the outer entrance act as filters to remove the dust from the inhaled air. The nose is also the organ of smell and the endings of the nerves of smell, or the olfactory nerves, are found in the mucous membrane. The eustachian tubes, connected with the ear, open into the space behind the nasal cavities. In the center of the rear wall is a mass of tissue called the adenoids. This mass is usually much larger in children than in adults and sometimes seriously interferes with breathing. If the mass gets large and becomes infected, it may be necessary to remove it by surgery. At the same time the tonsils are sometimes removed, and this is referred to as a tonsillectomy and adenoidectomy.

The pharynx is a tube-shaped structure behind the nose and mouth that serves as a passageway for both air and food. Air passes through the pharynx to the larynx and, in the act of swallowing, muscles lift the pharynx to receive the food and press it down into the esophagus. That part of the pharynx behind the mouth is called the throat. The tonsils lie at the back of the throat. The larynx is a boxlike structure that lies in front of the esophagus at the upper part of the neck and is moved by the muscles attached to it. In the act of swallowing, a small lid closes down over the upper end to shut out food. Inside this triangular box are two folds of mucous membrane, the vocal cords, extending from front to back. There is a space between these folds that changes in shape to become wider in breathing and narrower in speaking. The vibrations of these cords as air passes over them produces the sound of speaking or singing. When the cords vibrate slowly the voice is lower in pitch. If they vibrate rapidly, the pitch becomes higher. Voices differ because of differences in the length of the vocal cords and the size of the voice box. Vibrations are produced by the air breathed out, and the voice becomes louder and stronger if we force air out rapidly or in large amount. If the air passages are blocked in any way, the voice is usually affected. When the vocal cords become inflamed, the voice becomes hoarse.

The trachea

The trachea or windpipe is in front of the esophagus and is a tube held rigid by rings of cartilage and lined with mucous membrane filled with tiny hairlike processes. These processes move constantly to wave the mucus back and up into the throat and thus prevent dust and germs from entering the lungs. The upper end of the trachea joins the lower end of the larynx. At the lower end the trachea divides into the two branches of the bronchi. The *bronchi* are the divisions of the trachea that enter the right and left lungs and divide into many branches that grow smaller and thinner walled until they end in the air sacs.

The lungs

The lungs are two cone-shaped organs that lie in the chest cavity or rib cage. They are composed of spongy material containing the many small branches of the bronchi, numerous blood vessels, nerves, and air sacs. They are capable of holding seven or eight pints of air. A thin membrane, called the pleura, covers each lung and also lines the chest cavity. These two membranes are separated by a fluid that keeps the surfaces moist so they move smoothly against each other with the motion of the lungs in breathing. If these surfaces become inflamed or rough, they rub against each other and cause pain with every breath. This condition is known as pleurisy. Sometimes an abnormal amount of fluid forms, and if the amount becomes so great that it interferes with breathing, it has to be withdrawn. This condition is known as a pleural effusion. There is usually no air between the lung and the chest wall. If a defect in the chest wall or lung develops, a collection of air between the chest wall and the lining of the lung will be formed. This is called a pneumothorax.

THE EXCRETORY SYSTEM

Carbon dioxide, a waste product of cell activity, is eliminated by the lungs, although these organs are not usually considered parts of the eliminative system. The skin gives off water and some waste material that is important in elimination when other agencies are impaired, but in reality the skin is primarily a protective and heat-regulatory structure and not an important excretory organ. The waste left after digestion of food is not typically a product of the elimination system and is better considered under the digestive system, although this waste needs to be eliminated.

Much of the waste material is eliminated from the body in the urine through the combined action of the kidneys, ureters, bladder, and urethra (Fig. 21-6). The kidneys are two bean-shaped organs located in the upper back part of the abdomen on either side of the backbone slightly above the waist. They are imbedded in cushions of fat that help to keep them in place. The kidneys remove from the blood those salts, poisons, proteins, wastes, and water that are eliminated from the body as urine.

The urine is carried away from the kidneys by two tubes called the ureters. The

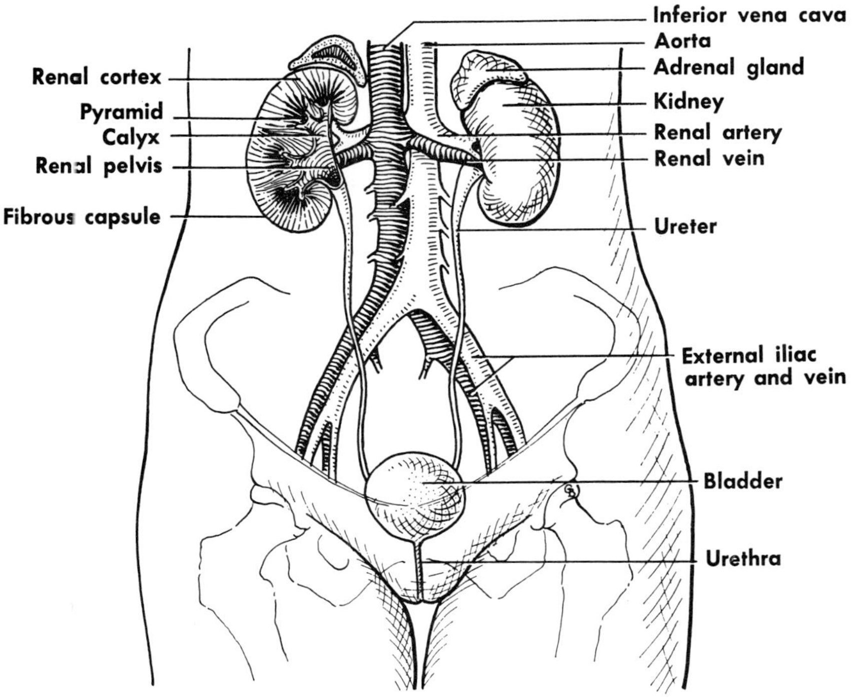

Fig. 21-6. Urinary system.

ureters are about ten inches long and contract to move the urine down into the bladder. The bladder lies in the pelvic cavity behind the pubic bone. It is in front of the rectum in the male and in front of the vagina and the neck of the uterus in the female. It is hollow and muscular and acts as a reservoir for the urine, normally holding about a pint. When it becomes full, pressure causes a desire to empty the contents. In order to prevent a constant leakage of urine, the opening into the urethra is provided with a tight, circular muscle that normally is contracted and relaxes only during the act of urination.

The urethra is the narrow passage from the bladder that ends in the outer opening through which urine is voided. This opening is at the end of the penis of the male and between the clitoris and the opening of the vagina in the female. Involuntary urination, or incontinence, is caused by lack of bladder control, which may in turn be caused by lack of consciousness, injury to the nerves that control the bladder, weak bladder muscles, bladder disease, or substances in the urine that cause irritation. Nervousness and the sight and sound of water will sometimes cause a desire to urinate. If the bladder cannot be emptied normally, it is sometimes necessary to draw the urine out by a catheter. This procedure requires careful training before it can be safely performed.

THE REPRODUCTIVE SYSTEM

The reproductive organs differ in the male and female and in general begin to function at the time of puberty. In boys, this development usually begins at about the age of 13 to 15 years, but in girls it is usually a year or two earlier. The growth of the organs of reproduction causes increased changes in general body growth and in the emotions. This period of change is called puberty.

The male reproductive system

The male reproductive organs consist of the testes, the urethra, and the prostate

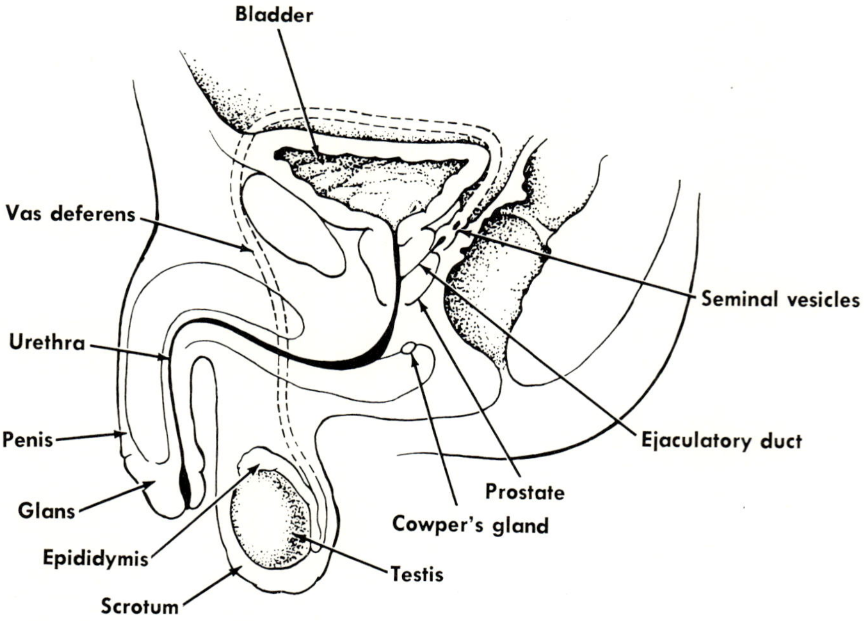

Fig. 21-7. Male reproductive organs. (From Iorio, J.: Childbirth: family-centered nursing, ed. 3, St. Louis, 1975, The C. V. Mosby Co.)

(Fig. 21-7). The testes are two oval-shaped glands suspended in and covered by the baglike sac known as the scrotum. The testes serve two main functions: to make male reproductive cells called spermatozoa and to secrete testosterone, the principal male hormone. Spermatozoa are carried from the testes through a narrow tube called the ductus deferens or vas deferens. During an operation called a vasectomy, which is performed to cause sterility, this tube is cut.

Before reaching the urethra within the penis, several glands contribute secretions that provide a vehicle for the spermatozoa. The largest of the glands is the prostate gland, which lies at the base of the urethra. This gland sometimes becomes enlarged and hard in later life and presses against the urethra and interferes with the passage of urine. Sometimes this gland becomes inflamed, a condition known as prostatitis. In older men, this gland must often be removed surgically, either because it has increased in size or because it has developed cancer. Another gland is located immediately above the testis and is called the epididymis. This gland sometimes becomes infected and extremely swollen and painful, a condition called epididymitis.

The penis consists of the shaft, an opening for urine and semen called the urethra, and the glans. The glans is highly sensitive and is located at the end of the penis. It is covered by a fold of skin, the prepuce, that is often removed for hygienic or religious reasons. This operation is called circumcision and when done in early childhood reduces the incidence of cancer of the penis in adults. During sexual stimulation, or under a variety of conditions involving involuntary reflexes, the penis may become engorged with blood, enlarged, hardened, and erect.

The female reproductive system

The female reproductive system (Fig. 21-8) contains the ovaries, which are two almond-shaped glands that lie near the back wall of the pelvic cavity and produce the female cells known as ova. Each cell is contained in a little sac, and when the cell or ovum is fully developed, the sac bursts and the ovum is discharged. The ovaries also secrete two important hormones: estrogen and progesterone. These are the principal female hormones and influence changes in menstruation and the growth of a fertilized ovum. During adult life the ovaries contain many eggs in various stages of development and one is discharged about every 28 days. This process begins at puberty and continues at regular intervals until late middle age when, during menopause, menstruation gradually ceases. There are two uterine tubes, also known as the fallopian tubes. They carry the ova from the ovaries to the uterus. The upper ends are near the ovaries and are provided with little fringes that catch the ovum as it leaves the ovary. The ovum passes through the tube into the uterus and, if it is not fertilized does not survive. Fertilization takes place in the tube when a male sperm cell penetrates the ovum. An impregnated ovum passes down into the uterus and becomes attached to the uterine wall. If, as occasionally happens, the impregnated ovum remains in the tube, its growth distends and may rupture the tube. This causes bleeding that may be fatal and necessitates an immediate surgical procedure. This condition is called a tubal or ectopic pregnancy. The uterus is a hollow, pear-shaped organ that is muscular and capable of great expansion. The lower part tapers to a narrow neck, the cervix, that extends into the vagina. The uterus is supported by ligaments and is easily tilted forward and backward. During pregnancy it rises upward into the abdominal cavity.

The vagina is the canal that lies between the bladder and the rectum. It surrounds the lower end of the uterus and opens into the vulva. Its inner surface is moistened by fluid secreted by glands within its walls. The vagina changes considerably under the influence of female hormones at puberty. After menopause, when the ovaries produce less estrogen, the vagina

A

B

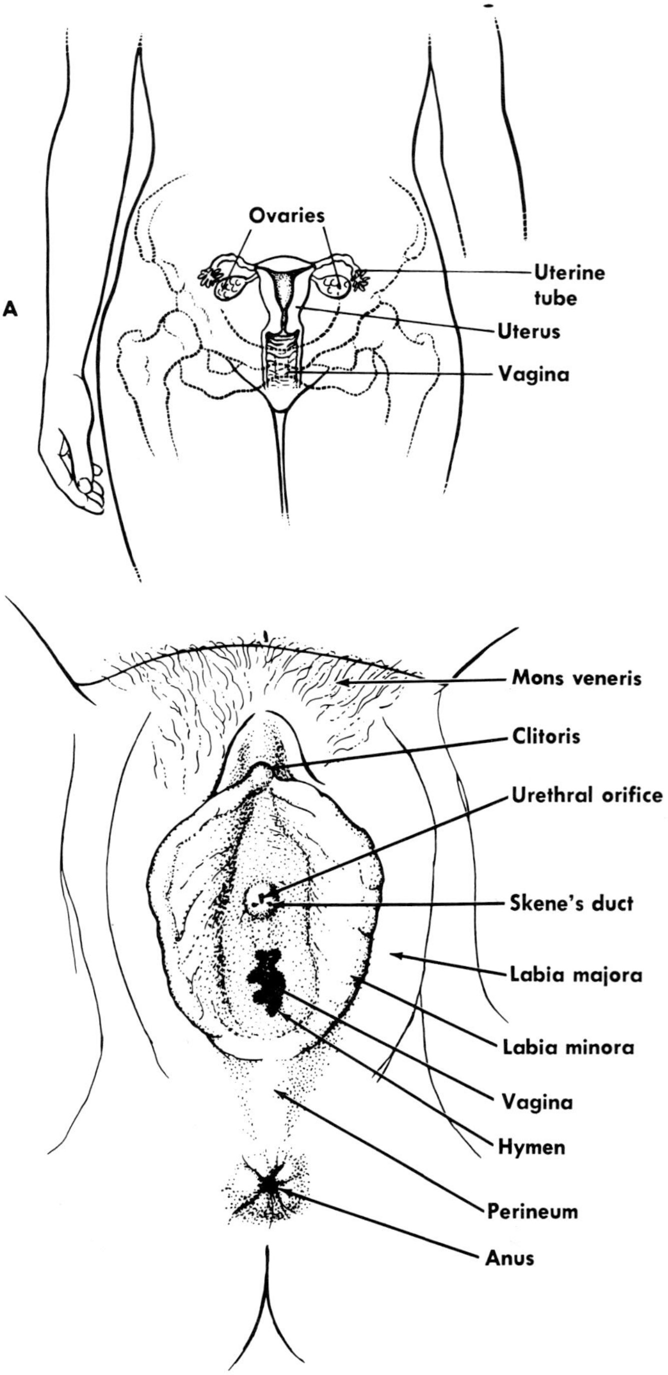

Fig. 21-8. A, Female pelvic area, schematic front view. **B,** External female genitalia. (**A** from Hubbard, C. W.: Family planning education, St. Louis, 1973, The C. V. Mosby Co. **B** from Iorio, J.: Childbirth: Family-centered nursing, ed. 3, St. Louis, 1975, The C. V. Mosby Co.)

becomes thin, less elastic, and produces less secretion.

The vulva (the external genitals) (see Fig. 21-8) consists of the labia, the clitoris, the hymen, and the pubis. The labia are two sets of liplike folds at the opening of the vagina. The clitoris is a small body containing many nerves and blood vessels; it is located at the upper meeting point of the labia majora and labia minora. Like the glans of the penis, it is very sensitive and subject to engorgement and enlargement during sexual stimulation. The hymen is a thin band of skin at the entrance to the vagina. It may be ruptured during sexual intercourse and is completely obliterated after childbirth. The pubis is the rounded fatty pad covered with skin and hair about the vaginal opening. The space between the lower end of the vagina and the rectum is called the perineum.

The *breasts* or *mammary glands* are an important part of the reproductive process in the female. They are present but undeveloped in the male. These two glands are located on the outer surface of the chest, are surrounded by fat, contain many blood vessels, and open into the nipples through many small canals. They secrete the milk that nourishes the child after it is born. Careful examination of the breasts for masses, retractions of the skin, or a bloody discharge from the nipples should be performed regularly in all women. Any of these may be early signs in cancer of the breast.

Menstruation. Through the influence of ovarian hormones, the lining of the adult uterus is prepared during each menstrual cycle to receive a fertilized ovum. If fertilization does not occur, a portion of the lining of the uterus is discarded as a bloody discharge called menstruation. In some women this occurs every 28 days while in others it is irregular. If a fertilized ovum nestles in the lining of the uterus it produces hormones that keep the uterine lining from being discarded. The fertilized ovum is thus able to grow on the surface of the uterus. As the embryo grows, a complex series of events eventually lead to a connection between the uterus and the embryo called the placenta. The embryo is later connected to the uterus by an umbilical cord.

During menstruation many women feel cramping sensations and varying degrees of discomfort. The severity of this discomfort (menstrual cramps) is highly variable among different women and for an individual woman may vary from month to month. Severe, prolonged, or incapacitating menstrual pain is sufficient reason for medical evaluation.

Menopause. The ovaries cease to ovulate when a woman is about 45 years old, although the age varies in individuals. This is called the menopause and menstruation ceases at this time. It is a difficult period for some women because of certain annoying and disturbing symptoms that appear in the form of a feeling of alternate heat and cold, a flushing and perspiring face, dizziness, headache, and mental depression that sometimes becomes serious. Estrogen is sometimes given to help the individual through this period of physical and mental adjustment. Today there are many products that aid in the menopausal period, and women should have very little difficulty during this period if properly attended by good medical advice.

THE ENDOCRINE SYSTEM

In recent years remarkable advances have been made in the knowledge about several glands in the body that have to do with vital phenomena of growth, development, and function. These glands are now grouped into a system known as the endocrine system. The glands involved are the pineal, pituitary, thyroid, parathyroids, thymus, pancreas, adrenals, ovaries, and testes. The secretions from these glands are released directly into the bloodstream and are called hormones.

The *pituitary gland* is located at the base of the brain and is divided into an anterior and posterior lobe. The anterior lobe of this gland produces a number of very important hormones that are released into the blood and regulate many important body functions. One hormone controls the thyroid gland, another the reproductive glands, and yet another the adrenal gland. Two hormones control growth and development of the breast during pregnancy. The posterior pituitary lobe secretes at least two hormones. One controls the elimination of water by the kidney while the other causes contractions of the womb during childbirth. Pituitary hormones can be given to individuals who do not produce them. For example, growth hormones can be given to promote growth in some types of dwarfs. Another pituitary hormone, oxytocin, is commonly given to pregnant women to induce labor or to contract the uterus after childbirth.

The *thyroid gland* is located in the neck below the voice box. It regulates the metabolic activity of the individual. This gland frequently produces either too much (hyperthyroidism) or too little thyroid (hypothyroidism). Hyperthyroidism is characterized by nervousness, weight loss, and a fast pulse. Hypothyroidism is characterized by sluggishness, weight gain, and a slow pulse. If the thyroid gland enlarges, the condition is known as a goiter. A goiter may be present with over- or underproduction of thyroid hormone.

The *parathyroid glands* are four in number and are located near the thyroid gland. These glands control calcium levels in the blood by secreting a parathyroid hormone. Excessive secretion of this hormone causes an elevation of blood calcium levels while underproduction of the hormone causes low calcium levels (hypocalcemia). This latter condition, if severe, results in tetany, a condition characterized by excessive muscular contractility.

There are two *adrenal glands* and they are located above the kidneys. These glands are divided into two sections. The outer section, known as the adrenal cortex, produces cortisone, which is an important hormone in adapting to stressful situations. The inner part of the gland is called the adrenal medulla and produces two closely related hormones called epinephrine and norepinephrine. These hormones are important in maintaining blood pressure and increasing the heart rate during stressful situations. Cortisone and a wide variety of drugs related to it are used in medicine for treatment of allergic, arthritic, and inflammatory disorders. Epinephrine, also known commercially as Adrenalin, is used in medical emergencies and should be available in every physician's office.

The *pancreas,* which was discussed under the digestive system, is a gland located behind the stomach. In addition to its digestive function, it secretes the hormone insulin. The lack of insulin results in diabetes mellitus, while too much insulin can cause the blood sugar to become too low. This is called hypoglycemia. Insulin is normally secreted after a meal and causes digested sugar and other nutrients absorbed from the intestines to be stored in muscle and fat tissues.

The *ovaries* and the two important female hormones, estrogen and progesterone, were described in the discussion of the female reproductive system. Estrogen is the main feminizing hormone and causes female sexual characteristics to develop at puberty. Estrogen and progesterone enable normal reproductive functions and are important in regulating the normal menstrual cycle.

The *testes* were described in the discussion of the male reproductive system. The male hormone, testosterone, causes male sexual development, promotes growth of the beard, male muscular development, and deepening of the voice.

The *thymus gland* is located behind the breast bone and is much larger in children than in adults. Although some of its functions are not quite clear it is well known that this gland is very important in creating cells capable of recognizing foreign substances in the body. These cells are called lymphocytes and are important in the body's ability to fight off infection.

THE SPECIAL SENSES

The ear

The ear is the organ of hearing and is divided into external, middle, and inner ear (Fig. 21-9). Cartilage forms the external ear and performs much the same function as the shell behind the band in the outdoor bandstand, serving to collect the sound waves and send them inward. The canal leading from the external to the internal ear is provided with glands that secrete a waxy substance that prevents objects from reaching the middle ear. The middle ear is a small cavity separated from the canal by a thin membrane called the eardrum. One end of a tiny bone known as the malleus is fastened to this membrane. The other end of the bone joins another small bone known as the incus, which in turn is joined to a third bone known as the stapes. The inner end of the stapes fits into the opening between the middle ear and the internal ear.

The eustachian tube leads from the middle ear to the throat, and the mastoid cells are located just behind the middle ear. The internal ear is a cavity containing fluid that catches the sound waves that strike the drum membrane and are carried by the chain of the three small bones across the middle ear. These sound waves are passed to the auditory nerve and carried to the hearing centers in the brain. The internal ear also contains three semicircular canals filled with fluid and communicating with the nervous system in regard to changes in position of the head. When they are not working well we become dizzy or we have an interference in our sense of equilibrium. Deafness is the result of injury to the hearing center, auditory nerve, drum membrane, or through poor vibration of the chain of small bones.

The eye

The structure and function of the eye resemble that of a camera except that the images of objects are permanently regis-

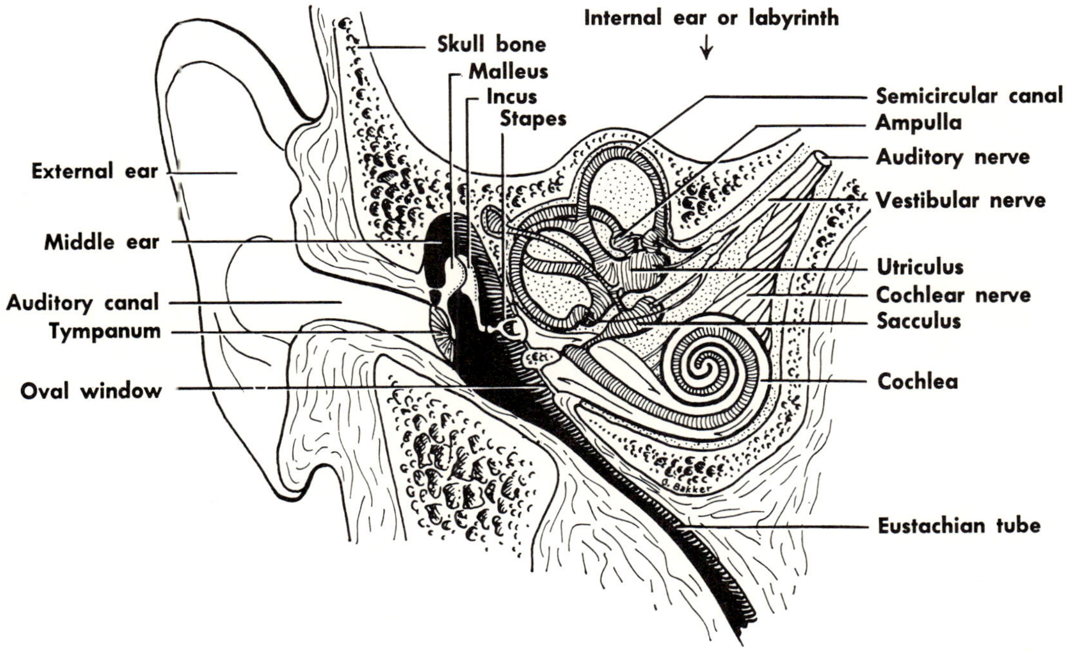

Fig. 21-9. External, middle, and internal portions of the right ear. The auditory tube leading to the middle ear is also shown.

tered on the camera film while those registered in the eye are constantly changing. The eyeball lies in the bony cavity and is protected by the eyebrows, the lids, and the lashes. It is connected at the back with the optic nerve, which communicates with the seeing center in the brain. The movements of the eyeball are controlled by six muscles that work in pairs in opposition to each other. Muscles in the lids control opening and shutting. The conjunctiva is the membrane that lines the lids and covers the forepart of the eyeball. The tear glands open on the underside of the upper lids and secrete a fluid that keeps the eyes moist. The excess is usually carried away by a small passage into the nose except at times of oversecretion in emotional upsets and in inflammation of the conjunctiva when the tears spill out over the cheeks.

The eyeball is divided into two chambers separated by the lens. The front chamber is in front of the lens and is small and filled with fluid. The back chamber behind the lens is much larger and contains a thicker fluid. The outer layer of the eyeball is the sclera or the white of the eye. It is a touch-protective layer and is transparent over the front of the eyeball. The transparent section is called the cornea. The next layer contains many blood vessels and the pigment that gives color to the eye. The pigmented section over the front of the eyeball is called the iris. The iris has an opening in the center, the pupil. The pupil varies in size with the amount of light admitted, contracting to shut out bright light and enlarging in dim light. It is like the opening in the shutter of the camera. The lens is a transparent body behind the pupil. The inner cone of the eyeball is the retina. The retina contains the nerve fibers of the optic nerve and cells sensitive to light. The light rays are brought to a focus by the lens, and the image it produces is reflected to the retina and carried by the optic nerve to the seeing center in the brain. The retina in each eye receives the image from a different angle. The sensations aroused by the image combine if they have fallen on corresponding points of the retina and give depth to the image. In order to make the image points identical the eyes must coordinate perfectly. The ability to see objects at different distances is known as accommodation and is accomplished by changing the curve of the lens inward and outward. Rays of light are bent as they enter the eye in order to make them meet on the retina (Fig. 21-10).

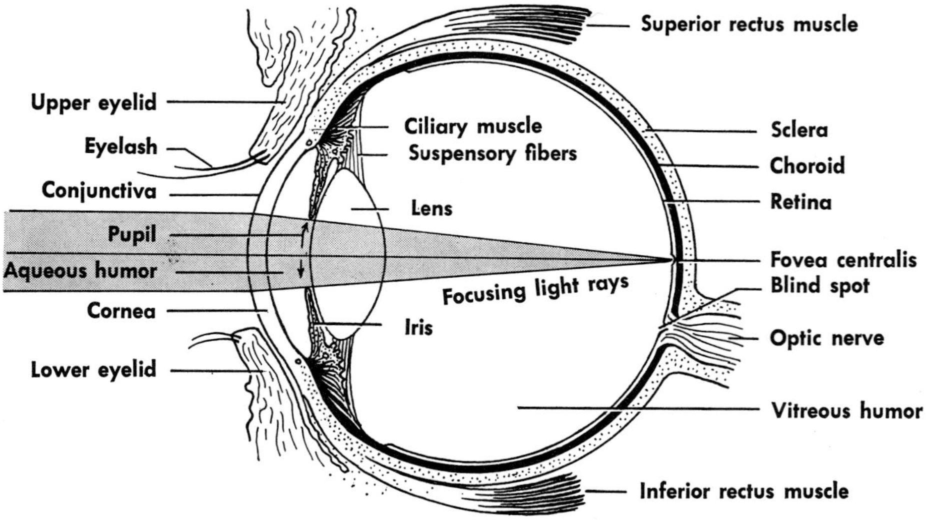

Fig. 21-10. Structure of the eye.

Review questions

1. Name the nine systems of the body.
2. Name the bones of the vertebral column.
3. What bones comprise the pelvis?
4. Describe the circulation of the blood.
5. Name the organs of digestion.
6. What is the function of the pancreas?
7. Name the organs of respiration.
8. Name the bones of the ear.
9. Discuss the physiology of the eye.
10. Compare the parts of the eye and the camera. In what three ways does the eye differ from the camera?

Suggested readings

Anthony, C. P.: Textbook of anatomy and physiology, ed. 8, St. Louis, 1971, The C. V. Mosby Co.

Dienhart, C. M.: Basic human anatomy and physiology, Philadelphia, 1973, W. B. Saunders Co.

Francis, C. C.: Introduction to human anatomy, ed. 6, St. Louis, 1973, The C. V. Mosby Co.

Goss, C. M., editor: Gray's anatomy, ed. 29, Philadelphia, 1973, Lea & Febiger.

chapter 22

Common medical terminology and a brief discussion of basic medical science

This chapter is designed to help medical assistants understand the language of medicine. The student must learn what amounts to a new language, often without the background that would help her understand and build medical words. However, many medical terms can easily be "translated" if the student knows the meanings of the commoner prefixes, suffixes, and combining forms that make up these words. For instance, *oophorocystectomy* seems a fairly formidable word, yet if one separates it into its component parts it immediately becomes intelligible. *Oophor* (egg-bearing; denoting an ovary; ovarian) plus *cyst* (a bladder or sac) plus *ectomy* (denoting surgical removal) equals the total meaning: removal of a cyst from the ovary.

Some combining forms are derived from more than one source; many of them stem from or are akin to several words foreign to the English-speaking reader. Usually only the original language source has been indicated, although a few are designated as having originated from both the Greek and the Latin.

This chapter is not intended in any way to take the place of a good medical dic-

Glossary

aneurysm a saclike dilation of a blood vessel

arrhythmia lack of rhythm; irregularity; usually used with reference to heartbeat

blepharitis inflammation of the edges of the eyelids involving hair follicles and glands opening on surface

cholecystitis inflammation of the gallbladder

encephalitis inflammation of the brain

endocrinology the science of the endocrine or ductless glands and their functions

enteritis inflammation of the intestines, more particularly of the mucous tissues

enterostomy surgical formation of a permanent opening into the intestine through the abdominal wall

esophagogastroscopy inspection of the esophagus and stomach by means of an illuminated instrument

gastrectomy surgical removal of a part or the whole of the stomach

glaucoma disease of the eye characterized by increase in intraocular pressure that may lead to atrophy of the optic nerve and blindness

keratitis inflammation of the cornea

myelitis inflammation of the spinal cord

myopia a defect in vision in which objects can only be seen distinctly when very close to the eyes; nearsightedness

necrosis death of areas of tissue surrounded by healthy parts

osteomalacia a disease marked by increasing softness of the bones so that they become weak and brittle

paresis partial or incomplete paralysis

pharmacology the study of drugs, their origin, nature, properties, and effects upon living organisms

phlebitis inflammation of a vein

splenectomy surgical excision of the spleen

thrombosis the formation of a blood clot

torticollis stiff neck caused by spasmodic contraction of neck muscles tionary, a constant requisite for everyone dealing with medical subjects. Rather, familiarity with its contents will give a clearer understanding of medical words and terms so that one may see at a glance the general meaning or class of any medical word and thus get greater enjoyment and better understanding from scientific reading and study.

Medicine is a very systematic science requiring a special vocabulary that is thoroughly systematic. The eternal effort of physicians is to be precise. They must describe the human body and its ailments with no chance for misunderstanding. The meanings of words in modern languages sometimes change. The noun *brain* has three distinct meanings. The noun *hand* has twenty-one distinct meanings. Therefore medical scientists often go to the Greek and Latin languages for descriptive terms that now have one and only one exact meaning.

Learning a medical vocabulary thus becomes a simple matter of memorizing a few score Greek and Latin words and then combining them systematically to make thousands of other precise terms.

The base word we call the root; the modifying term we call the prefix when we attach it before the root or the suffix when we attach it to the end of the root. Thus in the foregoing sentence *pre-* and *suf-* are prefixes to *-fix*. *Ophthalmo-* (eye) plus *-scope* (instrument for viewing) becomes *ophthalmoscope,* an instrument for studying the eye. *Oto-* (ear) plus *-scope* becomes *otoscope,* an instrument for examining the ear. Combining with *-itis,* a suffix meaning *inflammation,* are such words as *tonsillitis, peritonitis, otitis,* and *osteitis.*

Prefixes and suffixes, syllables added at the beginning and at the end of root words, give special meaning to the ideas the roots express. We have these in English, too. For example, *before*hand, handi*ness,* handi*craft.* As you memorize the following Greek and Latin prefixes and suffixes, you will quickly get the feel of their use in medical word construction.

Prefixes

a-, an-	without
ad-	to, at
ante-	before
antero-	in front of
anti-	against
brady-	slow
dia-	through
dys-, dis-	difficult, painful
ecto-	outside of
electro-	electric
endo-	within, inside
epi-	upon
ex-, ec-	out of, away from
hyper-	over, excessive
hypo-	under, below, less
infra-	below, after
intra-	within
mal-	bad
medio-	middle (halfway)
meso-	middle of
meta-	beyond, more than
para-	beside, beyond, unusual
peri-	surrounding
polio-	grayish
poly-	many, several
pseudo-	false
retro-	backward
sub-	beneath
super-, supra-	above
trans-	across, beyond
ultra-	beyond

Suffixes

-algia	pain
-centesis	puncturing
-clasia	breaking (to remedy a deformity)
-ectasis	dilation
-ectomy	cutting out, excision
-emia	blood
-iasis	a process or its result
-itis	inflammation
-lexy	fixation
-logy	knowledge of, science of
-lysis	gradual decline
-meter	measurer
-odynia	pain
-oma	tumor, swelling
-opia, -opsia	eye
-osis	condition of, state caused by
-pathy	disease
-plasty	molding, repairing
-rrhagia	bursting forth
-rrhaphy	suturing, sewing
-rrhea	flowing
-scope	instrument for examination
-scopy	examination by inspection

-sect	cutting
-stomy	making an opening
-thermy	use of heat
-tome	cutting instrument
-tomy	cutting
-trophy	nutrition
-uria	urine

Practical examples of word building

Using the suffixes *-itis,* inflammations, and *-oma,* swelling, let us consider the following examples of word building.

arthritis	arthros (joint)
bronchitis	bronchus (lung tube)
carditis	cardium (heart)
endocarditis	endo (within) cardium (heart)
dermatitis	derma (skin)
myelitis	myelos (marrow)
osteomyelitis	osteon (bone) myelos (marrow)
myositis	myos (muscle)
neuritis	neuron (nerve)
osteitis	osteon (bone)
phlebitis	phlebos (vein)
epithelioma	epithelium (skin)
carcinoma	carcina (cancer)
sarcoma	sarx (flesh)

DEFINITIONS AND EQUIVALENTS

This list defines many of the terms and abbreviation most commonly found in medical useage as well as many prefixes and suffixes that are employed as elements of medical words.

Knowing the definitions of the word elements in this list, the reader can easily dissect many medical words so that their meanings are automatically revealed. For example, *gastroenterostomy* can be dissected into *gastro-,* pertaining to the stomach, *entero-,* pertaining to the intestines, and *-stomy,* surgical opening; hence the word means a surgical opening between the stomach and the intestines.

Sometimes dissection of medical words is complicated slightly by the fact that the final vowel(s) of a prefix may be omitted before a suffix beginning with a vowel. For example, *myalgia* is to be dissected into *myo-* and *-algia,* the final vowel of the prefix *myo-* being omitted before the initial vowel of the suffix *-algia.* Similarly, *carditis* is to be dissected into *cardio-* and *-itis,* the final two vowels of *cardio-* being omitted before the initial vowel of *-itis.*

Despite occasional complications such as these, however, the reader will find this list generally quite easy to use, since alternative forms that are difficult to recognize are listed individually.

a-	a. absent b. deficient
adeno-	glandular
-algia	pain
an-	a. absent b. deficient
anorexia	loss or lack of appetite for food
antibiotic	a substance that interferes with the life processes of certain organisms. Examples: penicillin, streptomycin
apoth	abbreviation for apothecaries' measure or apothecaries' weight
apothecaries' measure	the old system of liquid measure often used by American pharmacists
apothecaries' weight	the old system of weight often used by American pharmacists
apoth meas	abbreviation for apothecaries' measure
apoth wt	abbreviation for apothecaries' weight
arthritis	inflammation of one or more joints
arthro-	pertaining to one or more joints
atrophy	the wasting away of an organ or a tissue
advp, avdp wt	abbreviations for avoirdupois weight
avoirdupois weight	the old system of weight in general use in the United States
benign	not malignant, i.e., not a threat to life
bilateral	pertaining to both sides of the body
carcinoma	cancer, i.e., a malignant tumor arising from epithelial tissue
cc	abbreviation for cubic centimeter(s)
centimeter	a. 0.01 m or 10 mm b. approximately 0.4 inch. Abbreviation: cm
chemotherapy	treatment with chemical compounds, e.g., often used in the treatment of cancer by drugs
cm	abbreviation for centimeter(s)

coronary thrombosis occurrence of a clot in one of the coronary arteries of the heart

cubic centimeter a. 1 ml or 0.001 L b. approximately 15 minims or 1/30 fluidounce. Abbreviation: cc

curettage or curettement the operation of scraping, especially the interior of the uterus, with a curette

derma-, dermato- pertaining to the skin

dermatology the field of medicine concerning the skin

dia- a. through b. between c. across d. apart

diagnosis a. the process of determining what disease is present b. the conclusion reached by such a process

differential diagnosis a list of possible causes for a given set of medical findings

disease entity an abnormal condition producing a group of symptoms and signs related by their common cause

dr abbreviation for dram

drachm variant spelling for dram

dram a. apoth wt: 60 gr or 3 scr or approximately 4 Gm b. avdp wt: 1/16 oz or approximately 2 Gm c. apoth meas: 1 fluidram. Abbreviation: dr or ʒ

drop a. approximately 1 minim b. approximately 0.06 cc. Abbreviations: gt (singular), gtt (plural)

-dynia pain

dys a. disorder b. difficult c. painful

ECG abbreviation for electrocardiogram

ecto- exterior

-ectomy surgical removal

EEG abbreviation for electroencephalogram

EKG abbreviation for electrocardiogram

electrocardiogram a record produced by an electrocardiograph. Abbreviation: ECG or EKG

electrocardiograph an instrument for recording the electric current that originates in the heart muscle

electroencephalogram a record produced by an electroencephalograph. Abbreviation: EEG

electroencephalograph an instrument for recording the electric current that originates in the brain

empirical based on knowledge derived solely from experience

endo- interior

endocrinology the field of medicine concerning the endocrine (ductless) glands

entero- pertaining to the intestines

etiology a. the study of causes, especially of disease b. loosely, a cause or a causative agent

fl dr abbreviation for fluidram

fl oz abbreviation for fluidounce

fluidounce a. 8 fl dr or 1/16 pt b. approximately 30 cc. Abbreviation: fl oz or fl ℥

fluidram a. 60 minims or ⅛ fl oz b. approximately 4 cc. Abbreviation: fl dr or fl ʒ

g unofficial abbreviation for: a. gram(s) (preferable abbreviation: Gm) b. grain(s) (preferable abbreviation: gr)

gamma same as microgram

gastro- pertaining to the stomach

gastrointestinal pertaining to the stomach and intestines. Abbreviation: GI

geriatrics or gerontology the field of medicine concerning conditions that are most common among aged people

GI abbreviation for gastrointestinal

Gm abbreviation for gram(s)

gr abbreviation for grain(s)

grain a. 1/60 dr or 1/480 oz apoth b. 1/7,000 lb or approximately 1/30 dr or 1/440 oz avdp c. approximately 60 mg or 1/15 Gm. Abbreviation: gr

gram a. 1,000 mg or 0.001 kg b. approximately 1/30 oz or 15 gr. Abbreviation: Gm

gt or gtt abbreviations for drop(s)

gynecology the field of medicine concerning conditions peculiar to women, especially diseases of the reproductive organs

hema-, hemato- pertaining to blood

hematology the field of medicine concerning the blood and the blood-forming organs

hemo- pertaining to blood

hernia rupture, e.g., protrusion of abdominal contents through a weak spot in the abdominal wall or the diaphragm

herniotomy a. strictly, cutting into a hernia b. loosely, herniorrhaphy, i.e., repairing a hernia

hormone a substance secreted by a ductless gland and regulating the functions of other organs

hydro- pertaining to: a. water b. hydrogen

hyper- a. above b. increased

hypertension high blood pressure

hypertrophy enlargement or overgrowth of a part of the body

hypo- a. below b. decreased

hypotension low blood pressure

-iatrist specialist

-iatry field of medicine

inter- between

intra- within

-itis inflammation

kg abbreviation for kilogram(s)

kilogram a. 0.001 Gm b. approximately 2.7 lb apoth or 2.2 lb avdp. Abbreviation: kg

L abbreviation for liter(s)

laryngology the field of medicine concerning the larynx (voice box) and associated structures

liter a. 1,000 ml or 1,000 cc b. approximately 1 qt. Abbreviation: L

-logist a. scholar b. specialist

-logy a. study b. field of medicine

m abbreviation for meter(s)

m^2 abbreviation for square meter(s)

mal- disordered

malignant a. virulent, i.e., dangerous to life b. pertaining to a tumor that tends to invade adjacent tissues and to spread to distant parts of the body

mcg abbreviation for microgram(s)

mcl abbreviation for microliter(s)

meno- pertaining to menstruation

meta- a. after b. changing

meter a. 100 cm or 1,000 mm b. approximately 3¼ ft or 39 in. Abbreviation: m

mg abbreviation for milligram(s)

milligram a. 1,000 Gm b. approximately 1/60 gr. Abbreviation: mg

milliliter a. 0.001 L or 1 cc b. approximately 15 minims or 1/30 fl oz. Abbreviation: ml

millimeter a. 0.001 m or 0.1 cm b. approximately 1/25 in. Abbreviation: mm

min unofficial abbreviation for: a. minute(s) b. minim(s)

minim a. 1/60 fl dr or 1/480 fl oz b. approximately 0.06 cc c. commonly regarded as equal to 1 drop. Abbreviation: m

ml abbreviation for milliliter(s)

mm abbreviation for millimeter(s)

mm^3 abbreviation for cubic millimeter(s)

myo- pertaining to muscle

nephritis inflammation of the kidneys

neuro- pertaining to nerves

neurology the field of medicine concerning the brain, the spinal cord, the peripheral nerves, and the neuromuscular system

obstetrics the field of medicine concerning care of pregnancy (normal or abnormal), including delivery of babies and aftercare

-oma tumor

ophthalmology the field of medicine concerning the eyes

orthopedics the field of medicine concerning bones, joints, tendons, and muscles

-osis a condition or a process, especially one that is abnormal

osteo- pertaining to one or more bones

otology the field of medicine concerning the ears

ounce a. apoth wt: 8 dr or 480 gr or approximately 30 Gm b. avdp wt: 16 dr or approximately 440 gr or 30 Gm c. apoth meas: 1 fl oz. Abbreviations: oz or ℥

oz abbreviation for ounce(s)

palliative affording relief but not cure

para- a. beside b. beyond

pathology the study of the manifestations of disease in tissues and organs

-pathy abnormality

pediatrics the field of medicine concerning conditions that are most common among children

peri- around

peritoneum the thin, smooth membrane lining the interior of the abdominal wall and covering the abdominal organs

phlebo- venous, i.e., pertaining to veins

-phobia morbid fear

pint a. 16 fl oz b. approximately 500 cc. Abbreviation: pt

pleura one of the two thin, smooth membranes lining the interior of the chest and covering the surface of the lungs

-pnea pertaining to: a. breathing b. breath

pneuma-, pneumato- pertaining to: a. air or gas b. breathing c. lung tissue or the lungs

pneumo- pertaining to: a. air or gas b. lung tissue or the lungs c. breathing

pneumono- pertaining to lung tissue or the lungs

post- after

pound a. apoth wt: 12 oz or 5,760 gr or approximately 360 Gm b. avdp wt: 16 oz or 7,000 gr or approximately 450 Gm. Abbreviation: lb

pre- before

proctology the field of medicine concerning the anus, the rectum, and the sigmoid colon

prognosis a forecast of the probable outcome of an illness

psychiatry the field of medicine concerning the mind and the personality

psycho- mental

psychosomatic pertaining to: a. both mind and body b. physical conditions resulting from mental causes

-ptosis falling

pyo- pertaining to pus

rhinology the field of medicine concerning the nose, especially the nasal passages

-rrhea a. flow b. discharge

sarcoma a tumor, often highly malignant, arising from connective or nonepithelial tissue

scr abbreviation for scruple(s)

scruple a. ⅓ dr apoth or 20 gr b. approximately 1.3 Gm. Abbreviation: scr

square meter a. 10,000 sq cm b. approximately 1,550 sq in. Abbreviation: m^2

stomato- pertaining to the mouth

-stomy surgical opening

sub- under

sulfonamides a group of chemotherapeutic drugs derived from sulfanilamide. Also called sulfa drugs or sulfas. Examples: sulfadiazine, sulfamerazine, and sulfamethazine

super- over

syndrome a group of symptoms and signs occurring together in such a way as to indicate the existence of a common cause. A specific syndrome is characteristic of a disease entity.

therapeutics the study of medical treatment

therapy medical treatment

thoraco- pertaining to the chest

-tomy surgical cutting

trauma a. a wound or injury b. in psychiatry, a horrifying or shocking experience

tumor a. a swelling; a morbid enlargement b. a neoplasm, i.e., a mass of new tissue, physiologically useless, growing independently of its surroundings

unilateral pertaining to one side of the body

-uria a. condition of the urine b. presence in the urine

urology the field of medicine concerning the kidneys, the ureters, the bladder, and the urethra as well as their accessory glands

WORD ELEMENTS

A suitable word to express a medical concept can often be quickly selected by following these rules.

1. Define the word for which you are looking. For example, suppose that you want a word that means a condition of the blood characterized by increased sugar.
2. Choose an appropriate suffix (a word element beginning with a hyphen) from the following list. For example, a suffix that means condition of the blood is *-emia.*
3. Choose one or more suitable prefixes (word elements ending with a hyphen). For example, a prefix meaning increased is *hyper-,* and one meaning sugar is *glyco-.*
4. Arrange prefixes in order of increasing importance, and put the suffix after the last of the prefixes. For example, since sugar is more important than increased, *glyco-* follows *hyper-;* thus *glyco-, hyper-,* and *-emia* are arranged in that order.
5. Drop all the hyphens and if the suffix begins with a vowel, drop the final vowel of the prefix directly before the suffix. For example, since *-emia* begins with a vowel, we drop the *o* in *glyco-* and the word we form is *hyperglycemia.*
6. To check on the word so obtained, look it up in a medical dictionary. For example, *hyperglycemia* is listed in all medical dictionaries and fits the definition with which we started.

Please note that in the following list alternative word elements of identical meaning are listed in order of preference.

abnormality	-pathy
above	hyper-, super-*
after	post-, meta-†
air	aero-, pneumo,* pneumato-†
anus	ano-
arm	brachio-
around	peri-
before	pre-
below	hypo-, sub-*
beside	para-
between	dia-, inter-*
beyond	para-
bladder	cysto-
blood	hemato-, hemo,* hema,‡ -emia
bone	osteo-
breathing	pneo- pneumato-,* pneumo-,† pneuma-‡
cecum	ceco-
chest	thoraco-
colon	colo-, colono-‡
condition	-osis
condition of the blood	-emia
condition of the urine	-uria
deficient	a-,§ an-,‖ ar-¶
decreased	hypo-
difficult	dys-
discharge	-rrhea
disease	-pathy
disordered	dys-, mal-‡
duodenum	duodeno-
ear	oto-, auriculo-‡
excreted in the urine	-uria
exterior	ecto-
eye	ophthalmo-, oculo-‡
falling	-ptosis
fear	-phobia
field of medicine	-logy, -iatrics†
flow	-rrhea
foot	podo-, pedi-‡
gallbladder	cholecysto-
gas	aero-, pneumo,* pneumato-†
gland	adeno-
head	cephalo-

*Often.
†Occasionally.
‡Rarely.
§Before any consonant but *h* or *r*.
‖Before *h* or any vowel.
¶Before *r*.

heart	cardio-, cordi-‡
ileum	ileo-
increased	hyper-
inflammation	-itis
interior	endo-
intestines	entero-; see also anus, cecum, colon, duodenum, ileum, jejunum, or rectum
jejunum	jejuno-
joint	arthro-
kidney	nephro-, reni-†
lacking	a-,§ an-,‖ ar-¶
larynx	laryngo-
liver	hepato-
lung	pneumono-, pneumo-,* pulmoni-‡
menstruation	meno-
mental	psycho-
mind	psycho-
mouth	stomato-, ori-†
muscle	myo-
neck	cervico-
nerve	neuro-
nose	rhino-, naso-*
ovary	oophoro-, ovario-†
over	hyper-, super-†
pain	-algia, -dynia
painful	dys-
pharynx	pharyngo-
presence in the blood	-emia
presence in the urine	-uria
pus	pyo-
rectum	recto-
respiration	pneumo-
science	-logy
skin	dermato-, derma-,‡ -derma
specialist	-logist, -iatrist,* -iatrician‡
stomach	gastro-
study	-logy
sugar	glyco-
surgical cutting	-tomy
surgical opening	-stomy
surgical removal	-ectomy
testical	orchio-, orchido-†
throat	see larynx, neck, pharynx, or trachea
trachea	tracheo-
tumor	-oma
under	hypo-, sub-†
urinary bladder	cysto-
urine	uri-, -uria
vein, venous	phlebo-
water	hydro-
within	endo-, intra-†

LIST OF COMMONLY USED WORDS

abortion	expulsion of embryo during first three months of pregnancy
abrasion	rubbing off of skin or lining of an organ
achlorhydria	lack of hydrochloric acid in stomach
adenoma	tumor of a glandular tissue
albuminuria	albumin in urine
-algia	pain, pertaining to
amnesia	lost or defective memory
andro-	pertaining to male
anemia	deficiency of hemoglobin in blood
aneurysm	sacular dilation of an artery
angina pectoris	chest pain caused by inadequate blood flow to the heart
angio-	pertaining to blood or lymph vessels
ankylosis	limitation of movement around a joint due to stiffness
anthropo-	mankind, pertaining to
arrhythmia	irregularity of heartbeat
arteriosclerosis	a degenerative process in arteries associated with aging; commonly referred to as hardening of the arteries
arthritis	inflammation of joint
arytenoid cartilage	a support for vocal cords
ascites	increased fluids in the abdominal cavity
asphyxia	suffocation
atelectasis	airless condition of lung
atrophy	waste of, diminution of a part
auditory	pertaining to hearing
auricular	pertaining to ear
avulsion	tearing off of a part
borborygmus	rumbling of bowels
bradycardia	slowness of heart
bronchiectasis	dilation of wall of bronchus
bronchus	main inlet to lung
caput	head
carcinoma	cancer of gland, mucous membrane, or bone
caries	decay, particularly of teeth
cautery	burning agent, as electric knife
centesis	puncturing of a cavity
cephalic	pertaining to head
cervix	neck
chole	gall
cholecystectomy	removal of the gallbladder
chorea	a neurologic disorder characterized by purposeless movements
cirrhosis	hardening, particularly of liver
colpo-	pertaining to vagina
coma	deep unconsciousness
contusion	bruise
craniotomy	operation on skull
crisis	sudden change in a disease usually for the better
crush	mangling injury
curettage	scraping, particularly of womb
cyanosis	blueness of body caused by lack of oxygen in blood
cyesis	pregnancy
cyst	pouch, sac
cyst-	pertaining to bladder
cystoma	cavity containing a fluid or semisolid substance
cyte	cell
delirium	disturbance of mind
delusion	faulty belief
diathermy	local elevation of temperature of high-frequency current
dysmenorrhea	painful menstruation
dyspnea	difficulty in breathing
edema	water accumulation in body tissues
electrocautery	electrically heated blade
electrosurgery	use of high-frequency current in surgical procedures
embolism	obstruction of blood vessel caused by a clot from another part of the body
empyema	pus in the chest
endarteritis	inflammation of artery lining
enteroptosis	sagging of intestines
enuresis	bed-wetting
epiphysitis	inflammation of bony prominences
epithelioma	cancer of skin
eructation	belching
erythema	redness
erythrocyte	red blood cell
fibroma	tumor with fibrous or connective tissue
fracture	breaking of a bone
gingivitis	inflammation of gums
glaucoma	increased eye pressure
glossitis	inflammation of tongue
gonad	sex gland
hematuria	blood in urine
hemophilia	abnormal tendency to bleed
hemorrhoids	piles
hernia	rupture
hordeolum	sty
hysterectomy	removal of womb (uterus)
infrared	heat rays from sun or infrared lamps that have healing properties
insomnia	inability to sleep
jaundice	yellowing of skin and eyes caused by liver dysfunction
keratitis	inflammation of cornea of eye
kyphosis	humpback

laceration	tearing of tissue
laparotomy	incision into abdomen
leukemia	cancer of blood cells
leukocyte	white blood cell
lipoma	fatty tissue
lordosis	swayback
lysis	subsidence of symptoms, destruction of tissue
mastitis	inflammation of breast
menopause	cessation of menstruation
menorrhagia	excessive menstrual flow
metritis	inflammation of womb
metrorrhagia	bleeding between menstrual cycles
miscarriage	expulsion of fetus from fourth to sixth month of pregnancy
myocarditis	inflammation of heart muscle
myoma	tumor of muscle
myopia	nearsightedness
myositis	muscle inflammation
myxoma	tumor of mucous membrane
necrosis	death of living tissue
nephritis	inflammation of kidneys
nephroptosis	floating kidneys
neuralgia	pain in a nerve
neuritis	inflammation of nerve
neuroma	tumor of nerve
neurosis	nervousness, often with odd behavior
nullipara	woman who has never given birth
onychectomy	removal of a nail
orchid-	pertaining to testes
osteitis	bone inflammation
osteoma	bone tumor
osteomyelitis	inflammation of a bone
otitis media	inflammation of middle ear
papilloma	wart, skin outgrowth
paranoia	psychosis with delusions
paresis	slight or incomplete paralysis
parous	giving birth to
paroxysm	spasm, convulsion
patho-, -pathy	pertaining to disease
-penia	shortage of
pericarditis	inflammation of heart covering
periostitis	inflammation of tissue covering bone
peritonitis	inflammation of abdominal lining
pexis	fixation
phlebitis	inflammation of vein
phobia	unreasoning fear
placenta	afterbirth
pneumothorax	air in chest between lungs and ribs
polio-	gray (matter of brain and spinal cord)
polyp	tumor with a stem
premature delivery	ending of pregnancy after seventh month
primigravida	woman pregnant for first time
procto-	pertaining to anus
pyrexia	high fever
rales	abnormal sounds in lungs
salivation	excessive secretion of saliva
salpinx	tube (of womb)
sarcoma	cancer of flesh
schisto-	condition of being split
schizophrenia	disorganized mentality
scoliosis	sidewise spinal curvature
sepsis	poisoning
somatic	pertaining to body
sprain	wrenching of a joint
strain	stretching of a muscle
syncope	faint
tachycardia	fast heartbeat
terato-	monster
thele	nipple
thorax	chest
tonic	normal and healthy vigor
torticollis	wryneck
trachoma	contagious eye disease
trephining	making round opening in skull
thrombosis	clot in blood vessel
ultraviolet	invisible light from sun or sunlamp that has healing properties
uremia	blood poisoning from unexpected nitrogen wastes
vas, vaso, vascular	vessel, duct
vertigo	dizziness
vesica	bladder

DISEASES

A brief discussion of the general causes of disease and of predisposing factors is found in the next chapter. It is suggested that the medical assistant refer to the many excellent textbooks available on the subject of medical sciences for a complete discussion of medical diseases. Such books as *Today's Health Guide,* published by the American Medical Association, and *An Introduction to Medical Science* by Young and Barger would be most helpful and educational.

CLASSIFICATION OF DRUGS

Taking care of the sick is a sacred trust, and the administration of medicine to alleviate pain or promote health is a very responsible duty. Since medical assistants frequently are called upon to administer drugs (under direct supervision of the physician) and also frequently order drugs from the supply houses, they should be familiar with the names and the effects of most drugs.

One way in which drugs are classified is according to the effect they produce. Among the most important groups are the following:

analgesics or anodynes drugs that relieve pain when absorbed into the blood
anesthetics drugs that produce insensibility to pain. A local anesthetic produces insensibility at the site of application; general anesthetics also produce unconsciousness
antacids drugs that neutralize acidity
anthelmintics drugs that destroy or expel worms
antipyretics or febrifuges drugs that reduce fever
antiseptics substances that destroy or check the growth of bacteria
antispasmodics drugs that relieve convulsions or spasmodic pain
astringents agents contracting or hardening tissues
carminatives drugs that relieve gas formation in the stomach and intestines
cathartics or evacuants drugs causing free movement of the bowels
caustics substances that burn or destroy tissues
deodorants agents used to neutralize unpleasant odors
depressants drugs that lessen functional activity
diaphoretic drugs causing increase of perspiration
digestants substances that aid in the digestion of food
disinfectants agents for checking bacterial growth
diuretics drugs that increase urine excretion
emetics substances that cause vomiting
emollients substances that soften or sooth irritated or inflamed surfaces
escharotics drugs that produce blisters
expectorants drugs that facilitate clearance of material from the air passages
hemostatics agents for arresting hemorrhage
hypnotics sleep-producing drugs
laxatives drugs that produce mild action of the bowels
mydriatics drugs that dilate the pupil of the eye
myotics drugs that contract the pupil of the eye
prophylactics agents to prevent the development of disease
purgatives drugs that produce active bowel movements
refrigerants agents that have cooling properties
rubefacients agents that produce reddening of the skin
sedatives drugs that have a quieting effect
specifics drugs that cure particular diseases
stimulants drugs that increase functional activity
styptics agents that arrest hemorrhage by contracting the blood vessels
tonics agents that increase the normal tone of a region or system

DIET THERAPY

Literally, we must eat to live, although quite a number of substantial-looking people might be accused of living to eat. It is possible to preserve the balance between the two extremes, that is, to find pleasure in eating the things we need to maintain healthy and efficient bodies and to enjoy some foods for their delightful taste, quite apart from the fact that they are food essentials.

Unfortunately, people do not always like the foods they need. Our food habits and tastes are influenced by early training, nationality, the part of the country in which we live, our mental attitudes, and our pocketbooks.

Essential foods

Foods provide the materials that make the body grow and keep it going from the time it begins as an individual cell. Foods burned in the body produce energy for work; they furnish the materials of which the body is made and supply those substances that regulate important body processes. By our choices of foods we provide wisely or foolishly for these body needs. Such choices can only be made intelligently by knowing what the required materials are, how much of each we need, and where they are to be found. These materials or food elements fall into six groups: carbohydrates, proteins, fats, minerals, water, and vitamins. Foods containing these essentials have been listed and the amounts contained in a given quantity of each have been estimated.

Carbohydrates. Carbohydrates are sugars and starches. They are energy sources and may be used up as fast as they are taken in if the body is active. Unused portions are stored as an emergency supply in the liver and as body fat.

Proteins. Proteins are also energy sources, but in addition they are necessary to the life of cells and furnish the building material for muscles.

Fats. Fats provide energy and material for body fat itself. They are greater energy-producers than either carbohydrates or proteins. A normal storage of fat is desirable for emergency use, protection against injury, padding for some of the organs of the body, and assistance in regulating body temperature. Excess fat may interfere with body processes and is unattractive.

Minerals. Minerals provide the essential materials for bone and other body structures. They assist in regulating important processes of the body; the action of one mineral is often dependent upon the presence of other minerals.

Water and cellulose. Water composes about two thirds of body weight; the body cannot live without it. It supplies a great part of the body fluids that bring food to the cells and carry away waste products, and it aids in regulating body temperature. The body loses about four and one-half pints in 24 hours; this loss must be replaced mainly by the fluids we drink. Six to eight glasses of fluid replace this loss, although the amount varies with individuals. Fluids are increased or restricted in some types of illness.

Vitamins. Vitamins are substances that are essential for health and growth of the body, for the regulation of many metabolic processes, and are essential factors in a large number of chemical reactions occurring within the body. Since the first vitamins were discovered in the early 1900s, our knowledge of these factors has grown considerably. As each new vitamin was discovered it was given a different letter and soon a large number of letters were assigned to many factors. In recent years, there has been a growing tendency to name new vitamins by their specific name rather than by letters.

It is convenient to divide the vitamins according to their ability to be dissolved in either water or fat. The water-soluble vitamins include the B complex vitamins and vitamin C. The fat-soluble vitamins include vitamins A, D, E, and K.

The B complex vitamins are composed of numerous vitamins with entirely different chemical structures; however, deficiency of one of these vitamins is frequently associated with deficiency in one or more of the others. Thiamine (vitamin B_1) is important in maintaining the normal function of the nervous system, heart, and skin. A severe thiamine deficiency produces the disease beriberi. Thiamine deficiency is usually seen in patients with chronic malnutrition or alcoholism. Brewer's yeast, wheat germ, and pork are good dietary sources of thiamine. Riboflavin (vitamin B_2) is an important factor in maintaining normal skin and the linings of the mouth, tongue, and eyes. Organ meats, milk, and green, leafy vegetables are key sources of riboflavin. Niacin (nicotinic acid) is a B vitamin that was originally found to be the specific deficiency in the disease pellegra, which in its severest form is characterized by diarrhea, dermatitis, dementia, and death. Meats are excellent sources of niacin. Pyridoxine, also called vitamin B_6, is important in normal blood production and the maintenance of normal skin. Pyridoxine deficiency is sometimes caused by certain antituberculous drugs. The sources of pyridoxine are meats, fish, beans, and wheat germ. Vitamin B_{12} is a water-soluble vitamin important in normal development of red blood cells. This vitamin is not absorbed in patients with pernicious anemia and must therefore be given by injection as treatment for this condition. Liver, kidneys, meat, and fish are important sources of vitamin B_{12}. Folic acid is another water-soluble vitamin important in the development of normal blood. Deficency of this vitamin causes anemia. Green, leafy vegetables are the main source of folic acid.

Vitamin C, also known as ascorbic acid, is an important factor in maintaining the integrity of the blood vessels. Severe vitamin C deficiency causes scurvy, a disease characterized by bleeding into the skin and internal organs and by severe joint deformity and pain. Citrus fruits are the primary sources of vitamin C.

Vitamin A is a fat-soluble vitamin that is important in night vision, health of the entire eye, and in the maintenance of normal skin. Fish liver oils, liver, and yellow vegetables are good sources of vitamin A.

Vitamin D is produced in normal skin on exposure to sunlight. It is also present in certain foods such as fish liver oils, liver, and fortified milk. Vitamin D deficiency causes rickets.

Vitamin E deficency in different animals causes anemia, muscle disease, and infertility. Vitamin E deficiency may be an important problem in premature infants and in some debilitated children. The value of vitamin E in heart disease, fertility, and other medical problems in humans is highly controversial. Wheat germ, vegetables, and eggs are important sources of vitamin E.

Vitamin K is an important vitamin in producing factors that enable the blood to clot. This vitamin is largely produced in the intestine by the bacteria that normally reside there. Severe vitamin K deficiency causes excessive bleeding and it is given routinely to newborn infants to reduce the incidence of hemorrhagic diseases that may occur. Vitamin K is found in cabbage, cauliflower, spinach, and other vegetables.

It is important to emphasize that vitamin supplements are not needed by most people who consume well-balanced, nutritious diets. Vitamin therapy is important when a specific vitamin deficiency exists. For example, vitamin D is essential in the treatment of rickets and vitamin B_{12} is needed for the treatment of pernicious anemia.

Large amounts of the B complex and C vitamins can be taken since they are water soluble and easily eliminated by the kidneys. Other vitamins, such as A and D are not readily eliminated by the body and accumulate in certain tissues such as the liver. Excessive amounts of vitamin A may cause severe headaches, convulsions, and even death. Excesses of vitamin D may produce abnormal elevation of the calcium levels in the blood and may lead to death. In general, vitamins should not be taken without consulting a physician, because usually only a physician is able to determine what specific vitamin deficiencies exist and what specific vitamin therapy is needed in a particular patient. Vitamin therapy is often given to children, pregnant women, and individuals with malnutrition.

Estimate of caloric level for weight loss

A gross estimate of total calories needed to maintain the present weight of a sedentary or moderately active adult may be achieved by multiplying present weight by 12 to 15 calories per pound. Thus a man leading a sedentary or moderately active life and who weighs 175 pounds needs between 2,100 and 2,625 calories to maintain his weight.

A deficit of 500 calories per day under maintenance needs allows loss of about one pound per week. In the absence of disease, satisfactory weight loss can be achieved in most men with 1,400 to 1,800 calories per day and in women with 1,000 to 1,400 calories per day. However, in a given patient, final selection of total calories for weight reduction will be arrived at by trial, with an increase in calories if the patient is losing too rapidly and a decrease if he is losing too slowly.

Nutrient content of diets

Table 2 shows the nutrient content of diets of 1,000, 1,200, 1,400 and 1,800 calories per day compared with the Recommended Dietary Allowances established by the Food and Nutrition Board, National Academy of Sciences–National Research Council.

The Food and Nutrition Board, in setting up the Recommended Dietary Allow-

Table 2. Summary of nutrient content of diets

Calorie level	CHO gm	Protein gm	Fat gm	Calcium gm	Iron mg	Vitamin A IU	Ascorbic acid mg	Thiamine mg	Riboflavin mg	Niacin equivalents mg
1,000	95	80	40	1.06	10.8	17,743	160	0.94	2.49	26.2
1,200	115	85	50	1.09	12.1	18,529	148	1.10	2.65	30.0
1,400	120	85	70	1.05	12.1	18,598	136	1.10	2.60	30.2
1,800	155	105	90	1.41	14.1	20,571	141	1.30	3.30	36.8

ances, relates the recommendation for thiamine to the total calories of the diet, providing 0.5 mg for each 1,000 calories for adults on ordinary levels of caloric intake, but holding to not less than 1 mg daily when the calorie intake is less than 2,000. The 1,200, 1,400, and 1,800 calorie diets provide more than 1 mg of thiamine daily and otherwise meet the Recommended Dietary Allowances.

When calories are restricted to a level of 1,000, the iron and thiamine content of the diet falls slightly below the recommended allowances for a 25-year-old woman. If a 1,000 calorie diet is prescribed for prolonged periods, the patient may benefit from a multivitamin and mineral supplement.

Review questions

1. What are some common diseases of the circulatory system?
2. What are the terms used for removal of the gallbladder, removal of the appendix, and partial removal of a portion of the small intestine?
3. Describe the conditions known as hypermetropia, astigmatism, glaucoma, conjunctivitis, and retinitis.
4. What is meant by splenectomy, myxedema, acromegaly, and hyperthyroidism?

Suggested readings

Sister Agnes Clare: Understanding medical terminology, ed. 5, St. Louis, 1973, Catholic Hospital Association.

Skinner, H. A.: The origin of medical terms, New York, 1961, Hafner Publishing Co., Inc.

Sloane, S. B.: The medical wordbook: a spelling and vocabulary guide to medical transcription, Philadelphia, 1973, W. B. Saunders Co.

Smith, G. L., and Davis, P. E.: Quick medical terminology, New York, 1972, John Wiley & Sons, Inc.

Young, C. G., and Barger, J. D.: Learning medical terminology step by step, ed. 3, St. Louis, 1975, The C. V. Mosby Co.

chapter 23

How the physician makes a diagnosis

One of the most complex and exciting aspects of medicine is the process of making a diagnosis. During many years of arduous training the physician develops the skills needed to be able to make a diagnosis and to choose appropriate treatment for a disease. Laymen often marvel at the ability of a physician to unravel a complex history, conduct an examination, and make a specific diagnosis. In this chapter the steps and the methods used by a physician in arriving at a diagnosis will be given and the role of the medical assistant in this process will be emphasized. At the end of the chapter several case histories will be presented illustrating some of the steps involved in making a diagnosis.

WHY PEOPLE GO TO PHYSICIANS

There are two main reasons why people go to see a physician. The most common is that they perceive themselves to be in poor health. The patient may go see a physician because of severe or unusual pain, fever, a disorder of the special senses, or the perception of an irregularity in one of the bod-

Glossary

anaphylaxis a severe, life-threatening allergic reaction; often caused by administration of drugs or by insect stings

CBC a complete blood count; the hemoglobin, hematocrit, white cell count, and differential count

chief complaint the patient's reason, in his own words, of why he has come to the physician

cholesterol a chemical substance in blood that is thought to be associated with heart disease

differential diagnosis a list of two or more diagnoses that could possibly be the cause of the patient's problem

ECG (EKG) an electrocardiogram; a test that measures the electrical activity of the heart

exudate a collection of pus-containing material

hypertension abnormally high blood pressure

hypotension abnormally low blood pressure

indurated an abnormal firmness of soft tissues

intradermal into the skin

ketone a sweet-smelling byproduct of fat metabolism produced in greater quantities during starvation or poorly controlled diabetes

ketonuria the presence of ketones in the urine

microaneurysms small changes in the blood vessels of the eye that occur in diabetics

podiatrist a foot specialist

polydipsia excessive water or fluid drinking

polyuria excessive urine production

primary diagnosis the cause of the patient's current, most important problem

secondary diagnosis a problem that is less important or urgent than the patient's primary diagnosis

serology a serologic test of the blood; most commonly a blood test for syphilis

streptococcal pharyngitis a specific, sometimes dangerous, form of throat infection; often referred to as "strep throat"

tachycardia an abnormally fast heart rate; a pulse of over 100 beats per minute

tachypnea an abnormally fast respiration

urinalysis a test for abnormalities in the urine

visual acuity a measure of eyesight

ily functions. In these cases the patient expects to be told what is wrong and given treatment for the disorder or expects that he will be told that the problem will resolve itself without treatment.

The second reason people go to a physician is because they desire to remain in good health. Examples of this are routine general physical examinations, special tests to check for specific diseases such as hypertension, cancer, and diabetes, and routine vaccinations. The patient expects to be reassured that all is well and to be given advice on how to remain well. The public is made aware of the benefits of routine visits to the physician by a variety of factors such as news reports of famous individuals who have particular diseases, magazine and newspaper articles discussing advances made in the early detection of various diseases, and educational programs sponsored by groups like the American Cancer Society, the American Heart Association, and the American Diabetes Association. The data below are from a widely distributed brochure of the American Cancer Society that attempts to educate the average person regarding protection against various forms of cancer.

The first question a physician's assistant or a physician asks when a patient comes for care is "Why did you come to the doctor today?" or "What can we do for you?" At times the reason for the visit is a chief complaint that the patient perceives to be a medical problem.

Common chief complaints

Pain is one of the most common chief complaints. Some of the factors that motivate patients to seek medical attention for pain are its severity, its duration, its location, or the worry that the pain may be a symptom of a serious medical problem. The

Safeguards against cancer

The American Cancer Society lists seven safeguards against cancer representing practical ways the average person can be protected against this disease. Each concentrates on a major cancer target and some aim at prevention while others aim at early detection.

Do-it-yourself safegards:

1. Lung—Don't smoke cigarettes. Twenty-nine million Americans have quit. They know it's the best way to prevent most lung cancer.
2. Skin—Avoid overexposure to sun. A broad-brimmed hat, a beach umbrella, protective lotion are ways to shield yourself.
3. Breast—Monthly self-exam. Monthly breast self-examination can detect cancer in an early curable stage.

Safeguards and your doctor:

4. Mouth—Exams regularly. Your physician or dentist can easily detect mouth cancer. See him regularly.
5. Uterus—Pap test once a year. Quick, simple, painless test can detect uterine cancer before symptoms appear when the disease is most curable.
6. Colon-Rectum—Procto annually (especially after 40). The most common internal cancer, which is highly curable, if detected and treated early.
7. Body—Annual health checkup. The most important safeguard. A complete checkup lets you know you are in good health.

assistant and physician will try to find out the location, duration, severity and character of the pain, and what, if anything, makes it better. For example, a headache that has been occurring in the same manner for twenty years, is brought on late in the day during pressure situations, is located in the back of the head, and is rapidly relieved by sleep or aspirin is most likely a tension headache rather than one caused by a brain tumor.

Fever is another chief complaint. Most patients are aware that most fevers are caused by viral infections such as the common cold. They may take aspirin and recover in a few days without seeking medical attention. A long-lasting fever or a fever accompanied by shaking chills or drenching sweats may make the patient suspect that something more than a simple viral infection is present. Fever is frequently the result of bacterial infections. The physician and assistant will always think of common causes of fever first and will try to get clues as to the location of the infection by trying to determine if other specific parts of the body are involved. For example, earache, sore throat, cough, abdominal pain, diarrhea, flank pain, or vaginal discharge may point to the ear, throat, lungs, intestines, kidneys, or pelvic organs as the origin of the fever.

Injuries are a frequent chief complaint. In some cases, the extent of an injury, as in a cut finger, may be obvious; in other cases, such as neck pain or headache several days after an auto accident, the extent may be much more complex. It is especially important to question the patient carefully after automobile or other serious injuries about possible multiple injuries involving the head, neck, chest, abdomen, and parts of the body covered with clothing. It is a mistake to concentrate too much on a simple laceration of the arm or leg in the patient involved in an automobile accident or after a serious fall.

Respiratory complaints frequently cause patients to see a physician. Difficulty in breathing is often an alarming symptom that may be caused by infection, asthma, lung disease, heart disease, or anxiety. A careful history is essential in making a diagnosis of the cause of the respiratory complaint.

Genital, urinary, and gastrointestinal complaints bring patients to doctors with great frequency. Pain, abnormal discharge or bleeding, irregularities of menstruation, diarrhea, and constipation are common.

Disorders of the special senses, especially vision and hearing, are frequent chief complaints. Once again, the number of possible causes for a chief complaint may be rapidly reduced by a careful history followed by a physical examination aimed at clarifying the findings in the history.

THE HISTORY

The present illness. The history begins with the patient telling his problem in his own way to the physician or assistant. After the patient has finished, certain specific aspects of the problem are questioned. It is important not to put words in a patient's mouth. Certain elements of the history such as duration, location, severity, prior treatment, and general symptoms are essential. The assistant should at all times be sensitive to what the patient thinks or feels about the illness. For example, a man whose brother died recently of a heart attack may come to the office complaining of "heartburn" when he is really concerned about a heart attack. A middle-aged woman who is having irregular menstruation may say that she is worried about the menopause when in actuality she is more concerned as to whether she has cancer of the uterus.

The system review and past medical history. In this step the general state of the patient's health is reviewed with particular attention to previous illnesses, injuries, operations, and allergies. It is important to record the names and locations of prior physicians and hospitals and the dates of previous medical treatment. This information is often needed in the future. At times a form for the release of medical information is needed and may be filled out by the assistant and signed by the patient.

The family history. Certain diseases are hereditary and individuals with family histories of these diseases are at increased risk to develop them. Common examples are diabetes, certain forms of heart and kidney disease, allergies, and certain blood diseases like sickle cell anemia. The state of health of parents, siblings, and children should be determined.

Occupational and social history. It is important to remember that each patient has individual social, economic, and personal characteristics. In both diagnosis and treatment of many illnesses the patient's job, financial and social background, level of education, marital status, hobbies and interests, and plans for the future can be significant. The history is not complete until there is a clear knowledge of the patient as a unique human being. Patients who have smoked or worked in coal mines for years are susceptible to lung disease so this information would be useful to the physician in diagnosing and treating a respiratory problem.

PHYSICAL EXAMINATION

The assistant will usually prepare the patient for examination by the physician. The degree of preparation will vary according to the purpose of the visit or chief complaint. A twisted ankle may need only removal of the stocking and shoe, a cough only disrobing to the waist, whereas a complete physical examination will require the patient to disrobe completely and wear an examining robe.

The assistant takes and records the vital signs (temperature, pulse, respirations, and blood pressure) and sometimes the height and weight. In some offices the assistant may also test the patient's visual acuity and hearing. The physician is usually not left alone with female patients undergoing complete physical examinations or examinations of the genitalia, rectum, or breast. The presence of a female assistant will usually make the anxious female patient more comfortable and will also protect a male physician against allegations of unethical behavior during the examination. The assistant will be needed to aid the physician during all proctoscopic and pelvic examinations and during most minor surgical procedures.

A physical examination may take as little as a few minutes or as long as an hour depending on the reason for the visit and the thoroughness of the examination. During the examination the physician tries to correlate the history with certain signs or physical findings that will enable the cause of the patient's complaints to be identified. In addition, during a complete physical examination, the condition of the various systems of the body (nervous, cardiac, pulmonary, special sensory, digestive, genitourinary, skeletal, and so on) will be evaluated. It is unrealistic to presume that a complete physical examination will be performed on all patients coming to the doctor's office. At times a patient may come with a chief complaint that can be handled in a few minutes but also desires a complete examination. Frequently these complete examinations are postponed until a later date and an appointment allowing more time is set up.

SUMMARY AND DIAGNOSIS

The physician will sometimes briefly outline the patient's problem in the medical record. The most serious problems and the problems related to the chief complaint are usually listed after the important findings in the history and physical examination are recorded. The physician, after integrating all of the findings, makes a *primary diagnosis,* a statement of what is considered to be the main problem. When a definitive diagnosis has not been made, the most likely diagnosis is listed first and other possible diagnoses are listed as *differential diagnoses. Secondary diagnoses* are written last and include significant abnormalities unrelated to the present illness.

DISPOSITION

The last part of the record will include further diagnostic tests. Commonly performed diagnostic tests include the CBC, urinalysis, serology, chemistry, x-rays, ECG, skin tests, and tests of the special senses. Also included will be medication, instructions for follow-up visits, and special orders regarding activity, diet, and so forth. At times the patient may be referred to another physician for further diagnostic evaluation or treatment.

Special skin tests

Many of the skin tests formerly used as diagnostic aids in medicine are no longer used or are used very infrequently. By far the most commonly performed skin test in modern medicine is the intradermal skin test for tuberculosis, which consists of the injection of a purified protein derivative (PPD) derived from tubercle bacilli. The reaction is read at 48 to 72 hours. The area of redness is ignored and the raised, indurated area is carefully measured with a ruler and its diameter recorded. A positive PPD implies that a patient has been previously exposed to tuberculosis. It gives no indication as to whether he has active disease. A negative skin test in otherwise healthy patients is very strong evidence against the possibility of tuberculosis. The PPD comes in three strengths: first strength, intermediate strength, and second strength. The intermediate strength PPD is most commonly used.

Other than the PPD, common skin tests used in modern medicine are diagnostic skin tests to determine hypersensitivity or allergies. These tests may be performed either by scratching the skin or by placing a patch over the area to be tested. The material to be tested is included in the patch or is allowed to come in contact with the scratched skin. Most of these skin tests are read in 15 to 30 minutes.

At times, reactions to certain substances like horse serum are tested by placing a drop of an extremely dilute solution of the drug in question directly on the eyelid. A positive test is indicated by redness and itching in 5 to 10 minutes.

The medical assistant is frequently required to perform and read the above tests. It should be emphasized that at all times precautions against possible anaphylaxis as described in Chapter 35 should be taken and that all of these tests should be performed only after careful instructions from the physician.

THE PROBLEM-ORIENTED RECORD (WEED SYSTEM)

In recent years a new system has been developed for recording histories, physical examinations, and laboratory data in medical records. This system is being widely taught at many medical and nursing schools, and is becoming increasingly popular with physicians in medical offices, clinics, and hospitals. It is especially useful in caring for patients with complex or multiple problems who are going to receive long-term medical care.

The patient's medical record is oriented around the patient's problems. After the history and physical examination have been performed, the patient's problems are listed. In succeeding visits each of the problems is brought up to date by including new symptoms, physical findings, laboratory tests, or treatment. New problems are added as the need arises.

An integral part of the Weed system is an up-to-date record of resolved and active problems. This information is kept in the front of the medical record. For example, an elderly woman with heart disease may fall and fracture a wrist. After the fracture has healed, the fractured wrist becomes a resolved problem. The heart disease continues to be an active problem. When a problem first appears or becomes resolved, its date of onset or resolution is recorded in the chart. A list is also kept of medications, their amount, and the duration of treatment. The Weed system makes progress notes easier to understand and relate to patients with multiple problems. It also serves as a quick reference by which to review a patient's complete medical history and the current management of each of his problems.

CASE HISTORIES

The following case histories illustrate the process by which the physician makes his diagnosis.

Case number 1

A 25-year-old bank teller is in apparent good health when he develops a sore throat, fever, and muscle aches over a two-day period. When the illness begins, he takes several aspirin and throat lozenges for his sore throat. These offer only temporary relief and on the second day of his illness he is forced to come home from work early. On the third day he calls his physician's office and gets an emergency appointment.

When he arrives at the physician's office, the physician's assistant fills out the appropriate forms and takes him to an examining room. The assistant asks what is wrong; and when he says that he "feels terrible," he is asked how long he has felt this way. He explains that he was well until three days previously when he developed a sore throat, fever, and muscle aching and upon being asked what he has taken for this problem, he replies that he has been taking aspirin. The answer to each question as to whether he has these problems frequently and whether he has had a rash, headache, cough, or earache, is no. The assistant next takes the oral temperature and the other "vital signs" and records these in the medical record. The patient is given an examining robe to put on and he then strips to the waist and waits for the physician.

The physician reads a brief account of the history and the medical record (or is told by the assistant the general nature of the problem), reviews the history, and examines the patient. No rash is noted on the skin. The ears are examined with the otoscope and they are normal. With the aid of a flashlight and a tongue depressor, the physician examines the patient's throat and finds that it is beefy red in color and that the tonsils are covered with a whitish exudate. The glands under the jaw are slightly enlarged and tender, but the rest of the glands of the neck appear normal. The physician percusses the chest, listens over both lungs, listens over the heart, and hears no abnormalities. The patient is asked to lie on the examining table and the physician proceeds to examine the abdomen where there is no tenderness or other abnormality noted.

The physician tells the patient that he has a throat infection that probably is streptococcal, and asks if the patient is allergic to penicillin. The patient is then told that some tests are going to be performed to confirm the diagnosis and that he should call back in three days. He is reassured that he should be better in two or three days and should be able to return to work at that time. He is given a prescription for penicillin tablets and told that he can take two aspirin every four hours for fever or pain. Before leaving, the patient is reminded that he should call back at any time if any problems develop.

Analysis of case number 1. The above history is an example of a patient who developed a problem, became concerned about his health, and went to the physician to find out what was wrong and to receive treatment. The patient came to the physician because he "felt terrible" but more specifically because he had a sore throat, fever, and muscle pains. These were the *symptoms* (what the patient felt). The medical assistant and doctor took a medical history to find out when these symptoms began, what they felt like, and what the treatment had been. The physical examination showed that the patient had fever, tachycardia, a red throat, an exudate on his tonsils, and that the glands under the jaw were tender. These were *signs* or positive physical findings that lead to a diagnosis. The physician analyzed the history and physical findings and came to a *tentative diagnosis* of a streptococcal pharyngitis; in order to make a *definitive diagnosis,* a throat culture was ordered. Penicillin, aspirin, and bed rest were prescribed as treatment. Medical follow-up was provided, which in this case necessitated only a telephone call to the office in three days. The treatment given, the instructions to the patient, and medical follow-up were the *disposition* of this case.

This case is an example of the importance of the chief complaint, symptoms, physical examination, diagnostic tests, treatment, and medical follow-up of a patient. If the patient had been having the sore throat for several weeks and had taken penicillin for two weeks, the history would have suggested a different diagnosis to the physician. Similarly, if there had been a rash, a tender liver, or enlarged spleen, more diagnostic tests would have been ordered and, instead of a *presumptive diagnosis,* a *differential diagnosis* would have been made. This would have consisted of a list of two or more possible diagnoses to account for the history or physical findings. Further tests would have been ordered to find out which of these possible diagnoses was correct. *Specific treatment* would then be delayed until the results were returned in a few days. Aspirin might have been ordered as *symptomatic treatment* if the illness was suspected as being caused by a virus.

Case number 2

A 46-year-old woman comes to the doctor because of weakness and a loss of 30 pounds over a three-month period. Her history reveals that she cannot remember exactly when her illness started but about three months previously she had noted a loss of 5 pounds from her usual weight. After further questioning, she states that during the last two months she has been eating normally but has been drinking a lot of fluids. She says that she awakes several times during the night to urinate and drink water. The physician asks her a long series of questions about her past medical problems, pain, headaches, and visual disturbances as well as about any shortness of breath, vomiting, bowel habits, eating patterns, and infections. No major problems are elicited. The patient is then asked her past medical history and she reveals that she has two children, each of whom weighed over 9 pounds at birth. The family history is obtained and it is learned that her mother had diabetes before she died of a heart attack and that her older sister has diabetes that is being treated with pills and a special diet.

A physical examination shows the patient to be a frail, anxious woman. Her vital signs are normal except that her respirations are 24 per minute. There is a sweet odor on her breath. She has microaneurysms on ophthalmoscopic examination. The lungs and heart are normal but her liver is slightly enlarged and somewhat tender. She has good pulses in her legs and feet but has lost the hair over the lower part of her legs. A neurologic examination, including the tendon reflexes of the knees and ankles, is normal.

The physician asks for an immediate urinalysis and a Dextrostix glucose measurement, which is done at once by the assistant. The urinalysis shows 2+ protein, 4+ glucose and 4+ acetone. The urine sediment is normal. The glucose measurement shows that the glucose was over 250 mg per 100 ml. The physician tells the patient that she has diabetes mellitus and that she will have to be hospitalized for a few days for treatment and instructions on how to care for her diabetes.

Analysis of case number 2. In this case the *chief complaints* that brought the patient to the doctor were her weight loss and weakness. She had *symptoms* of excessive water drinking (polydipsia) and urine production (polyuria). The *physical signs* were obvious weight loss, rapid breathing (tachypnea), microaneurysms in the retina, a tender and enlarged liver, and decreased hair over her legs. She had a *past history* of large babies, a condition frequently associated with diabetes, and several close relatives had diabetes. In any given patient there may be countless reasons why weight loss and weakness could occur. In this particular patient the physician was able to integrate the history and physical examination and was virtually certain that the patient had diabetes mellitus. When the diagnosis was confirmed, the severity of the diabetes was ascertained by two simple tests performed by the medical assistant. Although in most cases diabetes mellitus does not require immediate hospitalization, in this instance the diabetes was severe and immediate therapy and a hospital management was needed.

Several factors about the patient's history deserved attention. First, the patient was aware that she had lost weight and felt weak but did not associate these complaints in any way with her polyuria and polydipsia. This is an example of an assistant or a physician asking specific questions in order to focus on a possible diagnostic clue. Diabetes is one of the many causes of weight loss especially when associated with polydipsia and polyuria. Second, the patient was eating normally and did not have any complaints relating to her gastrointestinal system. A 30-pound weight loss could have been from a diet or some sort of gastrointestinal problem that interfered with normal food intake. Third, this patient demonstrates the importance of getting a past history. In this case a clue to her diagnosis was obtained when she stated that she had had unusually large babies, a common occurrence in diabetic women. The importance of getting a family history is demonstrated, since diabetes is an inherited disorder and there is frequently a family history of diabetes in diabetic patients.

Diabetes is the result of a deficiency of insulin, a key hormone involved in converting ingested carbohydrates, fat, and protein into their respective storage fuels of glycogen, fat, and muscle. A deficiency of insulin caused the patient to be unable to utilize ingested sugar, which built up in the blood and spilled over into the urine. Water accompanied the sugar spilled in the urine and created a need to urinate excessively. Because of the insulin deficiency, the patient's fat stores broke down and were converted into fatty acids, which were converted by the liver into ketones. The ketones, in turn, were eventually spilled over into the urine causing ketonuria and were also expelled by the lungs causing a sweet odor on the breath. Also, because of insulin deficiency, the muscles started to release stored amino acids, some of which were converted into sugar and caused a further elevation of the blood glucose level. The amino acids lost from the muscle were therefore converted to sugar and eventually eliminated in the urine. The combined breakdown of fat and muscle stores caused the patient to lose weight. An understanding of the pathophysiology of diabetes led the physician to order the appropriate tests to confirm the diagnosis and to evaluate the extent of the diabetes.

The patient had four additional findings in her physical examination that can be explained by her diabetes. The rapid breathing exhibited by the patient was caused by the body's attempt to discharge excessive acids. The excessive acids were due to the release and metabolism of fatty acids which in turn were caused by her insulin deficiency. The patient was trying to eliminate carbon dioxide and carbonic acid in an attempt to adjust to her acidosis. The enlarged tender liver was caused by the excessive amounts of fat present in the patient's liver, a result of the diabetes.

In addition to the above chemical abnormalities, the physician was aware of the fact that diabetes causes extensive changes in blood vessels. These changes lead to an increased incidence of degenerative changes in blood vessels of the brain, eyes, kidneys, legs, and other tissues. In this case the vessels of the eye were affected as evidenced by microaneurysms seen in the eye examination. It is possible that the kidneys were also affected by the diabetes since there was leakage of protein into the urine. A careful check was made for evidence of disease of the blood vessels and nerves of the legs and feet but none was found.

In future visits the patient's response to treatment will be carefully reviewed. During each subsequent visit the physician and assistant will take the opportunity to teach the patient more about her diabetes. They will also provide reading material for her and her family. Particular attention will be paid to the patient's eyes, heart, feet, weight, and diet. She will need careful evaluation at regular intervals by an ophthalmologist in order to prevent possible blindness resulting from her diabetes. She will be placed on insulin and will have to adjust her life so that she eats regularly and has a regular pattern of physical activity. Her physician or a podiatrist will carefully advise her about care of her feet. On numerous occasions during the next few years the assistant will help explain the importance of all these matters to the patient. The assistant will advise the patient to carry in her purse a card stating that she is a diabetic and giving instructions for emergency treatment.

Case number 3

A 51-year-old black man comes to the doctor because of chest pain and occasional headache. The headaches usually occur at the end of the day at work, are pulsating, and can be relieved by aspirin and rest. He describes the chest pain as a severe squeezing sensation of the left side of his chest, which sometimes radiates from his chest to the neck and left arm, lasts one or two minutes, and is relieved quickly by rest. It seems to be more frequent during episodes of anger or physical exercise. The patient states that he was once told that he had high blood pressure but stopped taking his blood pressure medicine several years ago and never returned to see his doctor since he felt completely well. The blood pressure is taken on several occasions after resting and the lowest blood pressure obtained is 190 over 110 mm Hg. Physical examination reveals an enlarged heart. The rest of the physical examination is unremarkable. A CBC and urinalysis are performed in the office and are both normal. An electrocardiogram is obtained and shows evidence of enlargement of the heart but demonstrates no evidence of a heart attack. The patient is asked to sign a release of information form and his previous medical records are requested. He is given a diuretic and another antihypertensive drug as well as nitroglycerin to take under his tongue for his chest pain. He is told that his headache was perhaps related to his hypertension but might also be caused by nervous tension. He is given a 5 gram salt, 1500 calorie diet and told the importance of losing weight and stopping his cigarette smoking. He is also told that he has high blood pressure and that this can be controlled with appropriate medication.

A chest x-ray film and routine blood chemistries show enlargement of the heart, elevation of the blood urea nitrogen (BUN) concentration, and a moderately elevated cholesterol. The patient is seen about six times during the next three months and every two months thereafter. His diet is modified slightly to lower his cholesterol. He loses weight and adjusts his working conditions and his chest pain reoccurs only two or three times during the next year. Each time it is rapidly relieved with nitroglycerin. On each follow-up visit he is weighed and his blood pressure is checked at least twice by the medical assistant. On one occasion the patient complains of light-headedness on rising in the morning and although his blood pressure is 130 over 86 mm Hg while sitting, it falls to 98 over 60 mm Hg on standing and he becomes light-headed again. This information is made known to the physician who adjusts the dose of the antihypertensive drugs. Urine and blood tests are performed several times during the year to check on kidney function and cholesterol. On one occasion the patient asks the assistant when the doctor will take him off his pills. This question is relayed to the physician and on the next visit it is then reemphasized to the patient that he will probably have to take his medication for the rest of his life even though he feels well.

Analysis of case number 3. The physician made several diagnoses after the patient's first visit: hypertension, coronary artery disease, and obesity.

About 25 to 30 million Americans have hypertension but only about half of them are aware of it with only half of that number being treated for it. Most people with hypertension feel fine for many years. When the disease becomes advanced, it produces damage to the heart, kidneys, and the brain. These three organs are the ones that suffer the most serious damage from hypertension and are the principal causes of death from this disease.

In the patient discussed the hypertension had produced symptoms (chest pain), physical signs (an enlarged heart), and laboratory evidence (elevated BUN) of heart and kidney damage. He was seen often in the office because there is good evidence that adequate medical treatment increases survival of patients with hypertension. Of importance also is the assistant's role in pointing out to the physician the side effects of the treatment (hypotension on standing) and the patient's lack of adequate understanding of the nature of his disease and its treatment. It is not unusual for patients to ask medical assistants questions that they would normally not ask the physician.

Coronary artery disease is the most common cause of death in the United States. Although its exact cause is not known, several factors are known to be associated with it. These include: diabetes, hypertension, high cholesterol, obesity, and cigarette smoking. This patient had all of these "risk factors" except diabetes. The high cholesterol was found on routine laboratory testing but a specific test for cholesterol might also have been ordered by the physician because of the suspicion raised on noting the patient's coronary artery disease at a relatively young age. Treatment was directed at trying to correct all of these "risk factors" and by treating the chest pain. This was accomplished by trying to adjust the patient's life style and by providing symptomatic treatment of his chest pain with nitroglycerin.

Two further points can be made in regard to this case. First, the patient was black and hypertension is known to be more common in blacks than in whites. Second, several years before, no effort was made to contact the patient when he failed to keep his doctor's appointments. A good physician's assistant will try to locate patients such as this to remind them of the need for continued medical treatment.

Review questions

1. What are the two main reasons people go to the physician?
2. What are some common "chief complaints"?
3. What is meant by the term differential diagnosis?
4. What is a PPD?

Suggested readings

Brams, W. A.: How to live your high pressure, New York, 1973, Arco Publishing Co., Inc.

Berni, R. and Readey, H.: Problem-oriented medical record implementation, St. Louis, 1974, The C. V. Mosby Co.

Dolger, H., and Seeman, B.: How to live with diabetes, ed. 3, New York, 1972, W. W. Norton & Co., Inc.

Young, C. G. and Barger, J. D.: Introduction to medical science, ed. 2, St. Louis, 1973, The C. V. Mosby Co.

chapter 24
Preparation of patients

No detail of the equipment or management of a physician's office can be considered unimportant when it is borne in mind that the sick are even more susceptible to impressions and atmosphere than the well and that the reception given a patient on his first visit to a physician has a definite influence upon his confidence in the treatment to be administered and therefore upon its results.

THE MEDICAL OFFICE

The usual medical suite includes a reception room, a consulting room, a room for examination and treatment, and a toilet and lavatory. Physicians engaged in group practice as a rule occupy more spacious quarters. In the consulting room are the physician's desk, the filing equipment, and the medical library; in the treatment room an adjustable examining table, cabinets and closets for instruments, drugs, and surgical supplies, the sterilizer, and such special apparatus as may be required in the physician's particular specialty.

The reception room

Although it is obvious that not all office suites can be so located as to receive sunshine during the greater part of the day, any office can be given a homelike and welcoming aspect. A medical assistant should study the possibilities of the reception room and its furnishings, and she may often make

---

Glossary

cautery an instrument used to destroy tissue or stop bleeding by the application of heat or chemicals
cervix the neck of the uterus
cystoscopy examination of the bladder by means of a special tube called a cystoscope
emesis vomiting
gastric pertaining to the stomach
hemostat a clamp for controlling or stopping hemorrhage
lavage the washing out of a cavity such as the stomach, bladder, ear, etc.
lithotomy incision into the bladder for removing a stone
otoscope device for the examination of the ear
ophthalmoscope an instrument used to examine the internal structure of the eye
Papanicolaou (Pap) smear a diagnostic test for cancer of the cervix
paracentesis the procedure of removing fluid from the chest or abdomen
percussion hammer an instrument used during a neurologic examination to test the tendon reflexes
perineum the region between the vulva or scrotum and the anus
procaine a local anesthetic
proctoscopy the examination of the rectum through a special tube called the proctoscope
prone the position of lying flat on the abdomen
pubis the lower anterior part of the pubic bone
sigmoidoscopy examination of the rectum and sigmoid colon by visualization through a special tube called a sigmoidoscope
Sims position a semiprone position used to examine the anus or perineum
speculum an instrument for examination of canals such as the nose and vagina
supine the position of lying on the back
trocar an instrument used for aspiration or removal of fluids from cavities

suggestions that will add to its attractiveness. Cut flowers in summer and stands with blossoming plants in winter add a pleasing touch. A table with magazines and papers is a usual feature, and if these are recent publications they will be much more appreciated by those who use them.

The consulting room

Keeping the physician's desk in order is usually a part of the assistant's duty. Clean desk blotters and small blotters, cleaned and filled fountain pens, well-sharpened pencils, a plentiful supply of all kinds of stationery that may be reqired, case history forms ready at hand, the memorandum calendar filled in with the day's appointments and engagements, and mail sorted into communications requiring immediate attention and those of less urgency are among the details for which a doctor depends upon the assistant. The case histories of patients who have made previous visits and who have appointments for the day should be laid out in proper order, or each case record may be handed separately to the doctor when the patient is ushered into the consulting room.

The treatment room

The furnishings of the room used for examination and treatment of patients will depend largely upon the special line of work in which the physician is engaged. The usual examining table is made in sections that can be adjusted so that either the upper or the lower part of the body can be elevated or depressed. The electrocardiograph is used in making graphic tracings of the heart action. Numerous devices for the testing of vision are a part of the equipment of the ophthalmologist. The sphygmomanometer, for testing blood pressure, the stethoscope, for listening to sounds in the chest, and the ophthalmoscope, for looking into the eye, are used by nearly all physicians. The contents of the instrument cabinet will vary but will in all cases include various types of knives, forceps, dilators, specula, needles, and ligature material. An assistant who is expected to help with the examination and treatment of patients should become familiar as rapidly as possible with the apparatus. The surgical supply closet will contain absorbent cotton, gauze, adhesive plaster of various widths, and an assortment of bandages and dressings. Preparation of folded dressings, cotton or gauze sponges, and so on is usually a responsibility of the medical assistant.

In addition to the iodine, alcohol, boric acid, sterile petroleum jelly, and other articles used in minor surgery, some doctors keep on hand a considerable supply of drugs, usually in the form of tablets, to be prescribed for their patients. The assistant may be expected to take charge of all medical and surgical supplies as well as stationery and other supplies for office use and to order a fresh supply of any article that needs replenishing. Instrument and drug cabinets should be kept locked when not in use.

OFFICE AND PATIENT

A physician's assistant is often called upon to help in the treatment room in the preparation of patients for various types of examinations and in such procedures as dressings, minor surgical operations, and spinal punctures. This should be done with dexterity and forethought, anticipating the physician's needs so that the examination may be expedited and the patient and physician may be inconvenienced as little as possible.

If the patient is a female, a female assistant should show her to the treatment room and aid her in preparing for the examination or treatment. A physical examination, especially a vaginal or rectal examination, is sometimes a trial to the patient, and a cheerful and matter-of-fact attitude on the part of the medical assistant can do much to allay nervousness or embarrassment. The assistant helps the patient to arrange her clothing in the required manner and to assume the proper position for examination, draping her with one or more sheets, as needed. A blanket may be added if the weather is cold, but a room used for examination and treatment should always be well warmed. Women patients coming for internal examinations should generally not be left alone with a male physician.

In chest examinations it is usually necessary to remove the clothing from the upper part of the body. All parts except the one immediately under examination should be protected from exposure. The usual procedures in chest examination require that the patient sit upright if he is able to do so. For an examination of the abdomen, the patient lies on his back with a small pillow under his head and his arms and legs extended. For a vaginal or rectal examination several positions are used. In the dorsal recumbent position the patient lies upon the back, the legs are slightly separated, the thighs are drawn up, and the knees are bent so that the soles of the feet rest upon the table. In what is known as the lithotomy position there is more extreme flexion of the thighs upon the body and the knees upon the thighs; for this position a table with upright rods furnished with stirrups in which the feet are supported is necessary. In the Sims position the patient lies on the left side with the left arm behind the back, the right arm in front, the thighs and knees flexed, and the buttocks at the edge of the mattress. In the knee-chest position the patient's chest and flexed knees rest upon the mattress and the head is turned to one side upon a small pillow. The abdomen is unsupported, as the intention is to allow the pelvic organs to fall forward.

For an internal examination the doctor may wear gloves or a glove for one hand only. Other articles used in examinations and in the making of uterine applications are specula, forceps, applicators, sponges or tampons, absorbent cotton and gauze, sterile lubricants, and various medicinal agents. Instruments for insertion into the body should be warmed before using. In a cystoscopy (direct inspection of the bladder), catheterization (instrumental removal of urine from the bladder), or any form of bladder treatment, the greatest care is necessary to avoid any possibility of infection; all articles used should be sterile, and the instruments needed for the procedure should not be removed from their sterile wrappings until the moment of use. The patient lies on the back, thighs and knees flexed and limbs well separated. Catheters or tubes for insertion into the urethra are usually of rubber or plastic. In addition, a sterile lubricant, sterile sponges or gauze wipes, and dressing forceps will be needed as well as an antiseptic solution if an irrigation of the bladder is to be performed. When an instillation of some drug into the bladder is to be performed, the drug should be placed in a sterile measuring glass.

In gastric lavage (the washing out of the stomach), the stomach tube and rubber sheets and other sheets for protection of the patient will be needed; for use in a lavage, a pitcher containing the solution and a pail for the return flow are required; in removal of a test meal, a special receptacle to hold the evacuated material that is to be analyzed is necessary. Since the swallowing of a stomach tube is difficult for some patients, the moral support given by the medical assistant may have much to do with the success of the procedure.

In eye examinations, irrigations, instillations and in examination and treatment of the ear, the assistant's principal duties are to place the patient in the proper position and light, to reassure nervous patients, to use gentle restraint in the case of unruly children, and to have at hand the necessary articles, which are highly specialized in such procedures.

In nose and throat examinations and treatments, specula and self-illuminating instruments for inspection may be required; tongue depressors, tubing, and other apparatus for the giving of irrigations, solutions, inhalants, and so on will also be needed.

A medical assistant, when required to prepare for and give aid in highly technical procedures, should make an intensive study of the work and its methods, becoming acquainted both with the reasons for and the details of each step of a procedure and with the name and use of every instrument and article that will be handled. The principles of antisepsis and asepsis should also become familiar and sight never lost of the unvarying necessity for infinite care in the details of their application.

MINOR SURGERY

Many minor surgical procedures, such as suture of lacerations, opening of abscesses, removal of infected nails, and excision of small growths, are performed in the physician's office. Much the same preparation and materials are used for all these procedures.

For suture of lacerations, the conventional materials for local sterilization are required—tincture of green soap, alcohol, iodine, or some other sterilizing solution. Sterile gauze, applicators, drapery material, and rubber gloves as well as a local anesthetic such as lidocaine or ethyl chloride are also essential. The instrument tray should contain an ample number of hemostats, forceps, large and small hypodermic syringes with large and small needles, a supply of suture needles and suture materials, such as silk, nylon, and catgut, as the occasion may warrant, and one or two needle holders. For incision of abscesses or dressings of infected wounds and burns, essentially the same materials are required, with the exception of sutures. As a rule, infected wounds are not closed.

Many physicians remove small tumors and warts and take biopsy specimens in the office. These procedures may be quite simple, requiring only local sterilization of the area followed by excision of the tissue with a knife or the cautery loop. A specimen removed for biopsy purposes should be placed immediately in a preservative or fixing solution. Biopsy specimens should not be placed on gauze, as small segments may become lost or enmeshed in the gauze, making a satisfactory microscopic study difficult.

Cauterizations, particularly of the uterine cervix, are often done in the office. These call for a cautery unit as well as instruments for pelvic examinations.

Occasionally the physician may remove fluid from a patient's chest or abdomen as an office procedure. For such measures trocars, cannulas, and paracentesis needles must be placed on the instrument tray.

Specialists in eye, ear, nose, and throat work and specialists in other branches of medicine perform a variety of minor operations in the office. In all these, the same general technique is followed, the proper instruments being added to meet the demands of the particular occasion.

SPINAL PUNCTURES

The tray for spinal punctures should include two puncture needles, a hypodermic syringe with needles, a larger needle for deep injections, lidocaine, gloves, gauze, two sterile towels, applicators, alcohol, iodine or other antiseptic solution, a spinal fluid manometer, and two or three sterile test tubes for the collection of the fluid.

The patient should remove all superfluous clothing and put on an examining gown or smock. If the patient is a man, the clothing is removed well below the lumbar area and fixed so it will not slide up over the spinal puncture area during the procedure. The patient is placed on his side with the knees drawn up toward the chest and the head bowed as close as possible to the knees. A good light should be available. An area on the patient's back extending from the first to the fourth lumbar vertebrae is cleansed with soap and water, then covered with antiseptic solution such as iodine. The excess solution is sponged off with alcohol. In removing the solution, the assistant should be careful not to pass from an unsterile area of the skin across the sterile area. It is best to begin in the middle of the sterilized area and clean from within outward, without touching the cleansed area with the hands. The physician may sterilize the area; in this event the assistant opens sterile gauze packages and pours the cleansing and antiseptic solutions.

In preparation for the spinal puncture, a sterile towel is placed on the table or in a large pan, and the puncture needles, syringe, hypodermic needles, and sterile gauze are laid on the towel. If not needed immediately, the instruments should be covered with one end of the towel to protect them from contamination.

When the physician is ready, the assistant opens sterile rubber gloves in a manner to prevent their contamination and assists in putting them on. The lidocaine is then poured or the ampule broken and held while the anesthetic is drawn into the syringe. As the puncture is being made, the patient is held in the proper position, and when the spinal canal is reached, the test tubes for collection of the specimen are passed.

After the puncture needle is withdrawn, the assistant should remove the excess antiseptic solution from the patient's skin and place a small dressing over the site of the puncture or cover it with collodion. The patient is usually required to lie flat in bed for several hours after this procedure to minimize any headache that sometimes follows the spinal puncture. The assistant should see that he is made comfortable.

The needles and syringe should be sterilized before being put away.

PELVIC EXAMINATIONS

Lithotomy position is used in almost all cases. Dorsal recumbent position can be used in those instances where it is impossible or impractical to put the patient in stirrups, but it is more difficult to use the speculum in this position.

1. Needed equipment includes clean rubber gloves and lubricant, vaginal speculum, cotton balls, uterine forceps (or a long sponge forceps), light, applicators, a stool for the physician, and slides, culture tubes, and other special equipment as ordered.
2. The patient removes outer clothing and lower garments such as girdles. The patient may be draped with a large sheet crosswise or a small sheet diagonally. Legs are placed in stirrups with knees flexed and apart; stirrups should be placed at as comfortable a distance as possible. Patient is placed low on table so buttocks are about one inch over the edge. Sheet is placed to cover legs and thighs and expose the perineum. Anchor the sheet under the feet in stirrups. It is of utmost importance that the bladder be empty; urge the patient to attempt to void. If patient has been having vaginal bleeding, clean the perineum before and after examination with cotton balls and soap and water if necessary.
3. Aid in securing patient cooperation and in manipulating drape. Head may be elevated during part of the exam to relax the abdomen. A female assistant should usually be in attendance when female patient is being examined. Mother

Fig. 24-1. Dorsal recumbent position for pelvic examination.

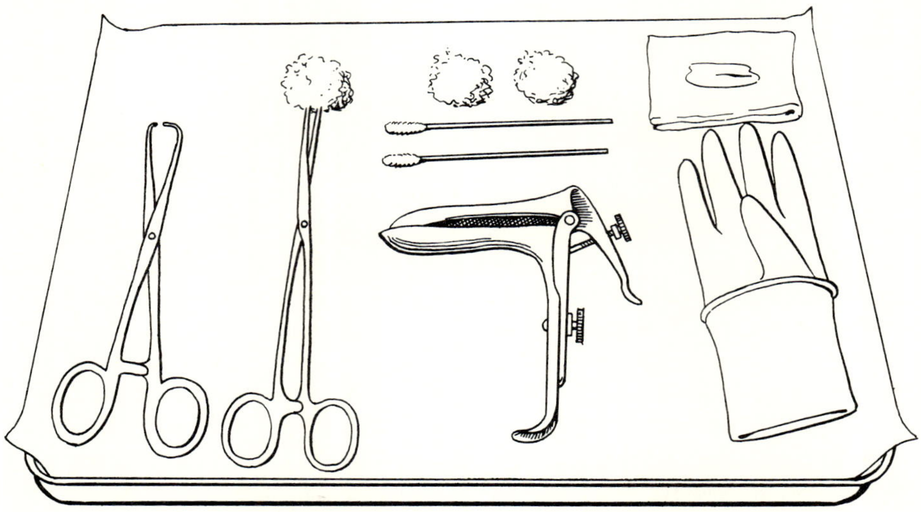

Fig. 24-2. Tray setup for pelvic examination.

or adult female relative is often present when pelvic examination of a minor must be made.

4. Equipment is washed thoroughly with soap and water. Disposable gloves are frequently used. Specula are boiled for ten minutes; both gloves and specula need more disinfection than just washing. Waste is disposed of by wrapping or placing in covered waste receptacle. If patient has been having vaginal bleeding or has a discharge, offer a perineal pad. Care for specimens in the proper manner; label accurately.

The female assistant should remain in the room during the examination. When the physician is ready, she should open a pair of gloves and hold them while he puts them on. She then applies a liberal amount of lubricant to his extended hand or applies it on a piece of sterile gauze within his reach. Thus the speculum and the gloved hand may be inserted without causing the patient pain. The medicaments used in treatments should be convenient so the assistant may pass them upon request.

The physician will sometimes want to take a bacterial culture specimen during the pelvic examination. If gonococcal cultures are desired they must be plated immediately on Thayer-Martin agar plates and placed in a candle jar. The physician may wish to examine vaginal secretions immediately under the microscope looking for fungi and *Trichomonas* (a common parasite of the vagina). A small bottle of saline, glass slides, and cover slips will be needed for this procedure.

Cancer of the cervix is a potentially deadly type of cancer that occurs commonly in middle-aged women. This common cancer can be universally cured if detected in its early stages. The most effective way of detecting cancer of the cervix in its early stages is through a Papanicolaou (Pap) smear. If a Papanicolaou smear is to be done, no lubricant is used on the vaginal speculum. Instead, the speculum is moistened with warm water and given to the physician. Two slides are usually prepared. The physician uses a special applicator and collects one sample from the cervix and one from the vagina and smears these on the appropriately labeled slides. The slides are *fixed immediately* with one of many available fixatives specially supplied for this purpose. A Pap smear is part of every routine physical examination of an adult female and should be performed once a year.

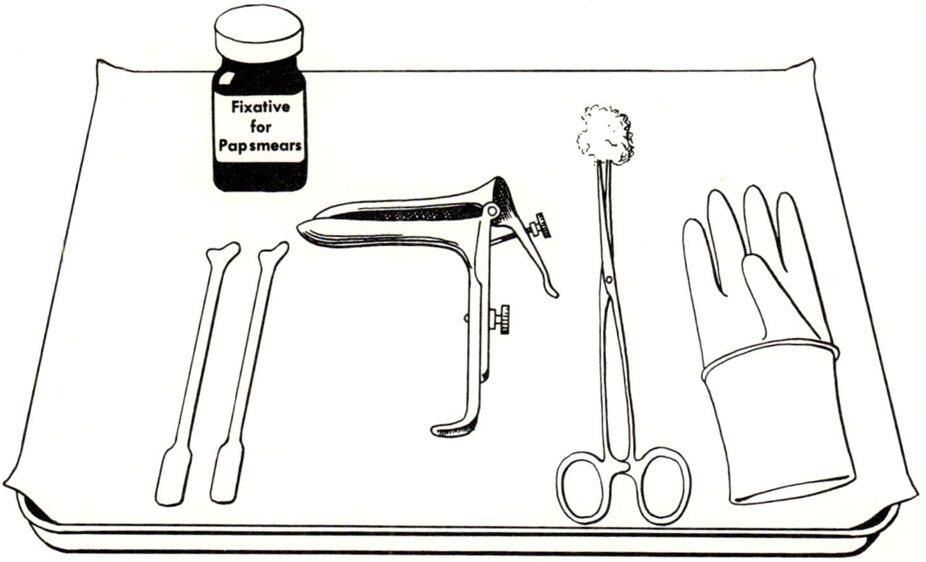

Fig. 24-3. Tray setup for Papanicolaou smear.

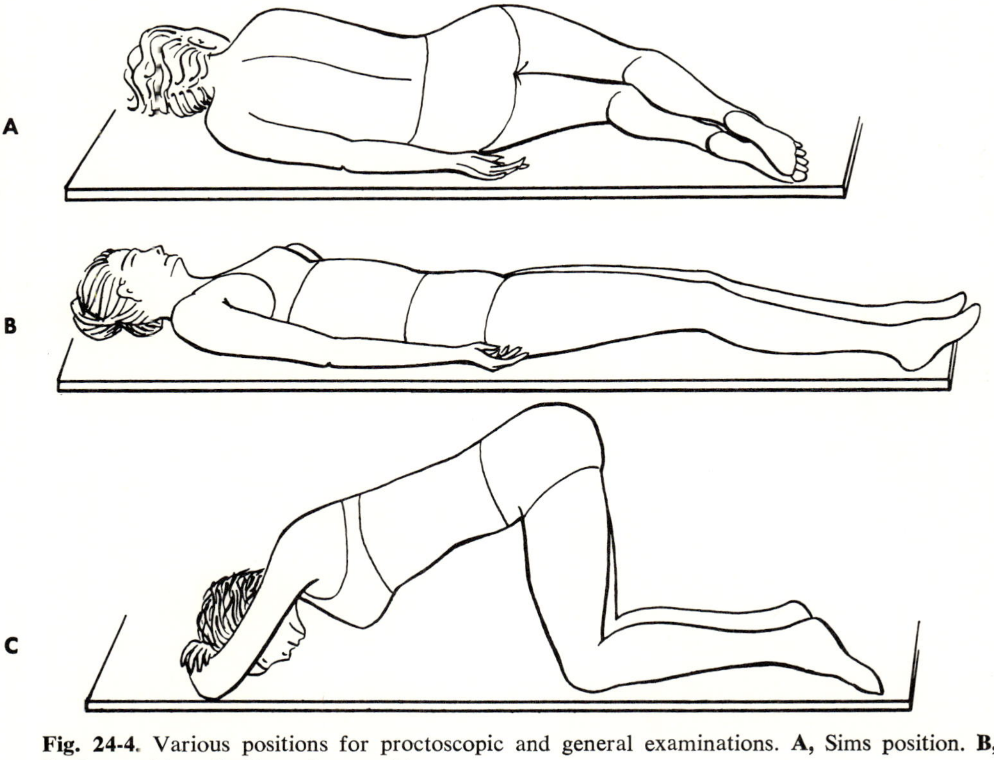

Fig. 24-4. Various positions for proctoscopic and general examinations. **A,** Sims position. **B,** Supine position. **C,** Knee-chest position.

PROCTOSCOPIC EXAMINATION

The female assistant is required to prepare women patients for proctoscopic examinations, having them first remove their clothing, as for a pelvic examination, and put on an examining gown. If a proctoscopic table is available, the table is inverted so the part to be examined is elevated and exposed. Drapes are applied around the patient to prevent unnecessary exposure. If a proctoscopic table is not available, the patient is placed upon a regular examination table in what is known as the knee-chest position—the patient kneels with her knees as near the end of the table as possible, and the shoulders are placed close to the knees, the head resting on the table on a pillow. This position affords the maximum exposure as well as good relaxation and is reasonably comfortable for the patient. Those who are unable to assume this position because of their age, weight, or a deformity may be placed on the left side with the knees drawn close to the chest. The assistant then separates the buttocks to permit good exposure.

The assistant should learn the routine of an examination and be prepared to pass the physician the proper instruments and other necessities as required. The patient having been prepared, the assistant holds gloves for the physician and applies lubricating jelly to the examining finger. Following digital examination, the physician usually inserts a small proctoscope, while the assistant turns on the rheostat and adjusts the light to the proper intensity. A sponge, forceps, or long applicators, and if necessary, bottles of medication that have been opened and a slide for smears are then passed. After the use of the short proctoscope, the physician may wish to insert a long one. In this event, the assistant lubricates the instrument before passing it. At the end of the examination the patient is cleansed and given a tissue or a pad to finish her cleansing. Proper cleansing will relieve a great deal of the patient's discomfort and embarrassment from these examinations.

If smears or biopsy specimens have been taken, they should be properly labeled and carried to the laboratory for examination. The instruments are then washed and sterilized.

The same procedures should be followed in the examination of male patients. The female assistant probably will not be called upon for aid, however, or at least not until the patient has been properly draped.

The knee-chest position is preferred, or a special table is used.

1. Necessary equipment includes scopes as needed, large applicators (about 15 inches), lubricants, waste basin, specimen bottles for biopsy if needed, and suction equipment if used. Check the light on the scope to be sure it is in order.
2. The patient is prepared as previously described. The patient is encouraged to have a bowel movement before coming to the office. Some doctors ask their patients to take a tap water or saline enema prior to the examination while others do not. Enemas are usually avoided in patients who have colitis or bleeding from the rectum.
3. Help instruct and reassure the patient and adjust the drape. Provide instruments and waste basin as needed. Observe patient for fatigue or fainting, as he might easily fall off the table from this position.
4. Help patient to get up and dress. Straighten table and drape sheet. Wash instruments and disinfect as usual. Do not boil the light attachment of the scope; wipe it with an alcohol sponge if necessary. Dispose of waste material by wrapping and putting in incinerator or covered waste container—not in examining room. Care for specimens, and handle biopsy specimens with utmost care. The patient, especially the elderly or weak, should usually rest for a few minutes, as getting up from this position may cause patient to faint if not feeling well.

X-RAY EXAMINATION

The preparation for x-ray examinations varies according to the region to be studied.

For examination of the skull, teeth, extremities, and chest no special preparation is needed. For x-ray photographs of the gastrointestinal tract, the patient is not allowed to eat for at least six hours prior to the examination. If the study is to be made in the morning, he omits breakfast and is observed between eight and ten o'clock. Another observation is made four or five hours later. Thereafter, the patient may have food, although it is desirable that he first take a laxative to assist in the elimination of barium that has been ingested. If a 24-hour observation is required, further restriction of diet may be necessary, and the patient is cautioned not to take a laxative until the study has been completed.

For an examination of the colon, preparation is made the night before. The patient is given a laxative that causes little formation of gas and does not tend to draw water into the intestinal tract. Different roentgenologists prefer different laxatives. The patient usually has a light meal the afternoon before, takes the powder at seven or eight o'clock in the evening, and omits breakfast. The examination may be made at any time thereafter. This is a good procedure to follow for cleansing the intestinal tract when x-ray photographs are to be made of the lower spine or kidney or bladder areas. Some variation will be necessary, depending upon the time of the different observations.

For x-ray photographs of the gallbladder, the patient is given specific instructions as to his diet the night before. He is also given some pills which he takes as directed the night before the examination. The dye having been taken, he omits food and water until the next day, following the preliminary x-ray films. He may then be allowed water but no food until the second observation has been completed, usually four to six hours later. Immediately following the second observation, the patient is sometimes given what is known as a fat meal, consisting of cream, one or two eggs, and bread with butter. A third observation may then be made approximately eight hours after the first.

There are other, more unusual x-ray examinations, for which special techniques are required. For these the physician will have his own methods of preparation.

EXAMINATIONS OF EYE, EAR, NOSE, AND THROAT

1. Instruments needed are specula, otoscope, ophthalmoscope, forceps, cotton-tipped applicators, slides, and culture tubes if needed, light, head mirror, basin for waste, syringes, medications, and other special equipment. Have alcohol lamp or hot water available if laryngeal mirror is to be used.
2. Drape patient's shoulder to protect clothing; a towel may be moved from side to side if needed. It is usually not necessary for the patient to remove more than outer clothing such as coat, hat, and so on. Glasses should be removed for some examinations and put in a safe place, preferably in a case in patient's pocket or purse. Dentures may be removed during examination of mouth and throat. It is also important to put these in a place where they will not be broken, as the office may be held responsible.

   Patients with hearing aids should usually remove them just for examination of the ear in order that they may understand questions and directions.
3. Assist physician by adjusting light, holding basins for irrigations, and so on. Warmed solutions (about body temperature or 100° to 105° F.) must be used in irrigating ears.
4. Wash and boil metal forceps, soiled basins, and other equipment. Instruments that may not be boiled may be washed and soaked with alcohol. Scopes may be wiped with alcohol sponge if soiled. Medication bottles and tubes are returned clean to their places; wipe off excess ointment. Care for specimens.

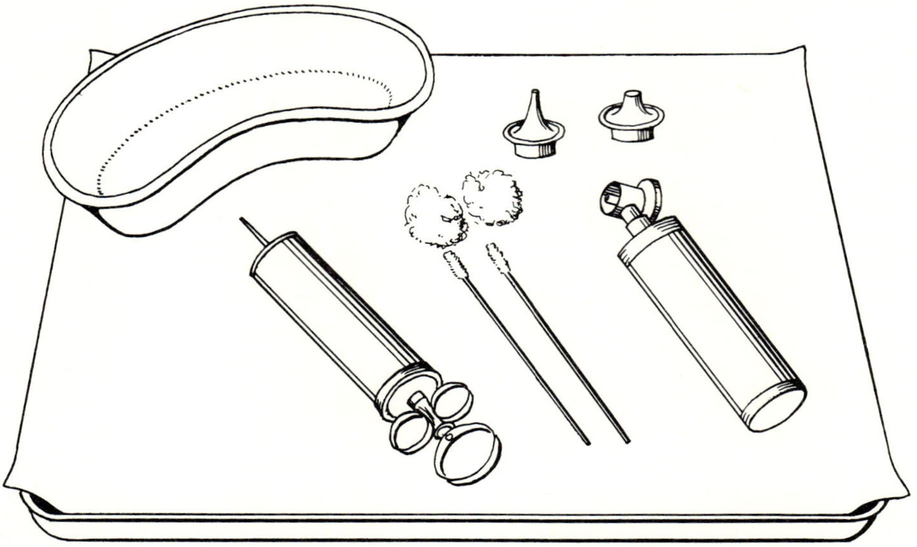

Fig. 24-5. Tray setup for otoscopic examination.

EYE EXAMINATION

The physician's assistant is often expected to perform visual acuity examinations as part of the routine physical examination. Many offices have charts with different sized letters on them called Snellen Charts (Fig. 24-6). The patient is placed exactly 20 feet from the chart and asked to read as many letters as possible with each eye separately, then with both eyes. If the patient wears glasses, he is asked to read the chart with his glasses on and then without his glasses. A person with normal eyesight will be able to read the line marked 20. When a patient can read only the very large letters, these are marked in higher numbers. For example, if a patient reads only the letters in the row marked "50" or "100," his vision is recorded as 20/50 or 20/100. This means that the patient can read at 20 feet what the normal person reads at 50 or 100 feet.

One of the most frequent causes of blindness in adults is glaucoma. This is a disease of the eye in which the pressure within the eyeball is increased. This pressure is measured with the aid of an instrument called a tonometer. All adults, especially those with a family history of glaucoma, should have a tonometry performed regularly.

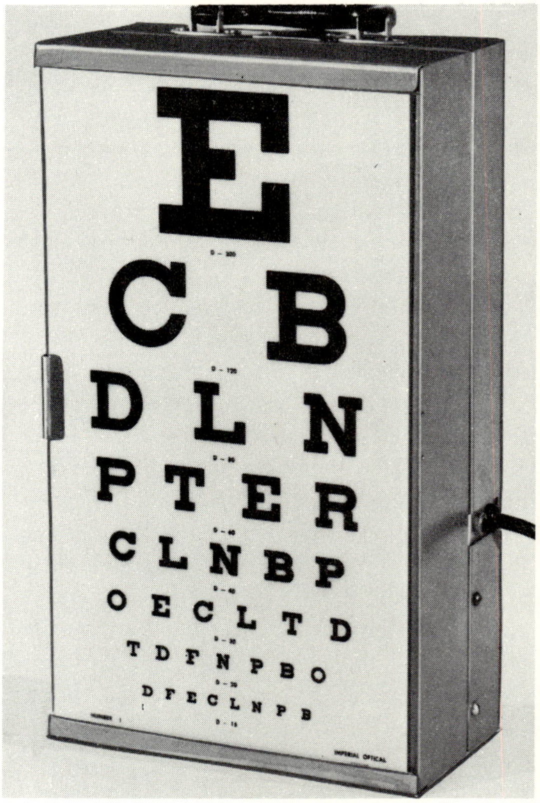

Fig. 24-6. Snellen visual acuity chart. (From Stein, H. A., and Slatt, B. J.: The ophthalmic assistant: fundamentals and clinical practice, ed. 2, St. Louis, 1971, The C. V. Mosby Co.)

CHEST EXAMINATION

Dorsal recumbent or supine position may be used, but it is usually preferred that the patient be sitting up if possible.

1. Stethoscope and manometer and other instruments as needed for special examination or treatments should be available.
2. The patient should usually be stripped to waist. Cover patient with sheet while lying on examining table. Cover chest with towel that may be moved about as patient is examined. Patient may either sit up or turn on side for examination of back or chest, depending on physician's preference and patient's condition. In sitting up, sheet may be held up by patient or assistant to cover chest while back is being examined.
3. Be ready to assist patient to move about and help physician as need arises. Keep

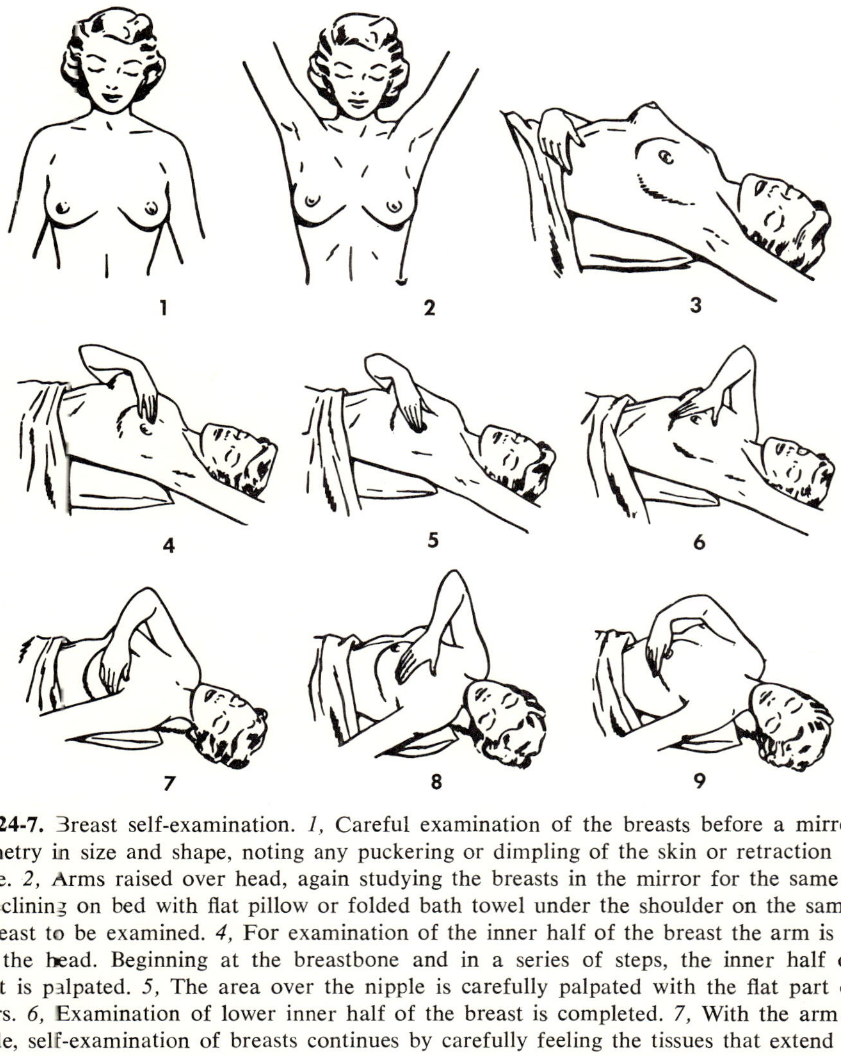

Fig. 24-7. Breast self-examination. *1,* Careful examination of the breasts before a mirror for symmetry in size and shape, noting any puckering or dimpling of the skin or retraction of the nipple. *2,* Arms raised over head, again studying the breasts in the mirror for the same signs. *3,* Reclining on bed with flat pillow or folded bath towel under the shoulder on the same side as breast to be examined. *4,* For examination of the inner half of the breast the arm is raised over the head. Beginning at the breastbone and in a series of steps, the inner half of the breast is palpated. *5,* The area over the nipple is carefully palpated with the flat part of the fingers. *6,* Examination of lower inner half of the breast is completed. *7,* With the arm down at side, self-examination of breasts continues by carefully feeling the tissues that extend to the armpit. *8,* The upper outer quadrant of the breast is examined with the flat part of the fingers. *9,* The lower outer quadrant of the breast is examined in successive stages with the flat part of the fingers. (From The nurse and breast self-examination, New York, American Cancer Society, Inc.)

patient's head turned away from physician to prevent breathing in the physician's face.
4. Help patient to dress if needed. Straighten up examining table and return instruments to usual place. Instruments may be wiped with an alcohol sponge if the patient just examined is suspected of having a communicable disease.

Approximately 25% of the female population will develop cancer during their lifetime and of this number about one fourth will develop breast cancer. The earlier a breast lesion is discovered, the greater the chances for recovery and survival. Therefore, a portion of the routine physical examination for adult females is a breast examination. The patient is prepared as for other chest examinations. At some point during or after the examination, the physician or the assistant may provide the patient with instructions on breast self-examination as outlined by the American Cancer Society in Fig. 24-7. It is suggested that the breasts be examined regularly each month after the menstrual period since there may be swelling, soreness, or lumps prior to ovulation. Postmenopausal women should examine the breasts on the same day each month.

EXAMINATION OF ABDOMEN

Examination of the abdomen is usually performed with the patient in a supine position.

1. Usually no special equipment except stethoscope is required.
2. Patient's clothing is removed to expose abdomen. Patient lies flat on back on table; knees may be slightly elevated to ease tension of abdomen if desired. Cover abdomen with sheet and cover chest with towel during examination. During examination of the abdomen, drape sheet may be folded back to pubis.
3. Be on hand to assist patient in moving about and to redrape as needed.
4. Help patient to dress; straighten examining table.

UPRIGHT POSITION

Upright postion is used for examination of skeletal system, part of neurologic examination, examination for hernia, and other examinations.

1. Have on hand equipment as ordered by physician for examination to be done. If part of neurologic examination, have percussion hammer, applicator with pin on one end, and tubes of hot and cold water; sometimes the physician will have a special gadget for checking pain and light touch to be used in place of applicator and pin. In an orthopedic examination, a tape measure and special equipment as desired by physician should be available.
2. All of patient's clothing is usually removed, including shoes. Place a towel or paper towels for patient to stand on. Patient may be draped with a sheet, which may be fastened on one shoulder and moved aside as examination progresses. Many offices will have an examining gown for the patient to wear, and disposable paper scuffs are on hand for the patient to stand or walk about in.
3. Assist patient to move about as physician directs and manipulate drape or gown to keep patient covered.
4. Return drape sheet and table cover to usual order. Replace equipment, which will require no disinfection.

DIGITAL RECTAL EXAM

The Sims position is usually used unless this is a part of a pelvic examination.

1. Rubber rectal glove (not sterile), lubricant, and specula as ordered by physician are needed.
2. Place patient on right side, preferably with clothing removed from lower part of body. Cover with drape sheet, which may be adjusted to cover body and expose rectal area. Left knee is flexed moderately; right knee is flexed sharply with thigh pulled up on abdomen. Body is tilted slightly forward. In men the rectal examination is often made by having the patient bend over, rest his

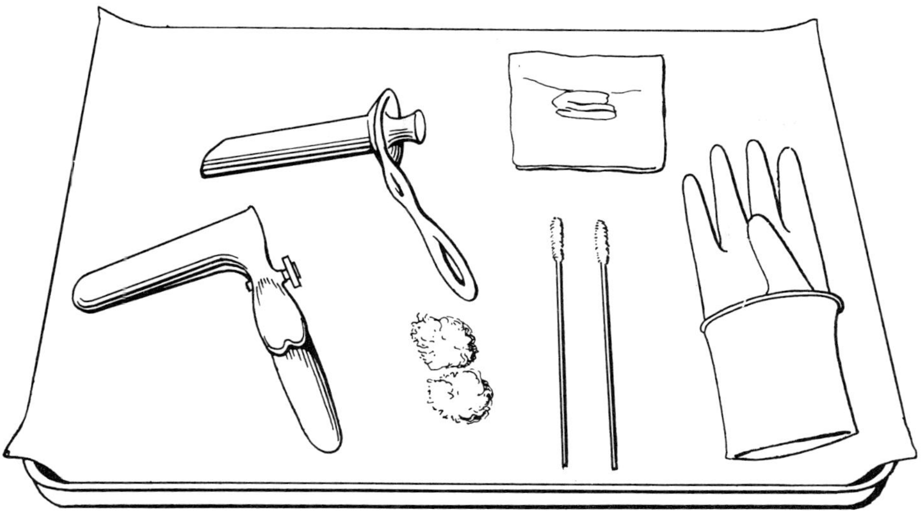

Fig. 24-8. Tray setup for rectal examination.

elbows on a table with his feet slightly apart.

3. Assist with instruments, provide lubricant as needed, and adjust drape.
4. Wash rectal glove and instruments and disinfect in routine manner. Seal lubricant. Hang gloves to dry; turn and powder and put away. Care for specimens if any.

POSITIONS

1. Supine or dorsal recumbent. Patient lies on back.
2. Prone. Patient lies on abdomen.
3. Sitting and upright.
4. Knee-chest. Patient rests on lower legs and chest; back is as relaxed as possible and thighs form a right angle to lower legs. Knees are about four inches apart.
5. Sims position. Patient lies on either side, but most often the right lower leg is extended and slightly flexed, upper leg is flexed sharply toward abdomen, and patient is tipped slightly forward, resting on knee of upper side.
6. Lithotomy or stirrups. Patient is positioned at very end of table with feet in stirrups; legs are relaxed and leaning outward with knees separated.

Avoid leaving the patient alone on a narrow examining table for any length of time; this particularly applies to the very weak patient, the confused patient, and any patient subject to convulsions. Also, many tables will be off balance if the patient sits on the very end. Check on this and caution the patient not to move around carelessly.

EQUIPMENT FOR SPECIAL PROCEDURES

Usual equipment for physical examination

1. Hand towel
2. Tongue depressors
3. Percussion hammer
4. Nasal speculum
5. Ear speculum
6. Ophthalmoscope
7. Otoscope
8. Sphygmomanometer
9. Stethoscope
10. Tape measure
11. Straight pin
12. Kidney basin

Equipment for dressing change of injury or operative wounds

1. Waste basin
2. Bandage scissors
3. Adhesive tape
4. Sterile equipment

a. Hemostat for handling material on the sterile field by the doctor
b. Gauze; 4-inch preferred by physicians; antiseptic for cleansing the skin may be put on tray in a sterile medicine glass if desired
c. Applicators or cotton balls for painting the skin with the antiseptic
d. Tissue forceps and suture scissors if sutures are to be removed; clip remover if wound has clips
e. Sterile gloves or forceps (In infected wounds, gloves should always be provided.)

Equipment for incision and drainage of infected wound or abscess

1. Waste basin; the refuse is wrapped and burned.
2. Bandage scissors.
3. Adhesive tape.
4. Sterile equipment.
   a. Sterile gloves (usually).
   b. Sterile gauze.
   c. Skin antiseptic and applicators or cotton balls.
   d. Scalpel; usually a No. 10 blade for excision; may be No. 15 for face.
   e. Sharp scissors and thumb forceps (often).
   f. After incision of abscesses there is frequently a tendency for the skin to close before the infected wound has had time to heal. In order to provide adequate drainage during healing, drains are often inserted for one or two days after incision. These drains greatly aid in total wound drainage. They can be rubber, gauze, or gauze impregnated with antibiotic solution.

Suture material

If suture material is needed in any procedure, it may be added to any surgical setup. It will include a sterile needle, according to the surgeon's preference, a sterile needle holder, and sterile suture as ordered. If linen or similar material that comes on a spool is used, the autoclaved piece of suture is placed on the sterile field; handle with sterile forceps. If gut suture or any suture material that comes in an ampule is to be used, the ampule is sterilized and placed on the sterile field; the surgeon breaks the ampule in a folded gauze or towel when needed. If the ampule is not used, it may be wiped clean with a sponge and returned to the supply. Silk suture is usually discarded if not used, although it may be autoclaved a second time without weakening it too much.

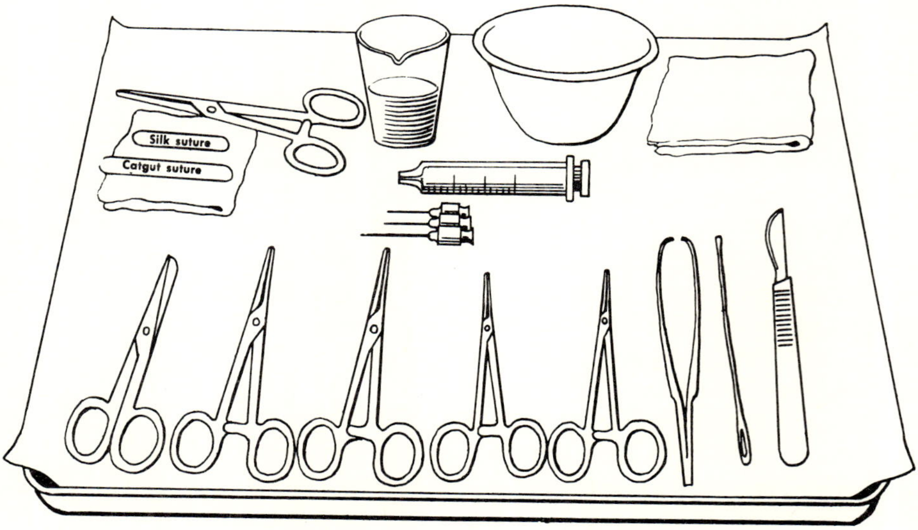

Fig. 24-9. Tray setup for minor surgery.

The size of the suture is measured in terms of 0's. The larger the number of 0's, the finer the suture. One- to three-0 sutures are used to obtain closure of very large wounds. Four- and five-0 sutures are often used to close skin lacerations. Very fine sutures of 6- to 8-0 are used for wounds of the face and during eye and ear surgery.

Local anesthesia

This setup may be prepared whenever the doctor indicates that a local anesthetic may be needed. It may be set up individually or simply added to the sterile tray to be used in the procedure.

1. Applicators or cotton balls and a forceps to be used in painting the skin.
2. Skin antiseptic in sterile medicine glass or to be poured as needed.
3. Syringe (2 cc or 5 cc usually best size).
4. Sterile 25-gauge needle and sterile 23- to 24-gauge needle about 1½ inches or longer if necessary, depending on area to be anesthesized.
5. Local anesthetic. Procaine hydrochloride 1 to 2% and Xylocaine 1 to 2% are most commonly used. They may be purchased in 2-ml and 5-ml ampules. If used a great deal, they may be purchased in a rubber-stoppered vial for multiple use. The glass ampules are best sterilized by soaking them in a chemical antiseptic for 20 to 30 minutes. The glass ampules may be autoclaved with the other equipment to be used if desired. The anesthetic may be poured into a sterile medicine glass if this is more convenient.
6. Most doctors will want sterile gloves when using a local anesthetic.

All of the aforementioned sterile trays will be set up on sterile towels that must be sterilized by autoclave. The towels will be handled by forceps and under sterile technique, as must all the equipment put on the tray. Putting liquids such as the antiseptic and anesthetic in sterile medicine glasses on the tray will make it possible for the physician to work alone if this should be necessary. If these are in the stock bottles, they should be poured by the assistant to avoid contaminating the physician's gloves during a sterile procedure.

Scrub hands thoroughly before starting to set up any sterile tray to reduce the possibility of contamination of supplies by hands.

Catheterization tray

1. With autoclave available.
   a. Sterile field with autoclaved towel.
   b. Sterile catheter, preferably autoclaved; usually about French (Fr.) 14 unless otherwise specified—the larger the French size, the larger the catheter.
   c. Sterile emesis basin and small basin —small basin with three or four cotton balls moistened with tincture of green soap or occasionally, 70% alcohol.
   d. Sterile gloves.
   e. Sterile culture tubes, specimen bottle, and so on.
   f. Paper or extra basin for discarded cotton balls.
   g. Lubricant such as K-Y jelly on sterile gauze or in sterile basin.
2. Without autoclave.
   a. Sterile field provided by boiled emesis basin.
   b. Boiled catheter, preferably boiled just before use.
   c. Boiled hemostat or other forceps (used to handle catheter).
   d. K-Y jelly—about 1 teaspoon dropped into the sterile emesis basin.
   e. Sterile gloves
   f. Culture tubes, specimen bottle, and so on.
   g. Small clean basin with clean cotton balls moistened with soap or alcohol.

Tray for gastric aspiration

The tray is usually clean, and disinfection is required after use only when there is a special indication, such as aspiration for tubercle bacillus.

1. Clean tray with clean towel.

2. Bib or apron for patient to protect clothing.
3. Basin of ice chips.
4. Levin tube as requested; usually four- or five-hole Levin; about Fr. 14. Tube should be placed in ice chips for about 15 or 20 minutes to chill and stiffen.
5. Lubricant for tube such as petroleum jelly, mineral oil on gauze square, or K-Y jelly.
6. Triumph syringe.
7. Paper cup of ice chips or a sip of water for patient if permitted.
8. Specimen bottles as needed, preferably labeled as to sequence of time.
9. Emesis basin.

CARE OF SPECIMENS

1. Try to obtain the proper bottles and solutions for specimens—the pathologist who will examine the specimens will be pleased to provide these if requested. In an emergency, any closed bottle with formaldehyde may usually be used. In an emergency some pathologists may prefer that the solution used simply be saline.
2. Deliver to pathologist or call for the laboratory to pick up as soon as possible. If there will be some delay, most specimens are best kept in a container in the refrigerator until sent.
3. The container with the specimen should be labeled with at least the name of the patient before taking from the room in which it was obtained.
4. Fill in requisition properly; it may be obtained from the laboratory if requested. The requisition usually includes the name of the patient, doctor, date, where the specimen is from, and what procedures are desired. Often you will also indicate whether the patient or doctor is to be billed. If the patient is being billed, be sure the patient's address is included.

DEPARTURE OF THE PATIENT

The patient leaving a doctor's office should be shown the same unvarying courtesy as is shown at his arrival. As is said elsewhere, a physician has no more effective advertisement than a satisfied patient.

Review questions

1. How would you prepare a patient for pelvic examination? What would you include in the tray setup for such an examination?
2. Describe the setup for a minor surgery tray.
3. Describe the preparation for a spinal puncture test in your office.
4. How would you assist in a proctoscopic examination?
5. Describe the setup for a local anesthetic tray.

Suggested readings

Bates, B.: A guide to physical examination, Philadelphia, 1974, J. B. Lippincott Co.

Young, C. G., and Barger, J. D.: Introduction to medical science, ed. 2, St. Louis, 1973, The C. V. Mosby Co.

chapter 25
Medical and surgical office procedures

When a patient arrives for a doctor's appointment the initial portion of the physical examination is often made by the physician's assistant. The assistant records the blood pressure, pulse, temperature, respiration, and often the weight and height in the patient's record. These measurements are an essential part of any routine physical examination and are often referred to collectively as the "vital signs." In this chapter we will describe the proper method for obtaining this information and briefly discuss the importance of the "vital signs" in medicine.

THE PHYSIOLOGY OF BLOOD PRESSURE

The circulatory system is composed of the heart, the arteries, the capillaries, and the veins. Blood is pumped through this system by the heart. When blood leaves the left side of the heart it does so under considerable pressure that is transmitted to the large arteries of the body. As blood enters the organs and tissues of the body, the pressure within the very numerous but small blood vessels diminishes rapidly so that by the time the blood reaches the veins it is under much less pressure than when it left the heart.

The arterial blood pressure is the pressure of the blood against the walls of the large arteries of the body. If a tube were connected directly into an artery one could measure the pressure within the vessel. Although this is done in rare instances in hospital intensive care units, it is a highly im-

---

Glossary

aneroid manometer a device used to measure blood pressure by means of compressed air and a pressure gauge
antecubital pertaining to the area at the junction of the forearm and arm.
apical pulse the pulse as determined by listening over the heart
auscultation act of listening with the aid of a stethoscope
axilla pertaining to the armpit
bradycardia an abnormally slow heart rate
carotid the principal artery of the neck
centigrade metric system of measuring heat
convalescence the period of recovery after the termination of a disease or operation
diastole the point of greatest cardiac relaxation
dyspnea difficult breathing
Fahrenheit a heat scale used in the United States and England.
femoral pertaining to the thighbone or femur
hypertension abnormal elevation of blood pressure
hypotension a condition in which the blood pressure is abnormally low
manometer a device for determining liquid or gaseous pressure
orthopnea difficulty in breathing when lying flat
pulse deficit the difference between the apical and radial pulse
sphygmomanometer instrument for determining blood pressure
systole the time during which the heart is contracting
tachycardia a heart rate greater than 100 beats per minute
vasomotor pertaining to the nervous control of the pressure within the blood vessels.
visceral refers to the internal and primarily the abdominal organs

practical way of measuring blood pressure. Feeling the character of an arterial pulsation may indicate a very vigorous or a very weak and feeble pulse but is generally totally unreliable in determining blood pressure. The simplest and most reliable method of measuring blood pressure involves using a stethoscope (Fig. 25-2) and a device called a sphygmomanometer (Fig. 25-1). Blood pressure measurements taken in this fashion are simple, reliable, and reproducible if taken correctly.

There are four factors that determine blood pressure. The first is the force of the pumping action of the heart. During exercise or stress the heart contracts more forcefully than at rest. After a massive heart attack the heart may produce only a feeble pumping action. In the former case the blood pressure would be higher while in the latter it would be lower than at rest. The second factor that determines blood pressure is the volume of blood within the arteries. If arterial blood volume is increased, the blood pressure may be elevated. If blood volume is decreased, as occurs during hemorrhage, the blood pressure decreases. The third factor that determines arterial blood pressure is the resistance offered by the small blood vessels that regulate the escape of blood out of the large arteries. There are many factors that control the resistance of these small blood vessels, some of which are are related to the same hormonal and neurologic factors that control the force of contraction of the heart. The fourth factor that influences the pressure within the arteries is the elasticity of the walls of the arteries. When blood is pumped out of the heart, it momentarily increases the pressure within the arteries. This pressure quickly falls as blood leaves the arteries. Unlike the rigid walls of pipes of a water pumping system, the arteries are elastic. This permits them to expand and contract slightly during each contraction of the heart. It also permits smooth, continuous flow of blood through the system rather than intermittent flow. If blood vessels become more rigid, as sometimes happens in old age, the pumping of blood out of the heart momentarily creates higher pressure than if the blood were pumped into a younger, more elastic arterial system.

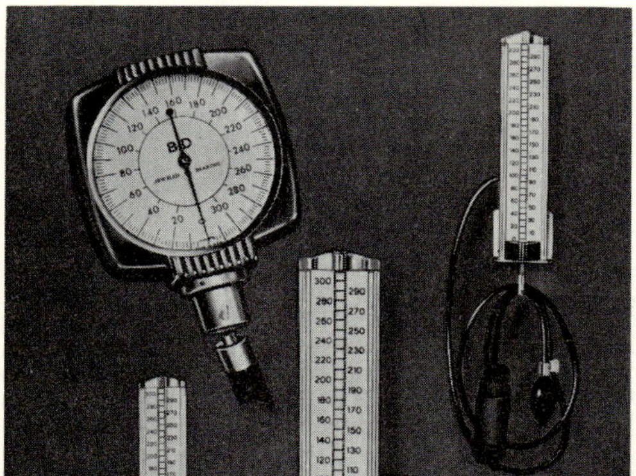

Fig. 25-1. Various types of sphygmomanometers used in medical offices. (Courtesy Becton, Dickinson & Co., Rutherford, New Jersey.)

From the preceding discussion several terms used in the measuring of blood pressure will be understood. The time during which the heart is pumping will correspond to the moment when the pressure within the arteries is greatest. This is called *systolic pressure* because it corresponds to the maximum pressure generated within the heart during its contraction (systole). Blood is rapidly drained from the arteries while the heart is refilling and resting between contractions. Pressure within the arteries therefore falls reaching its lowest point just before the heart contracts again. The lowest pressure in the arteries is called the *diastolic pressure* because it occurs when the heart is refilling (diastole). The difference between the systolic and the diastolic blood pressure is called the *pulse pressure.*

People are frequently confused when they are told or overhear two numbers instead of one for blood pressure. If it is permitted by the physician, the patient should be informed that it is important to remember that there are both systolic and diastolic blood pressures. In normal adults the systolic pressure is approximately 120 and the diastolic pressure is approximately 80 millimeters of mercury. These numbers are written with the systolic pressure as the numerator and the diastolic pressure as the denominator or stated as "120 over 80."

THE TECHNIQUE OF TAKING BLOOD PRESSURE

The equipment needed for a blood pressure reading includes a stethoscope and a sphygmomanometer, which may be of two types. One utilizes a column of mercury and the other uses compressed air to measure blood pressure. The mercury manometers are more reliable but more cumbersome and susceptible to loss of mercury from the column. The compressed air or *aneroid manometer* is more compact and less rugged, but must be tested at least once a year for accuracy.

The patient should be resting and preferably relaxed in a chair or reclining on a couch or examining table, with the arm and forearm both exposed. The forearm is slightly flexed. The blood pressure cuff is deflated completely and wrapped around the arm so that the rubber bag is over the inner aspect of the arm. It is adjusted so that its lower edge is about 1 inch over the crease between the arm and the forearm (antecubital space). The cuff is attached to the manometer if not already connected.

The antecubital space is felt for a pulse and a stethoscope is placed snugly directly over the pulse. Care is taken not to touch the stethoscope to the cuff. The air valve on the rubber bulb attached to the cuff is closed and the bulb is compressed until the

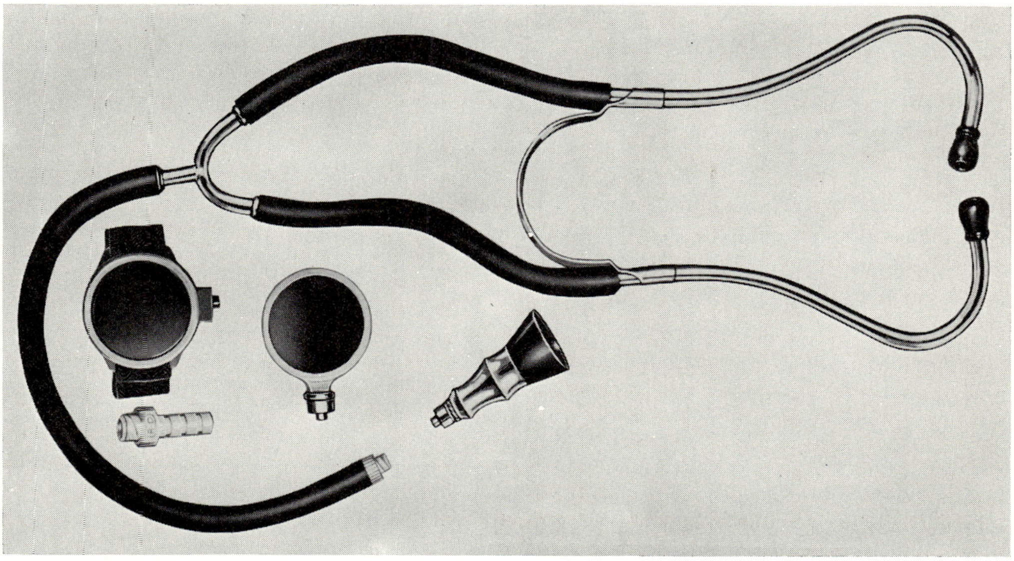

Fig. 25-2. Typical stethoscope used in medical offices. (Courtesy Becton, Dickinson & Co., Rutherford, New Jersey.)

pressure reaches approximately 220 to 240 mm Hg. The air valve is opened so that the pressure falls about 2 mm with each pulse. When sounds are first heard they are remembered and a note is made when the sounds suddenly acquire a different or muffled quality and again when they disappear completely. The reading at which sounds first appear is called the systolic pressure. Physicians' opinions differ as to whether the time of the muffling or the time of disappearance of the arterial sounds should be used as the diastolic pressure. In most cases the readings are similar. The preference of the physician should be sought and followed by the assistant. In some cases both numbers may be noted in the medical record, especially when they are highly different.

Some physicians prefer to raise the pressure to 220 to 240 mm Hg and rapidly estimate the general range of systolic blood pressure. They then completely deflate the cuff, wait several seconds, and carefully measure the exact blood pressure over the anticipated range obtained during the preliminary recording. Most physicians suggest that blood pressure measurements on new patients be taken in both arms. If a discrepancy exists, the arm with the higher pressure is used in all future recordings and the discrepancy is noted in the record.

COMMON ERRORS IN TAKING BLOOD PRESSURE

1. *Recording the first blood pressure.* The slight discomfort felt on initial compression, especially in an anxious or apprehensive patient, can cause the first blood pressure reading to be erroneously high. After the cuff has been applied, the medical assistant should talk quietly to the patient for a few minutes in an effort to make him relax before the blood pressure is recorded. Several measurements should be made at each examination; generally the third value recorded is the most reliable.
2. *Failing to raise the pressure well above systolic pressure at the outset.* It is important not to "creep up" on the cuff pressure in order to determine the systolic pressure.
3. *Failing to completely deflate the cuff between readings.* This produces erroneously high readings.
4. *Failing to use the correct cuff size.* The compression cuff must be the correct width for the diameter of the patient's arm. If it is too narrow the blood pressure readings will be erroneously high; if too wide, the reading will be too low. The inflatable rubber bladder should be long enough to encircle at least half the arm. The center of the rubber bladder should rest over the artery being compressed. For the average adult, an inflatable bladder 13 cm (5.1 inches) wide and 23 cm (9.1 inches) long is generally satisfactory. Corrections in the width of the compression cuff must be made for extremely obese or unusually thin arms. The general rule is that the width of the inflatable bladder be 20% greater than the diameter of the limb on which it is used (see Table 3).
5. *Failing to place the cuff snugly, correctly.*
6. *Failing to use recalibrated aneroid manometers or failing to keep mercury manometers erect during readings.*
7. *Failing to take the blood pressure in both arms on initial examination or in the arm with the highest pressure on follow-up examinations.*
8. *Telling a patient that his blood pressure is too high or too low or otherwise ex-*

Table 3. Recommended widths of compression cuffs

Age	Width of inflatable bladder
Newborn infants	2.5 cm (1 inch)
Children (1 to 4 yrs)	6 cm (2.3 inches)
Children (4 to 8 yrs)	9 cm (3.5 inches)
Adults	13 cm (5.1 inches)
Obese adults	20 cm (8 inches)

pressing surprise or concern about the findings.

HIGH BLOOD PRESSURE (HYPERTENSION)

Over 25 million Americans are thought to have hypertension. Only about one half of these are aware of this and probably less than one half of these are being adequately treated for their hypertension. Hypertension has many possible causes only some of which are known. Although it is usually a chronic disease that may require long-term care, hypertension at times can be extremely severe and require immediate hospitalization and treatment. Hypertension is more common among blacks and is frequently seen as a complication of renal disease. The most gratifying factor in the treatment of hypertension is that good medical care can greatly reduce the incidence of death from this potentially deadly disease.

In Table 4 the normal range of systolic and diastolic blood pressure for Americans is given. These tables have been compiled from life insurance data from large numbers of people of varying ages. As can be noted from the table, blood pressure usually increases with age. Although physicians vary in their criteria for hypertension, the World Health Organization defines hypertension as a systolic pressure of greater than 160 or a diastolic pressure greater than 95 mm Hg.

LOW BLOOD PRESSURE (HYPOTENSION)

To the laity, having "low blood pressure" is a well-acknowledged cause of weakness, fatigue, lassitude, and a host of other vague symptoms. This may indeed be the case in a new patient but, in general, most individuals with resting blood pressure of 90 to 100 systolic and 50 to 60 diastolic are otherwise healthy and content and cause no concern to the physician. Patients should therefore never be told by the assistant that their blood pressure is "too low."

The most important causes of hypotension are blood loss (hemorrhage), dehydration, adrenal insufficiency, drug treatment, and disorders of the nervous system. In many cases the assistant may be asked by the physician to take a patient's blood pressure in both the recumbent and sitting or standing position. The assistant should be ready to assist or even catch the patient in case severe dizziness or loss of consciousness occurs from this maneuver. At times physicians may ask that all patients on certain antihypertensive drugs have their blood pressure taken in both the sitting and standing positions.

TEMPERATURE

Temperature is the balance maintained between the heat produced and the heat lost by the body. The heat of the body

Table 4. Blood pressure averages

	Normal systolic range			Normal diastolic range (fourth phase)		
Age	Minimum	Average	Maximum	Minimum	Average	Maximum
15-19	100	118	136	60	75	90
20-24	102	120	137	62	77	91
25-29	104	122	138	64	79	92
30-34	106	124	139	66	81	93
35-39	108	126	140	68	83	94
40-44	110	128	142	70	84	95
45-49	112	130	144	72	86	96
50-54	115	133	146	74	88	97
55-59	118	136	148	77	90	98
60-64	121	139	150	80	92	100

is produced by the burning of food; most of it is generated in the muscles and internal organs, and it is distributed to other parts of the body by the blood and blood vessels. The heat of the body is eliminated through the skin by perspiration and its evaporation and by radiation; through the lungs by the breath; and through the saliva, urine, and feces. The balance between the heat produced and heat lost in the normal person is the normal temperature of the body. Any interference with this balance increases or decreases the temperature, according to the nature of the trouble or disease. There is usually only a slight variation of not more than one degree in the temperature of a normally healthy person.

The temperature is ascertained by means of the clinical thermometer. This is a small glass tube containing a column of mercury ending in a bulb. Thermometers are made with thin or fat bulbs; the fat bulb should always be used for taking a rectal temperature (Fig. 25-3). Mouth and rectal thermometers should never be used interchangeably. The mercury expands with heat and will remain at the point reached until shaken down. The clinical thermometer is divided into degrees and tenths of degrees, from 94° to 107° F.

Normal temperature. The temperature 98.6° F. is read as follows: ninety-eight and six tenths degrees Fahrenheit. Since the metric system is being used more frequently, it is important to know that the normal temperature in the centigrade scale is 37°. A table for the conversion of temperatures between Fahrenheit and centigrade scales is given on p. 308. To convert from centigrade to Fahrenheit, the formula is: $F = (C \times 9/5) + 32$. For example, if the temperature is 40.0° C, the Fahrenheit temperature is equal to the sum of the product of $40.0 \times 9/5$ (which is 72) plus 32 (which equals 104). To convert from Fahrenheit to centigrade, the formula is: $C = (F - 32) \times 5/9$. If the Fahrenheit temperature is 104°, $F - 32$ is 72; $72 \times 5/9$ equals 40.

Care of clinical thermometers. Clinical thermometers break easily and require particular care to insure their safety in taking temperatures. Individual thermometers should be washed with soap and water, rinsed with clear water (running water is preferable), dried, and put in a safe container. Before the thermometer can be used for another person it must be disinfected by soaking in a disinfectant solution for at least 10 minutes; 70% alcohol may be used. The thermometer should be laid in a flat dish and covered with the solution. When it is removed from the solution it should be washed with clear water. Always disin-

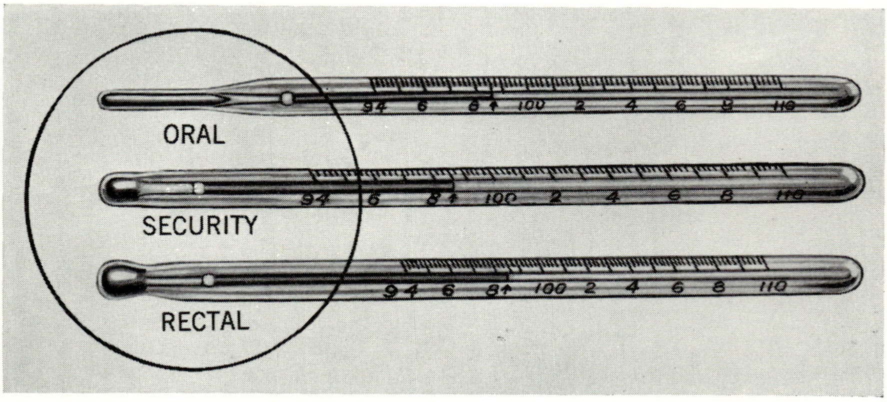

Fig. 25-3. Various types of clinical thermometers. (Courtesy Becton, Dickinson & Co., Rutherford, New Jersey.)

fect a thermometer before placing it in a tube container if the container cannot be sterilized by boiling or by a disinfectant. The thermometer may be kept in a covered box or jar with a piece of cotton in the bottom to protect the bulb.

Individual equipment tray. A small tray containing the following items is necessary for taking temperature.

1. One thermometer, rectal or oral (whichever is being used)
2. One jar of soap and water
3. One jar of clean water
4. A jar or glass of wipes (paper, cotton, or gauze)
5. A jar or tube of lubricant, if a rectal temperature is being taken (Petroleum jelly, oil, cold cream, or the lubricant that comes in tubes may be used.)

Normal daily variation of temperature. The daily avarage temperature varies in health from 97.6 to 99° F.; it is lowest in the early morning (two to six o'clock) and highest in the evening (five to eight o'clock). In women the temperature varies during certain days of the menstrual cycle.

Daily variation of temperature in illness. In illness, the temperature is also lowest in the early morning hours, about dawn or a little before, and is highest in the early evening. In convalescence, the temperature may be subnormal in the morning, reaching normal about noon or a little before. During infection, the temperature rises. At times, a rise in temperature may follow a chill.

Methods of taking temperature

The temperature is most frequently taken in one of three ways.

1. By mouth. The thermometer is placed under the tongue, lips closed.
2. By axilla. The thermometer is placed in the armpit.
3. By rectum. The thermometer is inserted about an inch into the rectum.

When taken by mouth, the record is about a degree lower than when taken by rectum and nearly a degree higher than when taken by axilla. The thermometer must be left in for a different length of time for each method. Normal temperature when taken by mouth is 98.6° F.; the thermometer should be left in two or three minutes. Normal temperature taken rectally is 99.6° F.; the thermometer should be left in five minutes. Normal axillary temperature is 97.6° F.; the thermometer should be left in ten minutes.

How to take temperature by mouth. This is the general method of taking the temperature of the adult under normal conditions.

Look at the thermometer to ascertain just where the mercury is, hold it firmly with the thumb and first two fingers (the hand slightly bending inward), and with a quick movement of the wrist downward and outward, shake it until the mercury registers 96° F. or below. Be careful when shaking a thermometer that your hand does not hit something or that you do not hit the thermometer itself against a table or chair.

Ask the patient to open the mouth and place the thermometer under the tongue at the center, the end coming out at the corner of the lips. Ask the patient to close the lips lightly and not to talk or open them, as the air coming in the mouth would cool the thermometer and an accurate temperature could not be obtained.

Leave the thermometer in at least two minutes, even if it is marked a "one minute" thermometer. It will take a minute for the mouth to become even in temperature and the other minute for the thermometer to register. Remove the thermometer at the end of the period, look at it carefully, and be sure that you read it accurately. Hold it horizontally between your thumb and first finger and rotate it slowly until you can see the bar of mercury.

Moisten the cleansing tissue in soap and water, wipe the thermometer, and discard the tissue. Moisten a clean piece of tissue in clean water, wipe the thermometer, discard the tissue, and place the thermometer in container or in disinfectant solution if it must be used for another person. Record the temperature.

Cautions to observe when taking the temperature by mouth. See that the patient has had nothing hot or cold in the mouth for at least ten minutes before the thermometer is put under the tongue; otherwise you cannot get an accurate temperature. See that the patient holds the thermometer for the prescribed time with the lips closed and that it is not held with the teeth. Do not take the temperature by mouth under the following circumstances.

1. If the patient cannot keep the lips closed because of difficulty in breathing, coughing, or weakness
2. If the mouth is very dry
3. If the patient is mentally unbalanced, delirious, unconscious, or has a mouth or nose injury
4. If an infant or a child is not old enough to know how to hold a thermometer properly in the mouth

In all these cases the temperature should be taken by rectum or axilla, as there is danger of the thermometer being broken and the patient swallowing small pieces of glass or some of the mercury.

Should a thermometer break while in the mouth, rinse the mouth out well with plenty of water to wash out all particles of glass and report at once.

When the mouth temperature is unexpectedly high or low. If the temperature is found to be remarkably high or low and there is no apparent reason for this, take it again, being sure the thermometer is well shaken down, and watch the patient carefully all the time it is in the mouth, or take it again by rectum, or use another thermometer.

How to take a temperature by axilla. The temperature is sometimes taken by axilla when the mouth or rectal method cannot be used.

Wipe the axilla (armpit) with a soft, dry washcloth or a ball of absorbent cotton to remove moisture. Do not rub. Put the bulb in the center with the end slanting toward the body and have the patient grasp the opposite shoulder with the hand. This will keep the arm close to the side and enclose the thermometer. Prevent contact with clothing. Leave it in place for ten minutes and read. Cleanse the thermometer and record the temperature.

Centrigrade and Fahrenheit temperature equivalents

Centigrade° (C.)	*Fahrenheit° (F.)*
35.0	95.0
35.5	95.9
36.0	96.8
36.5	97.7
37.0	98.6
37.5	99.5
38.0	100.4
38.5	101.3
39.0	102.2
39.5	103.1
40.0	104.0
40.5	104.9
41.0	105.8
41.5	106.7
42.0	107.6
42.5	108.5

Cautions to observe when taking an axillary temperature. A temperature taken under the arm is nearly a degree lower than that taken by mouth and the thermometer must be left in place ten minutes. The armpit must be dry and the thermometer so placed that it will not touch the clothing or be exposed to the air. When the patient is unable to put his hand on the opposite shoulder himself, place it there gently and hold it with your own hand or hold the patient's arm close to his side. When taking a child's temperature by axilla, hold the thermometer in place for the entire time. Sit down and do it comfortably.

Do not take an axillary temperature under the following circumstances.

1. When the patient is so thin that there is a hollow under the arm that it would be impossible to make airtight

2. When the patient is perspiring so freely that the axilla cannot be kept dry for the allotted ten minutes

How to take a rectal temperature. Rectal temperature is the most accurate and the most reliable of all the methods of taking temperatures. The mucous membrane lining of the rectum with which the thermometer comes in contact is not exposed to the air, and the conditions do not vary as do those of the mouth or axilla. The rectal temperature is usually employed when the patient is very ill, in fevers (where an accurate temperature is of the utmost importance), for infants and children, and when the patient is delirious, mentally unbalanced, or very restless.

The rectal thermometer differs from the mouth thermometer in that the bulb is usually slightly larger and often is colored.

Dip a tiny square of cleansing tissue in the lubricant or, if the lubricant comes in a tube, squeeze a small portion on the paper. Oil the bulb of the thermometer, previously having seen that it is well shaken down. Never dip the thermometer directly into the jar of petroleum jelly or oil. Gently insert the thermometer into the rectum about one inch. If the patient is perfectly able, he may insert the thermometer himself, but never allow a very sick person or a child to do this. Leave the thermometer in for three minutes, remove it, read it carefully, wipe it with a paper square, and cleanse in usual way. Record the temperature.

Cautions to observe in taking a rectal temperature. Be careful not to insert the thermometer too far. When taking the temperature of an infant or young child, hold the child on you lap face downward, lubricate the thermometer, and insert it gently, slanting it towards the navel. Hold the thermometer in place for three minutes.

PULSE

The pulse is the impulse of the heart's contraction transmitted to an artery. The pulse is most often felt in the arteries of the neck (carctid), wrist (radial), feet (dorsalis pedis), groin (femoral), or over the heart (apical).

Normal pulse rate (average number of pulsations in one minute)

Adults	60- 80
Children over seven	80- 90
Children from one to seven	80-120
Infants	110-130
At birth	130-160

The *character* of the pulse varies with the strength of contraction of the heart, the size and elasticity of the artery, and the tissues surrounding the artery. The physician will sometimes spend several minutes in examining a patient's pulses in order to obtain information that may reveal abnormalities of the circulation or the heart.

The *rate* of the pulse varies considerably among individuals. It is generally higher in children than in adults. The table above gives approximate normal pulse rates in adults and children at various ages. These values are only approximations, however; in athletes, for example, it is not unusual to obtain resting rates as low as 45 to 50 per minute.

Causes that increase or decrease pulse rates. The pulse rate is increased by fear, physical activity, fever, certain types of heart disease, hyperthyroidism, shock, and certain drugs. It is decreased during sleep or rest, certain types of heart disease, hypothyroidism, after certain brain injuries, and by certain drugs such as digitalis.

Varieties of pulse. The pulse may vary in intensity from the weak and feeble pulse seen in shock to the strong and bounding pulse seen after exercise.

A pulse may be irregular in either its timing or intensity. An irregularity of the pulse such as the skipping of an occasional beat occurs in all normal individuals especially during excitement, exercise, or after taking certain stimulants such as coffee or tea. Most of these irregularities go unnoticed but at times may concern a patient sufficiently so that he seeks medical advice. In certain individuals an irregularity of the pulse rate may be an important sign of heart disease. If the pulse has a highly irregular cadence or if there are frequent skips of beats, this should be noted in the medical record or, without alarming the patient, brought to the attention of the physician. In such cases, it is sometimes useful to count the pulse rate for one minute and then to record the apical rate by determining the heart rate by listening over the heart with a stethoscope. If the latter is greater, the difference is referred to as the *pulse deficit*. This pulse deficit is important in the examination of the patient with atrial fibrillation, one of the most common causes of a very irregular pulse.

A pulse may vary in intensity in association with irregularities in rhythm or cadence. A pulse that varies only in intensity but is otherwise perfectly regular is often a manifestation of heart disease. If the pulse rate is below 60 per minute and regular, it is called a *bradycardia;* if it is greater than 100 it is called a *tachycardia*. When the cause of a bradycardia or tachycardia is not readily apparent, an electrocardiogram is often performed to clarify the matter.

Arteries used for taking the pulse and their location. The radial artery, which comes down the forearm through the wrist a little below the base of the thumb, is accessible in most cases and can be pressed against the bones of the wrist and arm. The temporal artery on the side of the forehead is used for taking the pulse when the arms or hands are injured. Sometimes it is less noticeable to the patient if the pulse is taken at the temples, and the disturbance of getting at the hand is avoided. The carotid artery in the neck or the femoral artery in the groin may also be used.

Explanation. The pulse is usually taken by pressing an artery against a bone with the fingers and counting the heartbeats for a minute. The count should be accurate and repeated until you are sure it is correct, and at the same time the quality of the pulse and its regularity or irregularity should be noted. A watch with a second hand and pad and pencil are needed.

Procedure for taking the pulse at the wrist. Let the patient be in a comfortable position, with the arm and hand supported. Do not take the pulse immediately after the patient has been emotionally upset or after exertion. With the tips of the first two or three fingers of your hand, make a firm but gentle pressure on the artery inside the wrist just below the thumb. Never use your own thumb in taking a pulse, for there is an artery in it and the pulsations might be taken for those of the patient. When you can feel the pulse plainly (moving your fingers until you do so), begin to count the beats. Be careful not to press too hard or you may cut off the pulse entirely if it is week. Hold your watch in the other hand and count the number of beats for a full minute. Check by counting again if you are uncertain. Record the pulse on pad or bedside note as soon as taken. Do not trust your memory. Note on chart any unusual condition.

RESPIRATION

Respiration is the process whereby the body takes in oxygen and eliminates carbon dioxide. A respiration is one breath taken in (inspiration) and one breathed out (expiration). Oxygen, a gas composing 21% of air, is necessary to life and is taken up by the lungs and from there it is transferred to the blood and eventually to the tissues. The lungs also eliminate carbon dioxide, a metabolic waste product that is produced in the body tissues.

Causes of variations of normal respirations. All work in which the muscles are exercised causes a demand for more oxygen and increases the carbon dioxide that must be eliminated. This is accomplished by more frequent respirations, as may be easily seen by the way one breathes quickly after running or exercising vigorously in any way. Excitement, nervousness, and any strong

Rate of normal respirations

14-20 respirations in one minute in adults
20-26 respirations in one minute in children
30-38 respirations in one minute in infants

emotion have a direct effect upon the respirations and may increase them suddenly, as when one gasps with fright. The respirations are slower when asleep than when awake. Certain drugs have a marked effect upon the respirations, increasing or decreasing them according to the drug used. For example, opium or morphine (which comes from opium) slows the respirations, and in overdoses the respirations may fall as low as one or two to the minute. In certain diseases of the kidneys, in which there is coma, and in diseases and injuries that cause pressure on the brain, such as after a stroke or skull fracture, the respirations are lowered in rate. Diseases of the lungs and the circulatory system and those in which there is an elevation of temperature tend to increase the rapidity of the respirations. Pain, hemorrhage, shock, gas poisoning, high body temperature, high altitudes, and obstruction of the air passages are other causes of increase in respirations.

Varieties of respirations

Dyspnea simply means difficult breathing. When the respirations are labored from any cause and the patient cannot breathe easily or without great effort, he is suffering from dyspnea. The patient may sometimes become cyanotic from a lack of oxygen. There is dyspnea in asthma, chronic bronchitis, congestive heart failure, and pneumonia.

Orthopnea is breathing that is so difficult that the patient cannot lie down but has to sit up almost straight. In this condition, the patient often finds it more comfortable to lean forward a little, resting arms or shoulders on some support.

Stertorous breathing is the snoring sound made when inhaling the breath in certain conditions such as apoplexy or coma. This term comes from the Latin word meaning snore. Stertorous breathing is usually accompanied by a puffing out of the cheeks or lips with each expiration and is caused by a relaxation of the soft palate. It is not in itself a serious symptom.

Cheyne-Stokes respiration is a particular kind of breathing named after the two doctors who first described this condition. It must be seen and explained to be thoroughly understood, but is such an important sign that it will be described in the two forms in which it appears.

1. First form. The respirations begin by being rather short or shallow and gradually increase in strength and number up to a certain point when there is a slight pause, and then they decrease in the same manner as they increased until they cease with another slight pause, when the whole process is repeated.
2. Second form. After the respirations have gradually increased up to the pausing point, they suddenly stop and then begin over again.

Cheyne-Stokes respirations are usually found in serious conditions of diseases of the heart and kidney, various forms of meningitis, coma, and injuries of the brain; they are very grave signs.

Cheyne-Stokes respirations should not be confused with irregular breathing, and a close observance will avoid this mistake, for there is a regularity in the increase and decrease in the pauses and stopping in the Cheyne-Stokes type that is absent in irregular respirations.

Qualities that describe respirations. Besides the regular terms for peculiar types of breathing, there are many qualities that should be noted in order to describe respirations correctly.

1. Shallow or deep respirations depend upon the amount of air inhaled and exhaled, whether more or less than normal. Shallow respirations are those in which little air is inspired and are usually rapid, as

in pneumonia and other diseases of the lungs. Deep breathing is often seen in diabetics during severe diabetic acidosis.

2. The number of respirations per minute is of great importance. Rates of 12 and below are subnormal and should be considered serious symptoms. Rates between 14 and 20 are normal. Rates between 34 and 36 are above normal. Rates between 36 and 50 are rapid. Rates of 60 and above are extremely rapid and very dangerous. Rates above 40 should also be considered serious symptoms.
3. In regular breathing the inhalations and exhalations are the same in depth and rapidity, while in irregular breathing the inhalations and exhalations may be different in the amount of air taken in and breathed out and in the number of respirations per minute. Very rapid and shallow breathing may be perfectly regular, while a normal number of respirations per minute may vary greatly in depth and in rate.

How to count and take the respirations. The respirations are easily controlled by the patient under certain circumstances and just consciousness that they are being taken will influence the rate; thus they should always be counted without the patient's knowledge. When taking them, their character should be noted and described (if not normal) when charted. The position the patient assumes in some cases is significant, such as easier breathing when lying on one or the other side or when in a sitting position. Note the expansion of the chest and abdomen and the patient's color. A watch with a second hand and pad and pencil are needed. When taking the pulse, either before or after counting it, with your hand on the wrist, watch the respirations and count them by looking at the chest as it rises and falls so that the patient may think you are still taking the pulse. Count for a minute. When the breathing is irregular count one minute three times to be sure of correctness.

Never place your hand on the patient's chest and tell him that you are going to take his respirations, for the very consciousness that you are doing so will probably make him breathe unnaturally and you will not get an accurate count of his usual rate of breathing. Never take the respirations immediately after the patient has exercised or become excited. The respirations are usually taken with the pulse and temperature, but in conditions where there is a marked increase or decrease, the respirations should be carefully watched and taken very frequently. A good time to do this is while the patient is asleep, for then the breathing is not influenced by consciousness.

Review questions

1. What four factors determine blood pressure?
2. How would you take a blood pressure reading?
3. What is meant by systolic pressure, diastolic pressure, and pulse pressure?
4. What is considered normal temperature in an adult? In a child?
5. What could you include in an equipment tray for a temperature setup?
6. What is the difference in appearance of an oral and rectal thermometer?
7. Name several methods of taking a temperature reading.
8. How would you convert a temperature reading from centigrade to Fahrenheit? Fahrenheit to centigrade?
9. What may cause a variation in the pulse rate?
10. What is the normal respiration rate for adults? For children?

Suggested readings

Caldwell, E., and Hegner, B.: The health assistant, Albany, N. Y., 1969, Delmar Publishers.

Crowley, V.: Introductory concepts in pathology, Chicago, 1972, Year Book Medical Publishers, Inc.

McInnes, M. E.: The vital signs, St. Louis, 1970, The C. V. Mosby Co.

Prior, J. A., and Silberstein, J. S.: Physical diagnosis, ed. 4, St. Louis, 1973, The C. V. Mosby Co.

chapter 26

Drugs and solutions

The administration of medicines is one of the most responsible duties of the assistant in the office. They are prescribed by the physician, and the assistant is expected to know enough about them to administer them properly and to know what action to expect. In addition to giving medicines, the assistant is responsible for the care of all medications in the office. Medications are given commonly by several routes, but most medicines are given by mouth. The method of administration depends on the characteristics of the medication and the desired effect. In the office the assistant will be most concerned with the administration of medications by other than oral routes. Errors in medication may have very serious consequences, both in deleterious effects on the patient and in not producing the needed and expected effect.

BRAND AND GENERIC NAMES

Modern medicine has progressed in large measure because of the advances made by pharmaceutical firms in developing new and better drugs. When a pharmaceutical firm develops a drug it usually patents it and has exclusive rights over it. The drug is given a scientific name and is also given a brand name by which it is frequently identified

---

Glossary

ampicillin a penicillin derivative antibiotic
analgesic a drug that relieves pain
anticholinergic a drug that antagonizes certain actions of the autonomic nervous system
antiemetic a drug that reduces vomiting
antihistamine a drug that counteracts the effects of histamine; an antiallergy drug
antipruritic a drug used to reduce itching
bronchodilator drug used in the treatment of asthma by dilating bronchial passages
BNDD (Bureau of Narcotics and Dangerous Drugs) a federal agency that regulates the manufacture, sale, and administration of narcotic, habit-forming, and other dangerous drugs
digitalis a drug that improves the contraction of the heart
diuretic a drug that increases urine production
erythromycin an antibiotic drug
expectorant a drug that helps to liquefy secretions of the respiratory tract
FDA (Food and Drug Administration) a federal agency that regulates drug manufacture, safety, and administration in the United States
generic name the chemical name of a drug
hypnotic a sleeping pill
oral hypoglycemic a drug used to treat adult onset diabetes
parenteral by injection
penicillin an antibiotic drug
PDR (Physicians' Desk Reference) a reference source for information about drugs
phenothiazine a chemical whose derivatives are often used as tranquilizers
sulfonamide a type of antibiotic, often referred to as a "sulfa drug"
suppository a form of administering a drug so that it dissolves after placement in the rectum or vagina
tetracycline an antibiotic drug
tincture a solution that is made up with alcohol
trade name a commercial or brand name of a drug
tranquilizer a drug that reduces anxiety or agitation
USP (United States Pharmacopeia) contains a listing of minimum standards for purity of certain drugs; a term used to certify that a drug meets USP standards for purity

and that is registered as a trademark by the company. For example, chlordiazepoxide hydrochloride is most commonly known by its brand name Librium. Many drugs are better known by their trade or brand names than their chemical or generic names. This is especially true of drugs made only by one manufacturer. Often the generic drug, for example, tetracycline, may be made by a dozen or more companies under a dozen different brand names. The use of brand and generic names in prescribing drugs varies among physicians. In general, generic drugs are cheaper for the patient to purchase.

THE PHYSICIANS' DESK REFERENCE

Each physician's assistant should be familiar with the Physicians' Desk Reference (PDR). The PDR is published yearly by the Medical Economics Company and is available to all physicians. The book has six sections: (1) the names, addresses, and telephone numbers of all the drug manufacturers in the United States; (2) an alphabetical index of drugs produced by each manufacturer; (3) classification of drugs by broad categories such as anesthetics, antibiotics, and so forth; (4) generic or chemical name; (5) identification of drugs by means of color pictures of the most commonly prescribed pills and capsules (this list frequently permits the assistant or physician to identify a pill or capsule that is unfamiliar); (6) a detailed list of drugs and a discussion of the chemical nature, indications for use, contraindications, precautions, warnings, dosage, and administration of the drugs as well as information as to how the drugs are supplied.

The PDR has several supplements every year, which, when received, should be inserted in the book. An up-to-date PDR is an important reference source for the physician and his assistant.

FDA BULLETINS

At times the Federal Drug Administration will issue directives, advice, or warnings to physicians. These bulletins should be called to the physician's attention as soon as they are received so that they can be properly evaluated. Some physicians will keep a file of these bulletins for future reference.

CARE OF MEDICATIONS

1. Labels must be kept legible. At times bottles kept in refrigerators will become moist and the label will slip off the bottle. This problem may be eliminated by taping the entire label with transparent tape.
2. Drugs should not be kept in examining and waiting rooms where they are readily accessible to patients. Drugs classified as dangerous by the Bureau of Narcotics and Dangerous Drugs must be kept in a locked storage area.
3. Medicine cupboards should be cleaned regularly. Bottles should be kept clean and wiped clean after every use. When frost-free refrigerators are not used, the refrigerators should be defrosted on a regular basis. Highly volatile substances such as ether, acetone, and other organic solvents should never be kept in refrigerators because of the possibility of explosion.
4. Poisonous compounds and medication for external use only should be clearly labeled and kept apart from other medication.
5. Drugs on hand should be inventoried regularly and outdated drugs discarded. Care should be taken to note whether drugs should be frozen, refrigerated, or kept at room temperature.
6. Drugs needed during emergencies should be kept in a readily available location. Included near these medications should be syringes, alcohol sponges, and diluents needed for their immediate use. A checklist of emergency drugs and supplies should be made out by the physician and the medical assistant should be familiar with the indications and method of administration of each of the items on the list. This checklist will vary accord-

ing to the needs of the particular office or clinic and the preference of its physicians.

RULES OF ADMINISTERING MEDICATIONS

1. Wash hands before starting.
2. When selecting or preparing medications, give the job your undivided attention; this is the only way to avoid errors. If an error is made, report it promptly to the physician, never to the patient. Let the physician evaluate the seriousness of the error and tell the patient what is necessary.
3. Be certain that you have correctly understood the name of the drug and the dosage. Jot this information down on a slip of paper kept available for this purpose; do not trust your memory. If you are not certain that you have understood the name, dosage, or instructions, *ask*.
4. Read the label three times: first, when selecting the bottle from the supply cupboard; second, before measuring out the desired amount; and third, before replacing it in the supply cupboard. This should be done so faithfully that it becomes automatic.
5. The decision as to how a drug is to be administered is always made by the physician. The assistant should read the instructions on the label carefully to be sure that the drug can be given as directed by the physician.
6. Most medications come with a package insert with information about the drug such as its use, dose, storage, and method of administration. This information is also available in the PDR.
7. If the medication is not given immediately for any reason, label it carefully. If it is prepared for the doctor to give, further identify it by the bottle or empty ampule, which should be shown to the doctor before he administers the medication.
8. Adequate record keeping is one of the hallmarks of a well-run medical practice. All the medications given must be permanently recorded in the patient's medical record. The name and dose of the drug given as well as the date must be recorded and the entry in the record initialed by the assistant. If the patient is being seen for the first time and is already on medication, he should be encouraged to bring for identification all medication being taken.
9. If calculation of the amount of drug to be given is required, make the calculation carefully. If there is the slightest doubt as to a calculation of a dose of a drug, the physician must be consulted for further help.
10. Measure accurately.
11. The Bureau of Narcotics and Dangerous Drugs requires that all narcotics be accounted for. A log book with notations of the amount of these drugs dispensed, the date, and the name of the patient to whom the drug was dispensed should be kept locked with the drugs. These logs should also include a tally of the amount of drugs on hand at any given moment and the date on which an inventory of the drugs was last taken.

REASONS FOR ADMINISTRATION OF MEDICATIONS IN WAYS OTHER THAN BY MOUTH (PARENTERAL)

A drug may be given intramuscularly or intravenously for a variety of reasons; such administration of the drug is called parenteral. Some of the most common reasons for administering drugs parenterally are included below:

1. Some drugs are poorly absorbed by the body if given by mouth. Examples of these are certain antibiotics like streptomycin and some vaccines like tetanus toxoid.
2. Patients with vomiting or recent abdominal surgery frequently cannot be given drugs by mouth.
3. Under certain conditions it may be desir-

able to administer drugs parenterally to avoid irritation of the stomach or intestines.

4. In certain emergencies a rapid drug effect is needed that can best be achieved by parenteral administration. Under other conditions the concentration of drug needed in the body can be achieved only by parenteral administration. An example of this are antibiotics given during serious infections in hospitalized patients.
5. Certain patients cannot be relied upon to take medications reliably for extended periods of time. Others would be seriously inconvenienced by long-term or frequent drug administration. Long-acting drugs may, therefore, be given parenterally. An example of this is benzathine penicillin, a long-acting form of penicillin given to patients as prophylaxis against rheumatic fever or as treatment of syphilis.

FORMS OF MEDICATIONS PREPARED FOR PARENTERAL USE

Most drugs for parenteral administration come in prepared solutions for either single or multiple dose usage. Some come in vials whose tops may be broken off as directed; others come in rubber stopper bottles that should be scrubbed with an alcohol sponge before each use. Care must be taken that only sterile needles and syringes are used. The correct method for administering these drugs is discussed in Chapter 28. If for any reason there is reason to suspect that a bottle has been contaminated, it should be discarded.

Other drugs may be supplied in a concentrated, powder, or pill form that must be dissolved in a liquid or diluent. The type of diluent needed is always indicated on the label or the appropriate diluent may come with the drug. It is usually desirable to give intramuscular medications in amounts of less than 2.0 ml but more than 0.5 ml.

When a physician orders a parenteral drug, its name and amount and the patient's name should be written down. Concentration of the drug will appear on the label and is usually expressed in milligrams, grams, or units per cubic centimeter. A simple formula may be used to calculate the correct dose.

$$\frac{\text{Dose required}}{\text{Concentration}} = \text{ml's needed}$$

Example: The physician orders 75 mg of Demerol. The Demerol bottle is labeled 50 mg per ml. Therefore:

$$\frac{\text{Dose required (75)}}{\text{Concentration (50)}} = \text{ml's needed (1.5)}$$

The assistant will therefore give the patient 1.5 ml of Demerol. When using the formula both the dose and the concentration must be expressed in the same terms. If the order is given in grams, for example, the concentration must be in grams per ml also. An assistant who is not clearly familiar with the method of converting minims, grains, or other apothecary measures into the concentrations given on the label should ask for specific instructions as to preparing the medication or should let the physician make the calculations or preparations.

Fig. 26-1 gives a conversion table for approximate dose equivalents for grains, grams, and milligrams. This table is for reference only and no attempt should be made to memorize it except to remember that 1 grain equals 65 milligrams. The approximate fluid equivalents are given in Fig. 26-2. The key items to remember in this table are that a teaspoon equals approximately 5 ml's and a tablespoon, 15 ml's.

When writing a prescription, the physician must give the pharmacist the name of the patient, the name of the medication, the amount to be prepared, and instructions that should be printed on the label. The pharmacist must also receive instructions as to how many times, if any, the prescription may be renewed or if another brand may be substituted. For drugs specified by the Bureau of Narcotics and Dangerous Drugs, the physician's BNDD number will be needed. This number is the individual physician's registration and identification number with the Bureau of Narcotics and Dangerous Drugs and can be used only by him.

Most prescriptions written today are for pills, capsules, solutions, or ointments and creams already prepared by pharmaceutical companies. These preparations have largely eliminated the need for detailed instructions as to how the pharmacist is to prepare the solutions or medications and have greatly simplified prescription writing.

Approximate dosage equivalents for grains and grams

Grains *(gr.)*	*Grams* *(Gm.)*	*Milligrams* *(mg.)*
1/600	0.0001	0.1
1/500	0.00012	0.12
1/400	0.00015	0.15
1/300	0.0002	0.2
1/250	0.00025	0.25
1/200	0.0003	0.3
1/150	0.0004	0.4
1/120	0.0005	0.5
1/100	0.0006	0.6
1/80	0.0008	0.8
1/60	0.001	1
1/30	0.002	2
1/20	0.003	3
1/15	0.004	4
1/12	0.005	5
1/10	0.006	6
1/8	0.008	8
1/6	0.010	10
1/4	0.015	15
1/3	0.020	20
3/8	0.025	25
1/2	0.032	32
3/4	0.050	50
1	0.065	65

Fig. 26-1

Approximate household measures

1 teaspoonful	1 fl. dr.	4-5 cc.
1 tablespoonful	½ fl. oz.	15 cc.
1 glassful	8 fl. oz.	240 cc.

Fig. 26-2

Prescription abbreviations—weights and measures

gr.	grain or grains
gtt. (or gutta[e])	drop(s)
ʒ	dram
℥	ounce
$\overline{\text{ss}}$	one half
ʒ $\dot{\overline{\text{i}}}$	one dram
ʒ $\overline{\text{ss}}$	one half dram
ʒ $\overline{\dot{\text{i}}\text{ss}}$	one and one half drams
ʒ $\ddot{\overline{\text{ii}}}$	two drams
℥ $\dot{\text{i}}$	one ounce
℥ $\overline{\text{ss}}$	one half ounce
℥ $\overline{\dot{\text{i}}\text{ss}}$	one and one half ounces
℥ $\ddot{\overline{\text{ii}}}$	two ounces
cc.	cubic centimeter
Gm.	gram
mg.	milligram
mcg.	microgram

Fig. 26-3

Latin prescription abbreviations and meanings

ā ā	of each
a. c. (ante cibum)	before meals
b.i.d. (bis in die)	twice a day
caps	capsules
hora	an hour
h. s. (hora somni)	at bedtime
non. rep. (non repetatur)	do not repeat (do not refill)
omn. hor. (omni hora)	every hour
p. c. (post cibum)	after meals
p.r.n. (pro re nata)	as needed
q. s. (quantum sufficit)	a sufficient quantity
q.i.d. (quater in die)	four times a day
q.	every
℞	take (thou) a recipe
Sig. (signa)	directions
stat (statim)	immediately
t.i.d. (ter in die)	three times a day
ut dict.	as directed

Fig. 26-4

The prescription is usually written in a type of shorthand understood by the physician and pharmacist. In Figs. 26-3 and 26-4 are listed commonly used abbreviations in prescription writing. The assistant may need to refer to these figures if there is need to translate the physician's notes on a medical record or prescription.

There is a growing tendency toward conversion to the metric system in medicine, which, unfortunately, has not yet become universal. The abbreviations in Fig. 26-4 usually have Latin roots and may be difficult to learn. Only the most commonly used are included.

COMMONLY USED DRUGS

It is beyond the scope of this text to include a detailed discussion of medical pharmacology or therapeutics. The physician's assistant should be familiar with some general concepts of the nature and the use of certain common drugs. In the following pages, different drugs will be discussed under broad categories based on their common use.

Analgesics

Analgesics are drugs used to relieve pain. Table 5 lists some of the most commonly used analgesics.

One of the oldest and best analgesics is aspirin, which may be buffered to reduce gastric irritation. In addition to its role in the treatment of pain, aspirin reduces fever and is therefore called an antipyretic. It also helps to reduce the inflammation of many types of arthritis.

Phenacetin and acetaminophen are also good analgesics and antipyretics and are often used for patients who cannot take aspirin. Two other nonnarcotic analgesics that, unlike the above drugs, require a physician's prescription, are Darvon and Talwin. The latter is frequently given parenterally.

The most potent analgesics are narcotics. All are potentially habit forming and require a prescription. Two commonly used narcotics are morphine and meperidine, which may be given parenterally as well as orally. Other commonly prescribed narcotics that can be given by mouth are listed in Table 5. Codeine is frequently used in combination with nonnarcotic analgesics to form compounds, and sometimes as a cough suppressant in cough syrups.

Psychotherapeutic drugs

The two most commonly prescribed drugs in the United States in the early 1970s were both tranquilizers. The use of drugs aimed

Table 5. Analgesics

Generic category	Common brand names
Aspirin and aspirin compounds	Bayer, Bufferin, Empirin, Excedrin, Fiorinal, Phenaphen
Acetaminophen, phenacetin, and related compounds	Empirin, Excedrin, Fiorinal, Phenaphen, Tempra, Tylenol
Propoxyphene and related compounds	Darvocet-N, Darvon, Darvon Compound-65, Darvon N, Darvon N with A.S.A.
Pentazocine	Talwin
Narcotics	
Codeine and combinations	Empirin, Phenaphen, and Tylenol are all available with varying amounts of codeine
Meperidine	Demerol
Oxycodone	Percodan
Morphine and related drugs	Dilaudid

at reducing the tensions and stresses of modern life has become a significant part of our culture. All of the drugs described in this section need a physician's prescription and are either habit forming or have a serious potential for abuse.

The *barbiturates* are a group of drugs frequently used as sedatives, sleeping pills (hypnotics), and in the treatment of certain types of epilepsy (anticonvulsants). They are usually given by mouth except in emergencies or when they are used during induction of anesthesia. Some barbiturates are long acting (phenobarbital) while others are short acting (pentobarbital and secobarbital) (Table 6).

Diazepoxide derivatives include Valium and Librium, the two most commonly used sedative-tranquilizers in the United States. They are usually taken by mouth and may be somewhat less addictive than the barbiturates.

Phenothiazines are taken by mouth or parenterally and have a variety of uses ranging from their ability to reduce nausea and vomiting (antiemetics) to the ability to reduce itching (antipruritics). They are potent tranquilizers when given in high doses. Millions of psychotic patients who formerly had to be institutionalized are now treated as outpatients because of the development of the phenothiazine drugs. Examples of the most commonly used drugs in this category are given in Table 6.

The most commonly used *antidepressants* are also listed in Table 6. They often take weeks or more to have their desired effects and are not used to treat simple, transient episodes of sadness or tension.

Other commonly used sedatives and "sleeping pills," in addition to the barbiturates, include chloral hydrate and numerous other drugs that are almost always prescribed by their brand names (Table 6).

Table 6. Psychotherapeutic drugs

Generic category	Common brand names
Barbiturates	
Amobarbital	Amytal
Pentobarbital	Nembutal
Phenobarbital	Luminal
Secobarbital	Seconal
Diazepoxide derivatives	Librium, Librax, Valium
Phenothiazine derivatives	
Chlorpromazine	Thorazine
Others	Mellaril, Sparine, Compazine, Stelazine, Phenergan, Vistaril
Antidepressants	
Imipramine	Tofranil
Amitryptyline	Elavil, Triavil
Others	Ritalin, Dexedrine
Other hypnotics and tranquilizers	Dalmane, chloral hydrate, Doriden, Equanil, Etrafon, meprobamate, Miltown, Noludar, Norgesic, Placidyl, Quaalude, Serax, Tranxene, Sinequan

Antibiotics

Antibiotics (Table 7) enable physicians to treat a large number of infections that were often fatal forty or fifty years ago. Antibiotics work by interfering with the metabolism of bacteria. Only a minority of viruses can be treated with antibiotics.

The first drugs used to treat bacterial infections effectively were the *sulfonamides,* commonly referred to as the sulfa drugs. Sulfonamides are used today primarily to treat urinary tract infections. They are given only by mouth.

Penicillin was one of the first antibiotics discovered and remains one of the best drugs of modern medicine. It can be given orally or parenterally. Some drawbacks of this drug include its inability to act against many gram-negative bacteria, the tendency of certain bacteria such as staphylococci to become resistant to it, and its tendency to produce allergies in a small proportion of recipients.

Pharmaceutical manufacturers have been able to develop *derivatives of penicillin* that act against gram-negative organisms and that are effective in treating penicillin-resistant staphylococci. In general, however, penicillin allergy precludes the use of any of the penicillin derivatives except in very special cases.

The most commonly used *oral* penicillin preparations are derivatives of penicillin V. The most common *parenteral* forms of penicillin are derivatives of penicillin G, some of which provide antibiotic therapy for several days or weeks after a single parenteral administration (benzathine penicillin).

Ampicillin is a penicillin derivative that is effective against some gram-negative bacteria. The penicillinase-resistant penicillins are used in the treatment of penicillin-resistant staphylococci.

Table 7. Antibiotics

Generic category or name	Brand name
Sulfonamides	Bactrim, Gantanol, Gantrisin, Septra
Penicillin and derivatives	
Penicillin	Bicillin, Permapen, Pentids, Pen-Vee K, V-Cillin K
Ampicillin	Amcill, Omnipen, Penbritin, Polycillin, Principen
Penicillinase resistant penicillins	Prostaphlin, Unipen
	Keflex, Tegopen
Tetracyclines	Achromycin, Declomycin, Minocin, Mysteclin, Sumycin, Terramycin, Tetrex, Vibramycin
Erythromycins	E-Mycin, Erythrocin, Ilosone, Pediamycin
Erythromycin-related drugs	
Lincomycin	Lincocin
Clindamycin	Cleocin
Streptomycin-related antibiotics	Kantrex, Garamycin

Tetracyclines are among the most frequently used drugs in modern medicine. They have a wide spectrum of activity against many different bacteria and can be given both parenterally and by mouth and some derivatives have been developed that need be given only once a day. Because they cause discoloration of growing teeth, the tetracyclines are usually not given to children for prolonged periods. In adults the tetracyclines are often given to patients allergic to penicillin, to treat upper respiratory tract infections, and in the treatment of chronic bronchitis and urinary tract infection. Many forms of tetracycline have been developed that vary in their absorption by the digestive tract or in the presence of food.

The *erythromycins and related drugs* are usually given by mouth and are widely used in the treatment of infections in children and in patients allergic to penicillin.

The *streptomycin group* of drugs was developed to treat bacteria not responsive to penicillin. These drugs are also of great use in the treatment of tuberculosis. Since they must be given parenterally, they are most frequently used in hospitalized patients. Newer members of this group of antibiotics include kanamycin and gentamicin.

Antihypertensive and cardiac drugs

Fortunately our knowledge of the cause and complications of hypertension, one of the leading causes of death in the world, is rapidly expanding. Hypertention may be caused by a variety of factors and can therefore be treated with a variety of drugs.

Diuretics are drugs that increase urine production and are frequently used in the treatment of hypertension, heart failure, and diseases associated with abnormal water retention (edema).

The most commonly used diuretics include furosemide, the various thiazides, spironolactone, and triamterene. These drugs can be used alone, in combination with each

Table 8. Antihypertensive and cardiac drugs

Generic category or name	Brand name
Diuretics	
Thiazide diuretics	Diuril, Enduron, Esidrix, Hydro-Diuril, Hygroton
Furosemide	Lasix
Spironolactone	Aldactone
Spironolactone-thiazide	Aldactazide
Triamterene	Dyrenium
Triamterene-thiazide	Dyazide
Antihypertensives	
Methyldopa	Aldomet
Methyldopa-thiazide	Aldoril, Aldoclor
Hydralazine	Apresoline
Reserpine	Serpasil
Reserpine-thiazide	Diupres, Hydropres, Rauzide, Regroton, Salutensin
Reserpine-hydralazine-thiazide	Ser-Ap-Es
Guanethidine	Ismelin
Drugs for angina pectoris (coronary dilators)	
Nitroglycerine	Nitro-Bid, Nitrostat, Nitrospan
Other nitrates	Isordil, Peritrate
Propranolol	Inderal

other, or in combination with other drugs that reduce high blood pressure. Commonly used diuretics, antihypertensive and combinations of these drugs are listed in Table 8.

Various drugs containing potassium are often given with diuretics to prevent side reactions caused by the lowering of potassium in the body by diuretics. Examples of potassium preparations include potassium chloride, Kaon, and K-Lyte.

The most common cardiotonic drug is digitalis. Digitalis increases the effectiveness of the heart as a pump and is given for many types of heart failure. Digitalis is most often given by mouth although it can be given parenterally. The most common forms of digitalis are digoxin and digitoxin. (Digitalis leaf is still used by some physicians.) An excess of digitalis may cause a very slow pulse, irregular heart rate, or even death; instructions for taking digitalis must therefore always be clear, precise, and carefully followed.

There are many drugs given for the pain of coronary artery disease (angina pectoris). The most commonly used is nitroglycerine, a small pill that is placed under the tongue during attacks of chest pain. Other commonly used drugs are listed in Table 8. Many of these drugs may be taken by mouth.

A number of drugs are used to treat irregularities of the heart rate, the most common of which include quinidine and procaine amide. Certain drugs called anticoagulants are used to prevent blood clots in vessels, which may break off and lodge in the lung (pulmonary embolus). The most common anticoagulant used in outpatients is Coumadin.

Drugs used in the treatment of arthritis

For the treatment of arthritis, aspirin and the other nonnarcotic analgesics listed in Table 5 are the most frequently prescribed by physicians. Others often used include phenylbutazone and indomethacin (Butazolidin, Tandearil, Indocin). Gold is sometimes given by injection for rheumatoid arthritis.

Numerous cortisone derivatives are used as anti-inflammatory agents. Some of these are given by mouth while others are given directly into the painful joints. The most frequently prescribed cortisone derivatives include prednisone, Aristocort, Decadron, and Medrol. All cortisone derivatives in high doses are potentially dangerous drugs. Although these drugs when first introduced were thought to be "wonder drugs," it is now known that they must be given under very careful medical supervision. The experienced physician's assistant will be able to detect many patients who are taking cortisone by their typically round, ruddy faces with acne.

Colchicine, allopurinol, and probenecid are three drugs commonly used to treat gout.

Anticonvulsant drugs

Anticonvulsant drugs are used to treat the various forms of epilepsy. The most commonly used anticonvulsant drugs are phenobarbital and Dilantin. Other drugs, such as Valium and paraldehyde are used in emergencies.

Gastrointestinal drugs

Disorders of the gastrointestinal tract are among the most common reasons why patients seek medical attention. Gastrointestinal drugs are most frequently used to treat peptic ulcers and related disorders, diarrhea, and constipation. Peptic ulcer diseases are the result of the erosion of part of the lining of the lower esophagus, stomach, or duodenum by acid and digestive juices. Treatment of these disorders is first directed at avoiding or reducing certain factors such as stress, coffee, tea, alcohol, spices, and certain irritating drugs. The second aspect of treatment is to reduce the effect of acid upon the digestive organs. This is done either by neutralizing the acid produced by the stomach or by reducing its production. Substances that neutralize stomach acidity are called antacids or buffers.

One of the substances that can be used to buffer excess acidity is food. Milk and other bland foods have been used for centuries for this purpose. Antacid preparations are the mainstay for the treatment of ulcer diseases. The most commonly used antacids include sodium bicarbonate, aluminum and magnesium hydroxide, and calcium carbonate. Antacid therapy should be supervised by a physician since patients with heart or renal disease may be adversely affected by these drugs. Also, excessive consumption of milk and certain antacids may cause serious disease. The number of antacids available with and without a prescription is very large.

When we see or smell food, acid and gastric juice production is increased and this process continues when food enters the stomach. Production of acid and gastric juices is under the control of the autonomic nervous system. Acid production can be reduced with medications called anticholinergic drugs, which frequently affect many organs in addition to the intestinal tract. Because they can adversely affect the heart rate, bladder, pressure within the eyes, and nervous system, they should be given only by a physician.

The treatment of diarrhea may be as simple as eliminating certain foods, such as milk, from the diet or as complex as removing a tumor from the colon. The medical assistant must remember that diarrhea may be symptom or sign of some underlying disorder, which must be identified to determine the appropriate treatment. Except in mild, short-term diarrhea, the patient should be evaluated by a physician. Some drugs used to treat diarrhea increase the bulk of stool or act as absorbents and many of these can be purchased without a prescription. Other drugs reduce intestinal motility. Most of these require a prescription and all are potentially dangerous when used indiscriminately.

There are many drugs used to treat constipation. Once again a medical assistant should remember that constipation may be an early symptom of a serious medical disorder such as cancer of the rectum. Also, because laxative abuse may create a serious dependency on these drugs, the choice of a proper laxative should therefore be left to the physician.

Laxatives are of many different types. Mineral oil lubricates; other laxatives act as stool softeners; caster oil and derivatives of cascara directly stimulate the bowel; and various compounds of magnesium, such as milk of magnesia and magnesium citrate, increase the water content of the stool. Because patients with appendicitis and intestinal obstruction can be seriously harmed by the use of any laxative, anyone with vomiting or abdominal pains should therefore be strongly discouraged from using a laxative until they are evaluated by a physician.

Respiratory tract drugs

Decongestants, expectorants, antihistamines, and bronchodilators (Table 9) are used in the treatment of respiratory tract disorders. The upper respiratory tract includes the nose, throat, paranasal sinuses, and trachea. The most frequent disorders of this system are caused by viral illnesses such as common colds. Treatment of these disorders is entirely symptomatic, that is, directed to the symptoms that bother the patient. Bacterial infections of the upper respiratory tract frequently mimic the most common viral disorders but may be associated with more serious consequences if left untreated by antibiotics. At times bacterial infections may complicate what starts as a viral infection.

The lower respiratory tract includes the bronchi and the lungs. Infections of these organs produce bronchitis and pneumonia. Viral infections are common in these structures and are sometimes difficult to distinguish from potentially deadly bacterial infection. Symptoms frequently associated with upper respiratory disorders include nasal congestion, sore throat, sinus congestion, pain, fever, chills, and dry cough. Symptoms of lower respiratory tract disorders include cough, wheezing, shortness of breath, chest pains, fever, and chills.

In both upper and lower respiratory tract disorders, allergies may be the primary or aggravating problem. Allergies to a large variety of substances ranging from pollen, dust, foods, and articles of clothing may exist.

Decongestants are substances that reduce stoppage of the passages and sinuses of the upper respiratory tract by constricting the small blood vessels present in the mucous linings of the upper respiratory tract. They may be taken by mouth or administered by nasal drops or sprays. They are frequently combined with antiallergic drugs called antihistamines. A list of commonly used decongestants is included in Table 9.

Expectorants are drugs that stimulate the production of a watery secretion from the bronchi of the lower respiratory tract so that secretion in the bronchi and trachea can be readily coughed up and elimated. Commonly used expectorants are listed in Table 9.

Antihistamines are drugs that act against the effects of histamine, which is a chemical produced in the body during allergic reactions and is responsible for some of the problems associated with allergic disorders. Antihistaminics are most effective in disorders such as hay fever. All of the commonly used antihistamines may produce drowsiness, which may be dangerous while driving or operating machinery; therefore, a precaution against such activity is frequently given to patients taking antihistamines. Commonly used antihistamines are listed in Table 9.

Asthma is a condition caused by the abnormal narrowing of the air passages of the lower respiratory tract. It is frequently related to allergies, although in some individuals attacks may be associated with infections or with episodes of psychologic stress. Antibiotics, decongestants, and antihistamines are often used in asthmatic patients, either separately or as combinations of drugs. Drugs that act to relax abnormally narrowed air passages are called bronchodilators. Bronchodilators may be given as injections, inhaled as aerosols, or taken as suppositories or pills. Some commonly used bronchodilators are given in Table 9.

Table 9. Respiratory tract drugs

General category	Brand name
Decongestants, expectorants, and combinations	
Oral:	Actifed, Benylin, Chlor-Trimeton, Coricidin, Dimetane, Dimetapp, Drixoral, Elixophyllin, Naldecon, Novahistine, Ornade, Phenergan, Polaramine, Robitussin, Sinutab, Sudafed, Triaminic, Trind, Tuss-Ornade
Topical, nasal:	Afrin, Neo-Synephrine
Antihistamines and combinations	Actifed, Benadryl, Chlor-Trimeton, Coricidin, Dimetapp, Drixoral, Phenergan, Polaramine, Pyribenzamine, Tacaryl, Teldrin, Triaminic
Drugs used in asthma—Bronchodilators	
Oral:	Actifed, Brondecon, Choledyl, Elixophyllin, Isuprel, Marax, Quadrinal, Quibron, Tedral, Verequad
Inhalers:	Alupent, Isuprel, Medihaler

Hormones and endocrine drugs

Diabetes mellitus is a disease produced by an absolute or relative deficiency of insulin. Individuals who develop diabetes in childhood usually need insulin replacement for the rest of their lives. Many individuals who are diagnosed as having diabetes in adulthood frequently go for long periods of time without needing insulin because the pancreas produces enough insulin to prevent diabetic symptomatology except during periods of stress.

Insulin is a protein that is inactivated if taken orally and therefore can only be given by injection. In general all insulin preparations should be kept refrigerated. Insulin is measured in units and the average daily requirement of insulin in most diabetics varies between 20 and 60 units per day. The amount of insulin needed to control diabetes is greater during infections, certain forms of stress, and as a result of obesity. In the past insulin was prepared in two concentrations: 40 and 80 units per ml; 1 ml of U-40 insulin had half as much insulin as 1 ml of U-80 insulin. The terms U-40 and U-80 insulin refer to *concentration* and not the *type* of insulin being used. A specific syringe has to be used that is calibrated for use with U-40 and U-80 insulin.

Because of the confusion often created by having two different concentrations of insulin and two different types of syringes, there is a growing tendency to switch all diabetic patients to U-100 insulin, insulin that has 100 units per ml. It will take several years before the transition to exclusive use of U-100 insulin will be complete.

There are three basic categories of insulin based on the duration of their action: *short, intermediate* and *long-acting* insulin. Short-acting insulins are semilente and regular insulin. These insulin preparations have a significant effect starting 1 hour after administration. They peak at about 2 to 3 hours and are gone by 6 to 8 hours. The most frequently used type of insulin is the intermediate acting, which starts showing an effect in 2 to 3 hours, peaks between 4 to 8 hours, and lasts 12 to 24 hours. The two most common forms are Lente and NPH insulin. Long-acting insulins are the least often used. Two examples in this category are PZI (protamine zinc insulin) and Ultralente insulin. These insulin preparations have a somewhat less predictable duration of action.

Insulin is prepared from the pancreas of slaughterhouse animals. Because most commercial insulin preparations contain both pork and beef insulin, in individuals with insulin allergy, pork insulin alone is sometimes used, which must be specifically prescribed.

Juvenile diabetics tend to have "brittle" diabetes and need more frequent modifications of their insulin dosage than "stable" maturity onset diabetics. Also, juvenile diabetics tend to need more frequent administrations of insulin, often before each evening meal, to achieve good control of the diabetes. Although there are many general guidelines, each diabetic patient must be treated individually to adjust his requirements to his particular response to treatment. Treatment of all diabetics follows certain guidelines referred to as "good control," which are maintenance of good general nutrition and normal weight, avoidance of ketosis, avoidance of hypoglycemia, and avoidance of marked glucose loss in the urine. An integral part of establishing "good control" is a proper diet, regular physical exercise, and the maintenance of good general health. Good control of diabetes results in less time spent in the hospital and less limitations on normal activities. Despite good control, diabetics tend to develop more eye, kidney, and vascular diseases than non-diabetic patients.

Oral hypoglycemic agents are used in adult onset diabetics. The most commonly used oral hypoglycemic drugs act by stimulating insulin production by the pancreas and are therefore employed in diabetics who still have a significant amount of insulin production from their pancreas. They are of little value in most juvenile onset diabetics.

Table 10. Oral hypoglycemic agents

Generic name	Brand name
Phenformin	DBI, Meltrol
Chlorpropamide	Diabinese
Tolbutamide	Orinase
Tolazamide	Tolinase

Table 11. Oral contraceptive agents*

Demulen, Enovid, Norinyl,
Norlestrin, Oracon, Ortho-Novum,
Ovral, Ovulen

*These drugs are rarely referred to by generic names.

A list of commonly used oral hypoglycemic drugs is included in Table 10. Some of these agents such as tolbutamide must be taken several times a day, but most of the other agents may be taken once a day because of their longer duration of action.

It should be reemphasized that diet constitutes the mainstay of treatment of most adult onset diabetics and is essential in the treatment of juvenile diabetics. Although the diets vary in their complexity, in general, diabetics are encouraged to maintain an adequate state of nutrition, avoid irregular meals, and avoid excessive amounts of carbohydrates. Attainment and maintenance of a normal weight and regular physical activity are also encouraged.

Thyroid hormone is given to individuals who have thyroid deficiency (hypothyroidism). At times it is also given to individuals with certain types of goiter. Various forms of thyroid medication include desiccated thyroid, thyroid extract, thyroglobulin, Synthroid, Cytomel, and Liotrix.

Hyperthyroidism, the result of excessive amounts of circulating thyroid hormone, is treated with a variety of agents. These include propylthiouracil, Tapazole, iodine, and various sedatives.

Individuals with insufficient amounts of adrenal hormones are said to have adrenal insufficiency or Addison's disease. These individuals are treated with various derivatives of cortisone given by mouth.

Ovarian hormones and gynecologic drugs

Normal conception and pregnancy depends on a complex sequence of events in the ovary, fallopian tubes, and uterus. These events are controlled by hormones secreted from the pituitary gland and the ovary. Certain derivatives of the principal ovarian hormones, estrogen and progesterone, are used to interrupt the normal, complex series of events needed for conception. These drugs are commonly called birth control pills, some of which are listed in Table 11. In general women should take birth control pills only after consulting a physician. Although birth control pills are one of the most effective means of avoiding pregnancy, they can have serious side effects, such as thrombophlebitis, pulmonary embolism, and hypertension, in a minority of women. Women on birth control pills should have at least one pelvic examination a year.

Various forms of estrogen are commonly given to women when their normal ovarian function declines at the menopause. One commonly used form of estrogen is Premarin.

A large number of drugs can be used to treat fungal, bacterial, and protozoan infections of the vagina. All of these drugs should be used only after consulting a physician. Over-the-counter vaginal douches not infrequently produce allergic reactions to the genitalia and must be used with care.

Ointments

Ointments consist of an ointment base (usually petrolatum or lanolin) plus any medication that may be desired. Ointments may be sterilized in the autoclave if the medication contained is not harmed by being subjected to heat. Plain petroleum jelly ointment may be readily sterilized. If the ointment is sterile and it is desired to keep it that way, always use a sterile tongue depressor to handle material. Ointments that are sterile are often provided in tubes. These are sterile when opened and may be considered to be sterile if the tube remains unbroken and the first little bit squeezed from the tube each time is discarded. Most ointments are for use on skin or, occasionally, for rectal use. Only ointments marked ophthalmic may be used in the eye.

Anesthetics

Three general types of anesthetic are used: general, local, and spinal. The majority of general anesthetics are given by inhalation; ether, nitrous oxide, ethylene, and cyclopropane are in general use today. Sodium Pentothal, which is given intravenously, also produces general anesthesia. Local anesthetics are most frequently derivatives of novocaine and are given by injection into the specific area. Ethyl chloride, which is not used very often today, is given by spraying the area; it gives a "freezing" feeling. Spinal anesthetics are also most commonly drugs resembling novocaine; they may be administered by continuous spinal or continuous caudal injection or by only one injection. Curare is now used as an adjunct to many anesthesias to increase relaxation. The various anesthetic agents are frequently given in combination.

Review questions

1. State three basic rules that should always be followed in administering medications.
2. Give the equivalent of the following:
   a. ¼ grain = ____grams ____milligrams
   b. 1 teaspoon = _____ml
   c. 8 ounces = _____ml
   d. 1 milligram = ____grams ____grains
3. Amplify the following abbreviations:
   a. gr
   b. cc
   c. mg
   d. t.i.d.
   e. p.c.
   f. non. rep.
4. What is meant by parenteral administration of a drug?
5. What information may be obtained from the PDR?
6. What is an FDA bulletin?
7. What is the difference between the brand name and the generic name of a drug?

Suggested readings

Biddle, H. C., and Sitler, D. W.: Mathematics of drugs and solutions, ed. 7, Philadelphia, 1966, F. A. Davis Co.

Goodman, L. S., and Gilman, A., editors: The pharmacological basis of therapeutics, ed. 4, New York, 1970, The Macmillan Co.

Hart, L. K.: The arithmetic of dosages and solutions, ed. 3, St. Louis, 1973, The C. V. Mosby Co.

Keane, C. B., and Fletcher, S.: Drugs and solutions, Philadelphia, 1970, W. B. Saunders Co.

chapter 27

Sterilization procedures for the medical office

Sterilization is the complete destruction of all forms of microbial life. Objects must therefore be considered either sterile or unsterile. In a practical sense there can be no degrees of sterility. It is vital to make such a distinction because of the role sterilization plays in protecting health and life of patients who visit the medical or dental office.

As Pasteur demonstrated more than 100 years ago, we live in a virtual sea of microscopic organisms. The air around us, the objects we touch, and the substances we ingest all contain countless bacteria, fungi, and viruses. The healthy individual is normally protected from such organisms by the outer skin and inner mucous membranes that form the body's first line of defense. It is not unusual during injury, surgery, or even during simple procedures such as brushing the teeth for microorganisms to bypass the first barriers of defense against infection. In these cases two other important mechanisms serve as protection. One is the system of white blood cells that actively entrap and destroy microorganisms that have invaded the body. The other is a closely related mechanism in which the body's immunologic system recognizes the invading organism as a foreign substance and creates antibodies to it. These antibodies are proteins that enable the body to destroy specific invading organisms.

In many instances, the patient can be protected by the use of presterilized, disposable materials from reliable suppliers. Disposable syringe and needle systems, disposable gloves, drapes, and other materials that are discarded after use can eliminate the hazard of cross infection without the necessity for sterilization procedures. But materials that are used repeatedly with many patients can communicate infection or disease. Therefore the organisms that contaminate such medical or dental instruments must be controlled by appropriate measures.

METHODS OF CONTROLLING MICROBIAL LIFE

The three principal methods of combating microbial life are sanitization, disinfection,

---

Glossary

antiseptic an agent that will prevent the growth or arrest the development of microorganisms; also referred to as a germicide

autoclave apparatus for sterilization by steam heated under pressure, usually to 250° F.

catheter a tube for evacuating or injecting fluids

contaminate to soil, stain, or pollute; to make impure

disinfectant an agent used to kill or inhibit the growth of disease-causing bacteria

microbial a general term for organisms that can be seen only with the aid of a microscope

sterilization the destruction of all microorganisms by exposure to chemical or physical agents and sterilization. These represent different levels of decontamination and are often used jointly.

Sanitization is properly defined as a cleaning step preliminary to processes of actually destroying infectious organisms. A thorough cleaning eliminates most chemical impurities on medical supplies. It also significantly reduces the number of microorganisms on the surface. Sanitizing agents include water and various soaps, detergents, and chemicals.

Disinfection is any means by which most infectious organisms but not necessarily all resistant or spore-forming varieties are destroyed. Disinfecting agents include chemical germicides, of which there are several types for several purposes, and boiling water or flowing steam. Used properly, such agents are effective against ordinary pathogenic bacteria and some viruses. However, they may provide inadequate protection against spore-forming bacteria and organisms such as the virus of serum hepatitis.

Sterilization is the complete destruction of all forms of microbial life. Sterilization can be accomplished by a number of methods, such as dry heat, the use of moderately heated chemical-gas mixtures, and, in some instances, chemical germicides. Such methods, however, are limited to certain applications and usually require long exposure periods to bring about sterilization.

The most commonly used sterilizing method involves the autoclave, which employs moist heat in the form of saturated steam under pressure. Relatively simple to operate, rapid and reliable in its sterilizing action, the autoclave is widely considered the most practical answer to the sterilizing needs of the medical office (Fig. 27-1).

Sanitization of materials

Cleaning of instruments. The first step in sterilizing contaminated materials, such as instruments, is their prompt removal from the treatment area to a separate work space. There, away from contact with patients, the instruments should be cleaned in water containing a blood solvent or a low-sudsing detergent. Care should be exercised in handling sharp instruments to avoid infection of the operator and to prevent dulling of scissors or cutting edges.

If a double sink is not available, a sep-

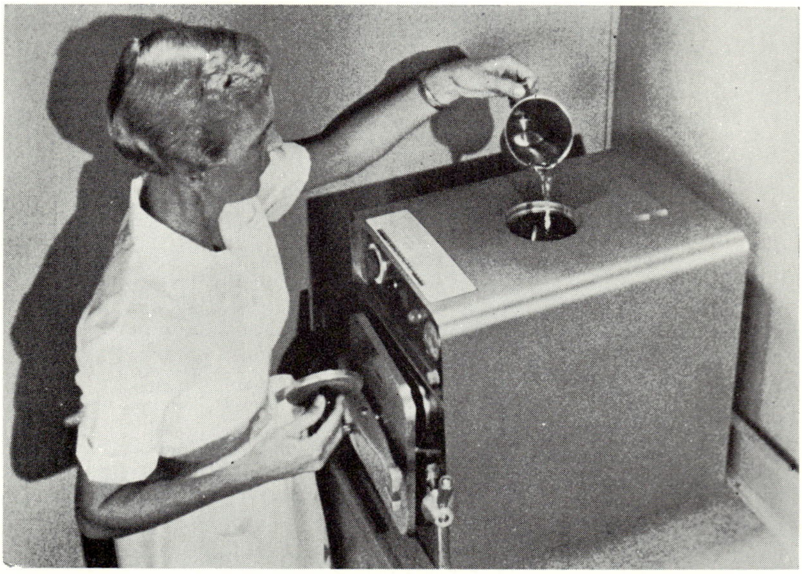

Fig. 27-1. Sterilization by autoclave method. (Courtesy Wyeth Laboratories, Philadelphia, Pennsylvania.)

arate rinse of fresh water is prepared. The instruments then are thoroughly brushed, with particular attention to serrated jaws, box locks, and other areas where oil, grease, or contamination may collect (Fig. 27-2). If instruments cannct be cleaned immediately, they should be kept in a solution containing an effective blood solvent. After thorough manual cleaning and rinsing in hot water, the instruments should then be checked for working condition. Such instruments should never be oiled, since lubricants may interfere with the sterilizing agent. After cleaning, the instruments will then be ready for wrapping and sterilization.

Cleaning syringes and needles. Reusable

Fig. 27-2. Cleaning syringes. (Courtesy Wyeth Laboratories, Philadelphia, Pennsylvania.)

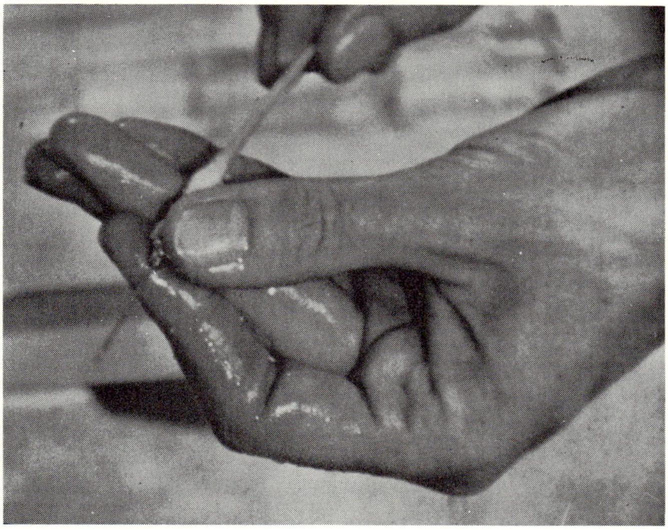

Fig. 27-3. Cleaning hub of a needle. (Courtesy Wyeth Laboratories, Philadelphia, Pennsylvania.)

syringes and needles are one of the most common means for transmission of serum hepatitis. Because of this, the use of disposable needles and plastic syringes have largely replaced reusable syringes and needles in most offices. If used, reusable syringes should always be rinsed immediately after use to prevent coagulation of materials in the syringe and needle. The syringe is filled with tap water, and the water is ejected through the needle. The contaminated needles are placed in a separate tray, and the syringe is filled with detergent or blood solvent. Then, to prevent infection of the operator, needles should be placed in the sterilizer for 30 minutes at 250° F. to sterilize them and render them safe for handling by the operator. Then, in water containing a low-sudsing, nonetching detergent, the interior of the syringe barrel is thoroughly brushed (Fig. 27-3).

The inside of the tip is also cleaned to remove possible foreign matter or contamination. The syringe plunger, of course, must also be thoroughly brushed. A tray of distilled water is then prepared. The components are flushed twice in tap water and once in distilled water. After the final rinse in distilled water, the syringes are then ready for wrapping and final sterilization.

When hypodermic needles are to be cleaned after having been contaminated, the inside of the needle hub is first carefully swabbed with a cotton applicator in water containing a blood solvent or detergent. Then a stylet is repeatedly passed through the interior of the needle to remove any tissue or foreign matter. The point of the needle is then carefully checked. If it is dull or damaged, it must be sharpened properly and recleaned completely before being sterilized. Next, being careful not to dull or damage the point, the exterior of the needle is also cleaned. The hub and outside of the needle are rinsed under running tap water; then the interior of the needle is flushed by ejecting tap water through it twice with a syringe. The procedure is repeated with distilled water to assure that all residual detergent is removed. The needle is then ready for wrapping and sterilization. The need for this lengthy procedure has been greatly reduced with the use of disposable syringes. It is still used when caring for special needles and syringes used in surgical procedures and in lumbar punctures.

Cleaning rubber goods. Rubber goods, such as drainage tubes, catheters, and gloves, also must be cleaned thoroughly before sterilization (Fig. 27-4). Rubber gloves, for example, should be washed in cold water immediately after use to remove particles of dry blood or other gross soil. A closable, waterproof receptacle should be used for storage of soiled gloves in the treatment room. Gloves should then be thoroughly washed in warm water containing a low-sudsing detergent. The glove is turned inside out and the process repeated. After washing, the glove should be rinsed thoroughly in fresh tap water to remove all detergent. The gloves are filled with water and inspected for punctures or unremoved soil. After inspection, the gloves are ready for drying. If air drying is used, the exposed surface will first be allowed to dry; then the glove must be turned to expose the inner surface for drying.

Technique of wrapping instruments. The next step before actual sterilization is wrapping of instruments or supplies in protective coverings. Materials such as clean muslin or disposable paper are used because they can be penetrated by steam but not by surface or airborne contaminants during handling and storage. The method for wrapping will be similar for instruments and supplies such as dressings or dry goods. Hinged instruments such as hemostats must always be opened.

All items are placed in the center, and the material is folded up from the bottom, doubling back a small corner. The right and then the left edges are folded over again, leaving the corners doubled back. The pack is folded up from the bottom and secured with pressure-sensitive tape and is then dated and labeled according to its

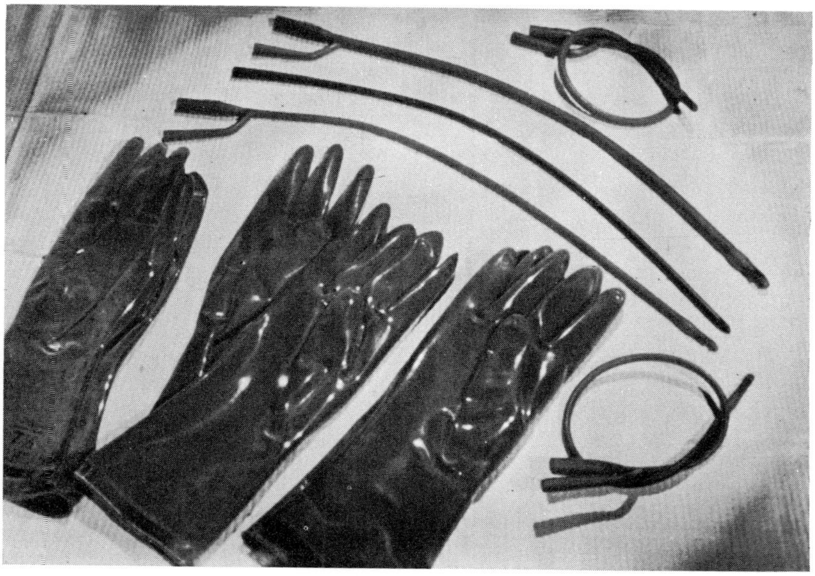

Fig. 27-4. Typical rubber goods to be cleaned. (Courtesy Wyeth Laboratories, Philadelphia, Pennsylvania.)

contents. The pack should be firm enough for handling but loose enough to permit proper circulation of steam. The materials included in each pack can be varied to suit the needs of each office, but the same wrapping pattern should be followed for all packs.

If instruments must be used immediately, they may be sterilized in trays without individual wrapping. Clean muslin or similar material is placed over the bottom of the perforated tray, and the instruments are positioned neatly. The material is folded over the instruments, and the tray is placed directly in the sterilizer.

Reusable syringes can best be wrapped in disposable paper wrappers, while needles may be sterilized individually in constriction tubes with cotton stoppers or in disposable paper forms when wrapped in envelopes with syringes. When syringes are to be wrapped, the envelope is first dated and labeled as to syringe size. Then the matched syringe and plunger are placed loosely inside. The envelope is folded securely, sealed, and placed in the tray horizontally. This allows steam to circulate more freely inside the syringe barrel.

If the needle is to be sterilized with the syringe, disposable paper forms should be used to protect the point and to provide a means for sterile handling of the needle when preparing an injection. Such forms provide better protection than gauze or cotton needle covers. Also, they prevent the needle from piercing the syringe envelope when placed inside (Fig. 27-5).

Needles may be sterilized individually in glass tubes with constricted sides, using gauze or cotton stoppers. Such tubes must be placed on their sides in trays to allow circulation of steam inside the tube.

When dried rubber gloves are to be wrapped, they should first be powdered with a nonirritating starch preparation. Then, using paper or gauze to separate the rubber surfaces from contact, the cuffs of the powdered gloves are folded over. The inside, or palm, is also held open by paper or gauze to allow free circulation of steam. The same procedure is repeated for both gloves. The gloves are positioned with the thumbs pointing away from the center, and the wrapper folded neatly to protect the gloves from contamination. An alternate method is the use of glove envelopes that

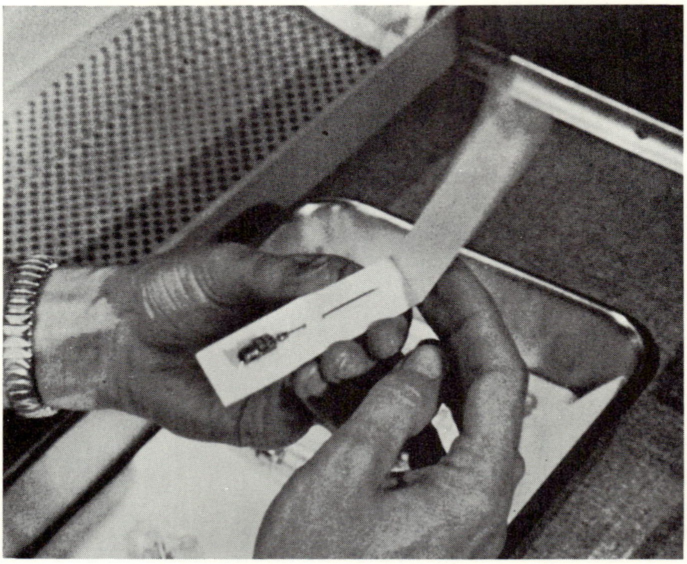

Fig. 27-5. Proper method of wrapping needle for sterilization. (Courtesy Wyeth Laboratories, Philadelphia, Pennsylvania.)

require an inner and outer wrapper. After the wrapper has been secured and labeled, the packets can then be placed in the sterilizer with the folded edges up. This will position the gloves so that steam can replace air in the thumbs for effective sterilization.

In some offices a small indicator is placed with the tools to be sterilized. This indicator will change color when adequate temperatures for sterilization have been reached. It serves as a check to determine if sterilization has been adequate.

Positioning loads in the autoclave. Proper positioning is important for all instruments and materials because of the pattern steam follows as it circulates through the autoclave. When the sterilizing cycle is begun, steam builds up at the top of the chamber, moving downward from the point of admission. Cool, dry air is forced downward and out an exhaust drain at the bottom front of the chamber. Therefore materials must be placed in the autoclave so that steam can penetrate along natural corridors or planes between and within packs. It is also necessary to avoid forming pockets in which air cannot drain out. Such air pockets prevent contact of the steam with all surfaces, and sterilization failure may result. Instead, utensils and similar objects should be positioned so that cool air can drain out in a downward direction to be replaced by steam.

When steam is in direct contact with all surfaces, 15 minutes at 250° F. is sufficient to kill all known microorganisms. In practice, however, longer periods are required to achieve such exposure. For fully wrapped surgical instruments, 30 minutes at 250° to 254° F. allows adequate time for sterilization with a satisfactory margin of safety. Hypodermic syringes and needles should be sterilized 30 minutes at 250° to 254° F. This minimum should never be compromised, since needles and syringes are one of the most common offenders in transmitting the virus of serum hepatitis.

Rubber goods should be sterilized for 20 minutes at 250° F. to avoid heat damage to the rubber. But all such loads must be properly spaced for full circulation of steam. Uncovered utensils, glassware, and similar items, if inverted or placed on edge, can be sterilized in 15 minutes at 250° F. When unwrapped instruments are sterilized in trays covered with muslin, 20 minutes at 250° F. is adequate for sterilization. These times may vary if paper or other fabric wrappers are used. Therefore correct exposure data must be obtained from suppliers of such materials to assure observance of adequate exposure periods. For all loads the exposure period must be timed after the sterilizer has come up to the proper temperature. Because temperature, not pressure, is the sterilizing influence, the thermometer in the autoclave and the temperature selection gauge should be checked frequently to ensure that sterilizing conditions have been reached in the chamber.

Removing loads from the sterilizer. At the end of the sterilizing period, the first step in removal of sterile materials is to exhaust steam pressure from the chamber. When the temperature has decreased to 212° F., and the pressure within the chamber reaches 0, the door of the sterilizer may be opened slightly. Care must be taken to avoid steam burns to the hands and face. Many modern autoclaves have eliminated the need for these steps by automatically carrying the sterilization process through a full cycle that includes drying. If this type of autoclave is not available, the load should be allowed to dry approximately 15 minutes before being removed. If materials have been wrapped in paper or muslin packs, they can be removed by an operator with clean, dry hands.

Storing sterile goods. Specific storage places should be established for each instrument or type of supply; the area should be away from areas where contaminated materials are handled. Sterile materials should be stored in clean, dustproof drawers or cabinets that are used only for dry, sterile goods. In well-protected, dust-free areas, properly wrapped materials can safely be stored for four weeks. After four weeks all packs should be reprocessed and resterilized before using. If instruments are sterilized loosely in trays, they must not be stored, but should remain covered and should be used immediately.

Let us now summarize steam sterilization before we discuss other matters.

1. All materials must be properly cleaned before sterilization.
2. They must be adequately wrapped or covered to protect them from recontamination.
3. They must be properly positioned in the sterilizer to allow contact with steam at all surfaces.
4. They must be exposed to saturated steam at 250° F. for 20 to 30 minutes.
5. After sterilization, materials must be allowed to dry before removal from the sterilizer.
6. All sterilized goods must be stored in clean, dustproof areas where they can be considered to remain sterile for four weeks.

Other methods of sterilization

Chemical sterilization (Fig. 27-6). In some instances, chemical germicides from reliable suppliers may be used to sterilize heat-sensitive materials. Items such as nonboilable sutures or delicate cutting instruments can be sterilized in strong formaldehyde and alcohol solution, provided they are completely immersed and exposed for three hours or more, depending upon the strength of the germicide. If instruments have been carefully cleaned and adequately exposed, such formaldehyde and alcohol solutions will destroy viruses and bacteria, including spore-forming types. Because such germicides are often toxic, instruments must be rinsed in fresh isopropyl alcohol or sterile distilled water before they are used.

Chemical disinfection procedures

There are, of course, many medical and dental procedures that do not require the use of sterile technique. Instruments and supplies used in contact with the outer skin or for shallow insertion into the body orifices can be safely disinfected, since they do not bypass the body's natural defenses. In disinfecting such objects, the surface is thoroughly washed, as with sterilization pro-

Fig. 27-6. Chemical sterilization. (Courtesy Wyeth Laboratories, Philadelphia, Pennsylvania.)

cedures. Then the instrument is thoroughly rinsed and dried, and its surface is disinfected by topical application of approximately 90% isopropyl alcohol or comparable germicidal solutions. Since the activity of alcohol drops sharply below 70%, fresh alcohol must be used to assure adequate strength. One hundred percent ethyl alcohol is a relatively poor disinfectant while a 70% solution is a good one. Other instruments such as percussion hammers or stethoscopes may also be safely disinfected by topical application of fresh isopropyl alcohol or similar antiseptics (Fig. 27-7).

Boiling water is another disinfectant method although it cannot be considered adequate for sterilization since it does not eliminate the danger of hepatitis infection or contamination with certain spore-forming bacteria. Consequently, boiling water should be used only for disinfection of instruments and supplies that do not penetrate into body tissues. With instruments that may be disinfected by this method, the basic steps are: proper cleaning to remove oil, grease, or other soil; complete immersion in the boiling water; and exposure for not less than 15 minutes after the water has reached the boiling point. When the cycle has been completed, the disinfectant instruments are then ready for use.

These disinfection procedures, applied to appropriate instruments and supplies, are adequate and useful in controlling many common forms of microbial life. But their limitations must be recognized. Disinfection must not be used as a substitute for sterilization. With known or suspected infectious cases, all materials should be sterilized rather than disinfected. But the presence of infectious organisms is often unknown. Millions of individuals carry the virus of hepatitis with no readily apparent symptoms. Some are in your community, where they receive routine medical treatment and unknowingly leave behind the cause for serious illness among the patients who follow. The spread of serum hepatitis and numerous harmful organisms can be prevented only through proper sterilization of reusable supplies or through the use of presterilized materials, such as the disposable injection systems, gloves, blades, and other items that are discarded after use, which cannot cross-infect patients. The importance of sterilization can sometimes be obscured by the

Fig. 27-7. Simple disinfection method of sterilization. (Courtesy Wyeth Laboratories, Philadelphia, Pennsylvania.)

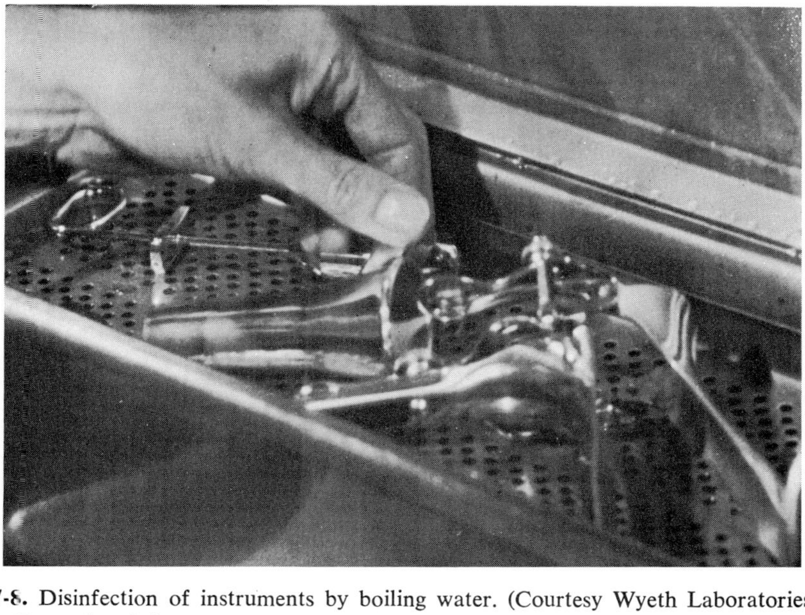

Fig. 27-8. Disinfection of instruments by boiling water. (Courtesy Wyeth Laboratories, Philadelphia, Pennsylvania.)

welter of tasks that must be performed in the busy medical office. Yet few procedures more directly affect the continued health of the patients you and your doctor serve. Because of that dependence, sterilization methods in the medical office should be periodically reexamined for their adequacy and must always receive conscientious attention from the individual who performs them.

Review questions

1. Name three methods for reducing microbial contamination of medical equipment.
2. What are the best methods of sterilizing glassware, instruments, and rubber gloves?
3. Why do disposable syringes and needles eliminate the hazard of cross-infection?
4. How would you properly clean a syringe and needle?
5. When is chemical sterilization indicated?

Suggested readings

Anderson, D. A.: Introduction to microbiology, St. Louis, 1973, The C. V. Mosby Co.

Perkins, J. J.: Principles and methods of sterilization in health sciences, ed. 2, Springfield, Ill., 1970, Charles C Thomas, Publisher.

chapter 28
Hypodermic injection technique

Giving injections is a serious and important part of medical treatment. In a very real sense the same kind of preparation and caution employed in an operating procedure must be exercised in giving injections. Two foreign objects, a hypodermic needle and the medication, are being introduced into the body, and this should be done with as much precision as a surgeon employs when using a scalpel. The accuracy of the choice of injection site and the excellence of injection technique help control the effectiveness of the medication. A misdirected injection or improper technique in administering the injection may prevent medication from acting most efficiently or, more important, may cause irreparable damage.

A physician orders an injection for a patient only when it is absolutely necessary or if it is the manner of treatment most suited to the existing circumstances. Some of the reasons and advantages for giving injections of medication (also referred to as parenteral therapy) are:

1. To administer medication when the mental or physical state of the patient makes any other route difficult or impossible
2. To achieve a quick response to the medication
3. To guarantee the accuracy of the amount of medication received
4. To obtain a sure response from the patient
5. To prevent irritation of the digestive system, loss of medication through involuntary ejection, or destruction by digestive acids
6. To anesthetize a specific area of the body
7. To concentrate medication at a specific location in the body

A hypodermic injection requires skillful technique, and it is often necessary for the medical assistant to give one. Diabetic children and adults who must take insulin are taught by doctors and nurses in hospitals and clinics to give this medicine to themselves by hypodermic injection. The medicines given in this way are usually given in small quantities and act much more quickly than when taken by mouth. The greatest care must be exercised to give the

---

Glossary

abscess a localized collection of pus in any part of the body
acromion the part of the scapula that connects with the clavicle
aspirate to remove or draw out by suction
brachial pertaining to blood vessels or nerves that supply the arm
clavicle collarbone; a bone curved like the letter *s* that connects the sternum and scapula
deltoid a muscle in the upper lateral arm
intradermal into the skin
intramuscular into a muscle
intravenous into a vein
PPD a commonly used skin test for tuberculosis
prone the position of lying horizontal with the face downward
scalpel a surgical knife
stylet a slender piece of metal for making permanent a canal after operation or for stiffening or clearing a cannula or catheter; a thin probe
subcutaneous beneath the level of the skin

exact amount ordered and to make no mistake in giving the correct drug. The equipment, its sterilization, and the important points to remember are practically the same in giving any hypodermic injection under the skin, although the medicines used may be in the form of tablets or liquid in sealed ampules or vials.

DISPOSING OF INJECTION MATERIALS

Discard any syringes and needles properly. Careless disposal of needles creates a major hepatitis hazard to those handling office trash. In some offices needles are broken off in special containers designed for this purpose. The tip of disposable syringes should be bent or crushed to make the syringe inoperable. It must be remembered that syringes and needles of any type are much sought after by drug addicts and drug abusers and must therefore be disposed of properly. It is the practice in some offices to dispose of syringes and needles separate from the usual office trash.

SUBCUTANEOUS INJECTION

Equipment

Syringes. Syringes are used with sterile precautions. They are usually of a disposable plastic type but may be reusable, sterilized glass syringes. They are supplied in 1-, 3-, 5- and 10-cc sizes. They also may be graduated for measuring insulin. The 1-cc tuberculin syringe is graduated to the hundredth of a cubic centimeter; it is used where a very fine measure is essential. Many syringes have either a plain tip on which the needle fits or are of the Luer-Lok variety (Fig. 28-1). There are some advantages to both types.

Needles. Needles are chosen with consideration for the proper length and width. They may be ½ inch, ¾ inch, 1 inch, 1½ inches, and so on. Gauge of the needle is designated by the number that is usually on the needle wrapper. The larger the gauge of the needle, the smaller its lumen or width. An 18-gauge needle has a large lumen whereas a 25-gauge needle has a much smaller lumen.

Disposable needles have almost totally replaced reusable needles. Under no circumstances may a needle be used on more than one patient without prior sterilization.

Antiseptic. Some sort of antiseptic to clean the skin is needed. The most commonly used is 70% ethyl or isopropyl alcohol. These may be applied with a cotton

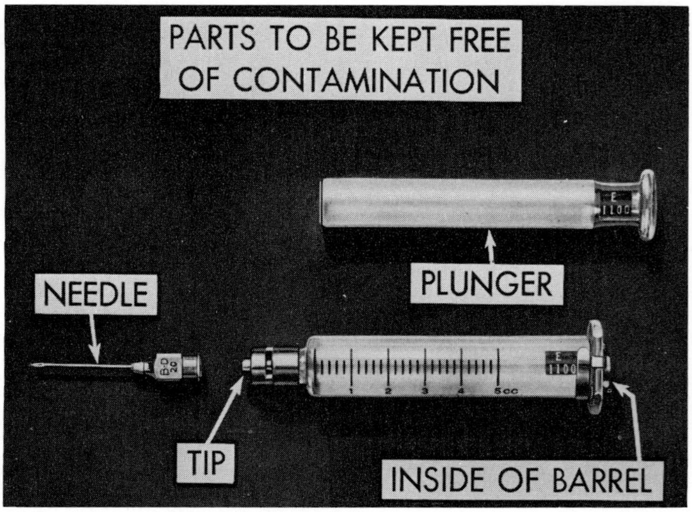

Fig. 28-1. Luer-Lok hypodermic syringe. (Courtesy Becton, Dickinson & Co., Rutherford, New Jersey.)

ball but it has become more convenient to use foil-wrapped antiseptic sponges impregnated with an alcohol solution.

Medication. If medication must be dissolved, have sterile water or saline at hand. Medication must be calculated exactly. Dosage should be dissolved so that the total amount of solution is between 0.5 and 1 ml, if possible. If a tablet is to be dissolved, a sterile field should be provided so that the tablet will not have to be handled. The drug is drawn into the syringe from the sterile bottle, vial, or ampule. Measure accurately. Check to be sure that the needle is securely fixed on the syringe to avoid possible waste of the drug. With the needle pointing upward, air is ejected from the syringe. It is wise to re-cover the disposable needle with its cover if it is carried any distance or if the drug is not to be administered immediately. The drugs to be administered should never be prepared in view of an anxious patient.

Administration

1. Cleanse the skin by rubbing with the alcohol sponge on a small circular area.
2. Hold the needle and syringe as you would hold a pencil and at about a 30- to 45-degree angle to the skin. Check to see that air bubbles have been ejected.
3. Grasp the skin between the thumb and forefinger on the left hand, raising a triangular fold.
4. Holding the syringe in the right hand, insert the needle through the skin at the base of the fold with a quick movement, holding the skin firm (Fig. 28-2).
5. Pull back on the plunger to ascertain that the needle has not entered a blood vessel. If no blood returns, the needle is not in a vein. If blood returns, remove the needle being careful not to inject any fluid. A new injection must then be prepared since injecting blood into the subcutaneous tissues may produce pain and discoloration at the injection site (Fig. 28-3).
6. Inject the medication and pull out the

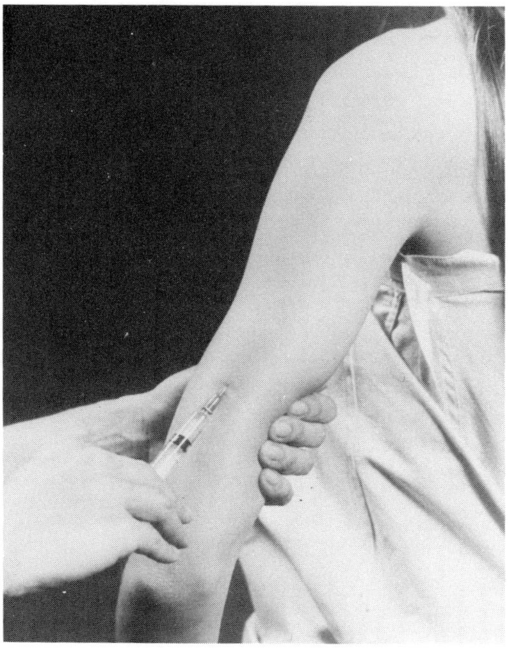

Fig. 28-2. Method of giving a subcutaneous injection. (Courtesy Pharmaseal Laboratories, Glendale, California.)

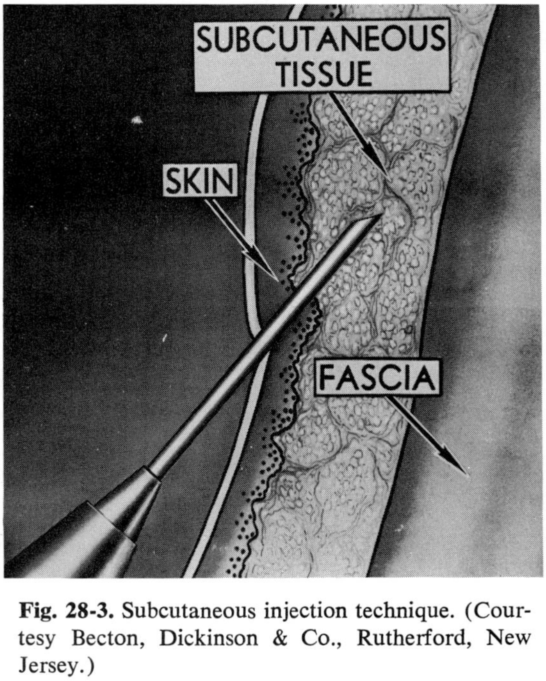

Fig. 28-3. Subcutaneous injection technique. (Courtesy Becton, Dickinson & Co., Rutherford, New Jersey.)

needle. Pressure is applied for several seconds with an alcohol sponge or until no blood flows from the injection site.

7. Discard the syringe and needle properly. If reusable syringes and needles are used, they must be rinsed properly after each use and prepared for initial sterilization.

Subcutaneous injections should be given in fleshy areas of the body to avoid the possibility of striking bones, large blood vessels, and nerves. Choose a site in which the blood supply is good, in which there is not too much subcutaneous fat, and at which a slight sore spot following the injection will not cause undue discomfort. The outer side of the upper arm or thigh is most commonly used. A different spot should be chosen each time if the injections are given frequently.

Cautions to observe when giving subcutaneous injections

Under some conditions, the tissues are very susceptible to infection, and unless a subcutaneous injection is given with strict attention to the sterilizing solution, syringe, needle, and skin and administered without contamination, an abscess may follow. An unsterile needle, a needle with a blunt point that would tear the tissues, or carelessness in cleaning the skin with alcohol may be the cause of an abscess.

INTRAMUSCULAR INJECTIONS

Intramuscular injections are given when a quick but prolonged action is preferred to an immediate effect of short duration. By injecting medication into the muscle, a deposit of medicine is formed, which is gradually absorbed into the bloodstream. Muscle tissue has a better blood supply than subcutaneous tissue, and the danger of an unabsorbed accumulation of drugs is avoided. When given properly, the intramuscular injection is probably the easiest, safest, and best tolerated of the several types of injections.

Medications for many intramuscular injections are in an aqueous solution or in a suspension, and a few are in an oil solution or suspenison. When suspensions or oil solutions are given, it is generally necessary to give them at a slower rate because of the thicker fluids.

Drugs given intramuscularly

All drugs in oil suspensions. Oily suspension is usually prepared to slow down the absorption and make the drug effective over a longer period of time. If not given in the muscular tissue where the blood supply is good, it might not be absorbed at all. Drugs that separate on standing should be shaken.

Drugs mixed with heavy metals. Drugs that are mixed with heavy metals (notably zinc and alum) to slow absorption are administered intramuscularly. Toxoids are usually given in this manner.

Very irritating drugs. Liver extracts, penicillin, streptomycin, and vitamins are good examples. If the drug is not absorbed thoroughly, the tissue may be very irritated, and a sterile abscess, or at least a great deal of discomfort, may develop.

Large doses of any drugs. Drugs in amounts of 2 ml and over are given intramuscularly. Again, prompt and complete absorption is necessary to prevent damage to the tissue.

Selection of site

The upper outer quadrant of the buttocks is the best site (Fig. 28-4). Here the muscle tissue is deep enough to permit the injection of fairly large amounts of material without danger of trauma to tissue. Any discomfort that may follow the injection is usually not too troublesome in this area. The muscle tissue is deep enough to protect the underlying bone and avoid striking the bone with a needle. Occasionally the injection may be given deep in the deltoid muscle of a well-developed patient. This area may be used for medications that are not too irritating or for an occasional injection where the discomfort may be less in this area. For further information on selection of site, see Figs. 28-5 and 28-6.

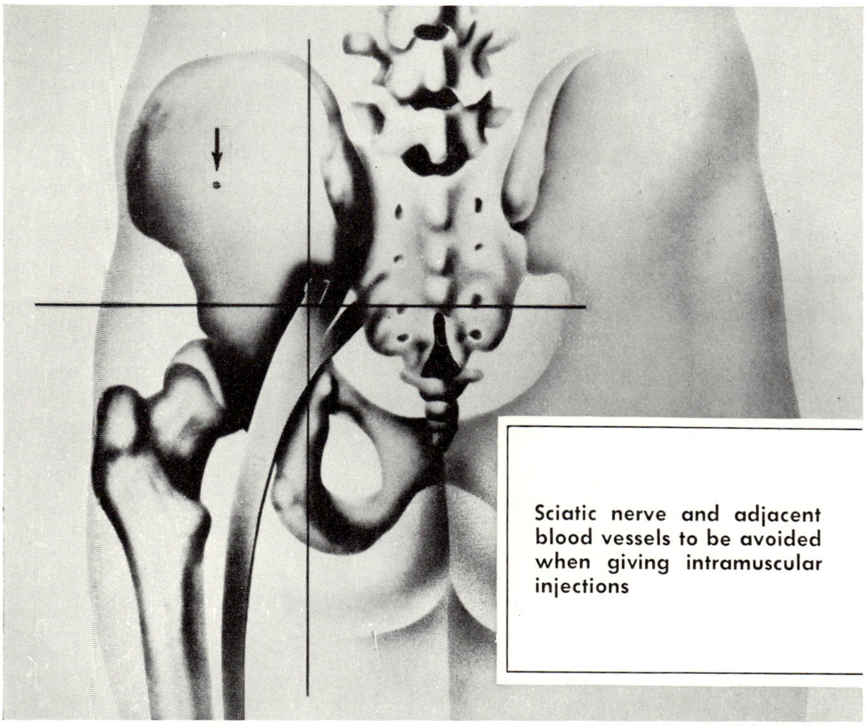

Fig. 28-4. Cautions to observe when giving intramuscular injections. (Courtesy Becton, Dickinson & Co., Rutherford, New Jersey.)

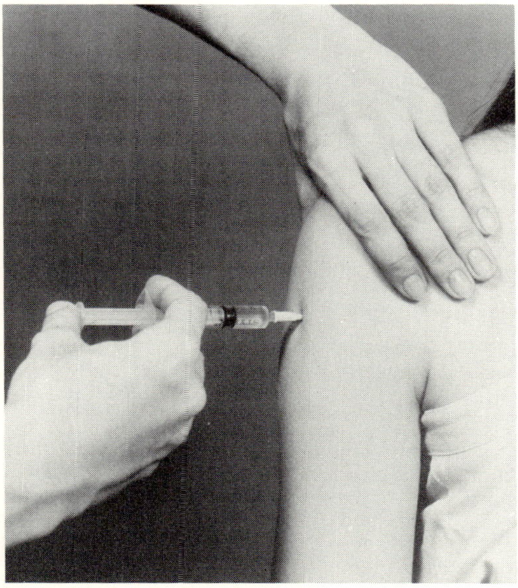

Fig. 28-5. Intramuscular injection—the middeltoid area. (Courtesy Pharmaseal Laboratories, Glendale, California.)

Equipment

The skin is prepared for a subcutaneous injection. A syringe is chosen to correspond with the amount of medication to be given. A 2-cc or 5-cc syringe will usually be large enough. A needle 1½ inches in length should be long enough to penetrate the muscle; 20 or 23 gauge should be large enough to permit the medication to flow through.

Procedure

1. Wash hands.
2. Assemble sterile syringe and needle.
3. Open ampule; swab rubber stopper if it is a multiple-dose ampule.
4. Insert needle and draw out proper amount. Injecting an equal amount of air into the ampule aids in withdrawing medication. If it is a heavy oil, it may be drawn into syringe with a large-gauge needle to save time. If medication

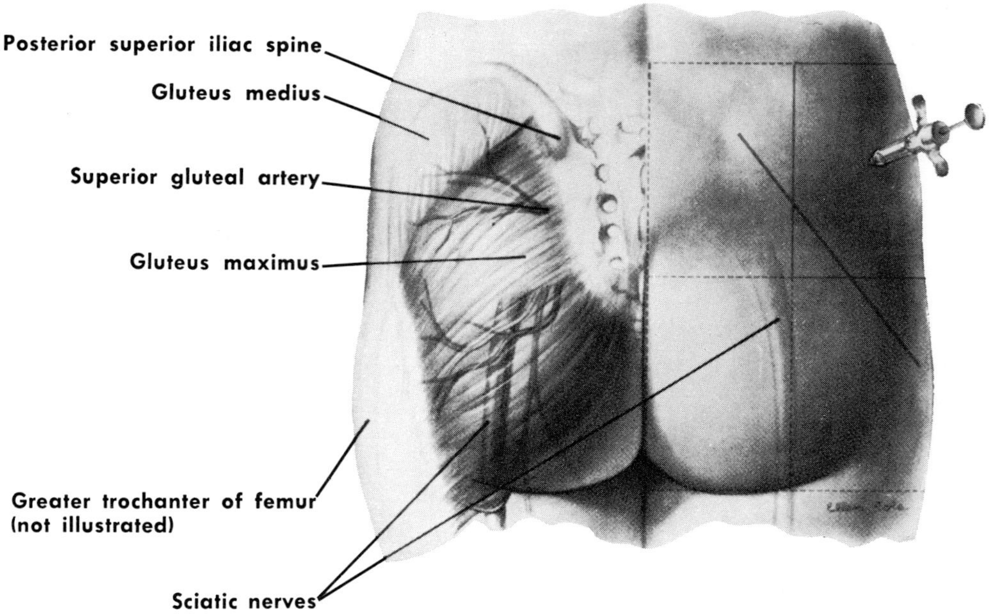

Fig. 28-6. Intramuscular injection—the gluteus area. (Courtesy Wyeth Laboratories, Philadelphia, Pennsylvania.)

is in powder form and must be mixed with solution, check literature to ascertain proper solvent and amount.

5. Wipe needle and check amount of drug and name of medication; if medication is prepared and set aside for any reason, for identification mark with name and amount and leave ampule beside it until it is given.
6. Explain the treatment to the patient. If the patient is warned when to expect to feel the needle and that the medication may burn, if such is the case, he is less likely to jump, thus pulling away and possibly breaking the needle.
7. Intramuscular medications are best given with the patient lying on his abdomen on a table or a bed. This relaxes the muscles and reduces the pain of the injection. A spot is chosen on the buttocks in the upper outer quadrant. This injection technique minimizes the chance that the patient might inadvertently jump when stuck with a needle. It also minimizes the danger of the patient fainting after the injection and falling on the floor.
8. Using an alcohol sponge or swab, cleanse an area approximately two inches square on and around the proposed injection site.
9. With the thumb and index finger of the left hand, spread or tense the skin in the injection area.
10. Holding the syringe like a dart or pencil, plunge the needle firmly and quickly into the site chosen at a right angle to the skin.
11. Once the surface of the skin has been punctured by the needle, the remainder of the penetration of the needle through the skin and into the muscle should be with a firm and steady pressure. In the case of average weight or heavy patients it is preferable to retain the pressure on the skin around the injection site with the thumb and index finger of the left hand for the entire time the needle is being inserted. In thin patients, it is often preferable to release the pressure of the left hand once the punc-

ture has been made and change to a slight pinching grip in order to firm the injection site and avoid the possibility of going too deep and striking a bone, nerve, or blood vessel.

12. Once the desired depth of insertion has been reached, steady the syringe tip with the left hand and with the right hand pull back or out on the plunger approximately one-quarter inch for a few seconds to see if any blood can be aspirated back into the syringe. This is especially important if you are giving heavy metals or oils. Should blood appear in the syringe, the needle should be withdrawn and a new injection site selected.
13. If no blood appears, the position of the fingers on the right hand can be shifted so that the thumb covers the head of the plunger and the index and middle fingers are hooked under the side grips on the syringe barrel. With a firm pressure on the thumb move the plunger downward into the syringe as far as it will go. In giving large amounts, inject more slowly to give the muscle tissue a chance to adjust to the distention by the fluid. In children inject rapidly, as they may move and dislodge the needle.
14. After the medication has been injected, apply pressure against the injection site with the alcohol sponge in the left hand as the needle is withdrawn by the right hand; this reduces the risk of medication leaking into the subcutaneous tissues and possibly forming abscesses.
15. Cleanse the injection site by massaging the area with the sponge to remove any blood or medication that might be present. If rapid absorption is desired, the massaging should be continued for about two minutes. If a small amount of bleeding occurs, this will usually be relieved by firm pressure with a fairly dry sponge for a moment or two. If a small amount of oozing persists, apply a bandage firmly to protect patient's clothing; this may be done routinely in many offices.
16. Undrape patient and help him to get ready to leave if necessary. Most physicians suggest that after penicillin or antibiotic injection patients should wait one-half hour in the office before leaving. Most anaphylactic reactions will occur during this period.
17. Disposable syringes and needles are handled as previously described. Reusable syringes and needles require more extensive care. Wash syringe thoroughly. Oily solutions may require some benzine or ether; be sure to rinse thoroughly. Place in sterilizer or container to await sterilization. Stylet needles to prevent stoppage. The heavy oily drugs will be easier to inject and also easier to get out of the syringe if dry syringes are used. Boiled syringes permitted to dry overnight in a sterile container will be fairly dry for use the next day. If alcohol is used for sterilization, rinse with water before using.
18. After the injection has been given, it is important that all the information be recorded on the patient's chart. This should include: the hour of injection, name of the medication, amount and strength, method of administration, specific site including which side of the body, any unusual reaction, and your signature. No injection is complete until this information has been recorded.

Intramuscular injection sites

Mid-deltoid area. A site often chosen for its ease of access is the deltoid area, which can be employed when the patient is in either standing, sitting, or prone position. While the deltoid muscle forms a fairly large triangle on the shoulder prominence, the actual area available to a shoulder injection is limited, since there are major bones, blood vessels, and nerves to be avoided. The recommended boundaries of the injection area form a rectangle bounded by the lower edge of the acromion on the top to a point on the lateral side of the arm opposite the axilla or armpit on the bottom. The two side boundaries are lines parallel to the arm one third and two thirds of the way around the outer lateral aspect of the arm.

Care should be taken to avoid not only the acromion, clavicle, and humerus but also the brachial veins and arteries and the radial nerve. It is recommended that the number and size of injections made at this site be limited. The area is small and cannot tolerate repeated injections and large quantities of medication.

Gluteus medius. Perhaps the most commonly used site for muscular injections is the posterior gluteus medius, a muscle located in the buttocks. Each buttock may be divided into quarters, or quadrants. Injections are usually given in the upper, outer quadrant. The other quadrants contain numerous blood vessels and nerves that may be damaged by intramuscular injection.

The patient should be lying face down with the injection site clearly exposed. Under no circumstances should there be any compromise with correct technique. Do not hurry, and do not let modesty tempt you to give this injection to a person who is bending over a table or whose clothing is only partially removed from the injection site. As a general rule the gluteal area is incompletely developed in infants and small children. It is therefore not considered to be the site of choice for this age group.

INTRAVENOUS INJECTIONS

Medical assistants are not usually expected to give medication intravenously. This route of administration is reserved for hospital use, administration of intravenous fluids, and emergency drugs. It should be given only by a licensed nurse or a physician.

INTRADERMAL ADMINISTRATION OF MEDICATIONS

The technique of intradermal diagnostic tests requires a production of two wheals, one for the test and one for the control, preferably with one on each arm. Intradermal injections are as a rule used for diagnostic purposes such as tuberculin skin testing and testing for allergies of various types.

Equipment

Syringe. Tuberculin syringe is used, as fine calibrations are needed.

Needles. Sharp fine needles are required. Each patient tested requires a new needle. Needles of 25 or 26 gauge may be purchased, which greatly facilitate work.

Skin preparation. Alcohol, Zephiran, or other preparations may be used. Acetone and ether are frequently used because they remove the skin oils well and dry rapidly, avoiding contamination of the drug.

Procedure

The inner side of the forearm is usually chosen if only a few intradermal tests are to be made. If multiple tests are to be made, the skin of the back may be used; this area is usually used for patch tests, however. Skin of the upper outer arm is also frequently used.

After the usual preparation of the syringe and needle and drawing the medication into the syringes, the skin is prepared. It is important that the skin be dry when the needle is inserted, or some of the skin preparation material may be carried on the needle and may result in a false reaction to the test. The medication must be measured very accurately.

The needle is inserted at an almost parallel angle between the layers of skin just under the epidermis (Fig. 28-7). It is inserted to the depth of the bevel or until the bevel is just under the epidermis. Care must be taken that the tip of the needle does not go into the underlying dermis, or the reaction will not be reliable. A short-beveled needle facilitates giving this type of injection. There is usually little or no bleeding; bleeding in any amount signifies an imperfect test.

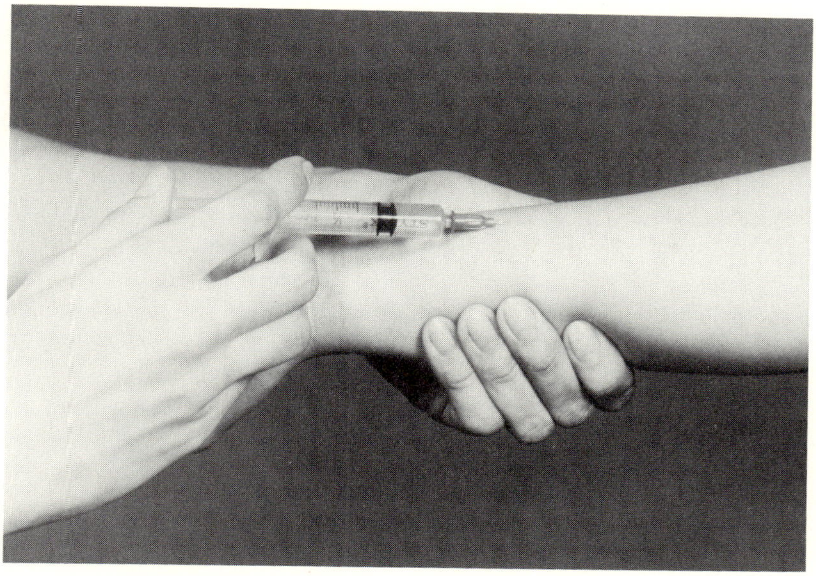

Fig. 28-7. Intradermal injection technique. (Courtesy Pharmaseal Laboratories, Glendale, California.)

This type of injection requires no aspiration. The medication is injected rather slowly in order to separate the two layers of skin and avoid leakage of the drug around the needle. A small wheal will rise at the point of needle insertion.

Remove the needle by applying very gentle pressure over the point of insertion. Too much pressure may result in leakage of the medication through the site of puncture. Do not massage. If the wheal does not rise as the medication is injected and if no medication can be seen leaking out on the skin, the needle has probably been inserted too deeply, and the test may be repeated at a different location in most cases.

It is very important that skin testing material be kept scrupulously clean, as contamination of an injection by some residual material from a previous injection will render the test valueless.

If several skin tests are given, it is imparative that a record of the site of injection of each be kept so that there will be no confusion in the reading of the tests.

The time of reading of the skin test will vary with the tests done, and information may usually be secured from the literature that will accompany the drug. Tuberculin skin tests are read at 24 to 48 hours while most skin tests for allergy will be read within 20 minutes. Reading the test requires that a comparison with the control be made whenever a control injection is used. Tests may be read as positive or negative or, in some cases, the assistant should carefully measure and record the area of erythema (redness) or induration (hardening).

Other sensitivity tests

Scratch test. A superficial scarification is made, the medication is placed on the skin, and some of the material is absorbed through the scratches. This test is usually read in about 30 minutes and is used most commonly when a prompt reaction is needed (for instance, in determining a possible drug allergy).

Patch test. A small amount of the material to be tested is placed on the cleaned skin and a gauze and adhesive patch is applied to cover the area. If several tests are to be made, the skin of the back is most commonly used. A plain patch is used as a control. These tests are most commonly read in 24 hours, although the proper interval will be determined by the doctor. Patch tests are used commonly by allergists to determine sensitivity to various substances.

Conjunctival test. This test is made by dropping about 0.1 ml on the conjunctiva. In half an hour or less, redness, irritation, and engorgement of the blood vessels of the eye will result if the reaction is positive. A strongly positive reaction may be relieved by dropping a drop or two of Adrenalin in the eye after the test has been read.

Anaphylaxis

Anaphylaxis is a severe allergic reaction to a foreign substance, which may result in shock and death. Although it may occur after any drug, it most commonly occurs after penicillin or other antibiotic injection and after the administration of some vaccines that contain horse serum. Any patient receiving a drug made from horse serum should be tested to determine hypersensitivity. A careful history of allergy should be taken as well as direct questioning as to any previous medication of this type. Adrenalin should be immediately available when any medication containing horse serum is administered or when any patient with a history of allergy is skin tested or drugs are administered, particularly by the intravenous route. Less severe reactions include mild itching, urticaria, angioneurotic edema, asthma, and serum sickness.

Other complications in parenteral administration of drugs

Allergic reactions. Physicians vary in their instructions to medical assistants on the handling of allergic reactions. It is important that the assistant know what treatment the doctor wishes administered if an allergic reaction should occur. Before injecting any medication, the assistant should tactfully question the patient as to a history of a previous reaction to that or any other drug. Any allergic reactions should be plainly and prominently marked on the patient's record since a repeated administration of the medication may cause a more severe reaction and could even possibly result in the patient's death. If any questions arise, the physician should be consulted before a drug is administered.

Abscess. A sterile abscess is usually caused by extreme irritation of the tissue by very irritating medication or too frequent injection in the same area. A septic abscess may result whenever there is any contamination of equipment or drug.

Breakage of needles. Breakage of needles should be reported promptly. Have patient remain in position and mark site of injection with pen or pencil.

Cautions

1. Be sure all equipment is sterile.
2. Double-check the dosage measured; drugs given by hypodermic injection act fairly quickly, and once given they cannot be aspirated or removed.
3. In case of error in medication or accidental breakage of the needle, report promptly to the physician, who may take any necessary steps. Let the physician tell the patient whatever he thinks advisable.
4. If the procedure is explained to the patient before administration of the drug, you will usually avoid any sudden movement when the needle is inserted through the skin—such sudden movement when the needle is inserted through the skin may result in the needle being broken. Have good control over the patient when giving injections.
5. Use special syringes whenever indicated (insulin, and so forth).
6. Choose site of injection carefully, and indicate area injected so that it will not be used on next visit.
7. Check equipment carefully. Be sure that the needle is securely attached to the syringe.

8. Never administer in the eye any ointment or medication not definitely marked "ophthalmic."
9. Medications prepared for intravenous administration must be prepared with sterile, *triple-distilled* water only. Check label for contraindications to giving the drug by this route. All intravenous medications must be clear and of watery consistency.
10. Discard any drug that has altered in color or consistency or about which you may have any doubts. Check with the pharmacist about doubtful drugs.

The Tubex cartridge unit and the reusable syringe

A number of medications are prepared for administration with a prefilled sterile cartridge-needle unit. An example of this type of unit is the Tubex system. In instances where an empty Tubex sterile cartridge-needle unit is used, additional preparation is necessary. First, the empty syringe must be assembled. After the vial of medication has been selected and the seal sterilized with alcohol, the needle is then inserted through the seal, the plunger of the syringe is depressed to expel the air into the vial, and the correct amount of medication is withdrawn into the syringe. The needle is then withdrawn from the vial, and in the case of an empty Tubex sterile cartridge-needle unit, the rubber needle sheath is replaced in order to maintain sterility.

Preparation for injection with prefilled Tubex sterile cartridge-needle unit

(Fig. 28-8)

1. Select the Tubex unit required.
2. To load the Tubex hypodermic syringe, grasp barrel of syringe in one hand. With the other hand, pull back firmly on plunger and swing the entire handle section downward so that it locks at right angle to the barrel.
3. Insert Tubex sterile cartridge-needle unit needle end first into the barrel. Engage needle ferrule by rotating it clockwise in the threads at front end of syringe.
4. Swing plunger back into place and attach end to the threaded shaft of the piston. Hold the syringe barrel with one hand and rotate plunger until both ends of Tubex sterile cartridge-needle unit are fully but lightly engaged. To maintain

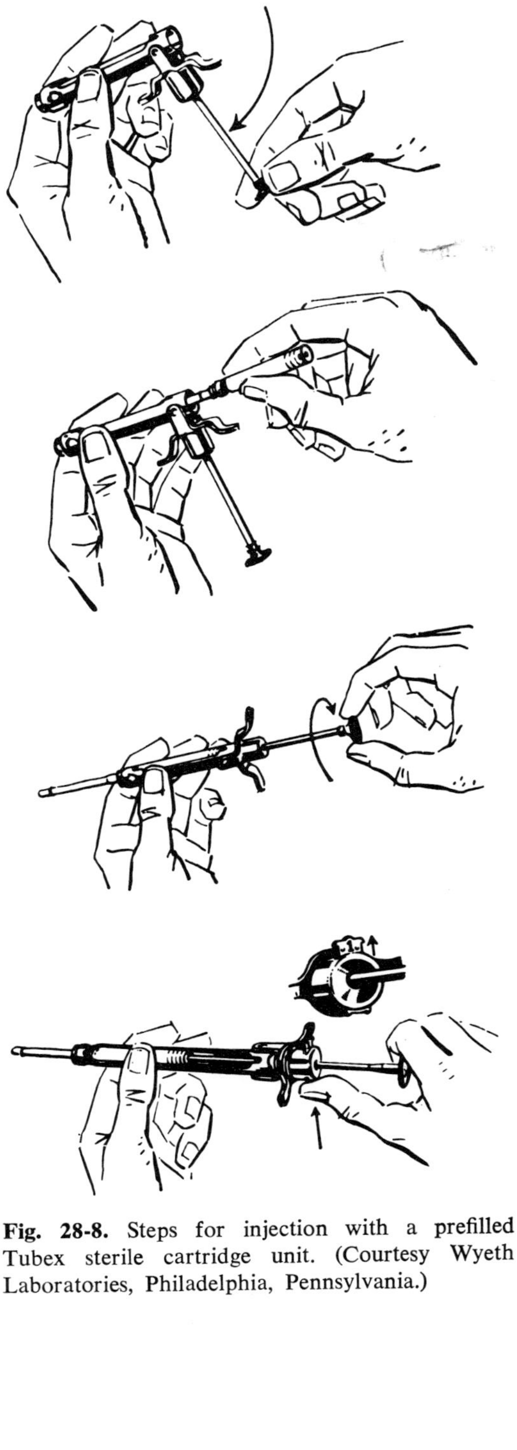

Fig. 28-8. Steps for injection with a prefilled Tubex sterile cartridge unit. (Courtesy Wyeth Laboratories, Philadelphia, Pennsylvania.)

sterility, leave the rubber sheath in place until just before use.

5. To adapt 2-cc syringe to 1-cc Tubex, engage both ends of Tubex and push the slide through so the number 1 appears. After use, the syringe automatically resets itself for 2-cc Tubex.

Procedure after injection with Tubex
(Fig. 28-9)

1. To remove the empty Tubex, replace sheath, using a twisting motion to avoid snagging. Disengage plunger from piston by rotating counterclockwise and open syringe. Do not pull plunger back before disengaging or syringe will jam. Rotate Tubex cartridge-needle unit counterclockwise to disengage at front end of syringe and remove from syringe.
2. Before discarding, the sheath-covered needle should be bent to seal the lumen in order to discourage pilferage or re-use. The syringe, never having come in contact with patient or medication, is returned to storage.

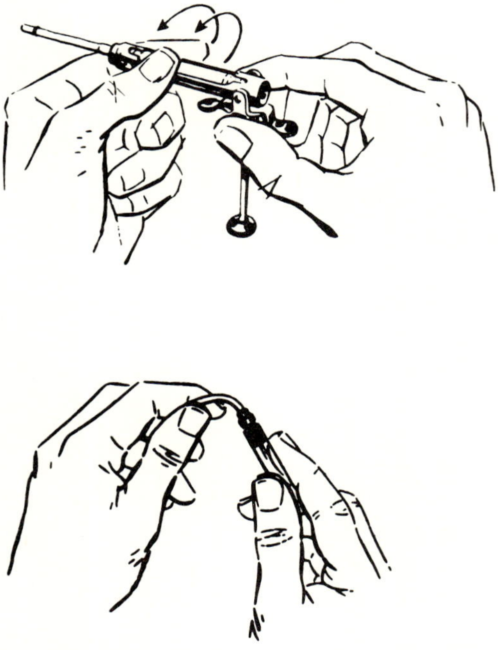

Fig. 28-9. Steps to take after injection with a Tubex sterile cartridge unit. (Courtesy Wyeth Laboratories, Philadelphia, Pennsylvania.)

CARE OF SYRINGES AND NEEDLES

How to separate a stuck syringe

1. To release, soak syringe for 5 to 20 minutes in a commercially accepted neutral (pH 7) cleaning solution. Do not force; let the cleaner do the work.
2. Fill air space of stuck syringe with warm water or cleaning solution. If you wish, this may be done with a syringe opener.
3. Fill the syringe opener with warm water or cleaning solution. Attach it firmly to the tip of the stuck syringe, holding the syringe at the barrel base when doing so. Apply gentle, steady pressure, gradually increasing the pressure until solution seeps around the plunger and reaches the top of the barrel. Do not grasp the stuck syringe, but let it remain suspended. Keep the pressure steady and the plunger will gradually be expelled from the barrel of the stuck syringe. Avoid expulsive force. A bunched towel beneath the syringe will prevent breakage if plunger pops out.

How to clean a syringe

1. Immediately after use, flush the syringe and needle two or three times with a commercially acceptable cleaning solution until all traces of medication disappear. If used for blood work, flush first with cold tap water to minimize getting blood into the cleaning solution. Use a stainless steel container for cleaning solution. Syringe and needle can be separated and left in solution. Enamel pans should be avoided, as small particles may chip off and clog the needle and syringe.
2. Separate the needle and syringe parts and soak in the neutral cleaning solution for 5 to 20 minutes. When used for most oily solutions they should be left soaking for 1½ hours. Brush or wipe away any soil not removed. Avoid use of abrasive cleaners.
3. After soaking, assemble syringe and flush with cleaning solution. Rinse thoroughly under running tap water, then flush with distilled water or alcohol. It is now ready for sterilization.

Removing a stuck needle

To remove a stuck needle, soak the syringe and the needle for 5 to 20 minutes in a commercially accepted neutral cleaning solution. Then grasp the square part of the needle hub firmly in a pair of pliers or with a forceps. Never grasp the round part of the hub. Hold the pliers or forceps firmly and rotate the syringe, not the forceps, counterclockwise, being careful not to use force.

How to remove stains and deposits from syringes

For alkali deposits use a 10% solution of nitric acid. For arsenic and iron stains use a 10% solution of hydrochloric acid. For gentian violet stains, use a 10% solution of nitric acid. For blood stains, use a 10% solution of nitric acid, sodium citrate, or concentrated ammonia. In such cases, swab carefully with cotton applicators dipped in the solution. Rinse thoroughly after each swabbing. Care must be used when using acid solution, particularly with a Becton-Dickinson lock syringe or any syringes with metal parts. Do not let the solution come in contact with any of the metal parts, not even the lumen of the metal tip. Never leave a glass syringe immersed in strong acids or alkali. Syringes with metal parts should never be left immersed in solutions containing mercury, any of its derivatives, or ammonia.

Sterilization of syringes

After cleaning, wrap the syringe with the barrel and plunger separated between layers of gauze. Then wrap a double layer of muslin and pin or tie. Mark the size of the syringe on the muslin for easy identification. Sterilize for 30 minutes under 15 to 17 pounds pressure at 250° to 254° F. unless specific instructions are given for a particular autoclave.

Rules in care of syringes

The following are some important cautions to observe for best syringe performance.

1. Don't wedge plunger into barrel at an angle.
2. Don't exert lateral pressure on glass syringe tip.
3. Don't test compression by covering tip hole, pulling back plunger, and suddenly releasing it. This will almost certainly knock out the barrel base.
4. Don't discard a "jumpy" syringe. Clean it.
5. Don't soak syringes in strong alkali solutions.
6. Don't play with syringes. They are medical instruments.
7. Don't stack syringes with other metal equipment.
8. Don't leave plunger in barrel intact after using until thoroughly clean and ready for sterilization.
9. Don't leave needles attached to syringe tips unless they are thoroughly cleansed.

Care of hypodermic needles

To clean a needle, flush with cold water immediately after use. Insert the stylet or a needle wire through the needle to make sure there is no clogging of the cannula. Always insert the wire through the hub, not from the point. Wash thoroughly inside and out with a commercial neutral cleaning soultion. Attach needle to the syringe and flush cleaner through the needle. Clean inside of hub with a tightly wound cotton applicator. Flush out needle and rinse with clear water.

To remove stains from a needle, use a fine powdered or caked household abrasive cleaner and rinse well. Soak the needles clogged with medications or blood for 5 to 20 minutes in cleaning solution before final washing and then flush the needle with alcohol or air. For a very quick drying, a Becton-Dickinson needle dryer may be used.

To autoclave a needle, put cotton in the bottom of a test tube. Place the needle in the tube point down. A Becton-Dickinson needle Steri-tube, which does not require cotton to protect the point, may be used. Cover the mouth of the test tube with a square of muslin and secure with a thread or rubber band. Mark the size of the needle on the muslin for easy identification. Sterilize for 15 to 20 minutes at 15 to 17 pounds pressure at about 250° F. unless specific instructions are given for a particular autoclave.

Aseptic assembling technique

To assemble a sterile syringe and needle, the plunger must be inserted into the barrel and the needle fitted without contaminating the inside surface of the barrel, plunger surface, syringe tip, or needle cannula. First pick up the syringe barrel and place between the thumb and fingers of the left hand, using a sterile forceps. Then pick up the plunger and insert into syringe barrel, using a sterile forceps, and then finally pick up a needle by the square part of the hub and place on the syringe tip firmly.

Ampule technique (Figs. 28-10 and 28-11)

With a knife or file, make a scratch on the glass and break off the tip of the ampule. Then hold the ampule in the left hand as near horizontal as possible without spilling the fluid. Hold syringe in the right hand, insert the needle in the vial, and then hold the syringe between the index and the middle fingers; plunger handle can be grasped by the thumb and third finger and medication withdrawn. Hold syringe perpendicular so that all air rises to the tip of syringe; then expel the air from the syringe and the needle.

Vial technique (Fig. 28-12)

To draw from a bottle, pour alcohol on a sterile piece of cotton and thoroughly wipe the top of the rubber stopper on the vial. Then fill the syringe with the same volume of air as the amount of medication to be withdrawn from the vial. Then hold the bottle in one hand and thrust the needle through the rubber stopper with the other hand. Inject the air from the syringe into the vial. This equalizes the pressure and facilitates filling of the syringe. Withdraw the medication by pulling back the plunger. Then hold the syringe perpendicular so that any air rises to the tip of the syringe. Expel the air from the syringe and needle.

DISPOSABLE SYRINGES AND NEEDLES

Within the past few years the use of disposable equipment such as syringes and

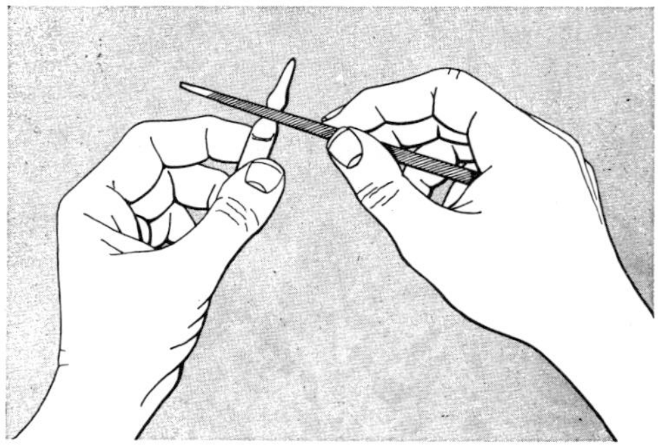

Fig. 28-10. Correct method of breaking an ampule.

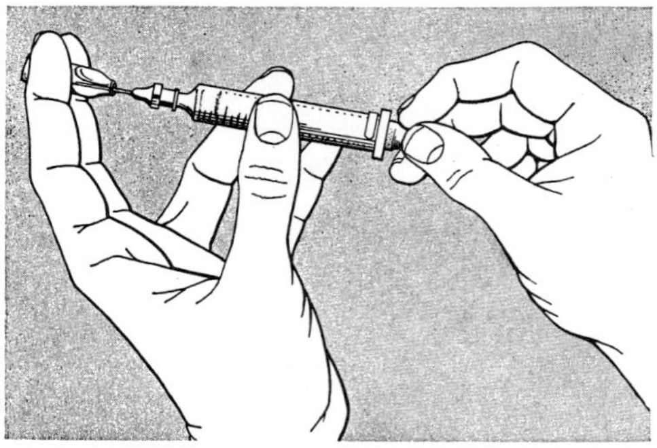

Fig. 28-11. Correct method of withdrawing solution from ampule.

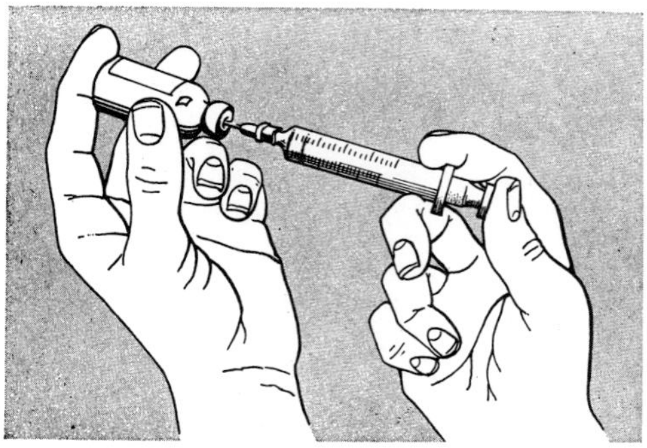

Fig. 28-12. Correct method of withdrawing solution from vial.

needles has increased in the modern medical office (Fig. 28-13). These items are made of plastic or some alloy. The needles can be made much sharper since they are not used for repeated injections. The disposable syringe and needle are individually packaged in a sterile container with a plastic guard over the needle. Syringes and needles are supplied in a wide range of sizes, and may be purchased individually or in combination with syringe and needle. A color-coded plastic hub makes it easy to identify the various gauges and lengths of needles.

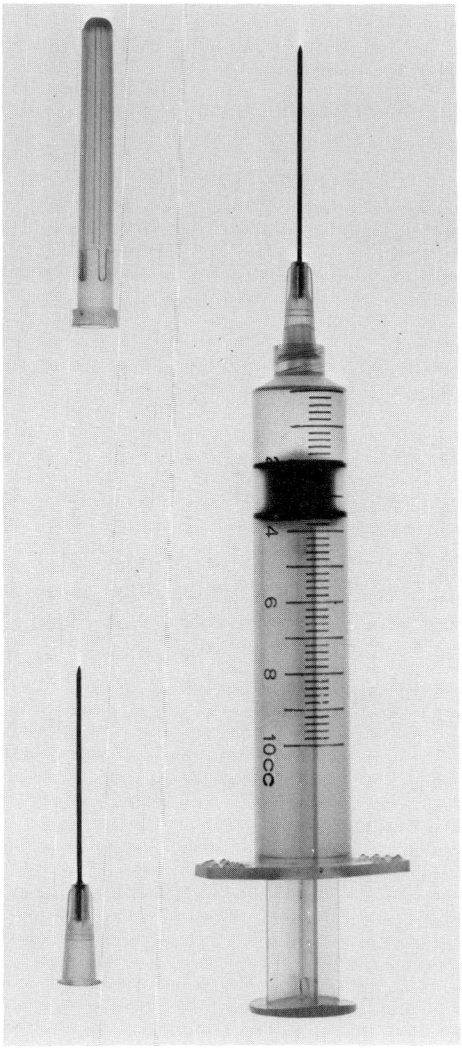

Fig. 28-13. Disposable syringe and needle. (Courtesy Becton, Dickinson & Co., Rutherford, New Jersey.)

Disposable syringes and needles save valuable time usually spent in cleaning and sterilizing and greatly decrease the transmission of hepatitis or any other infection to patients. The advantages of economy of time and safety to the patient greatly exceed the slight additional cost involved in the use of this type of equipment.

Review questions

1. What type and size needle would you use for a subcutaneous injection? An intravenous injection? An intramuscular injection?
2. Describe the procedure in giving an intramuscular injection, indicating the location of choice.
3. How is an intradermal injection administered? What size needle is best to use?
4. What is meant by a patch test? A scratch test?
5. What is meant by anaphylaxis? How would you handle such a case?
6. Why is the use of a disposable syringe and needle a convenience? What advantages does it have over the standard reusable syringes and needles?
7. How would you separate a stuck syringe? A stuck needle?
8. What is the best method of sterilizing syringes and needles?
9. How would you remove medication from an ampule? A vial?

Suggested readings

Dison, N. G.: An atlas of nursing techniques, ed. 2, St. Louis, 1971, The C. V. Mosby Co.

Squire, J. E., and Welch, J. M.: Basic pharmacology for nurses, ed. 5, St. Louis, 1973, The C. V. Mosby Co.

chapter 29

Technique of simple laboratory operations

A word of caution should be given to all laboratory workers. It is of greatest importance that the worker be on the alert to avoid errors that may creep into the performance of even the simplest test. One way to avoid this is by testing your techniques against known standards. For example, test your ability to do a red or white blood count against yourself or other normal individuals. The same procedure should also be used with the other tests you use. It is a good practice to check all laboratory methods at least once a month.

Caution should also be observed in the use of complicated apparatus, particularly the photoelectric colorimeter. This apparatus is capable of giving erroneous results if not properly adjusted, and no one should use it unless its proper calibration and care are understood.

The physician's office assistant should not attempt work without proper training. Some procedures, such as a differential blood count, appear simple, but they should not be undertaken without thorough work under a trained technologist.

We wish to emphasize that this textbook is not intended to be a substitute for a clinical laboratory textbook or an introduction to medical science. Laboratory functions for the medical assistant should be limited to those simple laboratory procedures generally done in the average physician's office. Complex laboratory procedures should only be done by qualified laboratory technicians or technologists.

GENERAL LABORATORY RULES

1. See that all laboratory equipment is kept in a clean and orderly manner.
2. Give complete attention to whatever you are doing and organize all necessary equipment before starting a procedure.
3. Have working area cleared of all unnecessary articles.
4. Observe all rules regarding use and proper cleaning of glassware and proper handling of chemical reagents.

Glossary

astigmatism a condition in which images do not properly focus on retina because of change in curvature of cornea

Bunsen burner a burner used in the laboratory that can be adjusted for luminous or nonluminous flame

burette a graduated tube for measuring a reagent

centrifuge a machine for the separation of heavier materials from lighter ones through the employment of centrifugal force

diaphragm in microscopy, an apparatus located beneath the opening in the stage by means of which the amount of light passing through the object can be regulated

substage attachment to the microscope beneath the stage by which attachments are held in place

5. Wear a laboratory apron when doing tests that might be messy.
6. Observe caution when using a Bunsen or alcohol burner and never leave it burning longer than necessary.
7. When disposing of stains make sure you pour them directly into the drain and not into the sink.
8. If you spill an acid of strong alkali on your skin, immediately douse with running water for ten minutes.

RULES WHEN USING REAGENTS

1. When removing a glass stopper from a bottle it should be grasped between first and second or second and third fingers from backside of hand and held in this position while pouring from bottle. If it is a screw cap place topside down on table. In either case always replace top immediately afterwards.
2. To avoid contamination never pipette a solution directly from a stock bottle, but instead pour a small amount of the solution into a clean beaker and pipette from there. Never pour back the unused quantity.
3. When extracting a dry chemical it is preferable to pour out a small quantity into a smaller container and withdraw desired amount from that.
4. Never inhale or smell a reagent.
5. Always read label three times: when it is removed from shelf, just prior to extracting substance, and when replacing bottle on shelf.

RULES WHEN MIXING REAGENTS OR MAKING SOLUTIONS

1. When it is necessary to mix an acid with water be sure that you *add the acid to the water and never add water to acid.*
2. Make sure that container used for combining reagents is absolutely clean.
3. When making solutions from solids make sure that all solid is dissolved. This may generally be hurried by stirring with a clean glass rod or by heating if indicated.
4. After solution is made up it should be filtered into a clean container, capped, and labeled as to name and date.

GLASSWARE

Common types of glassware employed in the laboratory

1. *The Erlenmeyer flask* is a Pyrex flask used in mixing or for temporary storage of reagents.
2. *The beaker* is a wide-mouthed Pyrex container used for holding or transferring reagents.
3. *The volumetric flask* is a Pyrex flask with a graduation mark on the long neck and accompanied by a glass stopper. It is used for mixing and storing reagents.
4. *Graduated cylinders* are glass cylinders with calibrations etched along their length, which are used primarily for rough or qualitative measurements and sometimes for making up percent solutions. They range in capacity from 10 ml to 1,000 ml.
5. *The petri dish* is a round, flat, glass dish with a cover; it is used as a container for culture media for bacterial growth.
6. *Transfer pipettes* are long, narrow glass tubes graduated in 1-ml, 0.1-ml, or 0.01-ml increments. They are used for transferring measured quantities of a liquid from one container to another.
7. *The volumetric pipette* has a bulb and only one graduation mark situated above the bulb; it is used for more accurate measurements.

Proper cleaning of glassware

1. Glassware should be rinsed out or soaked as soon after use as possible, until one has time to clean it properly.
2. It should be scrubbed with hot, soapy water, rinsed well, and finally rinsed with distilled water. For chemical work it is good to clean it by soaking in chromic sulfuric cleaning solution. This solution consists of strong sulfuric acid saturated with potassium or sodium dichromate. The proportions are potassium dichromate, 100 gm, concentrated sulfuric acid,

250 ml, and water, 750 ml. Dissolve the dichromate in water and then add the sulfuric acid slowly. It must be handled with great care since it is extremely corrosive to tissue, clothes, furniture, and books. It may be necessary to leave the glassware in the solution for several days. The cleaning mixture should be in a closed vessel when not in use. The solution is dangerous. It should never be heated, and it should be stored in a Pyrex container. Work with this solution should always be done at the sink. Glassware cleaned in the solution should be rinsed twice with tap water and six times with distilled water and dried by putting into alcohol and then ether or a drying oven.

3. It should then preferably be dried in a hot-air oven. Never dry the inside of glassware with a towel—a towel leaves lint.
4. Glass slides should be washed with soap and water (after scrubbing with cleanser, if stained), rinsed thoroughly, and finally placed in 95% alcohol, dried with a lint-free towel, and stored in a covered container. If slides are to be in the best possible condition, they should be flamed before being put away.
5. If the inside of a blood-counting pipette becomes stained, the pipette may be soaked in a dilute sulfuric acid solution.
6. Chipped and cracked glassware should be discarded. This is particularly true of pipettes. Do not use pipettes that have chipped ends.
7. After using a syringe, separate plunger from syringe as soon as possible after use to prevent sticking. This is very important if the syringe is used to draw blood.

USING REAGENTS

Handling the reagent bottle

In using liquid reagents it is well to know how to handle the reagent bottle (Fig. 29-1). The stopper of the bottle is removed by the right hand with the palm up. The stopper and the bottle are then held with the right hand, freeing the left hand to hold some other piece of apparatus. This procedure is done to protect the hands as well as the laboratory tabletop from the action of strong acids and alkalis. Never lay a stopper on the tabletop.

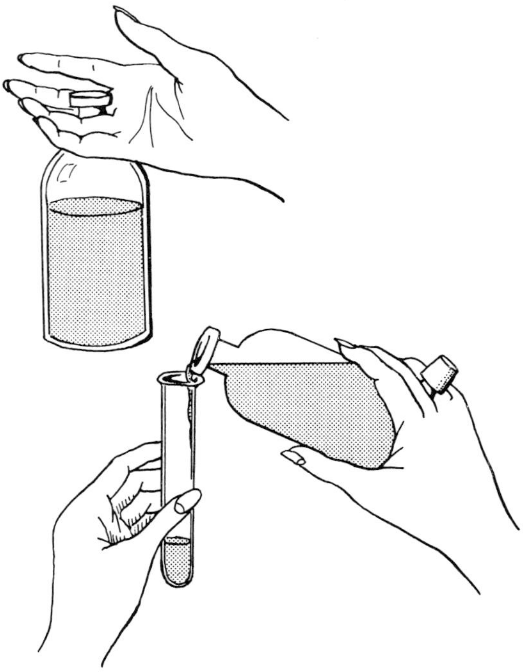

Fig. 29-1. Correct way to handle the reagent bottle

Smelling the bottle

It is never wise to smell the contents of any bottle. The material in the bottle may be extremely poisonous, or it may have a stifling or suffocating odor. The mucous membranes of the nose and throat may be permanently injured.

Reading labels

Always read the label on the bottle. Be sure that you have the correct reagent. If there is no label on the bottle, its contents should be destroyed. Using such a solution may cause an explosion, resulting in eye injury or lacerations.

Wasting reagents

Do not waste materials or reagents. Please remember that the materials in the solution or reagent are expensive. If an experiment calls for the use of 5 ml of a certain solution, use that amount.

Using dry chemicals

In the use of dry chemicals, be careful not to spill any of the material upon the hands, clothing, or laboratory tabletop. Some chemicals are very corrosive and will ruin anything that they touch.

Protecting reagents from contamination

Contamination of reagents is always fatal to laboratory work. When a reagent is removed from a bottle, never put any of it back into the bottle. It is much better to throw away the excess. Insert only clean pipettes into a reagent bottle.

HEATING LIQUID IN A TEST TUBE

Correct laboratory technique in heating liquid in a test tube is essential to safety. Observe these simple rules.

1. Never fill the test tube more than one third full of a liquid when heating.
2. Hold the tube by the test tube holder. Preheat the tube to prevent breakage. The tube is then held in the hottest part of the flame, at the junction of the two cones.
3. Always keep the open end of the test tube away from you or from anyone standing near you.
4. Obtain the right slant of the tube and its contents while the heating is taking place. Heat the liquid in the tube from the top downward instead of from the bottom upward. This prevents the "popping out" of the liquid.
5. Never hold the tube in an upright position, heating the bottom of the tube. The contents are very apt to boil out, causing severe burns (Fig. 29-2).

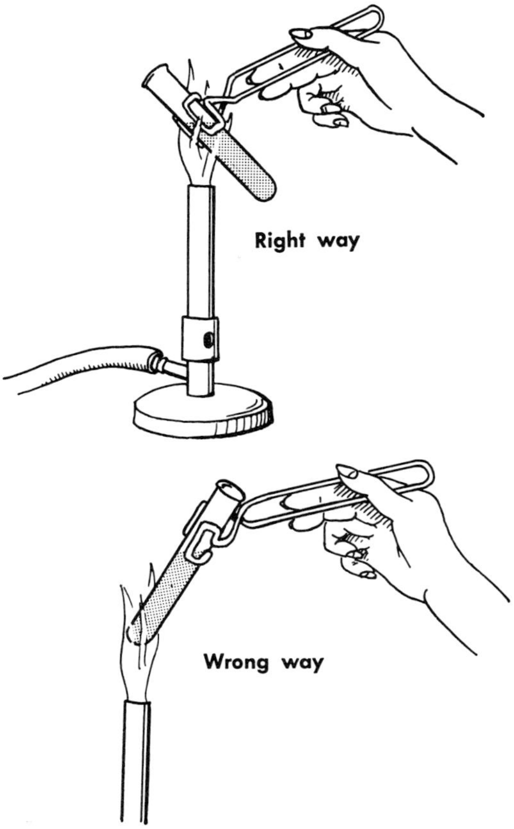

Fig. 29-2. Heating liquids in a test tube.

PREPARING A BOILING WATER BATH

A simple type of water bath may be prepared by using a large glass beaker or a granite pan filled about half full of hot water, a tripod, and a Bunsen burner and tubing. If a beaker is used, a wire gauze should be placed under the beaker. An electric stove or hot plate may be substituted for the Bunsen burner.

OVERLAYING ONE LIQUID WITH ANOTHER

One method in common use today is to run one liquid slowly down the side of a tube onto the other liquid. This is conveniently done by the use of a curved medicine dropper. This technique is applicable to those liquids having different specific gravities. In other words, the liquid in the tube must be heavier than the one that is to be added on top. If the gravities of the two liquids are the same, they will mix intimately, and it will be impossible to separate the two fluids.

The other way of overlaying is to fill a

1-cc pipette with one of the liquids. With the forefinger over the open end of the pipette containing the liquid of heavier gravity, insert the pipette into the bottom of the tube that holds the other liquid. Now slowly release the finger on the pipette, allowing the liquid in the pipette to flow into the bottom of the tube. If this is done carefully, there will be two liquids present in the same tube, and they will be not at all mixed. After the addition of the heavier liquid, the first or lighter fluid will rise to the top, and the heavier or added liquid will be on the bottom.

CLEARING VARIOUS MATERIALS TO BE TESTED

Filtration

Filtration is carried out by carefully pouring the liquid through a dry filter paper that has been properly placed in a funnel (Fig. 29-3). This is done by first folding the filter paper in half. It is again folded in half, or, in other words, it is quartered. Care must be taken not to rupture the paper at the tip by excess finger pressure. The half-opened filter paper should snugly fit the funnel bowl wall to about half its depth when placed in the funnel. The material that passes through the paper is called filtrate; the material which is caught on the filter paper is called the residue or the precipitate.

Heating

Simply heat the material to be tested over the flame of a Bunsen burner. This should be done very slowly. In many cases, the solution will become clear. This method is applicable to a urine specimen in which the earthy phosphates have precipitated. The material must not be heated too long nor become too hot because some compounds are precipitated by heat and this would ruin the analysis. Material in a flask or a test tube may be heated in a boiling water bath.

Centrifuging

Place equal portions of the liquid in two small test tubes and place them in the centrifuge. The tubes are now centrifuged from 10 to 15 minutes. This is done at a high rate of speed. By centrifugal force, the cloudy and heavier material is thrown to the bottom of the tube, and, of course, the clear liquid will be on the top.

In centrifuging it is important to be sure that each tube is correctly balanced. A second tube with a similar amount of water

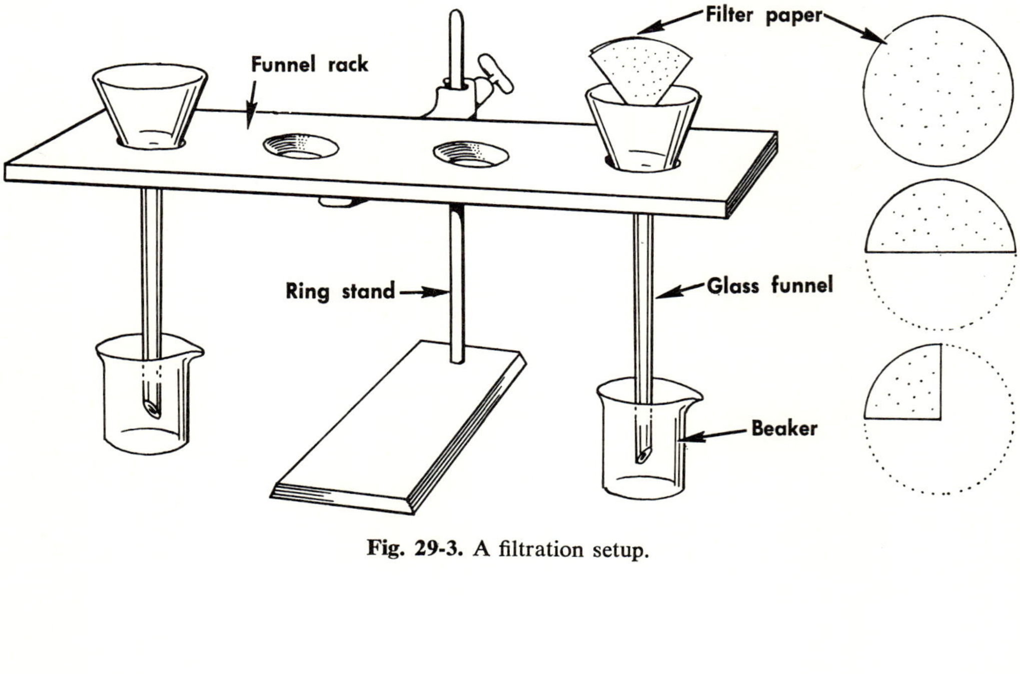

Fig. 29-3. A filtration setup.

as the tube containing the solution to be centrifuged is used for this purpose. A water-filled tube serves as a balance. Failure to do this will cause excessive vibration of the centrifuge and may damage it. If a centrifuge should start to vibrate excessively it must be stopped immediately, allowed to stop completely, and checked for proper balance.

MEASURING APPARATUS

Cylinders

Graduated cylinders are used for rough or qualitative work only. They are used to measure approximate amounts as well as corrosive and poisonous liquids. These cylinders are made in various capacities such as 10, 15, 25, 50, 100, 500, and 1,000 ml (Fig. 29-4). The cubic centimeters are then divided into fractions of a cubic centimeter.

Graduated flasks

Graduated flasks are used almost exclusively for the preparation of solutions of known concentration or strength. They may be graduated to contain or to deliver a given volume of a liquid. Flasks are usually of 100-, 200-, 250-, 500-, or 1,000-cc capacity (Fig. 29-5). There is a graduation mark on the neck of the flask, and the diluent (usually water) is added up to this mark.

Pipettes

Pipettes are long narrow tubes graduated in cubic centimeters, tenths of cubic centimeters, or finer calibrations (Fig. 29-6). On the upper part of the pipette there will be found a mark that is labeled 0. From this 0 the pipette is graduated as is shown by the numerous markings, the number of the letter varying with the size of the pipette. On a 1-ml pipette there are usually ten markings, each of which represents a tenth of a milliliter. On a 5-ml pipette there are five large marks, each of which denotes one milliliter. Between these marks are smaller ones representing tenths of milliliters. A pipette is filled by first sucking in the liquid with the mouth until it reaches a point above the upper graduation mark, then immediately placing the index finger of the right hand over the open end of the pipette. The excess liquid is then allowed to flow from the pipette by slightly releas-

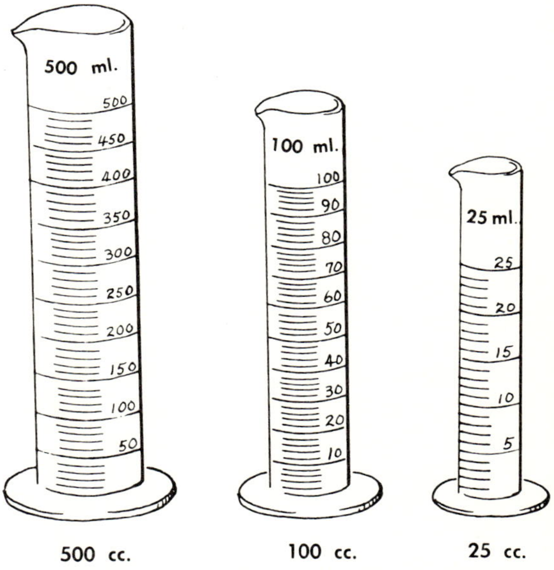

Fig. 29-4. Three sizes of graduated cylinders.

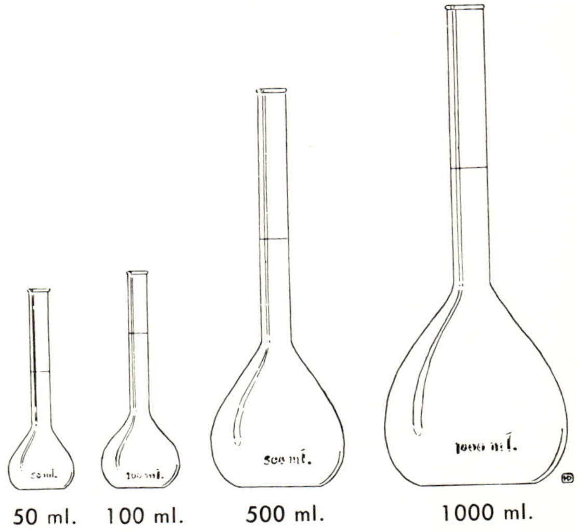

Fig. 29-5. Volumetric flasks. (From White, W., and Frankel, S.: Seiverd's chemistry for medical technologists, ed. 2, St. Louis, 1965, The C. V. Mosby Co.)

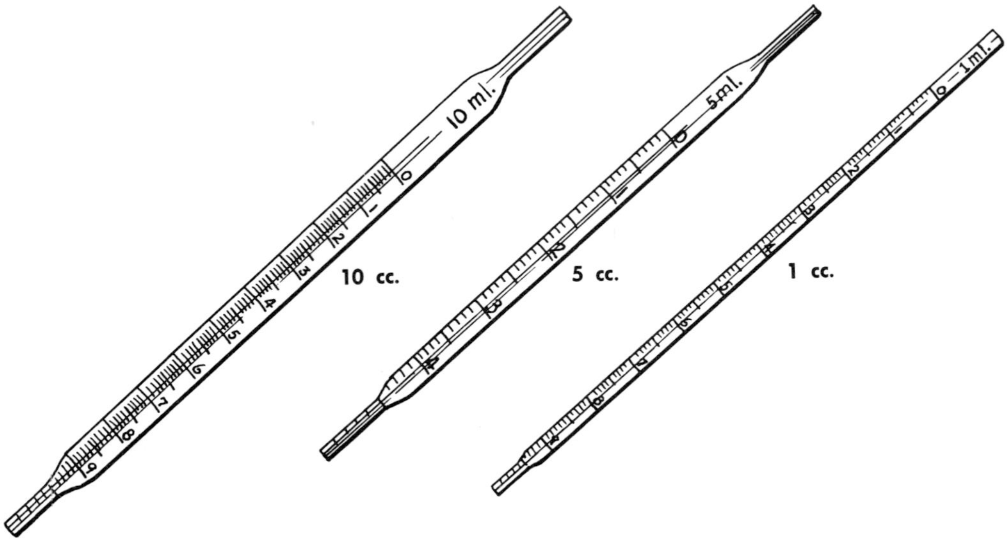

Fig. 29-6. Three sizes of pipettes.

ing the finger from the top of the pipette. Control of the flow, or dropping of liquids, is easier if the pipette top and the finger-tip are both dry. This must be slowly and carefully done, and some practice will be necessary to accomplish this with ease and accuracy. When the bottom of the meniscus (the curved surface of the liquid) is exactly tangent with the graduation mark of the pipette, the correct amount of liquid is then present in the pipette. Never suck acids or strong alkalies into pipettes, as severe oral burns may result. Instead, the pipette should be placed in the agent and the liquid allowed to rise by capillary attraction into the pipette. Special rubber suction bulbs are also available to perform this task. Pipettes with a frosted band near the top must have the last drops blown out. Those without this frosted band must have their tips touched to the side of the container to remove the necessary included drop. Some pipettes have their last marking above the tip. These pipettes should be emptied only to the last marking.

THE MICROSCOPE

The microscope is the chief tool of the laboratory worker, and for maximum efficiency its operation must be carefully studied. The best microscope is of little value to one not proficient in its use.

Choice of a microscope

Microscopes vary greatly in quality. Clinical microscopy is a difficult task and much is expected of its practitioners. Work of such importance should not suffer because of lack of good tools. The minimum equipment for clinical laboratory microscopy consists of a single-tube instrument with stand, coarse and fine adjustments, mirror, condenser, diaphragm, 16-mm, 4-mm, and 1.8-mm (oil-immersion) objectives, and oculars. A mechanical stage should be included with the microscope.

Kinds of microscopes

Monocular. The monocular microscope is, of course, made for just one eye (Fig. 29-7). It is a good plan when using this type of microscope to keep both eyes open. After a little practice, this will not be difficult to do, and the microscopist's eyes will not become overworked and tired.

Binocular. It will be evident at once that both eyes are used with this type of instrument (Fig. 29-8). For the beginner, it may

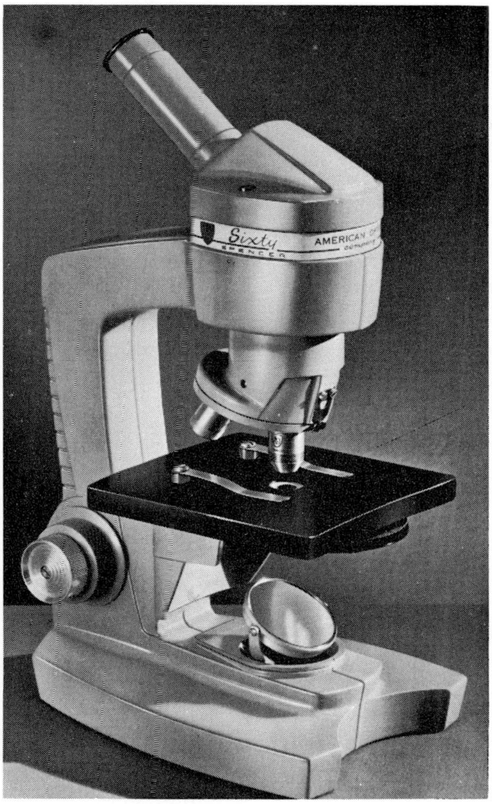

Fig. 29-7. Monocular microscope. (Courtesy American Optical Company, Buffalo, New York.)

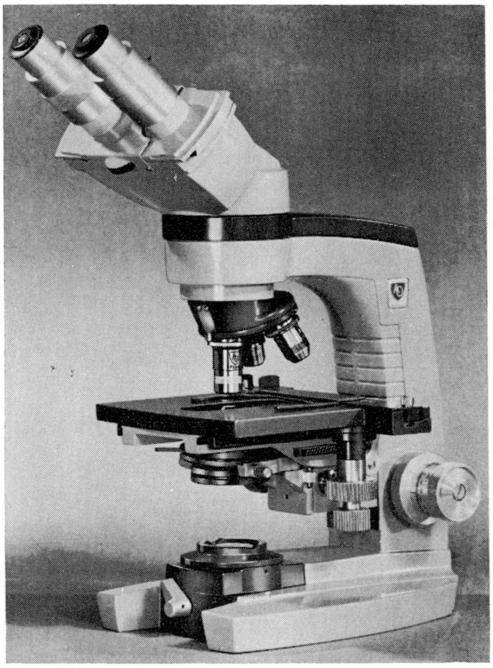

Fig. 29-8. Binocular microscope. (Courtesy American Optical Company, Buffalo, New York.)

be a little hard at first to use both eyepieces, but after a few hours' practice this difficulty is overcome, and the student will prefer using a binocular microscope. This type of microscope is the one of choice. It must be borne in mind now that it is poor economy to invest in a cheap microscope.

Parts of the microscope

Eyepieces. Eyepieces fit into the eyepiece tubes. The eyepieces in common use today are marked 5×, 6×, or 10×. The last has the greatest magnifying power. Since the exterior surface of the eyepiece is exposed, it is apt to become dusty; therefore it should be carefully cleaned before use. This cleaning can be done with a special lens paper or with a very soft cloth.

Objectives. The microscope will always be provided with a revolving nosepiece into which the various objectives are screwed. Care must be used in properly attaching the objective to the nosepiece; the following procedure is suggested. Hold the upper knurled edge of the objective between the thumb and forefinger of the left hand; bring the screw head into contact with the opening in the nosepiece, keeping the objective in line with the tube; gently revolve the objective with the thumb and forefinger of the right hand. *Never* at any time force the objective. Objectives also have different magnifying powers. The following are in common use.

1. The lowest power objective, which is marked 16 mm or 10×
2. The intermediate power, frequently called the high dry power, which is marked 4 mm, 43×, or 45×
3. The highest power, which is called the oil-immersion objective, and is marked 1.8 mm, 97×, or 100×

In becoming familiar with the different objectives, the student should remember

Examples of magnification

Eyepiece	Objective	Magnification
5×	10×	50
10×	10×	100
5×	45×	225
10×	45×	450
5×	100×	500
10×	100×	1,000

that the low power is the shortest of the three objectives, while the oil immersion is the longest of the three. Another point of differentiation is the size of the opening in the smaller end of the objectives. The objective with the greatest opening is the lowest power, and conversely the one with the smallest opening is the highest power or the oil immersion.

Stage. The stage is the flat heavy part upon which slides are placed for examination. Upon the stage are found two slide clips. In place of these clips, it is more convenient to use an attachable mechanical stage that is fitted upon the stage by means of set screws. This mechanical stage is almost indispensable in laboratory work, especially when the work involves and requires a high-power magnification.

Substage. Fitting into the opening on the stage and immediately below it is the substage. This part holds the substage condenser, a necessity in microscopic work. Its purpose is to condense the light upon the object under examination. For best results the proper amount of light is focused on the object by lowering and raising this substage by means of the pinion adjustment. On the lower part of the substage will be found the shutter or diaphragm. This shutter is to close off light or to admit more light. Since the amount of light required varies, adjustment of the substage in connection with specific uses of the microscope will be described.

Other parts of the microscope. The *pinion head* is used for coarse adjustment of the microscope. The *micrometer head* is used in fine adjustment and focusing. These two pinion heads are very important as they must be used every time the apparatus is used. When finding the field it is always necessary to lower the head of the microscope by means of the coarse adjustment. After this is accomplished, the fine adjustment is then used. This is absolutely essential when using high-power magnification. Other parts are a *mirror for indirect light* and a *microscopic light or lamp.* There are several varieties of microscopic lights on the market. One of the most important items in a lamp is the blue glass that accompanies the apparatus.

A convenient pointer for a microscope is made from a hair. Place a short piece of hair on the ledge within the eyepiece. This can be cemented in place by means of a very small amount of glue. When the eyepiece is in place, the hair appears as a black line, the end of which can easily be placed upon the object under observation.

Use of the microscope

The material to be examined is placed upon the microscopic slide. The latter is then placed upon the microscopic stage and fastened with the clips or held in place by the mechanical stage. Using the lowest power objective and a 10× eyepiece, slowly lower the microscope head by means of the coarse pinion head. When the field is found, the light is then adjusted by raising or lowering the pinion attached to the substage. Next, open or close the shutter in order to admit just the proper amount of light to give a clearer and distinct field. To make the field of vision clear, use the fine-adjustment pinion. From this point on, higher power of magnification can then be obtained by changing the objective.

Care in handling the microscope

1. Don't pick up the microscope by any part except the handle.

2. Don't drop a microscope. Even a small jar may permanently damage the instrument.
3. Don't try to adjust the microscope yourself if you do not fully understand its mechanism. You may throw the instrument out of balance and adjustment. This is especially true of the binocular instrument.
4. Handle a microscope carefully. Please remember that it is an expensive piece of apparatus.
5. Don't force the pinion heads if for some reason they seem to turn too hard. They may need a drop of oil or some simple adjustment.
6. Don't force a high-powered objective upon a microscopic slide. This may cause scratches on the objective or even permanently damage the lens.
7. Be sure that the lens of the objective is clean before attempting to do microscopic work. Be sure to wipe off the objective if it has been lowered into a liquid.
8. When not in use, the microscope should be put back into its case or covered with a bell jar or some close-meshed cloth.
9. Remove oil or balsam that may adhere to any part of the stand, stage, or substage. This can be done by using a small amount of xylene on a soft cloth.
10. Never use alcohol on any of the lacquered parts, as this will remove the finish.
11. Remove the eye lens at regular intervals to clean out dust and dirt particles.

Space for using the microscope. The microscope should be kept set up and ready for use. This will assure its being much more frequently called upon for aid than if it were stored away out of sight.

However limited the space, sufficient space must be allotted exclusively for the use of the microscope and its few accessories. It need be no more than a shelf wide enough to accommodate the equipment. To this should be added a convenient seat *of proper height.* A kitchen stool will suffice. Attempting work with the microscope handicapped by improper relationship between height of work table and stool is so intolerably fatiguing as to lead to unreliable work.

A suitable cover for the microscope is essential to keep out dust when it is not in use. A bell jar of glass or heavy cellophane-like material is quite satisfactory, or a bag with a drawstring may be used, placing it over the top of the microscope and drawing the string tight around the base. Certain accessories will be kept close at hand to minimize effort and save time. Since blood counts will be performed frequently, the counting chamber and cover glass are included in this equipment. They should be kept in a dustproof box, preferably the plush-lined case usually furnished by the manufacturer. This keeps them from harm. Immersion oil should be kept in a bottle having a glass rod inserted in the cork for applying it to the slide. The best immersion oil is some type of high-grade mineral oil such as Nujol. It does not gum up the lenses as does the commonly used cedar oil, and it is washed off the slides much more easily.

Keep a tumbler with cotton on the bottom three fourths full of distilled water for cleaning the counting chamber. Change this water frequently. Keep a number of clean, lintless handkerchiefs handy to wipe the counting chamber and cover glass after washing.

For wiping oil from the lenses after use we employ cleansing tissue. This material is inexpensive and takes the place of the more costly lens paper. *Remember never to use any strong solvent on the objectives. Material of this type will loosen the cement of the older type lens and cause it to become loose and worthless.*

A pad and pencil for recording results of examinations and a blue wax pencil for marking slides complete the list of accessories.

Proper adjustment of illumination. The

problem of obtaining maximum efficiency of illumination remains. Three factors enter into this: the light itself, the position of the mirror on the microscope (if a substage light is used, the mirror will be removed and adjustment is made in this case by moving the light), and, most important of all, the manipulation of the diaphragm, which controls the amount of light admitted to the condenser.

To know when the illumination has been properly adjusted place a slide on the microscope and focus the low-power lens upon it. Remove the ocular and look on the back lens of the objective. Move the mirror, *not the microscope or light,* until the back lens of the objective is evenly illuminated. If shadows of trees, windows, or other objects appear in this field, try to eliminate them by raising and lowering the condenser. Upon examination, the mirror will be found to have a concave and a plane side. Use the concave side with the low-power (4 mm and 16 mm) objectives and the plane side with the oil-immersion (1.8 mm) lens. The mirror should be kept thoroughly clean by frequent wiping with pieces of lens tissue.

The most difficult part of illumination for the novice to grasp seems to be the proper manipulation of the iris diaphragm. Two cardinal principles should be remembered. First, the lower the power of the objective used, the lower the light should be cut. In using the 16-mm lens to examine urine sediment or to count leukocytes, the diaphragm should be almost completely closed; when the 4-mm objective is brought into play, the opening should be slightly increased; and when using the oil-immersion objective, the diaphragm may be opened wide. Second, the more brilliantly stained the object being viewed the more light you can admit. As an example, if a differential blood count is being made with the 4-mm lens (the high dry), the diaphragm may be at least half open, whereas during the examination of urinary sediment, especially if seeking hyaline casts, the light should be cut almost completely off. If this is not done, these hyaline structures will not be seen. *The diaphragm should be constantly adjusted while making an examination to get the most revealing picture. It is controlled by a little lever under the condenser and you should learn to seek this out and manipulate it subconsciously, as the fine adjustment is kept in constant use while focusing. If you are having trouble with an examination and things are not seen as clearly as they should be, examine the amount of light being admitted. The trouble is not infrequently caused by improper adjustment of the diaphragm.*

Focusing. In the microscopes illustrated in Figs. 29-7 and 29-8, a coarse and fine adjustment control will be seen, the coarse adjustment being the larger nut and placed behind the smaller, which is for fine adjustment. The coarse adjustment is for finding the relative focus; the fine is for bringing out the details clearly. *Do not use these interchangeably.* Using the coarse for fine focusing will result in broken cover glasses and slides; *trying to find a field with the fine adjustment will place too much strain on it and quickly wear it out.*

Place a slide on the stage and bring the low or high dry objective down until it almost touches. Then, while looking into the microscope, slowly raise it with the coarse adjustment until the image is seen. Then, using the fine adjustment, bring out the details as described. It is a good plan never to turn the fine adjustment more than two thirds of a revolution. It is frequently desirable to keep the slide moving on the stage while attempting to focus. If this is not done, it may be found that you are trying to focus on a spot where there is no material.

If it is found impossible to obtain a clear image although the illumination has been found satisfactory, the eyepiece should be rotated. If the blur is seen to rotate with it, this is the source of the trouble. Remove it and wipe it thoroughly. The upper portion should be frequently cleaned, as it becomes soiled from contact with the eyelashes. In the event that the difficulty is not in the ocular, it is possible that the back of the objective has become fogged. This is not an infrequent occurrence if the instrument has been brought into a warm room from a cold one. Again, it is possible that the objective has been dipped into some fluid—immersion oil, balsam, or water—and this has dried and caused fogging. Water can be removed with moistened tissue and the lens then polished dry. If balsam or cedar oil has dried on the lens, it must be cautiously removed with the smallest possible amount of xylol and the excess of this reagent wiped away with lens tissue.

Never focus down while looking through the microscope. This is inviting disaster to slides and cover glasses as well as possible damage to the lens.

Use of objectives. Of the three objectives, designated 16 mm, 4 mm, and 1.8 mm respectively, the 16 mm is the shortest and has the largest lens. The objective is used for low-power work, principally urine sediment examinations, counting leukocytes, and for inspecting the counting chamber of red cells for irregularity of distribution (but only an expert should use it for counting these cells). The 4-mm lens, the high dry, is mostly used for close inspection of the urinary sediment, counting red blood cells, and making routine differential blood cell counts.

Always use a cover glass when using the high dry objective for examining urinary sediment. Do not dip the lens into the fluid without this protection. When using the 4-mm objective for differential blood counts, spread a thin film of mineral oil on the slide, over the stained blood, before making the examination.

The oil-immersion lens (1.8 mm) is used for obtaining the highest possible magnification. Used with the eyepiece that gives a magnification of 10 diameters (marked 10×) the object as seen is about 1,000 times its actual size. To use this lens, place a drop of mineral oil (such as Nujol) on the slide and focus down with coarse adjustment until the tip of the lens just touches the oil. Now, look through the microscope and focus upward very slowly with the coarse adjustment. When the object is seen, bring it into proper detail by use of the fine adjustment. This lens is used for all types of bacteriologic work, for seeking malarial parasites, and for all other purposes demanding the highest available magnification.

Making minor repairs and adjustments on the microscope. If anything of a serious nature happens to the instrument, the manufacturer's representative should be contacted. About once every three or four years the oil-immersion lens should be returned to the factory for inspection and regrinding. Occasionally, though less frequently, the other objectives need this same treatment. The objectives should not be taken apart, but the back lens may be cleaned with a bit of twisted lens paper or a camel's hair brush to remove dust particles.

If the fine adjustment refuses to function, it has probably run out. This can usually be corrected by turning it three or four complete revolutions.

If the tube slips down and will not stay where placed, the gears are probably worn. Manufacturers anticipate this wear and have placed screws at the back of the pinion box to be tightened when this difficulty is experienced. (A small screwdriver should be a part of the microscope kit.)

An occasional drop of mineral oil may be placed on the bearings after removing the body tube, but do not use too much oil on the instrument. Wipe it occasionally with a clean cloth. Keep the microscope covered when not in use.

If the microscope is to be carried, *do not* carry in such a manner that the weight of the instrument falls on the adjustments. One hand *under* the base should carry the major portion of the weight. Grasp the curved arm with the other hand to steady and support.

Practical pointers concerning use of the microscope. If a single-tube microscope is used, learn to work with both eyes open.

Squinting or closing one eye causes unnecessary strain. If much work is done, frequently shift from one eye to the other. An excellent system is to make the red and white cell counts with the right eye and shift to the left for making the differential. By so doing, it is not necessary to shift positions each time a notation is to be made on the pad. By inclining the head slightly, these figures can be kept in line of vision of the right eye.

If you wear glasses habitually, learn to do microscopy without them if possible. The instrument will focus to compensate for your visual defects if you are nearsighted or farsighted. On the other hand, if astigmatism is your difficulty, glasses will have to be worn, as this difficulty cannot be corrected by the microscopic lens. Find out the nature of your eye defect from the person who prescribed the glasses.

Review questions

1. Why is it important to know how to handle a reagent bottle?
2. Is it a good plan to smell or taste chemical reagents?
3. What is the correct method of heating a liquid in a test tube?
4. How may various liquids be clarified?
5. What is meant by overlaying a liquid?
6. How is the magnification power determined?
7. How is the amount of light regulated?
8. Name the parts of the microscope.
9. What don'ts about a microscope should be remembered?
10. How is an oil-immersion objective used?

Suggested readings

Bauer, J. D., Ackermann, P. G., and Toro, G.: Clinical laboratory methods, ed. 8, St. Louis, 1974, The C. V. Mosby Co.

Frankel, S., Reitman, S., and Sonnenwirth, A., editors: Gradwohl's clinical laboratory methods and diagnosis, ed. 7, St. Louis, 1970, The C. V. Mosby Co.

Hepler, O. E.: Manual of clinical laboratory methods, ed. 4, Springfield, Ill., 1970, Charles C Thomas, Publisher.

Lee, L. W.: Elementary principles of laboratory instruments, ed. 3, St. Louis, 1974, The C. V. Mosby Co.

chapter 30
Routine urinalysis

The kidneys are complex organs with many functions. They enable the body to eliminate metabolic waste products by filtering the blood and excreting waste products in the urine. In addition, the kidneys are important in maintaining normal salt, water, acid-base, and mineral metabolism and are essential in maintaining normal blood pressure and red blood cell production.

In the normal adult about 1,400 or more liters of blood pass through the kidneys over a 24-hour period. During this time more than 140 liters of plasma are filtered by about 2 million filtering units in the kidneys called *glomeruli*. Over 138 liters of this plasma filtrate are reabsorbed by the kidneys by means of small tubes, called renal tubules, attached to the glomeruli. The tubules reabsorb most of the water, minerals, and salt presented to them. Fluid not absorbed contains a high concentration of certain waste products and is called urine.

In this chapter the procedure for a routine urinalysis will be discussed. Before this is done, it is important to briefly describe the characteristics of normal urine and to point out the significance of certain abnormal findings in the urine.

COMPOSITION

Urine is a complex solution of water and a variety of organic and inorganic substances. The most important organic substances are urea, uric acid, and creatinine. Urea, the most abundant organic substance

---

Glossary

albuminuria presence of readily detectable amounts of albumin in urine
amorphous without definite structure
anuria the cessation of the flow of urine
glomerulus the part of the kidney that serves as its main filtration apparatus
glomerulonephritis the form of nephritis involving primarily the glomeruli (often referred to as nephritis)
glycosuria the presence of sugar in the urine
hematuria the presence of blood in the urine
ketonuria the presence of ketone bodies in the urine
meniscus the curved surface of water when it is in a narrow container
nephritis inflammation of the kidneys
oliguria the production of smaller than normal amounts of urine
pathology study of the nature and cause of disease; a condition produced by disease
polyuria the production of excessive amounts of urine
pyuria the presence of pus cells in the urine
renal pertaining to the kidneys
specific gravity a measure of the density of urine in relation to water
supernatant an overlying layer of fluid; the fluid above the sediment after centrifugation
tubule the portion of the kidney that collects urine after it has been filtered by the glomeruli
uremia a toxic condition associated with kidney failure
urinometer device for determining specific gravity of urine
urobilinogen a colorless pigment of bile metabolism that is excreted by the kidneys after absorption from the intestine

found in the urine, is produced in the liver and is the major waste product of protein metabolism. The most important inorganic substances are chlorides, phosphates, sulfates, and ammonia. The chlorides, mainly sodium chloride, make up about half the inorganic substances.

The kidney normally reabsorbs most of the amino acids and sugars that are filtered from the blood so that these substances are not normally seen in the urine. The filtering system of the kidneys usually does not allow large protein molecules, such as albumin and hemoglobin, to escape into the urine. Other substances, such as ketones and bilirubin are found in the urine only when they are present in abnormally high concentrations in the blood.

GENERAL PHYSICAL CHARACTERISTICS

Quantity

The quantity of urine normally produced over a 24-hour period is highly variable but averages about 1200 to 1500 ml. The amount of urine is dependent on the amount of liquid taken in and the amount of liquid lost in stools, as water vapor from the lungs, and as perspiration. Usually urine output is greater during the day than at night.

When urine production exceeds 3,000 ml per day, the condition is called *polyuria.* Polyuria may be caused by diabetes, kidney disease, a variety of metabolic disorders, or compulsive water drinking. It may also occur when treatment for excessive water retention is started by a doctor. *Oliguria* is the excretion of smaller than normal amounts of urine and may be due to kidney disease, dehydration of any type, or obstruction of the urinary tract. *Anuria* is the complete absence of urine and such a condition obviously requires immediate medical attention.

Color

The normal amber color of urine is due to the presence of bile pigments. The color of urine varies with its concentration, that is, dilute urine is pale while concentrated urine is dark.

An abnormal color of urine may be caused by the presence of a variety of pigments; for example, hemoglobin may make the urine red or smoky colored; and bile or bilirubin may give urine a brown color. Medications may also change the color of urine.

Appearance

The appearance of urine is important. It is essential to note if the urine is cloudy and, if so, the degree of cloudiness. A note should also be made if solid material, called sediment, is found in the urine after it has been standing. This is more common in the urine of females because of contamination by vaginal secretions. A white, cloudy urine in the presence of an alkaline or neutral urine often disappears on the addition of a small amount of acid to the urine. This material usually consists of phosphate crystals and is a normal finding. Cloudy urine in an acid urine that clears upon heating is often due to urate crystals and is also normal. Cloudy urine may also be caused by pus cells in the urine that indicate inflammation of the urinary tract and may be a very important finding.

Specific gravity

The concentration of urine is compared with water, which is given a concentration or specific gravity of 1.000. Dilute urine has a specific gravity of 1.002, moderately concentrated urine has a specific gravity of 1.015 to 1.025, and very concentrated urine has a specific gravity of 1.030 or above. At times patients are asked not to drink water for a given period of time in order to test the ability of their kidneys to concentrate urine.

Specific gravity of urine is measured in the office by a urinometer cylinder. The urinometer is partially filled with urine and a float is placed in it. The float is spun gently and care is taken so that the bulb does not touch the sides of the urinometer. The mark at which the bottom of the meniscus touches the scales of the float is the specific gravity.

Reaction

Urine can be characterized as acid, neutral, or alkaline. The acidity of a solution is measured by a chemical abbreviation called pH. Acid urine has a lower pH than alkaline urine; urine below 6.0 pH is called acid and above 7.0 alkaline. Although any given sample or urine may be acid, neutral, or alkaline, pooled 24-hour urine samples are usually acid.

Alkaline urine is normal after large meals and is frequently seen if it has been permitted to stand for a prolonged period. Acid urine may be found after ingesting certain drugs such as vitamin C, after large protein meals, or during fasting.

Although the urine reaction may be measured precisely with a pH meter it is usually measured with color strips described later in this chapter.

COLLECTION OF URINE

The time of urine collection is often of great importance. For example some urine tests, such as pregancy tests and tests for the the culture of bacteria, are best collected in the morning. Other tests, such as for pH and glucose, may be influenced by recent meals. Some tests are collected over a given period of time. For example, 24-hour collections are used to test for hormones, protein, or renal function.

Urine should be collected in clean containers and should be fresh when examined. If urine cannot be examined for several hours, it should be stored in a refrigerator. Urine for bacterial cultures should be collected in sterile containers and submitted to bacteriologic testing as soon after collection as possible.

Males should be instructed to collect a sample of urine from midstream during voiding. For females the procedure is more elaborate. The area of the urethra should be gently swabbed with an antiseptic solution at least twice. Care should be taken to separate the labia and maintain them separated during this procedure. Urine is collected from a midstream voiding sample. Failure to follow these techniques will create erroneous interpretations of urine sediments during microscopic examination or bacterial culture.

TESTS IN ROUTINE URINALYSIS

The routine urinalysis is divided into three steps. The first involves noting the physical properties such as color, appearance, and specific gravity. The second involves testing the urine with one of the popular laboratory reagent strips such as Clinistix, Labstix, or Multistix (Figs. 30-1 and 30-2). The third step involves examining the urine sediment with the aid of the microscope. This is sometimes checked by the physician and requires considerable training and experience by the medical assistant.

The development of convenient, solid state reagent systems has been a great advance in routine urinalysis because they have eliminated the need for time-consuming, unprecise, and elaborate laboratory procedures in the medical office. They consist of a transparent plastic strip with up to seven pieces of filter paper attached to one end. Each piece of filter paper is impregnated with chemical agents that change color depending on the concentration of the substance being measured.

The instructions on the bottle should be followed closely. For example, urine should be dipped, immediately removed, tapped against the side of the vessel and read as directed. Glucose is read at exactly 10 seconds after dipping, ketones at 15 seconds, bilirubin at 20 seconds, occult blood at 30 seconds, and urobilinogen at 60 seconds. The pH and protein may be read immediately after dipping. All readings are made by comparing the color developed with the charts on the cover of the container.

Urine pH

Values are read numerically in the range of pH 5 to pH 9; readings may be interpolated to one-half unit.

Protein

Before the development of reagent strips, the measurement of protein in the urine

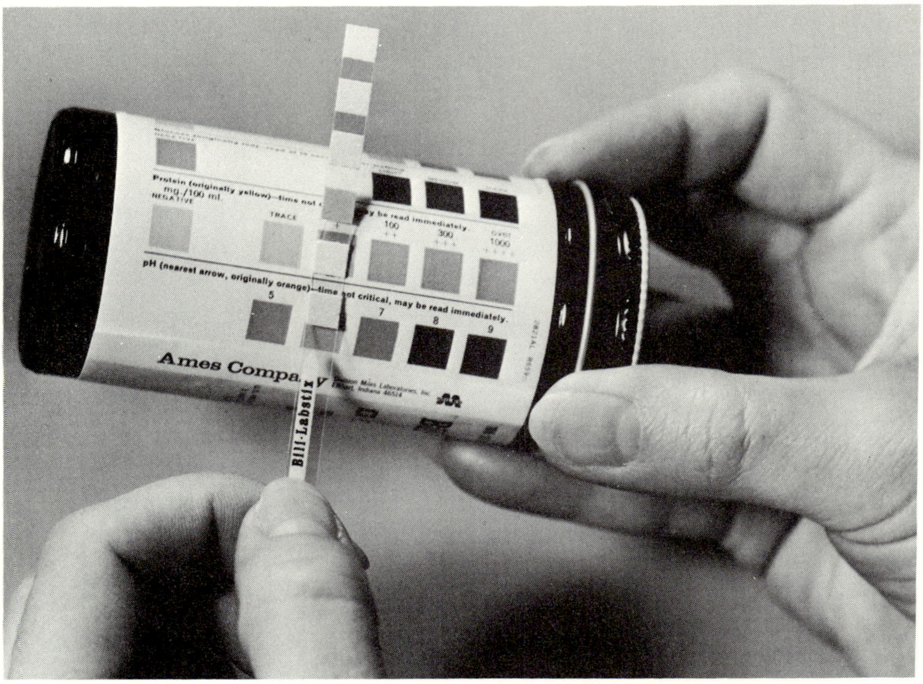

Fig. 30-1. Bili-Labstix strip procedure to determine the presence of glucose, occult blood, bilirubin, and protein in urine. (Courtesy Ames Company, Division Miles Laboratories, Inc., Elkhart, Indiana.)

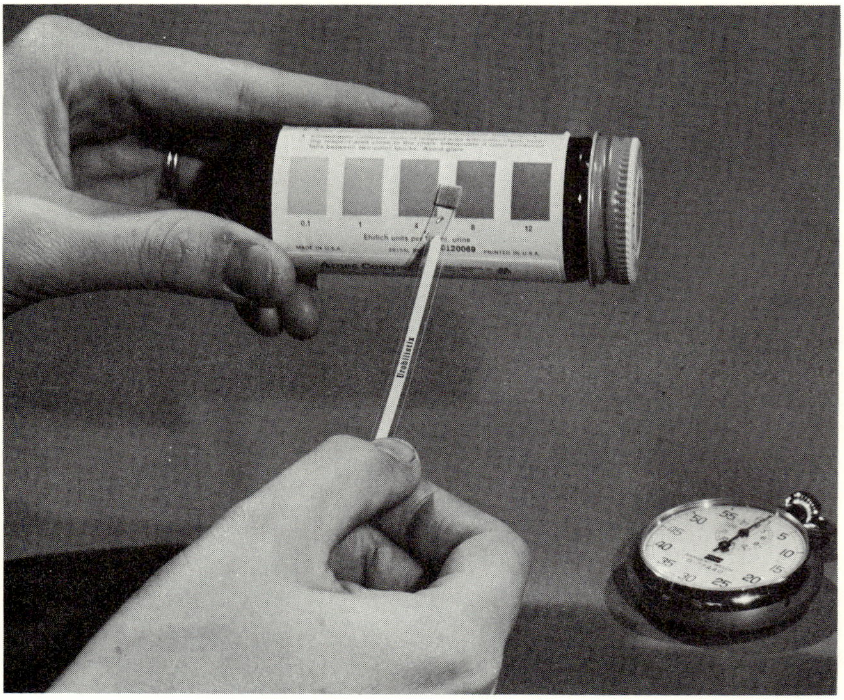

Fig. 30-2. Urobilistix strip procedure to determine the presence of urobilinogen in urine. (Courtesy Ames Company, Division Miles Laboratories, Inc., Elkhart, Indiana.)

was a tedious, time-consuming test involving several reagents and extensive laboratory equipment. These tests are no longer performed in this fashion except on special occasions or by medical laboratories.

Proteinuria is the presence of abnormal amounts of protein in the urine. The most frequently encountered protein in the urine is albumin. For this reason the terms albuminuria and proteinuria are often used interchangeably. Albumin is a protein that is normally found in large amounts in the blood and is of sufficient size that it is filtered out of the urine by the glomeruli. Large quantities of albuminuria or proteinuria therefore suggest that the kidneys' filtering mechanism is failing in its normal function. The most serious cause of proteinuria is kidney disease such as nephritis or nephrosis.

The urine is checked routinely for protein primarily as a screening test for possible kidney disease. It must be emphasized, however, that many individuals have small to moderate amounts of protein in their urine and yet have no serious kidney disease. This, like other laboratory tests, must be interpreted with caution by the physician.

The results of the protein portion of the reagent strip may be read either in a "plus" system or as milligram per 100 ml. Urine with trace or 1 plus protein must be interpreted with caution since it may be normal, especially in concentrated urine.

Glucose

In the normal individual glucose does not appear in the urine unless the concentration in the blood is above 160 to 180 mg per 100 ml. This value is called the threshold for glucose or the blood level at which it will start to spill over into the urine. Since blood concentrations of glucose above 160 or 180 mg% are usually seen only in diabetics, the presence of glucose in a urine sample should make one suspect that the patient has diabetes mellitus. The renal threshold for glucose varies considerably among individuals. In some individuals glucose may not be found in the urine until the blood glucose concentration is considerably higher than 180 mg per 100 ml, while in other individuals it may be present in the urine even with concentrations of glucose between 120 and 140 mg per 100 ml. These levels are commonly reached even by normal individuals after a meal. It is important, therefore, that in individuals not known to have diabetes, further tests involving the measurement of blood glucose be performed before making a diagnosis of diabetes.

The glucose concentration of the urine is made 10 seconds after wetting. A color that matches the light block generally indicates one-fourth gram of glucose per 100 ml of urine; a color that matches the dark block generally indicates more than one-half gram of glucose per 100 ml. When it is important to quantitate the amount of glucose present in the urine, other methods more precise than the reagent strips must be used. One popular method involves the use of Clinitest. This method will be described later in this chapter.

Ketones

When a person has not eaten for over twelve hours, the body starts to utilize stored fats for fuel. As stored fat is burned for energy, certain by-products are produced by the liver. Some of these by-products are called ketones. Ketones appear in normal individuals during starvation. They may also appear in the urine if certain low carbohydrate diets are ingested for prolonged periods. Perhaps the most important use of the ketone measurement, however, is in diabetes mellitus. Ketone bodies in the urine, especially with large amounts of glucose, may indicate that not enough insulin has been taken. The measurement of glucose and ketone bodies is an essential part of the management of all insulin-requiring diabetics.

The shade of lavendar or purple developed 15 seconds after dipping the urine indicates a small, moderate, or large concentration of ketones in the specimen. In diabetic patients a more precise, quantitative measurement of ketones in the urine may be desirable. If this is the case, ketones may be measured by means of an Acetest tablet, which will be described later in this chapter.

Bilirubin

Bilirubin is a pigment that is produced from the breakdown of hemoglobin. Although excessive levels of bilirubin may be the result of an increased breakdown of blood cells in the circulation, the most common causes of high bilirubin levels are liver diseases such as hepatitis and cirrhosis. When these occur the bilirubin is filtered by the kidneys and appears in the urine giving it a brownish appearance. Bilirubin levels are approximated at 20 seconds and are read as small, moderate, or large.

Occult blood

Any blood in a clean, well-collected urine specimen that has not been contaminated by vaginal secretion demands medical evaluation. Modern sticks and tapes have completely replaced older techniques for testing for small amounts of blood in the urine. Blood in the urine can have a variety of causes including injury, infection, kidney stones, tumors of any part of the urinary system, or nephritis. Great caution must be taken to ensure that urine collected from women with vaginal bleeding of any type not be contaminated with vaginal blood. Many physicians postpone routine urinalyses on women who are menstruating.

The shade of blue developed at 30 seconds indicates the urinary concentration of blood. This is usually described as small, moderate, or large. Since red blood cells are heavier than urine, they frequently settle at the bottom of the container after prolonged standing. It is therefore important that the urine be mixed before testing for occult blood. The presence of occult blood should lead to a careful examination of the urine sediment for red blood cells. If none are found, one should consider another substance producing a positive reaction, such as myoglobin, a protein found in muscles, that will also give a positive occult blood test.

Urobilinogen

Urobilinogen is a colorless bile pigment that is present in normal urine in small amounts. Increased amounts of urobilinogen are found with excessive destruction of blood in the circulation and in liver diseases such as viral hepatitis. In order for urobilinogen to appear in the urine, it must first pass through the liver and bile ducts and into the intestines where it is absorbed, enters the circulation, and is filtered by the kidneys. The total absence of urobilinogen in the urine should raise the suspicion of a total obstruction of bile flow. Urobilinogen is measured 60 seconds after dipping the tape in fresh urine. The color varies from light yellow to more intense shades of brown with increasing concentration of urobilinogen. The concentration in the urine should be recorded as 0.1, 1.0, 4.0, 8.0, and 12.0 units per 100 ml.

The urobilinogen measurement can be influenced by several drugs used to treat urinary tract infections. It is important that the urine samples be fresh as urobilinogen decomposes rapidly on standing.

Summary

The seven urine tests discussed provide valuable diagnostic information to the physician concerning the health status of the pancreas (diabetes), kidney, urinary tract, liver, and biliary tract. Furthermore, the dietary status (ketone) or the presence of hemolytic disorders may be indicated.

The procedures are easy to follow and all seven tests can be done in one minute on a given urine sample. However, good technique and close comparison with the color charts are important. The strips should be protected by keeping the cap tightly on the bottle and being sure the urine is fresh and well mixed when tested. There may be false positive or false negative results because of the presence of certain drugs or contaminants in the urine.

Urinalysis should be considered as a *screening* test for possible disease states that may lead to further tests and a final diagnosis by the physician. Development of the solid state, rapid tests now enables routine and repetitive urine testing that can provide more valuable clinical information than is available by any other means.

OTHER METHODS OF MEASURING GLUCOSE AND ACETONE

In addition to the multiple stix preparations two other urinary glucose measuring tests will be described. These are the Clinitest tablets and the Tes-Tape method.

Clinitest tablets are frequently used by diabetics to give an accurate measurement of the spill of glucose in the urine. The materials needed for the test include a test tube, a medicine dropper, water, and fresh urine. Five drops of the patient's urine are placed in the test tube. Ten drops of water are added and the solution is swirled gently. The Clinitest tablet is added and the test tube allowed to stand until the reaction is complete. Care must be taken to avoid touching the bottom of the test tube as intense heat is generated during the reaction. After the reaction is complete, the tube is gently agitated and the final color compared with a color chart. A brick red color indicates that more than 2 grams of glucose are present per 100 ml of urine.

Because of the relative inconvenience of

A

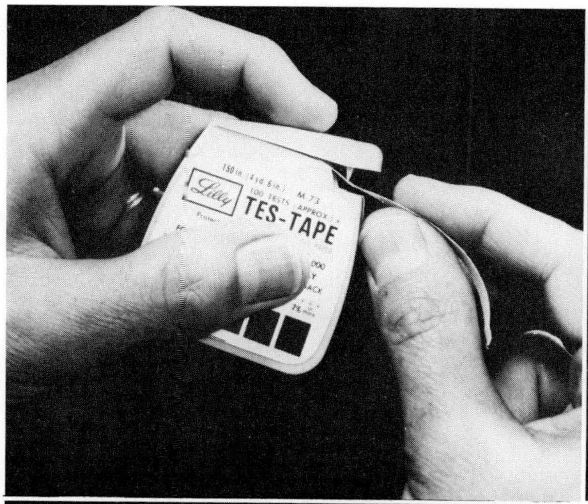

B

C

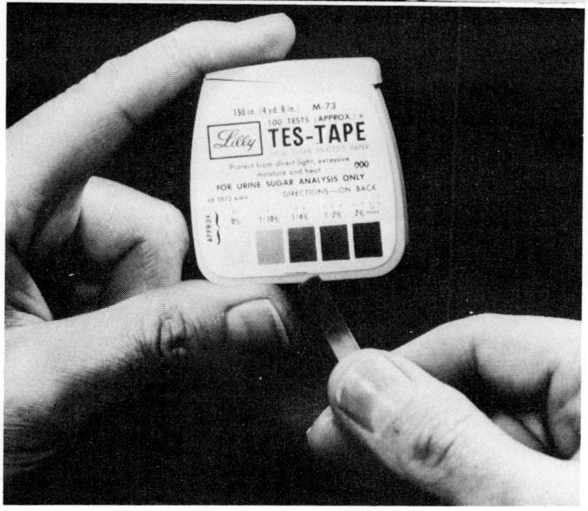

Fig. 30-3. A, Tes-Tape dispenser. **B,** Tes-Tape urine test. **C,** Tes-Tape color comparison chart. (Courtesy Eli Lilly and Co., Indianapolis, Indiana.)

the Clinitest tablet in testing as a means of determining urinary glucose in diabetics, the Tes-Tape method was developed and has achieved wide acceptance. The Tes-Tape method is a colorimetric test based on an enzyme reaction. Unlike the Clinitest method, it will not give positive reactions with a great number of other reducing sugars.

The Tes-Tape consists of a plastic dispenser containing a roll of specially treated test paper that indicates the presence of glucose in the urine (Fig. 30-3, *A*). Each tape dispenser contains sufficient test paper to make approximately 100 tests, provided about 1½ inches of paper are used for each test. The paper is torn, dipped in urine, and allowed to dry in air for one minute and then compared with a color chart on the dispenser (Fig. 30-3, *B* and *C*). If the tape indicates one-half percent or higher, an additional minute of developing time is allowed to elapse before a final reading.

It is important that the Tes-Tape not be placed on a foreign substance while drying. At times patients taking certain drugs may have difficulty correctly interpreting the tests. The tape should not be used if it has turned brown or if the expiration date printed on the carton has passed. The reliability of the Tes-Tape may be checked by dipping it into a non-dietetic cola or pop beverage. If a 4 plus reaction is not obtained, the tape has probably deteriorated and should not be used.

The Acetest tablet is frequently used to measure urine acetone in diabetics. This test is performed by wetting a tablet with several drops of urine and observing the color after 30 seconds. A light purple color will signify "small" amounts of acetone while a deep purple color that develops within 30 seconds signifies "large" amounts of acetone.

MICROSCOPIC EXAMINATION

A careful microscopic study is part of every routine urinalysis. It will often reveal structures of diagnostic importance. For the examination of organized sediments, the specimen should be as *fresh* as possible. If it is not to be examined immediately, it should be kept cold or a little formalin should be added. Red cells and casts disintegrate rapidly in warm specimens, particularly if dilute and alkaline. The microscopic examination should be performed on the sediment obtained by centrifugation, always following a standard procedure. The amount of sediment present is not necessarily indicative of the presence or absence of pathologic structures.

Procedure

Stir or shake the specimen to mix it thoroughly, then centrifuge it. Pour off the supernatant fluid and pour a few drops of the sediment onto a clean slide. Holding a clean cover slip between the fingers by the edges, touch a free edge of the slip to the urine on the slide and allow it to drop over the urine. This prevents formation of bubbles. Place the slide on the microscope stage, holding it in place with the clamps or mechanical stage attachment. Focus with the low-power objective and examine at least six different fields for casts. Then switch to high-power objective and differentiate between different structures. After examining six different fields, estimate the approximate number of the various structures per high-power field (HPF). With some structures, the numbers present may be indicated as: rare, occasional, numerous, or too numerous to count. Others of the more important structures must be estimated in figures, as: 1-4/HPF, and so on. The most important structures to be searched for in sediment are casts, erythrocytes, and leukocytes, although the presence of other structures must be noted in the report as well.

STRUCTURES TO BE SEARCHED FOR IN URINE SEDIMENT (Fig. 30-4)

Organized sediment

Epithelial cells. Skin cells or cells of mucous membranes for various parts of the urinary tract are searched for. The presence of certain types is considered normal, while other types are considered abnormal.

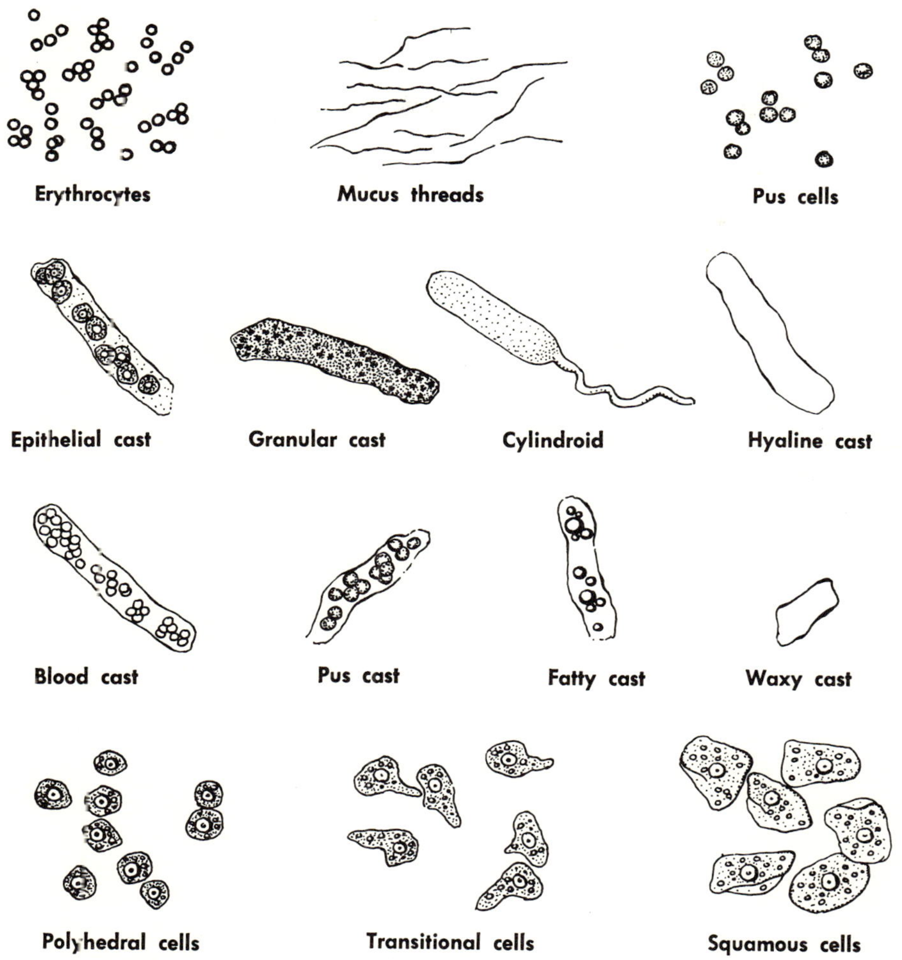

Fig. 30-4. Sediments found in urine under the microscope.

Among epithelial cells are the following types.

1. *Squamous epithelial cells.* These are large, flat, irregular cells with a distinct round or oval nucleus, derived from superficial layers of the urethra and vagina, which may normally be present in the urine.
2. *Small round epithelial cells.* These are small spherical cells about one third larger than leukocytes with a round nucleus, which may come from the deeper layers of any part of the tract. When they are polygonal in shape and granular with a large nucleus, they probably come from the renal tubules and are referred to as renal epithelial cells. The presence of more than a few is considered abnormal.
3. *Transitional epithelial cells.* These may be pear-shaped, spindle-shaped, large and round, or have tail-like processes. They all contain a small nucleus and are derived from the transitional epithelium in kidneys, ureters, and bladder. The presence of more than a few is considered abnormal.

Leukocytes (white blood cells). These are round or oval granular cells that sometimes appear with an irregular periphery. A few (0-3/HPF) are present in normal urine. They are numerous as a result of pathology and are then usually referred to as *pus cells,* or *pyuria.* This pyuria indicates inflammation in some part of the tract. An estimate must always be made, that is, 2-4 WBC/HPF. If they do not average one per field, you may record it as: *rare or occasional WBC.*

Erythrocytes (red blood cells). These usually appear as tiny, round or oval, slightly concave disks with no granulation and are usually one third to one half the size of leukocytes. They may be slightly swollen in alkaline urine and crenated in very acid urine. If present in urine for a long period of time, they may appear as faint rings. Normally, no more than one red blood cell should be found in the urine per high-power field. One should always estimate the number per HPF, just as with leukocytes. Large numbers of cells indicate bleeding in some part of the tract.

Albuminous casts of kidney tubules. These rarely occur in urine that does not contain, or that has not recently contained, albumin. Their presence indicates some abnormal change in the kidney, although this might be slight or transitory. They are searched for under low-power objective with slightly darkened field and usually appear as faint, tubular shadows with at least one rounded end.

1. *Hyaline casts.* These are colorless, semitransparent, cylindrical structures with rounded ends. They may vary greatly in length and width.
2. *Granular casts.* These are hyaline casts in which numerous granules are imbedded. These are designated as finely or coarsely granular casts, depending on the size of the granules.
3. *Fatty casts.* These are hyaline casts containing small refractile fat globlets.
4. *Waxy casts.* These are grayish or colorless and have a dull, waxy appearance, as if cut from paraffin. Those with a distinct yellow color are *fibrinous waxy casts.*
5. *Casts containing organized structures (those in which cells and other structures are imbedded).* The name of the prevalent structure is used to designate these, that is, *blood casts, pus casts, bacterial casts, epithelial casts,* and so on.

Mucous threads. Mucous threads appear in the form of very faint, often twisted, strands. Their presence in moderate amounts is normal.

Bacteria. Under normal conditions, urine is free of bacteria. The presence of more than a few bacteria in the urine sediment should be reported to the physician. The meticulous collection of urine, especially in females, is of great importance. Samples contaminated with vaginal secretions frequently have large amounts of bacteria, which sometimes lead to the erroneous diagnosis of a urinary tract infection.

Spermatozoa. Spermatozoa may sometimes appear as contaminants in urine. Their presence should be indicated if found.

Unorganized sediment (crystals) (Fig. 30-5)

Crystals found in normally acid urine

1. *Uric acid crystals.* These are usually yellow or reddish brown crystals forming rosettelike clusters or rhombic plates. They are of no significance unless found in a fresh specimen in the presence of blood cells, which may then indicate the presence of kidney stones.
2. *Calcium oxalate.* These are colorless, glistening crystals that have the appearance of small squares crossed by two intersecting, diagonal lines. Rarely they take the shape of a dumbbell. They are commonly found in urine after the ingestion of vegetables rich in oxalic acid, such as spinach, asparagus, and tomatoes. They are of importance only when present in clumps with signs of renal irritation, which may then suggest stones.
3. *Amorphous urates.* These appear as fine, yellowish, almost colorless granules and are very common in concentrated and strongly acid urine. They are of no clinical significance. If they are so abundant as to obscure other structures, the urine should be warmed before examining and they will disappear.

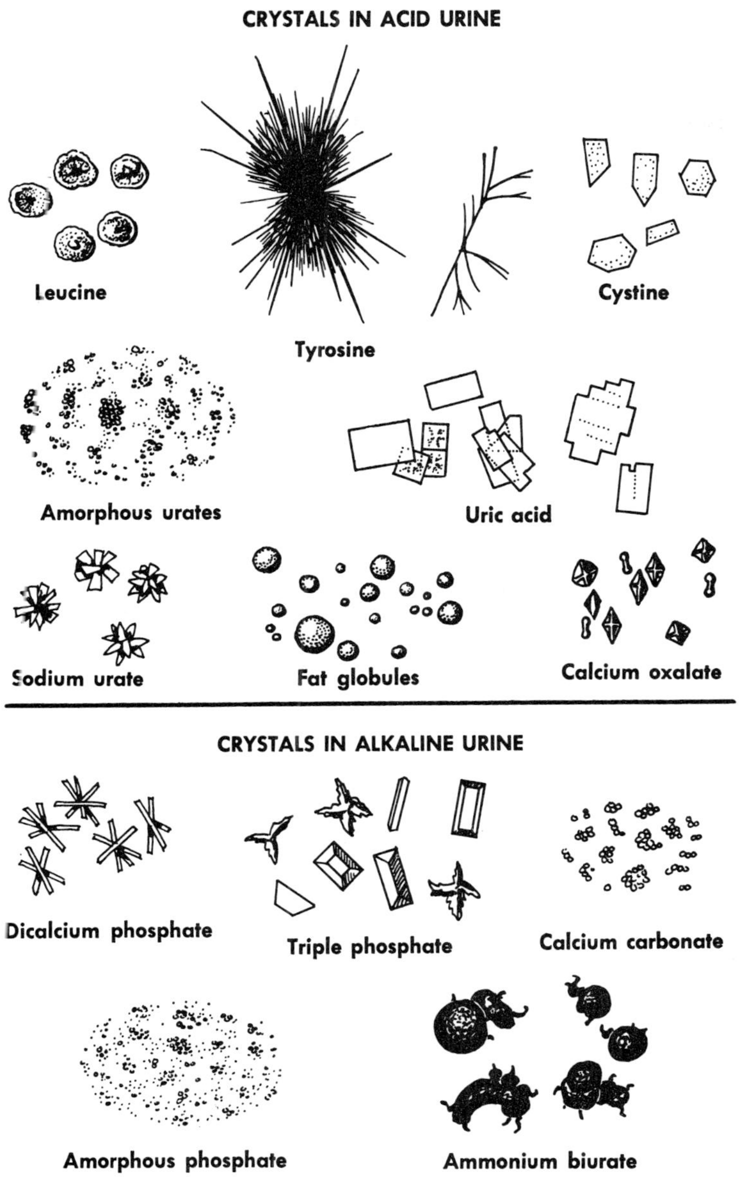

Fig. 30-5. Crystals found in urine under the microscope.

Crystals normal in alkaline urine

1. *Triple phosphate crystals.* These are colorless and may be shaped as a prism or arranged as stars or rosettes. When rapidly deposited, they may assume feathery, starlike, or leaflike forms. They are sometimes found in neutral, or even acid, urine.
2. *Calcium phosphate crystals.* These take the form of large, flat, colorless, jagged-edged crystals or tiny, colorless prisms.
3. *Ammonium biurate.* This is the only urate deposited in alkaline urine. It forms opaque yellow crystals, usually in the shape of spheres or compact sheaves of fine needles. They are generally found with phosphates in decomposed urine and have no significance.

Abnormal crystals found in acid urine

1. *Leucine.* These are slightly yellow, oily-looking spheres with radial striations.
2. *Tyrosine.* These are black sheaves of very fine needles constricted in the center.
3. *Cystine.* These are colorless, highly refractile, rather thick hexagonal plates.
4. *Cholesterol.* Cholesterol appears as large, flat, jagged-edged plates similar in appearance to calcium phosphate crystals.

Outside materials

1. *Trichomonas vaginalis.* These are protozoa that invade the vagina in women and the urethra in males and may be picked up as contaminants in urine.
2. *Yeast cells.* These are smooth, colorless, highly refractile, round or oval cells, frequently budding or seen in chains.
3. *Mold fungi.* These are commonly found in urine exposed to the air. They appear most commonly in branches and are highly refractile.

Review questions

1. What is the normal color of urine?
2. What is the normal reaction of urine?
3. What is the normal specific gravity? What is the significance of specific gravity?
4. Describe three tests for sugar in the urine.
5. When should a microscopic examination of the urine be made?
6. What is the significance of casts in the urine?
7. How is blood detected in the urine?

Suggested readings

Frankel, S., Reitman, S., and Sonnenwirth, A., editors: Gradwohl's clinical laboratory methods and diagnosis, ed. 7, St. Louis, 1970, The C. V. Mosby Co.

Hepler, O. E.: Manual of clinical laboratory methods, ed. 4, Springfield, Ill., 1970, Charles C Thomas, Publisher.

Oppenheim, I. A.: Textbook for laboratory assistants, St. Louis, 1972, The C. V. Mosby Co.

chapter 31

Hematology

One of the most common laboratory tests used in clinical medicine is the complete blood count (CBC). This test involves the determination of hemoglobin, hematocrit, white blood count, red blood count, and an estimate of the percent of various white blood cells present in the blood (differential count). Other tests such as the platelet count, sedimentation rate, reticulocyte count, and tests to detect abnormalities in the red blood cells are done under special conditions. Frequently these tests are performed by medical laboratories or are done by specially trained medical technologists.

In this chapter the physiology of the blood will be outlined and the procedures used in performing CBCs and other hematologic tests commonly performed by medical assistants in an office will be described. It should be emphasized that in some medical offices many of the procedures described are no longer performed. The development of modern laboratory techniques has made it feasible to perform many routine blood tests at a relatively low cost to the patient and with a minimal expenditure of time on the part of the medical assistant.

This textbook can serve only as an introduction to the skills needed to perform a CBC and other basic hematologic tests. It cannot substitute for well-supervised, practical experience in a school or a medical

Glossary

ABO type major determinant of the blood that permits its transfusion into donors

anemia a deficiency of red blood cells or hemoglobin or both

anticoagulant an agent that prevents or delays the clotting of blood

basophil a type of leukocyte; characterized by the presence of dense blue granules

bleeding time the time that it takes a puncture of the skin to stop bleeding

bone marrow the hallow cavity within bone that is responsible for production of blood cells

coagulation time the time it takes blood to clot in a tube

differential count an estimate of the relative percent of the various types of leukocytes in the blood

eosinophil a type of leukocyte found in certain allergic conditions; characterized by the presence of red-staining granules

erythroblastosis fetalis a hemolytic disease of the newborn infant characterized by hemolysis, jaundice, and potential brain damage

erythrocyte (red blood cell) the element of blood that contains hemoglobin

hemacytometer an instrument used in counting red and white blood cells

hemoglobin the substance in blood that gives it its characteristic red color and that transports oxygen from the lungs to the tissues

leukocyte (white blood cell) a normal constituent of blood responsible for providing protection against infection

lymphocyte a type of leukocyte that is important in combating infection and in immunity

neutrophil the most common type of leukocyte; characterized by neutral staining in granules

Rh a blood typing system that is important in transfusions

sedimentation rate the speed at which red blood cells settle over a given period of time

venipuncture insertion of a needle into a vein to remove blood or insert fluids laboratory. This text will not make the medical assistant a fully trained medical technologist.

PHYSIOLOGY OF BLOOD

Hematology is that branch of medicine that deals with the morphology of the blood cells and blood-forming tissues and the study of the blood, its functions, and its abnormalities. Blood is a tissue that makes up about 9% of body weight. An average man has from 5 to 6 liters of blood.

The blood circulates and comes in intimate contact with every tissue of the body, and changes in any tissue of the body are usually attended by changes in the circulating blood. The cells are not produced in the circulation but are derived from parent cells in various organs so that the blood is in the nature of a mixed secretion of a variety of organs.

The blood transports all the chemical nutritional elements and oxygen needed for the function of the tissue cells and removes the waste products of their metabolism. It also carries hormones and various substances needed to defend the body against injurious agents. Since it is the only tissue that can be examined frequently and with ease during life, blood examinations occupy a prominent place in the investigation and diagnosis of disease.

Blood cells are manufactured in the hematopoietic system (blood-forming organs). Erythrocytes are manufactured mainly by the red bone marrow of the short bones such as the sternum, vertebrae, ribs, and proximal epiphyses of the femur and humerus. Leukocytes are manufactured by lymph nodes and glands and by the yellow bone marrow.

The functions of the blood are so intimately associated with the processes of life that any discussion of the subject is necessarily extremely complex. Its functions include the following.

1. Conveying oxygen to the cells from the lungs and carbon dioxide from cells to lungs
2. Carrying food substances such as glucose, amino acids, fats, minerals, and vitamins to the body cells
3. Aiding in the defense of the body against bacteria and other organisms by means of the antibodies and leukocytes
4. Transporting waste products to the kidneys
5. Distributing hormones
6. Equalizing body temperature

EQUIPMENT NEEDED FOR ROUTINE BLOOD WORK

1. A sterile disposable stylet or lancet
2. Alcohol or some other disinfectant
3. Cotton balls or disposable gauze pads impregnated with disinfectant
4. Clean blood pipettes, hemacytometer counting chamber, cover glass, and appropriate diluting fluids if the CBC is to be performed in the office
5. A tourniquet, syringe, disposable needles, and a tube with an anticoagulant for venous blood if the tests are to be sent to a laboratory

STEPS FOR OBTAINING BLOOD SPECIMENS

Blood may be obtained either from the skin, as described later, or, if the tests are to be performed in a laboratory, from blood obtained from veins (venipuncture).

Venipuncture technique (Fig. 31-1)

1. The skin over a prominent vein at the crease of the elbow is cleansed with alcohol or a disposable sponge.
2. A tourniquet is placed around the arm above the elbow and the patient is asked to open and close the hand several times to produce engorgement of the vein.
3. A syringe that is appropriate for the volume of blood desired is used.
4. Generally a 1¼-inch 21-gauge needle with a medium bevel is used and is attached either to the syringe or to a hollow plastic device called a Vacu-

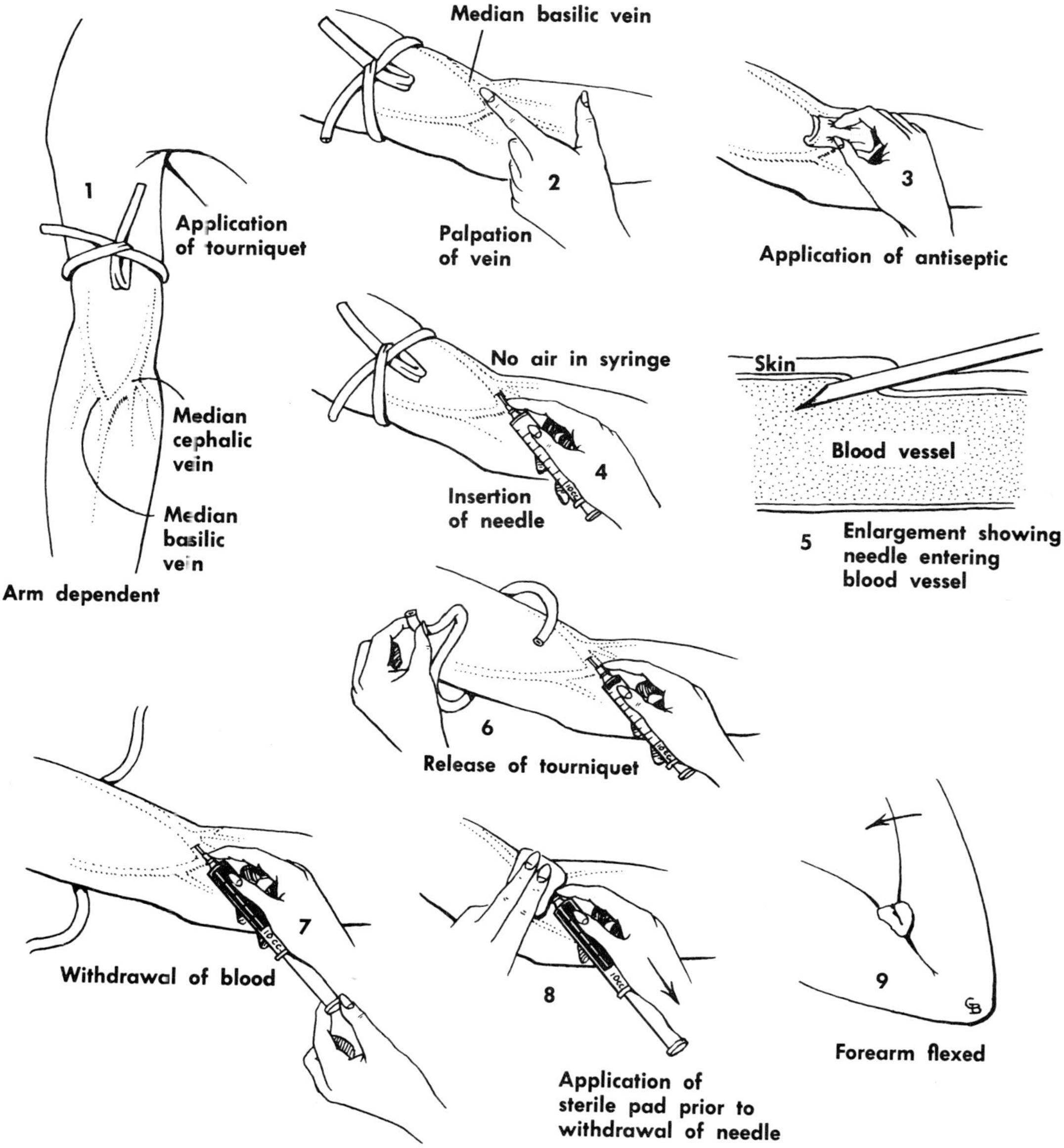

Fig. 31-1. Venipuncture technique.

tainer. A Vacutainer is used when tubes with a vacuum are available.

5. Both the needle and syringe must be sterile and dry. Disposable needles and syringes have replaced glass syringes in many offices.
6. The skin over the vein is drawn tense with the thumb of the left hand. The skin and vein are punctured with a quick thrust of the needle with the bevel of the needle facing up.
7. Once the vein is entered, the needle and syringe are kept from moving and the tourniquet is released.
8. Blood is drawn by slow traction on the plunger of the syringe. Too rapid withdrawal causes collapse of the vein and a temporary halt in flow. When the re-

quired blood has been withdrawn, a sterile sponge is placed over the needle, the needle is removed, and the patient is asked to place the sponge over the puncture wound for several minutes.

9. The needle is removed from the syringe and the blood is gently emptied into a sterile test tube or a tube containing an anticoagulant. If an anticoagulant is present in the tube, the tube is capped and the blood is mixed with the anticoagulant by inverting several times.
10. The syringe and needle should be disposed of properly and a final check made with the patient to ensure that bleeding has stopped completely.
11. If a Vacutainer is used, the Vacutainer tubes are inserted into the Vacutainer and blood is allowed to fill the tube. With this instrument several tubes of blood may be filled with one venipuncture. No syringes are needed. However, the Vacutainer does need special needles designed to screw into place in the Vacutainer. After it is used, the Vacutainer should be washed with tap water but need not be sterile since only the disposable needle comes in contact with the patient's skin.

Skin puncture technique

1. In an adult, use a finger as the puncture site, and in infants, the big toe or heel.
2. Open sterile lancet; cleanse finger briskly by rubbing thoroughly with an alcohol-dampened cotton ball.
3. Produce hyperemia by massaging blood from base of finger to the first joint; hold the finger tightly at that point to retain the blood in the fingertip.
4. When finger is dry (do not dry with cotton ball but allow to air dry), grasp disposable lancet in the proper manner and with a quick stab make a puncture on the tip of the finger with the length of the tiny puncture parallel with the length of the finger.
5. With a dry sterile cotton ball, always wipe off the first drop of blood.
6. If the puncture is of sufficient depth, a drop of blood should appear again. If the amount is insufficient, more blood may be massaged from the finger base up to the first joint. *Never* squeeze around the puncture site, as the tissue fluid will be expressed and the results of the tests will be erroneous. If not enough blood is obtained, the finger should be punctured again. If the patient has cold hands, ask him to rub them briskly to improve the circulation or have him hang the arm downward to bring more blood to the fingers by gravity.

ERYTHROCYTES (RED BLOOD CELLS)

Erythrocytes are biconcave disks containing an iron-bearing protein known as hemoglobin. They give the blood its red color. Normally, erythrocytes in the circulation have no nucleus. Nucleated erythrocytes are found normally only in the bone marrow and appear in the circulation only in blood diseases.

Normal erythrocyte count

The red blood count remains fairly stationary from day to day in normal individuals. A normal red cell count in men is 4,500,000 to 6,000,000 per mm^3. In women the normal red cell count is 4,000,000 to 5,500,000. In children the red cell count is about 7,000,000 at birth, falls during the first few months, and is similar to that of the adult by adolescence.

Technique for red blood count

In most medical laboratories the red cell count is performed by a special machine called a Coulter counter. A small amount of blood is placed in the Coulter counter and the machine within several seconds gives the red blood count on an electronic display. When the red blood count is performed in an office by the assistant, the following steps must be followed accurately and diligently if accurate results are to be obtained (Fig. 31-2).

1. After the puncture has been made and

the first drop wiped off, take a red pipette, and, holding it almost horizontally with the side of the tip resting against the finger, draw blood up to the 0.5 mark. If drawn up slightly above this mark, the blood may be brought down by tapping the tip of the pipette against a dry finger or by wiping the tip on a dampened towel.

2. Wipe the tip of the pipette off quickly

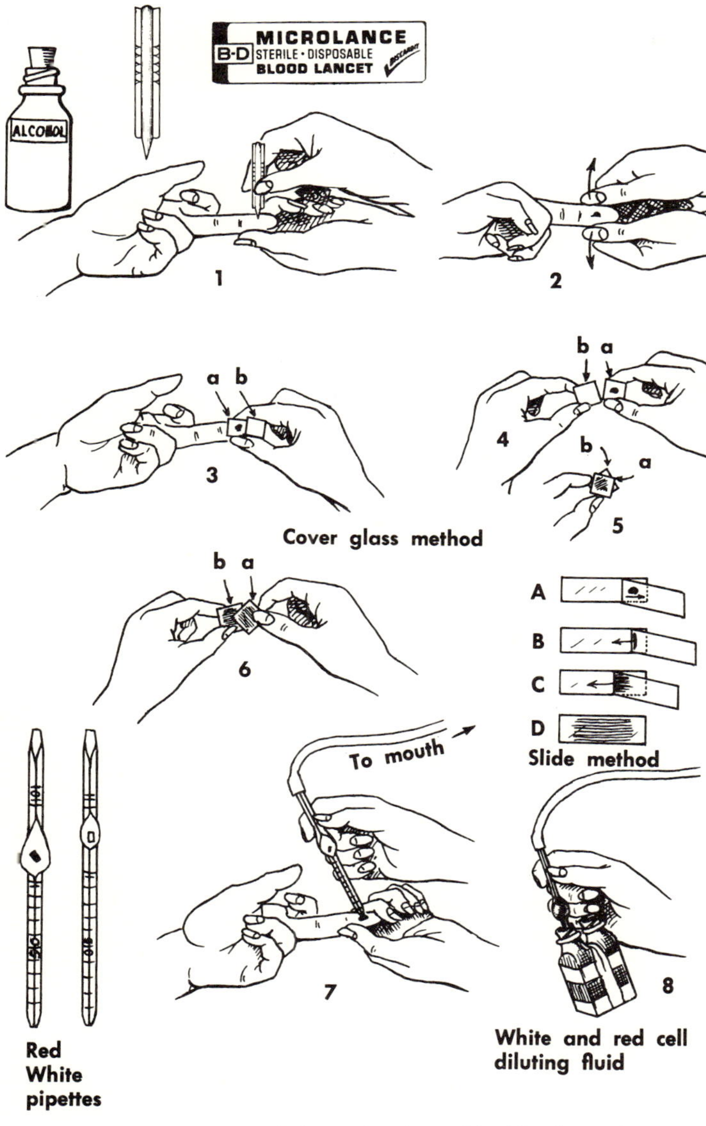

Fig. 31-2. Technique of red or white blood count.

Fig. 31-3. Red blood cell pipette. (Courtesy American Optical Company, Buffalo, New York.)

with cotton before placing into the diluting fluid.

3. Place the pipette immediately into the red diluting solution and draw up the solution exactly to the 101 mark (Fig. 31-3). Hold the pipette as vertical as possible. Rotate the pipette between the thumb and forefinger while diluting to avoid blood clots. This prevents the formation of bubbles. If the solution is drawn slightly past the mark, it may be brought down by tapping as previously described. Blood is diluted by a factor of 200 in the red pipette.
4. Place tongue over opening in tube to hold solution at the proper mark and withdraw pipette from the solution quickly, immediately placing it in a horizontal position and placing forefinger against the tip. Holding it thus, remove the rubber tube and place thumb over end, shake a few times, and then place pipette on table. Proceed to the next operation.
5. When ready to make the count, shake the pipette thoroughly for 1½ to 2 minutes, being sure not to shake along the long axis but in a circular or figure-eight motion.
6. After shaking, immediately blow out about five drops or perhaps even one third of the bulb's contents. The counting chamber should be charged immediately.
7. The counting chamber (Fig. 31-4) and cover glass should be checked previously to see that they are clean, dry, and lintless, and the cover glass should be placed in the proper position over the counting platform.

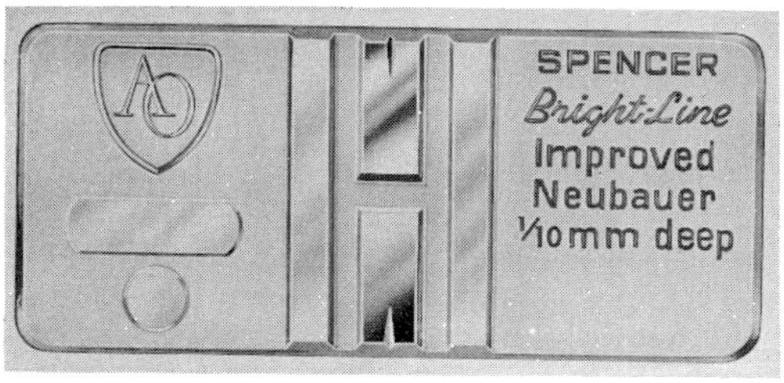

Fig. 31-4. Hemacytometer (counting chamber). (Courtesy American Optical Company, Buffalo, New York.)

8. Charge the counting chamber by placing the tip of the pipette at the edge of the cover glass at an angle, allowing the dilution to run under the cover glass by releasing the pressure of the finger slightly over the opening at the top of the pipette so that the dilution completely and exactly fills the space between the chamber and the cover glass. No bubbles or extraneous matter should be present.
9. Allow the cells to settle for 1 to 2 minutes before counting.
10. Place the chamber on the microscope stage and with low-power objective check for uniformity of distribution, air bubbles, and dirt particles. If satisfactory, locate the red counting area, consisting of twenty-five large squares, each of which contains sixteen small squares (Fig. 31-5). Then, the top left-hand corner square should be moved to the center of the field, and the objective switched to high power. Count all cells contained within the sixteen squares of the corner square as well as all cells contained within the remaining three corner squares plus the center square, making a total of five large squares (each containing sixteen smaller squares). To avoid confusion in counting, count all the cells touching the outer line on the left and top, but do not count those touching the inner line on the right and bottom of each of the five large squares. (When there are three lines instead of two bordering each large square, the center line is considered to be the outside line.)
11. To determine the final count, add the five counts together and add four zeros. This will represent the number of red blood cells per cubic millimeter of blood.

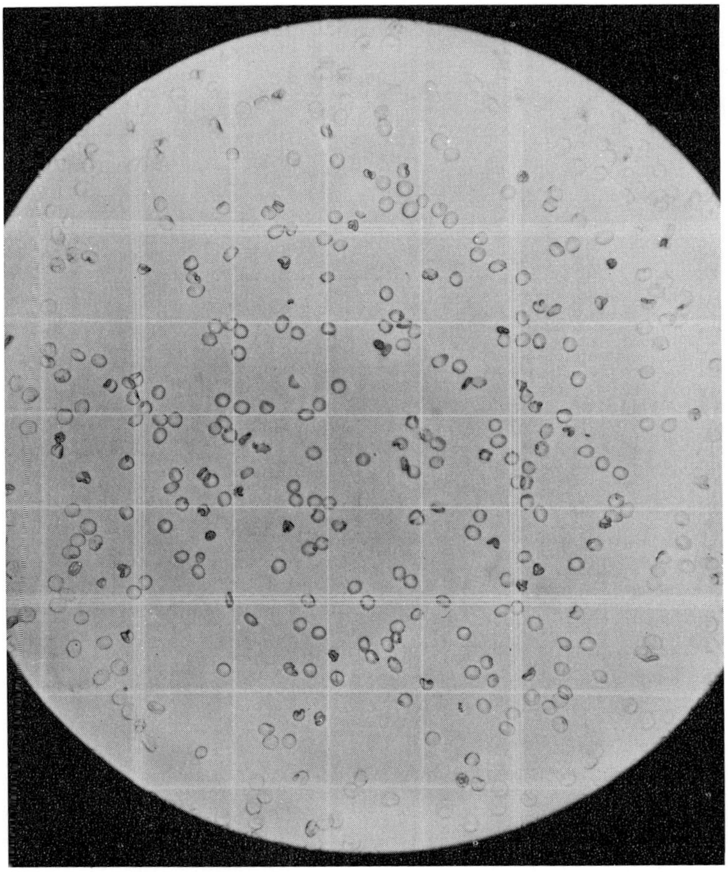

Fig. 31-5. Technique of counting red blood cells (16 squares).

Red cells diluting fluids

Diluting fluids are isotonic to red cells. They cause white blood cells to swell and disintegrate, leaving mainly red blood cells. Among fluids used are Hayem's solution, considered by most to be the best of the diluting solutions, Toison's solution, and physiologic saline, which should be used only in an emergency when other solutions are unavailable.

HEMOGLOBIN

Hemoglobin is composed of heme, an iron pigment, and globin, a large protein, and is normally found only in red blood cells. In the lungs, hemoglobin picks up oxygen, which is released in the tissues. Hemoglobin turns from a bright red to a darker color in the tissues with the loss of oxygen. Thus blood in an artery is red while blood in a vein may have a dark blue color.

In men the normal hemoglobin concentration is 14 to 18 grams per 100 ml of blood. In women the normal concentration is 12 to 16 grams per 100 ml. Values less than these are considered abnormal and this condition is known as anemia. In newborn infants the normal hemoglobin concentration is 20 to 22 grams per 100 ml of blood but falls rapidly during the first few weeks of life.

When blood is sent to a medical laboratory for a CBC, the test for hemoglobin concentration is always performed, which in most large laboratories takes only a few seconds.

When a CBC is performed in a medical office, the determination is frequently done with less sophisticated equipment but, if properly performed, can be very reliable. Most of the commonly performed tests convert hemoglobin into a chemical form that causes a color change in direct proportion to the amount of hemoglobin originally present in the blood. This color change is compared with standard solutions containing known quantities of hemoglobin. The instrument that measures the exact color change is called a photometer. Instructions for the use of various photometers and office procedures for the determination of hemoglobin are supplied by the manufacturers of the equipment.

Differential white count (leukocyte count)

A differential count is an estimation of the specific types of white blood cells found in the blood. This procedure requires that a thin smear of blood be prepared and that this smear be stained with dyes that will permit differentiation of the various forms of white blood cells. In order for this procedure to be performed it is essential that the smear be properly made and that the stain be adequate to distinguish the various types of white blood cells.

There are five types of leukocytes commonly found in blood. They are the neutrophil, eosinophil, basophil, lymphocyte, and monocytes (see Fig. 31-8).

During bacterial infections, there is often an increase in neutrophils with the appearance of immature forms of neutrophils in the circulation. After certain viral illnesses, it is common for an increased number of lymphocytes to be present in the blood. During certain types of allergic reactions or infestations with parasites, eosinophils may appear in increased numbers in circulation. The presence of extremely immature and bizarre-looking white blood cells, especially when the total leukocyte count is greatly increased, is the key finding in patients with certain types of leukemia.

LEUKOCYTES (WHITE BLOOD COUNT)

One of the main functions of leukocytes is to act as collectors of debris in circulation. When bacteria invade the bloodstream, they are engulfed and destroyed by leukcocytes. If an infection starts in a part of the body, leukocytes are mobilized and are attracted to the site of infection where an inflammatory reaction takes place and the bacteria are usually eliminated. At times this collection of leukocytes and debris forms a fluid that we refer to as pus. In addition to infection, there are other factors that produce inflammation and will cause an increase of leukocytes in the blood. In leukemia, a form of cancer of white blood cells, the leukocyte count may be extremely high. When leukocytes are deficient in the blood the patient is often unable to fight off infections effectively; an example of this is the patient who has a marked reduction of leukocytes after taking certain drugs. When the white blood count is above normal, the condition is called *leukocytosis* and when it is abnormally low it is called *leukopenia.*

Normal values

In adults, the normal range is from 5,000 to 10,000 per cubic millimeter of blood. The average normal is 7,500. At birth the count may be as high as 20,000, rapidly decreasing into the normal range for children within a few weeks; the normal range for children is usually considered to be from 8,000 to 11,000. The white count may vary from day to day. It is often higher after vigorous exercise.

Technique for white blood count

If blood is analyzed in a laboratory, it is placed in the Coulter counter with a special fluid that destroys the red blood cells. The remaining cells, the leukocytes, can be counted within several seconds. It is clear that the Coulter counter can perform a procedure in as little as one minute that might take the medical assistant up to half an hour. If blood is analyzed in the office the procedure (Fig. 31-2) below should be used:

1. After wiping off the first drop of blood,

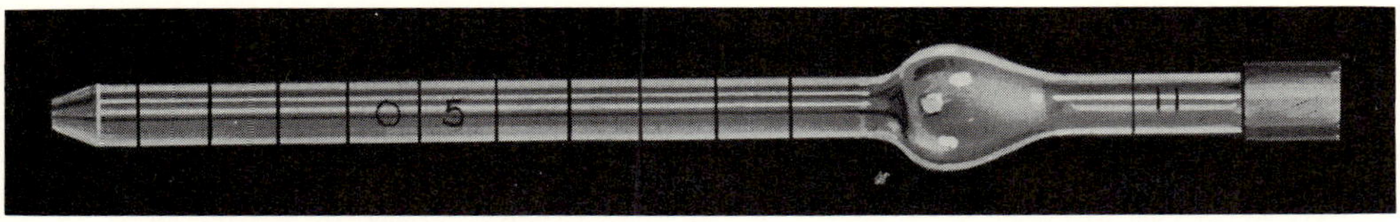

Fig. 31-6. White blood cell pipette. (Courtesy American Optical Company, Buffalo, New York.)

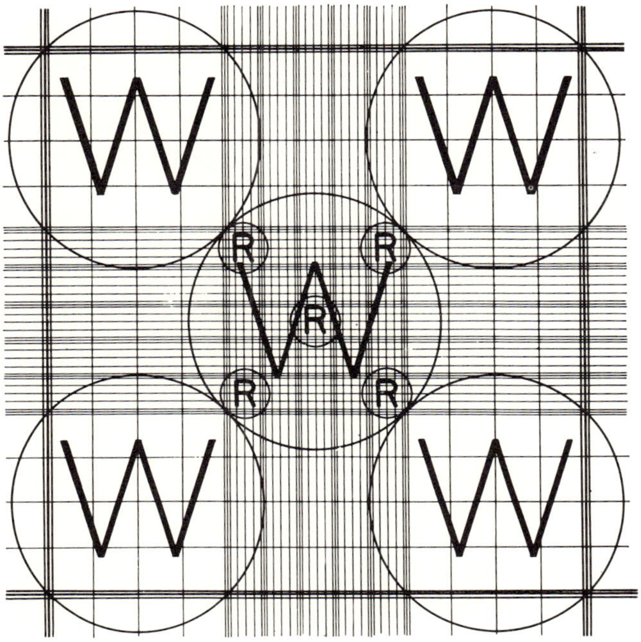

Fig. 31-7. Diagrammatic scheme for converting either red or white blood cells.

draw it up to the 0.5 mark in the white pipette (Fig. 31-6).

2. Wipe off the tip quickly and plunge it into the white diluting solution, drawing up to the 11 mark. This dilutes the blood twenty times.
3. Shake the pipette for 1½ to 2 minutes, and blow out or expel three drops.
4. Immediately charge the counting chamber and allow the cells to settle for one minute.
5. Locate the white counting squares with the low-power objective in the extreme corners of the entire ruled area, and count all the cells seen in the four corner squares (each containing sixteen smaller squares) (Fig. 31-7).
6. Multiply the total of all four squares by 50, and this will give the number of white blood cells per cubic millimeter of blood.

White cell diluting fluids

White cell diluting fluids are isotonic to white cells and hypotonic to red blood cells. They include N/10 hydrogen chloride and 1% to 2% acetic acid.

Preparation of smears

1. Using a clean glass slide, touch one end to a drop of blood on the finger, taking care not to touch the slide to the patient's finger.
2. Place the slide on a flat surface with the drop of blood to the right, and steady it with the left hand.
3. Take another slide in the right hand and, at about a 45 degree angle, touch

the end of that slide to the surface of the other slide to the left of the drop of blood. Then, with a free, steady motion, draw the slide up to the blood and allow it to spread almost the entire width of the slide. Then, with a steady, light, and even pressure, push the spreader to the other end. The blood will follow, making a smear. A thin to medium film of blood is preferable for making an accurate differential count. This is regulated by:

a. The angle by which the slide is held to spread the blood (The smaller the angle, the thinner the smear.)
b. Pressure of the spreader on the slide (The greater the pressure, the thinner the smear.)
c. The size of the drop of blood (The smaller the drop, usually the thinner the smear.)
d. The speed used in smearing

4. Write the patient's name and the date through the thick end of the blood smear with a pencil when blood is dry.
5. Place the slide on the staining bridges over the staining pan. Add Wright's stain quickly, drop by drop, until the slide is covered generously. Or, you may make a heavy wax ring with a marking pencil around the smear and place the stain within this area. Note the approximate number of drops used (usually about sixteen to twenty). Allow the stain to remain for 1 to 3 minutes. (The time depends on that particular batch of stain; whenever a new bottle is purchased, it should be tested to determine the best staining time, as the batches vary.)
6. At the end of the staining time, apply buffer solution (may be distilled water) over the stain, using the same number of drops. Then blow gently over the surface of the slide to mix the buffer with the stain until a metallic scum is visible on top. Allow the buffer to remain from 2 to 6 minutes (usually double the staining time).
7. Float off the stain and buffer by pouring a gentle stream of distilled water over the slide while it is still on the staining bridges. Continue rinsing thoroughly for about 10 seconds.
8. Prop the slide at an angle and allow it to dry, or place it between a folded sheet of smooth filter paper, right side up, and smooth the paper gently with the fingers to remove the water.
9. When it is ready to examine, place a drop of immersion oil on the smear near the thin end or toward the center of the smear, and place the slide under the oil-immersion objective, making certain that the objective is immersed in oil.
10. Following a pattern so that the same area is not covered twice, classify a total of 100 leukocytes. The total number of each type then represents the percentage of each. When making a pattern, moving the slide on the stage, it is considered preferable to start at the bottom edge of the smear, working to the top edge, then moving slightly to the right and down to the bottom again. The edges should always be included in the pattern, as there is a tendency for segmented neutrophils to be located there.

Main types of leukocytes

The following is an outline of the types of leukocytes (Fig. 31-8).

I. Granulocytes
   A. Neutrophils
      1. Segmented polys
      2. Stabs or bands
      3. Juveniles or metamyelocytes
      4. Myelocytes
   B. Eosinophils
   C. Basophils
II. Lymphocytes
   A. Mature
   B. Immature
III. Monocytes

Granulocytes—neutrophils

Segmented neutrophils. The segmented

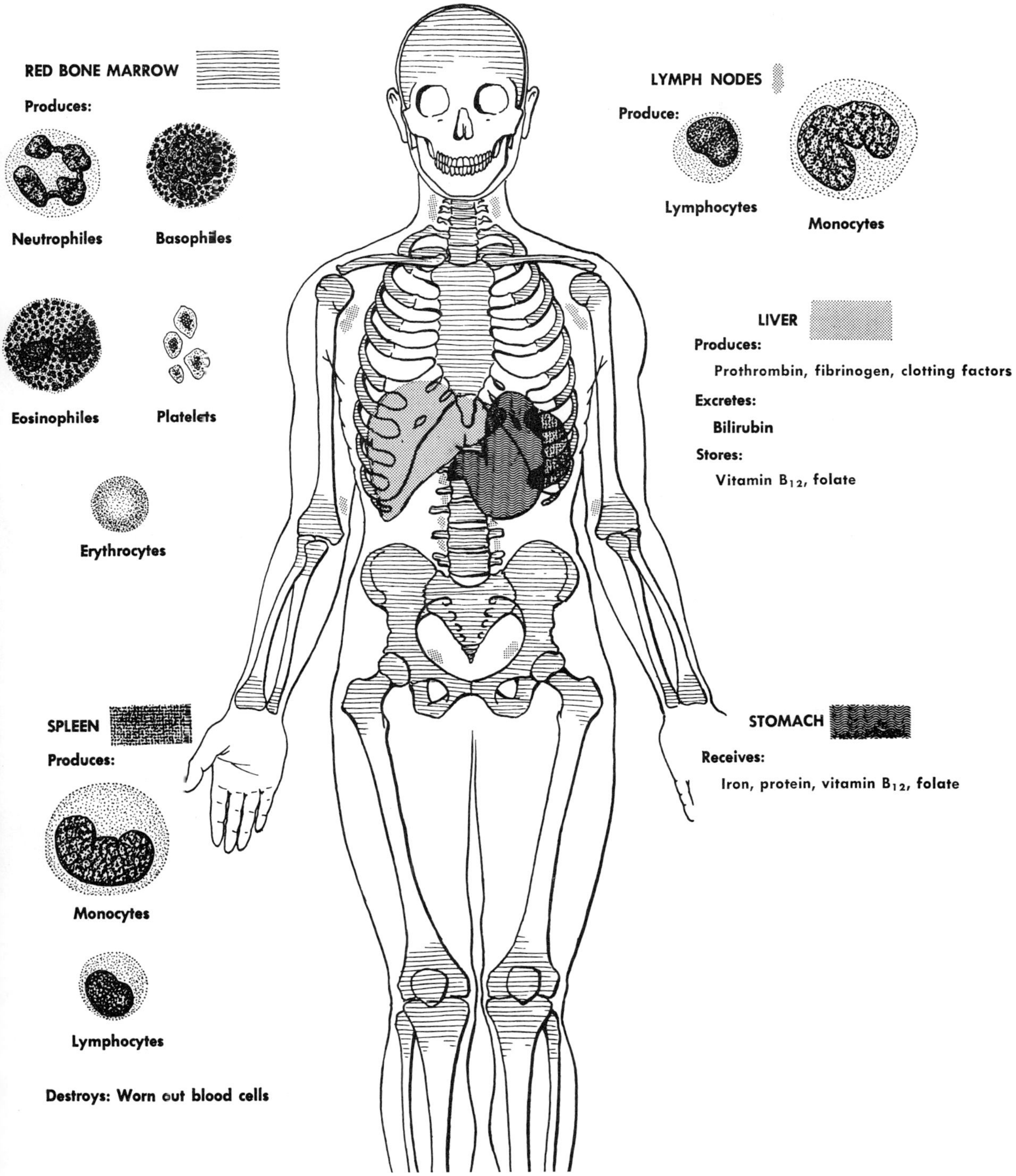

Fig. 31-8. The hematopoietic system.

neutrophils are commonly called segs or polys. Normal values are 55% to 69%. They are round or oval cells. The cytoplasm is a lavender or pink color, with pinkish or lavender granules. The nucleus is segmented, having from two to twelve segments, but usually three or four, and it stains a purplish or lavender color. It should be reported if cells with five or more segments are present in the smear.

Stab neutrophils. Stab neutrophils are commonly called stabs, bands, or rods. Normals are 2% to 5%. The cell is round or oval, with a cytoplasm similar in color to that of the segs, and contains fine granules that are pinkish or reddish violet. The nucleus is one continuous piece that looks like a flexible rod. It commonly forms letters, such as C, S, N, and U. The nucleus is colored a dark purple or lavender, and it occupies about one quarter of the cell.

Juvenile neutrophils. Juvenile neutrophils are commonly called juves. Normals are 0 to 1%. The cell is round or oval and the cytoplasm is usually a bluish pink, containing granules that may be definite or fine and of a purplish or reddish color. The nucleus is bean shaped and usually purplish in color. It usually occupies about half the cell.

Myelocyte neutrophils. These are commonly called myelos; they are not present in normal blood. The cytoplasm often takes an almost neutral stain, tinged with blue, and it, as well as the nucleus, is dotted with definite pinkish or purple granules. The nucleus is round or oval, ordinarily stains bluish purple, and takes up about two thirds of the cell.

Granulocytes—eosinophils. Eosinophils are commonly called eos. Normals are 1% to 3%. The cytoplasm has light blue tinges and is covered with coarse, round or oval, bright pink or red granules. The nucleus is usually segmented and stains a deep lavender to light blue.

Granulocytes—basophils. Basophils are commonly called basos. Normals are 0 to 1%. The cytoplasm takes a neutral or bluish tinted stain that is sprinkled with very coarse, dark purple granules that may also be found on the nucleus. The nucleus usually takes a lavender or purplish stain and may sometimes be segmented.

Lymphocytes. Lymphocytes are commonly called lymphs. Normals are 20% to 40% for adults and 35% to 60% for children. Mature lymphs are relatively small cells, often no larger than red cells. Cytoplasm is usually a bright blue and at times may be almost negligible, as the purple or lavender nucleus may take up almost the entire cell. Immature lymphs are larger than mature cells, having much more cytoplasm, which generally stains a very pale, glass-like blue. Occasionally, a few pink granules may appear in the cytoplasm. The nucleus is usually round or oval but may be indented as well. It stains a purple or lavender color.

Monocytes. Monocytes are commonly called monos. Normals are 2% to 6%. These are the largest of all the white cells and are also considered the most delicate. Very commonly they are quite irregular in shape and usually take a pale stain. The cytoplasm is usually a smoky blue-gray, sometimes sprinkled with a fine pink dust. The nucleus generally is horseshoe shaped or lobulated, staining a lavender color.

SEDIMENTATION RATE (WINTROBE METHOD)

In the sedimentation rate determination, the distance that the red corpuscles have fallen after a given interval of time is measured.

Needed equipment includes a Wintrobe hematocrit tube, pipette, and bulb or the metal pipette and 2-cc syringe, a test tube containing dried double oxalate mixture, and a centrifuge and Wintrobe rack.

Procedure

1. Venous blood is drawn and oxalated by expelling into oxalated tube, corking it, and repeatedly inverting tube at least ten times.
2. Blood is then withdrawn from tube by

means of the pipette and bulb or by pipette and syringe. The pipette is then passed to the bottom of the Wintrobe hematocrit tube, and the blood is gradually expelled as the pipette is raised, always keeping the tip below the surface of the blood. Fill the tube to the 0 mark, making sure that there are no bubbles present.

3. Immediately place the tube in the Wintrobe rack, allowing it to stand vertically for exactly one hour.
4. At the end of the hour read the level of the junction between the plasma and cells, which corresponds with a calibration mark.
5. For accurate results the sedimentation rate should be corrected. This is done by obtaining the hematocrit as described in the following section. The corrected rate is then found by the aid of the chart.
6. To correct the sedimentation rate find on the chart the horizontal line corresponding to the sedimentation rate for the patient. Find also the vertical line corresponding to the volume of packed red cells for the patient. Select the curved line nearest the point of junction of the horizontal and vertical lines, and follow this to the line representing the normal volume of packed red cells for men or women, as the case may be (42 cc line for women and 47 cc line for men). The horizontal line at this last point of junction leads to corrected sedimentation rate.
7. The normals for this method in females are 2 to 20 mm/hour (average 9.6 mm/hour). Male normals are 1 to 10 mm/hour (average 3.7 mm/hour).

The sedimentation rate is elevated during infections and in many types of inflammation. Increased sedimentation rates are also seen in many types of arthritis, malignancy, and during pregnancy. The sedimentation rate is an aid to the physician in determining the effectiveness of therapy for certain forms of arthritis.

HEMATOCRIT

Formerly, the hematocrit determination was a tedious procedure because it required 30 to 40 minutes of centrifugation. During this period the blood was spun in a tube and the heavier red blood cells collected at the bottom. Since large tubes were formerly used it took a long time to completely pack the red cells to the bottom.

In recent years extremely rapid, reliable and relatively inexpensive centrifuges have been developed that permit determination of the hematocrit in 3 to 4 minutes. These hematocrit centrifuges are designed to spin small capillary tubes at extremely high speeds for a relatively short period.

Procedure

1. Small, disposable hematocrit tubes are used.
2. The hematocrit tube is allowed to fill from the colored end by touching it to a drop of blood from the finger or the blood that has been collected in a tube with anticoagulant.
3. The tube is filled to about three quarters of capacity and is then capped with clay that is provided in a special dispenser.
4. The tube is then placed in the hematocrit centrifuge, secured in place with a special cover, and centrifuged for 3 or 4 minutes.
5. The hematocrit is read from a special scale. In normal people the hematocrit is about three times the hemoglobin concentration.

The hematocrit is the percentage of volume of total blood volume occupied by the red cells after they have been packed at the bottom of the tube. In men the normal hematocrit is about 42% to 54% and in women it is 36% to 48%. Other normal blood values are given in Fig. 31-9.

COAGULATION TESTS

Before a major surgical procedure, a physician frequently wants to be certain that the patient has the ability to coagulate blood normally. If this is not done, the patient may experience severe hemorrhage as a result of

Blood values for normal individuals

		Average	*Range*
Red cells	men	5.4 million/cu.mm.	4.6-6.2
	women	4.8 million/cu.mm.	4.2-5.4
Hemoglobin	men	16 gm./100 cc.	14-18
	women	14 gm./100 cc.	12-16
Hematocrit	men	47 cc./100	40-54
	women	42 cc./100	37-47
Mean corpuscular volume		87 cu. micra	80-94
Mean corpuscular hemoglobin		29 micromicrograms	27-32
Mean corpuscular hemoglobin concentration		34%	32-36
Reticulocytes		0.5%	0.1-0.8
Sedimentation rate (corrected)		0.20 mm./minute	0.08-0.35
Platelets		300,000 cu.mm.	250,000-350,000
Leukocytes		7,000 cu.mm.	5,000-10,000
Neutrophils			
Total		66%	50-70
Band forms		4%	3-5
Lymphocytes		26%	20-30
Monocytes		6%	3-9
Eosinophils		2%	0.5-3
Basophils		0.5%	0-1
Clotting time		3 minutes	2-6
Bleeding time		2 minutes	1-3

Fig. 31-9

routine surgical procedures. Even though most of the tests to determine coagulation are no longer done in the physician's office, but in large medical laboratories or in the hospital, the medical assistant should be familiar with some of the more frequently performed tests for coagulation.

Bleeding time

The bleeding time test is a test in which a puncture is made in the skin, usually on a finger, and the time that it takes for bleeding to stop is noted. In certain types of bleeding disorders the bleeding time may be markedly prolonged.

Coagulation time

This test gives the time it takes the blood to clot in a tube. In this procedure blood is removed from the vein of the patient and placed in two or more tubes that are tilted every 30 seconds until a clot appears. The time that it takes to coagulate the blood varies greatly with the size and type of the tube used as well as the method. Prolonged clotting times occur in certain types of hemophilia, or may be caused by liver disease, a deficiency of platelets, or certain drugs used to inhibit coagulation.

BLOOD TYPING

All humans have two major systems that determine if blood can be given to or received safely from another individual. One of these is called the ABO blood type system and the other is the Rh system, both of which are inherited from our parents. If a major discrepancy exists in either of these blood typing systems, a serious reaction may occur after a transfusion that could cause severe illness or even death.

The most important blood type system is called the ABO system. Individuals are either A, B, O, or AB in blood type. In addition, they are either Rh positive or negative. Thus an individual is classified both in terms of his ABO type and his Rh type. For example, a patient may be A positive, B positive, A negative, B negative, and so on. In general, transfusions are given to patients using blood that has the exact ABO and Rh characteristics as the recipient. In grave emergencies the blood of certain O-negative individuals may be given to anyone. This blood is known as universal donor blood.

In order for blood to be given safely, the blood type of both the donor and the recipient must be known. This is done routinely on all donor blood by the Red Cross or other collection agencies for blood. Because of the potential hazards involved in erroneous blood typing, these procedures are rarely done in general medical offices except by licensed medical technologists, by physicians, or by medical assistants under careful supervision of a physician.

Before a transfusion is given, serum from the patient is mixed in a test tube or on a slide with a small sample of red cells of a proposed donor. If abnormal precipitation or coagulation of the donor red cells occurs, the blood is not given because the patient's serum and the donor's blood do not match. This procedure, which is done immediately before a transfusion, is called cross-matching.

The Rh factor is especially important because Rh-negative women who are impregnated by Rh-positive men may produce fetuses that are susceptible to serious complications during pregnancy and immediately after delivery, causing a condition known as erythroblastosis fetalis. This is characterized by severe destruction of red blood cells, jaundice, and sometimes brain injury. Modern medical advances can almost entirely prevent these complications if proper medical care is given to pregnant women.

About 45% of Americans are type O; 40% are type A; 10% type B; and 5%, type AB. About 85% are Rh positive and 15% Rh negative.

BLOOD FOR CHEMICAL DETERMINATIONS (BLOOD CHEMISTRIES)

It is important for the medical assistant to be familiar with some of the terminology used in ordering and obtaining blood for chemical determinations. When a procedure calls for whole blood, the blood is collected in a tube containing an anticoagulant and is sent to the appropriate laboratory. Immediately after collection the blood should be mixed by tilting it several times to assure complete mixing with the anticoagulant. If coagulation has obviously occurred it is usually wise to bring this to the attention of the physician or to collect a second tube.

When the chemical procedure calls for plasma, blood is collected in a tube containing an appropriate anticoagulant. This unclotted blood is centrifuged and the clear supernatant fluid is called plasma. The separation is frequently performed in the medical laboratory but may sometimes be performed in the office.

When the procedure calls for a serum sample, the blood is collected in a plain tube without anticoagulant and allowed to clot, which takes from 30 to 60 minutes. After the clot has formed, the tube may be centrifuged and the resultant clear supernatant solution is the serum.

Although serum and plasma look alike, the basic difference is that serum has been obtained after the blood has spontaneously clotted. Chemically, the main difference between serum and plasma is that serum does not contain fibrinogen, a key factor used in clot formation. See Fig. 31-10 for an outline of the elements contained in normal blood.

Care should always be taken to label specimens with the appropriate name and date. It is also important to follow precisely the instructions of the laboratory in obtain-

Elements contained in normal blood

- Blood
  - Cellular elements
    - Erythrocytes
      - Hemoglobin
      - Lecithin
      - Salts
    - Leukocytes
      - Granulocytes
        - Neutrophils
        - Basophils
        - Eosinophils
      - Lymphocytes
      - Monocytes
    - Thrombocytes (platelets)
  - Plasma
    - Serum
      - Antibodies
      - Serum albumin
      - Serum globulin
      - Glucose
    - Fibrinogen . . . . . Yields fibrin

Fig. 31-10

ing the correct blood, plasma, or serum sample. In some instances refrigeration or freezing of the sample may be required.

Dextrostix*—blood sugar test. Dextrostix is a solid-state reagent strip that provides a rapid, 1-minute test for blood sugar (Fig. 31-11). The glucose in the blood reacts with the enzyme glucose oxidase, which is impregnated into the cellulose fibers of a reagent area at one end of a plastic strip. This reaction forms hydrogen peroxide, which in turn reacts with the indicator orthotolidine and the enzyme peroxidase, which are also impregnated into the reagent area so that orthotolidine is oxidized to a blue color, the intensity of which depends upon the level of glucose in the blood.

Being enzymatic, the reaction is specific for glucose. A blood sugar determination should measure glucose, since this is the sugar whose blood level is affected in diabetes. Dextrostix measures blood glucose over a range of 45 mg/100 ml of blood to 250 mg/100 ml (Fig. 31-11).

*Ames Company, Elkhart, Indiana.

The procedure calls for adding a large drop of whole blood onto the reagent area, waiting 60 seconds, washing the blood off with a sharp stream of water, and then comparing the color of the reagent area with a color chart. Color blocks are provided for 45, 90, 130, 175, and 250 mg/100 ml. Color development on the strip with an intensity that falls between two color blocks may be interpolated for more definitive answers.

The drop of blood used may be obtained by fingertip capillary puncture or, if desired, by venipuncture. The finger should be cleaned with an alcohol swab and allowed to dry prior to puncture. A large drop of blood should be allowed to form (may be aided by squeezing blood toward fingertip) prior to applying to the Dextrostix reagent area. If blood is obtained by venipuncture, fluoride-containing tubes should be avoided since fluoride inhibits the enzymatic reactions of the strip. Only fresh whole blood should be used.

If the drop of blood used is too small and only part of the reagent area is cov-

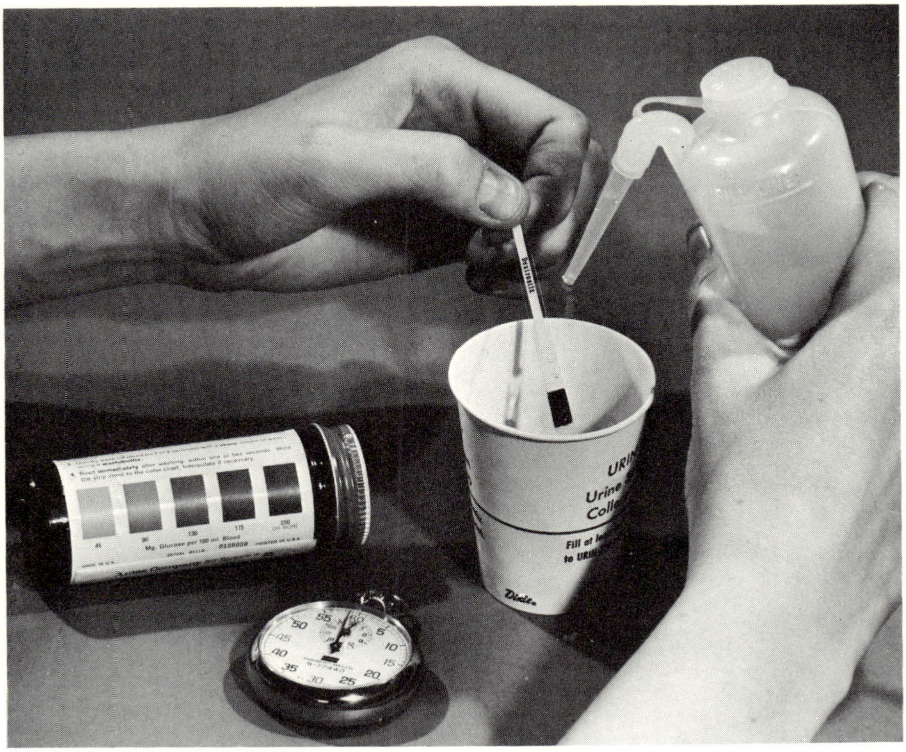

Fig. 31-11. Dextrostix strip procedure for rapid determination of blood glucose. (Courtesy Ames Company, Division Miles Laboratories, Inc., Elkhart, Indiana.)

ered, the color comparison step is made more difficult. If the reagent area is covered but with a thin film instead of a large drop, the blood tends to dry on the strip prior to the end of the sixty-second period, giving values that are too low. The blood used should be fresh, since on standing glucose in blood undergoes glycolysis and disappears. Again, only whole blood should be used and it should be mixed well prior to testing.

Timing is critical. Valid results are dependent upon washing the strip at exactly sixty seconds. If the strip is overwashed, color can be washed from the strip, giving values that are too low. If the strip is underwashed, the red blood on the strip will make reading the answer difficult. Therefore, a sharp stream of water and a rapid wash give the best results.

In recent years the manufacturers of the Dextrostix reagent strips have developed a relatively inexpensive and accurate method that has gained wide clinical acceptance for measuring blood sugar. This system uses a Dextrostix reagent strip and a special meter. Instructions for the use of this meter are supplied by the sales representative of the company.

Blood chemistry automated instrumentation systems. Several instruments have been developed that permit the determination of over eighteen different chemicals in a single blood specimen. These automated systems permit the analysis of what formerly would take several hours to be completed in a few minutes, resulting in a considerable saving to the patient. Because of the rapidity in which the tests can be performed, the relative economy in laboratory time required for their performance, and their high reliability, the tests have become almost universally accepted. The two most common forms of automated chemical instrumentation systems are Auto Analyzer or SMA systems and the Ames/BMI systems.

Review questions

1. What is the function of the blood?
2. Describe the steps in doing a complete blood count.
3. What is the normal range of red cell count? White cell count?
4. Describe the technique for a white blood cell count.
5. What is the normal hemoglobin in men, women, and children?
6. What is the significance of a differential blood count?
7. Describe the preparation of a blood smear.
8. What is meant by sedimentation rate and hematocrit?
9. State the difference between coagulation time and bleeding time.
10. Discuss the method of taking a venipuncture.

Suggested readings

Dougherty, W. M.: Introduction to hematology, St. Louis, 1971, The C. V. Mosby Co.

Seiverd, C. E.: Hematology for medical technologists, ed. 4, Philadelphia, 1972, Lea & Febiger.

Wintrobe, M. M.: Clinical hematology, ed. 6, Philadelphia, 1967, Lea & Febiger.

chapter 32

Medical office microbiology

The science of microbiology has developed so rapidly within recent years that it is impossible to more than mention certain phases of the subject in a book of this type. The branch that is of the greatest interest to the medical assistant, namely, the study of pathogenic microorganisms, will be dealt with in this chapter. Among the lowest forms of living things are organisms that are too small to be seen without the aid of a powerful microscope and that are of such simple structure that a single cell suffices for all their vital activities.

There have been many famous scientists who have been involved in the study of microbiology. Among the most famous to be considered is Louis Pasteur. As the result of the research of Pasteur, the study of the causal relation between bacteria and disease was taken up with renewed vigor. Investigations into the cause of certain infectious diseases in plants and insects placed a doctrine upon a firm foundation. Later it was demonstrated that microorganisms were responsible for certain infectious diseases in man and animals. The brilliant research of Pasteur may be regarded as the foundation of the science of bacteriology.

PREVENTIVE MEDICINE

The principles of microbiology are applied in many ways in the science of pre-

Glossary

acid-fast stain a stain used to identify tuberculosis bacilli
antibody a protein developed by the body that recognizes a foreign substance or infectious agent
culture medium a solution or preparation used to grow bacteria or fungi
empyema pus in a body cavity, especially the chest
epidemic the appearance of an infectious disease that attacks many people at the same time in the same area
evolution a process of orderly and gradual change or development
furuncle an infection of the skin forming small pockets of pus
gram stain a common test used to identify and characterize bacteria
immunity a protection provided against infection by specific antibodies produced during a previous exposure to an infectious organism
incubation the interval between exposure and the appearance of the first symptom of infection
morphology the science of external structure and form without regard to function
pasteurization the heating of a substance at a temperature that destroys objectionable organisms without major chemical alterations of the substance
pathogenic productive of disease
peritonitis inflammation of the lining of the abdominal cavity
poliomyelitis a viral disease that produces inflammation of the spinal cord
septicemia a toxic condition from the invasion of the blood stream by bacteria, viruses, or the products of microbes
thrush a fungal infection of the mouth or throat
VDRL a serologic test for syphilis
wheal a more or less rounded evanescent elevation of the skin that is usually white in the center and pink in the periphery and accompanied by itching

ventive medicine. Vaccines and antitoxins of every sort are the direct products of microbiologic methods. Tests for immunity such as the Schick test for susceptibility to diphtheria, the various tests for tuberculosis, tests for typhoid fever, and other tests that have been developed within recent years have made the science and study of microbiology a progressive field in medicine.

A characteristic of modern medical methods is the care with which diagnoses are made. In a great number of instances there is not the least need to guess whether or not a patient has a particular infection. The examination of sputum for tuberculosis will usually give information that is of tremendous aid to the physician in making a diagnosis. We have in mind cases in which the entire line of treatment was changed as a result of a diagnostic test that could not have been made except by one trained in the methods of microbiology. For example, if the pus drawn from a person with empyema contains a pneumococcus, the treatment given to that patient will be different from that given when the pus contains a bacillus. The life of the patient may depend upon just such a difference. A considerable part of the work of the medical assistant will lie in the collection and care of such samples as may need to be taken and sent to the laboratory. It is often very important for purposes of diagnosis and treatment to determine as soon as possible the nature of the microorganisms causing an infection.

CLASSIFICATION OF MICROBIAL INFECTIONS

Diseases caused by microbes are the most common causes of illness and death in the world. Since almost everyone will, during an average lifetime, acquire an illness caused by an infection, in this chapter we will concentrate on discussing the procedures most often used in a general medical office to identify the cause of infections. It is beyond the scope of this chapter to provide a comprehensive review of microbiological technique.

VIRAL DISEASES

The viruses are the smallest living organisms, most of which are not visible with light microscopes. All but a few do not respond to routine antibiotics.

Perhaps the most common infectious disease is the common cold, which may be caused by any one of over one hundred different viruses. Most of us become infected with a common cold virus, develop antibodies to that virus, and recover from the infection within two weeks. The antibodies developed against the virus protect us against it in the future but do not protect us against the dozens of other viruses that may cause a similar illness. It is not unusual, therefore, for one person to develop several colds every year and dozens of colds in a lifetime.

Other common diseases caused by viruses are chickenpox, mumps, smallpox, poliomyelitis, measles, and German measles. All of these diseases are caused by specific viruses. In addition, certain viral infections may produce sore throat, bronchitis, and gastroenteritis.

Most of the office microbiology performed on patients with infections is done to ensure that a bacterial infection is not causing the illness. For example, throat cultures are taken to be sure a sore throat is not caused by a streptococcal bacterial infection.

In general, viral cultures are tedious and complicated procedures performed only in large medical laboratories. At times physicians will order diagnostic viral studies that measure the amount of antibodies the patient has against a given virus during an illness and again several weeks after recovery from the illness. If there is a marked increase in antibodies, the physician can look back and presume that the illness was caused by a given virus. Since this information is of no help to the physician in treating an individual patient, these tests are not commonly performed in a medical office practice. These tests are, however, important in studying epidemics of viral diseases by public health authorities.

Vaccines have recently been developed against many viruses that were formerly major causes of death and disease, such as those causing smallpox, poliomyelitis, measles, German measles, and mumps. Other vaccines, for example, those given for rabies and yellow fever, are used under special circumstances.

FUNGAL DISEASES

Fungi, which can be seen with the aid of a microscope and can be grown in a culture medium, are less important as a cause of disease than are either bacteria or viruses. They are resistant to most antibiotics but can be treated with specific drugs.

One of the most common fungal diseases, thrush, is due to infection by the fungus *Candida* and causes white plaques to appear on the throats of infants. This fungus is also responsible for many cases of vaginal infection in women and skin and nail infection in patients of all ages. Another group of skin infections caused by fungi is ringworm, which commonly occurs on the scalp, between the toes (athlete's foot), and in the groin.

Some fungal infections can affect the lungs, heart, and brain and cause death. Patients with cancer and other chronic illnesses, especially those treated with anticancer drugs, are especially susceptible to serious fungal infections.

BACTERIA IN EVERYDAY LIFE

In everyday life we are constantly working with or against bacteria. We wash our hands because they have bacteria on them. We disinfect a wound for the same reason. We cover our sneezes. We wash fruit before eating it. We try to keep the flies off our food. We have sanitary sewers and carefully controlled water supplies. We pasteurize milk. We have refrigerators and sealed cans in which to keep our food. We avoid dust and use vacuum cleaners. We do a hundred things a day that we would not need to do if there were not billions of these microorganisms constantly about us.

The good medical assistant is a master of applied bacteriology, although perhaps without knowing the exact reason for doing a great many things. Needless to say, understanding the underlying principles could make a good medical assistant become even better. Since the discovery of bacteria as a cause of disease and wound infection it has been possible to explain a great many things that had been previously shrouded in mystery. With the true explanation in mind, it has been comparatively easy to avoid accidents that would have been inevitable in the old days.

CLASSIFICATION OF BACTERIA

Bacteria may be divided into two subgroups: a lower, simpler form and a higher,

Classification of bacteria

Classes in which pathogenic species occur		*Genera in which chief pathogenic species occur*
Bacteria (Schizomycetes)	Cocci	*Micrococcus, Diplococcus, Streptococcus, Staphylococcus, Meningococcus*
	Bacilli	*Bacillus*
	Spirilla	*Vibrio, Spirillum (Spirochaeta, Treponema)*

Fig. 32-1

more developed form. The members of the lower form are minute masses of protoplasm surrounded by an envelope, each cell a living unit containing all the vital capacities of an independent organism. Although there are hundreds of different species, they can be divided into three general forms as follows: spheres known as cocci, rods known as bacilli, and spirals known as spirilla (Fig. 32-1).

In addition to their form, bacteria are commonly divided into two broad categories depending on their staining characteristics with a special stain called the gram stain. This will be described later in the chapter. At times the gram-stain characteristics of bacteria are known before the organism is identified by more elaborate methods. Knowledge of the results of the gram stain will sometimes influence the choice of antibiotics by a physician before the results of bacterial cultures are available.

The forms of bacteria

Bacteria commonly assume one of three forms, and it is customary to give attention to this fact before other methods of identification are attempted (Fig. 32-2). Each of these general forms shows variations that are of much value in making preliminary attempts at identification.

The coccus. The coccus is round or practically so when it is free from other organisms. Several types of them are capable of producing disease and are of immense medical importance. By virtue of the different arrangement of the cells, the following subgroups are distinguished.

The staphylococcus. The pus-producing cocci are known as the staphylococci. These cocci constitute one of the most important group of bacteria. Sometimes these organisms are known as the pus-producing or pyogenic cocci. They are commonly described as appearing in grapelike clusters.

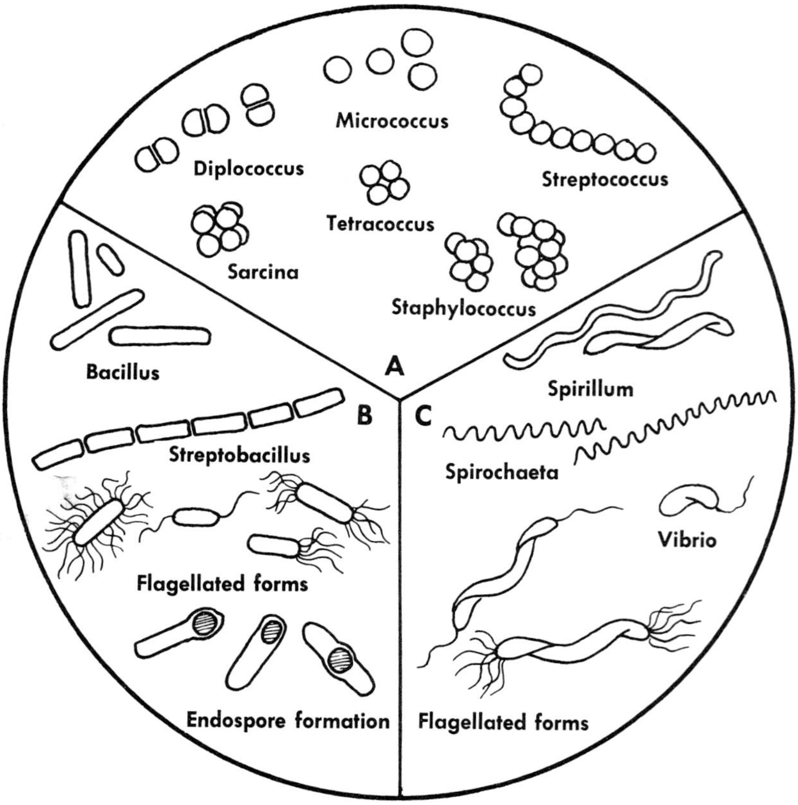

Fig. 32-2. The forms of bacteria. **A,** Cocci. **B,** Bacilli. **C,** Spirilla.

When smeared on a slide they appear to be like marbles that have been rolled out on a flat surface and yet are sticking together as though they were moist. They may appear in short chains of three or four or may be in pairs or in tetrads. They are gram positive. They do not produce spores and therefore are easily killed by various disinfecting agents.

Different strains of staphylococcus show widely varying powers of virulence. Most of the strains that are found widely distributed are quite harmless except possibly under unusual conditions. They typically produce boils; they also aggravate acne by infecting pimples, and producing pockets of infection called furuncles. Wound infections are more often caused by the staphylococcus than by all other bacteria combined. The infections may be quite destructive, but there is usually no danger to life from staphylococcus wound infections unless they are left untreated or there are other complications such as septicemia and spread of the infection.

When penicillin was first introduced virtually all staphylococci were susceptible to its action. In recent years the widespread use of penicillin has been associated with an increased number of staphylococci resistant to penicillin. So common is this problem that many physicians presume that staphylococcal infections acquired in the hospital are resistant to penicillin until bacterial cultures and tests for sensitivity prove otherwise.

The streptococcus. This group of bacteria undoubtedly causes more disease than does any other group. The organisms are comparatively easily recognized as streptococci but present extremely difficult problems when it comes to practical classification of the members of this group. All of the streptococci are gram positive. Streptococci are prone to break body defenses and invade the blood stream, causing septicemia, which in some cases is followed by rapidly fatal blood poisoning and the patient may die within a few days. In other instances recovery may come quickly. The infection may become entrenched on heart valves causing endocarditis, which may produce chronic, progressive disease.

Streptococci are frequently responsible for ear infections (otitis media), sore throat ("strep" throat), skin infection (impetigo), and, less frequently, peritonitis and pneumonia.

Other than the danger of their causing septicemia, by far the greatest importance of streptococci is that they are the primary cause of rheumatic fever and the most common cause of glomerulonephritis in man. These diseases can produce permanent, serious damage to the heart and kidneys but are preventable by appropriate treatment of streptococcal infections. Rheumatic fever is not produced by all types of streptococci, however, but by a type called beta hemolytic because of a characteristic of producing a peculiar growth pattern on blood agar. A physician will want to know if a throat culture performed on a patient has beta-hemolytic streptococci as this will necessitate treatment with penicillin to prevent rheumatic fever.

Almost all streptococci are susceptible to penicillin. Development of penicillin resistance, so common among staphylococci, is unusual with streptococci.

The pneumococcus. It must not be supposed that pneumonia is caused only by the bacteria bearing the name of pneumococcus. As a matter of fact, pneumonia is really the name of a group of diseases of the lung. However, when no qualifying term is used to designate the type of pneumonia, it is commonly supposed that lobar pneumonia is being considered. Lobar pneumonia is a descriptive term for a pneumonia that involves a single lobe of a lung. The pneumococcus is a frequent cause of lobar pneumonia. It is a gram-positive organism usually found in pairs, although it may occasionally grow as a short chain. The individual bacteria are shaped like the tip of the old-fashioned surgeon's lance. The pair commonly is surrounded by a capsule of varying thickness. The most common diseases caused by the pneumococcus organism are lobar pneumonia, bronchial pneumonia, empyema, and some forms of meningitis.

The meningococcus. Meningococci are organisms that predominantly cause meningitis. However, meningitis may be caused by many different bacteria, such as staphylococcus (following injury to the skull), streptococcus (following injury or septicemia), or pneumococcus (following pneumonia). The meningococcus grows in pairs; the individual members of the pair fit together like two coffee beans. They are gram negative, have no spores, and are nonmotile.

The gonococcus. The gonococcus is the cause of gonorrhea. The bacteria was first described by Neisser, whose name is often used with the organism and the corresponding disease. It is a gram negative organism and usually is found in pairs within pus cells.

Gonorrhea in men produces a thick, yellow discharge from the penis *(urethritis)* and at times infection of the prostate and epididymis. Gonorrheal infection, even when treated appropriately, may produce urethral stricture many years after the original infection. Some men are carriers of this organism without any apparent disease. The use of a condom greatly reduces the incidence of gonorrhea.

Gonorrhea in women is a frequent cause of pelvic and genital infections. It is more common for women than men to be carriers of gonorrhea without any symptoms and in women the disease is sometimes difficult to diagnose with bacterial cultures.

Certain strains of gonorrhea are resistant to penicillin except in very high dosages. Newborn infants are routinely treated with silver nitrate eyedrops to avoid blindness from gonorrheal infection of the eyes.

In men the diagnosis of gonorrhea is made either by stains that demonstrate the characteristic intracellular diplococci in pus cells or by culture. In women the diagnosis can be made only by culture. Cultures for gonorrhea are unusual because they must be placed upon the appropriate culture media immediately after they are obtained. These cultures also require specific culture media and careful, specialized attention, such as placing them in covered jars in which a candle is permitted to burn out.

Most states require that all cases of gonorrhea be reported to the local public health authorities. Informing the physician of positive gonorrhea reports and filling in the appropriate venereal disease reports is one part of the medical assistant's job.

The bacillus. The second major classification of bacteria is known as the bacillus. There are more species in this group than in all the others combined. Many of the different kinds of bacilli are practically identical so far as can be determined by staining, measuring, or other morphologic methods. All of the members of this group are longer than they are wide and are best described as being rod shaped. The rods may be relatively long or short, plump or slender, curved or straight, smooth or beaded, and motile or nonmotile.

The colon bacillus. The colon bacillus (also known as *Escherichia coli* or *E. coli*) is found in enormous numbers in the normal bowel of humans and animals. Its predominance there is such that it is hard to isolate other species belonging to the group because the colon bacillus dominates the picture as seen in smears. We are accustomed to consider the colon bacillus nonpathogenic, but it is not unlikely that it kills and injures more people, at least in the temperate zones, than all of the other members of the group combined. It is, for example, the common cause of peritonitis following a perforation or rupture of the bowel. It causes a great many cases of cystitis and infections of the kidney. Many cases of colitis are thought to be caused by the irritation of this organism, also certain types of diarrhea in infants. Some types of *E. coli* are more likely to cause disease than others. The colon bacilli are gram negative.

The typhoid bacillus. The typhoid bacillus is the most important one in the group.

Typhoid bacteria are found in nature in the human bowel and in materials recently contaminated with feces. Such contaminated material will not cause the disease unless it is taken into the mouth, either with food or contaminated water. With the advent of modern sewage and water treatment facilities, there is very little typhoid fever in developed countries. A vaccine is available for those who are traveling to underdeveloped areas of the world.

In certain states food handlers are required to have a stool culture to ensure they are not carriers of the typhoid bacillus.

The spirillum. The spirillum is characterized by the fact that the organisms are curved in a spiral manner. The spiral may show several corkscrewlike turns, or, in the case of the bacteria of cholera, a portion of a single coil. Few of the bacteria that cause disease belong to this group.

Spirochetes. The organisms that cause syphilis belong to a class of microbes called spirochetes. Because these microorganisms cannot be grown in bacterial cultures, diagnosis of syphilis is made by the use of serologic tests. There are numerous types of tests for syphilis and more than one test may be needed to make a definite diagnosis or to follow a patient's response to treatment.

Syphilis is a particularly treacherous disease because, if untreated, its early manifestations completely disappear and the disease may be latent for decades. In many individuals the disease reappears years later and may produce insanity, brain or heart damage, and even death. Treatment in this stage of the disease is often of no value.

The physician's assistant will at times receive tests from laboratories or public health authorities indicating that a given serologic test for syphilis is positive. Many states require that a detailed report be made of every case of a positive serology. It is important to realize that not all patients with a positive serology will require treatment or are capable of transmitting syphilis. Indeed some patients with chronic disease have positive test for syphilis without ever having had the disease. These tests are called biologic false positive tests for syphilis.

THE STAINING OF BACTERIA

The best of microscopes can reveal comparatively little of the structure and form of most bacteria until they are stained by some means or another. All bacteria seem to contain substances that have a chemical affinity for basic dyes; acidic dyes will stain bacteria faintly or not at all. Furthermore, many bacteria may be destained by covering the stained specimen with a weak acid solution, such as acid alcohol, since the acid combines with the stain and takes it out of the bacteria. It is frequently convenient or useful to stain a given smear by more than one method. This can be easily accomplished by removing the first stain by acid alcohol, rinsing out the acid, and staining it again as if it were the first time.

Preparation for staining

Before bacteria can be stained, they must be put through a process to prepare them for the operation. A clean glass slide, free from greasy film, is used. Usually it is well to make a circle on the slide with a colored wax pencil. This circle will enable the operator to find the smear quickly and serve to aid him in focusing the oil-immersion lens. A drop of clean water is put within the circle. Into this drop of water is mixed a very small amount of the culture to be studied, care being taken not to get too much material or too thick a smear. If the material to be tested is already in a liquid state, the water need not be used, of course. When thoroughly and evenly spread about, the smear is allowed to dry in the air. When dry, the slide is fixed by passing it two or three times through the tip of a Bunsen burner flame. After the smear is made and fixed, it is customary to lay the slide on a rack over some sort of receptacle to catch excess stain.

Special stains

If it is merely desired to make an organism visible under the microscope, a wide variety of basic dyes might be used. It is usually possible, however, to serve two purposes at the same time, and to stain the specimen in such a way that additional information can be secured. For this purpose a great many special or differential stains have been developed. Most of the routine procedures of the practical bacteriologic laboratory depend more or less upon some stain of this sort. All of these stains are merely presumptive evidence of the idenitity of the organism rather than proof of it. It is not possible to identify positively any organism by staining methods alone. Differential stains are tremendously useful in bacteriology, but they must not be considered final proof. For example, an acid-fast stain-

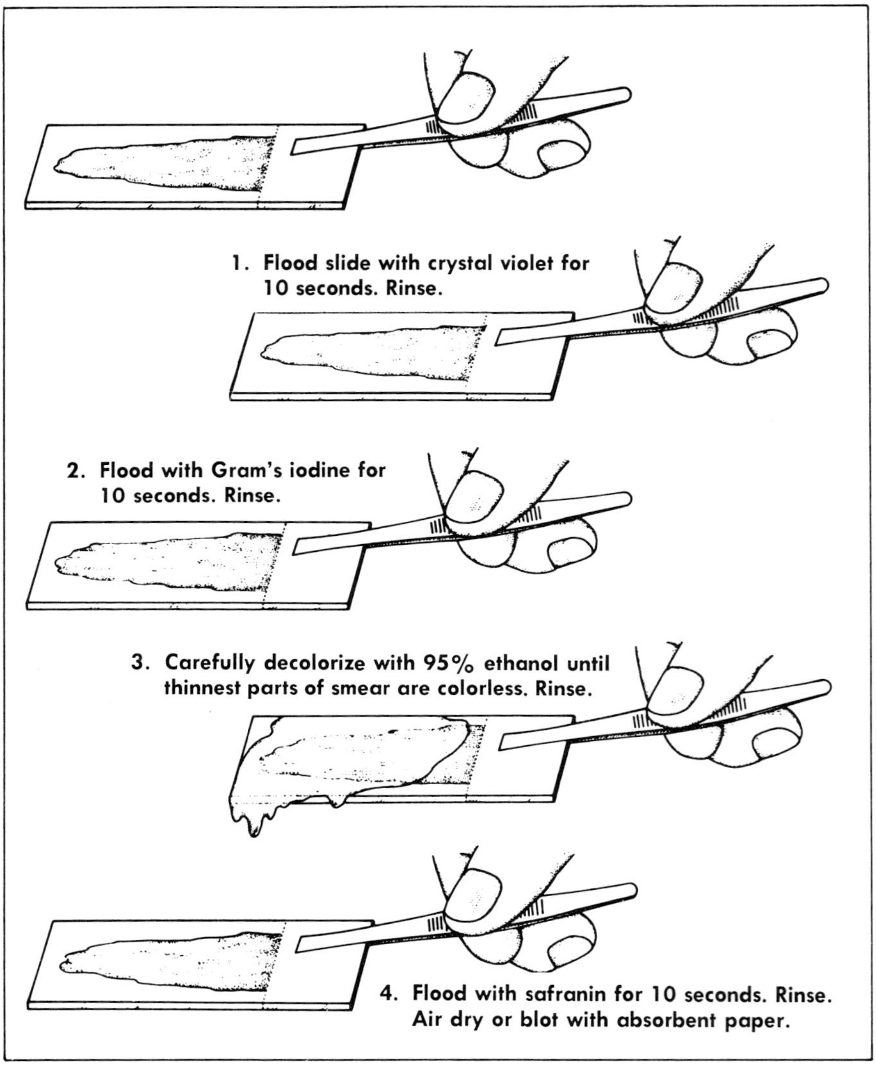

Fig. 32-3. Four steps of the Gram-stain method. Each step entails a tap-water rinse. The smear should be thin, air dried, and gently heat fixed. In step 3, the critical step, ethanol-acetone or acetone may be substituted for ethanol. (From Provine, H., and Gardner, P.: Hospital Practice **9:**86, Oct. 1974.)

ing bacterium, which morphologically seems identical to the tubercle bacillus and is found in sputum, may still be some other quite harmless species. It is presumed, however, with great likelihood of being correct, that it is tubercle bacillus.

The gram stain. The gram stain is the most useful of the special stains. It seems that practically all bacteria fall into one or the other of two categories in regard to their ability or inability to retain gentian or crystal violet after being treated with an iodine solution and then washed with alcohol or acetone. Those that hold the violet stain are known as gram positive, and those that lose it are gram negative. This relation to the gram stain is not an accident but seems to be a rather fundamental division of bacteria, inasmuch as there are many other properties that go along with it. The most reliable method of making the gram stain that we have found is described in Fig. 32-3.

Care of the stained smear

Once the stain is made, the slide must be thoroughly dried and then may be preserved by either of two general methods.

With cover glass. Film may be covered with balsam with a very thin cover glass placed over it. The cover glass must be so thin that an oil-immersion lens will have sufficient working distance. Such slides are permanent.

Without cover glass. The immersion oil can be put directly upon the dry smear and the smear examined without a cover glass. This is the method usually used, but the slides are more easily spoiled. Such slides may have the immersion oil removed with xylol, or they may be stored for some time with the oil left on them. They catch dust in such cases, of course, and the oil may become hardened, but otherwise they are quite satisfactory.

HOW BACTERIA CAUSE DISEASE

It must not be supposed that all bacteria can cause disease or even that the dangerous ones cause it unless certain definite conditions are met. The determination of these conditions and finding ways by which they can be avoided are among the most important reasons for the study of bacteria. In order for disease to be present in the body, there must be some sort of vehicle to carry the bacteria into the body. Prevention of disease consists very largely in prohibiting these carriers from serving in the capacity of introducing the bacteria into the body.

There are four major ways in which bacteria can get into the body and cause disease. One is from contamination with feces. The diseases spread by fecal contamination include typhoid fever, cholera, dysentery, infantile diarrheas, poliomyelitis, and infectious hepatitis.

Another method of disease transmission is discharge. By this term we include mainly secretions from the mouth and nose, the ears, or running sores. Most diseases spread in this manner are those of the respiratory system. Living conditions, the hygienic precautions, and the general intelligence and enlightenment of the community are of the utmost importance in controlling such infections.

Another method of transmission of disease is contact. Diseases spread by contact are mostly those of the skin and eyes, such as ringworm, conjunctivitis, trachoma, wound infections such as tetanus, gas gangrene, rabies, and, of course, the venereal diseases such as syphilis and gonorrhea. The contact may be between two persons, or between an animal and a person, or between a contaminated object and a person. The more intimate and prolonged the contact, the greater the danger. Contaminated objects are far more infectious if they have remained wet since being soiled.

The fourth method of spread of diseases is the bite of insects and these diseases are commonly seen in underdeveloped areas of the world. Tropical regions are noted for such infections, but this is so largely because sanitation development in such regions has lagged. The more common insects and diseases involved are as follows: mosquitoes, which produce malaria and yellow fever; flies, which can produce sleeping sickness and other infections; fleas, which can produce bubonic plague; and lice, which can produce typhus fever, Texas tick fever, and other diseases.

The bacteria must find a suitable portal of entry. Before an invading army can cause real damage to an enemy country, it is necessary that it have some means of transportation to the country it is expecting to invade. Having arrived at its shores, no harm will result unless the soldiers can gain entrance. Bacteria must meet the same requirements so different kinds require different kinds of portals. The bacteria causing the various wound infections must depend upon a break in the skin. For this reason a scratch or cut opens wide the gates. On the other hand, many bacteria that would cause no injury under such circumstances must get into the throat or the bowel in order to produce typical diseases with which their names are associated. Microorganisms that are not able to invade tissues of the normal throat may easily cause trouble in a congested or inflamed throat.

Surgical wounds and the injuries of childbirth must be considered as enormous portals whereby bacteria can gain access to the tissues of the body. Modern surgery and obstetrics owe a great part of their success to the fact that we have learned to regard surgical and obstetric procedures as opportunities for the entrance of infection. Surgical dressings for all sorts are nothing more than means of closing the gate after it has been opened.

In order for disease to occur, bacteria must enter in adequate numbers. Some bacteria are capable of causing disease in animals or man in small numbers; in other diseases, the number required is enormous, and in such cases infection occurs only in the presence of massive contamination. Carrying out the comparison with the invading army, it is obvious that a mere handful of men would do no harm even if they found a suitable portal of entrance. On the other hand, an army of a million men would demand respect and an army of ten million would probably be invincible if other conditions were favorable. Whether a few or many bacteria will be needed to bring about infection will of course depend upon the virulence of the bacteria and on the susceptibility of the host. Most of the sanitary procedures serve merely to reduce the number of bacteria present rather than to do away with all of them.

Surgical operations are theoretically carried out in a sterile manner; however, there are always a few bacteria present in prolonged operative procedures. If the number is less than that required to produce infection, no harm results. In actual life we are constantly exposed to a wide variety of microorganisms but rather rarely have serious infections. As a matter of fact, these subinfectious exposures tend to cause us to become immune by giving us experience with the microorganisms.

The bacteria must be able to grow and reproduce in the body. If the invading army cannot maintain itself in the new territory it will soon be unable to go forward no matter what its size or power may have been in the beginning. Rarely do enough bacteria get into the body at one time to cause serious trouble immediately. Disease develops only when the bacteria have increased in number so that there are many times the original number. This increase necessitates a certain period of time, which accounts for at least part of the incubation period that all infections require. This incubation period varies widely according to particular disease and also according to the number of microorganisms gaining admission and the susceptibility of the host. In order for disease to develop, the bacteria must be able to cause injury to the body. If the invading army does not injure the invaded country, there will be little reason to resist it. Disease is an expression of the inner action of the body and the injurious agent. The injury to the tissue may be produced in various ways that need not be discussed here in detail.

HOW THE BODY RESISTS INFECTIONS

Every day of our lives hundreds and perhaps millions of bacteria, viruses, and fungi penetrate the skin or linings of our lungs and intestines and enter the body. Most of these microbes do not find a satisfactory environment. Many are engulfed by our white blood cells and are killed soon after entry into the body.

In addition to these protective mechanisms, the body possesses a remarkable ability to detect foreign proteins. As soon as a foreign protein substance enters the body, it is recognized as such and complex proteins, called *antibodies,* are made against that specific protein. Most antibodies are proteins that are classified as *gamma globulins* that enable the body to neutralize or kill offending organisms or toxins.

Once the body has eliminated the foreign organism, it has a remarkable memory for the organism and if it encounters it again, antibodies directed against it prevent a disease. When this happens the individual is protected or immune from infection by this particular organism.

Immunity is common with many viral infections such as mumps, chicken pox, measles, or poliomyelitis. It is also common against certain bacterial infections such as pertussis and diptheria and certain toxins such as that produced by tetanus.

It is possible to kill or in some way weaken or modify many viruses and bacteria so that they do not cause serious disease. If sufficient viral, bacterial, or toxin protein is given, the body will produce antibodies to it as effectively as if it had been invaded by the offending organism and an illness produced. This is the most common technique used in immunization. A viral or bacterial protein is given and the body produces antibodies against it. This process is called *active immunization.* Some common forms of active immunization are given at the end of this chapter.

Another method for producing immunity is sidestepping the process by which the body takes days or weeks to make antibodies, to give large amounts of specific antibodies to the patient as an injection. In the past this was done by developing in horses antibodies to various substances. The horse serum, rich in specific antibodies, was given to the patient who got immediate immunity without waiting for his body to make its own antibodies. This process of immunization is called *passive immunization.*

Passive immunization with horse serum has two faults. First, it provides protection for only a few weeks or as long as the horse serum antibodies last in the body. Second, since all the antibodies are proteins, the individual recognizes the horse serum as a foreign protein and makes antibodies against it. Because of the prolonged memory of the body associated with antibody production, the stage is set for future problems. If the same patient is given horse serum months or even a year later, he may develop large amounts of antibodies to this protein very quickly. Sometimes this causes a prolonged illness called serum sickness or a severe, sudden reaction called anaphylaxis.

The medical assistant should remember two important points from the above discussion. The first is that extreme caution must be used when giving horse serum to anyone, especially to those known to have had horse serum injections in the past. Careful tests for allergy or sensitivity to horse serum are needed, which must be performed with the utmost precaution since the tests themselves can sometimes cause an anaphylactic reaction. The second point to be remembered is that passive immunization with antibodies made in humans is always preferable to horse serum. Because of this, vaccines for passive immunization against tetanus and human gamma globulin preparations with large amounts of antibodies specific against certain diseases have come into widespread use. Unfortunately, it may still be necessary to use serum obtained from horses in certain cases such as in snake bites. Individuals receiving vaccines that are made in fertilized eggs (such as the rabies vaccine) should be carefully screened for a history of allergy to eggs.

IMMUNIZATION FOR INFANTS AND CHILDREN

Routine immunization for infants and young children: Administer diphtheria and tetanus toxoids and pertussis vaccine (DPT)—three doses of 0.5 ml each of the trivalent preparation—intramuscularly at intervals of not less than four weeks starting at 1 to 3 months of age. Administer 0.5 ml 8 months after third dose and 0.25 or 0.5 ml in three years. Pertussis vaccine need not be given to children who are past 5 to 10 years of age. Because allergic reactions to one or more protein components of the diphtheria and pertussis organisms are more common in older children, administer toxoids "for adult use" to children over 10 years of age. Give tetanus toxoid in a dose of 0.5 ml every 5 to 10 years depending on how much risk of tetanus the patient is exposed to.

Smallpox vaccination is usually given at eight to twelve months and repeated until a primary "take" is obtained. Revaccinate every four to seven years.

Poliomyelitis vaccine

Inactivated virus. Give four injections of 1 ml each at 2, 3, 4, and 12 months. Give a fifth dose one or two years later.

Live attenuated virus. Starting at 3 to 4 months of age, Type I is given *orally,* Type III six weeks later, and Type II six weeks after Type III. Types I, II, and III may be given together in two doses at least eight weeks apart beginning at 6 weeks to 6 months of age. A third dose is given eight to twelve months after the second. A booster dose is given when the child enters elementary school. Infants may be given three doses along with the DPT injections starting at 2 months of age, and a fourth dose at 15 to 18 months of age.

In general, live virus vaccines should not be given within one month of each other.

Other vaccines

Mumps vaccine is seldom indicated during childhood.

Measles (rubeola) vaccine is a live attenuated virus vaccine. A single subcutaneous or intramuscular injection of 0.5 ml is given children 9 months of age or older. There is a better response among children who are at least 11 years of age.

German measles (rubella) vaccine is a live attenuated virus vaccine. Inject a single 0.5 ml subcutaneous dose in children 1 year of age or older.

Vaccines are also available for the following diseases: cholera, plague, Rocky Mountain spotted fever, typhoid fever, paratyphoid, typhus fever, and tuberculosis.

Many of the readers of this book will have been vaccinated against smallpox. Because smallpox vaccination is seen by some to be a greater threat than the disease itself, many public health officials in the United States no longer recommend routine smallpox vaccination of small children.

Review questions

1. What relation does Pasteur have to the science of bacteriology?
2. Name three types of bacteria that can cause disease.
3. What is meant by passive immunization?
4. State briefly a simple method to stain a bacterial slide.
5. Name five common viral diseases.
6. Name three common fungal diseases.
7. Name two common venereal diseases and explain how they are diagnosed.

Suggested readings

Gebhardt, L. P.: Microbiology, ed. 4, St. Louis, 1970, The C. V. Mosby Co.

Smith, A. L.: Principles of microbiology, ed. 7, St. Louis, 1973, The C. V. Mosby Co.

chapter 33
Electrocardiography

Electrocardiography has advanced so much recently that it has become a necessary instrument to the physician in everyday practice. Most physicians do only the interpretation and leave the taking of the record to the assistant or the technician in the office. Only a perfect record will give the physician and cardiologist the utmost information. This chapter is written to help the medical assistant who is inexperienced in electrocardiography with no attempt to include instructions concerning interpretation. Standard electrocardiographic techniques will be discussed. No cardiographic machines or their individual instruction will be described because extensive literature is furnished by the manufacturers, and their technical representatives will give information on the proper handling of any specific instrument.

As this chapter is intended particularly for the assistant not trained in the field of electrocardiography, the language will be kept as simple as possible. For the same reason, the positioning of the precordial electrodes is described in relation to the landmarks of the chest wall rather than to the outlines of the heart. Aside from the advantage in diagnostic purpose that many authors see, it should not be expected of the assistant to determine the apex and left border of the heart, which is often difficult even for the experienced physician.

THE HUMAN HEART

The Latin word for heart is *cor;* anything pertaining to the heart may be called cardiac. The heart, a hollow organ of specialized muscles, is shaped like a slightly flattened cone. The inside is lined with a membrane called endocardium. The whole heart is enclosed in a fibroserous sac, the pericardium, which contains a lubricating fluid. The cavity of the heart is divided longitudinally into the right and left halves by a septum, and each half consists of two chambers: an atrium and a ventricle.

Between the atria and the ventricles on

Glossary

atrium one of the chambers of the heart that receives blood from the body or the lungs before sending it to the ventricles
auricle an archaic term for the atrium
cardiologist a specialist in treatment of heart disease
coronary arteries a pair of arteries that supply blood to the heart
diaphragm the muscular wall between the thoracic and abdominal cavities
digitalis a cardiotonic drug originally derived from the leaf of the foxglove plant
electrode that part of an electrocardiograph that is used to pick up electrical impulses from the patient
intercostal pertaining to the space between two ribs
midclavicular pertaining to a point on a line drawn perpendicularly to the middle of the clavicle
millivolt (mv) one thousandth of a volt
myocardium muscular tissue of the heart
precordial pertaining to the precordium or the area of the chest wall over the heart
stylus the part of an electrocardiograph that records electrical impulses on paper

each side of the heart there are valves that allow blood to flow in only one direction: from the atrium to the ventricle. On the right side this valve is called the tricuspid valve and on the left, the mitral valve.

The heart is an extremely efficient muscular pump that can rest only between heart beats. In order for it to function efficiently, it needs a continuous supply of blood. There are two main coronary arteries that arise from the aorta just beyond the aortic valve, one of which, the left coronary artery, divides into two large branches. Disease of these blood vessels is called arteriosclerotic heart disease or coronary artery disease and is a leading cause of death in the United States.

In addition to its remarkable properties as a mechanical pump, the heart has an elaborate electrical system. In order for a muscle to contract, it needs electrical stimulation. The electrical activity that initiates heart contraction arises from a specialized area of heart cells located in the right atrium. This is the normal pacemaker of the heart and is referred to as the sino-atrial (SA) node. From the atria and the SA node the electrical signal is carried to a node of tissue between the atria and the ventricles known as the atrioventricular (AV) node. From there the electrical impulse is carried to both ventricles.

Electrical overactivity of the cardiac pacemaker may result in a fast heart rate whereas underactivity will cause a slow heart rate. If the normal pacemaker fails, the heart has two "backup systems" that can assume the role of pacemaker. One is located in the AV node. This system takes over and keeps the heart beating at a rate of about 40 to 50 beats per minute. The last "backup system" is located anywhere within the walls of the ventricles. This system keeps the heart beating at 30 to 40 beats per minute, a rate that is usually insufficient for normal health. Individuals with a pacemaker originating in the ventricles are said to suffer from complete heart block and are often given an artificial pacemaker to pace their hearts at an acceptable rate.

During a normal contraction of the heart, the atria, being closest to the pacemaker in the SA node, contract first. This pumps blood into the ventricles. The electrical signal is delayed in the AV node while the ventricles fill with blood. The ventricles contract when the electrical signal reaches them. Ventricular contraction closes the valves to the atria and forces blood out of the heart and into the lungs or body.

It is not unusual for minor breakdowns to occur in the electrical system of the heart. These minor breakdowns may result in a few dozen beats falling out of place during a day. Most of these beats are unnoticed. At times they will be noted on feeling the pulse or will be felt by the patient as a skipping of the heart beat called a palpitation. An irregularity of the pulse or heart beat may therefore be totally harmless. On the other hand, an irregular heart rate in a patient with heart disease or chest pain may be the cause of great concern under certain circumstances. The electrocardiogram is an important tool in determining the nature and severity of irregular heart activity.

At times the electrical activity of the atria or ventricles suffers a major breakdown and results in a chaotic electrical activity that produces no useful pumping action. This chaotic electrical activity is called fibrillation. If only the atria are fibrillating, this is called atrial fibrillation. If the ventricles also fibrillate, all pumping stops and death ensues. In recent years it has become known that ventricular fibrillation is the single most common cause of death after a heart attack. It is also known that if ventricular fibrillation occurs it can be corrected by shocking the heart with a large electrical current delivered over the chest wall. Machines for this purpose are found in all hospitals and in some doctor's offices and are called electrical defibrillators.

The electrocardiogram permits the physician to detect disorders of many of the systems described above. It is often used to detect enlargement of the heart or one of its chambers. It can tell us where the heart's pacemaker is located and its condition, if one of the arteries to the heart is partly occluded or if part of the heart muscle has died because of a heart attack, or if there are abnormalities in specific portions of the electrical conducting system of the heart. Lastly, since the electrical activity of the heart can be influenced by many drugs and abnormalities of the body's metabolism, the electrocardiogram frequently provides clues as to the effect or toxicity of many drugs and may offer clues of derangements of body metabolism.

THE ELECTROCARDIOGRAPH (ECG OR EKG)

The electrocardiograph (ECG or EKG) is an instrument devised for the measurement and recording of the minute electrical currents arising from the heart muscle. These electrical voltages or potentials are ordinarily fractions of a millivolt, a thousandth of a volt.

Because they are so small, they must be properly magnified or amplified so that their variations may be readily seen when converted into a graph or record. This graph, which provides visual permanent evidence of the heart's electrical activity for diagnostic analysis, is called an electrocardiogram.

The first practical electrocardiograph was a string galvanometer type of apparatus developed in 1903 by a Dutch physiologist named Einthoven. He devised an instrument in which the force of the heart currents, applied directly to a coarse fiber (often called a string) suspended in a magnetic gap, caused the string to deflect. The deflections of the string were magnified by an optical system projected through a camera and recorded on a photographic paper.

This type of electrocardiograph embodied factors requiring arduous manipulation and delicate handling. The years since 1903 have produced some notable advances in accuracy, sensitivity, speed, simplicity of operation, economy, portability, and freedom from external interference—advantages that are embodied in the amplifier type of electrocardiograph that we are now using. The modern type of electrocardiograph is known as a direct writing recorder. In this type of instrument, the heart voltages from the patient are led through a lead selector to an amplifier and thence to a galvanometer coil, which is attached to a writing arm and stylus ribbon. As the coil moves in response to the electrical activity of the heart, the writing arm with its attached stylus ribbon moves also. The movements or deflections of the stylus, which is heated, are recorded on the moving paper, which is sensitive to heat. There are two layers or coatings of plastic material on this paper, including a black coating beneath the white coating that is readily visible. The heat of the stylus ribbon melts away the white plastic, and the black shows through. The result is a permanent recording of the writing arm's excursions, or electrocardiogram, which is also called a heart record or tracing.

The most common type of electrocardiograph machine in use today is the amplifier instrument (Figs. 33-1 and 33-2). With this type, the action current of the heart transmitted to the electrodes is amplified by vacuum tubes, and the amplified current moves a small mirror. The record is obtained with the aid of a light beam that is reflected by the moving mirror and thus projected on the moving sensitized paper. A detailed description of the many different electrocardiographic machines is not included here. Manufacturers have published profusely illustrated booklets that give the exact instructions for operation of their particular instruments, and well-trained and dependable technicians employed by the manufacturers will give additional information whenever needed. These service representatives will also take care of adjustments, and no repairs should ever be attempted by an untrained person on these very delicate instruments. Although the various ECG machines

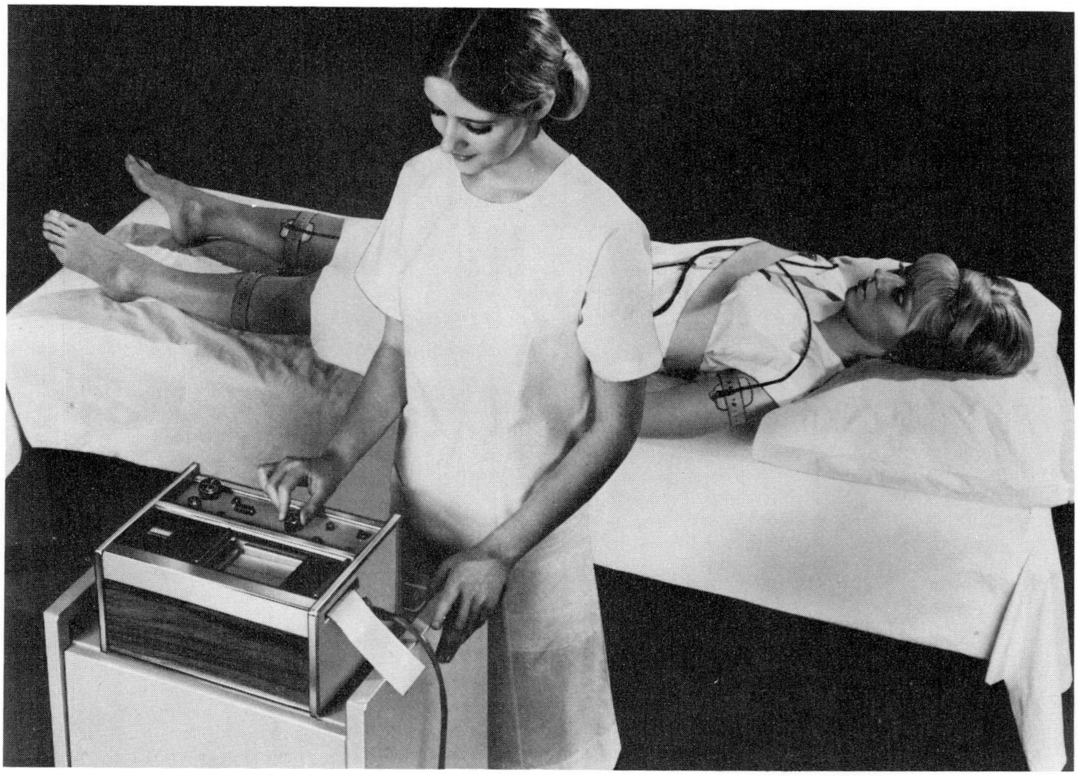

Fig. 33-1. Modern direct writer electrocardiograph. (Courtesy The Burdick Corporation, Milton, Wisconsin.)

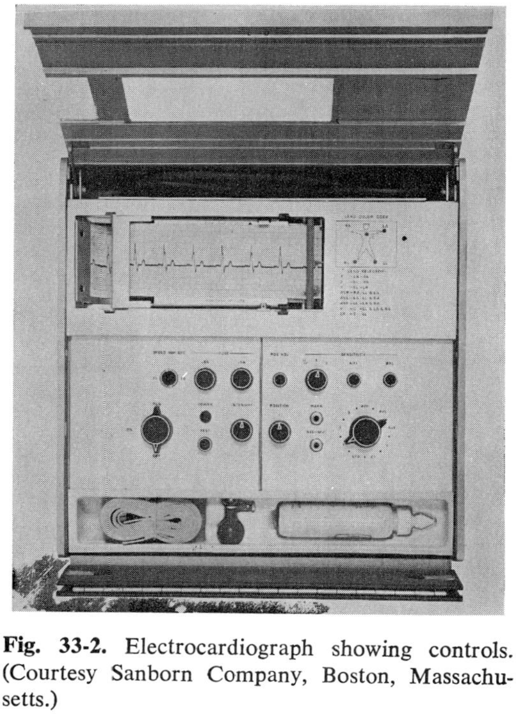

Fig. 33-2. Electrocardiograph showing controls. (Courtesy Sanborn Company, Boston, Massachusetts.)

differ greatly in appearance, arrangement of switches, buttons, and special features, there are several accessories that are common to all instruments: (1) the sensitivity control, (2) the centering device, (3) the lead selector, (4) the lead marker, (5) the cables and electrodes, and (6) the paper or film on which the graph is recorded.

STANDARDIZATION

In order to compare electrocardiograph records properly, it is necessary that a certain height in deflection always correspond to a certain electrical potential of the human heart. For this reason and because the height of the waves in the cardiogram plays an important role in the interpretation, it is conventional that, for all routine records, the machine is standardized so that a current of 1 mv causes a deflection of

10 mm in the record. If the standardization value is too high or too low, the heart waves will show the same aberration, and this to be taken into consideration when the record is interpreted.

To control and record the sensitivity, the standardization button is momentarily depressed several times while the lead selector is on standard and the recorder switch is on record or run. This depression introduces 1 mv to the machine, which should cause a 10-mm deflection on the record—the height of two large squares on the writing paper.

If the deflection is smaller or larger, adjustments must be made by turning the sensitivity control switch until proper standardization is obtained. Modern machines will rarely need correction, but a record of the stardardization has to be included in every electrocardiogram to assure the physician of proper technique.

Occasionally, the voltage of the precordial leads exceeds the width of the cardiograph paper. In these cases, the instrument is standardized at half sensitivity by setting the standardization height at 0.5 cm. The resulting record will then be reduced to half size, but the shape and timing will be unchanged.

The stardardization may be done at the start and at the end of the recording. Many cardiologists, however, want the standardization included in every lead.

The centering device

The centering device controls the position of the base line of the electrocardiogram. For the standardization and most tracings the center line should be kept near the center of the paper. If very high waves appear, as is frequently seen in certain leads, the center line must be dropped close to the botton of the recording paper to obtain the complete tracing. If the waves are very deep, the center line must be moved to the upper margin of the paper; otherwise the full wave will not be registered or might even be distorted.

The lead selector

The lead selector is marked for standard or 1 mv and the various leads. Most modern instruments offer the possibility of selecting up to ten leads without changing the electrode wires.

The lead marker

The lead marker permits the operator to use a type of code to mark the lead being recorded. After the electrocardiogram has been completed, the code may be interpreted and the leads marked off with appropriate numbers and letters. With direct writing instruments, the leads can be marked with pencil as soon as the paper appears, and this method should be used in any case to write down directly on the record the name, age, and other important data of the patient. Whether the lead marker is used or not and whether a code is used or not, the technician or assistant should always make the routine leads in a certain order. An example of a frequently used code is a system of dots and dashes. The first three leads taken are leads 1, 2, and 3. These leads are represented by one, two, and three dots respectively. The next three leads taken are leads AVR, AVL, and AVF. These leads are noted by marking them with four, five, or six dots respectively. The next leads taken are the precordial or chest leads or leads V1 to V6 as they are frequently called. These leads are marked with a dash followed by a single dot for lead 1, a dash followed by two dots for lead 2, a dash followed by three dots for lead 3, and so on.

Cables and electrodes

The power cord connects the instrument with the electric line. The patient cable is divided into five electrode wires, and the ends of the wires are marked with the letters LA for the left arm, RA for the right arm, LL for the left leg, RL for the right leg, and C for the chest.

The four limb electrodes and the chest electrode are intended to assure good contact of the lead wires with the patient. They are manufactured from a special alloy to assure good contact and a minimum of interference. Electrodes of different makes should never be used on the same patient because production of a galvanic current may be the result. The normal limb electrode is an oblong about 3 to 5 cm in size. The chest electrode is round, usually around 3 cm in diameter. Electrodes of about half that size are available if tracings of infants or small children are to be taken. Rubber straps fasten the electrodes to the patient and a suction cup attaches the chest electrode.

A ground wire is delivered with some machines. Many of the electrocardiograph machines being made at the present time have built-in grounding devices and do not need external grounding wires. Grounding may be necessary with any instrument to eliminate interference.

Electrode jelly is used to reduce the skin resistance.

The electrocardiographic paper

As previously mentioned, direct writing instruments or machines that record by means of a heated stylus require a paper with a heat-sensitive surface (Fig. 33-3). The background of every finished record is formed by a network of horizontal and vertical lines. The paper moves during the recording at a constant speed of 25 mm per second. Many machines provide a 50-mm-per-second speed for specialized use in studying irregularities in normal electrical activity. In routine use only the 25-mm-per-second speed is used. Since the lines on the paper form squares 1 mm high and 1 mm long, each millimeter of the horizontal line represents 0.04 second in time. The heavier lines after each fifth square represents 0.2 second, and five large squares represent 1 second.

The vertical lines are also divided into millimeters, and their purpose is to register the amount of the cardiac action current, each millimeter representing 0.1 mv.

THE ELECTROCARDIOGRAPHIC ROOM AND PREPARATION OF THE PATIENT

Although an electrocardiogram may be taken in any place and in emergency cases may have to be taken in a patient's home, often under the most adverse conditions, the physician should assign a permanent room in the office for taking electrocardiograms. This room should be as far away as possible from all x-ray, short-wave, and other electrophysiotherapy equipment and should not contain any electrical apparatus such as electric fans, centrifuge, refrigerator, and so on. An electric heater will not interfere, but other apparatus, if in operation, may cause

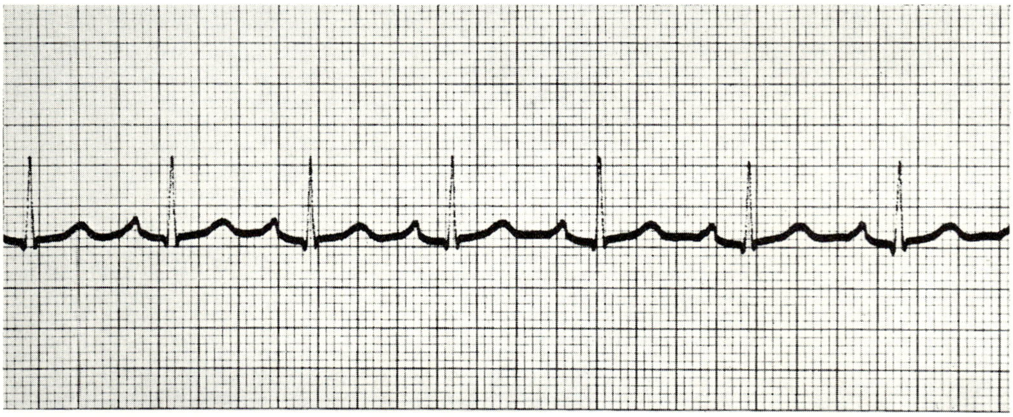

Fig. 33-3. Electrocardiograph paper. (Courtesy Sanborn Company, Boston, Massachusetts.)

severe distortion of the electrocardiographic record.

The room should be quiet and pleasant, not only in the interest of the perfect record, but also for the benefit of the patient, who should be relaxed and rested whenever possible. The room should be warm so that the patient does not shiver. Because tremors and excessive muscular contractions interfere with the taking of a good electrocardiogram, a blanket or sheet may have to be used to reduce shivering.

The bed or couch should be comfortable and long and wide enough so that the patient can rest his body and extremities. Examining tables should not be used because they are generally too hard, too narrow, and have too many bare metal parts that interfere with the recording should the patient touch them.

If the patient is very short of breath, he should be placed in a semirecumbent position. In some cases, the record must be taken with the patient sitting in a chair.

Instructions for patient prior to the taking of an electrocardiogram

Mr.
Mrs.
Miss ____:

A.M.
Your cardiogram will be taken on ____________________ at __________ P.M.
(Date) (Time)

at ____.
(Name and address)

1. There is no pain nor discomfort in taking an electrocardiogram. There is no sensation for the patient whatsoever; no electricity is put into the patient. Tiny silver plates are placed on the patient on the calf of each leg, on each wrist, and at different points on the chest. Tiny electrical currents generated by the heart itself are simply picked up by these plates, and a record is made by the machine.

2. You will be asked to lie down on a comfortable table while the test is being made.

3. For your own comfort and convenience, please wear loose clothing, as you will be asked to take off clothing from the waist up to expose the bare skin of your chest. It will be also necessary to have your legs bare from the knees down to the ankles and your arms bare from elbow to hands. The actual taking of the electrocardiogram requires only five or six minutes, but please allow a half hour for your visit.

4. If the person taking the electrocardiogram is not the physician but is a trained nurse or technician, please do not expect that person to tell you the results of the test, as he has neither been trained nor authorized to make an interpretation of the cardiogram. That is the job of your physician.

5. During the taking of the cardiogram, please lie absolutely still, as any muscle movement interferes with a clear tracing. Do not talk.

6. The skin of the chest, sides, back, arms, and legs must be absolutely free of any skin ointments, tissue creams, oils, or medications of any kind whatsoever.

Fig. 33-4

The chair should also be as comfortable as possible and should have armrests, and the feet of the patient should not touch the floor but rest on a nonmetallic footstool.

The electrocardiogram is taken with the patient in a recumbent position whenever possible. A small pillow may support the head but not the shoulders. The arms are at the sides, and the legs do not touch each other. Any change of this standard position of the patient should be brought to the attention of the physician who interprets the records.

The arms, legs, and chest are exposed, and the areas that are used in the electrocardiographic examination are cleaned if necessary, as dirt and greasy ointments interfere with the recording. Watches should be removed from the patient.

If the electrocardiographic examination is a new experience to the patient, the assistant should explain the purpose and principle of the test (Fig. 33-4). The patient should be assured that no shock or other sensation will be felt and that only the very weak current of the patient's heart is registered.

Certain drugs, especially digitalis, may cause changes in the electrocardiogram. It is, therefore, necessary for the assistant to ask the patient if he has been taking digitalis and, if so, to note the type, amount, and duration of any drugs being taken. This information is included with the data giving the patient's name, age, height, weight, and the date of the examination.

THE RECORDING OF THE ELECTROCARDIOGRAM

If two electrodes connected to a cardiographic machine are placed on different parts of the human body, a record of the electric current produced by the heart may be obtained. The possibilities of placing the electrodes are unlimited, and therefore certain combinations of the electrodes have been agreed upon by international convention. One such combination, for instance, is obtained by placing one electrode on the left and the other on the right arm. The record of any such combinations is called a lead.

We distinguish the limb leads if both electrodes are connected to different extremities; chest extremity leads if one electrode is connected to the chest and the other to an extremity; unipolar chest leads if one electrode is placed upon the chest and the other one connected with the central terminal; and unipolar limb leads if electrode is connected to the extremity and the other to the central terminal.

THE LIMB LEADS (LEADS 1, 2, AND 3)

The patient is prepared as described previously. A small amount of electrode jelly, about the size of a pea, is placed on the electrode and rubbed with the edge into the skin on the inner side of the left forearm, in the center of the arm between the elbow and the wrist.

The area so prepared should not be much larger than the size of the electrode, and the skin should be slightly reddened by the rubbing. Then the electrode is fastened to the prepared area with the help of a rubber strap to assure good contact. Too loose an electrode may spoil the record since it may slide on the skin. If applied too tightly, muscle tremor appears and distorts the record. Ask the patient if the strap seems too tight for comfort. Try to move the electrode about after the electrode and strap have been applied. Should it slip or slide on the limb, the strap is too loose and should be tightened slightly. Should it appear that the skin is being pinched on either side of the electrode, then no doubt the connection is too tight and should be slightly loosened. The jelly around the electrode is wiped off with paper toweling or a piece of cotton.

The same procedure is repeated on the right arm and on the left leg. For the latter, we choose the lateral side halfway between the ankle and knee. Care should be taken that no electrode touches the bed or couch upon which the patient is reclining. The lead wires, which are marked LA (left arm), RA (right arm), LL (left leg), and RL (right leg), are firmly attached to their corresponding limbs.

Before the limb leads are taken, these connections should be routinely checked again because any mistake caused by interchange of the wires would change the contour of the record and would lead to erroneous interpretation. The lead selector is now set on No. 1 and the first lead recorded. With the knob on No. 2 and No. 3, two more leads are taken. These three leads represent the standard limb leads. Lead 1 forms a connection between the left and right arm; lead 2 between the right arm and the left leg; and lead 3 between the left arm and the left leg. In addition, there is a provision for a connection of the right leg with the purpose of grounding the patient and thus eliminating interference in certain leads.

THE STEPS IN TAKING THE LIMB LEADS

1. The limb electrodes are attached as previously described and the chest electrodes may be left unattached.
2. Set lead selector switch to standard. Start the recorder. Center the base line. Adjust the standardization. Turn the recorder off.
3. Set lead selector switch to lead 1. Wait several seconds.
4. Turn the recorder on to run or record. Run for a few heartbeats; depress the standardization button momentarily.
5. Mark for identification (lead marker).
6. Allow to record for about 8 seconds.
7. Turn the recorder switch off.
8. Turn the lead selector to lead 2. Wait several seconds.
9. Repeat steps 4, 5, 6, and 7 with leads 2 and 3.

THE CHEST EXTREMITY LEADS

(Fig. 33-5)

After recording the limb leads, the wires remain attached. The chest electrode consists of a circular metal plate or suction cup about one inch in diameter with an insulating handle. This chest electrode is connected to the wire marked C and is placed in succession over all of the following six standard positions for the chest leads (see Fig. 33-5).

1. The fourth intercostal space, right sternal margin
2. The fourth intercostal space, left sternal margin
3. Midway between positions 2 and 4
4. Fifth intercostal space, midclavicular line

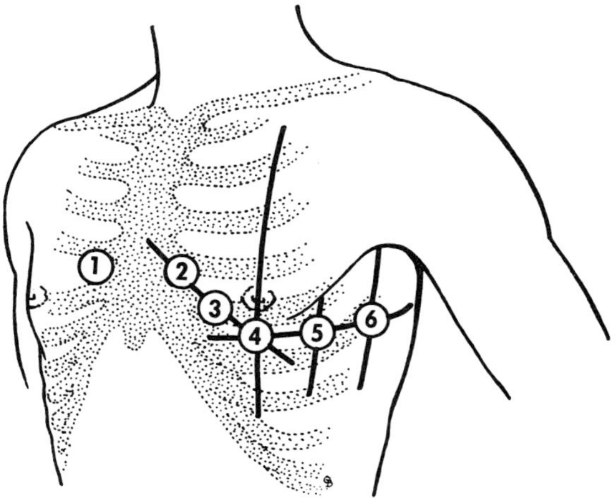

Fig. 33-5. Standard positions for C or V leads. **1,** Fourth intercostal space, at right border of sternum. **2,** Same interspace, at left sternal border. **3,** Midway between positions 2 and 4. **4,** At outer border of apex-beat area. **5,** Same level as 4, in anterior axillary line. **6,** Same level as 4 and 5, in midaxillary line. (Courtesy Sanborn Company, Boston, Massachusetts.)

5. Level of position 4, anterior axillary line
6. Level of position 4, midaxillary line

The most difficult part in taking an electrocardiogram is the correct positioning of the chest leads. One way of doing this accurately is to feel for the ridge on the sternum (breast bone) that joins the upper and middle parts of this bone. Immediately lateral and just below this point is the second intercostal space (space between the second and third rib). The fingers are then gently run down two spaces on the side of the sternum until the fourth intercostal space is felt, which is the level where the first and second chest leads, V1 and V2 are placed. V1 is placed on the right and V2 on the left border of the sternum. This level corresponds to a point just above the level of the nipple of the breast in men. The nipple, however, cannot be used as an accurate guideline for lead placement in women. Chest lead 4 is placed in the fifth intercostal space at a point that meets an imaginary line perpendicular to the middle of the clavicle (the midclavicular line), which in most men falls just below the nipple. Chest lead 3 is placed midway between V2 and V4. Leads 5 and 6 are placed on the anterior and midaxillary lines at the same level as lead 4. The anterior and midaxillary lines are the imaginary lines drawn from the front fold and the middle of the axilla (armpit).

Other positions may be used if requested by the cardiologist. In women with heavy breasts, lift the left breast and place the chest electrode on the spot where the midclavicular line crosses the fourth intercostal space.

Careful technique is more important with chest leads than with limb leads, because any deviation from the correct localization of the electrode may impair the reading or the comparison if records are repeated on the same patient. Furthermore, poor electrical contact is more likely because of the small size of the electrode, respiratory movement, and uneven surface of the chest wall, especially in thin patients.

Apply a small amount of jelly to the chest electrode, and with the edge of the electrode rub it into the skin until a slight reddening appears. Place the electrode in the correct position and remove the excess jelly with paper toweling or cotton.

FINISHING THE RECORD

After the electrocardiogram is taken, about six inches of the paper are run through the machine to avoid damage to the last part of the record and the strip is cut or torn off. All control buttons and the main switch are turned off, and the instrument is disconnected. The electrodes are removed from the patient; the remaining electrode jelly is removed with a damp towel. The electrodes and straps are immediately cleaned with soap and water or alcohol and are dried and stored away ready for further use.

Records taken with a direct writing machine do not need further manipulation and may be read and mounted immediately.

Mounting and filing

Years ago, many physicians wrote the report on the back of the record and filed a roll of three leads in a drawer or filing cabinet. Today, however, flexible cardboard forms are used to mount the records. Different types of boards and folders are manufactured by the various companies that are most suitable for the corresponding type of electrocardiogram paper, but some of them provide space for only four leads. With the slotted type, the leads are inserted in slots or under tabs without trimming, and no pasting or fastening is necessary. Most mounts today have adequate space to mount all of the leads taken in modern electrocardiography.

AUTOMATIC CASSETTE ELECTROCARDIOGRAPHS

Recent advancements enable the electrocardiographic recordings to be made on a cassette electronic tape (Fig. 33-6). This can be used to write a standard record or it can be transmitted over the telephone to

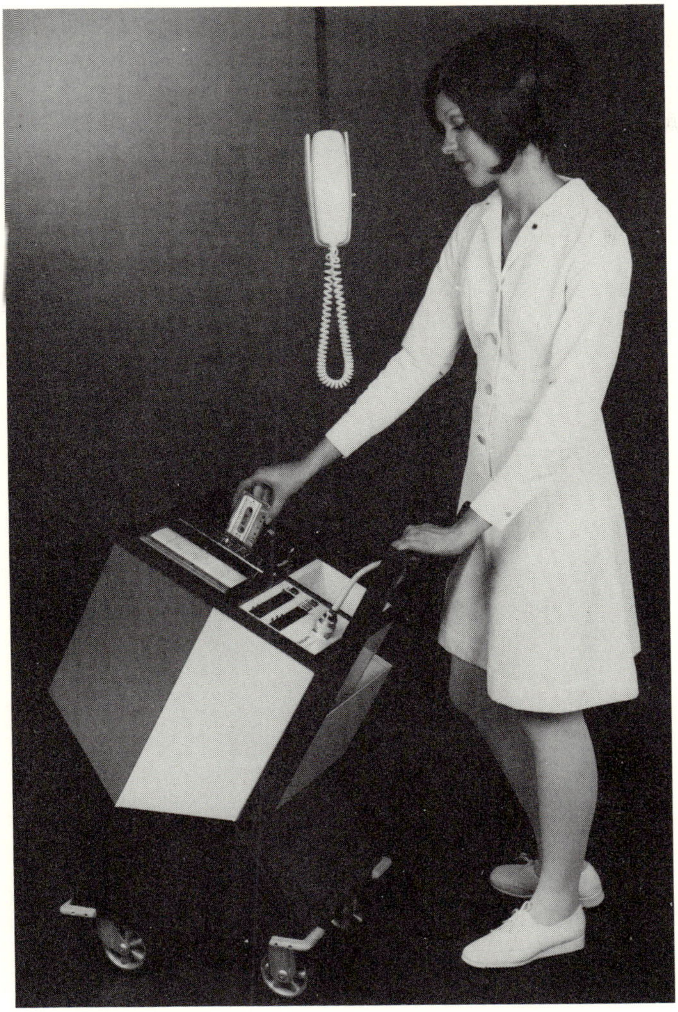

Fig. 33-6. Automatic cassette electrocardiograph. (Courtesy Marquette Electronics, Inc., Milwaukee, Wisconsin.)

distant locations that may provide centralized interpretation of routine or complicated electrocardiograms. Such a system has been developed by the Marquette Electronics Corporation of Milwaukee, Wisconsin. Detailed description and instructions of these machines are provided by the manufacturer.

EXERCISE AND MASTER'S TESTING

In patients suspected of having coronary artery disease, the electrocardiogram may be perfectly normal during resting. If, however, the patient is asked to climb a series of steps or walk a treadmill that is moving at a specific speed, the heart's rate and work load increase. During these episodes of stress and increased work, abnormal electrocardiographic patterns may appear that were not present previously. Such testing was developed by Dr. Master and is frequently called Master's Test. More recently treadmills have replaced the steps used in exercising the patient and the tests are referred to as Treadmill Tests. These tests are usually performed in the offices of internists or cardiologists or in hospitals.

Review questions

1. How do you standardize an electrocardiograph machine?
2. What is the centering device?
3. Discuss briefly the limb leads required in taking an electrocardiograph.
4. How many chest leads are usually taken?
5. What instructions could you give a patient in preparation for an electrocardiograph?

Suggested readings

Andreoli, K. G., et al.: Comprehensive cardiac care, ed. 2, St. Louis, 1971, The C. V. Mosby Co.

Burch, G. E., and Winsor, T.: Primer of electrocardiography, ed. 6, Philadelphia, 1972, Lea & Febiger.

Hurst, J. W., and Myerburg, R. J.: Introduction to electrocardiography, ed. 2, New York, 1973, McGraw-Hill Book Co.

Phibbs, B.: The human heart, ed. 2, St. Louis, 1971, The C. V. Mosby Co.

Zalis, E. G., and Conover, M. H.: Understanding electrocardiography, St. Louis, 1972, The C. V. Mosby Co.

chapter 34

Medical office x-ray procedure

The medical assistant can study x-ray technique, learn the mechanics of making a radiograph, get the film and patient ready, place the x-ray tube, operate the controls, and put the film through the various solutions. But that would not mean becoming an x-ray technician. For radiography is much more than a series of procedures; it is a science and an art. It is a science in that it embodies the sciences of physics, geometry, and chemistry; it is an art in that it requires practice and experience to attain the desired skill.

Anyone who proposes to make use of radiography, therefore, must study three equally important and interrelated matters: (1) the principles that govern radiography techniques, (2) the means by which those principles are applied, and (3) the sympathetic, careful, and correct handling of sick or injured people.

The purpose of this chapter is to provide a practical groundwork for the student that will give meaning to the mechanics of technique to be learned later. With that in mind, the discussion has been kept as simple and as brief as possible.

THE DISCOVERY OF X-RAYS

Wilhelm Conrad Röntgen, a physicist at the University of Würzburg, Germany, discovered a "new kind of ray" on November 8, 1895. He called this radiation x-rays, which is the common term in usage today. The name roentgen rays, in honor of the discoverer, is also frequently used, especially in medicine.

In the history of diagnostic medicine, no individual has made a more momentous contribution to the armamentarium of the physician. The immediate acceptance and application of x-ray technique in medicine and the widespread use of this diagnostic tool today bear eloquent witness to the value of Röntgen's discovery.

Glossary

Bucky diaphragm a radiographic device with alternating strips of lead and wood in grid formation whose function is to reduce the effect of secondary radiation

cervical pertaining to the neck

contrast medium a radiopaque substance used in the radiography of hollow organs or soft tissues

costal pertaining to the ribs

dorsal pertaining to the back

epiphysis the structure, at the end of a bone, from which the bone grows

fluoroscopy the visualization of internal organs either directly or indirectly by means of a screen in a darkened room

foramen a hole in a bone for the transmission of nerves, vessels, and other structures

fracture a break in the continuity of a bone

kilo prefix meaning one thousand

radiograph x-ray film that has been exposed to x-rays

radiography science that deals with taking of x-ray pictures

radiologist a doctor who specializes in radiology and its allied fields

roentgenogram an x-ray picture

roentgenologist a doctor who specializes in roentgenology and its allied fields

QUALITIES AND BASIC REQUIREMENTS OF A GOOD X-RAY ASSISTANT

A good assistant is ever aware that the work is entirely technical and that, as such, it is important not to attempt to practice medicine by either venturing a diagnosis of a roentgenogram or by giving advice to patients. Such action can only be a display of ethical ignorance and has no place in the conduct of the assistant's chosen profession. In many instances the roentgenologist does not personally see the patient. The assistant is the representative and should at all times behave in a manner deserving of this responsibility. These qualities are of great importance and even though an x-ray assistant has basic qualifications, a generous measure of technical education and experience must be acquired in addition.

FUNDAMENTAL FACTORS OF A GOOD RADIOGRAPH

Each radiograph must present to the diagnostician a vivid picture of the part in which he is interested. Therefore, in setting a standard of radiographic qualities, be guided by the roentgenologist or the physician's opinion. To be able to take a good radiograph is commendable; to be able to take a good radiograph consistently is wonderful.

First you must center the film that is in the holder (either cardboard holder or cassette) to the table (Fig. 34-1). Center the part of anatomy to be x-rayed to the film. Then center the tube to the anatomy and the film. Always mark the film with a right or left mark, the name of the patient, date, portion x-rayed, and the views taken.

X-ray photographs are taken of two types of patients: those who are very sick and those who come in for an x-ray for diagnostic purposes. The sympathetic, careful, and correct handling of a sick or injured patient is very important. In handling a sick patient handle him carefully and do not expose him more than necessary. Carefully drape the patient with a sheet to prevent chills. Articles such as jewelry should be removed from the patient when taking an x-ray photograph; hair pins should be removed when the head is x-rayed, but only on a physician's order should you remove splints, plaster casts, braces, or adhesive strips.

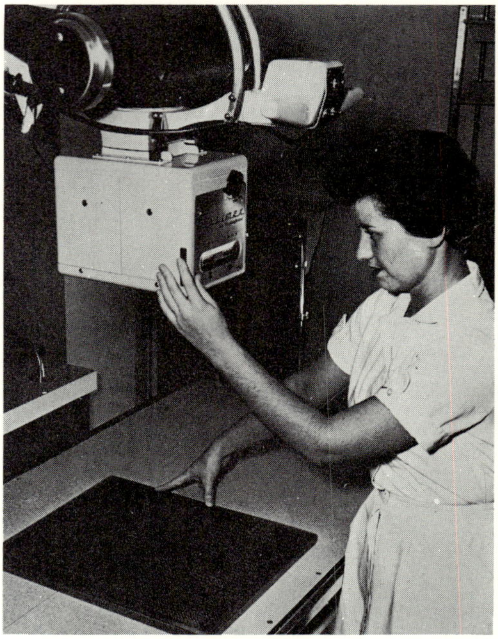

Fig. 34-1. Proper way to center film on x-ray table. (Courtesy Continental X-Ray Company, New York, New York.)

X-RAYS AND THEIR PRODUCTION

Before one can understand what x-rays are, a little background must be acquired.

A ray can be defined as a beam of light or radiant energy that travels as a wave and can be measured in terms of energy and wavelength. To get the concept of waves and wavelength think of the disturbance created when a stone is tossed into a quiet pond. As the stone strikes the water, some of its energy produces waves that travel outward in ever widening circles. Although the water is in motion it does not travel anywhere, as may be seen by the motion of a floating chip that rises and falls with the waves but only oscillates about its original location. The energy of the waves proceeds outward from the center. The wavelength of water waves is the distance from crest to crest. In any system of waves, wavelength is the distance between two successive corresponding locations in the moving energy pattern.

Light waves, radio waves, and x-rays are energy waves of electric and magnetic influences. They are appropriately called electromagnetic waves. All these forms of electromagnetic radiation are grouped according to their wavelength in what is called the electromagnetic spectrum.

X-RAYS

X-rays are an invisible form of radiant energy of very short wavelength. We know now that x-rays are a part of the electromagnetic spectrum, that is, they are related to radio waves, visible light rays, and gamma rays. Gamma rays are given off by radium and other active elements. All electromagnetic waves travel through space at the same speed, about 186,000 miles per second. X-rays are quite similar to light in that they travel at the same speed and obey many of the same laws.

A distinguishing feature of x-rays is their extremely short wavelength—only about 1/10,000 the wavelength of visible light. It is this charatceristic that is responsible for the ability of the x-ray to penetrate materials that ordinarily would absorb and reflect light. When lengthy exposures are employed, x-rays have the power to change many chemicals. Another important characteristic is the ability of x-rays to excite fluorescence in many substances such as barium preparations, zinc sulfide, and others. This activity makes possible the use of fluoroscopic and intensifying screens and reduction of x-ray exposure in radiology. Therapeutically, x-rays are a powerful agent in the treatment of cancer, tumors, and other lesions. Radiation therapy is the treatment of disease by the use of x-rays or radioactive isotopes. The doctors of medicine specializing in this field are known as radiation therapists or radiologists.

ELECTRICAL TERMS IN X-RAY TECHNIQUE

ampere a unit of strength of electricity. Electricity, like water, is capable of flowing through a conductor. This flow of current is measured in amperes.

volt unit of force for electricity to flow. It must be under pressure.

watt unit of power. The number of amperes or volts, respectively, does not indicate the amount of power in the circuit; however, when both amperes and volts are multiplied, the product is the unit of power called watt.

milliampere 1/1000 amperes equal 1 milliampere. The ampere is too large a unit to employ in radiology. Therefore the milliampere is used instead.

kilovolt 1,000 volts equal a kilovolt. Thousands of volts are required when making exposures. The term usually employed is the kilovolt.

kilowatt 1,000 watts equal one kilowatt. Thousands of watts are used by x-ray apparatus. Therefore the term kilowatt is more commonly employed.

X-RAY TUBES

An x-ray tube consists of a highly evacuated glass bulb into which are sealed two electrodes. The negative electrode, which is called the cathode, is the source of electrons. It is usually a filament of tungsten steel wire at the end of the cathode wound into a spiral wire. The positive electrode is called the anode or target. It is made of some heavy metal such as wolfram or tungsten because it must be able to withstand tremendous heat without melting. Ordinarily the target is attached to a molybdenum rod and supported by an iron sleeve that helps to radiate the heat.

When an electric current of high voltage is turned on, the cathode is heated and while hot sends out a stream of electrons or cathode rays that are pulled through the vacuum by the high voltage until they reach a speed of thousands of miles per second. They slam against the atoms of the target which is the anode, and as they strike a spurt of x-rays splashes out. The stream of electrons from cathode to anode constitutes the tube current and is measured in milliamperes by a milliammeter.

There are a number of x-ray tubes in

use, such as (1) the *simple Crookes tube* (the modern x-ray tube works on the same principle), (2) the *Coolidge tube,* and (3) the *Machlect tube,* which is the largest tube and which has a rotating anode. There are two types of x-ray tubes: the stationary anode tube (Fig. 34-2) and the rotating anode tube.

The stationary anode tube is the conventional type that has been most extensively used. The limitations of the stationary tubes have been largely overcome in the rotating anode tube that permits the use of a smaller focal spot for a longer period of time. The tube focal spot from which the x-ray beam emanates should be as small as conditions permit in order to secure the sharpest possible definition in the radiographic image.

X-rays are like light in that they radiate in straight lines in all directions from the focal spot and are stopped by an efficient absorber. For that reason the tube is enclosed in a lead housing that stops most of the radiation except the useful rays called the *primary rays* or *central rays,* which are permitted to leave the tube through a window. The central ray or primary ray of the focal spot of the tube is an imaginary straight line that begins at a focal point in the tube and passes to the center of the x-ray beam outside. An important point to remember is that *the shorter the wavelength, the greater the energy of the ray and the more penetrating the ray will be.* For that reason x-rays and the tubes that produce them are classified as hard or soft. Hard rays have the shorter wavelength and thus are more penetrating. Nearly all the energy applied to the x-ray tube is transformed into heat at the focal spot. Different voltages are applied to the x-ray tube to meet the demands of various classes of radiographic work. The higher the voltage, the greater the speed of electrons striking the focal spot. The result is a decrease in wavelength of the x-ray emitted and an increase in both their intensity and penetrating power.

TECHNICAL FACTORS IN X-RAY TERMINOLOGY

Kilovolt peak (KVP) is the kilovolt maximum. It is important to remember that the amount of KVP to be used *depends upon the measurements of the anatomic area to be x-rayed.* The thicker or larger the part to be x-rayed, the more KVP will be used. The low focus has a capacity of 50 milliamperes (ma); however, we never use the capacity *except for chest x-ray.* All extremities and small bones use approximately 25 ma at low focus for 1 second at a time. High focus has a capacity of 100 to 200 ma. High focus is used for large or thick bones such as the spine, hipbones, and pelvis. The basic fac-

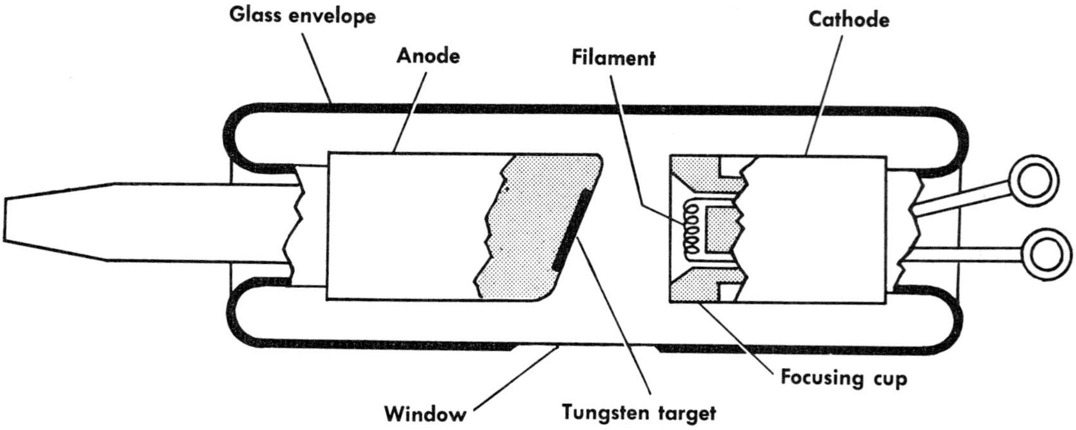

Fig. 34-2. Diagram of stationary anode x-ray tube showing relation of anode and cathode. (Courtesy Eastman Kodak Company, Rochester, New York.)

tor is MAS, which means milliampere second = milliampere × time (always in seconds). The faster the time, the better the picture. The higher the concentration of milliamperes, the faster the picture is taken.

TRANSFORMATION OF ENERGY

The transformation of energy is accomplished by means of a transformer. There are two types of transformers: (1) the step-down transformer such as is used in doorbells (the voltage is reduced from 110 V to 6 to 12 V) and (2) the step-up transformer such as is used in x-ray procedures. The step-up transformer produces a high voltage necessary for the generation of x-rays. In other words, the transformer steps up or increases the voltage. The amount of current the transformer will produce will depend on the number of windings of the coil in the transformer.

POSITIONS USED IN X-RAY PHOTOGRAPHY

1. The AP or anterior posterior position. The anterior is near the tube and the posterior near the film.
2. The PA or posterior anterior position. The posterior is near the tube and the anterior near the film.
3. The lateral position of a hand or foot. The hand is on the side with the little finger near the film.
4. The RL (right lateral). The right side of the body is near the film.
5. The LL (left lateral). The left side of the body is near the film.
6. The supine position. The patient is on his back with his face upward.
7. The prone position. The face and abdomen are down on the table.
8. The oblique position is halfway between the AP or PA and lateral positions.

CONTROL PANEL

Every machine has a control panel, which is the brain of the x-ray machine (Fig. 34-4). To operate an x-ray machine, first turn on the wall switch, then turn on the main switch. Be sure that the exposure switch is set at radiography. Regulate the milliampere and focus switches to high or low focus, as desired. Measure the patient or the portion that is to be x-rayed for the proper KVP. Adjust KV as required. For a thick area use more KV to penetrate the area. The major KV dial moves 10 points up or down in one turn. The minor dial moves 1 point up or down in one turn. Set the time for the proper exposure and check

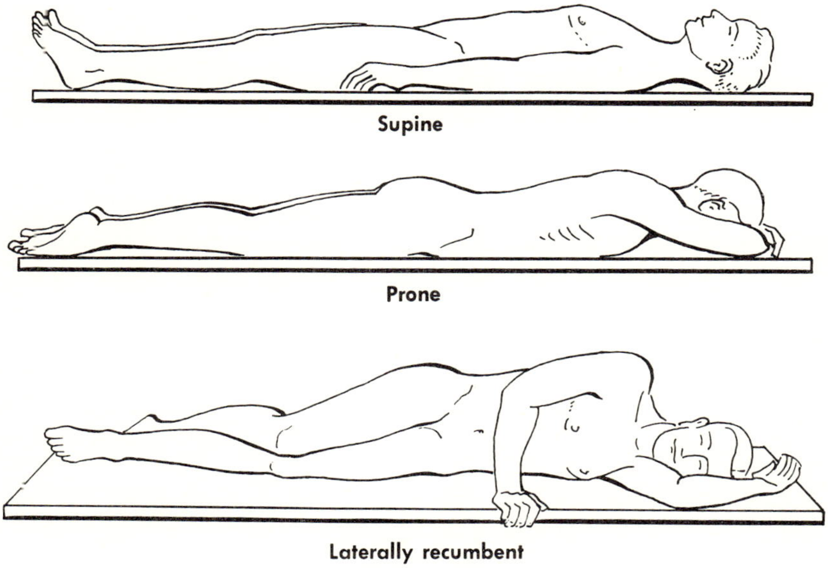

Fig. 34-3. Common positions for x-ray examination.

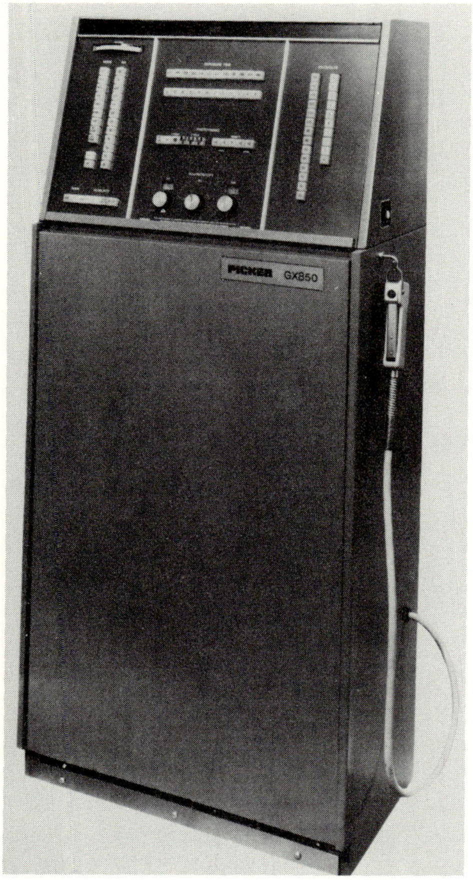

Fig. 34-4. Modern x-ray generator control console. (Courtesy Picker Corporation, Cleveland, Ohio.)

the circuit breaker to see that it is in all the way. Position the patient and center the tube to the film and anatomy. Then adjust the filament setting for milliamperage required. Complete the exposure by pressing the time switch button until a click is heard. (Always caution the patient to be still.) Then turn off the main switch on the panel. At the end of the day pull the wall switch off.

SCATTERED RADIATION IN REFERENCE TO BUCKY TECHNIQUE

Up to this point two things have been taken for granted: (1) that all rays that come out of the object have come straight from the focal spot or primary beam and have traveled through the part to form a well-defined, clear-cut image and (2) that all rays that do not penetrate are absorbed and could be forgotten. Unfortunately this is not the case. Some of the radiation is scattered in all directions by the atoms of the object struck. These secondary rays are scattered radiation or scattered x-rays. The object is thus a source of effective but unwanted radiation. It is unwanted because it does not contribute to the formation of the useful image. On the contrary, it produces an overall haziness superimposed on the useful image.

The most effective way to cope with scattered radiation is through the use of a grid. This device is composed of alternating strips of lead and radiotransparent materials, so arranged that when the focal spot is centered over the grid the plane of each strip is in line with the primary beam. The lead strips absorb a considerable amount of the oblique scattered radiation, that is, the rays not traveling in the direction of the primary beam. The radiotransparent strips are usually about eight times as deep as they are wide. The relation of the depth of the lead strips to the width of the radiotransparent strips represents the grid ratio. To illustrate, if the depth is eight times the width, the grid ratio is 8:1; if the depth is six times the width, the ratio is 6:1, and so on. *The greater the ratio, the more effectively the grid will absorb scattered radiation.*

When a grid is used, the shadows of the lead strips are superimposed on the useful image. This is tolerated when a stationary grid with very thin narrow strips is used. To eliminate this grid pattern, which tends to break up useful image detail, it is only necessary to move the grid during exposure; then the lines are blurred and not distinguishable. *A device comprising a grid and its moving mechanism is called a Potter-Bucky diaphragm* or sometimes simply a Bucky.

BUCKY TECHNIQUE

The Bucky technique was developed by a German radiologist. He developed this technique for work on the spine and the skull and for heavy detail work using metal cassettes that are placed on the tray that moves along with the tube. *The principle of the Bucky is to draw in more of the secondary rays along with the central ray.* There are three points to remember: (1) The Bucky has its own timer. (2) The Bucky has its own switch on the machine for making exposures. This is labeled Bucky release. This switch releases the Bucky mechanism to and fro and turns on the high-tension current. This procedure is called synchronization. It has a synchronizing Bucky timer and Bucky switch. (3) The Bucky must be set or cocked after each exposure. This is done by pulling the lever or spring out as far as it will go.

GENERAL TECHNIQUE FOR BUCKY GRID

1. Always center the patient's entire body on the table with the white line.
2. Pull Bucky tray out and place the right size cassette in it.
3. Lock the cassette in the tray by using the clamps on the tray.
4. Bring the tray with the cassette in it to the desired part of the anatomy to be x-rayed.
5. Measure the part to be x-rayed.

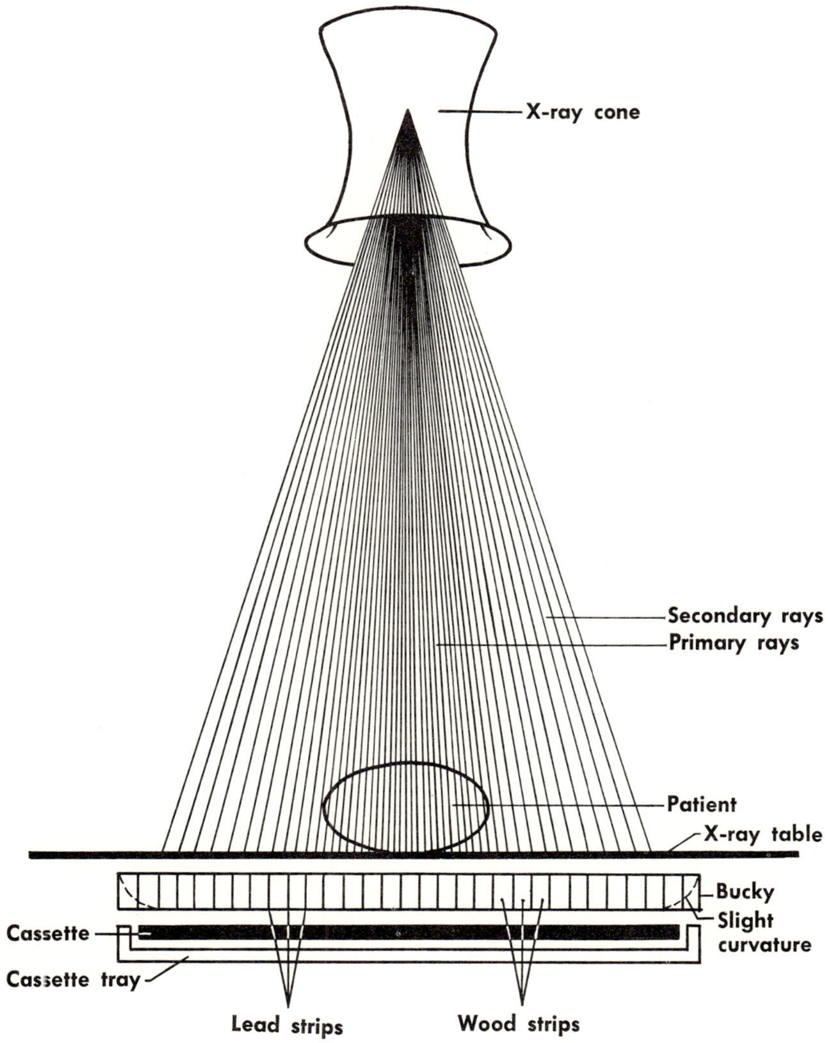

Fig. 34-5. Diagrammatic scheme of Bucky grid showing scattered radiation.

6. Set the machine up and be sure to check the Bucky timer.
7. Center the tube to the center of the cassette and then push the tray as far in as it will go.
8. Cock the Bucky and make the exposure.

X-RAY PROTECTION

Because x-rays are not harmless, overexposure to x-ray has many possible ill effects. Massive exposure (several hundred Rads) can cause severe burns or even frank necrosis (death) of tissue akin to a delayed reaction to a burn. Massive radiation exposure to limited areas of the body are used to kill malignant (cancer) tissues and normal tissues are often affected by this radiation either directly or by the scattering of x-rays from tissues along the path of the x-ray beam. Massive radiation exposure produces severe suppression of the bone marrow as evidenced by a decrease in the red cells (anemia), white cells (leucopenia), and platelets (thrombocytopenia). Massive radiation also causes damage to the lining of the gastrointestinal tract with resultant vomiting and diarrhea. Many organs like the lungs, heart, and kidneys are severely affected by excessive radiation.

Doses of radiation are measured in Rads. A single chest x-ray produces less than one thousandth of a Rad of radiation. In treating cancer, as much as 4,000 to 5,000 Rads may be given to a small area of the body. This amount of radiation, if delivered directly to the bone marrow, intestines, and other tissues, causes severe damage and may result in death.

Over the last fifty years there has been a growing awareness of the danger of less than massive doses of radiation. For example, leukemia is more common among radiologists than among any other groups of physicians. Thirty or forty years ago it was not uncommon for physicians to treat patients with ringworm infections of the scalp or enlarged tonsils, adenoids, or lymph nodes with radiation. At the time these treatments were thought to produce no ill effects. In recent years it has been noted that these patients, twenty to forty years after treatment, are developing tumors of the neck and head at a significant rate.

In general, tissues with rapidly dividing cells, such as the reproductive organs, the bone marrow, and embryonic tissues, are most likely to suffer radiation damage and subsequently to develop tumors. Exposure of pregnant women or the genitalia of children to x-rays carries with it a small but definite risk. These procedures should therefore be performed only for sound medical reasons.

X-ray technicians or medical assistants are constantly being exposed to possible radiation. They should adhere to the following rules:

1. Wear, at all times during the working day, an exposure monitoring badge that is submitted several times during the year for reading. An overexposure to x-rays will be picked up by these badges before the technician or assistant is exposed to dangerous amounts of radiation. Similar badges are to be worn by any medical assistant or x-ray technician who has any contact with radioactive isotopes of any type.
2. Never hold a patient who is being x-rayed unless protective gloves and a gown are being worn.
3. Ascertain that the area where x-rays are being taken is fully guarded with lead-lined walls, and so forth.
4. Have the x-ray equipment checked periodically by qualified persons to assure that the equipment is not emitting dangerous amounts of radiation.

In order to protect the patient from unnecessary radiation, the following guidelines may be used:

1. Always ask a female patient if it is possible that she could be in the first three months of pregnancy. If it is possible and the physician is not aware of it, check with him before taking an x-ray.

2. In patients who are known to be pregnant, shield the abdomen to avoid unnecessary radiation. Usually upper GI series, intravenous pyelograms, cystograms, and similar procedures are avoided during pregnancy. It must be stressed that the most dangerous period for x-ray exposure to the fetus is during the first three months of pregnancy when the patient is least likely to know that she is pregnant.
3. Whenever possible shield the gonads of the children undergoing x-rays of the abdomen or pelvis.
4. Learn x-ray techniques that will spare overpenetrating the patient with x-rays (especially children and pregnant women).
5. Know what you are doing; be proficient so that you never repeat an exposure to the patient because of your lack of knowledge.

CHEST X-RAY PHOTOGRAPHS

The only time the full capacity of the tube is used is for a chest x-ray. The exposure is done at the fastest possible time because there are so many movements in the chest. If using 100 ma use 1/10 second of time; for 200 ma use 1/20 second of time; and for 400 ma use 1/40 second of time. Chest x-rays are taken at six-feet distance and in a standing position with a 14-by-17 film. Measure the patient for KVP setting. The exposure should either be taken on a deep inspiration and held or on a deep expiration and held.

DARKROOM TECHNIQUE AND PROCESSING

Once you have a clear idea of the principles of exposure it is time to consider the principles relating to film processing. Processing is the term for the various operations that collectively produce a visible, permanent image on an exposed film. These operations are developing, rinsing, fixing, washing, and drying. The finished product is, of course, called a radiograph.

The care taken in the exposure room must be followed by equally painstaking work in the processing room if radiographs of acceptable quality are to be obtained. Anyone can do a job better by understanding what it is all about. For that reason a quick review is included here to make clear the purpose of each solution, its chemical composition, and how it works.

It is said that about 90% of radiographic failures are traceable to the darkroom, and the importance of meticulous care in this phase of radiology cannot be overemphasized.

The darkroom should be close to the x-ray machine. There must be sufficient facilities, brackets, and an electrical switch for safelights and timer. Circulating water facilities must be adequate, with hot and cold running water available. There should be sufficient ventilation of some form in the darkroom, depending on its size, and there should be enough room to allow movement. The size of the darkroom will depend upon the number of x-ray photographs taken. The colors of the walls of the darkroom should be very dark green or black and as lightproof as possible. The safelights should have 15-watt bulbs and be amber in color. The supply of x-ray film in the bin must be closed after obtaining a film for a cassette or a cardboard holder; otherwise the whole supply will be exposed to light and ruined. *The loading bench or table must always be kept spotlessly clean or your films will be damaged.* The film hangers should be stored in a convenient place. Hangers should be washed and kept clean at all times. *Never use dusty hangers.* The size of the tanks will depend on the amount of work that you will have. The thermometer should be kept clean and should float in the developing tank. If possible, it should not come in contact with the films. The timer or clock should be accurate and loud enough to hear. The films can be hung up on a film rack and dried overnight, or there are electric film dryers that may be purchased. Be sure to turn off the water before leaving for the day.

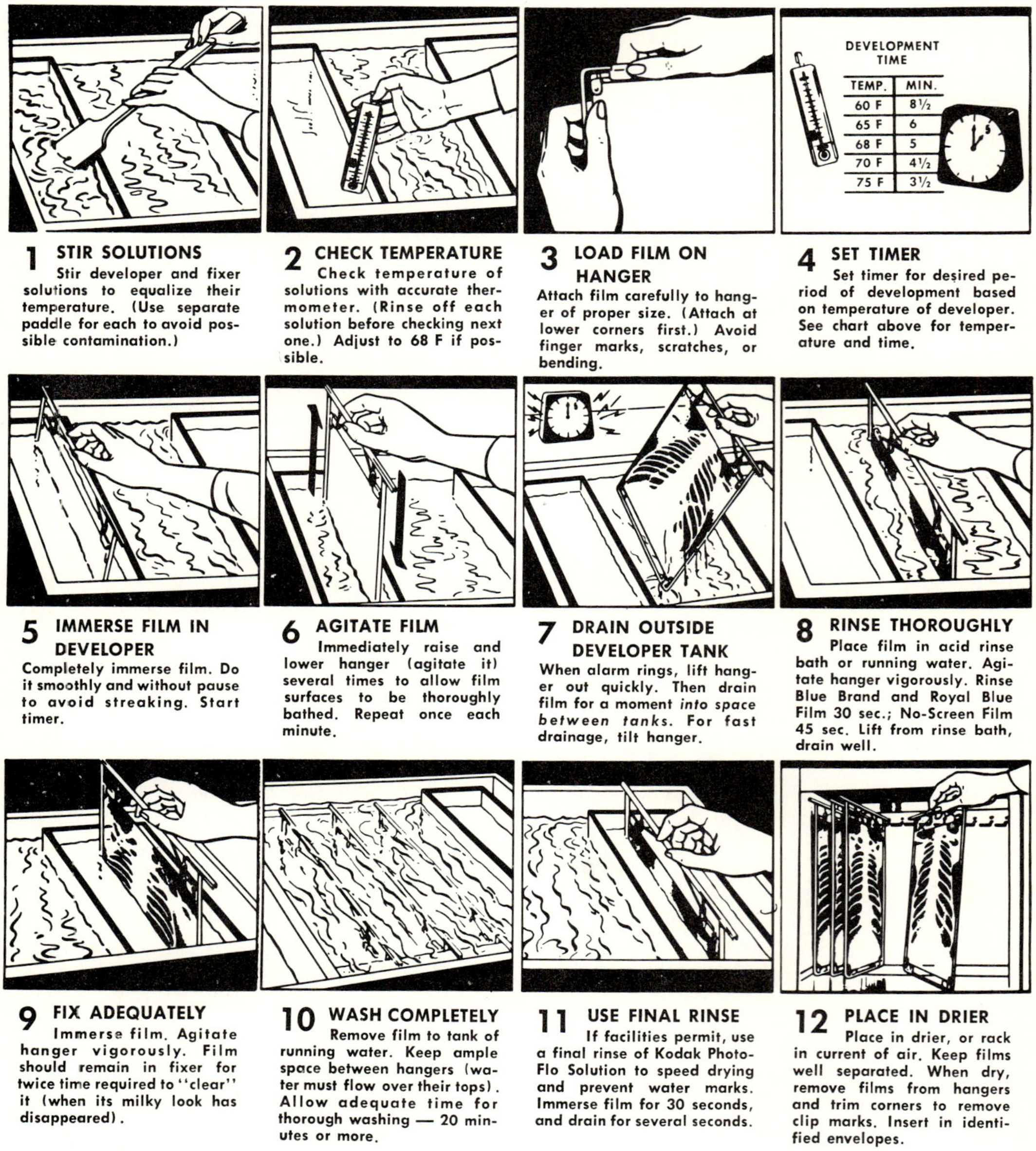

Fig. 34-6. Basic steps in processing x-ray film. (Courtesy Eastman Kodak Company, Rochester, New York.)

DEVELOPING SOLUTION

An x-ray film is constituted of a transparent cellulose sheet, often lightly tinted blue. It is coated on both sides with a gelatinous emulsion containing a silver salt known as halide. When exposed to x-rays or a light, a change effected in the silver halide crystals renders them reducible to a black metallic silver. It is subjected to the chemical action of the reducing agent, which in this case is the developing solution. Developing must be done in the prescribed time recommended by the time indicator chart. The time of developing cannot be speeded up. The temperature of the solution is an important element. In time the developing solution will become weak and contaminated; however, replenishers sold on the market will rejuvenate them to a certain amount of strength. Age will discolor the developer also. It will gradually turn yellow and then will continue to turn dark brown. A brown developer will produce fogging and stains on the film. The chemical processing of films is very definitely accelerated or retarded by the temperature changes. The optimum temperature for film processing has been established by film manufacturers at about 68° F. Solution temperature below this point requires a longer developing time. A simple but important step in processing is one frequently neglected: *thoroughly stirring the solution before use.* Remove the scum first with tissues or paper towels. Concentrates tend to settle to the bottom of the compartment, leaving weaker solutions near the top. Thus, especially during the developing stage, the effect may vary over the entire surface of the film, producing areas of unequal density. *Separate stirring paddles must be used for the developer and the fixer.* They must not be interchanged.

RINSING PROCESS AND FIXING OF THE FILM

The rinsing process after developing is merely a quick washing of the film in clear running water after developing and before transferring to the fixer solution. The rinse should not be continued for more than 4 or 5 seconds, as the developing process continues until stopped by the fixer. Fixing of the film constitutes a chemical process that dissolves the unexposed silver halide crystals in the emulsion. It clears the yellow coating and hardens the surface. The film should be in the fixer solution for twice as long as it was in the developing solution. The film should never be subjected to white light at any time until after it has been in the fixer for at least 3 to 4 minutes. The final processing before drying and storage of the film is a thorough washing in running water for not less than 30 minutes. A longer period of time is not harmful.

BEFORE EXPOSURE

Be sure to have the room dark with only the safelights on. Take the film box out of the storage bin and take your film out (take only one film out at a time). Make sure that the lid of the box is replaced after the removal of the film. Have the cassette or cardboard holder ready. Then remove the paper from the film without handling the film too much, or, if using a cardboard holder, leave the paper on the film. Place the film in the cassette or cardboard holder very carefully, avoiding friction. Then close or lock the cassette or cardboard holder. The film is now ready to be used.

LOADING THE FILM (Fig. 34-7)

All film comes wrapped in paper. The screen type or Blue Brand film is used in cassette. The paper of the screen-type film should be removed before placing in the cassette. In removing the paper, let the paper fall away from the film. This is accomplished by taking the film out with the right hand and separating the film from the paper with the left hand. Then place the film in the cassette and close. This method minimizes the static or pressure. The paper that encloses the nonscreen-type film is used in cardboard holders. Always be sure the top or cover is put back on the box of films. Press the sides of the film box to release air.

AFTER EXPOSURE (Fig. 34-8)

Have the developing solution at the correct temperature (usually 68° F.). Be sure to have only the safelights on. Remove the film from the cassette or cardboard holder. Then put the name, date, part taken, and other pertinent data on the film with the electric nameplate or otherwise identify with lead markers. Place the film lightly on the film hanger. Be sure there are no bulges. Place the film, which is on the hanger, in the developing solution for the necessary developing time. Set the timer or clock for the correct time. The time of the developer depends on the temperature of the develop-

Fig. 34-7. Loading x-ray film in cassette. (Courtesy Eastman Kodak Company, Rochester, New York.)

ing solution. After the film has been developed for the allotted time, remove it and shake off the excess and put it in the rinse water, lifting up and down several times. Then place the rinsed film in the hypo or fixer solution for the allotted time (Fig. 34-9). Remove the film from the hypo solution and place in the rinse water for about 30 to 60 minutes. After it has been in the water for the necessary time, remove and place the hanger with the film on the film rack to dry overnight. The next morning remove the film from the rack and cut off the corners with a scissors or film cutter.

TYPES OF FILM

There are two types of films: a nonscreen-type film that is used in a cardboard holder, and the screen type or Blue Brand that is used in a cassette. Films are usually bought in boxes of twenty-five or seventy-five and are always dated. Always be sure to check the date.

POINTERS ABOUT INTENSIFYING SCREENS OR CASSETTES

When x-rays strike the emulsion of an x-ray film, only about 1% of their energy is absorbed. The remaining 99% passes through without causing any effect. To make effective use of that 99% of wasted energy and to shorten the time of exposure, the intensifying screens are used.

An intensifying screen is a flexible sheet of cardboard coated with a thin layer of calcium tungstate crystals suspended in an emulsion. When this calcium emulsion is acted upon by x-rays, it emits light, which, when the screen is in contact with the film, speeds up the time of photographic effect and lessens the time of exposure. Because of this faculty of speeding up the exposure time, the use of intensifying screens is a necessity in all exposure of heavy parts, although their use is optional in radiography of the extremities (you may use either screen or nonscreen technique). They do offer a

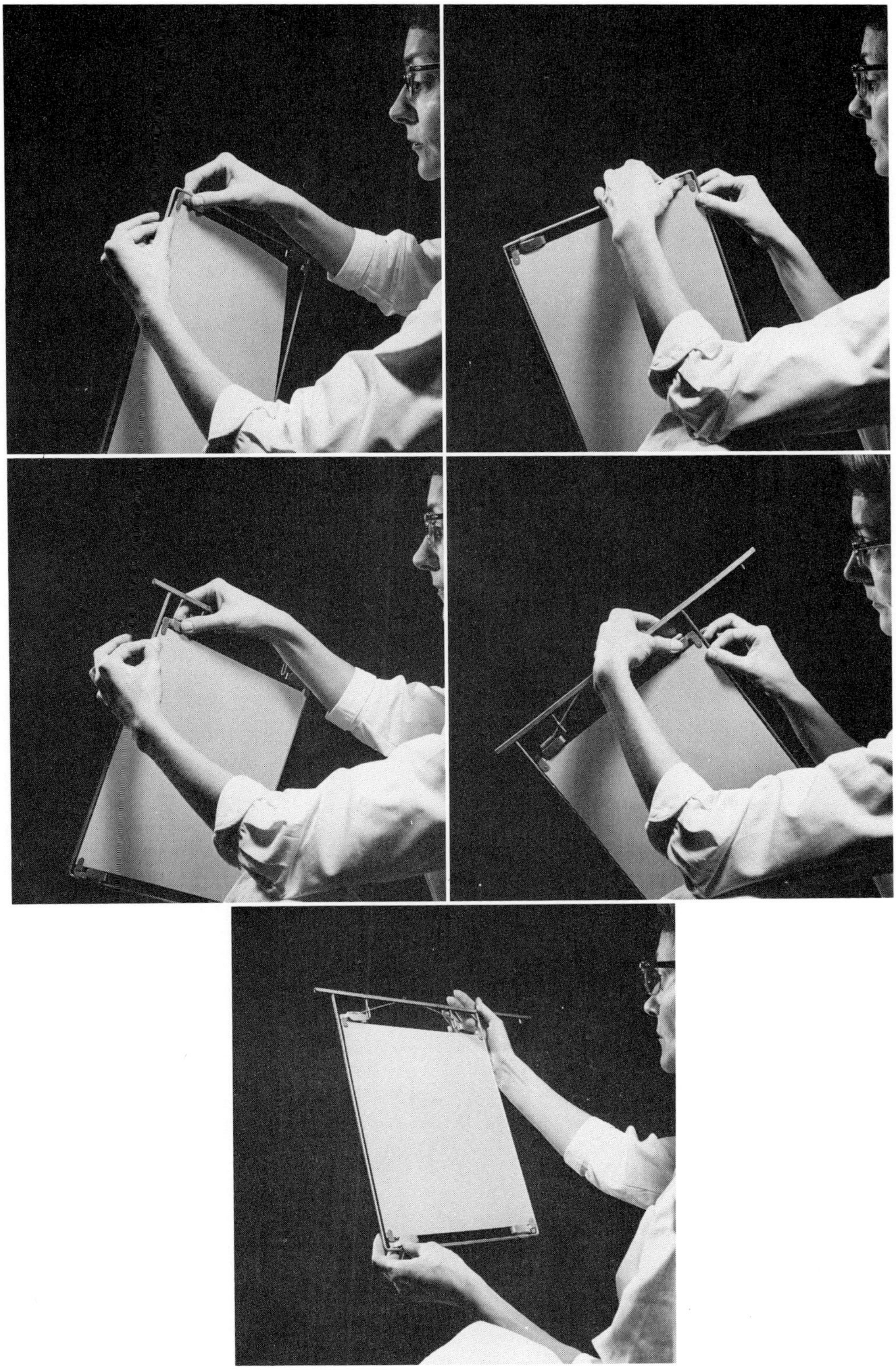

Fig. 34-8. Steps in loading a processing hanger. (Courtesy Eastman Kodak Company, Rochester, New York.)

Fig. 34-9. Modern x-ray developing and fixing tank. (Courtesy E. I. Dupont & Company, Wilmington, Delaware.)

most convenient and useful method of speeding up the exposure time to overcome motion in nervous patients and children. The ratio of exposure time between screen and nonscreen exposure using regular films is 1:4 or 1:5.

Intensifying screens materially increase the amount of contrast on a film. Because of the added speed, it is possible to reduce the amount of KV used. The use of intensifying screens likewise increases the speed of exposure to a point where it is possible to use a Bucky grid, thereby eliminating some fog and secondary radiation.

SCREEN CARE

Next to the patient, intensifying screens are the most fragile and expensive items we handle. For that reason and because a slight defect ruins the screen for further use, time spent in the proper care of screens is money in the bank. With proper care they will last indefinitely, although a busy laboratory expects to change screens at least every five years.

Proper care of screens means that they are never exposed to the possibility of being spotted by splashes of solution from the tank. Cassettes are never left open on the

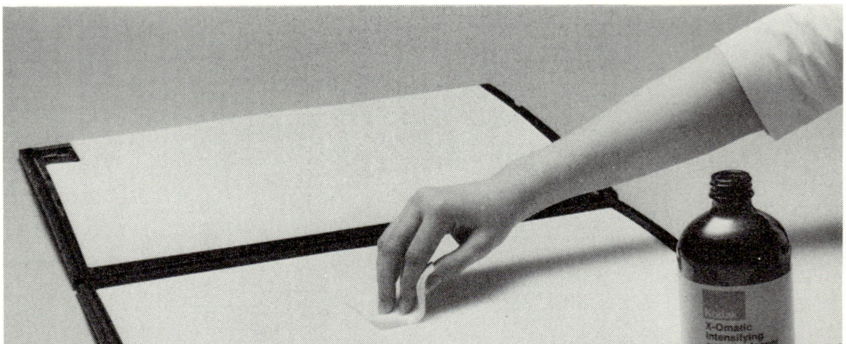

Fig. 34-10. Proper care of intensifying screens. (Courtesy Eastman Kodak Company, Rochester, New York.)

loading bench where there is a possibility of foreign substances falling on the screens.

Screens are never handled with wet hands. Films are removed from the cassette by digging a corner free with the fingernail. Screens are dusted periodically with a camel's-hair brush. Screens are washed according to the manufacturer's directions at least once a month or every six weeks. It depends somewhat upon the amount of usage to which they are submitted.

Cleaning of the screens is a process that requires meticulous care. A pure soap, cotton, and a small amount of water are used. Be sure to rinse the soap from the screen and dry well with cotton, allowing the cassette to remain open sufficiently long after washing to assure drying before films are placed in position and the cassettes closed.

Another manufacturer suggests pure grain alcohol (denatured alcohol is not satisfactory for washing screens). They should first be wiped with a soft cloth and then the entire screen gone over with an alcohol-soaked cotton swab. If the screen is very dirty, the cotton should be changed frequently. Allow 2 or 3 minutes for drying and then go over the screen lightly with a piece of lintless cloth, soft flannel, or cotton. It is most important when washing a screen with alcohol to avoid the identifying trademark imprinted on the face of the screen. The ink is soluble in alcohol, and will smear and possibly damage the screen.

Never attempt to scrape off any foreign substance that may be embedded in the screen. If it cannot be dissolved or removed by washing, it should be left and accepted as an imperfection on the screen from then on. Rubbing alcohol or any other cleaning compound should never be used for cleaning cassettes.

THE X-RAY AS A DIAGNOSTIC TOOL

X-rays may be taken by physicians either to ascertain a patient's state of health or to help make a specific diagnosis. In former years because tuberculosis was a leading cause of death in the United States, routine yearly chest x-rays were generally recommended for all. But with the marked decline in tuberculosis and because routine yearly chest x-rays have been shown not to alter the course of lung cancer, routine chest x-rays are no longer as widely used as in the past. Routine chest x-rays are taken of all patients known to have positive tuberculin tests, individuals exposed to tuberculosis, and of medical personnel coming in contact with sick patients.

Although the use of x-rays varies considerably among physicians in different types of medical practice, in the following section those x-rays commonly performed in a general medical office will be described.

Head. X-rays are often taken of the head after injuries, for severe headaches, or to check for possible tumors or metabolic diseases. Skull x-rays are frequently referred to as a "skull series."

Chest. X-rays of the chest may be ordered to detect abnormalities of the lungs, heart, great blood vessels, or the bones of the thorax. In looking for rib fractures, the x-rays are frequently ordered as "rib details." Routine chest x-rays are taken in full inspiration with the patient's back to the x-ray film (PA view) and sometimes in a lateral view.

Gastrointestinal x-rays. Patients with ulcer diseases frequently have x-rays of the upper gastrointestinal system after swallowing barium or some other contrast medium. This is called an "upper GI series." X-rays of the colon use "barium enemas." Both of these x-rays are extremely valuable in diagnosing cancer of the stomach and colon. X-rays of the gallbladder are called "cholecystograms" and are taken to ascertain the function of the gallbladder and the presence of cholelithiasis (gallstones).

The urinary system. The kidneys can be x-rayed by injecting a dye into a vein and obtaining x-rays of the kidneys as they pick up, concentrate, and excrete the dye into the ureters and bladder. This is called an "intravenous pyelogram" (IVP). The bladder and lower urinary tract may be x-rayed by injecting dye through a tube directly into the bladder. This is called a "cystogram." The amount of urine left in the bladder after voiding may be estimated by taking "post-voiding" x-rays.

Abdominal x-rays. A plain x-ray of the abdomen may be ordered to check for evidence of abdominal disease. Two frequent type of x-rays in this category are the plain film that includes the kidney, ureters, and bladder (KUB) and the "obstructive series."

Bone x-rays. Bone x-rays usually require no special patient preparation. When fractures are suspected, however, extreme care must be excised in moving a patient to avoid serious damage from the fracture. Splints and bandages that have immobilized a potential fracture should never be removed except under the specific instructions of the physician.

X-rays of the spine are frequently ordered. Neck x-rays are referred to as cervical or "C-spine" x-rays and low back x-rays as lumbosacral spine or "LS-spine" x-rays.

Radioisotope scans. Certain soft tissues of the body are not readily visualized by x-rays. These tissues (brain, thyroid, liver, spleen, and so forth) can be visualized by the use of radioisotopes. The function of the specific tissue can be determined by the amount and distribution of the radioactivity within the tissue. Instead of using x-ray film the radioactivity is recorded by a special scanning device and the tests are therefore called radioisotope scans of the respective tissue. This rapidly expanding field of radiology is referred to as nuclear medicine.

COMMON CAUSES OF UNSATISFACTORY RADIOGRAPHS

The experienced medical assistant will view radiographs to check their quality before submitting them to the physician. At times the assistant will notice, or the doctor will point out, that there is something wrong or less than optimal in the radiograph. Fig. 34-11 outlines the most frequent causes of unsatisfactory radiographs.

TERMINOLOGY

abduction to lead away from the body

acetabulum socket of the pelvis that receives the head of the femur

adduction to lead to the body

ampere unit of strength of electricity

angiogram x-ray photograph of the blood vessels

anode positive electrode in the x-ray tube

anterior front

arteriography radiographic visualization of the arteries for example, carotid, coronary, femoral

atrophy wasting away of tissue or a part

bronchography roentgenographic examination of the chest after intratracheal injection of opaque solution (Lipiodol)

cassette container with two intensifying screens in which the x-ray film is placed

cathode negative side of x-ray tube

cholecystogram x-rays of the gallbladder obtained after taking special contrast medium, usually in the form of pills

curie the quantity of radium emanation in equilibrium with 1 gm of radium element; used as a unit of measurement

cystogram x-ray photograph of the bladder

cystoscope instrument of interior examination of the bladder

Diodrast radiopaque dye

distal further away from the midline or the very end

dorsal knuckle surface of the wrist, hand, or foot

encephalography examination of head following the introduction of air into the subarachnoid space as a means of diagnosis

esophagram x-ray photograph of the esophagus

eversion outward rotation

extension straight positions of the joints

flat film taken without any contrast medium

flexion bend in the joint

GI series x-ray photograph examination of the gastrointestinal tract

hysterosalpingography x-ray photograph of the uterus and oviducts

inferior lower portion of the body

innominate bones hipbones

intercostal between the ribs

intervertebral disk broad and flattened disk of fibrocartilage between the bodies of vertebrae

intravenous pyelogram x-ray photograph of the kidney after injection of radiopaque material into the veins

inversion inward rotation

Iopax dye used for intravenous injections in pyelography

irradiation treatment by roentgen rays or other forms of radioactivity

KUB an x-ray of the abdomen that includes the kidney, ureters, and bladder

Common causes of unsatisfactory radiographs

Underexposure	Kilovoltage too low Milliamperage too low Exposure time too short Too great a focal film distance Central ray of x-ray tube not directed on film
Underdevelopment	Time too short Temperature too low Exhausted developer (chemical activity has been used up or the activity has been destroyed by contamination) Diluted developer by addition of water instead of fresh developer to raise level Melted ice from cooling attempt, or overflow of water from wash tank
Overexposure	Too high kilovoltage Too high milliamperage Too long exposure Too short a focal film distance
Overdevelopment	Time too long Temperature too high Inaccurate thermometer
Fog	Light leaks into the processing room through the doors, windows, etc. Safelight bulb is too bright Turn on light before fixation is complete
Stains on radiographs	Yellow spots are caused by exhausted developer (old developer) Covers left off the tanks Scum on developer surface Insufficient rinsing Exhausted fixer
Lack of details or fuzziness	Motion of the tube, film, or patient Too long exposure Poor contact of intensifying screens Too large a focal point

Fig. 34-11. Troubleshooting unsatisfactory radiographs.

kymography a method for recording of rhythmic movement of an organ

kyphosis a concave backward curvature of the spine

lateral recumbent lying on one side

medial nearest to the midline of the body

myelography a method of taking radiographs of the spinal subarachnoid space usually after injecting contrast material

palmar palm surface of the wrist or hand

plantar undersurface of foot

pneumoencephalography a method of taking x-rays of the brain after cerebral spinal fluid has been replaced by air

posterior back

pyelogram x-ray photograph of the kidney

pyelography roentgenographic examination of the kidneys after injection of opaque material

radiation emission of rays in all directions from a common center

radiolucent property of being partly or wholly permeable to radiant energy

radiopaque impenetrable to x-rays or other forms of radiation

retrograde urogram x-ray photograph of the urinary tract when the radiopaque material is injected directly into the ureters through the bladder

sagittal plane cutting the body in half or dividing it right to left

scoliosis lateral curvature of the spine. Usually consists of two curves, the original one and a compensatory curve in the opposite direction

sialogram x-ray photograph of the salivary ducts and glands

skull series a series of x-rays of the skull

spondylolisthesis forward subluxation of the lower lumbar vertebrae, usually on the sacrum, with consequent pelvic deformity

stereoscope instrument that combines two radiographs in such a way that the eyes see the picture in three dimensions

superior higher portion of the body

urethrocystogram x-ray photograph of the urethra and bladder

urography roentgenography of any part of the urinary tract after introduction of an opaque medium

Review questions

1. Name the fundamental factors of a good radiograph.
2. How are x-rays produced?
3. Define the following terms: ampere, kilovolt, KVP, milliampere seconds, and volt.
4. Name three types of x-ray tubes. What is meant by a rotating anode tube?
5. Discuss procedure in operating the control panel on any x-ray machine.
6. What is meant by scattered radiation? How does the Bucky grid absorb scattered radiation?
7. At what distance are chest x-rays taken? What is the best technique to use?
8. How should you protect yourself against x-ray overexposure? What are some of the risks involved in x-ray exposure?
9. Discuss briefly the proper procedure to process an x-ray film in the dark room.
10. Name some of the common causes of unsatisfactory radiographs.

Suggested readings

Cullinan, J. E.: Illustrated guide to x-ray technics, Philadelphia, 1972, J. B. Lippincott Co.

Jacobi, C. A., and Paris, D. Q.: Textbook of radiologic technology, ed. 5, St. Louis, 1972, The C. V. Mosby Co.

Watson, J. C.: Patient care and special procedures in radiologic technology, ed. 4, St. Louis, 1974, The C. V. Mosby Co.

chapter 35

Emergencies in the medical office

It is frequently the responsibility of the medical assistant to deal with an emergency in the absence of the physician. Most of the so-called emergency cases seen in a physician's office, although accompanied by a great deal of excitement, are not actually grave in nature. In most instances the competent medical assistant can recognize the real emergency. It is important to be constantly alert for all alarming symptoms, since certain acute and urgent conditions may require prompt recognition and treatment. In the physician's absence the medical assistant who can exercise good judgment and who is familiar with the necessary procedures can render real service not only to the patient and the patient's family but also to the physician.

Certainly the medical assistant is not expected to practice medicine or act as a fully qualified physician. The first duty is to summon the physician and then to take certain definitive steps prior to the physician's arrival or further instructions. The main task is to calm excitement and hysteria, allay fear, administer relief, and intelligently prepare for the doctor's arrival. The location of the doctor's practice considerably qualifies the type of emergency instructions to be given the medical assistant. If the physician practices in a large community with other physicians and ambulance service available, the medical assistant has no justification for undertaking the responsibility of treatment other than that preparatory to the doctor's arrival. In a rural community, if life is at stake and no authorized medical assistance is at hand, different measures are necessary. A medical assistant must bear in mind that with any emergency treatment, especially the giving of hypodermic injections in a critical case, the family may ascribe any bad outcome to that particular injection. Whenever possible, the authorization of the physician should be sought.

Situations the medical assistant may be

Glossary

abortion termination of pregnancy

antidote a substance that neutralizes a poison or its effects

aseptic a condition or area free of any bacterial contamination

asphyxia a failure in respiration causing a decrease in oxygen and increase in carbon dioxide in the blood

cyanosis the bluish discoloration seen in individuals whose blood contains excessive amounts of poorly oxygenated blood

epinephrine a hormone of the medulla of the adrenal gland sometimes used medicinally; often referred to as adrenaline

epistaxis a nosebleed

exsanguinate to drain of blood

fistula an abnormal connection between two spaces or cavities

giddiness state of dizziness or lightheadedness

Iodoform a type of iodine disinfectant

ipecac a drug often used to induce vomiting

speculum an instrument for examination of canals such as the ears, vagina, and anus

styptic contracting a blood vessel

tourniquet any device used on an extremity to place pressure so as to control hemorrhage or produce filling of the veins called upon to face alone fall roughly into three classifications: (1) cases of injury, either major or minor, such as the results of automobile accidents, fire, industrial mishaps, and so on, (2) cases of sudden collapse, and (3) alarming postoperative symptoms following a minor operation that has been performed in the physician's office. In each of these cases, the medical assistant's first duty is to notify the physician. If the physician is not expected momentarily and the case appears alarming with an immediate serious outlook, it is best to notify some nearby medical colleague of the doctor or, if none is in reach, to call for an ambulance.

Following is a list of the emergencies that arise most frequently in the physician's office; suggestions to the medical assistant concerning the most effective procedure in each specific instance are also included.

CARDIOPULMONARY RESUSCITATION

In the United States more than 650,000 people die every year of heart attacks. Since more than half of these deaths occur suddenly or within two hours of the onset of symptoms, sudden death from heart attacks is the most important medical emergency in the United States. A large number of these deaths can be prevented by prompt, appropriate treatment.

Medical assistants should be prepared to initiate and assist the physician in providing emergency care for a dying patient with a heart attack. In order to do so the assistant must understand why death occurs after a heart attack and what can be done to save a patient's life, and must feel confident enought to initiate care for the dying patient without the physician's aid if necessary.

When a patient has a heart attack, a portion of the heart muscle dies and the area around the dead heart muscle frequently interferes with the normal electrical activity of the heart. The ventricles may suddenly develop a chaotic electrical activity called ventricular fibrillation. Whether the heart undergoes ventricular fibrillation or completely stops all electrical activity, the result is the same—all pumping of blood stops. A fresh supply of oxygen to the brain is lost and the patient loses consciousness. As the centers of the brain that control breathing do not get enough oxygen, the patient stops breathing and dies.

Cardiopulmonary resuscitation involves rescuing a patient who has entered into this process of dying. In order for this emergency rescue process to occur successfully, a series of steps, called the ABCs of cardiopulmonary resuscitation, have to be taken. First, an Airway must be opened to supply oxygen to the lungs. Second, Breathing must be started for the patient. Third, Circulation of blood out of the heart and into the lungs and brain must be started (Fig. 35-1 *a* to *c*). The technique used to perform these actions is called cardiopulmonary resuscitation.

Airway

The patient should be placed flat on his back on a hard surface. If the patient is in bed, a hard board is placed under his shoulders or if this is not available, the patient must be placed on the floor. The head is tilted backward as far as possible by one hand on the forehead and another on the back of the neck.

Breathing

If the patient does not start breathing immediately, mouth-to-mouth breathing is started. To perform mouth-to-mouth ventilation, the assistant uses one hand behind the patient's neck to maintain the head in the position of maximum backward tilt and pinches the victim's nostrils together with the thumb and index finger of the other hand, which also continues to exert pressure on the forehead to maintain the backward head tilt. The rescuer then opens his mouth widely, takes a deep breath, makes a tight seal with his mouth around the victim's mouth and blows into the victim's mouth. He then removes his mouth and allows the victim to exhale passively, watching the vic-

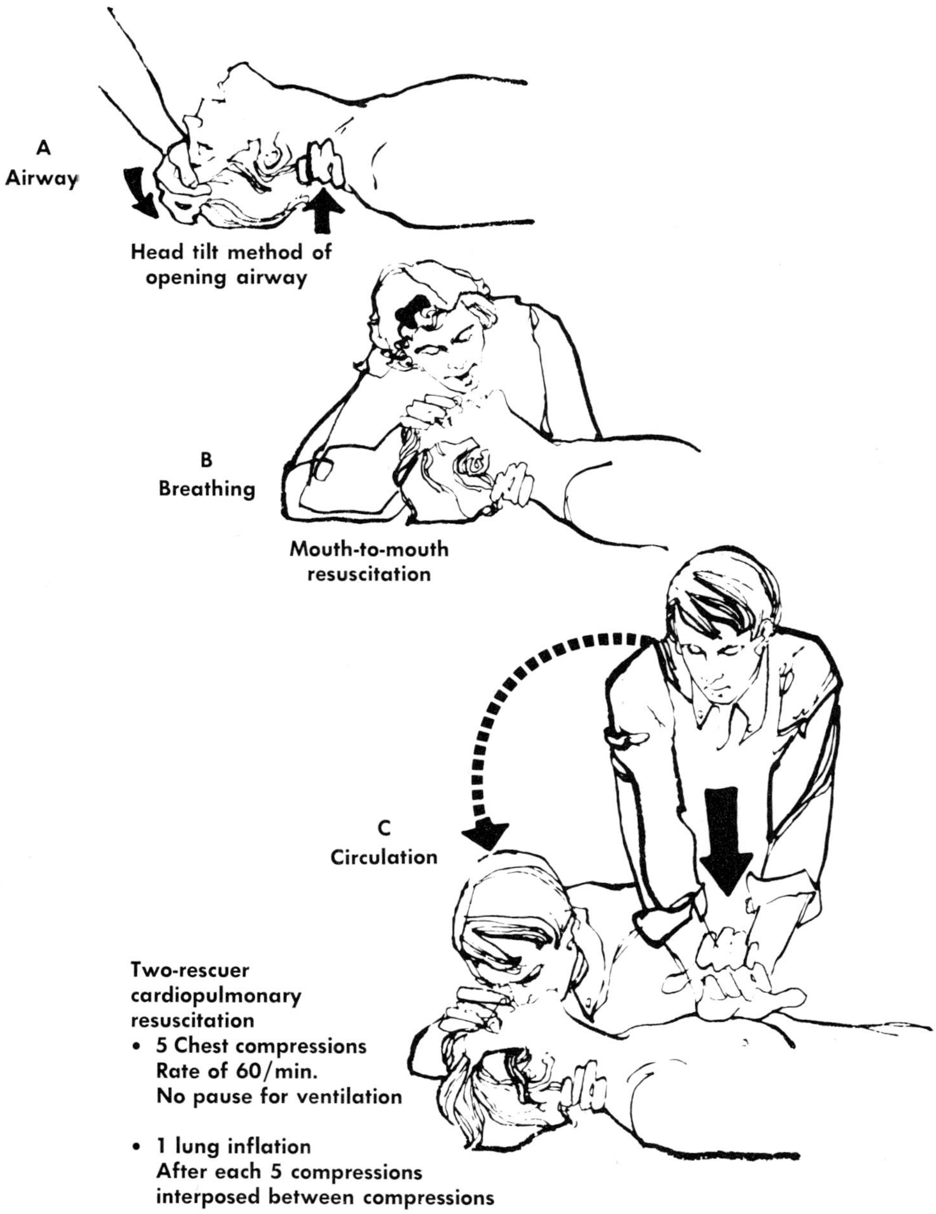

Fig. 35-1. Cardiopulmonary resuscitation (CPR) for basic life support. (Modified from J.A.M.A. **227**(Suppl.):835, Feb. 18, 1974. Reprinted with permission, American Heart Association, New York.)

tim's chest fall. This cycle is repeated once every 5 seconds as long as respiratory inadequacy persists. Adequate ventilation is ensured on every breath by the rescuer by observing the following: (1) seeing the chest rise and fall, (2) feeling in his own airway the resistance and compliance of the victim's lungs as they expand, and (3) hearing and feeling the air escape during exhalation. The initial ventilatory maneuvers should be four quick, full breaths without allowing time for full lung deflation between breaths.

Infants and children. Opening the airway

and performing artificial ventilation are essentially the same for children as for adults. There are some differences, however. The rescuer covers both the mouth and nose of the child with his mouth and uses small breaths with less volume to inflate the lungs once every 3 seconds. Care must be taken to force the head only slightly backward so as not to obstruct the breathing passages. Thus, in children, the main differences in pulmonary resuscitation are that the nose and mouth are both covered, that the amount of air delivered is in small breaths and puffs every 3 seconds, and that care is taken not to force the neck backward.

Accident cases. Whenever the possibility exists that a victim may have sustained a neck injury, extreme care must be taken not to extend the neck as this may cause severe and irreversible damage. In this situation the rescuer maintains the victim's head in a fixed, neutral position without extension. The index fingers are used to displace the lower jaw forward.

If at any time severe resistance develops during ventilation and the patient's chest is not moving, the possibility of a foreign body in the upper airway must be considered. An attempt should be made immediately to clear the airway with the fingers. In this way vomitus, loose teeth, or other obstructing objects may be removed from the upper airway.

Circulation

The third step in cardiopulmonary resuscitation is circulation. When circulation ceases the patient is said to be in cardiac arrest. This is recognized by pulselessness of the carotid arteries, large arteries located on either side of the neck, in an unconscious victim who has a deathlike appearance and whose breathing is absent. The carotid artery is located between the larynx (voice box) and the muscles of the side of the neck and is used to determine if the patient is in cardiac arrest.

With the patient flat on his back on a hard surface, circulation is started. The rescuer positions himself close to the victim's side and places the heel of one hand over the lower half of the sternum or breast bone. Care must be taken to avoid placing the hand over the lower 1⅓ inches of the breast bone. The other hand is then placed on top of the first one, the shoulders of the rescuer are brought directly over the victim's breast bone, the arms are kept straight as in a piston, and pressure is exerted directly downward to depress the lower half of the breast bone a minimum of 1½ to 2 inches. The compressions must be regular, smooth, and uninterrupted. In order to avoid fatigue, the rescuer must use the weight of his upper torso and shoulders to assist in the compression of the chest.

Since artificial circulation must be combined with simultaneous artificial ventilation, it is desirable to have two rescuers. One rescuer, usually the assistant, performs the breathing task while the other, usually the physician, handles the circulation. Breathing is continued in an uninterrupted fashion every 5 seconds and chest compression sixty times per minute without interruption for breathing.

The ABC method can sustain the life of a patient for several minutes. With the arrival of a physician and under appropriate conditions, other measures may be needed such as the application of an electrical current to the chest wall (defibrillation), insertion of a tube into the trachea to assist in breathing (intubation), and the administration of various drugs into a vein or even directly into the heart. All these steps require a physician and emergency care equipment. Many communities have all the equipment necessary for a successful cardiopulmonary resuscitation in ambulances.

It is important to remember that cardiopulmonary resuscitation can be successful only if started within minutes of an emergency. If a patient is brought to the office and it is definitely known that he has not been breathing for more than 10 minutes, cardiac resuscitation is not attempted. If any doubt exists, the victim is given the benefit of the doubt and resuscitation may be attempted until the attending physician arrives.

Training in cardiopulmonary resuscitation is provided by physicians, hospitals, the American Red Cross, and a variety of other qualified groups. Every physician's assistant should at least be able to secure an airway and conduct mouth to mouth breathing. This training may be used for children, accident victims, drowning victims, and other emergencies associated with cardiopulmonary arrest.

FOREIGN BODIES

Foreign bodies in the eye

Cinders, sawdust, or any foreign substance may become lodged in the eye, either under the lids or on the cornea, causing immediate and marked distress. It is best that the medical assistant make no effort to remove the particle without medical supervision. The patient should be made as comfortable as possible and cold compresses applied to the eye. If the pain is excessive, a drop or two of local anesthetic may be instilled into the eye, preferably after consulting the doctor over the telephone. It is essential that the assistant realize that the temporary relief of pain by this procedure must in all cases be followed by a careful examination of the patient by a physician.

Foreign bodies in the ear

Seldom do foreign bodies in the ear constitute a real emergency. Medical assistants should not attempt to use an instrument in the ear except in rare instances where they have been trained and specifically requested to do so by the physician. If the foreign body is a bug, roach, or other insect, a few drops of a bland sterile oil, which will asphyxiate the intruder and stop its movement, may be instilled. If the obstruction is a bean or a wooden object, care must be taken not to inject any fluid, which would cause these objects to swell and thus render their removal more difficult.

Foreign bodies in the nose

As a rule, a case of this sort is not an urgent one. Usually children are the victims or perhaps perpetrators of accidents of this type. The medical assistant may introduce some mildly medicated liquid petrolatum into the nostril or occasionally cleanse and irrigate the nasal passages with a warm saline solution. An attempt should be made to calm the patient and get him to breathe through the mouth. Under no circumstances should the assistant attempt to remove the obstruction instrumentally, as this may only push it farther back into the nose.

Foreign bodies in the pharynx, larynx, lungs, and esophagus

Numerous types of foreign bodies may become lodged in the throat, trachea, lungs, or the esophagus. Often these items will be immediately eliminated by vigorous coughing spasms. Frequently there is no evidence of respiratory difficulty at all but there is a history of swallowing a foreign body. When the patient is not exceedingly uncomfortable, the medical assistant must allay the fears of the immediate family by assuring them that prompt removal of the obstruction is not absolutely essential and that the patient will suffer no serious harm before the doctor's return. If, however, the obstruction has lodged in the larynx or trachea and interferes seriously with breathing and the patient is suffering distress and near suffocation, the medical assistant must recognize the urgency of the situation. If the patient is rapidly becoming cyanotic and the doctor has not yet arrived, one of his medical colleagues should be summoned.

FAINTING

Fainting is a broad term used to describe a sudden decrease in the level of consciousness. When consciousness is completely lost, it is called syncope. The causes of fainting are numerous and vary from fright on seeing a mouse to fatal stroke.

If a patient should faint in the office, lower the head in either of the following ways. If the patient is sitting and still conscious, bend the back forward until the head is between the knees; this will increase the blood supply to the brain. Keep him in this position a few minutes until the faint feeling has passed. An attack may often be stopped or prevented by this method. If the patient is lying down, has fallen, or is entirely unconscious, remove all pillows, keep head and shoulders flat, and raise the legs from the hips by elevating them. A chair, books, or whatever is immediately available will do for this purpose. Loosen the clothing, especially around the neck and waist. Some physicians will want you to use smelling salts, others will not. Keep the patient lying down until the condition improves. This is evidenced by the color coming back into the face and the pulse and respiration becoming normal. It is essential that the assistant note if there was any abnormal movement of the eyes or the rest of the body prior to a fainting episode. It is also helpful to determine the blood pressure and rate and regularity of the pulse and respiration during or immediately after the fainting episode.

Common fainting spells often occur in anxious patients within seconds of having blood drawn, seeing an unpleasant incident or injury, getting an injection, or otherwise experiencing pain or strong emotions. During these episodes the skin is cold and clammy, the pulse is somewhat slow but regular, and there is prompt recovery.

ACUTE POISONING

The medical assistant's most important role in poisoning emergencies is to determine when, what, and how much poison was taken and under what circumstances the poisoning occurred. Each poisoning must be treated as an individual case and the answers to the above questions will be crucial in determining further action by the assistant or the physician. Time is important. If the poison was taken within minutes of seeking medical attention, the treatment may be very different than if it was taken hours before. Knowing what specific poison was taken will determine if an antidote is needed. In general, patients or their families should be asked to bring to the office for further identification a sample of the poison or the empty container in which it was kept. An estimate of the quantity of poison taken should be made. The circumstances of the poisoning may be important, as, for example, in suicide attempts and in industrial poisonings.

Poison centers have been established throughout the country; these centers have up-to-date information on antidotes and treatments of accidental poisonings, which occur primarily in children. The medical assistant should obtain the telephone number of the nearest poison center and have it immediately available, not necessarily for the purpose of instituting treatment but for finding out specific antidotes and treatments for specific types of poisons. When the call comes that a child has swallowed a certain type of insecticide or solvent, the medical assistant should do everything possible to obtain the exact brand name and, if possible, any ingredients listed on the label. This will facilitate the work of the poison center in providing the medical assistant with the information that will be most useful to the physician in the treatment of an accidental poisoning.

Some substances, like lye or corrosive acids, should not be treated with induction of vomiting. Other poisonings, such as pills or medicines of any type, should be treated with induction of vomiting if the patient is alert and if the poison was recently taken. Vomiting can be induced by a variety of means such as stimulating the throat, giving mustard in water, or by giving a drug called ipecac. It should be stressed that patients with markedly reduced levels of consciousness should never be made to vomit for fear of aspiration of vomit into the lungs. In some cases the insertion of a tube into the stomach may be indicated. However, if the amount or nature of the poisoning is known to be trivial or not potentially serious this procedure will not be necessary. Also, neither vomiting nor the insertion of a stomach tube will help if the poison was taken several hours before seeking medical help.

In general, medical assistants should be concerned primarily with obtaining as much information as possible in a rapid and efficient manner. It is more important that the assistant realize the different types of treatment that may be used rather than worrying about how to treat an individual poisoning case. In most instances the physician or a colleague will be available to give specific instructions for treatment if provided with the proper information.

BURNS

Burns may be classified either by the extent of the injury they produce or the nature of the agent that causes the burn. First-degree burns cause reddening of the skin and pain. Second-degree burns cause blistering and loss of some of the skin tissues and are always painful. Third-degree burns extend through the entire depth of the skin, are painless, and may take a long time to heal. Burns may also be described in relation to the agent that produces them. Common causes of burns are fire, hot liquids, chemicals, or electricity. Most burns should be covered by a sterile gauze or a gauze impregnated with an antibacterial or antibiotic ointment. The choice of covering varies greatly among physicians and first-degree burns frequently need no covering at all. Pain medications may be used after consulting a physician.

Chemical burns

A strong acid or alkali that covers a large surface often rapidly causes a burn more severe than that caused by heat. All the excess chemicals should be wiped or rinsed off immediately. Some alkali, such as bicarbonate of soda, should be applied to an acid burn. If the burn has been caused by strong alkali, such as caustic soda, potash, or lye, a weak acid solution such as vinegar may be used. It is important for the medical assistant to realize that a large amount of water promptly applied is the single most important agent that can be used in a chemical burn.

Should the injured area be the eye, haste is essential since eye tissue is subject to rapid injury by many chemicals. As much of the chemical as possible should be removed by everting the lid and irrigating the eye with sterile water or saline.

HEMORRHAGE

Hemorrhages result from a multitude of causes and can be treated in various ways. The method to be used depends upon the source of the flow. The keen medical assistant will soon discover the bleeding point and will be able to differentiate between a serious and a trivial flow. Suggested treatment for the most frequently encountered types of hemorrhage are described in the following paragraphs.

Wounds

Treatment of wounds aims at two specific end results: (1) the arrest of hemorrhage, and (2) the prevention of infection. Clothing should be carefully removed and the injured surface exposed. If the hemorrhage is mild in character, a pad of sterile gauze pressed against the bleeding surface is usually sufficient. Profuse arterial or venous bleeding, however, is dangerous. Specific methods of controlling hemorrhage are direct pressure, elevation, styptics, and a tourniquet. By washing the skin surface, the bleeding point can be accurately established, and a sterile gauze compress may be applied with pressure.

If the bleeding is from a limb, elevation of the limb plus pressure will often help to accomplish the desired end. A tourniquet, perhaps the most widely known instrument of first aid, carries the potential of being one of the most dangerous. A simple tourniquet is devised by loosely tying a strip of strong cloth on the injured limb and placing a hard object or pad of some sort over the main artery under the cloth. A stick is passed into the knot of the bandage and twisted to constrict the pad over the artery. The tourniquet, however, is not to be employed indiscriminately in cases in which other methods of arresting bleeding might be successful, since a certain knowledge of anatomy is essential to the effective use, and much valuable time may be wasted in the attempt to apply it correctly. If the tourniquet is left on too long, gangrene may set in.

Once bleeding has been essentially arrested in the case of open wounds, the cut surface must immediately be sterilized by the medical assistant. If it is apparently clean, it should be painted with tincture of iodine solution. Irrigation with sterile water or saline may be used especially if the wound has been contaminated or has foreign particles embedded in it. In animal bites, where hemorrhage is slight but the chance of other toxic complications is great, immediate sterilization of the wound is important. Local health authorities' recommendations for reporting animal bites should be followed closely. Every effort should be made to identify the animal so that appropriate measures, such as rabies vaccine under certain circumstances, can be taken.

Every effort should be made to document the victim's immunization status against tetanus. Unimmunized individuals will need tetanus antitoxin as well as commencement of immunization against tetanus. Previously immunized patients will need a booster of tetanus toxoid if they have not been immunized for a given amount of time. This time varies between one and five years depending on the nature of the wound and the preferences of the physician. It is important to remind patients receiving tetanus toxoid for the first time that their immunization is not complete until the immunization injections are repeated at a later date.

Nasal hemorrhage

Nasal hemorrhage or nosebleed is sometimes referred to as epistaxis. In cases of severe nasal blood flow, the medical assistant must always bear in mind the fact that the best hemostatic is pressure. In 90% of all cases of this kind, the source of flow will be found on the anterior portion of the cartilaginous area of the septum. Sometimes these nasal hemorrhages point to systemic diseases. Postoperative hemorrhages are more serious and require more immediate attention.

The correct procedure is to have the patient in a sitting or semisitting position, with the head inclined forward. Pressure is to be applied with both fingers by the medical assistant or the patient himself to the anterior part of the nose. This usually suffices to stop the bleeding, thus controlling the immediate emergency. When bleeding is more or less severe, the medical assistant may saturate sterile absorbent cotton with some epinephrine solution (1:1,000) and insert it into the lower part of each nostril. An iced cloth, placed over the nose, may also be effective. If the blood still continues to flow, especially if it drips into the posterior portion of the throat, blood may be coming from the posterior portion of the nose and postnasal packing will be necessary. If the medical assistant has summoned the doctor and is expecting his arrival, it would be wise to prepare these necessary implements: (1) a proper light facility or a headlight, (2) a tongue depressor, (3) a nasal speculum, (4) dressing forceps, (5) a catheter, (6) Vaseline or gauze impregnated with Vaseline, (7) sterile gauze 1½ inches wide by 3 inches long, and (8) some gauze about 1 inch wide.

Mouth and throat hemorrhages

If the bleeding comes from a wound in the region of the tongue, the medical assistant may pull the tongue forward and press a finger to the base of the tongue. Some hemorrhages from the throat are postoperative tonsil hemorrhages, which usually take place within four to six hours after the operation but also frequently occur up to the eleventh day afterward. Of the two types of postoperative bleeding, late hemorrhages are very rarely of very great import. The immediate postoperative hemorrhages are more apt to do serious damage, and frequently the life of the patient may be saved by a watchful and intelligent medical assistant. The primary duty is to recognize the hemorrhage at its inception; the earlier it is discovered the better are the opportunities for quick action.

Uterine hemorrhage

When uterine hemorrhage is copious and sustained, it is of grave consequence, and every effort should be made by the medical assistant to secure efficient medical aid. It is of particular import to discover whether an abortion has been performed; if this is the case, the medical assistant may be unwittingly involved in a serious situation in which she may be held unjustly responsible for the outcome. If, however, the assistant is in a rural district where help is not obtainable and life depends upon quick action, there is no other course but for her to attempt to arrest the flow herself. First of all, she must make every possible attempt to ensure asepsis. She may insert a sterile vaginal speculum and pack the vagina as tightly as possible, preferably with iodoform gauze. If this is not at hand, sterile cotton, any sterile gauze, or even sterile bandage may be used. Too much stress cannot be laid upon the importance of discretion if there is some suspicion of attempted or performed abortion, especially where there is elevation of temperature. Under no circumstances should the assistant make an attempt to pack the uterus. She may subsequently be blamed for a perforation of the uterine wall that was present before her manipulation.

Rectal hemorrhage

Rectal hemorrhages after operation for hemorrhoids, fistulas, abscesses, and other conditions sometimes occur as late as the eighteenth postoperative day. The hemorrhage may be moderate or profuse and intermittent or continuous. If the operation has been performed on the lower rectum, wash out the rectum with ice cold water to remove stool and blood clots and to cleanse the mucous membrane. The cold douche contracts the tissue and aids in the control of the bleeding. Pressure by means of a bandage or gauze roll held tightly in the anal cleft by means of a tight binder usually stops the flow.

When the seat of operation was higher up, such as in a tumor, carcinoma, and so on, there is little that the assistant can do without being familiar with the methods of packing the rectum.

FRACTURES

In the case of suspected fracture, there is not the same urgency that there is in the presence of hemorrhage or wounds; the patient can rest quietly for some time without any serious harm. Under no circumstances should the medical assistant attempt to establish with certainty the presence of a break. By attempting manipulation she may thereby increase the displacement.

The patient should be moved as little as possible. If it is absolutely necessary to lift the patient, a splint should be improvised to keep the injured area rigid. If the break is a complete one, every effort must be made to prevent the jagged edge of the bone from penetrating the tissue and causing further damage. The limb should be supported by a soft cushion until the arrival of the physician. Cold compresses applied to the injured part will ease the pain and may reduce swelling. If the assistant is familiar with x-ray technique and if the apparatus is at hand, she will be performing a real service to the doctor if she takes x-ray pictures of the injured area in anticipation of his arrival. If the fracture is open and the tissues are torn, the external injuries should be treated in the same manner as a wound.

CONVULSIONS

Few experiences can be as dramatic and as frightening to the lay person as a convulsion by an epileptic patient. The medical assistant should always recognize that most convulsive seizures will end spontaneously and that the role of the assistant is to ensure that the patient does not asphyxiate or harm himself inadvertently during the episode. If the patient has vomited, he should be turned off his back and onto his side with his face down. In any case the assistant should wrap gauze or a clean handkerchief or a napkin about a tongue depressor and, after prying open the patient's jaw as gently as possible, introduce it into the side of the mouth between the teeth to prevent the patient from biting his tongue and to provide an adequate airway.

After the seizure, the patient will often be confused and disoriented for several minutes and must be closely watched. With the arrival of the physician, further treatment can be considered. If the convulsion is unusually prolonged, it may be necessary to give certain drugs to the patient intravenously. If there are repeated seizures, it is important that the physician be told if the patient regained consciousness between seizures.

SHOCK

Shock is a clinical condition characterized by insufficient blood flow to the internal organs. Shock may be caused by excessive loss of blood, by a heart attack or other cardiac problems, or may be the result of an infection or an allergic reaction. Individuals in shock are usually pale, cold, and clammy. They have a weak and fast pulse and low blood pressure. They may be confused or unconscious. The patient in shock should be placed in a reclining position with the legs elevated.

The medical assistant will be asked to take the patient's pulse and blood pressure frequently and to carefully observe the patient's mental status and breathing. Intravenous fluids will usually be started and drugs to treat the cause of the shock may be needed. Shock requires immediate medical attention. The physician will usually transfer the patient to the nearest hospital as soon as the patient's condition permits.

INSULIN REACTION

A common emergency is the insulin reaction of a diabetic patient. Patients vary in the type of reaction or the manner in which they begin an insulin reaction. For the most part, the patient begins to feel weak, sweats excessively, and experiences palpitation. Occasionally this reaction may progress so rapidly that the patient will become unconscious in a matter of minutes; usually, however, there is sufficient warning so that unconsciousness can be avoided. If the patient is rational, cooperative, and responsive, he should be given a high carbohydrate drink such as sweet orange juice. If the patient is able to eat, and chew, a candy bar will usually suffice.

If the patient is uncooperative and unable to drink or chew, the assistant will have to pursue a more heroic course. A substance known as glucagon is available in kit form*; each kit contains two vials, one containing the crystalline glucagon material, the other a diluent to be added to the glucagon for injection. The glucagon should not be used after the expiration date and should always be stored in a cool, dry place, since excessive heat will destroy its activity. The assistant should obtain one of these kits and become familiar with its use before attempting to use it in an actual emergency.

After administration of glucagon the physician should be called immediately. Once the patient responds adequately, he should be fed high carbohydrate drinks or candy, as previously mentioned. The unconscious patient receiving glucagon for an insulin reaction usually awakens within 15 minutes; if the patient does not awaken, he may be in a diabetic coma and not having an insulin reaction. In any case, it is urgent that a physician be notified immediately if the patient is unconscious.

ACUTE ALLERGIC REACTIONS

Another common emergency in many medical offices is the acute allergic reaction

*Eli Lilly & Company, Indianapolis, Indiana.

caused by an insect bite or by a drug reaction. The patient with the insect bite—usually the bite of a bee, wasp, or hornet—will undoubtedly present a history of a recent sting and the sudden development of hives, which are usually still apparent when the patient presents himself. He may also have respiratory distress and, in some instances, may go into shock. When this occurs, the allergic reaction is called an anaphylactic reaction. Some patients have become aware of their sensitivity to insect bites or drugs through previous experience. However, the first reaction is a rather frightening experience and this patient seeks immediate medical attention.

A subcutaneous injection of epinephrine (0.5 ml) will usually combat the immediate severe effects of an anaphylactic reaction following an insect bite until the aid of a physician can be obtained. This injection may be repeated in 5 to 10 minutes if the situation warrants. Loss of consciousness, respiratory difficulty, or shock after an injection should make the assistant think about anaphylaxis. A much more common reaction is the development of hives or a rash several hours or days after a drug is taken. Such reactions are called delayed allergic reactions and usually do not need the emergency measures taken during an anaphylactic reaction.

An allergic reaction after the injection or ingestion of certain drugs may occur immediately, when the doctor is giving the drug in the office, or it may begin sometime after the patient has left the office. The symptoms are similar to those of a reaction from an insect bite, plus an asthmatic type of breathing. Again, 0.5 ml of epinephrine injected subcutaneously will prevent progression of the severe manifestations.

While epinephrine injected immediately in the proper amounts can be life-saving, the assistant should be aware of the reaction this drug produces. The patient will usually experience flushing of the face, a period of excitement, a fast pulse, and a throbbing headache, which sometimes can be severe.

RESPIRATORY EMERGENCIES

There are many conditions that may cause a patient to suffer distress in breathing—cardiac disease (a condition known as pulmonary edema), pneumonia, a variety of diseases of the lungs, pulmonary emboli, or inhalation of noxious agents such as smoke, industrial fumes, and industrial gases. The patient with respiratory distress usually breathes best in a sitting or recumbent position. He should be made as comfortable as possible by being allowed to choose the position in which respiration is easiest for him. Tight clothing such as ties, belts, or girdles should be loosened to allow free respiratory exchange.

Oxygen should be administered with extreme caution to patients with severe, chronic pulmonary diseases such as emphysema. Administration of large amounts of oxygen to these patients may cause them to stop breathing. Oxygen, if it is necessary, can be administered, usually by mask, from a number of different sources. A portable disposable unit (Life-O-Gen) can prove to be very useful in an emergency.* The unit does not last too long, since it contains approximately seven gallons of pure oxygen; but it is equipped with a mask for administration of the oxygen and easy-to-follow directions. In many offices there are small tanks of oxygen together with a regulator and mask; this equipment makes prolonged administration of oxygen easier. In any event, a source of oxygen should be available in the office for a patient with respiratory distress. In all cases of respiratory embarrassment, however, the physician should be notified immediately and the emergency measures described should be carried out.

• • •

There is an infinite variety of emergency cases that may be brought into the doctor's office. The medical assistant should be well versed in the primary principles of first aid

---

*Linde Company, a division of Union Carbide, St. Louis, Missouri.

treatment, the necessity for asepsis, means of controlling hemorrhage, the alleviation of excessive pain, and the like. The medical assistant who at all times exercises intelligence and acts with dispatch may be of inestimable value in the prevention of a sad outcome to many injuries or medical emergencies.

Review questions

1. How would you handle a suspected fracture?
2. Name several methods of controlling nasal bleeding.
3. A patient faints in your office. What would you do?
4. A child has difficulty in breathing because of an obstruction in the throat. What would you do?
5. How would you handle a suspected acute poisoning?
6. What would you do for a patient having an insulin reaction?

Suggested readings

American National Red Cross: Advanced first aid and emergency care, ed. 2, Garden City, N. Y., 1974, Doubleday & Company, Inc.

Henderson, J.: Emergency medical guide, New York, 1973, McGraw-Hill Book Co.

Kennedy, R. H.: Emergency care of the sick and injured, Philadelphia, 1966, W. B. Saunders Co.

Index

G